Oracle Database 10g RMAN Backup & Recovery

Matthew Hart
Robert G. Freeman

New York   Chicago   San Francisco
Lisbon   London   Madrid   Mexico City   Milan
New Delhi   San Juan   Seoul   Singapore   Sydney   Toronto

Oracle Database 10g RMAN Backup & Recovery

234567890 DOC DOC 01987

ISBN-13: 978-0-07-226317-6
ISBN-10:   0-07-226317-2

Sponsoring Editor
Lisa McClain

Editorial Supervisor
Janet Walden

Project Editor
Sophia Ho

Acquisitions Coordinator
Alexander McDonald

Technical Editor
Matt Arrocha

Contributors
Keith Bingham
Bob Bryla
Aditya Gupta
Ashoke Mandal
Monica Penshorn
Cliff Sowa

Copy Editor
Bill McManus

Proofreader
Susie Elkind

Indexer
Karin Arrigoni

Production Supervisor
Jean Bodeaux

Composition
International Typesetting
and Composition

Illustration
International Typesetting
and Composition

Art Director, Cover
Jeff Weeks

Cover Designer
Pattie Lee

This book is dedicated to the hard-working men and women at Oracle Support Services.
—Matthew

This work is dedicated to the important people/creatures in my life: my wife Lisa, my five kids (Felicia, Sarah, Jacob, Jared, and Lizzie), and my animals Denali, Clifford, and Fonzie. Poor Fonzie went through a traumatic event during the writing of this book, for which I apologize...but at least now we won't be having any little Fonzies running around the house. There are so many others to thank for just being a part of my life that I know I will miss names, but Dave, Mark, Bill, Joel, Michael, and Kent all deserve recognition. Finally, thanks to my father for all he's been in my life, thanks to my Heavenly Father for all He's been in my life, and thanks to France and Italy, who have both made my wife the most interesting person around.
—Robert

About the Authors

Matthew Hart is the co-author of three books for Oracle Press, *Oracle9i for Windows 2000: Tips & Techniques*, *Oracle9i RMAN Backup & Recovery,* and most recently *Oracle 10g High Availability with RAC, Flashback, and DataGuard*. He has worked with high availability technologies in Oracle since version 7.3, and has worked with RMAN since its inception. He has spent considerable time perfecting backup and recovery strategies for Oracle customers. Matthew currently works and lives in Kansas City, Missouri. Matthew has also co-authored two children and an extensive domestic To-Do list.

Robert G. Freeman has been an Oracle DBA for so long he can't remember now when he actually entered SQL*Plus for the first time. In his spare time (what's that?) Robert flies airplanes and (when his knee allows) works out at the local ATA Karate Center (Master Barnum in Chicago is the best). Among the other books Robert has written are the best-selling titles *Oracle Database 10g New Features*, *Oracle9i RMAN Backup & Recovery,* and *Oracle9i New Features*. Robert also wrote the Oracle Press book *Portable DBA: Oracle*, which is a great book; go buy a copy and see for yourself!

Contents at a Glance

PART IV
RMAN in the Oracle Ecosystem

PART V
Appendixes

Contents

PART I
Getting Started with RMAN in Oracle Database 10*g*

PART II

Setup Principles and Practices

PART III
Using RMAN Effectively

PART IV
RMAN in the Oracle Ecosystem

PART V
Appendixes

Acknowledgments

o book is written by a single person, or even a pair of co-authors. For this second foray into RMAN, this was literally true. Robert and I reached out to a larger community to author the media management sections of this book, and a few great individuals rose to the challenge and surpassed our expectations. Cliff Sowa, one of the hardest-working men over at Oracle Support Services, pitched in (at late notice) with the Oracle Secure Backup chapter. Monica Penshorn, Aditya Gupta, and Ashoke Mandal, up at Medtronic in Minneapolis, came together to do the NetBackup chapter. Keith Bingham, Oracle Consulting, updated and delivered the EMC NetWorker chapter. Bob Bryla from Land's End wrote the Tivoli chapter for us. Without these contributors, the book would not have maintained the breadth that made *Oracle9i RMAN Backup & Recovery* such a comprehensive reference. I cannot thank you enough.

This is the second time Robert and I have worked on a book together, and I look forward to the third. Both Robert and I had huge personal transitions during the writing of this book, and it is no small feat to get it out the door and on the shelf. Thanks again, Robert.

Matt Arrocha at Oracle did our technical edit on this book again. Matt continues to be the real RMAN guru, and without his review I would have missed a few key features from the 10g update. It was my privilege to work with Matt closely for many years, and it was truly an enriching experience.

The staff at Oracle Press, as always, has done a spectacular job of getting this book to production. Lisa McClain organized the whole thing and got it moving. Alex McDonald and Sophia Ho were tasked with keeping us on deadline. Bill McManus worked his usual copy edit magic. It takes a village. Or sometimes just daily e-mail reminders.

I need to thank a few people who have continued to provide the kind of friendship and technical mentorship that someone like me needs to get by. That list has to include Scott Jesse, Tim Floyde, John Sobecki, Farouk Abushaban, and Werner de Gruyter.

As always, my good friend Martin Ingram continues to provide the kind of personal and professional support that keeps me pushing hard, every day. I also wanted to throw out a big thanks to all the folks in the Twin Cities Oracle Users Group, who have invited me twice up to their neck of the woods to talk about what I know. It's been a pleasure to be involved with such a vital grassroots organization.

This book, as with all projects that don't fit into my typical workday, could never have been completed without the continued support and determination of my wife. Every success for which I can boast came about because Beth believed in me and helped me create the time and space to excel. Thank you.

I need to thank my bug and my monster, for whom all this is done, and who patiently wait outside my office door for me to wrap up every day. They provide me the energy to stay focused, and the insight to not take any of it too seriously.

Thanks to you, the reader, for picking up this book and making it useful.

—Matthew Hart

I want to think my wife Lisa for putting up with me during the writing and editing process. I want to think Lisa McClain and Alexander McDonald for putting up with my terrible schedule, and Matthew as well. They really deserve a reward. Thanks to all the people at McGraw-Hill Professional, including Lisa McClain, Alex McDonald, Janet Walden, Sophia Ho, and Bill McManus.

—Robert Freeman

Introduction

Answering the Question ... and Asking a New One

In our *Oracle9i RMAN Backup & Recovery book*, we posed the following question in this same space: how can I balance availability with recoverability? We hoped to answer that question with a full coverage of Oracle's backup and recovery solution, and the number of copies sold tells us that many people liked the answer.

The subquestion, when looking to balance availability with disaster recovery, was stated thus: how can I keep my database up and available, free from performance-sucking monsters, but still make that database disaster-proof? Again, RMAN is the answer to this question, and you hold in your hot little hands the definitive guide to Recovery Manager.

Time marches on. Databases get bigger. Enterprises grow more complex. New paradigms take hold, and the business needs updates overnight, or at least it seems that way in the server room. The future looms, and overshadows a to-do list that grows longer each day, no matter how many items you scratch off. As the DBAs, we have moved past simple questions of availability, and have implemented multiple enterprise-wide solutions to keep our database up and disaster-proof. If our data is correct, most of us are already using RMAN.

But with the march of time comes new marching orders. RMAN is backing up and recovering our database, but the amount of data grows larger daily, and the tapes are not getting any faster. Meanwhile, massive disk storage arrays are getting bought at a dizzying rate, and the price is dropping faster than you can say Moore's law. No one is interested in slowing down backups, but as the vocabulary of availability has become entrenched in CIOs' minds, a new term is being brought to the forefront: mean time to recovery.

So a new question is posed: how can the mean time to recovery be minimized after the failure has occurred?

Well, if you haven't already guessed, our answer to this question is the same as in our last book: RMAN, RMAN, and RMAN. Oracle bundles tightly with every copy of its flagship database software Oracle Recovery Manager, or RMAN for short. As you probably already know, RMAN provides an interface for backing up and recovering your database. But this book is about RMAN in Oracle 10*g*; this book is for RMAN in grid computing.

RMAN still provides the extremely useful features for those of you who need to take their backup and recovery strategies to the next level. You can still

- recover a single block and avoid work stoppage on anything but a single table
- create a standby database for protecting your system from disaster-related outages
- back up directly to tape to ease the load on your disk storage system
- manage the backup and recovery work for a number of enterprise-wide databases

But RMAN in Oracle 10*g* has evolved along with the enterprise, to take advantage of new developments in database and storage technology. RMAN has evolved to focus on disk backups, and has evolved into a reliable partner during testing and development phases. It has been modified for heightened security concerns (insert SOX buzzword here) and for backup resource management (insert provisioning buzzword here). Most importantly, RMAN has maintained its focus on one critical business need: minimizing downtime after some type of failure has occurred.

Because of this evolution, this book extends a bit beyond just RMAN to discuss the new Flashback Technology offered by Oracle to help recover from user-induced failures—one of the harder bits for a media backup tool like RMAN to deal with.

A Book for the DBA and the Sys Admin

Perhaps the most frustrating part of formulating a solid, reliable backup strategy for an Oracle database is that it usually overlaps two different kinds of people: the database administrator and the system administrator. Formulating an RMAN strategy is no different. Its tight integration with the Oracle RDBMS means a system administrator must establish a working knowledge of an Oracle database. But, the reliance on external tape storage systems and the network topology makes it critical that the DBA be able to administer networked computer systems. This makes for an interesting separation of duties, and for headaches on each side.

Furthermore, business demands are fusing the role descriptions of the DBA and the Sys Admin. Or, more precisely, DBAs are finding their work increasingly expanding into Sys Admin work, and Sys Admins find themselves spending more time learning SQL commands.

This book addresses this overlap by offering how-to advice in the areas where the overlap is most acute: database backups.

RMAN: An Evolution into Excellence

RMAN was introduced in version 8.0.3, the first production release of Oracle8. Prior to this, the Oracle-provided interface for streaming backups directly to tape involved logical backups using the Export utility, or use of the Enterprise Backup Utility (EBU). Ah, EBU. May it rest it peace, and we promise this is the last time we will ever mention it. *Ever.*

As an initial release, RMAN had its pratfalls and quirks. But with every release since its rollout, new features have been added, bugs have been fixed, and the interface has been polished. The best way to visualize the progress is to think of the traditional poster showing the evolution of humans: on the left, we see a monkey, walking on all four. Then, moving to the right, we see an increasingly more upright version of a human, until we arrive at the left, where we see a fully upright, modern homo sapiens.

With the release of Oracle9*i*, RMAN reached a fully upright walking position. It has truly become a necessary component in any serious strategy for a highly available database system.

Now that RMAN has been through two 10*g* releases, it has moved beyond a simple upright position, and has picked up a tablet and learned to read. Belabored metaphor aside, RMAN has continued its evolution into a fully functional availability partner.

What This Book Covers

This handbook was written to utilize the latest features included in Oracle Database 10*g* Release 2 (version 10.2.0.1.0). It therefore takes advantage of the latest enhancements to the RMAN interface and explains the newest features available. If a particular topic is not available in Oracle 10*g* Release 1, we will try to point this out in the text. But all code examples and architectural explanations are based on the 10*g*R2 release of RMAN.

If you are still using Oracle9*i* or (heaven forbid) Oracle8*i*, we have another book for you: Oracle9*i RMAN Backup & Recovery*. The book you are currently reading makes no attempt to cover functionality as it existed in previous versions. Obviously, this book is comprehensive about how everything works in 10*g*, but we will not point out or make any reference to previous versions, except when talking about something wicked cool you only get in 10*g*.

Using This Book Effectively

Like all technical manuals worth their weight, this book is meant to be readable, cover to cover, as a way to familiarize yourself with RMAN and its role in any high availability or disaster recovery solution. The topics are approached in a format that allows each complex subject to build on previous chapters, slowly working forward from principles, to setup, to backups, and then beyond backups to advanced functionality and practices.

As such, Part I is dedicated to an introduction to backup and recovery principles in the Oracle RDBMS. It gives an important conceptual understanding of RMAN and how it does that mojo that it does. These two chapters lay the foundation for all future chapters, and we encourage you to read them carefully and understand the concepts being discussed. If you can understand the concepts and internal workings, then the rest of the book will be a breeze.

Part II is dedicated to setting up RMAN for initial usage. We cover all possible RMAN configuration options. Then, we discuss the integration with a media manager, the layer that allows you to write your backups directly to a tape device. While there are many products on the market, we will discuss four of the media management products: Oracle's own Secure Backup, VERITAS NetBackup, EMC NetWorker Module for Oracle, and IBM Tivoli Storage Manager.

In Part III, we provide the basics for RMAN usage, from the most basic backup operation to the most advanced recovery option. We discuss catalog maintenance and how to keep an eye on the catalog so that you can effectively manage the backups that are accumulating. Here is where we discuss using Oracle's redesigned Enterprise Manager product, as well as cover Flashback Technology for recovery from logical errors. Finally, there is a discussion on tuning RMAN backups and restores for optimal performance when it counts.

Part IV moves past backup and recovery, discussing how RMAN can assist you in tasks other than just simple backups. It runs through how to use the RMAN backups to make a cloned copy of your database, as well as how to use the backups to create a standby database for Oracle Data Guard. Then it discusses using RMAN in a Real Application Clusters (RAC) environment, with its special needs and requirements. Finally, this section ends with a series of RMAN case studies, which delve into common (and not so common) situations that require RMAN.

The appendixes in Part V include an RMAN syntax reference, for building a successful RMAN command, and an exploration of the RMAN catalog, both in v$views in the database and rc_* views in the Recovery Catalog. In addition, Appendix C goes into some detail about how to set up an RMAN test environment to put this book to work with minimal busywork.

RMAN Workshops

Not everyone reads a book cover to cover. We know this. Sometimes that's not the higher calling of a good technical book. A good book lives next to the computer, with pages dog-eared, sections highlighted, and little yellow Post-its hanging off the side.

This book is meant to be a reference guide in addition to a conceptual explanation. We've packed this thing with useful techniques and timesaving practices that you can implement now, even if you're a little spotty on the architecture. Sometimes you just need to know *how to do it*, right? Especially when it comes to backup and recovery. No one wants to get stuck in the middle of a weekend recovery binge, trying to figure out the exact syntax for a particular restore operation while the production database sits idly by, bleeding revenue at a spectacular rate.

So, to help with the highlighting and dog-earing of pages, we utilize RMAN Workshop sections, which readers of our Oracle9*i* book will recognize. Whenever we provide useful code for performing a specific operation, or a series of steps to complete a certain project, we put it in a gray RMAN Workshop box. When you see this box, you know the following pages will be filled with the actual steps you need to follow to get your job done fast. Think of RMAN Workshops as recipes, providing the ingredients and the mixing instructions for a quick and easy meal. And to make your life even easier, we've highlighted each RMAN Workshop, with its descriptive title and the page number, in the main Contents.

In addition to the RMAN Workshops, the final chapter of this book is a series of case studies that discuss actual backup and recovery scenarios, along with the best means of dealing with those scenarios. These scenarios are as simple as preserving backup metadata while re-creating the control file, or as complex as recovering a database through a **resetlogs** operation.

Again, we encourage you to read the book chapter for chapter. Nothing can replace a conceptual understanding of a product, especially when that product is protecting your most valuable asset: the database.

So, enjoy the book! RMAN is a challenging and rewarding product to dig into and utilize. It can save you time and energy, and help avoid health problems related to insomnia, outage stress, and paranoia. We haven't got a Surgeon General's label yet, but we're working on it.

PART
I

Getting Started
with RMAN in
Oracle Database 10g

CHAPTER
1

Oracle Database 10g
Backup and Recovery
Architecture Tour

elcome to *Oracle Database 10*g *RMAN Backup & Recovery*. If you purchased our previous book, *Oracle Database9*i *RMAN Backup & Recovery*, you have an idea of what to expect from this text. However, this book is more than just a simple revision. RMAN in Oracle Database 10*g* has so many new features that this book has a lot of new and revised content.

If you are already using RMAN and are concerned that the changes in Oracle Database 10*g* will adversely affect your backup and recovery strategies, don't worry. RMAN is fully backward compatible, so your existing backup and recovery strategies will not have to change when you move to Oracle Database 10*g*.

If you are just starting with RMAN, then welcome aboard! RMAN is a great choice for Oracle database backup and recovery. In this book, we give you all the information you need to use RMAN successfully. The book is designed to help you get started using RMAN as quickly as possible.

Before we get deep into RMAN, though, we thought you would like to take a tour of the base Oracle backup and recovery landscape, which actually has not changed a great deal in Oracle Database 10*g*. The real changes are in RMAN, though there are a few new wrinkles here and there in Oracle Database 10*g*. So, for some of you, the landscape may be familiar, in which case you can either ride along to refresh your memory or proceed straight to Chapter 2. If you are new to Oracle, this tour will really help you prepare for the onslaught of RMAN information you will be getting in subsequent chapters. So, jump on the bus, keep your feet and hands inside at all times, and we will be off.

In this tour of the Oracle database backup and recovery architecture, you will encounter the following:

- Backup and recovery essentials

- A few Oracle terms to know

- Oracle database physical architecture

- Oracle operational internals

- ARCHIVELOG vs. NOARCHIVELOG mode operations

- Oracle recovery modes

- Manual backup operations in Oracle

- Manual recovery operations in Oracle

As we proceed through this tour of Oracle, you will learn that it is important to understand how the Oracle product works so that you can properly apply the techniques that will be documented in this book to bring your wayward database back to life. You will also see that there is more to backing up and recovering a database than just entering a few commands and putting tapes in the tape drive.

The direct results of misapplying a technique, or not understanding a principle of the architecture, may be an extended outage or even loss of data. The old adage that you must walk before you can run certainly applies when it comes to backup and recovery. Finally, we are only going to cover basics and any additional information that you need to know with regard to RMAN and recovering your database. If you need more information on these subject areas, there are several good Oracle Press titles that can help you. You can find these titles at www.oraclepressbooks.com.

Backup and Recovery Essentials

Okay, getting on our way, our first stop is in the area of backup and recovery essentials. There are two different areas that need to be dealt with when crafting plans to execute in the event your database goes bottom up. The first architectural question is one of high availability, which is loosely coupled with the second question, which is one of backup and recovery. Let's look at these questions of high availability and backup and recovery in more detail.

High Availability

High availability (HA) implies an architecture that prevents the users from being aware of partial or total system (database, network, hardware, and so forth) failure. HA solutions can include such elements as mirrored drives, RAID architectures, database clustering, database failover schemes, and, of course, backup and recovery. HA adds additional costs to the overall database architectural solution, over and above the costs of the backup and recovery solution selected. RMAN is really not an HA solution, but it is part of an overall database solution that can include HA. Backup and recovery of your database is not superseded by HA solutions. Rather, how you will back up and recover your database is one of a collection of HA decisions you need to make.

If you are interested in looking at HA solutions, there are a number of them out there, including:

- Data Guard

- Real Application Clusters

- Oracle Replication

- RAID and mirrored drives

Various other vendors provide HA solutions as well. Because HA options are really a separate topic from RMAN, we do not cover them in this book. Oracle Press does offer a book that includes coverage on HA solutions: *Oracle Database 10g High Availability with RAC, Flashback, & Data Guard* (McGraw-Hill/Osborne, 2004) by Matthew Hart, one of the authors of this very text!

Backup and Recovery

As we continue our tour (anyone want to stop at the snack bar?), we move to backup and recovery, which is getting us close to the main topic of this book, RMAN. We will talk in detail throughout this chapter about the different kinds of backups that can be done in Oracle, but for now, let's talk about the primary types of backups: offline (cold) and online (hot).

Offline backups are done with the database down, which means that it is also unavailable to users. Online backups, on the other hand, are done with the database up and running, so users can continue with their business. RMAN supports both types of backups. In fact, as you will see in later chapters, some of the features of RMAN make it the preferable method for performing online database backups.

You shouldn't just "decide" that it's time to back up your database. This is particularly true in the case of production databases, where the users have certain levels of expectations for protection of their data. Before you decide when and how to back up your database, you should gather some of your users' requirements and consider your company's general backup policy. Only after you have gathered those requirements can you craft that backup plan. Let's look in some more detail at how you gather those requirements.

Backup and Recovery Strategy Requirements Gathering

In gathering user requirements, you really want to find out from them what their needs are. Users need to be asked a number of questions, and as the database administrator (DBA), you should take the lead in asking them. To collect backup and recovery requirements, you need to ask your customers a few questions, like the following:

- How much data loss can you afford in the event of a database failure?

- What is the maximum length of time you are able to allow for recovery of your database?

- How much are you willing to spend to ensure that your data is recoverable?

- Can the system be down during the backup?

Quickly, let's look at each of these questions in more detail.

How Much Data Loss Can You Afford?   This is probably the most important question of all. All backup and recovery plans have some risk of data loss associated with them, and as you move closer to a zero data loss solution, the costs of the backup and recovery plan can skyrocket. Just as was the case with HA, the organization needs to quantify the cost of data loss and, based on that cost, craft a cost-effective backup and recovery plan. It is critical that the customer understand how much data loss risk they are taking with the chosen backup and recovery plan. Of course, each database has an allowable amount of loss, too, and one database may be much more tolerant of data loss than another.

What Is the Maximum Length of Time You Are Able to Allow for Recovery?   Different technologies perform in different ways and vary widely in price. Generally, the faster you wish your recovery to go, the more expensive the technology ends up being. For example, recoveries directly from disk tend to be a bit more expensive than recoveries from tape, but also tend to be faster. It is important that the customer understand how long recovery of the database will take in the event of a complete outage.

How Much Can You Spend on Recovery?   There is a direct relationship between how much data loss you can tolerate, how long it will take to actually recover the database, and how much it will cost to provide a given level of protection. It is important, early on, to understand just how much the customer is willing to spend on architecture to support your proposed backup and recovery plan. Nothing is more embarrassing than proposing a massive architecture with a high dollar cost, and having the customer look at you and laugh at the projected expense.

Can the System Be Down During the Backup?   Another key piece of information to determine is what the state of the database needs to be during the backup. Can an outage be afforded to do backups, or do those backups need to be done online? The answer to this question impacts your total overall cost and your decisions in choosing a backup strategy.

Backup and Recovery: Crafting the Plan

Now that you have gathered your requirements, you can begin to craft your backup and recovery plan. You need to make a number of decisions, including:

- Based on the user (and business) requirements, do you need to do offline or online backups of the database?

- If you are going to use online backups, how often do you need to back up archived redo logs? How will you protect the archived redo logs from loss between backup sessions?

■ What are the company policies and standards with regard to recoverability?

■ How are you going to ensure that your system is recoverable in the event of a disaster?

Each of these questions is important. Disasters are important to plan for, and they do happen. Company policies may well supersede the needs of the users. Backup policies and standards are important to implement and enforce. Managing one database backup and recovery policy is easy. Managing many different databases with different methods of doing backup and recovery becomes cumbersome and dangerous.

Managing archived redo logs is important because they are critical to recovery, and you want to be able to support your users as much as you can. After all, the users are the reason you are there! To really be able to determine how to craft your backup strategy, you need to understand how Oracle works and how Oracle backup and recovery works; we will talk about that shortly. First, just to make sure we are all on the same page, let's discuss some basic Oracle terms.

A Few Oracle Terms to Know

It is always a bit hard to decide where to start when discussing the Oracle architecture because so many of the different components are interrelated. This makes it hard to talk about one without making reference to the other. So that we can have a common point of reference for some basic terms, in this section, we quickly define those terms. We will be using these terms throughout the rest of this book, so it is really important that you clearly understand them (we also define them in more depth as this chapter progresses). So, if you are a bit hazy on Oracle internal terms, please review the following until you know what they are without hesitation:

■ **Alert log** A text log file in which the database maintains error and status messages. The alert log can be a critical structure when trying to determine the nature of a database failure. Typically, the alert log is in the background dump destination directory, as defined by the database parameter BACKGROUND_DUMP_DEST, and is called alert<sid>.log.

■ **Archived redo logs** When the database is in ARCHIVELOG mode, archived redo logs are generated each time Oracle switches online redo logs by the LGWR process. Archived redo logs are used during database recovery. Copies of the archived redo logs can be written to as many as ten different directories, defined by the Oracle parameter LOG_ARCHIVE_DEST_n in the database parameter file. Also, Oracle Database 10*g* allows you to store archived redo logs in a new location called the flash recovery area, which we discuss in more detail in Chapter 3.

■ **Backup control file**   A backup of the control file generated as the result of using the **alter database backup controlfile to 'file_name'** command or the **alter database backup control file to trace** command.

■ **Block**   The most atomic unit of storage in Oracle. The default block size is determined by the parameter DB_BLOCK_SIZE in the database parameter file, and it is set permanently when a database is created. Oracle Database 10g allows tablespaces to be different block sizes than the default.

■ **Checkpoint**   A database event that causes the database to flush dirty (used) blocks from memory and write them to disk.

■ **Database**   Consists of the different components that make up an Oracle database (tablespaces, redo logs, and so forth). A database is much different than an instance. A database is where the data lives, and what you will be backing up and recovering with RMAN.

■ **Database consistency**   Implies that each object in the database is consistent to the same point in time.

■ **Database datafile**   A physical entity that is related to a tablespace. A database consists of at least one database datafile (which would be assigned to the SYSTEM tablespace), and most databases consist of many different database datafiles. Whereas a tablespace can have many different database datafiles associated with it, a given database datafile can have only one tablespace associated with it.

■ **Database parameter file**   Contains instance and database configuration information, and comes in two, mutually exclusive, flavors: init.ora, which is a text file, and spfile.ora, which allows for persistent settings of database parameters via the **alter system** command.

■ **Flash recovery area (FRA)**   An optionally configured area of disk that is used to store various recovery-related files. RMAN backup files, archived redo logs, online redo logs, and control files can be stored in this area. You can find more details on the FRA in Chapter 2 and find setup information in Chapter 3. You'll see examples of the use of the FRA in most chapters of this book.

■ **Granule**   A unit of Oracle contiguous memory. All System Global Area (SGA) memory allocations are rounded to the nearest granule units. The size of a granule is dependent on the overall expected size of the SGA, and it may be 4MB or 16MB. An SGA size of greater than 128MB tends to be the break point when Oracle uses the larger granule sizes. The number of granules allocated to the database is determined at database startup.

■ **Instance**   The collection of Oracle memory and processes. When the SGA (memory) is allocated and each of the required Oracle processes is up and running successfully, then the Oracle instance is considered started. Note that just because the Oracle instance is running, this does not mean that the database itself is open. An instance is associated with one, and only one, database at any given time.

■ **Online redo logs**   When redo is generated, it is physically stored in the online redo logs of the database. Oracle requires that at least two online redo logs be created for a database to operate. These online redo logs can have multiple mirrored copies for protection of the redo. This is known as *multiplexing* the redo log. As an online redo log fills with redo, Oracle switches to the next online redo log, which is known as a *log switch* operation.

Each online redo log file has a unique *log sequence number* associated with it that uniquely identifies it and, if it's archived, its associated archived redo log file. You can find the log sequence number of the online redo logs by querying the V$LOG view. The sequence number of a given archived redo log can be found in the V$ARCHIVED_LOG view.

Additionally, an online redo log (and an archived redo log) contains a range of database System Change Numbers (SCNs) that is unique to that redo log. During recovery, Oracle applies the undo in the archived/online redo logs in order of log sequence number.

■ **Processes**   The programs that do the actual work of the Oracle database. There are five required processes in Oracle Database 10*g,* and there are a number of others.

■ **Redo**   A record of all changes made to a given database. For almost any change in the database, an associated redo record is generated.

■ **Schema**   Owns the various logical objects in Oracle, such as tables and indexes, and is really synonymous with the user.

■ **SGA (System Global Area)**   An area of shared memory that is allocated by Oracle as it is started. Memory in the SGA can be shared by all Oracle processes.

■ **System Change Number (SCN)**   A counter that represents the current state of the database at a given point in time. Like the counter on your VCR, as time progresses, the SCN increases. Each SCN atomically represents a point in the life of the database. Thus, at 11 A.M., the database SCN might be 10ffx0 (4351 decimal), and at 12 P.M., it might be 11f0x0 (4592 decimal).

- **Tablespace** A physi-logical entity. It is a logical entity because it is the place that Oracle logical objects (such as tables and indexes) are stored. It is a physical entity because it is made up of one or more database datafiles. A database must contain at least one tablespace, the SYSTEM tablespace, but most databases consist of many different tablespaces.

- **Trace files** Generated by the database in a number of different situations, including process errors. Each database process also generates its own trace file. Trace files can be important when trying to resolve the nature of a database failure.

Controlling the Database Software

During various recovery operations, you need to control the state of the Oracle database and its associated instance. Let's quickly review how to start and stop Oracle databases.

To start the Oracle Database 10g database, you use the SQL*Plus Oracle utility. Log in as the user system using the SYSDBA login ID. At the SQL*Plus prompt, issue the **startup** command, as you can see in this example:

```
/usr/oracle>sqlplus / as sysdba
SQL*Plus: Release 10.2.0.1.0 - Production on Tue Aug 22 18:36:33 2006
Copyright (c) 1982, 2005, Oracle.  All rights reserved.
Enter password:
Connected to:
Oracle Database 10g Enterprise Edition Release 10.2.0.1.0 - Production
With the Partitioning, OLAP and Data Mining options
Connected to an idle instance.
SQL> startup
```

When you start an Oracle database with the **startup** command, the operation goes through three different phases:

- **Instance startup** The Oracle database instance is started.

- **Database mount** The Oracle database is mounted.

- **Database open** The Oracle database is opened for user activity.

NOTE
*You should be aware that the RMAN client, which we will discuss in later chapters, has the ability to shut down and start up the Oracle database on its own. You will not need to move from RMAN to SQL*Plus during a recovery operation in most cases.*

The **startup** command has several different variations (which is important to know for several different RMAN operations), some of which include the following:

- **startup**   Causes Oracle to go through each of the three startup phases, and open to the user community.

- **startup restrict**   Causes Oracle to go through each of the three startup phases, and open in restricted mode. Only those users with restricted privileges can access the database.

- **startup nomount**   Causes the startup process to stop after it has successfully started the database instance. You will often use this command to start the database instance prior to actually creating a database. This command is also handy to have if you need to re-create the control file. Note that in order to be able to use RMAN with a given database, you must be able to successfully start the instance with the **startup nomount** command.

- **startup mount**   Causes the startup process to stop after it has successfully started the database instance and then mounted it. This command is helpful if you need to recover the SYSTEM tablespace.

- **startup read only**   Causes your Oracle database (or standby database) to open in READ ONLY mode. Thus, DML operations are not supported, but you can query the database. This is handy if you are doing point-in-time recovery and you want to make sure you have recovered the database to the correct point in time before you commit to the new database incarnation with the **resetlogs** command.

- **startup force**   Causes the database to be shut down with a **shutdown abort** (discussed in the next list). This command can be followed by the mode you wish the database to be opened in again. Examples include

  - **startup force restrict**

  - **startup force mount**

  - **startup force nomount**

Of course, now that you know how to start up the database, you need to know how to shut it down. Again, from SQL*Plus, you can use the **shutdown** command, which comes in these flavors:

- **shutdown** (also **shutdown normal**)   Causes Oracle to wait for all user processes to disconnect from the database. Once this has occurred, the database will be completely shut down. Use of this option avoids instance recovery. After the **shutdown** command is executed, no new user processes are able to connect to the database.

- **shutdown immediate**   Kills all existing user sessions and rolls back all uncommitted transactions. Use of this option avoids instance recovery. After **shutdown immediate** is executed, no new user processes are able to connect to the database.

- **shutdown abort**   Basically, crashes the database. Use of this option requires instance (but not media) recovery. After **shutdown abort** is executed, no new user processes are able to connect to the database.

- **shutdown transactional**   Causes Oracle to wait for all user processes to commit their current transactions and then disconnects the user processes and shuts down the database. While it is waiting for these transactions to complete, no new user sessions are allowed to connect to the database.

As we proceed through this book, we use many of these commands, and it is important to understand what state the database and its associated instance are in when the command has completed.

Oracle Architecture

Our tour continues now as we begin looking at the physical components of Oracle. First, we take a look at the processes that make up an Oracle database. Then, we look at Oracle memory structures and the different logical, physical, and physi-logical structures that make up an Oracle database. Finally, we discuss the differences between an instance and an Oracle database.

The Oracle Processes

When the **startup nomount** command is issued, Oracle attempts to start an Oracle *instance.* An Oracle instance is started after several required operating system processes (programs) are started and the SGA memory area is allocated. In this section, we are going to take a look at the processes that get Oracle started. First, we look at the basic five Oracle processes required for any Oracle database to be functional. Next, we look at user and server processes. Finally, we look at other, optional Oracle processes that you might see from time to time.

NOTE
This is just a basic introduction to the Oracle processes. If you want more in-depth detail on them, please refer to the Oracle documentation.

The Five Required Oracle Processes

If an Oracle Database 10*g* instance has successfully started, there will be a minimum of five different processes started. Of course, on certain systems (such as Microsoft-based OSs), the five different processes are really just threads of a single Oracle process, but the basic idea is still the same. These required processes are as follows:

- **PMON**   Also known as the process monitor process (and one of what I call the "Jamaican processes").

- **SMON**   Also known as the system monitor process (and the other "Jamaican process").

- **DBWn**   Known as the database writer processes. An instance can be configured with up to nine of these processes in Oracle Database 10*g* (but generally no more than one is required). DBWn is responsible for writing information to the database datafiles from the database buffer cache structure in the SGA.

- **LGWR**   The log writer process is responsible for writing generated redo to the database online redo logs from the log buffer. LGWR is signaled to do these writes when a user session is committed, when the redo log buffer is nearly full, and at other times as required.

- **CKPT**   During a checkpoint operation, the CKPT process notifies DBWn of the checkpoint. The CKPT process also updates database datafile headers with current checkpoint information.

The User and Server Processes

When a user connects to the database, a user process is spawned (or a new thread is started on Windows NT) that connects to a separately spawned server process. These processes communicate with each other using various protocols, such as Bequeath or TCP/IP.

Other Optional Oracle Processes

A number of other Oracle processes may be launched as well when the Oracle instance is started (and in some cases, optional processes may actually be started much later on demand), depending on the configuration of the Oracle database parameter file. Most of these processes have little bearing on RMAN and database backup and recovery (unless the failure of one of the processes causes the database to crash, which is rare), so we won't spend much time on them. All of the optional processes are described in the Oracle documentation, online at otn.oracle.com, as well as in several Oracle Press books.

One set of optional processes that does have some bearing on RMAN and backup and recovery are the ARCHn processes. These processes (and, in reality, there may be one or many of them) are critical to the backup and recovery process if you are doing online backups. See the section titled "ARCHIVELOG Mode vs. NOARCHIVELOG Mode," later in the chapter, for more on the ARCHn process(es).

Oracle Memory and RMAN

In this section, we look at the memory areas that we need to be concerned with in relationship to RMAN. As with any process, RMAN does require memory for its own operations and as a part of its database interactions. First, we describe the Oracle SGA in more detail, and then we look at the Private Global Area (PGA).

The Oracle System Global Area

The principal memory structure that we are concerned with in terms of RMAN and backup and recovery is the System Global Area (SGA). The SGA consists of one large allocation of shared memory that can be broken down into several memory substructures:

- The database buffer cache
- The shared pool
- The redo log buffer
- The large pool
- The Java pool
- The Streams pool

Of particular interest to the RMAN user are the shared pool and the large pool. RMAN uses several Oracle PL/SQL packages as it goes through its paces (as you will read in Chapter 2). These packages are like any other Oracle PL/SQL packages in that they must be loaded into the shared pool. If the shared pool is not large enough, or if it becomes fragmented, it is possible that the RMAN packages will not be able to execute. Thus, it is important to allocate enough memory to the shared pool for RMAN operations.

The large pool is used by RMAN in specific cases and is not used by default, even if it is configured. RMAN allows you to duplex RMAN backups (or make concurrent copies of the same backup in different places) if either of the database parameters, BACKUP_TAPE_IO_SLAVES or DBWR_IO_SLAVES, is set to TRUE. In this case, Oracle can use the large pool memory rather than local memory (PGA). The use of the PGA is the default, so don't get confused and allocate tons of memory to the large pool when in fact it will never get used.

Defining Memory Allocations in the SGA

The individual sizes of the SGA components are allocated based on the settings of parameters in the database parameter file. These parameters include DB_CACHE_SIZE, DB_nK_CACHE_SIZE, LOG_BUFFER, SGA_MAX_SIZE, SGA_TARGET, SHARED_POOL_SIZE, LARGE_POOL_SIZE, and JAVA_POOL_SIZE (and there are several others). Each of these is defined in the Oracle documentation, so refer to it if you need more information on them. In Chapter 2, we will cover in detail the main parameters that have some bearing in terms of RMAN usage.

To recap quickly, we have discussed the makings of an Oracle instance in the last several pages. We have talked about the different Oracle processes and the different Oracle memory structures. When the processes and the memory all come together, an Oracle instance is formed. Now that we have an instance, we are ready for a database. In the next section, we discuss the various structures that make up an Oracle database.

The Oracle Database

Our tour now moves its attention to the Oracle database architecture itself. An Oracle database is made up of a number of different structures—some physical, some logical, and some physi-logical. In this section, we look at each of these types of structures and discuss each of the individual components of the Oracle database. We will conclude this section by looking at the flash recovery area (FRA) and Automatic Storage Management (ASM).

Oracle Physical Components

The Oracle database physical architecture includes the following components:

- Database datafiles
- Online redo logs
- Archived redo logs
- Database control files
- Flashback logs (optional)
- Oracle tablespaces

Each of these items is physically located on a storage device that is connected to your computer. These objects make up the physical existence of your Oracle database, and to recover your database, you may need to restore and recover one or more of these objects from a backup (except the flashback log). Let's look at each of these objects in a bit more detail.

Database Datafiles   The database datafiles are the data storage medium of the database and are related to tablespaces, as you will see shortly. When information is stored in the database, it ultimately gets stored in these physical files. Each database datafile contains a *datafile header* that contains information to help track the current state of that datafile. This datafile header is updated during checkpoint operations to reflect the current state of the datafile.

Database datafiles can have a number of different statuses assigned to them. The primary statuses we are interested in are ONLINE, which is the normal status, and OFFLINE, which is generally an abnormal status. A database datafile might take on the RECOVER status, as well, indicating that there is a problem with it and that recovery is required.

If the database is in ARCHIVELOG mode (more on this later), you can take a datafile offline, which may be required for certain recovery operations. If the database is in NOARCHIVELOG mode, then you can only take the database datafile offline by dropping it. Offline dropping of a datafile can have some nasty effects on your database (such as loss of data), so drop datafiles with care.

Online Redo Logs   If the Oracle SCN can be likened to the counter on your VCR, then the redo logs can be likened to the videotape (this analogy becomes harder and harder with DVDs somehow!). The online redo logs are responsible for recording every single atomic change that occurs in the database. Each Oracle database must have a minimum of two different online redo log groups, and most databases generally have many more than that, for performance and data preservation reasons.

Each online redo log group can have multiple members located on different disk drives for protection purposes. Oracle writes to the different members in parallel, making the write process more efficient. Oracle writes to one redo log group at a time, in round-robin fashion. When the group has been filled, the LGWR process closes those redo logs and then opens the next online redo log for processing.

Within redo logs are records called *change vectors.* Each change vector represents an atomic database change, in SCN order. During recovery (RMAN or manual), Oracle applies those change vectors to the database. This has the effect of applying all change records to the database in order, thus recovering it to the point in time of the failure (or another, earlier time if required). The LGWR process is responsible for writing the change vectors (cumulatively known as redo) to the online redo logs from the redo log buffer. We discuss this in more detail shortly in the "The Combined Picture" section of this chapter.

Archived Redo Logs   A *log switch* occurs when Oracle stops writing to one online redo log and begins to write to another. As the result of a log switch, if the database is in ARCHIVELOG mode and the ARCH process is running, a copy of the online redo log will be made. This copy of the online redo log is called an archived redo log.

Oracle can actually copy the archived redo log files to up to ten different destinations. During media recovery, the archived redo logs are applied to the database to recover it. We discuss this in more detail shortly, in "The Combined Picture."

Database Control Files   Each Oracle database has one or more database control files. The control file contains various database information, such as the current SCN, the state of the database datafiles, and the status of the database. Of interest to the RMAN DBA is the fact that the control file also stores critical information on various RMAN operations, such as the backup status of each database datafile. If you loose your control file, you will need to follow specific procedures to re-create the RMAN catalog within it.

Oracle Tablespaces   Our tour continues into a somewhat metaphysical part of Oracle. Tablespaces are the link between the physical world of Oracle, in the form of the database datafiles, and the logical world, in the form of the Oracle tablespace. Often, we refer to a tablespace as a physi-logical structure. Oracle stores objects within tablespaces, such as tables and indexes.

   A tablespace is physically made up of one or more Oracle database datafiles. Thus, the overall space allocation available in a tablespace is dependent on the overall allocated size of these database datafiles. A tablespace can be OFFLINE or ONLINE, and may also be in either READ WRITE or READ ONLY mode. If a tablespace is in READ ONLY mode, the contents of the tablespace will not change. Because the contents of a READ ONLY tablespace do not change, DBAs often only back up READ ONLY tablespace database datafiles once, immediately after they are made read only. Of course, if the tablespace is ever taken out of READ ONLY mode, you need to start backing up the tablespace again.

Flashback Logs   Oracle Database 10*g* introduces the capability to flash back the Oracle database to a point in time other than the current point in time. This capability is facilitated through the use of flashback logs. Flashback logs are stored in the FRA. Oracle is solely responsible for the management of flashback logs, so it will create, remove, and resize them as required. Also note that flashback logs are not archived by Oracle and are not needed for recovery.

The Flash Recovery Area

Oracle Database 10*g* introduces the concept of the FRA, which allows you to define a central area of disk space for recovery-related files such as RMAN backups and archived redo logs. The following structures can be stored in the FRA:

- Archived redo logs
- RMAN backup set pieces

■   RMAN datafile copies

■   Flashback logs

■   A copy of the database control file

■   One member of each redo log group

■   Control file autobackups and copies

We will discuss the FRA in much more detail in Chapters 2 and 3.

Oracle Automatic Storage Management

Oracle ASM is Oracle's answer to the need for an integrated system to manage database files. ASM supports a number of different file system types, from cooked disk drives, to raw disk drives, to NetFiler devices. The idea of ASM is to simplify the life of the DBA by making Oracle responsible for basic disk management operations such as load balancing and data protection. RMAN supports the ASM infrastructure in that you can place your database FRA on ASM disks, or you can back up directly to ASM disks.

While ASM has its place, we feel that it is mega-overkill for most Oracle installations. If you have a single, non-RAC server with two or three databases, you do not need ASM. In this book, we provide ASM coverage so that if you are using RMAN and ASM, you can back up and recover using ASM.

ARCHIVELOG Mode vs. NOARCHIVELOG Mode

An Oracle database can run in one of two modes. By default, the database is created in NOARCHIVELOG mode. This mode permits normal database operations, but does not provide the capability to perform point-in-time recovery operations or online backups. If you want to do online (or hot) backups, then run the database in ARCHIVELOG mode. In ARCHIVELOG mode, the database makes copies of all online redo logs via the ARCH process, to one or more archive log destination directories.

The use of ARCHIVELOG mode requires some configuration of the database beyond simply putting it in ARCHIVELOG mode. You must also configure the ARCH process and prepare the archived redo log destination directories. Note that once an Oracle database is in ARCHIVELOG mode, that database activity will be suspended once all available online redo logs have been used. The database will remain suspended until those online redo logs have been archived. Thus, incorrect configuration of the database when it is in ARCHIVELOG mode can eventually lead to the database suspending operations because it cannot archive the current online redo logs.

More coverage on the implications of ARCHIVELOG mode, how to implement it (and disable it), and configuration for ARCHIVELOG operations can be found in Chapter 3.

Oracle Logical Structures

There are several different logical structures within Oracle. These structures include tables, indexes, views, clusters, user-defined objects, and other objects within the database. Schemas own these objects, and if storage is required for the objects, that storage is allocated from a tablespace.

It is the ultimate goal of an Oracle backup and recovery strategy to be able to recover these logical structures to a given point in time. Also, it is important to recover the data in these different objects in such a way that the state of the data is consistent to a given point in time. Consider the impact, for example, if you were to recover a table as it looked at 10 A.M., but only recover its associated index as it looked at 9 A.M. The impact of such an inconsistent recovery could be awful. It is this idea of a consistent recovery that really drives Oracle's backup and recovery mechanism, and RMAN fits nicely into this backup and recovery architectural framework.

The Combined Picture

Now that we have introduced you to the various components of the Oracle database—and there are a number of them—let's quickly put together a couple of narratives that demonstrate how they all work together. First, we look at the overall database startup process, which is followed by a narrative of the basic operational use of the database.

Startup and Shutdown of the Database

Our DBA, Eliza, has just finished some work on the database, and it's time to restart it. She starts SQL*Plus and connects as sys using the sysdba account. At the SQL prompt, Eliza issues the **startup** command to open the database. The following shows an example of the results of this command:

```
SQL> startup
ORACLE instance started.
Total System Global Area    84700976 bytes
Fixed Size                    282416 bytes
Variable Size               71303168 bytes
Database Buffers            12582912 bytes
Redo Buffers                  532480 bytes
Database mounted.
Database opened.
```

Recall the different phases that occur after the **startup** command is issued: instance startup, database mount, and then database open. Let's look at each of these stages now in a bit more detail.

Instance Startup (startup nomount)

The first thing that occurs when starting the database is instance startup. It is here that Oracle parses the database parameter file, and makes sure that the instance is not already running by trying to acquire an instance lock. Then, the various database processes (as described in "The Oracle Processes," earlier in this chapter), such as DBWn and LGWR, are started. Also, Oracle allocates memory needed for the SGA. Once the instance has been started, Oracle reports to the user who has started it that the instance has been started back, and how much memory has been allocated to the SGA.

Had Eliza issued the command **startup nomount**, then Oracle would have stopped the database startup process after the instance was started. She might have started the instance in order to perform certain types of recovery, such as control file re-creation.

Mounting the Database (startup mount)

The next stage in the startup process is the mount stage. As Oracle passes through the mount stage, it opens the database control file. Having done that successfully, Oracle extracts the database datafile names from the control file in preparation for opening them. Note that Oracle does not actually check for the existence of the datafiles at this point, but only identifies their location from the control file. Having completed this step, Oracle reports back that it has mounted the database.

At this point, had Eliza issued the command **startup mount**, Oracle would have stopped opening the database and waited for further direction. When the Oracle instance is started and the database is mounted but not open, certain types of recovery operations may be performed, including renaming the location of database datafiles and recovery system tablespace datafiles.

Opening the Database

Eliza issued the **startup** command, however, so Oracle moves on and tries to open the database. During this stage, Oracle verifies the presence of the database datafiles and opens them. As it opens them, it checks the datafile headers and compares the SCN information contained in those headers with the SCN stored in the control files. Let's talk about these SCNs for a second.

SCNs are Oracle's method of tracking the state of the database. As changes occur in the database, they are associated with a given SCN. As these changes are flushed to the database datafiles (which occurs during a *checkpoint* operation), the headers of the datafiles are updated with the current SCN. The current SCN is also recorded in the database control file.

When Oracle tries to open a database, it checks the SCNs in each datafile and in the database control file. If the SCNs are the same and the bitmapped flags are set correctly, then the database is considered to be consistent, and the database is opened for use.

NOTE
Think of SCNs as being kind of like the counter on your VCR. As time goes on, the counter continues to increment, indicating a temporal point in time that the tape is currently at. So, if you want to watch a program on the tape, you can simply rewind (or fast forward) the tape to the counter number, and there is the beginning of the program. SCNs are the same way. When Oracle needs to recover a database, it "rewinds" to the SCN it needs to start with and then replays all of the transactions after that SCN until the database is recovered.

If the SCNs are different, then Oracle automatically performs *crash or instance recovery*, if possible. Crash or instance recovery occurs if the redo needed to generate a consistent image is in the online redo log files. If crash or instance recovery is not possible, because of a corrupted datafile or because the redo required to recover is not in the online redo logs, then Oracle requests that the DBA perform *media recovery*. Media recovery involves recovering one or more database datafiles from a backup taken of the database, and is a manual process, unlike instance recovery. Assisting in media recovery is where RMAN comes in, as you will see in later chapters. Once the database open process is completed successfully (with no recovery, crash recovery, or media recovery), then the database is open for business.

Shutting Down the Database

Of course, Eliza will probably want to shut down the database at some point in time. To do so, she could issue the **shutdown** command. This command closes the database, unmounts it, and then shuts down the instance in almost the reverse order as the startup process already discussed. There are several options to the **shutdown** command.

Note in particular that a **shutdown abort** of a database is basically like simulating a database crash. This command is used often, and it rarely causes problems. Oracle generally recommends that your database be shut down in a consistent manner, if at all possible.

If you must use the **shutdown abort** command to shut down the database (and in the real world, this does happen with frequency because of outage constraints), then you should reopen the database with the **startup** command (or even better, **startup restrict**).

Following this, do the final shutdown on the database using the **shutdown immediate** command before performing any offline backup operations. Note that even this method may result in delays shutting down the database because of the length of time it takes to roll back transactions during the shutdown process.

NOTE
*As long as your backup and recovery strategy is correct, it really doesn't matter whether the database is in a consistent state (as with a normal **shutdown**) or an inconsistent state (as with a **shutdown abort**) when an offline backup occurs. Oracle does recommend that you do cold backups with the database in a consistent state, and we recommend that, too (because the online redo logs will not be getting backed up by RMAN). Finally, note that online backups eliminate this issue completely!*

Using the Database and Internals

In this section, we are going to follow some users performing some different transactions in an Oracle database. First, we provide you with a graphical road map that puts together all the processes, memory structures, and other components of the database for you. Then, we follow a user as the user makes changes to the database. We then look at commits and how they operate. Finally, we look at database checkpoints and how they work.

Process and Database Relationships

We have discussed a number of different processes, memory structures, and other objects that make up the whole of the Oracle database. Figure 1-1 provides a graphic that might help you better understand the interrelationships between the different components in Oracle.

Changing Data in the Database

Now, assume the database is open. Let's say that Fred needs to add a new record to the DEPT table for the janitorial department. So, Fred might issue a SQL statement like this:

```
INSERT INTO DEPT VALUES (60, 'JANITOR','DALLAS');
```

The **insert** statements (as well as **update** and **delete** commands) are collectively known as Data Manipulation Language (DML). As a statement is executed, redo is generated and stored in the redo log buffer in the Oracle SGA. Note that redo is generated by this command, regardless of the presence of the **commit** command. The **delete** and **update** commands work generally the same way.

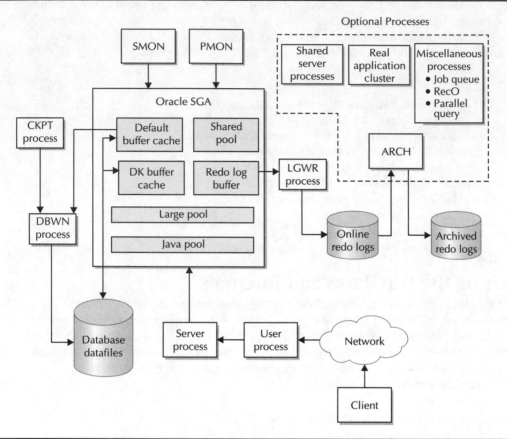

FIGURE 1-1. *A typical Oracle database*

One of the results of DML is that undo is generated and stored in *rollback segments.* **Undo** consists of instructions that allow Oracle to undo (or roll back) the statement being executed. Using undo, Oracle can roll back the database changes and provide *read consistent images* (also known as read consistency) to other users. Let's look a bit more at the **commit** command and read consistency.

Committing the Change

Having issued the **insert** command, Fred wants to ensure that this change is committed to the database, so he issues the **commit** command:

```
COMMIT;
```

The effects of issuing the **commit** command include the following:

■   The change becomes visible to all users who query the table at a point in time after the commit occurs. If Eliza queries the DEPT table after the commit occurs, then she will see department 60. However, if Eliza had already started a query before the commit, then this query would not see the changes to the table.

■   The change is recoverable if the database is in NOARCHIVELOG mode and crash or instance recovery is required.

■   The change is recoverable if the database is in ARCHIVELOG mode (assuming a valid backup and recovery strategy) and media recovery is required and all archived and online redo logs are available.

The **commit** command causes the Oracle LGWR process to flush the online redo log buffer to the online redo logs. Uncommitted redo is flushed to the online redo logs regardless of a commit (in fact, uncommitted changes can be written to the datafiles, too). When a commit is issued, Oracle writes a *commit vector* to the redo log buffer, and the buffer is flushed to disk before the commit returns. It is this commit vector, and the fact that the commit issued by Fred's session will not return until his redo has been flushed to the online redo logs successfully, that will ensure that Fred's changes will be recoverable.

The commit Command and Read Consistency   Did you notice that Eliza was not able to see Fred's change until he issued the **commit** command? This is known as *read consistency*. Another example of read consistency would be a case where Eliza started a report before Fred committed his change. Assume that Fred committed the change during Eliza's report. In this case, it would be inconsistent for department 60 to show up in Eliza's report, since it did not exist at the time that her report started. As Eliza's report continues to run, Oracle checks the start SCN of the report query against the SCNs of the blocks being read in Oracle to produce the report output. If the time of the report is earlier than the current SCN on the data block, then Oracle goes to the rollback segments and finds undo for that block that will allow Oracle to construct an image consistent with the time that the report started.

As Fred continues other work on the database, the LGWR process writes to the online redo logs on a regular basis. At some point in time, an online redo log will fill up, and LGWR will close that log file, open the next log file, and begin writing to it. During this transition period, LGWR also signals the ARCH process to begin copying the log file that it just finished using to the archive log backup directories.

Checkpoints

Now, you might be wondering, when does this data actually get written out to the database datafiles? Recall that a checkpoint is an event in which Oracle (through DBWR) writes data out to the datafiles. There are several different kinds of checkpoints. Some of the events that result in a checkpoint are the following:

- A redo log switch

- Normal database shutdowns

- When a tablespace is taken in or out of online backup mode (see "Oracle Physical Backup and Recovery" later in this chapter)

Note that ongoing incremental checkpoints occur throughout the lifetime of the database, providing a method for Oracle to decrease the overall time required when performing crash recovery. As the database operates, Oracle is constantly writing out streams of data to the database datafiles. These writes occur in such a way as to not impede performance of the database. Oracle provides certain database parameters to assist in determining how frequently Oracle must process incremental checkpoints.

Oracle Backup and Recovery Primer

Before you use RMAN, you should understand some general backup and recovery concepts in Oracle. Backups in Oracle come in two general categories, logical and physical. In the following sections, we quickly look at logical backup and recovery and then give Oracle physical backup and recovery a full treatment.

Logical Backup and Recovery

Oracle Database 10*g* uses the Oracle Data Pump architecture to support logical backup and recovery. These utilities include the Data Pump Export program (**expdp**) and the Data Pump Import program (**impdp**). With logical backups, point-in-time recovery is not possible. RMAN does not do logical backup and recovery, so this topic is beyond the scope of this book.

Oracle Physical Backup and Recovery

Physical backups are what RMAN is all about. Before we really delve into RMAN in the remaining chapters of this book, let's first look at what is required to manually do physical backups and recoveries of an Oracle database. While RMAN removes you from much of the work involved in backup and recovery, some of the principles remain the same. Understanding the basics of manual backup and recovery will help you understand what is going on with RMAN and will help us contrast the benefits of RMAN versus previous methods of backing up Oracle.

We have already discussed ARCHIVELOG mode and NOARCHIVELOG mode in Oracle. In either mode, Oracle can do an offline backup. Further, if the database is in ARCHIVELOG mode, then Oracle can do offline or online backups. We will cover the specifics of these operations with RMAN in later chapters of this book.

Of course, if you back up a database, it would be nice to be able to recover it. Following the sections on online and offline backups, we will discuss the different Oracle recovery options available. Finally, in these sections, we take a very quick, cursory look at Oracle manual backup and recovery.

NOARCHIVELOG Mode Physical Backups

We have already discussed NOARCHIVELOG mode in the Oracle database. This mode of database operations supports backups of the database only when the database is shut down. Also, only full recovery of the database up to the point of the backup is possible in NOARCHIVELOG mode. To perform a manual backup of a database in NOARCHIVELOG mode, follow these steps (note that these steps are different if you are using RMAN, which we will cover in later chapters):

1. Shut down the database completely.

2. Back up all database datafiles, the control files, and the online redo logs.

3. Restart the database.

ARCHIVELOG Mode Physical Backups

If you are running your database in ARCHIVELOG mode, you can continue to perform full backups of your database with the database either running or shut down. Even if you perform the backup with the database shut down, you will want to use a slightly different cold backup procedure:

1. Shut down the database completely.

2. Back up all database datafiles.

3. Restart the database.

4. Force an online redo log switch with the **alter system switch logfile** command. Once the online redo logs have been archived, back up all archived redo logs.

5. Create a backup of the control file using the **alter database backup control file to trace** and **alter database backup controlfile to 'file_name'** commands.

Of course, with your database in ARCHIVELOG mode, you may well want to do online, or hot, backups of your database. With the database in ARCHIVELOG mode, Oracle allows you to back up each individual tablespace and its datafiles while the database is up and running. The nice thing about this is that you can back up selective parts of your database at different times. To do an online backup of your tablespaces, follow this procedure:

1. Use the **alter tablespace begin backup** command to put the tablespaces and datafiles that you wish to back up in online backup mode. If you want to back up the entire database, you can use the **alter database begin backup** command to put all the database tablespaces in hot backup mode.

2. Back up the datafiles associated with the tablespace you have just put in hot backup mode. (You can opt to just back up specific datafiles.)

3. Take the tablespaces out of hot backup mode by issuing the **alter tablespace end backup** command for each tablespace you put in online backup mode in Step 1. If you want to take all tablespaces out of hot backup mode, use the **alter database end backup** command.

4. Force an online redo log switch with the **alter system switch logfile** command.

5. Once the log switch has completed and the current online redo log has been archived, back up all the archived redo logs.

Note the log switch and backup of archived redo logs in Step 5. This is required, because all redo generated during the backup must be available to apply should a recovery be required. While Oracle continues to physically update the datafiles during the online backup (except for the datafile headers), there is a possibility of block splitting during backup operations, which will make the backed up datafile inconsistent. Further, since a database datafile might be written after it has been backed up but before the end of the overall backup process, it is important to have the redo generated during the backup to apply during recovery because each datafile on the backup might well be current as of a different SCN, and thus the datafile backup images will be inconsistent.

Redo generation changes when you issue the **alter tablespace begin backup** command or **alter database begin backup** command. Typically, Oracle only stores change vectors as redo records. These are small records that just define the change that has taken place. When a datafile is in online backup mode, Oracle will record the entire block that is being changed rather than just the change vectors. This means total redo generation during online backups can increase significantly. This can impact disk space requirements and CPU overhead during the hot backup process. RMAN enables you to perform hot backups without having to put a tablespace in hot backup mode, thus eliminating the additional I/O you would otherwise experience. Things return to normal when you end the online backup status of the datafiles.

Note that in both backups in ARCHIVELOG mode (online and offline), we do not back up the online redo logs, and instead back up the archived redo logs of the database. In addition, we do not back up the control file, but rather create backup control files. We do this because we never want to run the risk of overwriting the online redo logs or control files during a recovery.

You might wonder why we don't want to recover the online redo logs. During a recovery in ARCHIVELOG mode, the most current redo is likely to be available in the online redo logs, and thus the current online redo log will be required for full point-in-time recovery. Because of this, we do not overwrite the online redo logs during a recovery of a database that is in ARCHIVELOG mode. If the online redo logs are lost as a result of the loss of the database (and hopefully this will not be the case), then you will have to do point-in-time recovery with all available archived redo logs.

For much the same reason that we don't back up the online redo logs, we don't back up the control files. Because the current control file contains the latest online and archived redo log information, we do not want to overwrite that information with earlier information on these objects. In case we lose all of our control files, we will use a backup control file to recover the database.

Finally, consider performing supplemental backups of archived redo log files and other means of protecting the archived redo logs from loss. Loss of an archived redo log directly impacts your ability to recover your database to the point of failure. If you lose an archived redo log and that log sequence number is no longer part of the online redo log groups, then you will not be able to recover your database beyond the archived redo log sequence prior to the sequence number of the lost archived redo log.

NOARCHIVELOG Mode Recoveries

If you need to recover a backup taken in NOARCHIVELOG mode, doing so is as simple as recovering all the database datafiles, the control files, and the online redo logs and starting the database. Of course, a total recovery may require such things as recovering the Oracle RDBMS software, the parameter file, and other required Oracle items, which we will discuss in the last section of this chapter.

Note that a recovery in NOARCHIVELOG mode is only possible to the point in time that you took your last backup. If you are recovering a database backed up in NOARCHIVELOG mode, you can only recover the database to the point of the backup. No database changes after the point of the backup can be recovered if your database is in NOARCHIVELOG mode.

ARCHIVELOG Mode Recoveries

A database that is in ARCHIVELOG mode can be backed up using online or offline backups. The fortunate thing about ARCHIVELOG mode, as opposed to NOARCHIVELOG mode, is that you can recover the database to the point of the failure that occurred. In addition, you can choose to recover the database to a specific point in time, or to a specific point in time based on the change number.

ARCHIVELOG mode recoveries also allow you to do specific recoveries on datafiles, tablespaces, or the entire database. In addition, you can do point-in-time recovery or recovery to a specific SCN. Let's quickly look at each of these options.

More detail on each of these options is available in Oracle Press's *Oracle Backup and Recovery 101* (McGraw-Hill/Osborne, 2002).

In this section, we briefly cover full database recoveries in ARCHIVELOG mode. We then look at tablespace and datafile recoveries, followed by point-in-time recoveries.

ARCHIVELOG Mode Full Recovery You can recover a database backup in ARCHIVELOG mode up to the point of failure, assuming that the failure of the database did not compromise at least one member of each of your current online redo log groups and any archived redo logs that were not backed up. If you have lost your archived redo logs or online redo logs, then you will need to perform some form of point-in-time recovery, as discussed later in this section. Also, if you have lost all copies of your current control file, you will need to recover it and perform incomplete recovery.

To perform full database recovery from a backup of a database in ARCHIVELOG mode, follow this procedure:

1. Restore all the database datafiles from your backup.

2. Restore all backed up archived redo logs.

3. Mount the database (**startup mount**).

4. Recover the database (**recover database**).

5. Oracle prompts you to apply redo from the archived redo logs. Simply enter **AUTO** at the prompt and Oracle will automatically apply all redo logs.

6. Once all redo logs have been applied, open the recovered database (**alter database open**).

ARCHIVELOG Tablespace and Datafile Recovery Tablespace and datafile recovery can be performed with the database mounted or open. To perform a recovery of a tablespace in Oracle with the database open, follow these steps:

1. Take the tablespace offline (**alter tablespace offline**).

2. Restore all datafiles associated with the tablespace to be recovered.

3. Recover the tablespace (**recover tablespace**) online.

4. Once recovery has completed, bring the tablespace online (**alter tablespace online**).

Just as you can recover a tablespace, you can also recover specific datafiles. This has the benefit of leaving the tablespace online. Only data that resides in the offline datafiles will be unavailable during the recovery process. The rest of the database will remain available during the recovery. Here is a basic outline of a datafile recovery:

1. Take the datafile offline (**alter database datafile 'file_name' offline**).

2. Restore all datafiles to be recovered.

3. Recover the tablespace (**recover datafile**) online.

4. Once recovery has completed, bring the datafile online (**alter database datafile 'file_name' online**).

ARCHIVELOG Point-In-Time Recoveries   Another benefit of ARCHIVELOG mode is the capability to recover a database to a given point in time rather than to the point of failure. This capability is used often when creating a clone database (perhaps for testing or reporting purposes) or in the event of major application or user error. You can recover a database to either a specific point in time or a specific database SCN.

If you want to recover a tablespace to a point in time, you need to recover the entire database to the same point in time (unless you perform tablespace point-in-time recovery, which is a different topic). For example, assume that you have an accounting database, that most of your data is in the ACCT tablespace, and that you wish to recover the database back in time two days. You cannot just restore the ACCT tablespace and recover it to a point in time two days ago, because the remaining tablespaces (SYSTEM, TEMP, and RBS, for example) will still be consistent to the current point in time, and the database will fail to open because it will be inconsistent.

To recover a database to a point in time, follow these steps:

1. Recover all database datafiles from a backup that ended before the point in time that you want to recover the database to.

2. Recover the database to the point in time that you wish it to be recovered to. Use the command **recover database until time '01-01-2006 21:00:00'** and apply the redo logs as required.

3. Once the recovery is complete, open the database.

You can also choose to recover the database using an SCN number:

1. Recover all database datafiles from a backup that ended before the point in time that you want to recover the database to.

2. Recover the database to the SCN that you wish it to be recovered to. Use the command **recover database until change '221122'** and apply the redo logs as required.

3. Once the recovery is complete, open the database.

Further, you can apply changes to the database and manually cancel the process after a specific archived redo log has been applied:

1. Recover all database datafiles from a backup that ended before the point in time that you want to recover the database to.

2. Recover the database to the point in time that you wish it to be recovered to. Use the command **recover database until cancel** and apply the redo logs as required. When you have applied the last archived redo log, simply issue the **cancel** command to finish applying redo.

3. Once the recovery is complete, open the database.

Keep in mind the concept of database consistency when doing point-in-time recovery (or any recovery, for that matter). If you are going to recover a database to a given point in time, you must do so with a backup that finished before the point in time that you wish to recover to. Also, you must have all the archived redo logs (and possibly the remaining online redo logs) available to complete recovery.

A Word About Flashback Database   Another recovery method available to you is the use of Oracle's flashback features. We will cover Oracle's flashback features in more depth in Chapter 13, but know that with the various flashback functionality, you can significantly reduce the overall time it takes to recover your database from user- and application-level errors. RMAN supports some of the Oracle Database 10*g* flashback features, so it is most appropriate to cover those in this book.

Backing Up Other Oracle Components

We have quickly covered the essentials of backup and recovery for Oracle. One last issue that remains to be covered are the things that need to be backed up. These are items that generally are backed up with less frequency because they change rarely. These items include

■ The Oracle RDBMS software (Oracle Home and the Oracle Inventory).

■ Network parameter files (names.ora, sqlnet.ora, and tnsnames.ora).

■ Database parameter files (init.ora, INI files, and so forth). Note that RMAN does allow you to back up the database parameter file (only if it's a SPFILE) along with the control file!

■ The system oratab file and other system Oracle-related files (for example, all rc startup scripts for Oracle).

It is important that these items be backed up on a regular basis as a part of your backup and recovery process. You need to plan to back up these items regardless of whether you do manual backups or RMAN backups, because RMAN does not back up these items either.

As you can see, the process of backup and recovery of an Oracle database can involve a number of steps. Since DBAs want to make sure they do backups correctly every time, they generally write a number of scripts for this purpose. There are a few problems with this. First of all, scripts can break. When the script breaks, who is going to support it, particularly when the DBA who wrote it moves to a new position somewhere in the inaccessible tundra in northern Alaska? Second, either you have to write the script to keep track of when you add or remove datafiles, or you have to manually add or remove datafiles from the script as required.

With RMAN, you get a backup and recovery product that is included with the base database product for free, and that reduces the complexity of the backup and recovery process. Also, you get the benefit of Oracle support when you run into a problem. Finally, with RMAN, you get additional features that no other backup and recovery process can match. We will look at those in coming chapters.

RMAN solves all of these problems and adds additional features that make its use even more beneficial for the DBA. In this book, we will look at these features, and how they can help make your life easier and make your database backups more reliable.

Summary

We didn't discuss RMAN much in this chapter, but we laid some important groundwork for future discussions of RMAN that you will find in later chapters. As promised, we covered some essential backup and recovery concepts, such as high availability and backup and recovery planning, that are central to the purpose of RMAN. We then defined several Oracle terms that you need to be familiar with later in this text. We then reviewed the Oracle database architecture and internal operations. It cannot be stressed enough how important it is to have an understanding of how Oracle works inside when it comes time to actually recover your database in an emergency situation. Finally, we discussed manual backup and recovery operations in Oracle. Contrast these to the same RMAN operations that you will find in later chapters, and you will find that RMAN is ultimately an easy solution to backup and recovery of your Oracle database.

CHAPTER
2

Introduction to the
RMAN Architecture

his chapter will take you through each of the components in the RMAN architecture one by one, explaining the role each plays in a successful backup or recovery of the Oracle database. Most of this discussion assumes that you have a good understanding of the Oracle RDBMS architecture. If you are not familiar at a basic level with the different components of an Oracle database, you might want to read the brief introduction in Chapter 1, or pick up a beginner's guide to database administration, before continuing. After we discuss the different components for backup and recovery, we walk through a simple backup procedure to disk and talk about each component in action.

Server-Managed Recovery

In the previous chapter, you learned the principles and practices of backup and recovery in the old world. It involved creating and running scripts to capture the filenames, associate them with tablespaces, get the tablespaces into backup mode, get an OS utility to perform the copy, and then stop backup mode.

But this book is really about using Recovery Manager, or RMAN for short. Recovery Manager implements a type of *server-managed recovery*, or SMR. SMR refers to the ability of the database to perform the operations required to keep itself backed up successfully. It does so by relying on built-in code in the Oracle RDBMS kernel. Who knows more about the schematics of the database than the database itself?

The power of SMR comes from what details it can eliminate on your behalf. As the degree of enterprise complexity increases, and the number of databases that a single DBA is responsible for increases, the ability to personally troubleshoot dozens or even hundreds of individual scripts begins to become too burdensome to be realistic. In other words, as the move to "grid computing" becomes more mainstreamed, the days of personally eyeballing all the little details of each database backup become a thing of the past. Instead, many of the nitpicky details of backup management get handled by the database itself, allowing us to take a step back from the day-to-day upkeep and concentrate on more important things. Granted, the utilization of RMAN introduces certain complexities that overshadow the complete level of ease that might be promised by SMR—why else would you be reading this book? But the blood, sweat, and tears you pour into RMAN will give you huge payoffs. You'll see.

The RMAN Utility

RMAN is the specific implementation of SMR provided by Oracle. RMAN is a stand-alone application that makes a client connection to the Oracle database to access internal backup and recovery packages. It is, at its very core, nothing more than a command interpreter that takes simplified commands you type and turns those commands into remote procedure calls (RPCs) that are executed at the database.

We point this out primarily to make one thing very clear: RMAN does very little work. Sure, the coordination of events is important, but the real work of actually backing up and recovering a database is performed by processes at the target database itself. The *target database* refers to the database that is being backed up. The Oracle database has internal packages that actually take the PL/SQL blocks passed from RMAN and turn them into system calls to read from, and write to, the disk subsystem of your database server.

The RMAN utility is installed as part of the Database Utilities suite of command-line utilities. This suite includes import, export, t*loader, and dbverify. During a typical Oracle installation, RMAN will be installed. It is included with Enterprise and Standard Edition, although there are restrictions if you only have a license for Standard Edition: without Enterprise Edition, RMAN can only allocate a single channel for backups. If you are performing a client installation, it will be installed if you choose the Administrator option instead of the Runtime client option.

The RMAN utility is made up of two pieces: the executable file and the recover.bsq file. The recover.bsq file is essentially the library file, from which the executable file extracts code for creating PL/SQL calls to the target. The recover.bsq file is the brains of the whole operation. These two files are invariably linked, and logically make up the RMAN client utility. It is worth pointing out that the recover.bsq file and the executable file must be the same version or nothing will work.

The RMAN utility serves a distinct, orderly, and predictable purpose: it interprets commands you provide into PL/SQL calls that are remotely executed at the target database. The command language is unique to RMAN, and using it takes a little practice. It is essentially a stripped-down list of all the things you need to do to back up, restore, or recover databases, or manipulate those backups in some way. These commands are interpreted by the executable translator, then matched to PL/SQL blocks in the recover.bsq file. RMAN then passes these RPCs to the database to gather information based on what you have requested. If your command requires an I/O operation (in other words, a backup command or a restore command), then when this information is returned, RMAN prepares another block of procedures and passes it back to the target database. These blocks are responsible for engaging the system calls to the OS for specific read or write operations.

RMAN and Database Privileges

RMAN needs to access packages at the target database that exist in the SYS schema. In addition, RMAN requires the privileges necessary to start up and shut down the target database. Therefore, RMAN always connects to the target database as a sysdba user. Don't worry, you do not need to specify this as you would from SQL*Plus; because RMAN requires it for every target database connection, it is assumed. Therefore, when you connect to the target, RMAN automatically supplies the "as sysdba" to the connection:

```
RMAN> connect target sys/password
connected to target database: PROD (DBID=4159396170)
```

If you try to connect as someone who does not have sysdba privileges, RMAN will give you an error:

```
RMAN> connect target /
RMAN-00571: ===========================================================
RMAN-00569: =============== ERROR MESSAGE STACK FOLLOWS =============
RMAN-00571: ===========================================================
ORA-01031: insufficient privileges
```

This is a common error during the setup and configuration phase of RMAN. It is encountered when you are not logged in to your server as a member of the dba group. This OS group controls the authentication of sysdba privileges to all Oracle databases on the server. (The name dba is the default and is not required. Some OS installs use a different name, and you are by no means obligated to use dba.) Typically, most Unix systems have a user named oracle that is a member of the group dba. This is the user that installs the Oracle software to begin with, and if you are logged in as oracle, it doesn't matter who you connect as within RMAN—you will always be connected as a sysdba user, with access to the SYS schema and the ability to start up and shut down the database. On Windows platforms, Oracle creates a local group called ORA_DBA and adds the installing user to the group.

If you are logged in as a user who does not have dba group membership, and you will need to use RMAN, then you must create and use a password file for your target database. If you will be connecting RMAN from a client system across the network, you need to create and use a password file. The configuration steps for this can be found in Chapter 3.

The Network Topology
of RMAN Backups

The client/server architecture of RMAN inevitably leads to hours of confusion. The reasons have to do with how the human mind stores spatial information; if you're good at spatial puzzles, RMAN will seem simple. If those tests in grade school were always baffling, read carefully.

This confusion is based entirely on where RMAN is being executed, versus where the backup work is actually being done. RMAN is a client application that attaches to the target database via an Oracle Net connection. If you are running the RMAN executable in the same ORACLE_HOME as your target database, then this Oracle Net connection can be a bequeath, or local, connection and won't require you to provide an Oracle Net alias—so long as you have the appropriate ORACLE_SID variable set in your environment. Otherwise, you will need to configure your tnsnames.ora file with an entry for your target database, and you will need to do this from the location where you will be running RMAN. Figure 2-1 provides an illustration of the network topology of different RMAN locations.

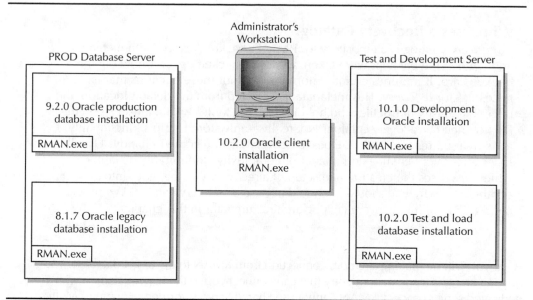

Administrator's
Workstation

PROD Database Server

9.2.0 Oracle production
database installation

RMAN.exe

8.1.7 Oracle legacy
database installation

RMAN.exe

10.2.0 Oracle client
installation
RMAN.exe

Test and Development Server

10.1.0 Development
Oracle installation

RMAN.exe

10.2.0 Test and load
database installation

RMAN.exe

FIGURE 2-1.   *Five different locations (and versions) for the RMAN executable*

TIP
*It is preferable to run RMAN from the target
database's ORACLE_HOME, if you can. This is
the simplest, most straightforward way to avoid
compatibility headaches in a hybrid environment
where you are responsible for backups that span
multiple Oracle databases and versions. This is how
Oracle Enterprise Manager handles the situation,
and we recommend it where it is feasible.*

Running RMAN Remotely

If you are responsible for many databases spread over the enterprise, it makes sense
to consolidate your application at a single client system, where you can better
manage your tnsnames.ora entries. All your RMAN scripts can be consolidated, and
you have no confusion later on where RMAN is running. You know exactly where
it is running: on your laptop, your desktop, or your Linux workstation. This client/
server model makes sense, as well, if you will be using a recovery catalog in your
RMAN configuration, as you will be making more than one Oracle Net connection
each time you operate RMAN. On the other hand, running RMAN from a different
system (or even a different ORACLE_HOME) than the target database means you
will be required to set up a password file, leading to more configuration and
management at each of your target databases.

> ### Who Uses a Recovery Catalog?
> A recovery catalog is a repository for RMAN's backup history, with metadata about when the backups were taken, what was backed up, and how big the backups are. It includes crucial information about these backups that is necessary for recovery. This metadata is extracted from the default location, the target database control file, and held in database tables within a user's schema. Do you need a recovery catalog? Not really—only stored scripts functionality actually requires the catalog. Does a recovery catalog come in handy? Usually. Does a recovery catalog add a layer of complexity? Indubitably. Chapter 3, which discusses the creation and setup of a recovery catalog, goes into greater depth about why you should or should not use a recovery catalog. We provide a discussion of the recovery catalog architecture later in this chapter.

If you will be making a remote connection from RMAN to the target database, you need to create a tnsnames.ora entry that can connect you to the target database with a dedicated server process. RMAN cannot use Shared Servers (formerly known as Multi-Threaded Server, or MTS) to make a database connection. So if you use Shared Servers, which is the default setup on all new installations, then you need to create a separate Oracle Net alias that uses a dedicated server process. The difference between the two can be seen in the following sample tnsnames.ora file. Note that the first alias entry is for dedicated server processes, and the second uses the Shared Server architecture.

```
PROD_RMAN =
  (DESCRIPTION =
    (ADDRESS_LIST =
      (ADDRESS = (PROTOCOL = TCP)(HOST = cervantes)(PORT = 1521))
    )
    (CONNECT_DATA =
      (SERVER = DEDICATED)
      (SERVICE_NAME = prod)
    )
  )
PROD =
  (DESCRIPTION =
    (ADDRESS_LIST =
      (ADDRESS = (PROTOCOL = TCP)(HOST = cervantes)(PORT = 1521))
    )
    (CONNECT_DATA =
      (SERVER = SHARED)
      (SERVICE_NAME = prod)
    )
  )
```

Running RMAN Locally from the Target Database's ORACLE_HOME

In *Oracle9i RMAN Backup & Recovery*, we insisted that running RMAN locally from each target database's own ORACLE_HOME was primarily for people with simple operations, or no recovery catalog.

We would like to retract that statement completely.

Running RMAN locally from each target database is really the *only* way to manage a large enterprise with hundreds (or thousands) of database targets. Because of RMAN's legendary compatibility headaches, keeping the rman.exe bundled tightly to the target database will save you time in the long run. There are drawbacks to deploying your RMAN backups in this fashion, but with a few more years of deployments under our belt, we feel that it is the best way to go.

Running RMAN locally means you can always make a bequeath connection to the database, requiring no password file setup and no tnsnames.ora configuration. Bear in mind that the simplicity of this option is also its drawback: as soon as you want to introduce a recovery catalog, or perform a database duplication operation, you introduce all the elements that you are trying to avoid in the first place. This option can also lead to confusion during usage: because you always make a local connection to the database, it is easy to connect to the wrong target database. It can also be confusing to know which environment you are connecting from; if you have more than one Oracle software installation on your system (and who doesn't?), then you can go down a time-sucking rat hole if you assume you are connecting to your PROD instance, when in fact you set up your ORACLE_HOME and ORACLE_SID environment variables for the TEST instance.

Perhaps the true difference between running RMAN from your desktop workstation and running it locally at each target database server comes down to OS host security. To run RMAN locally, you always have to be able to log in to each database server as the oracle user at the OS level, and have privileges defined for such. However, if you always make an Oracle Net connection to the database from a remote RMAN executable, you need never have host login credentials.

By any estimation, choose your option wisely. We've stated our preference, and then given you its bad news. As Figure 2-2 depicts, even our simplification into two options—client RMAN or server RMAN—can be tinkered with, giving you a hybrid model that fits your needs. In Figure 2-2, there are five different scenarios:

1. RMAN runs as a client connection from the DBA's workstation, because the DBA in charge of backing up PRODWB and DW_PROD does not have the oracle user password on the production database server.

2. RMAN backs up DW_PROD remotely, as with PRODWB, due to security restrictions on the database production server.

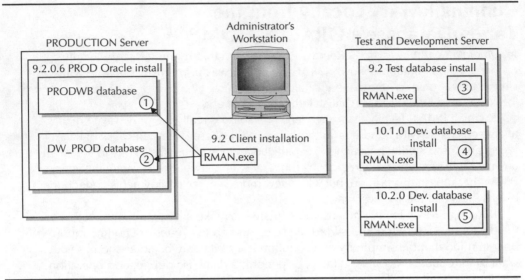

FIGURE 2-2. *Running different versions of the RMAN executable in the enterprise*

3. The 9.2 TEST database is backed up with a local RMAN executable that runs from the TEST $ORACLE_HOME.

4. The 10.1.0 DEV database is backed up locally. Because the DBA has oracle user privileges on the Test and Dev Server, this is feasible, and it minimizes the number of client installs to maintain at the local workstation.

5. The 10.2.0 DEV database is backed up locally as well, for the same reasons as the 10.1.0. DEV database.

Remember to remain flexible in your RMAN topology. There will be times when you will need to run your backups in NOCATALOG mode, using the local RMAN executable. And there may come a time when you need to run a remote RMAN job as well.

The Database Control File

So far, we have discussed the RMAN executable and its role in the process of using server-managed recovery with Oracle 10*g*. As we said, the real work is being done at the target database—it's backing itself up. Next, we must discuss the role of the control file in an RMAN backup or recovery process.

The control file has a day job already; it is responsible for the physical schematics of the database. The name says it all: the control file controls where the physical files of a database can be found, and what header information each file currently contains (or should contain). Its contents include datafile information, redo log information, and archive log information. It has a snapshot of each file header for the critical files associated with the database. Because of this wealth of information, the control file has been the primary component of any recovery operation prior to RMAN (Chapter 1 discusses this in greater detail).

Because of its role as the repository of database file information, it makes sense that RMAN would utilize the control file to pull information about what needs to be backed up. And that's just what it does: RMAN uses the control file to compile file lists, obtain checkpoint information, and determine recoverability. By accessing the control file directly, RMAN can compile file lists without a user having to create the list herself, eliminating one of the most tiresome steps of backup scripting. And it does not require that the script be modified when a new file is added. It already knows about your new file. RMAN knows this because the control file knows this.

The control file also moonlights as an RMAN data repository. After RMAN completes a backup of any portion of the database, it writes a record of that backup to the control file, along with checkpoint information about when the backup was started and completed. This is one of the primary reasons that the control file grew exponentially in size between Oracle version 7 and Oracle version 8—RMAN tables in the control file. These records are often referred to as *metadata*—data about the data recorded in the actual backup. This metadata will also be stored in a recovery catalog, when one is used (see Chapter 3).

Record Reuse in the Control File

The control file can grow to meet space demands. When a new record is added for a new datafile, a new log file, or a new RMAN backup, the control file can expand to meet these demands. However, there are limitations. As most databases live a life that spans years, in which thousands of redo logs switch and thousands of checkpoints occur, the control file has to be able to eliminate some data that is no longer necessary. So, it ages information out as it needs space, and reuses certain "slots" in tables in round-robin fashion. However, there is some information that cannot be eliminated—for instance, the list of datafiles. This information is critical for the minute-to-minute database operation, and new space *must* be made available for these records.

The control file thus separates its internal data into two types of records: circular reuse records and noncircular reuse records. *Circular reuse records* are records that include information that can be aged out of the control file, if push comes to shove. This includes, for instance, archive log history information, which can be removed without affecting the production database. *Noncircular reuse records* are those records that cannot be sacrificed. If the control file runs out of space for these records, the file expands to make more room. This includes datafile and log file lists.

The record of RMAN backups in the control file falls into the category of circular reuse records, meaning that the records will get aged out if the control file section that contains them becomes full. This can be catastrophic to a recovery situation: without the record of the backups in the control file, it is as though the backups never took place. Remember this: if the control file does not have a record of your RMAN backup, the backup cannot easily be used by RMAN for recovery (we'll explain how to re-add backups to the control file records in Chapter 12). This makes the control file a critical piece in the RMAN equation. Without one, we have nothing. If records get aged out, then we have created a lot of manual labor to rediscover the backups.

Fear not, though. Often, it is never that important when records get aged out; it takes so long for the control file to fill up, the backups that are removed are so old they are obsolete. You can also set a larger timeframe for when the control file will age out records. This is controlled by the init.ora parameter CONTROL FILE_RECORD_KEEP_ TIME. By default, this parameter is set to 7 (in days). This means that if a record is less than seven days old, the control file will not delete it, but rather expand the control file section. You can set this to a higher value, say, 30 days, so that the control file always expands, until only records older than a month will be overwritten when necessary. Setting this to a higher day value is a good idea, but the reverse is not true. Setting this parameter to 0 means that the record section never expands, in which case you are flirting with disaster.

In addition, if you will be implementing a recovery catalog, you need not worry about circular reuse records. As long as you resync your catalog at least once within the timeframe specified by the CONTROL FILE_RECORD_KEEP_TIME parameter, then let those records age out—the recovery catalog never ages records out.

The Snapshot Control File

As you can tell, the control file is a busy little file. It's responsible for schematic information about the database, which includes checkpoint SCN information for recovery. This constant SCN and file management is critical to the livelihood of your database, so the control file must be available for usage by the RDBMS on a constant basis.

This poses a problem for RMAN. RMAN needs to get a consistent view of the control file when it sets out to make a backup of every datafile. It only needs to know the most recent checkpoint information and file schematic information at the time the backup begins. After the backup starts, RMAN needs this information to stay consistent for the duration of the backup operation; in other words, it needs a *read consistent* view of the control file. With the constant updates from the database, this is nearly impossible—unless RMAN were to lock the control file for the duration of the backup. But that would mean the database could not advance the checkpoint or switch logs or produce new archive logs. Impossible.

To get around this, RMAN uses the *snapshot control file*, an exact copy of your control file that is only used by RMAN during backup and resync operations.

Re-Creating the Control File: RMAN Users Beware!

It used to be that certain conditions required the occasional rebuild of the database control file, such as resetting the MAXLOGFILES parameter or the MAXLOGHISTORY parameter. Certain parameters cannot be set unless you rebuild the control file, because these parameters define the size of the internal control file tables that hold noncircular reuse records. Therefore, if you need that section to be larger, you have to rebuild the control file.

If you use RMAN, and you do not use a recovery catalog, be very careful of the control file rebuild. When you issue the command

```
alter database backup control file to trace;
```

the script that is generated does not include the information in the control file that identifies your backups. *Without these backup records, you cannot access the backups when they are needed for recovery.* All RMAN information is lost, and you cannot get it back. The only RMAN information that gets rebuilt when you rebuild the control file is any permanent configuration parameters you have set with RMAN. In Oracle 10g, there is a new mechanism for generating limited backup metadata within a control file, but you are still building in a lot of manual work that never used to exist. Therefore, we encourage you to avoid a control file rebuild at all costs.

If you back up the control file to a binary file, instead of to trace, then all backup information is preserved. This command looks like the following:

```
alter database backup controlfile to '/u01/backup/bkup_cfile.ctl';
```

At the beginning of these operations, RMAN refreshes the snapshot control file from the actual control file, thus putting a momentary lock on the control file. Then, RMAN switches to the snapshot and uses it for the duration of the backup; in this way, it has read consistency without holding up database activity.

By default, the snapshot control file exists in the ORACLE_HOME/dbs directory on Unix platforms and in the ORACLE_HOME/database directory on Windows. It has a default name of SNCF<ORACLE_SID>.ORA. This can be modified or changed at any time by using the **configure snapshot controlfile** command:

```
configure snapshot controlfile name to '<location\file_name>';
```

There are certain conditions that might lead to the following error on the snapshot control file, which is typically the first time a person ever notices the file even exists:

```
RMAN-08512: waiting for snapshot controlfile enqueue
```

This error happens when the snapshot control file header is locked by a process other than the one requesting the enqueue. If you have multiple backup jobs, it may be that you are trying to run two backup jobs simultaneously from two different RMAN sessions. To troubleshoot this error, open a SQL*Plus session and run the following SQL statement:

```
SELECT s.sid, username AS "User", program, module, action, logon_time
"Logon", l.*
FROM v$session s, v$enqueue_lock l
WHERE l.sid = s.sid and l.type = 'CF' AND l.id1 = 0 and l.id2 = 2;
```

The RMAN Server Processes

RMAN makes a client connection to the target database, and two server processes are spawned. The primary process is used to make calls to packages in the SYS schema in order to perform the backup or recovery operations. This process coordinates the work of the channel processes during backups and restores.

The secondary, or shadow, process polls any long-running transactions in RMAN and logs the information internally. You can view the results of this polling in the view V$SESSION_LONGOPS:

```
SELECT SID, SERIAL#, CONTEXT, SOFAR, TOTALWORK,
        ROUND(SOFAR/TOTALWORK*100,2) "%_COMPLETE"
FROM V$SESSION_LONGOPS
WHERE OPNAME LIKE 'RMAN%'
AND OPNAME NOT LIKE '%aggregate%'
AND TOTALWORK != 0
AND SOFAR <> TOTALWORK
/
```

You can also view these processes in the V$SESSION view. When RMAN allocates a channel, it provides the session ID information in the output:

```
allocated channel: ORA_DISK_1
channel ORA_DISK_1: sid=16 devtype=DISK
```

The "sid" information corresponds to the SID column in V$SESSION. So you could construct a query such as this:

```
SQL> column client_info format a30
SQL> column program format a15
SQL> select sid, saddr, paddr, program, client_info
     from v$session where sid=16;
     SID SADDR    PADDR    PROGRAM         CLIENT_INFO
---------- -------- -------- --------------- ------------------------
      16 682144E8 681E82BC RMAN.EXE        rman channel=ORA_DISK_1
```

RMAN Channel Processes

In addition to the two default processes, an individual process is created for every channel that you allocate during a backup or restore operation. In RMAN lingo, the *channel* is the server process at the target database that coordinates the reads from the datafiles and the writes to the specified location during backup. During a restore, the channel coordinates reads from the backup location and the writing of data blocks to the datafile locations. There are only two kinds of channels: disk channels and tape channels. You cannot allocate both kinds of channels for a single backup operation— you are writing the backup either to disk or to tape. Like the background RMAN process, the channel processes can be tracked from the data dictionary, and then correlated with a SID at the OS level. It is the activity of these channel processes that gets logged by the polling shadow process into the V$SESSION_LONGOPS view.

RMAN and I/O Slaves

RMAN can utilize I/O slaves if they are configured on the target database. For the purposes of RMAN backups and restores, there are two kinds of slaves that are used: disk I/O slaves and tape I/O slaves.

Disk I/O slaves are configured using the parameter DBWR_IO_SLAVES. This parameter can be set to any number of values, and its primary use in life is to wake up extra DBWR slaves for disk writes when the dirty buffers are flushed to disk from the buffer cache. However, if this parameter is set to any non-zero value, be it 1 or 12 or 32, RMAN throws a switch that will automatically engage four I/O slaves per channel to assist with reading data blocks into RMAN memory buffers. This is a nice feature, but it changes considerably the way in which RMAN allocates memory. Using DBWR_IO_SLAVES is only important if your OS platform does not support native asynchronous I/O, or if you have disabled asynchronous I/O for the Oracle RDBMS. If you have asynchronous I/O enabled, then you do not need to use disk I/O slaves.

Tape I/O slaves assist with server process access to the tape device. If you have the parameter BACKUP_TAPE_IO_SLAVES set to TRUE, then RMAN will allocate a single I/O slave per tape channel process to assist with writes to the tape location. Unlike disk I/O slaves, this parameter affects no part of the database other than RMAN tape backups. Because there is no native asynchronous I/O to tape devices, we recommend you set this parameter to TRUE. It will help keep your tape drives streaming, meaning better performance on backups and restores. Chapter 16 discusses tape streaming in more depth.

The SYS Packages Used by RMAN

The RMAN server process that coordinates the work of the channels has access to two packages in the SYS schema: DBMS_RCVMAN and DBMS_BACKUP_RESTORE. These two packages comprise the entirety of the RMAN functionality in the target database.

SYS.DBMS_RCVMAN

DBMS_RCVMAN is the package that is used to access the tables in the control file and pass this information to RMAN so it can build backup and restore operations that accurately reflect the database schematics. This package is responsible for setting TIME operators and verifying checkpoint information in the datafile headers prior to running any operation. It also checks file locations and sizes, along with other information concerning node affinity (in a RAC environment) and disk affinity. This kind of information affects performance, and RMAN has automatic load-balancing and performance-enhancing algorithms that it runs through prior to building the actual backup/restore commands. Chapter 16 talks in depth about these performance gains. Stay tuned.

SYS.DBMS_BACKUP_RESTORE

SYS.DBMS_RCVMAN accesses the control file and verifies all the requisite information. It passes this information back to the RMAN server process, which can then create PL/SQL blocks based on code in the recover.bsq file. These PL/SQL blocks are made up of calls to the package DBMS_BACKUP_RESTORE, the true workhorse of RMAN. DBMS_BACKUP_RESTORE is the actual package that creates system calls to back up datafiles, control files, and archived redo logs. RMAN takes the information returned from DBMS_RCVMAN, divvies out the work among the channels based on the load-balancing algorithm, and then creates a series of calls to DBMS_BACKUP_RESTORE.

It is the work of DBMS_BACKUP_RESTORE that you can track in V$SESSION_LONGOPS. It performs the backup and restore operations. In addition, it accesses the control file, but only in a very limited way. It accesses it to back it up (actually, it backs up the snapshot control file), and to write backup information to it after backups have completed. Once it has completed a backup set, it writes to tables in the control file the information about when the backup was taken, how long it took to complete, and the size and name of the backup.

RMAN Packages in the Kernel

Both of these RMAN packages are installed by default by running the catproc.sql script when the database is created. There is no way to omit them during database creation, and therefore they exist in every Oracle database since version 8.0.3. What this means to you is that there is no configuration required by you for RMAN to work. You can run RMAN right now and start backing up your database.

These packages have another important trait: they are hard-coded into the Oracle software library files, so they can be called even when the database is not open. Most packages, as you know, would only be available when the database is open. However, RMAN can write calls to DBMS_BACKUP_RESTORE when the database instance is in nomount or mount mode. This is a critical element, and the reason is clear: we need to be able to back up and restore the database even when it is not open.

Which brings us to an interesting point: what state must the target be in if we are to connect to it using RMAN? Does the instance need to be started, or do we need to mount it, or must it be open? The answer is that RMAN can connect to the target database in any of these three states, but it must at least be in nomount mode (otherwise, there's no *there* there!).

Backing Up the Data Block

As you learned in Chapter 1, even when you used advanced techniques for backups, the units you were backing up were datafiles. The OS utility that ultimately made the backup was looking at the entire file and backing it up, and because of this, you had to go to extraordinary lengths to protect the integrity of the Oracle data blocks. RMAN, however, is different. Because RMAN is integrated into the RDBMS, it has access to your data at the same level that the database itself uses: the data block.

Block-level access is what distinguishes RMAN from any other backup utility, and even if you didn't already know this, it's why you are reading this book and implementing an RMAN backup strategy. This is an extremely powerful level of access that provides nearly all the benefits that you will get from using RMAN. It is because of this access that we can utilize the data block for more efficient backup and recovery.

The Data Block Backup Overview

Here's how it works: RMAN compiles the list of files to be backed up, based on the backup algorithm rules. Based on the number of channels and the number of files being simultaneously backed up, RMAN creates memory buffers in the Oracle shared memory segment. This is typically in the Private Global Area (PGA), but there are circumstances that push the memory buffers into the Shared Global Area (SGA). The channel server process then begins reading the datafiles and filling the RMAN buffers with these blocks. When a buffer is full, it pushes the blocks from an input buffer into an output buffer. This memory-to-memory write occurs for each individual data block in the datafile. If the block meets the criteria for being backed up, and the memory-to-memory write detected no corruption, then the block remains in the output buffer until the output buffer is full. Once full, the output buffer is pushed to the backup location—a disk or a tape, whichever it may be.

Once the entire set of files has been filtered through the memory buffers, the backup piece is finished and RMAN writes the completion time and name of the backup piece to the target database control file.

The Benefits of Block-Level Backups

Memory-to-memory writes occur for each block that is moved from disk into memory. During this operation, the block can be checked for corruption. Corruption checking is one of the nicest features of RMAN, and we discuss it in more detail in Chapter 12. Be aware that block checking is not used if you are performing a proxy copy.

Null compression becomes an option when we have access to the data block. We can eliminate blocks that have never been used (have a zeroed header) and discard them during the memory-to-memory write. Therefore, we only back up blocks that have been used and have a more efficient backup.

Misconceptions About Null Compression

This is a good place to mention the different misconceptions related to null compression. The first misconception is that we eliminate empty blocks. This means discussing the two access points that RMAN has to the database: the file header and the block header. RMAN can only draw conclusions about the contents of a block from its header or the file header information. Why no space management information? Well, space management information is only available when the database is open, and RMAN cannot rely on the database being open. We must only rely on that information that we can get without an open database: namely, file headers and block headers. So, if you truncate a table, all the blocks that had information in them, but are now empty, will be backed up, because RMAN only knows that the block has been initialized by a segment. It does not know that the block is empty.

The second common misconception about null compression is that an incremental backup can save time during the backup, as less is being backed up. This is true, to a certain extent, but only if your backup device is an extremely bad bottleneck. If you stream very quickly to your disk or tape backup location, then the act of eliminating blocks in memory saves little time, because RMAN is still reading every block in the file into memory—it just is not writing every block to the output device. Even during incremental backups, which eliminate blocks based on an incremental checkpoint SCN, we still have to check the header of each block to discover if it has changed since the last incremental backup. Incremental backups, then, save space in our backup location, and they provide a faster form of recovery, but they are not meant to be a significant or reliable time-saver during the actual backup.

In version 10*g*, RMAN has finally made available a version of whitespace compression, as would be done by a ZIP utility. This provides actual compression of the backed up blocks themselves. In addition, the new block-change tracking file allows RMAN to skip some blocks during backup without reading them into a memory buffer—so incremental backups begin to save time, if the change tracking is turned on. For more on compression and block change tracking, see the full coverage in Chapter 9.

And even newer to 10g, in Release 2 Patchset 1, RMAN is finally doing empty block compression. So, everything we've just described about backing up empty blocks no longer applies. So, with a block change tracking file and the latest patchset, you can skip null blocks and remove empty blocks from the backup. Only one word for that: score! And you may now have all your misconceptions back. We are through with them.

Block-level backup also provides performance gains from the perspective of redo generation. As you learned in Chapter 1, if you use old-school hot backup methodology, the amount of redo that you generate while you are running with a tablespace in hot backup mode can sometimes grow exponentially. This causes excess redo log switching, checkpoint failure, and massive amounts of archive log generation that can further cascade into space management challenges in your log archive destination.

RMAN, on the other hand, does not require hot backup mode, because it does not need to guarantee block consistency during a backup. RMAN's access to the data block allows it to coordinate with DBWR processes writing dirty buffers, and it can wait until the block is consistent before it reads the block into memory. So, blocks aren't being dumped to redo, and we always have consistent blocks in our backup.

RMAN does require ARCHIVELOG mode, of course. In fact, RMAN will not allow you to back up a datafile while the database is open unless you are in ARCHIVELOG mode. It gives you the following polite error:

```
ORA-19602: cannot backup or copy active file in NOARCHIVELOG mode
```

RMAN also leverages block-level backups to provide an often-overlooked but extremely useful recovery option: block media recovery. Now, if you were to receive the stomach-turning "ora-1578: block corruption detected" error, instead of recovering the entire file and performing recovery, RMAN can simply recover the bad block and perform recovery, meaning the rest of the data in the datafile is available during the recovery. More information on this appears in Chapter 12.

This just touches the surface of all the benefits you get from RMAN, but you get the point. The payoff is enormous when RMAN is utilized for block-level backups. The rest of this book is dedicated to utilizing this to your advantage.

RMAN in Memory

RMAN builds buffers in memory through which it streams data blocks for potential backup. This memory utilization counts against the total size of the PGA and, sometimes, the SGA. There are two kinds of memory buffers. *Input buffers* are the buffers that are filled with data blocks read from files that are being backed up. *Output buffers* are the buffers that are filled when the memory-to-memory write occurs to determine whether or not a particular block needs to be backed up. When the output buffer is filled, it is written to the backup location. There is a difference in the memory buffers depending on whether you are backing up to or restoring from disk or tape. Figure 2-3 illustrates input and output buffer allocation. It illustrates a backup of two datafiles being multiplexed into a single backup set.

Input Memory Buffers

When you are backing up the database, the size and number of input memory buffers depends on the exact backup command being executed. Primarily, it depends on the number of files being multiplexed into a single backup. *Multiplexing* refers to the number of files that will have their blocks backed up to the same backup piece. In order to keep the memory allocation within reason, the following rules are applied to the memory buffer sizes based on the number of files being backed up together:

■ If the number of files going into the backup set is four or less, then RMAN allocates four buffers per file at 1MB per buffer. The total will be 16MB or less.

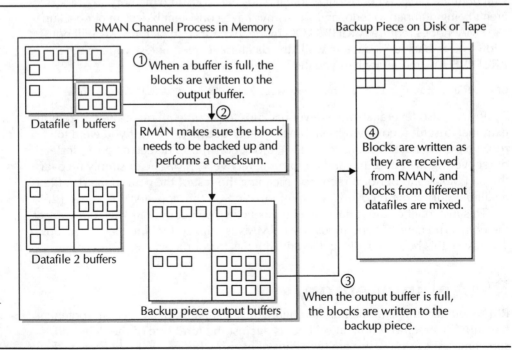

FIGURE 2-3. *Input and output buffers in memory*

■ If the number of files going into the backup set is greater than four, but no greater than eight, then each file gets four buffers, each of size 512KB. This ensures that the total remains at 16MB or less total.

■ If the number of files being multiplexed is greater than eight, then RMAN allocates four buffers of size 128KB. This ensures that each file being backed up will account for 512KB of buffer memory.

Bear in mind that these memory amounts are on a per-channel basis. So, if you allocate two channels to back up a database with 32 datafiles, for instance, then RMAN will load-balance the files between the two channels and may not end up with 16 files per channel. If some files are significantly larger than others, you may end up with only 8 files going into one backup set and 24 files going into the other. If this were the case, then the buffers for the first channel with 8 files would allocate 16MB of memory for input buffers (four buffers multiplied by 512KB each, multiplied by 8 files), and the second channel would allocate 12MB of memory buffers (521KB per file multiplied by 24 files).

You can use the following query to monitor the size of buffers on a per-file basis while the backup is running:

```
SELECT set_count, device_type, type, filename,
buffer_size, buffer_count, open_time, close_time
FROM v$backup_async_io
ORDER BY set_count,type, open_time, close_time;
```

Output Buffers when Backing Up to Disk

In addition to input buffers, RMAN allocates output buffers, depending on what the output source is. If you are backing up to disk, then RMAN allocates output buffers that must fill up with data blocks from the input buffers before being flushed to the backup piece on your file system. Per channel, there will be four output buffers, each of which is 1MB in size. So, the memory footprint per channel will always be 4MB.

Output Memory Buffers when Backing Up to Tape

Memory allocation is different when backing up to tape, to account for the slower I/O rates that we expect from tape devices. When you are backing up to or restoring from tape, RMAN allocates four buffers per channel process, each of which is 256KB in size, so that the total memory footprint per channel is 1MB.

Memory Buffers on Restore

Memory utilization during restore operations is slightly different than during backups. This is due to the fact that the roles are reversed: instead of reading from the datafiles and writing to the backup location, we are reading from the backup location and writing to the datafiles. During a restore from a disk backup, the input buffers will be 1MB in size, and RMAN will allocate four buffers per channel. When restoring from tape, RMAN allocates four input buffers with a size of BLKSIZE, which defaults to 256KB. The output buffers on restore are always 128KB, and there will be four of them per channel.

RMAN Memory Utilization: PGA vs. SGA

Backups to disk use PGA memory space for backup buffers, which is allocated out of the memory space for the channel processes. If your operating system is not configured for native asynchronous I/O, then you can utilize the parameter DBWR_IO_SLAVES to use I/O slaves for filling up the input buffers in memory. If this parameter is set to any non-zero value, RMAN automatically allocates four I/O slaves to coordinate the load of blocks into the input memory buffer. To coordinate this work, RMAN must utilize a shared memory location. So, the memory buffers for disk backups are pushed into the shared pool, or the large pool if one exists.

Memory for tape output buffers is allocated in the PGA, unless you are using tape I/O slaves. To enable tape I/O slaves, you set the init.ora parameter BACKUP_TAPE_IO_SLAVES to TRUE. This can be done dynamically and set in the SPFILE if you desire. When this is set to TRUE, RMAN creates a single slave process per channel to assist with the backup workload. To coordinate this work, RMAN pushes the memory allocation into the SGA.

If either of these I/O slave options is configured, memory will be pulled from the shared pool area in the SGA, unless you have a large pool configured. If you

The Large Pool in the Oracle SGA

The large pool is a specific area in the SGA of Oracle's memory space. It is configured using the LARGE_POOL_SIZE parameter in your init.ora or SPFILE, and the value is specified in bytes. The large pool is utilized for certain memory activities that require shared space but tend to walk all over the usual operations in the shared pool. It's occupants are primarily restricted to RMAN memory buffers, if I/O slaves are used, and Shared Servers for connection pooling. There are times that the large pool is used for Java connections, and it will also house parallel query slaves if you set PARALLEL_AUTOMATIC_TUNING to TRUE (this is deprecated in 10*g*).

Do you need a large pool? No. Without one, all of its potential occupants simply take up space in the shared pool. This is not the end of the world, but it's highly desirable to separate out RMAN buffers into their own space in the PGA. That way, SQL and PL/SQL parsing and other normal shared pool operations are not affected by RMAN backups, and vice versa. It also makes tuning the Oracle memory space for RMAN simpler and more straightforward.

do not have a large pool configured, and you expect to use I/O slaves, we highly recommend that you create a large pool with a size based on the total number of channels you expect to allocate for your backups, plus 1MB for overhead. How many channels makes sense? Chapter 16 will tell you. If you already have a large pool for Shared Servers (formerly MTS), JDBC connection pooling, or because you have PARALLEL_AUTOMATIC_TUNING set to TRUE, then increase the size of the pool to account for the RMAN memory buffers.

This introduction to the RMAN memory architecture does not include much information on tuning your system to cope with RMAN backups. Obviously, there is a resource hit that takes place while RMAN is running. In fact, you can tune RMAN to use more or less resources, depending on your needs. Chapter 16 discusses how to do this in greater detail.

One last note on memory utilization: If you are backing up to tape, you will be using a media management server product. If you are running your media manager from the same system as your target database, there will be additional system resources needed for the tape subsystem. Be sure to factor this in when tuning for backups.

The Recovery Catalog

So far, we have discussed the two most important RMAN components: the RMAN client utility and the internal database packages. However, there is another component that is involved with RMAN backups, although its usage is entirely optional: the recovery catalog.

The recovery catalog is a repository for metadata about RMAN backups. In a sense, you can think of the recovery catalog as merely a copy of the pertinent information out of the control file that RMAN requires for backup and recovery purposes. You create the recovery catalog in a user's schema in an Oracle database, and it is no more than a few packages, tables, indexes, and views. These tables contain data that is refreshed from the target database control file upon a resync command from within RMAN. The difference, of course, is that the recovery catalog can contain information about all the databases in your enterprise—and the control file holds only information about its own database.

To use a recovery catalog, you first connect from RMAN to the target database. Then, you make a second Net connection to the recovery catalog from within RMAN, like this:

```
rman>connect target /
rman>connect catalog rman/password@rcat
```

In the connect string to the catalog, you pass the username and password for the user that owns the RMAN catalog. Unlike the target, the connection to the catalog is not a sysdba connection and does not need this privilege granted to it.

Once connected, you can manually resync the catalog, or it will be implicitly resynchronized on any backup operation. A *resync* refers to the refreshing of the information from the target database control file to the tables in the recovery catalog.

A recovery catalog can serve as a repository for more than one target database, and as such can help centralize the administration of backups of many different databases. It has views that can be queried from SQL*Plus to determine the number, size, and range of backups for each target database that has been registered in that catalog.

Figure 2-4 details the network topology when a catalog is used. Inside of the recovery catalog, there are two packages: DBMS_RCVMAN and DBMS_RCVCAT. The first one, DBMS_RCVMAN, is identical in form to that same package in the SYS schema. It is in this way that the RMAN utility can use either the recovery catalog or the target database control file for information about backup and recovery, and not worry about different implementations.

The existence of the package name DBMS_RCVMAN in the recovery catalog can lead to some confusion on the database that houses the recovery catalog. This database is usually referred to as the *catalog database*. The catalog database is also a potential target database, and so it also has a package in the SYS schema called DBMS_RCVMAN; thus, if you select from DBA_OBJECTS on your catalog database, there are two packages with the same name, in two different schemas. This is not a mistake or a problem. One of them is built by the catproc.sql at the time of database creation (in the SYS schema), and the other is built when we create the recovery catalog (in a regular user schema).

The second package in the recovery catalog is DBMS_RCVCAT, and it is only used to perform operations specific to the recovery catalog during RMAN operations. In essence, you can think of this package as being the recovery catalog implementation of DBMS_BACKUP_RESTORE; whereas DBMS_BACKUP_RESTORE writes backup

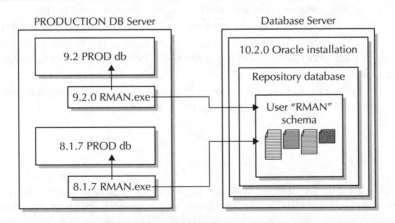

FIGURE 2-4. *Connecting to a recovery catalog*

completion information to the target database control file, DBMS_RCVCAT does this in the recovery catalog.

The base tables that contain information in the recovery catalog are unimportant, really, as you do not want to manually modify them. Instead, for the catalog's protection, Oracle created a series of views, all prefixed with RC_, that can be used to extract information from the catalog. Manually issuing any DML against catalog objects is a dangerous prospect, and we don't recommend it. The RC_* views, and what you can get from them, are outlined in Appendix B. As noted there, these views are different implementations of corresponding v$views in the database control file.

One final note on the recovery catalog: Starting in version 9.0.1, the default databases that get copied to your system when Oracle is installed all contain a user schema named RMAN. By default, this account is locked. Once unlocked, you can utilize this schema for recovery catalog purposes (for example, connect to the user and issue the **create catalog** command), or you can build your own user. However, due to security concerns and rampart confusion, the default RMAN user has been removed from 10*g*R2 default databases.

The Auxiliary Database

The *auxiliary database* refers to the instance that will become host to restored files from the target database in the event of a tablespace point-in-time recovery (TSPITR), a duplication operation (cloning the database), or the creation of a standby database using RMAN backups. When you perform any of these tasks, you will be connecting to the target database and the auxiliary database at the same time from within RMAN. In this way, you can utilize the information about the backups in the target database control file to coordinate the restore of those backups to the auxiliary database location. The following shows the connection to both the target database (locally) and the auxiliary database (using an Oracle Net connection):

```
rman>connect target /
rman>connect auxiliary sys/pwd@aux1
```

RMAN makes a simultaneous connection to each database and requires access to the SYS.DBMS_BACKUP_RESTORE and SYS.DBMS_RCVMAN packages in both the target database and the auxiliary database. As such, RMAN requires sysdba privileges at the auxiliary, just as it does at the target. Because RMAN must make a sysdba connection to two separate databases, it is required that you configure at least one of them with a password file and make an Oracle Net connection to it—there is no way to connect locally to two different databases.

We discuss the exact auxiliary database setup in great detail in Chapter 17. Figure 2-5 shows the network topology of an RMAN configuration when an auxiliary database is used. In Oracle8*i*, a recovery catalog was required in order to perform any actions at the auxiliary database, so this figure shows the topology with a catalog, as well.

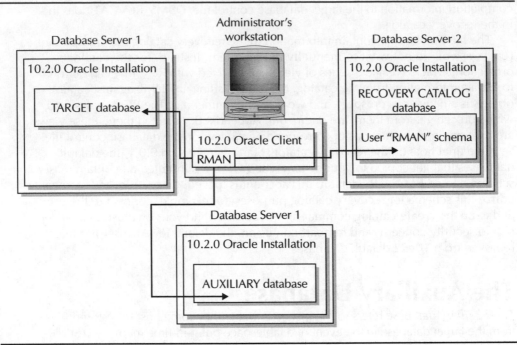

FIGURE 2-5. *Network topology with an auxiliary database in the mix*

Compatibility Issues

Given the number of different components that we have to work with, there are database version restrictions that you must stick with when working with RMAN. There are five different pieces of the compatibility puzzle, each of which has a version number:

- The RMAN executable version (the client utility)

- The target database

- The recovery catalog schema

- The recovery catalog database

- The auxiliary database (for duplication, TSPITR, and standby creation)

The easiest answer, of course, is to make sure all of these components are on the latest version, 10.2. If they are all at the same level, then there is no problem, right?

Of course, in the world where all of your databases are at the same level, everyone has their very own pony, fairies roam the earth, babies never cry, and no one ever has to take backups because failures never occur. But for the world we live in, there are some things to understand about RMAN version compatibility.

The Target and the RMAN Executable

The first general rule to stick with is to try and make sure that the target database and the RMAN executable are the same version. This is easy, if you will always be running RMAN from the target database environment. It gets trickier if you will be running all of your RMAN jobs from a centralized client interface. It means your client system will have to have an ORACLE_HOME client installation that corresponds in version to every database version that you will need to connect to and back up. The level of complexity is pretty high with this solution. This can also be avoided by using Oracle Enterprise Manager 10g. This allows a centralized interface so you can use the remote RMAN executables from a single console, or more consoles if the backup tasks are divided among DBAs. We discuss the Enterprise Manager interface in Chapter 11.

The Catalog Database and Catalog Schema

There are essentially three tiers to worry about with compatibility: Oracle8i, Oracle9i, and Oracle 10g. From the perspective of the catalog database and the catalog schema, there's a simpler answer: If you create a 10.2 recovery catalog in a 10.2 database, all databases down to 8.1.7.4 can be registered in it. If that is not possible, then read closely: All Oracle8 versions can be registered in an 8.1.x catalog. However, a 9.0.1 or 9.2.0 database cannot be registered in an 8i catalog. So, if you do not have an available database to use for the 10g recovery catalog, you will need to run it in NOCATALOG mode until one becomes available.

The Auxiliary Database

From a compatibility standpoint, the auxiliary database must be the same version as the target database that it will be cloned from. In fact, we would go so far as to encourage that you patch the ORACLE_HOME to which you will duplicate to the same level as the target database's ORACLE_HOME. In Chapter 17, we discuss in greater detail the use of an auxiliary database.

The RMAN Process: From Start to Finish

So far, we have discussed the different architectural components of taking a backup using Recovery Manager. As you may have noticed, there are a number of pieces to keep straight. To put it into a little perspective, we will run through a typical backup operation and explain the underlying RMAN activity at every step that it takes.

By doing so, you should be able to associate the lengthy expository in this chapter to the actual steps that you will take to perform a backup.

The following example illustrates a backup of a database called PROD. The backup will be going to a disk location; at this point in the book, the discussion of setting up and utilizing a media manager for backups to tape will be deferred to Chapters 4 through 8. The target database PROD has 20 datafiles and is running in ARCHIVELOG mode. The database is up and running during this operation. Here is our backup command:

```
C$>rman
rman>connect target /
rman>backup database;
```

That's it. That's all it takes. The following discussion explains what happens.

RMAN makes the bequeath connection to the target database that we have set up in our environment. This means it checks the variable ORACLE_SID for an instance name, then spawns a server process at that instance, logging in as a sysdba user. This connects as the internal database user SYS. RMAN immediately spawns the channel processes that will be used to perform the backup. In this case, we are using default settings, so only one channel is allocated. We are not using I/O slaves, so the process allocates memory in the PGA.

Next, RMAN compiles a call to SYS.DBMS_RCVMAN to request database schematic information from the target database control file, starting with a determination of the target database version. It gathers version information from the control file, along with control file information itself: What type of control file is it? What is the sequence number current in it? When was it created?

Because we have specified a full database backup, RMAN requests information for each datafile in the database and determines if any files are offline. As part of this information, it gathers which disk each file is on and how to dole out the work. Because we are using default settings, there will be only one channel and only one backup set. Therefore, RMAN ignores all disk affinity information and concentrates on compiling the list of files for inclusion in the backup set.

After the list is compiled, RMAN is ready to begin the backup process itself. To guarantee consistency, it then builds the snapshot control file. If one already exists, it overwrites it with a new one. Then RMAN creates the call to the DBMS_BACKUP_ RESTORE package to create the backup piece. The backup piece will be built in the default file location; on Unix, this is ORACLE_HOME/dbs, and on Windows, it is ORACLE_HOME/database. RMAN has the file list, so it can allocate the memory buffers for performing the read from disk. With 20 files, RMAN allocates input buffers of size 128KB. There will be four buffers per file, for a total memory utilization of 10MB for input buffers. RMAN will only allocate four output buffers, each of size 1MB. This brings our total memory utilization to 14MB for the backup.

After the memory is allocated, RMAN initializes the backup piece. The backup piece will be given a default name that guarantees uniqueness. RMAN then begins the backup. In database versions 9.2,10.1, and 10.2, RMAN allocates disk space in 50MB increments: 50MB is allocated on disk and filled with output buffers; when full, another 50MB is grabbed, until the last block is dumped to the backup piece. When the backup is complete, any remaining space in the final 50MB chunk is freed. It is worth pointing out that RMAN no longer does a check to see if there is enough space to complete the entire backup at the onset. This is due to the fact that null compression, and new 10g whitespace compression, will significantly reduce the backup from being the size of the datafiles. Instead, RMAN will run its backup until it runs out of space, and then fail.

Once the backup piece is initiated, the channel process can begin the database backup process. RMAN determines if you are using an SPFILE, and if so, it backs it up automatically as part of your backup set. Then RMAN will back up the current control file to the backup set. This control file backup is automatic whenever the SYSTEM tablespace is backed up; this behavior is changed if you have control file autobackup turned on (see Chapter 9).

So, we have the SPFILE and the control file backed up, and it is time to begin the datafile reads to pull data blocks into memory. The channel process does this by doing a read-ahead on the disk and pulling several blocks into memory at the same time. Then, the memory-to-memory write from input buffer to output buffer occurs. During this write, RMAN determines if the block has ever been initialized, or if the block header information is still zeroed out. If it is an unused block, the write to the output buffer never occurs and the block is discarded. If the block has been used, RMAN performs a checksum on the block. If the header and footer of the block do not match, RMAN indicates a corrupt block and aborts the backup. If the block has been initialized, and it passes the checksum, then that block is written to the output buffer.

Once the output buffer fills to capacity, we dump the buffer to the backup file location. The RMAN buffers are being filled up with blocks from all of the datafiles, so there is no order to the blocks in the dump file. The file is merely a bucket, and only RMAN will be able to restore the blocks to their proper location upon restore. While the blocks are being written out to the backup piece, the status of the backup is being polled by the RMAN shadow process. It checks in on the RPCs at the target and passes that information to V$SESSION_LONGOPS for your review. Based on the information gathered at the beginning of the backup operation, RMAN has an estimated completion percentage for each channel process. This can be viewed in V$SESSION_LONGOPS:

```
SELECT SID, SERIAL#, CONTEXT, SOFAR, TOTALWORK,
       ROUND(SOFAR/TOTALWORK*100,2) "%_COMPLETE"
FROM V$SESSION_LONGOPS
WHERE OPNAME LIKE 'RMAN%'
AND OPNAME NOT LIKE '%aggregate%'
AND TOTALWORK != 0
```

```
AND SOFAR <> TOTALWORK
/
       SID     SERIAL#    CONTEXT       SOFAR  TOTALWORK % COMPLETE
---------- ---------- ---------- ---------- ---------- ----------
        17        167          1        4784     116328       4.11
```

You can reissue this query throughout the backup process to get an update on the work still needing to be completed:

```
       SID     SERIAL#    CONTEXT       SOFAR  TOTALWORK % COMPLETE
---------- ---------- ---------- ---------- ---------- ----------
        17        167          1       96999     116328      83.38
```

Once every block in a datafile has been read into an input buffer and its status determined, then RMAN completes the file backup by writing the datafile header out to the backup piece. After all the files have their file headers written to the backup piece, RMAN makes a final call to SYS.DBMS_BACKUP_RESTORE, which writes backup information to the control file. This information includes the name of the backup piece, the checkpoint SCN at the time it started, and the time it completed.

And that is the entire process. Obviously, it gets more complex if we exercise more backup options, such as using multiple channels, using the FILESPERSET parameter, and backing up to tape. But each of these configurations shares the same fundamental process as previously described. If at any time during your study or testing of RMAN you want a more intimate look at the internal steps RMAN takes during backup, you can turn the debug option on for the backup and get a complete list of the entire process:

```
rman target / debug trace=/u02/oradata/trace/rmanbkup.out
```

Be warned, though, that this output is extremely verbose, and it can hamper backup performance. Only use debug for learning purposes on TEST instances, unless otherwise instructed to do so by Oracle Support Services when you are troubleshooting a production backup problem.

The Flash Recovery Area

The flash recovery area (FRA) is not a requirement for using RMAN, but it should be. New to 10g, the FRA is a specific location on disk that you set up to house all the Oracle recovery files. *Recovery files* refers to all files that might be required for a media recovery operation: full datafile backups, incremental backups, datafile copies, backup control files, and archive logs. The FRA also functions as a repository for mirrored copies of online redo log files, the block-change tracking file, and a current control file. If set up, flashback logs for using the flashback database option also live in the FRA. (We discuss flashback technologies in Chapter 13.)

The concept behind the FRA is to simplify the management of your backup and recovery duties by consolidating the requisite files into a single location that Oracle and RMAN can then micromanage, while the DBA moves on to other important duties. This simplification is based on some underlying principles of a solid backup strategy that focuses on availability:

- At least one copy of important datafiles, if not the entire database, should be kept on disks that are locally accessible to the database.

- Backups past a certain age should be moved to tape based on storage pressure on local disks.

- Long-term backup management should be almost completely automatic, based on business rules.

The FRA that you set up can be either a directory on a normal disk volume or an Automatic Storage Management (ASM) disk group. The FRA is determined by two initialization parameters: DB_RECOVERY_FILE_DEST and DB_RECOVERY_FLE_ DEST_SIZE. The first determines the location and the second the size. These can be set in your init.ora file, if you still use one, or in the SPFILE via an **alter system set** command.

With an FRA configured, you are not required to set any other LOG_ARCHIVE_ DEST_*n* parameter for archive logs; by default, with an FRA, Oracle will default LOG_ARCHIVE_DEST_10 to the FRA. It should also be noted that with an FRA in use, you cannot use LOG_ARCHIVE_DEST or LOG_ARCHIVE_DUPLEX_DEST— but, of course, you rid yourself of these outdated parameters long ago…right?

The FRA manages recovery files internally first based on database name, then types of files, and then by the dates the files are generated. The files themselves are named according to Oracle Managed Files (OMF) format. As such, the files are hard to decipher (except for archive logs, which still maintain the structure you give them with the LOG_ARCHIVE_FORMAT parameter). There are significant internal directory structures that exist for file management. However, the point of an FRA is that you don't need to spend much time worrying about the files. That being said, it's worth taking note of the internal structure and familiarizing yourself with where the files go. Sooner or later, you will end up digging for a particular file manually. Trust us.

The same FRA can be used by multiple databases. This can provide significant advantages, particularly for a Data Guard configuration, but also if you have a large ASM disk group and multiple databases on the same system. It can come in handy, as well, when it comes time to clone production for test purposes. Here's the catch: all the databases that share the FRA either have a different value for DB_NAME or have a different name for the value DB_UNIQUE_NAME.

Summary

In this chapter, we discussed the underlying architecture employed by RMAN to perform backups of an Oracle Database 10g database. We covered the RMAN executable, the target database packages, and the control file. We discussed in detail the process architecture and how memory is allocated for RMAN backups. We discussed the usage of an RMAN recovery catalog and how to connect to an auxiliary database. After discussing the different architectural components, we gave a brief run-through of a typical backup operation to show the different components in use.

PART
II

Setup Principles and Practices

CHAPTER
3

RMAN Setup and Configuration

ell, let's get started with this RMAN thing, shall we? I'll just reach down, pull on the handle…. I said pull on the handle…and, it doesn't start. Like many other things, we first need to set up RMAN and our database for backup and recovery operations before we can actually do anything. In this chapter, we look at initial RMAN setup requirements and options. First, we look at putting the database in ARCHIVELOG mode, in case you want to do online backups. We then look at the basic RMAN interface, so that you can get into RMAN itself. Next, we discuss configuring RMAN for database backup operations. Finally, we discuss the RMAN recovery catalog, including why you might want to use it and how to configure it for use.

Configuring Your Database to Run in ARCHIVELOG Mode

The first thing you need to decide when setting up RMAN for backups is what mode you are going to run your database in, ARCHIVELOG mode or NOARCHIVELOG mode. Chapter 1 discussed the benefits of running in each of these modes. In this section, we address the configuration of ARCHIVELOG mode.

Prior to Oracle Database 10*g*, a common mistake that new DBAs made was to fail to enable the ARCH process after putting the database in ARCHIVELOG mode. Setting the parameter LOG_ARCHIVE_START to TRUE did this. Oracle Database 10*g* eliminates the need to do this. Now, when the database is in ARCHIVELOG mode, Oracle automatically starts the ARCH process for you—handy if you are a forgetful DBA.

The ARCH process is called by the LGWR process. Once an online redo log fills up, LGWR switches to another online redo log group. At that time, if the database is in ARCHIVELOG mode, LGWR also signals ARCH to wake up and start working. ARCH responds to the call from LGWR by making copies of the online redo log in the locations defined by the Oracle database parameter LOG_ARCHIVE_DEST_*n* and/or to the defined flash recovery area (which we discuss shortly). Until the ARCH process has completed the creation of the archived redo log's copies, that online redo log file cannot be reused by Oracle.

As mentioned, Oracle Database 10*g* offers two different types of locations where you can store your archived redo logs: the ARCHIVELOG destination directories and the new flash recovery area. Let's look at each of these locations in more detail next.

ARCHIVELOG Destination Directories

You can use the LOG_ARCHIVE_DEST_*n* parameter to define up to ten different archive log destinations. These destinations can be local directories, network directories (for example, NT folders), or even a defined database service name if you are using Standby Database/Dataguard. You can define each location as a mandatory or optional location.

Along with configuring the LOG_ARCHIVE_DEST parameter, you may want to consider configuring the following parameters related to database archiving:

- **LOG_ARCHIVE_STATE_*n*** Defines one of two different states for each archive log destination. If set to ENABLE, the ARCH process will consider the destination associated with this state as a valid archive log destination. If set to DEFER, the ARCH process will not archive logs to the related LOG_ARCHIVE_DEST_*n* location.

- **LOG_ARCHIVE_FORMAT** Provides a template for Oracle to use when naming archived redo logs. As Oracle creates the archived redo logs, it renames them in such a way that each of the archived redo logs has a unique name assigned to it. Using the LOG_ARCHIVE_FORMAT parameter, you can manipulate the default naming standard as you require.

- **LOG_ARCHIVE_MIN_SUCCEED_DEST** Allows the DBA to define a minimum number of archive log destination copies that must succeed in order for Oracle to be able to reuse the associated online redo log again.

- **LOG_ARCHIVE_START** This parameter is obsolete in Oracle Database 10*g*. Oracle will now start the ARCH process for you automatically.

Each of the different parameters mentioned thus far is defined in the *Oracle Database 10g Reference Manual* (which is part of the overall Oracle documentation), should you need further information on them.

In the following example, we have a database we want to put in ARCHIVELOG mode. We will create three different archive log destination directories, including one to a service name that supports an Oracle standby database. We will also enforce the requirements that at least two of these destinations must be written to in order for the movement of the archived redo log to be considered complete, and that the standby database must be one of those two locations. Here is an example of the use of the various database parameter file parameters related to ARCHIVELOG mode operations:

```
log_archive_dest_1='location=d:\oracle\oraarc\robt mandatory'
log_archive_dest_2='location=z:\oracle\oraarc\robt optional'
log_archive_dest_3='service=recover1 mandatory'
log_archive_min_succeed_dest=2
log_archive_format="robt_%s_%t.arc"
```

In this example, our first archive log destination goes to d:\oracle\oraarc\robt. The second archive log destination is to a secondary location on the Z: drive. We have made this an optional archiving location because it is a networking device (which may not be all that reliable). The third destination is to an Oracle Net service (probably a standby database) called recover1. This will cause Oracle to send the archived redo logs through Oracle Net as they are generated.

Proceeding through the example, by using the LOG_ARCHIVE_MIN_SUCCEED_ DEST parameter, we have indicated that the archived redo logs must be successfully copied to at least two different locations. The format of the archived redo log is defined with the LOG_ARCHIVE_FORMAT parameter.

The Flash Recovery Area

The flash recovery area (FRA) allows you to centralize storage of all recovery-related files. The FRA can use locally attached storage, Oracle's Cluster File System (OCFS), or Oracle Database 10*g*'s new Automatic Storage Management (ASM) features. Table 3-1 lists the file types that are backed up within the FRA.

The FRA helps with the management of overall disk space allocation and provides a centralized storage area for all recovery-related files. The FRA also provides for much faster backup and restore operations as well.

Retention for files in the FRA is determined by the RMAN retention policy. This is set via the RMAN **configure retention policy** command. If a file does not have a retention policy associated with it, or it's a permanent file, then it will never be deleted. If a file is not yet obsolete under the RMAN retention policy, then it will not be deleted. Finally, archived logs are eligible for deletion once they are obsolete.

The FRA is created in a specific location defined by the parameter DB_RECOVERY_ FILE_DEST. This location can be a file system or an ASM volume. You define the

File Type	Notes
Archived redo logs	Archived redo logs will be stored in the FRA.
Control file	One copy of the control file is created in the FRA when the database is created.
Control file autobackups	The default location for the RMAN control file autobackups will be the FRA, if it is defined.
Flashback logs	Flashback logs (discussed later in this chapter) will be stored in the FRA, if it is defined.
Redo log	One copy of each redo log group member can be stored in the FRA.
RMAN datafile copies	The default location for the RMAN datafile copies will be the FRA, if it is defined.
RMAN backup and other related files	The default location for the RMAN files in general (backup set pieces, etc.) will be the FRA, if it is defined.

TABLE 3-1. *File Types Found in the Flash Recovery Area*

maximum size of the FRA by using the DB_RECOVERY_FILE_DEST_SIZE parameter. This is an Oracle-controlled file space limitation, independent of the overall space available in the file system itself. Oracle monitors the space available in the FRA, and once the amount of available space in the FRA starts to diminish to unsafe levels, Oracle generates a warning in the alert log (at 90 percent used and again at 95 percent used). Also, when there is less than 10 percent free space available in the FRA, Oracle removes files that are on the obsolete-file list.

NOTE
Running out of space in the FRA can be troublesome if that area is your only archive log destination, as this can cause your database to eventually halt. If the FRA is going to be your only archive log destination, monitor space availability carefully.

If you find that the FRA has run out of space, there are some different ways to respond to the problem:

1. If the problem is one of insufficient space allocation via the parameter DB_RECOVERY_FILE_DEST_SIZE and sufficient physical disk space exists to increase the space allocated to the FRA, increase the size of the parameter. This will immediately add additional space to the FRA. Of course, you cannot increase this parameter to a value that is greater than the amount of space that is physically available on the file system.

2. If you need more physical space, allocate additional physical space to the file system and then increase the size of the DB_RECOVERY_FILE_ DEST_SIZE parameter.

3. If additional space is not available, you can move the FRA to another file system where more space is available.

4. You can also make room in the FRA by using the RMAN **backup recovery area** command to move the contents of the FRA to another location. We will discuss the **backup recovery area** command and its limitations during discussions on performing RMAN backups.

5. As a last-ditch effort, physically remove older backup set pieces and/or archived redo logs from the FRA and then use the RMAN **crosscheck** command to get the database to recognize that the files have been removed.

NOTE
If you find yourself queasy at the idea of removing physical files from the FRA, then your gut instincts are good. Essentially this means that either your retention policy is not correct or that you have not allocated enough space to support the retention policy established for your database. Also, removing files potentially compromises the recoverability of your database, so exercise extreme caution when removing files.

Setting Up the Flash Recovery Area

To set up the FRA, you will want to configure the following parameters:

Parameter	Example	Purpose
DB_RECOVERY _FILE_DEST_ SIZE	Alter system set db_ recovery_file_dest_ size=20G scope=both;	Sets the allocated size of the FRA, in bytes, and must be defined in order to enable the FRA. This allows you to control how much disk space is allocated to the FRA. You should not set this value to a size that is greater than the total amount of available disk space.
DB_RECOVERY _FILE_DEST	Alter system set db_recovery_file_dest= '/u01/oracle/flash_recovery' scope=both;	Specifies the location of the FRA. This can be a file system, an ASM disk location, or an OMF location.

Note that you must specify the DB_RECOVERY_FILE_DEST_SIZE parameter before you specify the DB_RECOVERY_FILE_DEST parameter. Failure to do so will result in an ORA-32001 error message. In a similar fashion, you must disable the DB_ RECOVERY_FILE_DEST parameter before you reset the DB_RECOVERY_FILE_ DEST_SIZE parameter. Leaving DB_RECOVERY_FILE_DEST empty will serve to disable the FRA. Here is an example of disabling the FRA by resetting the DB_ RECOVERY_FILE_DEST parameter:

```
alter system set db_recovery_file_dest=' ' scope=both;
```

Oracle allows you to archive to both the FRA and one or more additional locations through the use of the LOG_ARCHIVE_DEST_*n* parameters. To do this, you do not use the standard FRA parameter DB_RECOVERY_FILE_DEST. Rather, you define the various LOG_ARCHIVE_DEST_*n* parameters as you normally would. Then, you define an additional LOG_ARCHIVE_DEST_*n* parameter for the FRA using the Oracle-supplied constant USE_DB_RECOVERY_FILE_DEST for the location of that archiving destination, as shown in this example:

```
SQL> alter system set
log_archive_dest_10='LOCATION=USE_DB_RECOVERY_FILE_DEST';
```

In this case, the LOG_ARCHIVE_DEST_10 parameter will cause ARCH to archive the archive log destination. Note that you still need to set the DB_RECOVERY_FILE_DEST parameter. What happens if you set the DB_RECOVERY_FILE_DEST parameter and you set any of the LOG_ARCHIVE_DEST_*n* parameters? Oracle will only archive to the LOG_ARCHIVE_DEST_*n* locations, and will not archive to the FRA unless you have set one of the LOG_ARCHIVE_DEST_*n* parameters to a location of USE_DB_RECOVERY_FILE_DEST.

Flash Recovery Area Views

Several views are available to help you manage the FRA. These views include the following:

- DBA_OUTSTANDING_ALERTS

- V$RECOVERY_FILE_DEST

- V$FLASH_RECOVERY_AREA_USAGE

Also, columns are available in several other views that help you to manage the FRA. Let's look at each of these views and columns in more detail.

The DBA_OUTSTANDING_ALERTS View   As files are added or removed from the FRA, records of these events are logged in the database alert log. You can check the new DBA view, DBA_OUTSTANDING_ALERTS, for information on outstanding issues with the FRA. Note that there is somewhat of a lag between the time a space-related issue occurs and the warning appears in the DBA_OUTSTANDING_ALERTS view.

The following is an example where the FRA has run out of space and is posting an alert to the DBA_OUTSTANDING_ALERTS view. You would need to deal with this situation quickly or risk the database coming to a complete halt. In this case, we used the **alter system** command to increase the amount of space allocated to the FRA.

```
SQL> select reason from dba_outstanding_alerts;
REASON
--------------------------------------------------------------
db_recovery_file_dest_size of 524288000 bytes is 100.00% used
and has 0 remaining bytes available.

SQL> alter system set db_recovery_file_dest_size=800m;
```

The V$RECOVERY_FILE_DEST View   The V$RECOVERY_FILE_DEST view provides an overview of the FRA that is defined in your database. It provides the size that the FRA is configured for, the amount of space used, how much space can be reclaimed, and the number of files in the FRA. In the following example, we can see that the increase in space to the FRA to 800MB has been recorded (SPACE_LIMIT). However, we still have used too much space (SPACE_USED) and the FRA is still full.

```
SQL> select * from v$recovery_file_dest;
NAME
-------------------------------------------------------------------------
    SPACE_LIMIT           SPACE_USED  SPACE_RECLAIMABLE NUMBER_OF_FILES
-------------- ---------------------- ------------------ ---------------
c:\oracle\product\10.2.0\flash_recovery_area
    838,860,800          1,057,116,672        338,081,280              11
```

One nice thing about Oracle is that it manages the FRA space for us as much as it can, and if there is reclaimable space available, it will free it as required. Note that in the previous query, Oracle indicated we were out of FRA space. Did you notice the SPACE_RECLAIMABLE column, though? This column indicates that there is reclaimable space available. This is space that is taken up by archived redo logs or backup set pieces that are no longer needed by virtue of whatever retention criteria we have selected (we will discuss retention criteria and setting that criteria later in this chapter). When Oracle needs space in the FRA (say, for example, we force a log switch), it will remove any files that are reclaimable and free up space. In the next query, we can see that this has occurred. After we ran the previous query that indicated we were out of FRA space, we forced a log switch. This caused Oracle to reclaim space from the FRA for re-use, and it then was able to write out the archived redo log. We can query the V$RECOVERY_FILE_DEST view and see that this has indeed occurred:

```
SQL> alter system switch logfile;
System altered.
SQL> select * from v$recovery_file_dest;
NAME
```

```
-------------------------------------------------------------------
    SPACE_LIMIT          SPACE_USED  SPACE_RECLAIMABLE NUMBER_OF_FILES
 ------------- --------------------- ------------------- ---------------
c:\oracle\product\10.2.0\flash_recovery_area
    838,860,800          719,412,736              64,000              7
```

The V$FLASH_RECOVERY_AREA_USAGE View   The V$FLASH_RECOVERY_
AREA_USAGE view provides more detailed information on which types of files are
occupying space in the FRA. This view groups the file types, and then provides the
percentage of space that is used by each file type, the percentage of the total FRA
reclaimable space that comes from that group, and the number of files in the FRA
that come from that group. Here is a query of the V$FLASH_RECOVERY_AREA_
USAGE view:

```
SQL> SELECT * FROM V$FLASH_RECOVERY_AREA_USAGE;

FILE_TYPE      PERCENT_SPACE_USED PERCENT_SPACE_RECLAIMABLE NUMBER_OF_FILES
------------   ------------------ ------------------------- ---------------
CONTROLFILE                     0                         0               0
ONLINELOG                       0                         0               0
ARCHIVELOG                  17.14                     17.09               7
BACKUPPIECE                108.88                     23.22               4
IMAGECOPY                       0                         0               0
FLASHBACKLOG                    0                         0               0
```

In this example, we notice a few things:

■   We are over our defined space allocation (the PERCENT_SPACE_USED of
   all the rows > 100 percent).

■   The backup set pieces are consuming most of that space, and 23.22 percent
   of that space is reclaimable.

■   The archived redo logs consume only 17 percent of the space allocated
   to the FRA, and even if we were to remove all of the archived redo logs,
   we would not free up enough space to bring the FRA under the amount of
   space allocated to it.

Other Views with FRA Columns   The column IS_RECOVERY_DEST_FILE can be
found in a number of Oracle Database 10g's V$ views such as V$CONTROLFILE,
V$LOGFILE, V$ARCHIVED_LOG, V$DATAFILE_COPY, V$DATAFILE, and
V$BACKUP_PIECE. This column is a Boolean that indicates whether or not the file
is in the FRA.

Another column, BYTES, can be found in the V$BACKUP_PIECE and RC_BACKUP_PIECE (an RMAN recovery catalog view) views. This column indicates the size of the backup set piece in bytes.

NOTE
*Manually removing fixed files from the FRA can have unexpected consequences. Oracle does not immediately detect the removal of these files, and thus the space is not reclaimed. If you end up manually removing files (or loose a disk perhaps), use the RMAN **crosscheck** command along with the **delete** command to cause Oracle to update the current control file information on the FRA. The folks at Oracle recommend that you not manually remove files managed by Oracle if at all possible.*

Other Flash Recovery Area Features

In Oracle Database 10*g*, the **alter database add logfile** and **alter database add standby logfile** commands create an online redo log member in the FRA if the OMF-related DB_CREATE_ONLINE_LOG_DEST_*n* parameter is not set. The **alter database drop logfile** and **alter database rename file** commands also support files in the FRA.

During database creation, Oracle can use the FRA to store the database control file and online redo logs. If the OMF-related parameter DB_CREATE_ONLINE_LOG_DEST_*n* is defined, then the control file and redo logs will be created in those locations, but will not be created in the FRA, even if the FRA is defined. If DB_CREATE_ONLINE_LOG_DEST_*n* is not defined, but CREATE_FILE_DEST is defined, then the control file and online redo logs will be created in the location defined by CREATE_FILE_DEST. If DB_RECOVERY_FILE_DEST is also defined, then a copy of the control file and online redo logs will get created there as well. Finally, if only DB_RECOVERY_FILE_DEST is defined, then the control file will get created in that location. If none of these parameters is defined, then the control file and online redo logs will be created to a default location, which is OS specific.

The FRA and ASM

RMAN supports the use of Automated Storage Management (ASM) for the storage of RMAN backups. What is ASM? ASM is a disk management tool that eliminates the need for the DBA to manage the physical files associated with a given database. ASM is somewhat like the logical volume groups you might be used to in Unix. ASM uses *ASM disk groups,* which are logical units of storage. Physical disks are assigned to an ASM disk group, providing the overall storage capability of that ASM disk group. ASM disk groups can exist on previously allocated file systems or on RAW disk. Combined with OCFS, clustered servers can share ASM disks in RAC configurations.

Having configured ASM and having defined the various disk groups, you can then assign datafiles, control files, online redo logs, and various RMAN backup files to the ASM disk groups.

ASM offers a number of features including load balancing, data redundancy, and easy addition and removal of new disks to the ASM disk groups. It is beyond the scope of this book to discuss configuration of ASM in general. However, be aware that RMAN does support ASM disk groups should you wish to use them. We are not necessarily recommending ASM in this book. Most non-RAC sites probably will find little value in an ASM implementation. However, if you are a RAC site, you might want to consider ASM coupled with OCFS as an alternative to other clustering options, depending on your platform.

If you are using ASM, you can configure the FRA such that it will be created in the ASM file system, as shown in this example:

```
alter system set db_recovery_file_dest='+ASMV01';
```

In this case, Oracle will use the ASM disk volume ASMV01 for the FRA. We can then use RMAN to back up to the FRA. We will discuss backups in Chapter 9.

NOTE
ASM has its own little quirks here and there, and sometimes managing space within an ASM disk group can get tricky. We will address ASM issues as we come to them throughout the book.

Should You Use the FRA?

We think the idea behind the FRA is a good one. We also like to copy those backups to some other media, such as tape, so we can send them offsite for disaster recovery purposes (nothing like a good flood, bomb, or tornado to make your disaster recovery planning seem really important).

We also like the FRA for the archived redo logs, but we also like the idea of copying archived redo logs to more than one location (and more specifically, more than one disk). Keep in mind that the archived redo logs are critical to database recovery, and if you loose one, all the others after that one are pretty much worthless. So, we tend to configure our 10*g* databases using FRA and at least one other archive log destination that is on a different disk. This means that we use the LOG_ARCHIVE_DEST_*n* parameters to configure the database to use both the FRA and another, separate, file system to store our archived redo logs.

We could go beyond this and tell you how much we like things such as standby databases and the like, but that's not what this book is about. The bottom line is that you need to protect the data in your charge because there is no worse feeling than coming into work on Monday morning and finding out the system crashed over the weekend and that the entire database is lost...along with all your backups.

Switching Between ARCHIVELOG Modes

Once you have configured the database to run in ARCHIVELOG mode, you can switch it between NOARCHIVELOG and ARCHIVELOG mode quite easily. To put the database in ARCHIVELOG mode, you must first shut down the database in a consistent state using one of these commands: **shutdown**, **shutdown immediate**, or **shutdown transactional**. Once the database has been cleanly shut down, mount the database by issuing the **startup mount** command. Once the database is mounted, issue the command **alter database archivelog** to put the database in ARCHIVELOG mode. You can then open the database with the **alter database open** command.

If you wish to take the database out of ARCHIVELOG mode, reverse the process. First shut down the database. Once the database has been shut down, mount the database by issuing the **startup mount** command. Once the database is mounted, issue the command **alter database noarchivelog** to put the database in NOARCHIVELOG mode. You can then open the database with the **alter database open** command.

If You Created Your Database with the Oracle Database Configuration Assistant

If you created your database with the Oracle Database Configuration Assistant (ODBCA), it is likely that Oracle has configured much of RMAN for you. ODBCA will configure the database in ARCHIVELOG mode, configure the FRA, and even offer you the chance to schedule RMAN backups. For smaller installations, this may well be all that is needed, and you will not need to worry about any other basic RMAN configuration issues. Still, it's a good idea to be aware of all the options that RMAN offers. For example, encryption of backups is not enabled when you create a database with the ODBCA, and you might want to enable that feature.

RMAN Workshop: *Put the Database in ARCHIVELOG Mode*

Workshop Notes

For this workshop, you need an installation of the Oracle software, and a database that is up and running in NOARCHIVELOG mode. Before you start the workshop, determine where you want Oracle to copy the archived redo logs to.

Putting the database in ARCHIVELOG mode will add some additional overhead onto the system in terms of CPU and disk I/O requirements. This additional overhead should be minimal.

Step 1. Configure both the FRA and a separate archive log destination for the archived redo logs. First, set the FRA parameters DB_RECOVERY_FILE_DEST_ SIZE and DB_RECOVERY_FILE_DEST:

```
SQL> alter system set db_recovery_file_dest_size=2G;
System altered.
SQL> alter system set
db_recovery_file_dest='c:\oracle\product\10.2.0\flash_recovery_area';
System altered.
```

Step 2. Now, define two archive log destination directories, one of which will be the FRA. Set the database parameter file and set the LOG_ARCHIVE_DEST_1 parameter so that it is pointing to a predefined file system that will be our first archive log directory. Set LOG_ARCHIVE_DEST_10 to point to the FRA. Use the **show parameter** command to verify that the settings are correct:

```
SQL> alter system set log_archive_dest_1='location=d:\archive\rob10R2';
System altered.
SQL> alter system set
log_archive_dest_10='LOCATION=USE_DB_RECOVERY_FILE_DEST';
SQL> show parameter log_archive_dest
NAME                    TYPE        VALUE
--------------------- ----------- --------
log_archive_dest_1      string
location=d:\archive\rob10R2
log_archive_dest_10     string
LOCATION=USE_DB_RECOVERY_FILE_DEST
```

Step 3. Shut down the database:

```
SQL> shutdown immediate
Database closed.
Database dismounted.
ORACLE instance shut down.
```

Step 4. Mount the database:

```
SQL> startup mount
ORACLE instance started.
Total System Global Area    84700976 bytes
Fixed Size                    282416 bytes
Variable Size               71303168 bytes
Database Buffers            12582912 bytes
Redo Buffers                  532480 bytes
Database mounted.
```

Step 5. Put the database in ARCHIVELOG mode:

```
SQL> alter database archivelog ;
Database altered.
```

Step 6. Open the database:

```
SQL> alter database open;
Database altered.
```

Although it is not part of the workshop, the process of taking the database out of ARCHIVELOG mode is as simple as reversing the process described in the workshop. Shut down the database, restart the database instance by issuing the **startup mount** command, and put the database in NOARCHIVELOG mode by issuing the command **alter database noarchivelog**. Note that there is no requirement to shut down the database in a consistent manner when moving from ARCHIVELOG mode to NOARCHIVELOG mode. Here is an example of switching back into NOARCHIVELOG mode:

```
SQL> shutdown
ORACLE instance shut down.
SQL> startup mount
ORACLE instance started.
Total System Global Area    84700976 bytes
Fixed Size                    282416 bytes
Variable Size               71303168 bytes
Database Buffers            12582912 bytes
Redo Buffers                  532480 bytes
Database mounted.
SQL> alter database noarchivelog;
Database altered.
SQL> alter database open;
Database altered.
```

Finally, you should do a backup of the database once you have completed either task.

The RMAN Command Line

Now that the database is in ARCHIVELOG mode (if you are going to do online backups), you are ready to configure RMAN and your database for backups. Before you can do that, it would be nice to actually know how to use the RMAN executable. So, let's take a slight detour in our setup discussion to look at the RMAN command-line interface (CLI) and how to use it.

There are two different ways to get to RMAN. The first is from the command line and the second is by using OEM. We will deal with the OEM interface in more detail in Chapter 11. Most of the examples you will see in this book, however, will be done using the CLI. We figure that if you can do it from the command line, you can do it from anywhere. In the next sections, we will look at how to connect to databases with the RMAN command line and also how to use the **connect** command.

Connecting via the RMAN Command Line

You can start RMAN from the OS prompt simply by typing the command **rman**. Once you have started the RMAN command interpreter, you can perform whatever operations you might need to perform. Often, it's much easier to get some of the preliminary work done by using command-line parameters. Thus, when we start RMAN, we can pass several command-line parameters. You can use the command-line parameters to connect RMAN to the database you are going to back up (known as the *target database*), the recovery catalog, or a number of other tasks. Table 3-2 provides a list of the command-line parameters, the data type for the argument of the parameter (if there is one), and the purpose of the parameter.

RMAN Command-Line Parameter	Parameter Argument Type	Purpose
target	Character string	Defines the username, password, and service name of the target database to connect to.
catalog	Character string	Defines the username, password, and service name of the recovery catalog.
nocatalog	No arguments	Indicates that no recovery catalog is going to be used by this session. This parameter is the default parameter in Oracle8*i* and Oracle9*i*.
cmdfile	Character string	Indicates the name of a command file script to execute.
log	Character string	Indicates that the RMAN session should be logged. The log file will take the name of the argument to this parameter. Also causes all RMAN messages to the screen to be suppressed (except the RMAN prompt).
trace	Character string	Indicates that the RMAN session should be traced. The trace file will take the name of the argument to this parameter.
append	No arguments	Indicates that the log file (defined by the log parameter) should be appended to.
debug	Various arguments	Indicates that RMAN should be started in debug mode.
msgno	No arguments	Indicates that the RMAN- prefix should be shown with each error message. If this option is not selected, then certain non-error messages will not include a message number with them.
send	Character string	Sends the character string message to the media management layer.
pipe	String	Invokes the RMAN pipe interface.
timeout	Integer	Indicates the number of seconds to wait for pipe input.
Auxiliary	Character string	Defines the username, password, and service name of the auxiliary database to connect to.

TABLE 3-2. *RMAN Command-Line Parameters*

Here are some examples of starting RMAN with some command-line parameters (and you will see others later):

```
RMAN target=system/manager@robt nocatalog
RMAN target='sys/robert as sysdba@robt' nocatalog
RMAN target=system/manager@robt
catalog=system/manager@catalog log="RMAN.log"
RMAN target system/manager@robt nocatalog log "RMAN.log"
```

NOTE
The = sign between the command-line parameter and the value of that parameter is optional. Also, if you are running Oracle Database 10g Real Application Clusters, you can only connect to one instance of that cluster.

Note that RMAN *always* connects as SYSDBA to the target database. This is good to know because it implies that the account we connect to has to have the SYSDBA privileges.

If you forget the command-line arguments to RMAN (and somehow manage to leave this book and your documentation at home), then there is a way to get RMAN to display the valid command-line parameters. Simply start RMAN with an invalid parameter. As you can see in the following example, RMAN will return an error, but will also provide you with a list of valid command-line parameters (we removed some of the errors at the bottom of the listing for brevity):

```
C:\Documents and Settings\Robert>rman help
Argument      Value           Description
----------------------------------------------------------------------
target        quoted-string   connect-string for target database
catalog       quoted-string   connect-string for recovery catalog
nocatalog     none            if specified, then no recovery catalog
cmdfile       quoted-string   name of input command file
log           quoted-string   name of output message log file
trace         quoted-string   name of output debugging message log file
append        none            if specified, log is opened in append mode
debug         optional-args   activate debugging
msgno         none            show RMAN-nnnn prefix for all messages
send          quoted-string   send a command to the media manager
pipe          string          building block for pipe names
timeout       integer         number of seconds to wait for pipe input
checksyntax   none            check the command file for syntax errors
----------------------------------------------------------------------
Both single and double quotes (' or ") are accepted for a quoted-string.
Quotes are not required unless the string contains embedded white-space.
```

RMAN offers the **checksyntax** parameter, which allows you to check the RMAN commands you want to issue for errors. Here is an example of the use of the **checksyntax** parameter:

```
C:\Documents and Settings\Robert>rman checksyntax
Recovery Manager:Release 10.2.0.1.0
Production on Tue Oct 18 23:27:51 2005
Copyright (c) 1982, 2005, Oracle.  All rights reserved.

RMAN> backup database pls archivelog;
RMAN-00571: ============================================================
RMAN-00569: =============== ERROR MESSAGE STACK FOLLOWS ===============
RMAN-00571: ============================================================
RMAN-00558: error encountered while parsing input commands
-- various error messages here have been removed

RMAN> backup database plus archivelog;
The command has no syntax errors
```

Note that a lot can be divined from RMAN error messages. Often, within the message, you can see that RMAN was expecting a particular keyword or phrase.

Using the RMAN connect Command

If you start RMAN and realize that you either have not connected to the correct database or wish to connect to a different database (target, catalog, or auxiliary), you can use the **connect** command to change which database RMAN is connected to. To change to another target database, use the **connect target** command. To change to a different recovery catalog, use the **connect catalog** command. To connect to a different auxiliary database, use the **connect auxiliary** command. Here are some examples of the use of the **connect** command:

```
connect target sys/password@testdb;
connect catalog rcat_user/password@robdb;
```

Exiting the RMAN Client

When you are done with RMAN, it's time to get out of the client. RMAN offers two commands, the **quit** and the **exit** command. These commands will return you to the OS prompt. RMAN also allows you to shell out to the OS with the host command. Here are some examples:

```
C:\>rman target=/
Recovery Manager: Release 10.2.0.1.0-Production on Wed Oct 4 22:49:14 2006
Copyright (c) 1982, 2005, Oracle. All rights reserved.
connected to target database: ORCL2 (DBID=582838926)
```

```
RMAN> host;
Microsoft Windows XP [Version 5.1.2600]
(C) Copyright 1985-2001 Microsoft Corp.
C:\>exit
host command complete
RMAN> exit
Recovery Manager complete.
```

Configuring the Database for RMAN Operations

Now that you know how to start RMAN, we need to deal with some configuration issues. While it is possible to just fire up RMAN and do a backup, it's a better idea to deal with some configuration questions before you do so. First, you need to set up the database user that RMAN will be using. Next, you can configure RMAN to use several settings by default, so we will look at those settings as well.

Setting Up the Database User

By default, you can use RMAN with the SYS account (as sysdba) without any configuration required. Of course, that's probably not the best account to use when you are doing production backups. We recommend, before you use RMAN to do a backup, that you create a separate account that is designated for RMAN backups.

RMAN Workshop: *Create the Target Database RMAN Backup Account*

Workshop Notes
For this workshop, you need an installation of the Oracle software and a database that is up and running. You need administrative privileges on this database.

Step 1.   Determine the user account name that you want to use, and create it with the database **create user** command:

```
CREATE USER backup_admin IDENTIFIED BY backupuserpassword
DEFAULT TABLESPACE users;
```

Step 2.   Grant the sysdba privilege to the BACKUP_ADMIN user. You need to grant this privilege because RMAN always connects to the database using the sysdba login. Here is an example of granting the sysdba privilege to the BACKUP_ADMIN account:

```
GRANT sysdba TO backup_admin;
```

> **Regarding Databases Created with the Oracle Database Configuration Assistant**
>
> If you created your database with the ODBCA, you were offered an option to set up automated daily backups. If you selected this option, Oracle will do some initial RMAN configuration for you (it will configure the FRA, for example). While this RMAN configuration is sufficient for databases that are not of consequence, if you are managing databases that are mission critical, you should still follow the steps outlined in this chapter and ensure that your database is properly configured for RMAN operations.

So, what happens if you try to connect RMAN to an account that is not properly created? The following error will occur:

```
D:\oracle\oradata\robt>RMAN target=backup/backup@robt
Recovery Manager: Release 10.2.0.1.0
Production on Tue Aug 22 21:40:51 2006
Copyright (c) 1982, 2005, Oracle.  All rights reserved.
RMAN-00571: ===========================================================
RMAN-00569: =============== ERROR MESSAGE STACK FOLLOWS ===============
RMAN-00571: ===========================================================
RMAN-00554: initialization of internal recovery manager package failed
RMAN-04005: error from target database:
ORA-01031: insufficient privileges
```

Now that we have created the user and granted it the privileges it will need, we are a step closer to being ready to use RMAN. Still, we have some RMAN default settings we need to configure, so let's look at those next.

Setting Up Database Security

We need to discuss briefly the differences between connecting to RMAN on the local server and connecting to it via Oracle Net. When you start RMAN, you might be logged on to the same server as the database. In this case, if you are logged on using a privileged OS user account, you do not need to do anything beyond Steps 1 and 2 in the preceding RMAN Workshop. How do you know whether your user account is a privileged one? It depends on the OS you are using. If you are using Unix, there is generally a Unix group called dba (though it may be called something else) that is created when the Oracle-owning account (usually called Oracle) is created. If your Unix user account is assigned to this group, then you will be able to connect to a target database without any additional work. If you are using Windows platforms, then the privileged users are assigned to an NT group, generally called ORA_DBA.

If you are not logging on to the local server using a privileged account, or if you are connecting to the target database using Oracle Net from a client workstation (for example, you are connecting using system/manager@testdb), then you need to configure your database to use a password file. To do so, you first need to create the password file, and then configure the database so that it knows to use it. Let's look at each of these steps in detail.

Create the Password File

To create the database password file, you use the Oracle utility **orapwd**. This command takes three parameters:

- **file** The password filename

- **password** The password for the sys user

- **entries** Any number of entries to reserve for additional privileged Oracle user accounts

By default, the Oracle database (on NT) will expect the password file to take on the naming standard PWD*sid*.ora, where *sid* is your database name. Here is an example of the creation of a password file:

```
orapwd file=PWDrobt.ora password=robert entries=20
```

So, now that we have created the password file, we need to configure the database to use it, and thus allow us to do remote backups via Oracle Net.

Configure the Database to Use the Password File

By default, an Oracle database is not configured to use the password file (unless you have used the ODBCA to create your database). To configure the database, edit the parameter file (init.ora) in your favorite editor. The parameter we are interested in is REMOTE_LOGIN_PASSWORDFILE. This parameter can be set to one of three values in Oracle Database 10*g*:

- **none** The default value. In this case, Oracle will ignore the password file, and only local privileged logins will be recognized for sysdba access.

- **shared** This parameter indicates that multiple databases can use the same password file. When in this mode, only the SYS user account password can be stored.

- **exclusive** This parameter indicates that the password file is used by only one database. In this mode, the password file can contain passwords for several privileged Oracle accounts. This is the recommend mode of operation, particularly when running RMAN. If you wish to connect RMAN to your database from a remote client, you must use this parameter setting.

If you are using Oracle Database 10g's SPFILE instead of a text-based parameter file, then use the **alter system** command to modify this parameter setting:

```
alter system set REMOTE_LOGIN_PASSWORDFILE=EXCLUSIVE scope=spfile;
```

Finally, the REMOTE_LOGIN_PASSWORDFILE parameter is not dynamic, so you cannot change it with the database up and running.

Setting the CONTROL_FILE_ RECORD_KEEP_TIME Parameter

When configuring your database for RMAN, you should consider how long you wish backup records to be stored in the control file. This includes records of full database backups and specific datafile, control file, parameter file, and archive log backups. The database parameter CONTROL_FILE_RECORD_KEEP_TIME is defined in days (the default is **7**). Thus, by default, Oracle will maintain RMAN backup and recovery records for a period of seven days. You can set this parameter to any value between 0 and 365 days.

This parameter can have a number of operational database impacts. First, it directly impacts the size of the database control file, because as RMAN backups occur, records relating to these backups are stored in the control file. As records are saved in the control file, the control file might well run out of space. In this case, Oracle will expand the control file to accommodate the storage of the required number of backup records. Setting this parameter to **0** will disallow any control file growth but has the negative impact of making the RMAN backup history retention period uncertain.

We suggest that you set CONTROL_FILE_RECORD_KEEP_TIME to a value no less than your selected database backup retention period. Otherwise, you risk having database backups available on your backup media without related backup records available in the control file. This can cause serious complications if you need to recover these older backups for some reason!

Configuring RMAN Default Settings

RMAN allows you to perform automated database backup and recovery, as you will see in later chapters. To support this feature, RMAN allows you to define default values for a number of settings, such as channel configuration. In this section, we look at the configuration of default RMAN settings. Of course, if you can configure something, you will want to be able to change that configuration, and even remove it completely if required. We will look at that, too. So, what will be the benefit of all of this configuration work? It will make the process of actually doing backups much easier in the end. First, we will quickly examine the **configure** command in RMAN and all that it provides us. Then, we will look at several of the different defaults you might want to configure using the **configure** command.

Throughout this section, we use a number of terms that you might not yet be familiar with, because they are covered in later chapters. Many of the terms were introduced in Chapter 2, though others may not be quite clear to you yet. That's okay, because to use RMAN, none of the default configuration options are really required. We suggest that you skim this section to get a feel for the various default values that you can set, and then, after you have read later chapters, return here and reread this section. At that point, you will be ready to decide what defaults you want to apply to your Oracle database.

Introducing the configure Command

RMAN provides the **configure** command, which allows you to define default values to be applied when executing backup and recovery sessions. Using the **configure** command, RMAN allows you to make changes to the default values of the various parameters that are persistent until cleared or changed again. The ability to customize default configuration settings allows you to execute automated RMAN operations. The following are several of the different settings that you can configure:

- A default device type, such as disk or SBT (tape device), to use for RMAN jobs.

- The number of channels that are automatically allocated when performing automated backup and restore jobs.

- A tablespace exclusion policy to configure specific tablespaces to be excluded during full database backup operations.

- The maximum size for any given backup piece and the size of any backup set when doing an automated backup.

- Backup optimization to default to ON or OFF. Backup optimization eliminates duplicate backups of identical datafiles (for example, those associated with read-only tablespaces) and archived redo logs.

- The default filename for the snapshot control file (refer to Chapter 2 for more details on the snapshot control file).

- The default for automated backups of the control file to ON or OFF, as well as the default format for the control file backup output files and the default device on which to create these backups.

- The default filenames for files of an auxiliary database.

- A default retention policy, which determines which backups and copies are eligible for deletion because they are no longer needed.

- The default encryption value and the associated encryption algorithm.

Each configurable setting has a default value assigned to it. The defaults are stored in the database control file (as are any configured values). This is true even if you are connecting to a recovery catalog. You can see the currently configured values for the various RMAN parameters by using the **show** command. Any nondefault RMAN-configured settings are also listed in the V$RMAN_CONFIGURATION database view. Here are some examples of the **show** command's use:

```
show default device type;
show maxsetsize;
show retention policy;
show all;
```

Configuring Various RMAN Default Settings

This section looks at setting RMAN defaults. First, let's look at configuration of channel default settings. You can configure channels in different ways. You can configure defaults for all channels with the **configure channel device type** command, or configure defaults for specific default channels with the **configure channel *n* device type** command.

You can clear channel defaults for all channels with the **configure channel device type clear** command, and clear channel defaults for specific default channels with the **configure channel *n* device type clear** command.

When you allocate a channel with the **allocate channel** command, you can specify the assigned names to the channels that you allocate. For example, the **allocate channel d1 device type disk** command will create a channel called d1. When automated channels are allocated, Oracle assigns default names to these channels. These default names depend on the type of default device used. The following table provides an example of the default name format that will be used.

Device Type	Default Name Format	Example
Disk	ORA_DISK_*n*	ORA_DISK_1 ORA_DISK_2
Tape	ORA_SBT_TAPE_*n*	ORA_SBT_TAPE_1 ORA_SBT_TAPE_2

The number of channels that are automatically allocated depends on the default level of parallelism defined (which we will discuss later in this chapter).

When you issue the **configure** command, Oracle displays the previous configuration settings, followed by the new configuration setting. Now, let's look at some of the number of ways that you can use the **configure** command to automate the backup and restore process with RMAN.

Examples of Using the configure Command

This section presents some examples of using the **configure** command to define default values. In this section, we cover a number of topics revolving around the **configure** command, including:

■ Configuring channel default settings

■ Using the format string

■ Configuring default automated backups of the control file and the SPFILE

■ Configuring default retention policies

■ Configuring default levels of encryption

■ Configuring archive log deletion policies

Configuring Channel Default Settings   Let's start with an example of configuring the default backup/restore device to tape or to disk. In this case, all channels assigned to backups will be allocated to disk:

```
CONFIGURE DEFAULT DEVICE TYPE TO SBT;
CONFIGURE DEFAULT DEVICE TYPE TO DISK;
```

When default device types are configured, Oracle will use that default channel unless you override the default using the **backup device type** parameter. Maintenance channels for **delete** commands and auxiliary channels for duplicate operations will also be automatically allocated.

Once we have configured a default device type, we can configure defaults for the specific type of backup that should occur when that device is used. For example, when doing backups to disk, we can opt to have Oracle back up the database by default using the standard Oracle backup set methodology, or we can have it default to using copies (which can only go to disk). You can also indicate that backup sets should be compressed by default and indicate the degree of parallelism (which represents the number of channels that will be allocated for that backup). Here are examples of configuring for these different options:

```
CONFIGURE DEVICE TYPE DISK BACKUP TYPE TO BACKUPSET;
CONFIGURE DEVICE TYPE DISK BACKUP TYPE TO COMPRESSED BACKUPSET;
CONFIGURE DEVICE TYPE DISK BACKUP TYPE TO COPY;
CONFIGURE DEVICE TYPE DISK PARALLELISM 2;
```

One word about compression, which is a new feature of RMAN in Oracle Database 10*g*. Compression provides real compression of your Oracle backup sets, not unlike zip compression. This can make your backup sets much smaller. Of course, the compression itself consumes resources and will make the backups take longer to complete or restore.

Now let's look at an example of configuring the number of channels to be allocated during an automated backup or recovery operation. Also in this example, we have set the default level of parallelism for disk operations to two. Thus, if you start an automated backup, two channels will be allocated to perform the backup in parallel.

```
CONFIGURE CHANNEL 1 DEVICE TYPE DISK FORMAT 'd:\backup\robt\backup_%U';
CONFIGURE CHANNEL 2 DEVICE TYPE DISK FORMAT 'e:\backup\robt\backup_%U';
```

NOTE
Generally, when setting the default level of parallelism, you should set it to the number of disks or tape drives attached to which you will be backing up.

Several options are available when configuring channels. With the **maxpiecesize** parameter, you can control the size of a backup set piece. You can control the maximum number of files that RMAN can open at one time with the **maxopenfiles** parameter. The **rate** parameter allows you to throttle RMAN and control the rate at which a backup occurs in either bytes, kilobytes, megabytes, or gigabytes per second.

In this example, we put all these options to use. We limit channel 1 to create each individual backup piece at a maximum size of 100MB, and we limit RMAN to opening a maximum of eight files on this channel. Finally, we have constrained the channel such that it cannot have a throughput of more than 100MB.

```
CONFIGURE CHANNEL 1 DEVICE TYPE DISK MAXPIECESIZE 100m maxopenfiles 8
rate 100MB;
```

NOTE
*Don't get confused about the difference between the **maxpiecesize** parameter and the **maxsetsize** parameter: **maxpiecesize** limits the size of the individual backup set pieces and has no impact on the overall cumulative size of the backup. The **maxsetsize** parameter, on the other hand, can and will limit the overall size of your backup, so use it carefully!*

If we had wished to limit all channels, we could have issued the command slightly differently:

```
CONFIGURE CHANNEL DEVICE TYPE DISK MAXPIECESIZE 100m;
```

So, why might we want to change the maximum size that a given backup set piece can be? First, we might have some specific file size limitations that we have to deal with. Tapes can only handle so much data, and some disk file systems have limits on how large a given datafile can be.

We might also want to set a tape device as the default device for all channels, along with some specific parameter settings. In this case, our **configure** command might look like this:

```
-- Note that we could have used the = sign after the PARMS clause if
-- we preferred like this PARMS='ENV=(NB_ORA_CLASS=RMAN_rs100_tape).
-- This is true with many parameters.
CONFIGURE CHANNEL DEVICE TYPE sbt MAXPIECESIZE 100m
PARMS 'ENV=(NB_ORA_CLASS=RMAN_rs100_tape)';
```

You may wish to configure a default maximum size for an entire backup set, in which case you would use this slightly modified syntax (it is followed by an example of resetting this value back to the default, which is unlimited):

```
CONFIGURE MAXSETSIZE TO 7500K;
CONFIGURE MAXSETSIZE CLEAR;
```

CAUTION
*Be careful when using **maxsetsize** to limit the size of the entire backup that is being created. While your database might be smaller than the **maxsetsize** defined initially, it could quickly grow beyond the **maxsetsize**, causing your database backups to fail.*

When using the **configure** command, you may find that you need to clear a given configuration so that you can use the default. To do this, use the **configure** command with the **clear** option. In this example, we are clearing out the default options set for default channel 1:

```
CONFIGURE CHANNEL 1 DEVICE TYPE DISK CLEAR;
```

As you will see in later chapters, you can configure the backup process to create duplexed backups; in other words, multiple copies of the backup can be created at different locations. You can also configure database default settings such that automatic backups will be duplexed using the **configure** command.

Here is an example where we have defined that all backups to disk by default will be duplexed, with two copies:

```
configure datafile backup copies for device type disk to 2;
```

We discussed the snapshot control file in Chapter 2. This file is a point-in-time copy of the database control file that is taken during RMAN backup operations. The snapshot control file ensures that the backup is consistent to a given point in time. Thus, if you add a tablespace or datafile to a database after the backup has started (assuming an online backup, of course), that tablespace or datafile will not be included in the backup. Sometimes it is desirable to have RMAN create the backup control file in a location other than the default location. In this event, you can use the **configure** command to define a new default location for the snapshot control file:

```
configure snapshot control file name to 'd:\oracle\backup\scontrolf';
```

Note that Oracle does not create the snapshot control file in the FRA even if the FRA is configured.

You may wish to exclude specific tablespaces during an automated backup, which Oracle allows you to do with the **configure** command. Here is an example of excluding a tablespace by default:

```
configure exclude for tablespace old_data;
```

The **configure** command allows you to enable or disable backup optimization. When enabled, *backup optimization* will cause Oracle to skip backups of files that already have identical backups on the device being backed up to. Here is an example of configuring backup optimization:

```
configure backup optimization on;
```

Note that for optimization to occur, you must have enabled it. In addition, you must issue the **backup database** or **backup archivelog** command with the **like** or **all** option. Alternatively, you can use the **backup backupset all** command (more information on these types of backups is provided in later chapters). Finally, you can disable the setting for backup optimization by using the **force** parameter of the **backup** command.

Using the Format String Note in previous examples that in several places we defined one or more disk locations and filename formats. This is known as the *format string specification*. You will see the format string specification used a great deal in this book, and you will use it a great deal when working with RMAN. Most of the examples you will see in this book will be from Oracle on Windows. Regardless of the platform you are using, though, the format string will look pretty much the same. For example, if we were using a Unix system, our format string might look like this:

```
CONFIGURE CHANNEL 1 DEVICE TYPE DISK FORMAT
'/u01/opt/oracle/backup/robt/backup_%U';
CONFIGURE CHANNEL 2 DEVICE TYPE DISK FORMAT
'/u01/opt/oracle/backup/robt/backup_%U';
```

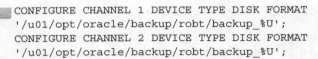

NOTE
*Oracle will not manage your backup files if you use the **format** parameter, even if you are backing up to the FRA, because the backup is not managed by Oracle. If the FORMAT option is used, then the retention policy will have to remove the formatted backups. If FORMAT is not used, then OMF names are used and the files are created in the FRA.*

The format string is used a lot in the **configure** command. You will also see it in other RMAN commands such as the **backup**, **restore**, and **allocate channel** commands. RMAN offers several *syntax elements* associated with the format string specification. These elements are placeholders that will cause RMAN to replace the format string with the associated defined values. For example, the %U syntax element in the previous example tells RMAN to substitute a system-generated unique identifier for the filename. %U then keeps each backup filename unique. Table 3-3 lists the valid syntax elements and gives a quick description of their use.

Element	Description
%a	Indicates that the activation ID of the database should be substituted.
%c	Specifies that the copy number of the backup piece within a set of duplexed backup pieces, with a maximum value of 256, should be substituted. This number will be 1 for nonduplexed backup sets and 0 for proxy copies.
%d	Indicates that the name of the database should be substituted.
%D	Indicates that the current day of the month from the Gregorian calendar in the format DD should be substituted.
%e	Indicates that the archived log sequence number should be substituted.
%f	Indicates that the absolute file number should be substituted.

TABLE 3-3. *Format String Specification Descriptions*

Element	Description
%F	Provides a unique and repeatable name that combines the database ID (DBID), day, month, year, and sequence.
%h	Indicates that the archived redo log thread number should be substituted.
%I	Indicates that the DBID should be substituted.
%M	Indicates that the month in the Gregorian calendar in the format MM should be substituted.
%N	Indicates that the tablespace name should be substituted.
%n	Indicates that the name of the database, padded on the right with x characters to a total length of eight characters, should be substituted. For example, if ROBDB is the database name, then the padded name is ROBDBxxx.
%p	Indicates that the piece number within the backup set should be substituted. This value starts at 1 for each backup set and is incremented by 1 as each backup piece is created.
%s	Indicates that the backup set number should be substituted. This number is a counter in the control file that is incremented for each backup set. The counter value starts at 1. This number will be unique for the lifetime of the control file (thus, it is reset at RESETLOGS or when the control file is restored or re-created).
%t	Indicates that the backup set time stamp, which is a 4-byte value derived as the number of seconds elapsed since a fixed reference time, should be substituted. %s and %t combined can be used to form a unique name for the backup set.
%T	Indicates that the year, month, and day from the Gregorian calendar in the format YYYYMMDD should be substituted.
%u	Indicates that an eight-character name, consisting of compressed representations of the backup set or image copy number and the time the backup set or image copy was created, should be substituted.
%U	This is the default file-naming pattern and provides a system-generated unique filename for RMAN-related files. The meaning of this substitution string differs when dealing with image copies or backup pieces. When using backup set pieces, %U specifies a convenient shorthand for %u_%p_%c that guarantees uniqueness in generated backup filenames. The meaning differs when using image copies, and depending on the type of image copy. Meaning when used with an image copy of datafiles: `data-D-%d_id-%I_TS-%N_FNO-%f_%u` Meaning when used with an image copy of an archived redo log: `arch-D_%d-id-%I_S-%e_T-%h_A-%a_%u` Meaning when used with an image copy of a control file: `cf-D_%d-id-%I_%u`
%Y	Indicates that the year in the format YYYY should be substituted.
%%	Indicates that you wish to actually use the % character; for example, %%Y.

TABLE 3-3. *Format String Specification Descriptions* (continued)

Configuring Default Automated Backups of the Control File and the SPFILE RMAN in Oracle Database 10g offers the ability to back up the control file and the database parameter file, and you can configure these backups to take place by default. Again, you can use the **configure** command to configure this automated backup process to happen automatically during a backup. Here is an example of configuring automated backups of these important database files, and an example of turning the default configuration off:

```
configure controlfile autobackup on;
configure controlfile autobackup off;
```

When autobackup of the control and parameter files is configured, the following rules apply:

- The control file and the server parameter file will be automatically backed up with each RMAN **backup** or **copy** command issued that is not included in a **run** block.

- If a **run** block is used, then the control files and parameter files will be backed up at the end of the **run** block if the last command is not **backup** or **copy**.

In addition to the last two types of automated control file backups, a special type of control file backup can be configured to occur as a direct result of database changes such as adding new tablespaces, adding datafiles, adding online redo logs, and so on. This type of automatic backup can only happen to disk. A special option of the **configure controlfile autobackup** command can be used to facilitate this backup. Here is an example:

```
RMAN> configure controlfile autobackup format for device type
disk to 'd:\backup\contf\robt_%F'
```

When this option is used, the Oracle RDBMS will automatically back up the control file during database structure changes that impact the control file. These changes might include adding a new tablespace, altering the state of a tablespace or datafile (for example, bringing it online), adding a new online redo log, renaming a file, adding a new redo thread, and so forth. Note that this automated backup can only be to disk, because tape is not supported. These backups can get a bit large (since the control file contains a history of many of the past backups), so make sure you allocate enough disk space to the backup directory. In spite of the additional space that will be required, these backups can be incredibly handy to have for recovery. Finally, be aware that if the backup fails for any reason, the database operation itself will not fail.

NOTE
If you are not going to use a recovery catalog, and
you wish to be able to recover your control file after
an automated control file backup, you must know
the DBID of the database. You should, as a part of
your initial setup and configuration of RMAN, note
the DBIDs of the databases that you will be backing
up and save that list somewhere safe. The DBID of
the database is available from the V$DATABASE
view in the DBID column. The DBID of the database
is also displayed when you start RMAN and connect
to a target database, as shown in this example:

```
C:\ t>rman targot=/
Recovery Manager: Release 10.2.0.1.0 -
Production on Sun Oct 23 11:00:49 2005
Copyright (c) 1982, 2005, Oracle.  All rights reserved.
connected to target database: ROB10R2 (DBID=3753137102)
```

Configuring Default Retention Policies   So, how long do you want to keep your
database backups? RMAN enables you to configure a backup retention policy, using
the **configure retention policy** command. Configuring a retention policy will not
cause backups to be deleted automatically, but will cause expired backup sets to
appear when the **report obsolete** command is executed. See Chapter 15 for more
on **report obsolete**.

Let's look at an example of how a backup retention policy works. First, let's
configure a retention policy of three days:

```
RMAN> configure retention policy to recovery window of 3 days;
new RMAN configuration parameters:
CONFIGURE RETENTION POLICY TO RECOVERY WINDOW OF 3 DAYS;
new RMAN configuration parameters are successfully stored
```

Now that we have configured our retention policy, let's see which backups that
we might have already done are reported to be obsolete:

```
RMAN> report obsolete;
RMAN retention policy will be applied to the command
RMAN retention policy is set to recovery window of 3 days
Report of obsolete backups and copies
Type                 Key    Completion Time    Filename/Handle
-------------------- ------ ------------------ --------------------
Backup Set           4      02-JUN-02
Backup Piece         4      02-JUN-02
D:\ORACLE\ORA102\DATABASE\0ADQ1RV0_1_1
Backup Piece         5      02-JUN-02
D:\ORACLE\ORA102\DATABASE\0ADQ1RV0_1_2
```

```
Backup Set            5        02-JUN-02
Backup Piece          6        02-JUN-02
D:\BACKUP\ROBT\BACKUP_0BDQ1SA2_1_1
Backup Piece          7        02-JUN-02
D:\BACKUP\ROBT\BACKUP_0BDQ1SA2_1_2
Archive Log           4        02-JUN-02
D:\ORACLE\ADMIN\ROBT\ARCH\ROBT_201.ARC
Archive Log           3        02-JUN-02
D:\ORACLE\ADMIN\ROBT\ARCH\ROBT_200.ARC
Archive Log           2        02-JUN-02
D:\ORACLE\ADMIN\ROBT\ARCH\ROBT_199.ARC
```

In this example, we have two backup sets and four related backup pieces that are obsolete based on our backup retention policy. Additionally, we have three archived redo logs that are ready to be removed as well. You can easily remove the backup sets by using the **delete obsolete** command:

```
RMAN> delete obsolete;
RMAN retention policy will be applied to the command
RMAN retention policy is set to recovery window of 3 days
using channel ORA_DISK_1
using channel ORA_DISK_2
Deleting the following obsolete backups and copies:
Type                  Key     Completion Time     Filename/Handle
-------------------   ------  ------------------  --------------------
Backup Set            4        02-JUN-02
Backup Piece          4        02-JUN-02
D:\ORACLE\ORA102\DATABASE\0ADQ1RV0_1_1
Backup Piece          5        02-JUN-02
D:\ORACLE\ORA102\DATABASE\0ADQ1RV0_1_2
Backup Set            5        02-JUN-02
Backup Piece          6        02-JUN-02
D:\BACKUP\ROBT\BACKUP_0BDQ1SA2_1_1
Backup Piece          7        02-JUN-02
D:\BACKUP\ROBT\BACKUP_0BDQ1SA2_1_2
Archive Log           4        02-JUN-02
D:\ORACLE\ADMIN\ROBT\ARCH\ROBT_201.ARC
Archive Log           3        02-JUN-02
D:\ORACLE\ADMIN\ROBT\ARCH\ROBT_200.ARC
Archive Log           2        02-JUN-02
D:\ORACLE\ADMIN\ROBT\ARCH\ROBT_199.ARC
Do you really want to delete the above objects (enter YES or NO)? yes
deleted backup piece
backup piece
handle=D:\BACKUP\ROBT\BACKUP_05DQ1NJ7_1_1 recid=1 stamp=463527534
deleted backup piece
backup piece
handle=D:\ORACLE\ORA102\DATABASE\08DQ1P0T_1_1 recid=2 stamp=463529047
deleted backup piece
```

```
backup piece
handle=D:\ORACLE\ORA102\DATABASE\07DQ1P0R_1_1 recid=3 stamp=463528990
deleted backup piece
backup piece
handle=D:\ORACLE\ORA102\DATABASE\0ADQ1RV0_1_1 recid=4 stamp=463532002
<additional output removed for brevity>
deleted backup piece
backup piece
handle=D:\ORACLE\ORA102\DATABASE\0ADQ1RV0_1_2 recid=5 stamp=463532002
deleted archive log
archive log filename=D:\ORACLE\ADMIN\ROBT\ARCH\ROBT_349.ARC recid=11
stamp=463524691
Deleted 11 objects
```

Note in the preceding example that the system will ask you to confirm that you really want to remove the objects that are slated to be removed. If any of the listed objects are not available to be removed, then you will need to run the **crosscheck** command (discussed in Chapter 14). Otherwise, each item listed as deleted in the **delete obsolete** output will be deleted by Oracle.

If you back up your database infrequently, you probably will prefer a redundancy policy that is stated in terms of number of backups rather than backups later than *x* days old. In this case, you can use the **configure** command again, this time using the **redundancy** parameter:

```
RMAN> configure retention policy to redundancy 3;
old RMAN configuration parameters:
CONFIGURE RETENTION POLICY TO RECOVERY WINDOW OF 2 DAYS;
new RMAN configuration parameters:
CONFIGURE RETENTION POLICY TO REDUNDANCY 3;
new RMAN configuration parameters are successfully stored
```

The **report obsolete** and **delete obsolete** commands work just the same when using this retention policy.

Finally, if you want to disable the retention policy, you use the command **configure retention policy to none**, and no retention policy will be applicable. Use the **configure retention policy clear** command to reset the retention policy to the default value, which is a redundancy of 1.

NOTE
If you are using a tape management system, it may have its own retention policy. If the tape management system's retention policy is in conflict with the backup retention policy that you have defined in RMAN, the tape management system's retention policy will take precedence and your ability to recover a backup will be in jeopardy.

Configuring Default Levels of Encryption   RMAN can create encrypted backups in Oracle Database 10g release 2 and later. During the backup, the backup sets are encrypted as they are created. When the backups are restored, Oracle will decrypt the backup sets. In this section, we discuss the types of encryption that are available and then look at how to configure RMAN so that it can use encryption.

Oracle offers three different encryption modes:

- **Transparent mode**   Transparent mode encryption requires no DBA interaction. To use this mode, you must have configured the Oracle Encryption Wallet.

- **Password mode**   Password mode encryption requires that a password be supplied when creating backups to be encrypted or when restoring backups that were encrypted when they were created. The password is supplied using the command **set encryption on identified by password only** in your RMAN backup scripts. This is the encryption mode we will use in this text.

- **Dual mode**   Dual mode backups can be restored either by password or by the presence of the Oracle Encryption Wallet. This makes offsite restores of backups easier, since the install of the Oracle Encryption Wallet is not required. To create a dual mode encrypted backup, you use the **set encryption on identified by password** command (note that the **only** keyword is missing).

Use the **configure** command to configure various persistent settings related to RMAN encryption of backups. You can use the RMAN **configure** command to indicate the following:

- Whether all database files should be encrypted

- Whether specific tablespaces should be encrypted

- Which of the available encryption algorithms should be used to encrypt your backups

If you are using Oracle Encryption Wallet–based security, then you only need to set the persistent RMAN settings required by the **configure** command. If you wish to use password mode encryption or dual mode encryption, you need to configure the persistent security defaults with the configure **command**, and then use the **set** command when starting your backups to set the correct password for the backup. RMAN does not persistently set the backup password, so it must be entered for each RMAN backup or recovery session. The **set** command, and how to use it during backups, is covered in much more detail in Chapter 9. In the following command, we configure and enable backup encryption for the entire database. Notice that if we have not configured the Oracle Encryption Wallet, any subsequent backups will fail unless we use the **set** command to establish an encryption password for the session (we are jumping the gun just a bit, but we provide an example of using the **set** command to set the backup password for appropriate context).

```
-- Configures default encryption.
-- Uses transparent mode encryption by default.
RMAN> CONFIGURE ENCRYPTION FOR DATABASE ON;
-- For this session, we want password mode encryption,
-- so we have to set the
-- password. This is good only for this session, until we exit RMAN or
issue-- another connect command.
RMAN> SET ENCRYPTION ON IDENTIFIED BY robert ONLY;
-- Way ahead of ourselves, but this backs up the database!
RMAN> BACKUP DATABASE PLUS ARCHIVELOG;
```

Archived redo log backups are backed up using encryption if the following are true:

- The **set encryption on** command is in effect at the time that the backup of the archived redo logs is occurring.

- Encryption has been configured for the entire database, or at least one tablespace of the database.

Configuring Archive Log Deletion Policies   You can configure RMAN to manage your archived redo log deletion policy for you. By default, Oracle applies the configured backup retention policy to the archived redo logs. However, if you are using the FRA and a standby database, you can configure RMAN to mark archived redo logs as eligible for removal, after they have been applied to a mandatory standby database using the **configure archivelog deletion policy to applied on standby** command. In this case, once the archived redo log has been successfully applied to a mandatory standby database location, it is eligible for removal from the FRA by Oracle.

If You Are Using Shared Servers

If you are using Oracle's Shared Servers option (known as Multi-Threaded Server, or MTS, in previous Oracle versions), then you have to configure a dedicated server for use with RMAN because RMAN cannot use a Shared Servers session to connect to the database. If you are using a Shared Servers architecture, refer to Chapter 5 of the *Oracle Database Backup and Recovery Advanced Users Guide (10g Release 2)* for more information on how to configure RMAN for use with the Oracle Database 10g Shared Servers option.

Essentially, you must configure a dedicated connection in Oracle Net for your server using the SERVER=DEDICATED syntax, as shown in this example (note that Oracle Net configurations vary greatly, so what may be required of you might differ):

```
Rob1_ded =
  (DESCRIPTION=
    (ADDRESS=(PROTOCOL=tcp)(HOST=robpc)(port1521))
    (CONNECT_DATA=(SERVICE_NAME=rob1_ded)(SERVER=dedicated)))
```

Summary of RMAN Configuration Tasks

We have thrown a great deal of information at you in this chapter. Let's summarize some of the tasks that we suggest you perform on any database on which you intend to perform backups using RMAN:

1. Determine whether you wish to run the database in ARCHIVELOG mode or NOARCHIVELOG mode. Configure the database accordingly.

2. Configure the FRA.

3. Set up a separate database user account (not sys) for use with RMAN.

4. In the database parameter file, set the CONTROL_FILE_RECORD_KEEP_TIME parameter to a number of days equivalent to or greater than the number of days you wish to retain database backups.

5. If you are using shared servers, set up a dedicated server address for RMAN to connect to.

6. Using RMAN, connect to the target database to ensure that the database is set up correctly (error messages will appear if your RMAN account is not correctly set up).

7. Use the **configure** command to establish your default RMAN values. In particular, consider configuring the following:

    ■ The default degree of parallelism for tape or disk backups. Set it to a default value equivalent to the number of disks or tape drives that you will be backing up to.

    ■ Automatic channels and device types. Configure as many channels as you have individual devices.

    ■ Automated control file/database parameter file autobackups.

    ■ Database backup encryption.

8. Configure the retention policy as required. Make sure this retention policy is in sync with any other retention policies, such as those associated with tape management systems.

9. Configure RMAN for control file and SPFILE automatic backups.

10. Before you use it for production database backups, test your RMAN configuration by doing a backup and recovery as demonstrated in later chapters.

The Recovery Catalog

Oracle maintains all of the metadata related to RMAN operations in the *RMAN repository*. The RMAN repository is *always* stored in the control file of the target databases. There may be cases where you will want to store the RMAN repository for your database in another location. This location is called the RMAN *recovery catalog*.

RMAN does not require the recovery catalog for most operations, so in many cases it is truly an optional component. Because the recovery catalog is largely optional, RMAN actually defaults to a configuration with no recovery catalog. In this section, first we look at what the recovery catalog is and when you need to use it. Then, we look at how you create a recovery catalog and discuss backup and recovery of the recovery catalog.

What Is the Recovery Catalog?

The *recovery catalog* is an optional component of RMAN that stores historical backup information from RMAN backups. Unlike the database control file's RMAN information, the recovery catalog data is not purged on a regular basis. Thus, the historical information in the recovery catalog tends to be more comprehensive and date further back than the historical information in the control file. Using a recovery catalog does have a few additional benefits over just using the database control file:

- You must use a recovery catalog if you wish to use stored RMAN scripts.

- A recovery catalog offers a single, enterprise-wide repository of RMAN information. This provides an easier and more flexible central repository of enterprise backup information.

- A recovery catalog allows more flexibility when doing reporting, since you can report on the target database at a time other than the current time.

- With a recovery catalog, certain default database RMAN channel configuration information will still be maintained.

If you are an old hand at RMAN, you may have noticed some bullets missing here. First, Oracle Database 10*g* easily supports recovery though **resetlogs** now without a recovery catalog. Also, if you are using control file autobackups (which we strongly suggest), the need for a recovery catalog for control file recoveries is pretty much removed.

> **NOTE**
> *If you are not going to use a recovery catalog, keep a record of your database DBIDs. While this is not required, and you can work around it, having the DBIDs for your databases will make recovery operations much easier.*

Should you use a recovery catalog? If you have just a few databases, then the recovery catalog is probably not worth the extra effort and hassle. If you have a database environment with many databases in it, you should consider using a recovery catalog. Generally, the added flexibility and centralized enterprise-wide reporting benefits of the recovery catalog outweigh the additional maintenance and administrative requirements that are added with the use of a recovery catalog. One downside to using a recovery catalog, though, is that if the catalog database is down, *your backups will all fail* unless you have coded your backup scripts to perform a backup without the recovery catalog in cases where the first backup with the recovery catalog fails.

Additionally, a recovery catalog is an essential part of a Data Guard backup environment and Split mirror backups. In these configurations, when you back up the database from the backup host, the recovery catalog is considered the most current information, so it is the brains behind the strategy and becomes a single point of failure if not maintained properly. The bottom line is that you need to decide for yourself whether your environment calls for a recovery catalog.

When connecting to RMAN, you must use the **catalog** command-line parameter to indicate that you want RMAN to connect to a recovery catalog. By default, RMAN uses the **nocatalog** option, which indicates that a recovery catalog will not be used. After using the **catalog** parameter, indicate the userid and password of the recovery catalog schema that contains the recovery catalog objects. Here is an example of connecting to the recovery catalog using the RMAN command line:

```
RMAN target='sys/robert as sysdba@robt'
catalog='cataloguser/password@bcatalog'
```

Creating the Recovery Catalog

As you might expect, some setup is required before we can actually connect to the recovery catalog. First, we need to create the recovery catalog user and grant it the appropriate privileges. Then, we need to connect to it and create the recovery catalog schema objects. Let's look at each of these steps next.

Configuring the Database for the Recovery Catalog

The recovery catalog database should, if possible, exist on its own database. However, in our experience, many sites use an active database as the recovery catalog database, which is fine as long as you take precautions when backing up that database.

Oracle makes the following suggestions with regard to space allocations for a recovery catalog database that would maintain recovery catalog records for one year:

Tablespace Name	Size Requirement
SYSTEM	90MB
TEMP	5MB
UNDO	5MB
RECOVERY CATALOG SCHEMA	15MB per registered database
ONLINE REDO LOGS	1MB per online redo log file

Creating the Recovery Catalog User

Generally, the recovery catalog should reside in its own database, because the recovery catalog is pretty useless if it is in the same database that you are trying to recover. The next RMAN Workshop provides a set of detailed instructions on creating the recovery catalog user account.

RMAN Workshop: *Create the Recovery Catalog User Account*

Workshop Notes

For this workshop, you need an installation of the Oracle software. You also need to identify a database to create the recovery catalog schema in. You need administrative privileges in this database to create the recovery catalog user account. Finally, determine the name and password you will assign to the recovery catalog user account.

You should create a tablespace for the recovery catalog schema objects. We suggest that you size the tablespace at about 15MB to start.

Step 1. Create the recovery catalog user. Make sure you do not use the SYSTEM tablespace as the temporary tablespace (check out the new Oracle Database 10*g* default temporary tablespace feature!). Assign the recovery catalog tablespace that you have created (as suggested in the Workshop Notes) to this schema as its default tablespace. Also, assign the recovery catalog user to an **unlimited quota** on the recovery catalog tablespace. Here is an example of this operation:

```
CREATE USER rcat_user IDENTIFIED BY rcat_password
DEFAULT TABLESPACE catalog;
```

Step 2.   Grant the following roles to the recovery catalog user:

- connect
- resource
- recovery_catalog_owner

Here is an example of granting the RCAT_USER user we created earlier the roles it requires:

```
GRANT connect, resource, recovery_catalog_owner TO rcat_user;
```

NOTE
The recovery catalog user account is somewhat of a privileged database account. Secure it as you would sys or system.

Creating the Recovery Catalog Schema Objects

Now that you have created the recovery catalog database and user, it's time to actually create the recovery catalog. This is a pretty simple process in Oracle Database 10*g*. All you need to do is use RMAN. When you start RMAN, use the **target** parameter to connect to the target database, and use the **catalog** parameter to connect to the recovery catalog database schema (which you just created).

At the RMAN prompt, you then issue the **create catalog** command. Optionally, you can use the **tablespace** parameter to define a tablespace in which to create the RMAN schema objects. The next RMAN Workshop provides an example of using the **create catalog** command to create the recovery catalog schema.

Register the Database with the Recovery Catalog

Now that you have prepared the recovery catalog for use, you need to register databases with it. This is required before you can perform an RMAN backup of a database using the recovery catalog. This is a rather simple process, as you can see in the associated RMAN Workshop.

RMAN Workshop: *Create the Recovery Catalog*

Workshop Notes

For this workshop, you should have completed the previous RMAN Workshop ("Create the Recovery Catalog User Account"). Also, we assume that you have created a tablespace called CATALOG_TBS, and we will be creating the RMAN schema objects in that tablespace.

Step 1.   Connect to the recovery catalog with RMAN:

```
RMAN catalog=rcat_user/rcat_password
```

Step 2.   Issue the **create catalog** command from the RMAN prompt:

```
create catalog tablespace catalog_tbs;
```

RMAN Workshop: *Register Your Database in the Recovery Catalog*

Workshop Notes

For this workshop, you should have completed the previous RMAN Workshop ("Create the Recovery Catalog").

Step 1.   Using RMAN, sign into the database and the recovery catalog at the same time:

```
set ORACLE_SID=main_db
RMAN target=backup_admin/backupuserpassword
CATALOG=rcat_user/rcat_password@recover
```

Step 2.   Register the database with the recovery catalog:

```
RMAN> Register database;
```

Step 3. (optional)   Verify that the registration of the database was successful by issuing the **report schema** command from the RMAN prompt when connected to the target database:

```
RMAN> Report Schema;
```

Dropping the Recovery Catalog

Just as you can create the recovery catalog schema, you may wish to drop it. Use the **drop catalog** command to drop the recovery catalog schema. Of course, you should understand that all the information contained in the schema is going to be lost, so you should consider backing up the recovery catalog database before you drop the catalog schema.

Adding RMAN Backups to the Recovery Catalog

If you have already executed RMAN backups without a recovery catalog and you wish to add them to the recovery catalog later, you can use the **catalog** command. You can catalog datafile copies, backup set pieces, archive log backups, and even whole directories of backups, as shown in the following examples:

```
RMAN> CATALOG DATAFILECOPY 'D:\ORACLE\ORA102\DATABASE\system01.dbf';
RMAN> CATALOG ARCHIVELOG 'D:\ORACLE\ORA102\DATABASE\arch_988.arc',
      'D:\ORACLE\ORA102\DATABASE\arch_988.arc';
RMAN> CATALOG BACKUPPIECE 'D:\ORACLE\ORA102\DATABASE\backup_820.bkp';
RMAN> CATALOG START WITH 'D:\ORACLE\ORA102\DATABASE\';
```

> **NOTE**
> *Beware of the **catalog start with** command. You must have the trailing backslash at the end of the directory path. If you used D:\ORACLE\ORA102\ DATABASE instead, Oracle will traverse all possible directory combinations of DATABASE that are available in C:\ORACLE\ORA102. This might include directories such as C:\ORACLE\ORA102\ DATABASE, C:\ORACLE\ORA102\DATABASE-123, and C:\ORACLE\ORA102\DATABASE-OLD. Use the trailing backslash to indicate that you just want C:\ORACLE\ORA102\DATABASE\.*

Unregistering a Database from the Recovery Catalog

You can use the **unregister database** command in RMAN to unregister a database. If you wish to unregister an existing database, simply connect to that database and to the recovery catalog and issue the **unregister database** command:

```
RMAN>unregister database;
```

If the database has been removed and you wish to remove it from the recovery catalog, you simply need to know the name of the database you wish to unregister in most cases. If you wish to unregister the OLDROB database, you would issue this command after connecting to the recovery catalog:

```
RMAN> Unregister database OLDROB;
```

In cases where multiple databases with the same name are registered in the recovery catalog, you need to know the DBID for the database that you wish to unregister. You then need to run the **unregister database** command in a **run** block, while also using the **set dbid** command, as shown in this example:

```
rman CATALOG rman/rman@catdb
RMAN> RUN
{   SET DBID 2414555533;    # specifies the database by DBID
    UNREGISTER DATABASE ROBOLD NOPROMPT;
}
```

Backing Up and Recovering the Recovery Catalog

We will look at how to actually use the recovery catalog in later chapters as we discuss RMAN backups in general. Since RMAN can back up databases without a recovery catalog, it makes sense that you can use RMAN to actually back up the recovery catalog itself. If you choose to use RMAN to back up your recovery catalog, it would be a very good idea to create backups of your control file and store them in a separate location from your RMAN backups of the recovery catalog. Since recovering the control file can be a time-consuming process during a non–recovery catalog restore of your database, a separate backup of the control file is something to consider.

Other Backup and Recovery Setup and Configuration Considerations

Finally, let's consider the other backup and recovery implications of your database. There are certain things that RMAN will not back up that you need to consider as a part of your overall backup and recovery strategy planning. These include such things as the base Oracle RDBMS software and the parameter files (tnsnames.ora, names.ora, sqlnet.ora, and so on). You need to make plans to back up and recover these files as a part of your overall backup and recovery planning.

You also need to consider your disaster planning with regard to RMAN and non-RMAN backups. How will you protect these backups from flood, fire, and earthquake? The beginning is a very good time to consider these questions, not when the fire is burning two flights below!

Summary

Whew! We have covered a great deal of ground in this chapter, and indeed there are several things you need to do before you start using RMAN. First, we described how to set up the database in ARCHIVELOG mode, if that is what you wish to do. Next, we looked at the RMAN command line and at how to configure your database for use with RMAN, including setting up the password file and configuring a user account for use with RMAN. We also looked at configuring RMAN default settings. We strongly suggest you take advantage of this feature in RMAN, as it can make your life much easier. We then provided you with a summary of RMAN configuration tasks. Finally, we discussed the recovery catalog, including configuration and backup issues.

CHAPTER
4

Media Management
Considerations

he focus of the RMAN utility in Oracle Database 10g is on the best way to leverage disk backups as the media recovery solution. With the price of disks falling, massive storage area networks (SANs) have found a permanent place in many data centers. With the business evolving toward cheaper and larger disks, upgrades in RMAN functionality (such as the flash recovery area) were implemented to make best use of the available storage space.

It's a logical progression for the RMAN backup utility, and of course writing to disk is something that the Oracle database is extremely good at. So anytime it gets to leverage its disk-writing muscle, the RDBMS will do so for performance improvements.

But, for many customers, the world of unlimited disk storage has not arrived. For many, the size of the database, or its location, keeps it from being backed up to disk. Or, there is still a business requirement to make a copy of the data and archive it offsite. So, what does RMAN do if it needs to write to good old-fashioned tape?

Tape backups of the Oracle database require third-party assistance. This is primarily due to the disparate nature of the different sequential media subsystems that are on the market and put to use every day. Instead of trying to employ different system calls for each of these different types of tape devices, RMAN's development team decided to employ those software vendors that already earn a living by selling products that can read and write from tape.

Oracle has its own media management software solution, named Oracle Secure Backup (OSB). OSB is a fully integrated, RMAN-to-tape solution that does not require any third-party vendor software plug-in. But OSB is still in its infancy, although it is certainly priced for rapid uptake in the market. However, until it fully matures, most customers will continue to purchase a license from any one of the number of certified backup providers that have an Oracle RMAN plug-in (more on this in a minute).

This chapter covers the conceptual architecture of employing a media manager to back up your database directly to disk. It does so from a generic standpoint, by staying focused on the RMAN side of the equation and speaking in grand sweeping generalizations about the media management products themselves. We will talk about the setup from the RMAN side, how it all works, and what changes when you use tape for your output device. Chapters 6, 7, and 8 go into detail about three of the most popular media management products on the market, and talk about configuring and using them specifically. Chapter 5 provides an overview of the new Oracle-produced media management product, Oracle Secure Backup (OSB).

In Oracle9i, there was a stripped-down version of the Legato Networker product, Legato Single Server Version (LSSV), that was shipped with the database. This was a free product that allowed you to back up a database to a local tape drive only. Starting with Oracle Database 10g Release 2, LSSV is a thing of the past. It no longer ships with Oracle products, so there is no out-of-the-box tape backup solution. You will have to purchase a product from a media management vendor in order to do any tape backups or download OSB from Oracle.

Tape Backups in a Disk Backup World

In the world of Oracle databases, size does matter. In fact, less than a decade ago, a database a few gigabytes in size was considered very large. Now, databases range upward into the terabytes, the first pedabyte database has been reported, and the average database is 100GB and growing. So when it comes to backups, the idea of trying to find enough contiguous space on disk to get the thing backed up can be difficult, even with the massive number of SANs being deployed in the enterprise.

Thus, the first reason for tape backups is the size of the database. The size of a database determines whether you need to back up to tape: buying more hard drives can get pricey, but tapes? Even with disk prices dropping radically, tapes are still cheaper in volume, and reliable, considering their purpose is to hold copies of data—copies that by the law of averages will rarely ever get used. Of course, there are times when disk backups become a critical piece of a strategy that stresses quick recovery—tape backups are much slower than disk backups on both the backup and the restore. The price point of a tape, compared to disks, remains a compelling reason for tape backups.

The second reason to use tape backups is manageability. Typically, enterprise-wide backup strategies are implemented and executed by a centralized person on a centralized system. And this is a good thing—economy of scale and all of that. It allows your company to invest in large tape storage jukeboxes that can stream data from multiple different sources. Then, the data backups can be cataloged and removed without having someone trek all over the enterprise distributing tapes, troubleshooting individual tape devices, or training users on new software rollouts.

A third and frequently disregarded reason for tape backups is their portability. A pile of tapes can easily be moved offsite for archival and disaster-proofing reasons. Hard drives just don't transport that well.

The drawback to pooling backup resources is that it leads to complications, especially in regard to Oracle databases. The tricky nature of Oracle datafiles, log files, and control files means that we cannot simply let an OS job step in and copy the files at its leisure. Instead, we have to prepare the database for the backup job, signal the copy to begin, and then reconfigure the database afterward. Or so it was in the old-school world (refer to Chapter 1).

Using RMAN means that this database configuration is eliminated and that backups can occur anytime, under any circumstances. However, to get the backups to stream to your centralized tape backup location, you have to do some RMAN-specific configuration.

RMAN and the Media Manager: An Overview

RMAN streams backups to tape by engaging a media manager. A *media manager* is software provided by a third-party vendor that takes the data stream of blocks passed from the RMAN channel process and redirects it to the appropriate tape.

Most often, a media management server exists in an enterprise network. A *media management server* is a centralized system that handles all enterprise-wide backup operations to tape devices that are managed there.

To engage a media manager, a computer system must have the corresponding media management client software installed on it. This is the software that makes the connection to the media management server and passes the data to it over the network. For RMAN to engage the media management server, an additional software component is needed. After you install the client software, you must also install the Oracle module for the media manager. The *Oracle module* is a software plug-in for the Oracle RDBMS that connects RMAN to the client media management software, which can then make the pass to the media management server. This plug-in for Oracle is referred to as the *Media Management Library (MML)*. Figure 4-1 shows a generalized overview of the backup topology when a media manager is used to back up to tape.

The Media Manager Catalog

The media manager is a separate subsystem in the overall backup system you will use. It has three essential components, as previously described: the Media Management Library that integrates with Oracle, the media management client, and the media management server. The media management server has multiple components, the specifics of which are dependent upon the vendor. But all media management servers must have a few similar components, the most important of which (from the perspective of this chapter) is the media manager catalog.

The media manager catalog is the database of information at the media management server that holds information about the physical tapes, who has

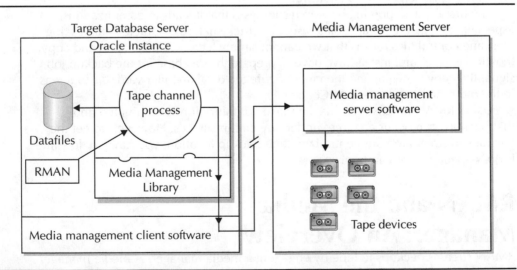

FIGURE 4-1. *Network topology when backing up to tape*

access to those tapes, and what is being stored on those tapes. It is this catalog that records the RMAN file handle when a backup is complete. The *handle* refers to the name of the backup piece that gets created when you perform a backup with RMAN. When you back up to disk, the handle is the physical filename. When you back up to tape, the handle is used in the media manager catalog to refer to a location on tape where the backups can be located.

RMAN completes a backup to tape by providing the handle name to the media manager, which records that handle in the catalog. When a restore is required, RMAN requests a specific handle (based on its own catalog) from the media manager. The media manager looks for that handle, associates it with a specific tape, and determines if that tape is available. If the tape is available, the media manager engages the tape and begins to stream the data back to RMAN so that you can rebuild the datafiles.

The Media Manager: Other Software Components

In addition to the catalog, the media management server comprises two essential pieces:

- **Device agent**   The component that is responsible for engaging the actual tape device and passing data to and from it.

- **Robotic interface**   The software that controls any robotics that are responsible for changing tapes when they are full, or when a request is made for a tape that has been filled in the past.

From the Oracle perspective, RMAN is blind to these components. RMAN simply sends a command request to its MML, and the media management software handles the coordination of all events after that. However, it is important to be familiar with these software components because your backup and recovery success depends on them. Many problems that come from using RMAN are related to the device agent or the robotic interface, but from the RMAN interface these problems are nearly impossible to discern.

Media Management Library

The MML is simply a library file that interprets generic requests from RMAN for a particular backup or restore operation, and interprets that request into the specific system call necessary at the media management server to turn that request into reality. The MML is provided by the same vendor that supplies the media management client and server software, but you purchase and license the MML separately from the client and server software.

The MML is loaded into the Oracle memory space as an integrated library file when a tape channel is first allocated, and it is logically part of the Oracle RDBMS software, so that RMAN can make the correct calls to the media management client software. The integration is simple, really: When a channel to tape is allocated, Oracle looks to load a file called libobk.so. This file, located in the ORACLE_HOME/bin directory, is just a symbolic link to whichever MML file you will be using. On the Windows platform, Oracle looks for a file called orasbt.dll in the searchable path. Regardless of which media management provider you use, its media management DLL will be named orasbt.dll, and media management providers usually write it to the WINDOWS\ system32 directory. If your media management provider does not do this, it will append the system path environment variable with a searchable path that leads to orasbt.dll.

In the next four chapters, we discuss the linking process by which you can establish your vendor's MML file as the one RMAN initiates when a channel is allocated. For testing purposes, Oracle provides a test MML file. This library file allows you to allocate a channel to tape but then write the backup to disk. In the following RMAN Workshop, we show you how to use this test MML.

RMAN Workshop: *Test Tape Channels with the Oracle Default SBT Interface*

Workshop Notes

You need access to a sufficient amount of disk space, and you need to create a directory in which to place the backup piece. In our example, we use the mount point u04, on which we created a directory called backup. Make sure you have sufficient memory available for the backup, as outlined in Chapter 2, and be aware of the disk I/O that goes to the backup location. Try to allocate space on a different controller from those that house your actual database.

Step 1. Build your backup directory:

```
$>cd /u04
mkdir backup
```

Step 2. Make sure permissions are established so that the oracle database, which operates as the user that installed the software, can write to this location:

```
ls -l backup
```

Step 3. Initiate RMAN and connect to the target. In the following example, we are connecting locally to the target PROD. This means that an **env** command shows us that ORACLE_SID=PROD.

```
$>Rman
Rman> connect target
```

Step 4.   Run your backup, using the PARMS parameter during channel allocation to specify the oracle test library file. You also need to specify a BACKUP_DIR directory, which is the location that RMAN will write the backup to. Here, we specify this as /u04/backup:

```
<RMAN> run {
2> allocate channel x1 type 'sbt_tape'
3> PARMS="SBT_LIBRARY=oracle.disksbt,
4> ENV=(BACKUP_DIR=/u04/backup)";
5> backup datafile 1 format='%U';}
```

Alternatively, you can use a permanent configuration command to set the oracle library (but remember that you've done it, and don't leave it lying around for too long):

```
CONFIGURE CHANNEL DEVICE TYPE 'SBT_TAPE' PARMS
'SBT_LIBRARY=oracle.disksbt,ENV=(BACKUP_DIR=/u04/backup)';
```

Here's the output from the preceding command:

```
using target database control file instead of recovery catalog
allocated channel: x1
channel x1: sid=144 devtype=SBT_TAPE
channel x1: WARNING: Oracle Test Disk API
Starting backup at 05-DEC-05
channel x1: starting full datafile backupset
channel x1: specifying datafile(s) in backupset
input datafile fno=00001
     name=/u01/app/oracle/oradata/v102/system01.dbf
channel x1: starting piece 1 at 05-DEC-05
channel x1: finished piece 1 at 05-DEC-05
piece handle=07h5ikqv_1_1 tag=TAG20051205T213631
   comment=API Version 2.0,MMS Version 8.1.3.0
channel x1: backup set complete, elapsed time: 00:00:25
channel x1: starting full datafile backupset
channel x1: specifying datafile(s) in backupset
including current control file in backupset
including current SPFILE in backupset
channel x1: starting piece 1 at 05-DEC-05
channel x1: finished piece 1 at 05-DEC-05
piece handle=08h5ikrp_1_1 tag=TAG20051205T213631
     comment=API Version 2.0,MMS Version 8.1.3.0
channel x1: backup set complete, elapsed time: 00:00:01
Finished backup at 05-DEC-05
released channel: x1
```

This is a great test if you are trying to troubleshoot possible problems with your media manager backup solution and cannot get the backups to work. By allocating a "fake" tape channel, you can rest assured that RMAN is not configured incorrectly.

CAUTION
Do not use the test MML file for production backups. If you will be backing up to disk in a production environment, allocate a disk channel. The performance of the fake MML is terrible, because RMAN is allocating memory buffers for tape, not disk, and therefore is not taking advantage of the speed of disk writes versus tape writes.

If you have not successfully loaded your vendor's MML file and you do not specify in the PARMS section of the channel allocation that you want to use Oracle's disk SBT interface, you will receive an error when you try to allocate a channel to tape:

```
RMAN-00571: ===========================================================
RMAN-00569: =============== ERROR MESSAGE STACK FOLLOWS =====
RMAN-00571: ===========================================================
RMAN-03009: failure of allocate command on x channel
    at 12/05/2005 21:26:43
ORA-19554: error allocating device, device type: SBT_TAPE, device name
ORA-27211: Failed to load Media Management Library
```

Interfacing with the MML

When you are linking Oracle and the MML, you are establishing the means by which RMAN can pass a command that engages the MML and, by extension, the media management client software installed on the database server. But how do you know which media management server to engage?

To specify the media management server, you must pass an environment variable within the RMAN session to specify the server name. Specifically, we specify the server name as an environment variable when we allocate our tape channel. As you saw in the previous RMAN Workshop, you pass the environment variable using the PARMS option of the **allocate channel** command. Different media management products have different environment variables that they accept. Veritas NetBackup, for example, requires the parameter NB_ORA_SERV:

```
allocate channel t1 type 'sbt_tape'
PARMS="ENV=(NB_ORA_SERV=storage1)";
```

In the preceding example, the name of the media management server is storage1, and our database server has already been registered in this server and has permissions to write to its tape devices.

In addition to the name of the server, there are numerous other parameters that we can pass at the time of the channel allocation to take advantage of management functions at the server. For instance, NetBackup offers the ability to specify the class or the schedule to use for this backup, whereas EMC Networker allows you to specify the resource pool. More details on these parameters are given in Chapter 6 and Chapter 7.

The SBT API

RMAN can engage different media managers with impunity because it sends the same marching orders no matter what MML has been loaded. Oracle developed RMAN with a generic API called the SBT API, which is provided to third-party vendors that wish to write integration products for Oracle database backups. This API is the means by which RMAN sends commands to the media manager.

The SBT API is responsible for sending the commands to the media management server to initiate the creation of backup files on tape. It also send commands to search for previous backups based on the file handle in the media manager catalog. It can send commands to remove these backups, as well as write new backups and, of course, read from the backup location. There are two versions of the Oracle RMAN SBT API: 1.1 and 2.0. Version 1.1 was published and used with Oracle 8.0.x, and that's it. Since then, RMAN has made calls to the media manager using the specifications of version 2.0. You can see this version in RMAN's output when you run a backup:

```
channel x1: finished piece 1 at 05-DEC-05
piece handle=08h5ikrp_1_1 tag=TAG20051205T213631
     comment=API Version 2.0,MMS Version 8.1.3.0
channel x1: backup set complete, elapsed time: 00:00:01
Finished backup at 05-DEC-05
```

RMAN also returns the version of the MML that it initializes at channel allocation time. This is seen during channel allocation in the RMAN output:

```
allocated channel: x
channel x: sid=12 devtype=SBT_TAPE
channel x: VERITAS NetBackup for Oracle8 - Release 3.4GA (030800)
```

Not only is this a good way to determine your MML version, but it also means that you have successfully linked your MML in with RMAN—otherwise, it would not be able to extract the version information.

Back Up to Tape: From Start to Finish

In this section, we do a walk-through of a backup to tape, and show the different calls made to the SBT API and how they are handled by the media manager. Again, please note that we are giving you a very generic overview, and the specifics are handled by the vendor that writes the integration MML.

When you allocate a tape channel, RMAN spawns a server process at your target database. This server process then makes a call to the SBT API of sbtinit( ). This call initializes the MML file and loads it into memory. It also returns to RMAN the version of SBT API supported by that MML. After calling sbtinit( ), RMAN calls sbtinit2( ), which supplies further configuration details to the media manager software.

After RMAN has parsed your backup command, it executes the RPC that makes the call to sys.dbms_backup_restore.backuppiececreate. At this time, the channel process calls sbtbackup( ), which handles the creation of the backup piece at the specified tape location. This call informs the media manager that Oracle will begin pushing the flow of data blocks to it, so it should prepare the tape device for the onslaught.

The RMAN input buffers fill up and make the memory-to-memory write to the output buffer. When the output buffer fills, the channel process calls sbtwrite2( ), which performs the write of filled output buffers to the tape location (for more on input buffers, see Chapter 2). Typically, this means engaging the device agent at the media management server in order to access the tape itself.

When all the output buffers for a particular backupset have been cleared out, and there is no more work for sbtwrite2( ), the channel session calls sbtclose2( ). This flushes out any media manager buffers and commits the backup piece to tape.

After we complete the backup piece, the channel process invokes sbtinfo2( ), to make sure the media manager catalog has documented the backup piece. It requests the tape, the tape location, and the expiration time of the backup from the catalog. Then, it writes the backup piece handle to the catalog.

After confirming the backup piece location, the channel process calls sbtend( ), which cleans up any remaining resources and releases them for other database use. The final action performed is the deallocation of the channel process, which is terminated at the target database.

Restore from Tape: From Start to Finish

Of course, sooner or later all that backing up you've been doing will get put to the test, and you will need to perform a restore. As with a backup, the SBT API has a specific series of steps that it goes through during a restore operation in order to get the backups on tape back into place for your database. In this section, we take a brief run-through of the SBT API during a restore operation.

When you allocate the tape channel for restore, RMAN creates a server process at the target database. This channel then calls sbtinit( ) to initialize the media manager software. This is identical to the initialization that would take place for a backup: the MML file is loaded into memory.

Based on the parameters of our **restore** command in RMAN, RMAN will have checked its catalog to determine the handle name of the backup required for the restore. It then takes this requested backup piece handle and passes it to the media manager using sbtrestore( ). The sbtrestore( ) function instructs the media manager to prepare the appropriate tape for a restore operation. This means engaging the media manager catalog and finding the appropriate tape, and then (if necessary) passing the command to the robotic instruction set to get the tape. After the tape is loaded, it will need to be rewound to the backup piece starting point.

After preparing the tape for the restore, the channel process calls the sbtread2( ) function to read the data from the tape device and stream it to the Oracle process. This data is loaded into the input buffers, written to the output buffers, and finally written to the datafile locations as specified by the control file.

When the end of a backup piece is detected on tape, the tape channel process calls the sbtclose( ) function to disengage the particular tape that had that piece on it. This signals that Oracle is done with the tape. If there are more backup pieces that need to be read for the restore operation, then the channel process returns to the second step and calls sbtrestore( ) for a different backup piece.

After the restore is complete and RMAN requests no more backup pieces, the channel process calls the sbtend( ) function, which cleans up the channel resources and releases them for other use. Then the channel process is terminated, after which the media manager is free to unload any tapes that had been requested.

Using sbttest and loadsbt.exe

As we mentioned previously, there are always indications as to whether you have successfully linked your MML with Oracle. The information from the channel allocation shows the MML version, for instance. However, these sorts of indicators do not guarantee success, as a failure may occur farther down the topology: at the media management client level or at the media management server. Oracle provides a utility called sbttest that can test to make sure that RMAN will be able to perform backups to tape using your media management configuration. This utility is called from a command line and performs a complete test: it writes a block to tape and then requests a read of that block. In this way, it runs through the entire gamut of SBT API functions that would occur during backup and makes sure they will all be successful.

Using sbttest is simple. After making sure that you have completed the full configuration of your media management configuration, go to the command prompt within the environment from which you will run RMAN and type **sbttest** and a test filename. The following code walks you through each of the sbt( ) calls previously listed in the "Restore from Tape: From Start to Finish" section and provides output on whether or not each call succeeded:

```
/u02/home/usupport> sbttest oratest_061902
The sbt function pointers are loaded from libobk.so library.
NetWorker: Cannot contact nsrexecd service on horatio.hadba.com,
Service not available.-- sbtinit succeeded
NetWorker: Cannot contact nsrexecd service on horatio.hadba.com,
Service not available.-- sbtinit (2nd time) succeeded
sbtinit: Media manager supports SBT API version 2.0
sbtinit: vendor description string=NMO v3.5.0.1
sbtinit: allocated sbt context area of 536 bytes
sbtinit: Media manager is version 3.5.0.1
sbtinit: proxy copy is supported
sbtinit: maximum concurrent proxy copy files is 0
-- sbtinit2 succeeded
-- regular_backup_restore starts ...............................
MMAPI error from sbtbackup: 7501, nwora_index_ssinfo:
index connect to cervantes.windba.com failed for client
horatio.hadba.com: Program not registered
-- sbtbackup failed
```

The sbttest utility has matured impressively since its inception as a simple binary indicator of success or failure. Now, a number of parameters can be passed to tweak the exact test you would like to take your media management system through. This includes naming the database you want to test, changing the number of blocks that are written by sbttest, and specifying how to further handle the file that sbttest writes to tape. Simply typing **sbttest** at the command prompt will give you all the switches you can use, along with simple text descriptions.

The sbttest utility is only available for Unix platforms; on Windows, you can request the utility loadsbt.exe from Oracle Support. Unfortunately, this utility does not have the same capabilities as sbttest, and instead simply checks the searchable path for a file called orasbt.dll. If it finds this file, it will try to load it the same way that Oracle will during a tape backup. It will tell you if it can be loaded, but it will not attempt to write a block to tape, and so it does not "swim downstream" very far to see if the entire configuration works. As such, it is not as useful as sbttest.

Media Management Errors

Error reporting in RMAN looks much the same when reporting media management problems as it does when reporting any other problem, and this can lead to some confusion. It is critical when troubleshooting RMAN errors to be able to determine where exactly the error is coming from: is it RMAN, the target database, the catalog database, or the media manager?

There are specific ways to determine if an error that is being returned in RMAN is related to the media manager. Some of them are obvious, particularly if you have not linked the MML correctly. We've shown examples of these errors already. However, if you have properly linked the MML with your Oracle installation, how can you tell if an error is related to the MML?

There are a number of different errors, but the most common error you will see related to the media manager is ORA-19511. This error is actually a *blank error*, meaning that Oracle supplies no text; instead, Oracle provides this as an error trap for media management errors. So if you see the following error, there is no doubt that you have linked your MML correctly and that the problem you are having is irrefutably a problem with the media manager.

```
ORA-19511: sbtbackup: Failed to process backup file
```

Other indicators of media management problems are not so clear, but just as telling. For instance, if you ever see in the error stack RMAN referring to a "sequential file," then you are dealing with a tape backup, and the problem is due to a failed read or write to the sequential file on tape. Another common error is ORA-27206:

```
RMAN-10035: exception raised in RPC: ORA-27206: requested file
not found in media management catalog
```

Again, the wording indicates a problem communicating with the media management catalog, which is where you would need to look to resolve the problem.

In addition to actual errors, any hang you might encounter in RMAN is *usually* related to media management problems. Usually. When RMAN makes an sbtwrite( ) call to the media manager, for instance, RMAN cannot possibly know how long this will take to complete. Therefore, RMAN does not provide any sort of time out for the operation—it will wait indefinitely for the media manager to return with either a successful write or an error. If the media manager is waiting on a particular event that has no time out, such as a tape switch or a tape load, the media manager waits, and so RMAN waits. And so you wait. And wait. Like we said, RMAN will not time out, so if you notice that RMAN is taking a particularly long time to complete and you see no progress in V$SESSION_LONGOPS (see Chapter 2), then your first instinct should be to check the media manager for an untrapped error or for an event such as a tape load or tape switch.

Summary

In this chapter, we discussed the concepts behind how RMAN utilizes the media management software of a third-party vendor to make backups to tape. We walked through the specific steps that RMAN makes using the SBT API. We also briefly discussed media management errors in RMAN.

CHAPTER
5

Oracle Secure Backup

racle Secure Backup (OSB), based on version 4 of the Reliaty engine, provides an end-to-end backup solution for Oracle environments, including centrally managed tape backup and restore operations of distributed, mixed-platform environments. OSB delivers secure tape data protection for the entire Oracle environment with the reliability you have come to expect from Oracle. Reducing the cost and complexity of enterprise tape backup software, OSB further increases the return on investment (ROI) for Oracle customers.

This chapter discusses features of OSB, components of OSB, installing OSB, and OSB screens available in Enterprise Manager.

Features of Oracle Secure Backup

- Designed to protect the Oracle database and other file system data running on heterogeneous file systems, including Microsoft Windows, Linux, and Solaris.

- Support for all major tape drives and tape libraries in SAN, Gigabit Ethernet, and SCSI environments.

- Ability to access local and remote file systems and devices from any location in a network without using NFS or CIFS.

- Substantial cost savings over comparable tape backup products by low-cost per tape drive pricing.

- Tight RMAN integration.

- A fast database backup solution, including optional database backup encryption to tape and encryption of backup information for transfer across a network.

- Support for a variety of tertiary devices such as tape drives, tape libraries, and network-attached storage (NAS) devices.

- Integrated directly from Enterprise Manager' Database Control or Grid Control.

- To reduce idle tape drive write periods, OSB and restore jobs are automatically allocated any available tape drive that shares tape resources with multiple servers.

- Oracle Secure Backup Express, available at no charge with the Oracle Database and Oracle Applications, may be employed for backup and restore of one server to a single tape drive.

- Single point of contact for issues involving Recovery Manager and the media manager.

- Back up to and restore data from Oracle Cluster File System (OCFS) on Linux and Microsoft Windows systems.

- Wildcards and exclusion lists to specify the files for backup.

- Multilevel incremental backups, duplexed database backups, backups that span multiple volumes, and direct-to-block positioning to avoid reading tape blocks to locate a backup.

Oracle Secure Backup and Recovery Manager

Oracle Secure Backup is able to back up all types of files on the file system. Although OSB has no specific knowledge of database backup and recovery procedures, it can serve as the media management layer for RMAN through the SBT interface. OSB furnishes the same services for RMAN as other supported third-party SBT libraries. OSB is better integrated with Oracle Enterprise Manager (OEM) as compared to other media managers. If your database backup strategy requires storage resources other than disk resources, you must employ RMAN together with a general-purpose network backup tool such as OSB.

Differences Between OSB and OSB Express

The following are the common features for Oracle Secure Backup and Oracle Secure Backup Express:

- Integrated with RMAN for online tape backup and restore of the Oracle Database

- Backup and restore of file system data

- Integrated with Oracle Enterprise Manager (version 10.2.0.1.0 and higher)

These features are available only with Oracle Secure Backup:

- Integrated with Oracle Enterprise Manager Grid Control (version 10.2.0.1.0 and higher)

- Support for multiple tape drives

- Support for virtual tape devices

- Fibre Channel support

■ Database backup encryption to tape (version 10.2.0.1.0 and higher)

■ Networked backups

Backup Encryption

Encrypted RMAN backups are available starting with Oracle Database 10.2.0.1.0. A special license is required to write an encrypted backup directly from the database to tape. For encrypted disk backups, a special license is required for the Oracle Database Advanced Security Option (ASO).

Oracle Secure Backup Interfaces

Figure 5-1 illustrates the interfaces you may use to access Oracle Secure Backup, described here:

■ **Oracle Secure Backup Web tool** This interface is a browser-based GUI that enables you to configure an administrative domain, browse the backup catalog, and manage backup and restore of file system data. The Web tool employs an Apache web server running on the administrative server. You may access the Web tool via any web browser that is able to connect to this server.

■ **Oracle Secure Backup command-line interface (obtool)** This command-line program offers an alternative to the Web tool. Using obtool, you may log in to the administrative domain to back up and restore file system data as well as perform configuration and administrative tasks. You may run obtool on any host within the administrative domain.

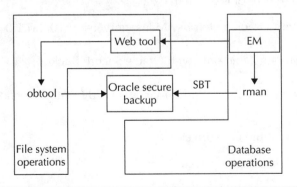

FIGURE 5-1. *OSB interfaces*

■ **Oracle Enterprise Manager Database Control and Grid Control** A set of GUI-based tools, Oracle Enterprise Manager was designed to manage the Oracle environment. OEM allows the scheduling of RMAN tape backups through the OSB interface. Administrative tasks such as managing devices and media within the OSB administrative domain may be performed via OEM. A link to the OSB Web tool is included within OEM. Backup Storage Selectors may be configured via OEM under the Backup Settings option.

You may use Oracle Enterprise Manager Database Control to backup or restore a single database. Using Oracle Enterprise Manager Grid Control allows the backup and restore of multiple databases.

■ **Recovery Manager command-line interface** The RMAN command-line interface may be used to configure and initiate backup and restore operations for utilization of OSB. The RMAN utility is located in the bin directory of an ORACLE_HOME directory. The RMAN command-line client will run on any database host so long as the client is able to connect to the target database. The OSB SBT library must exist on the same host as the target database in order for RMAN to make backups using OSB.

Oracle Secure Backup Components

An administrative domain is a group of hosts managed as a common unit for performing backup and restore operations. When configuring OSB, roles are assigned to each host in the domain. A single host may consist of one or more of the following roles:

■ **Administrative server** Starting and monitoring backup and recovery jobs is accomplished by the administrator server running within an administrative domain. The administrative server may also run other applications in addition to OSB.

■ **Media server** Houses secondary storage devices such as tape drives or tape libraries. At least one media server will be defined for each administrative domain.

■ **Client** A host whose local data is backed up by OSB. One or more clients will be defined in each administrative domain. Most hosts in the administrative domain are clients.

Figure 5-2 illustrates an OSB administrative domain. The domain includes an administrative server, a media server with an attached tape library, three clients, and five hosts.

Figure 5-3 demonstrates an OSB administrative domain containing a single Linux host. This Linux host assumes the roles of administrative server, media server, and client. An Oracle database with a locally attached tape library is configured for the Linux host. Note that this is the configuration used in the installation examples that follow.

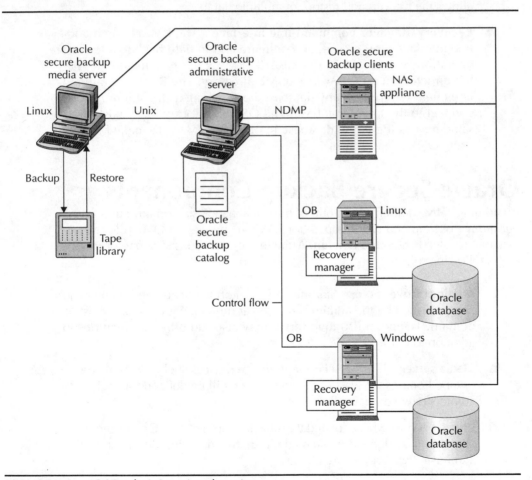

FIGURE 5-2. *OSB administrative domain*

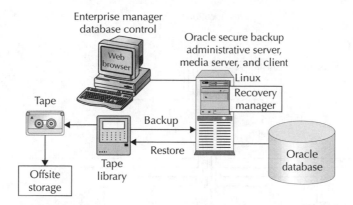

FIGURE 5-3. *OSB administrative domain with a single host*

Host Access Modes

Communicating to a host in an administrative domain is possible through two access modes:

- **Primary**   For primary access mode, OSB is installed on a host. Running in the background as daemons are the programming components of OSB. An Oracle database typically exists on a host accessed via this mode.

- **NDMP**   The Network Data Management Protocol host is a storage appliance provided by third-party vendors such as DinoStor, Mirapoint, and Network Appliance. Using a vendor-specific implementation, the NDMP host uses the NDMP protocol to back up and restore file systems. OSB is accessible via NDMP although OSB software is not installed on an NDMP host.

Using obtool, we can see from the output of the **lshost** command the access modes in use:

```
ob> lshost
filer_br    client                  (via NDMP) in service
oracle1     admin,mediaserver,client (via OB)  in service
```

Administrative Data

OSB arranges information for the administrative domain as a hierarchy of files in the OSB home on the administrative server. The directory into which OSB installed is the OSB home.

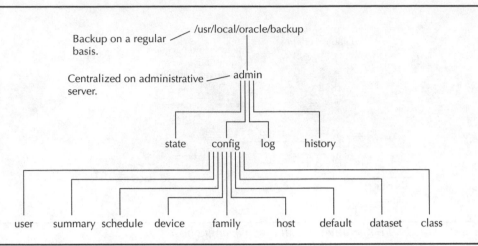

FIGURE 5-4. *Administrative server directories*

Figure 5-4 illustrates the directory structure for an OSB home. All platforms have the same directory structure, although the default home is /usr/local/oracle/backup for Unix and Linux systems but C:\Program\Files\Oracle\Backup for Microsoft Windows systems.

Domain-wide entities such as media families, classes, and devices are included within the administrative data. Figure 5-4 illustrates how the config directory contains several subdirectories. These subdirectories each represent an object maintained by OSB. For each object directory, OSB creates files describing the characteristics for the corresponding object.

The OSB catalog houses backup-related information. Beneath the admin/history/ host directory are subdirectories named after the hosts in the administrative domain. Within each of these subdirectories is a file containing catalog data. In addition, OSB creates backup sections, backup pieces, and volume catalogs in a subdirectory named admin/state/general.

Only in rare circumstances would it be necessary to access the administrative database directly from the file system. The Web tool and obtool interfaces are commonly used to access catalogs and configuration data.

Oracle Secure Backup Users and Classes

To enable OSB to maintain consistent user identities across the administrative domain, OSB saves information for OSB users and their rights on the administrative server.

On the administrative server, each OSB user has an account and an encrypted password. Using Web tool or obtool, an operating system user may enter their username and password. Using an encrypted SSL connection, the client program transmits the password to the administrative server.

Operating System Accounts

For OSB users, the namespace is distinct from the namespaces for Linux, Unix, and Microsoft Windows users. Therefore, if you access a host in the administrative domain as the operating system user matt, for example, and if the OSB user in the domain is named matt, these accounts will be managed separately though the names are identical. You may find it convenient to create the OSB user with the same name and password and as an operating system user.

At the time you create an OSB user, you may associate the user with Unix and Microsoft Windows accounts. Accounts of this type are used with an unprivileged backup, which is a backup that is not run with root privileges. Privileged backup and restore operations use a client with root (Unix) or Local System (Microsoft Windows) permissions.

If you were to create an OSB user named johnq and associate it with Unix account u_usr and Microsoft Windows account d_usr, when johnq uses the **backup -- unprivileged** command to back up a client, the jobs will run under the operating system account associated with johnq. Therefore, johnq is only able to back up files on a Unix client accessible to u_usr and files on a Microsoft Windows client accessible to d_usr.

With the "modify administrative domain's configuration" right, you may configure the preauthorization attribute for an OSB user. This right allows you to preauthorize operating system users to create RMAN backups or access the OSB command-line utilities.

NDMP Hosts

When setting up an OSB user account, you may configure user access to NDMP. You may set up the host to use a user-defined text password, a null password, or the default NDMP password. A password for an NDMP host is associated with the host, not the user. You may configure a password authentication method such as MD5-encrypted or text.

Oracle Secure Backup Rights and Classes

A defined set of rights granted to an OSB user is considered an OSB class. Though similar to a Unix group, an OSB class has a finer granularity of access rights specific for the needs of OSB. As shown in Figure 5-5, multiple users may be assigned to a class while each user is a member of a single class.

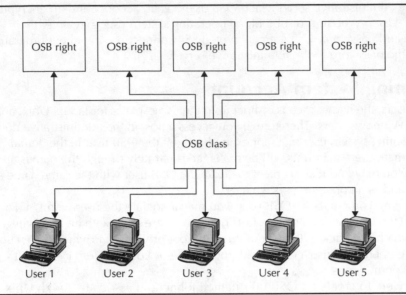

FIGURE 5-5. *Rights and classes*

These classes are important to understanding the rights of an OSB user:

■ **admin**   Utilized for overall administration of a domain, consists of all rights necessary to change domain configurations and complete backup and restore operations.

■ **operator**   For standard day-to-day operations, has no configuration rights but consists of all the rights needed for backup and restore operations. This right allows the user to control and query the state of primary and secondary storage devices.

■ **oracle**   Much like the operator class but with rights enabling the user to change Oracle database configuration settings and perform Oracle database backups. Members of this class usually are OSB users mapped to operating system accounts of an Oracle database installation.

■ **reader**   Allows members to browse the OSB catalog. Readers may only modify the name and password for their OSB user accounts.

■ **user**   Assigned to users to allow them rights to interact in limited ways with their domains. This class allows users to browse their own data within the OSB catalog and perform user-based restores.

Installing Oracle Secure Backup

Because OSB is designed for RMAN specifically, linking OSB with Oracle is quick and easy. OSB is available for delivery on CD-ROM or may be downloaded from the Oracle Technology Network (OTN) website at the following address:

http://www.oracle.com/database/secure-backup.html

The disk space requirements for OSB with Microsoft Windows are as follows:

Administrative server (may include the client or media server, or both)	20MB
Media server or client, or both (no administrative server)	15MB

The following are the disk space requirements for OSB with Unix or Linux:

Administrative server for Unix (may include the client or media server, or both)	60MB
Administrative server for Linux (may include the client or media server, or both)	40MB
Common files for all operating systems	10MB
Copy of each install package loaded for network installations to other Unix hosts	60MB
Package files built for network installations to other Linux hosts	40MB
Client or media server, or both	50MB

The following are the steps and considerations for installing OSB:

- Determine which hosts will house the administrative server, media server, and client(s).

- For Linux servers, verify that the SCSI Generic (SG) driver is installed.

- Download OSB into a staging directory and then unzip the downloaded file. Alternatively, you may order the OSB CD-ROM.

- Decide the name of the directory into which you will install OSB and then create that directory.

- Determine the SCSI settings for your tape drives and tape libraries.

- Determine whether you will perform an interactive install or a batch install.

- Verify that each host has a network connection and is running TCP/IP.

■ When performing a push installation, configure the destination hosts to allow access via **rsh** for the root user from the administrative server without a password.

■ Verify that you are able to log in as the root user for each host.

■ Run the OSB **setup** command.

Note that each node of a RAC cluster using OSB will require an installation of OSB.

RMAN Workshop: *Install Oracle Secure Backup*

Workshop Notes

The following example uses the Linux operating system. OSB is downloaded from OTN. The recommended directory for the installation of OSB on Linux is /usr/local/oracle/backup. For simplification of the example, the administrative server, media server, and client are all installed on the same machine.

Step 1. As the root user, create a directory for the download and then issue the change directory command to that directory:

```
[root@oracle-us /]#    mkdir /download
[root@oracle-us /]#    cd /download
```

Step 2. Download OSB into the download directory and then unzip the product:

```
 root@oracle-us download]#    unzip osb_10_1cdrom.zip
 extracting: osb_10_1cdrom/osb.10.1.060420.rel
  inflating: osb_10_1cdrom/doc/index.htm
  inflating: osb_10_1cdrom/doc/index.pdx
  inflating: osb_10_1cdrom/doc/nav/portal_1.htm
  . . .
  inflating: osb_10_1cdrom/solaris64/client.tz
  inflating: osb_10_1cdrom/solaris64/db2asc
  inflating: osb_10_1cdrom/solaris64/asc2db
  inflating: osb_10_1cdrom/solaris64/server.tz
```

Step 3. Create the directory where the install will place OSB files:

```
[root@oracle-us download]#    mkdir -p /usr/local/oracle/backup
```

Step 4. Issue the change directory command to the OSB destination:

```
[root@oracle-us download]#    cd /usr/local/oracle/backup
```

Step 5. Run **setup** from the destination directory:

```
[root@oracle-us /usr/local/oracle/backup]#
  /download/osb_10_1cdrom/setup
```

The following details are returned:

```
Welcome to Oracle's setup program for Oracle Secure Backup. This
program loads Oracle Secure Backup software from the CD-ROM to a
filesystem directory of your choosing.

This CD-ROM contains Oracle Secure Backup version 10.1.060420.

Please wait a moment while I learn about this host... done.
You may load any of the following Oracle Secure Backup packages:
     1. linux32 (RH 2.1, RHEL 3, RHEL 4, SuSE 8, SuSE 9)
        administrative server, media server, client
     2. solaris64 (Solaris 2.8 and later, SPARC)
        administrative server, media server, client

Enter a space-separated list of packages you'd like to load.
To load all packages, enter 'all' [1]: 1
```

Step 6. Because this is a Linux operating system, choose option 1. The
following output is returned:

```
- - - - - - - - - - - - - - - - - - - - - - - - - - -

Loading Oracle Secure Backup installation tools... done.
Loading linux32 administrative server, media server, client... done.


- - - - - - - - - - - - - - - - - - - - - - - - - - -

Loading of Oracle Secure Backup software from CD-ROM is complete.
You may unmount and remove the CD-ROM.

Would you like to continue Oracle Secure Backup installation with
'installob' now?  (The Oracle Secure Backup Installation Guide
contains complete information about installob.)
Please answer 'yes' or 'no' [yes]: yes
```

To continue the installation, answer **yes**. You then see the following output:

```
Welcome to installob, Oracle Secure Backup's UNIX installation
program. It installs Oracle Secure Backup onto one or more UNIX,
Linux, or other supported open-source systems on your network.
```

```
(Install Oracle Secure Backup for Windows using the CD-ROM from
which you loaded this software.) For most questions, a default
answer appears enclosed in square brackets.
Press Enter to select this answer.

Please wait a few seconds while I learn about this machine... done.

Have you already reviewed and customized install/obparameters for
your Oracle Secure Backup installation [yes]? No
Would you like to do this now [yes]? yes
```

Step 7.   Oracle Secure Backup allows you at this point to modify the obparameters file, which is where you indicate your desire to have the OSB client created automatically with the installation of OSB. You modify the obparameters file as follows using the vi editor:

```
[root@oracle-us /usr/local/oracle/backup]# vi install/obparameters
This "create pre-authorized oracle user" option is changed from no to
yes:
   create pre-authorized oracle user: yes
```

After saving our change we exit the file editor. We then return to the setup as follows:

```
[root@oracle-us /usr/local/oracle/backup]#   install/installob
```

Next you see the following output:

```
Welcome to installob, Oracle Secure Backup's UNIX installation
program.

It installs Oracle Secure Backup onto one or more UNIX, Linux, or
other supported open-source systems on your network. (Install Oracle
Secure Backup for Windows using the CD-ROM from which you loaded this
software.)

For most questions, a default answer appears enclosed in square
brackets.
Press Enter to select this answer.

Please wait a few seconds while I learn about this machine... done.

Have you already reviewed and customized install/obparameters for
your Oracle Secure Backup installation [yes]? Yes
```

Step 8.   This time answer **yes**. You then see

```
You can choose to install Oracle Secure Backup in one of two ways:
    (a) interactively, by answering questions asked by this program,
    or
    (b) in batch mode, by preparing a network description file
```

```
Use interactive mode to install Oracle Secure Backup on a small
number of hosts. Use batch mode to install Oracle Secure Backup
on any number of hosts.

Which installation method .would you like to use (a or b) [a]? a
```

Step 9.   Choose interactive mode, option a, so that you're prompted for the configuration options:

```
Oracle Secure Backup is not yet installed on this machine.

Oracle Secure Backup's Web server has been loaded, but is not yet
configured.

You can install this host one of three ways:
    (a) administrative server
        (the host will also be able to act as a media server or
        client)
    (b) media server
        (the host will also be able to act as a client)
    (c) client

If you are not sure which way to install, please refer to the Oracle
Secure Backup Installation Guide. (a,b or c) [a]? a
```

Step 10.   Select the administrative server option. The client will be installed automatically due to your change to the obparameters file, as shown next. The media server will be installed when you answer **yes** to the tape hardware prompts that follow in Step 12.

```
Beginning the installation. This will take just a minute and will
produce several lines of informational output.

Installing Oracle Secure Backup on oracle-us (Linux version
2.4.21-32.ELsmp)

You must now enter a password for the Oracle Secure Backup 'admin'
user. Oracle suggests you choose a password of at least 8 characters
in length, containing a mixture of alphabetic and numeric characters.

Please enter the admin password:
Re-type password for verification:
```

Step 11.   Enter the OSB password twice. The password is not displayed. You will see the following output:

```
generating links for admin installation with Web server
updating /etc/ld.so.conf
```

```
checking Oracle Secure Backup's configuration file
(/etc/obconfig)
setting Oracle Secure Backup directory to
/usr/local/oracle/backup in /etc/o
setting local database directory to /usr/etc/ob in /etc/obconfig
setting temp directory to /usr/tmp in /etc/obconfig
setting administrative directory to
/usr/local/oracle/backup/admin in /etc/o
protecting the Oracle Secure Backup directory
removing /etc/rc.d/init.d/qrserviced
creating /etc/rc.d/init.d/observiced
activating observiced via chkconfig
initializing the administrative domain
```

```
Is oracle-us connected to any tape libraries that you'd like to use
with Oracle Secure Backup [no]? yes
```

Step 12. Here you are prompted for details needed for the media server. Because you are installing the media server with this installation, answer **yes**. Using the configuration details for your SCSI tape hardware obtained earlier, answer as follows:

```
How many Oracle Secure Backup tape libraries are attached to
oracle-us [1]? 1
Please describe each tape library by answering the following
questions.
    Oracle Secure Backup logical unit number [0]: 0
    Host SCSI adapter number 0-15 [0]: 4
    SCSI bus address [0]: 0
    SCSI target ID [3]: 1
    SCSI lun 0-7 [0]: 0
Is the information you entered correct [yes]? Yes
How many Oracle Secure Backup tape drives are attached to oracle-us
[1]? 1
Please describe each tape drive by answering the following questions.
    Oracle Secure Backup logical unit number [0]: 0
    Host SCSI adapter number 0-15 [0]: 4
    SCSI bus address [0]: 0
    SCSI target ID [4]: 2
    SCSI lun 0-7 [0]: 0
Is the information you entered correct [yes]? yes
```

The following information is then returned:

```
Beginning device driver configuration and device special file
creation.
NOTE: No driver installation is required for Linux.
/dev/obt0 created
/dev/obl0 created
```

```
- - - - - - - - - - - - - - - - - - - - - - - - - - -

NOTE: You must configure the new devices via the Web interface or via
      the command line using the obtool 'mkdev' command.

- - - - - - - - - - - - - - - - - - - - - - - - - - -

Would you like to install Oracle Secure Backup on any other machine
[yes]? no
```

Step 13.   Because this is the only installation for now, answer **no** to the preceding prompt. The following summary is returned:

```
Installation summary:

    Installation  Host            OS          Driver     OS Move
    Reboot
        Mode      Name            Name        Installed? Required?
        Required?

    admin         oracle-us       Linux       yes        no
    no

Oracle Secure Backup will be ready for your use after you do the
following:
    On oracle-us:
        No further action is needed; Oracle Secure Backup is ready
        for your use on
        oracle-us.
```

The OSB administrative server, media server, and client are now installed and ready for use.

Enterprise Manager and Oracle Secure Backup

In versions 10.2.0.1 and 10.2.0.2, the OEM console Maintenance page does not include the OSB links by default. The option "osb_enabled" must be set to make the OEM links active for Oracle Security Backup. If you do not see the Oracle Secure Backup section on the OEM Maintenance page, you need to modify OEM as described in the next RMAN Workshop.

RMAN Workshop: *Configuring and Using Enterprise Manager for OSB Backups*

Workshop Notes

This workshop configures OEM for OSB usage and then schedules an OSB backup.

Step 1. Edit the file named emoms.properties in the directory named $ORACLE_HOME/hostname_SID/sysman/config. Set osb_enabled=true and then save the emoms.properties file.

Step 2. Stop and start the OEM Database Control console as follows:

```
emctl stop dbconsole
emctl start dbconsole
```

Step 3. Upon successful login to OEM, you'll see the following screen:

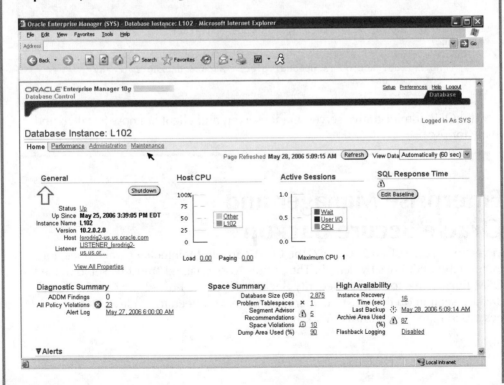

Step 4.   From the Maintenance tab, choose Schedule Backup.

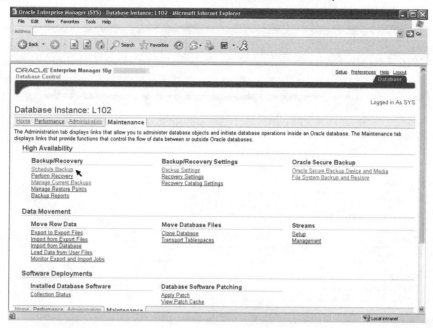

Step 5.   On the Schedule Backup page, click Schedule Customized Backup.

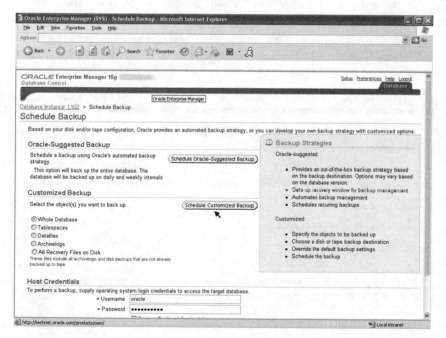

Step 6. On the Schedule Customized Backup: Options page, accept the default settings by clicking Next.

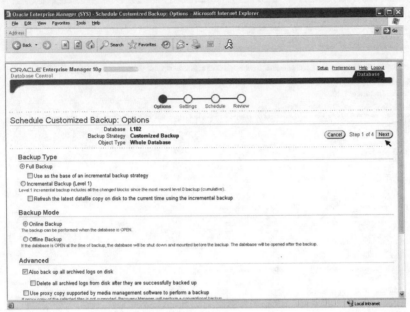

Step 7. On the Schedule Customized Backup: Settings page, select the Tape option and then click Next.

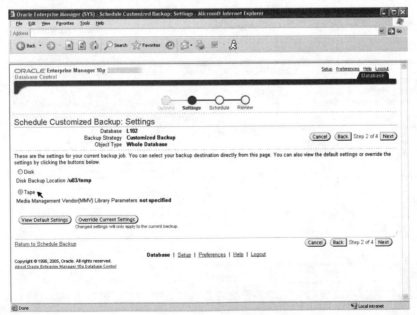

Step 8.   On the Schedule Customized Backup: Schedule page, click Next for immediate submission of the backup with a one-time-only schedule.

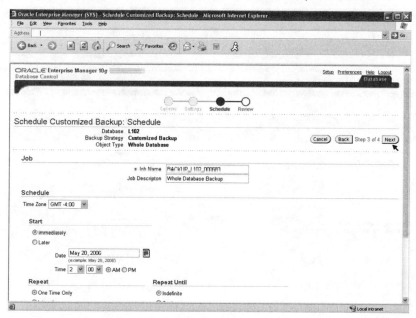

Step 9.   On the Schedule Customized Backup: Review page, click Submit Job.

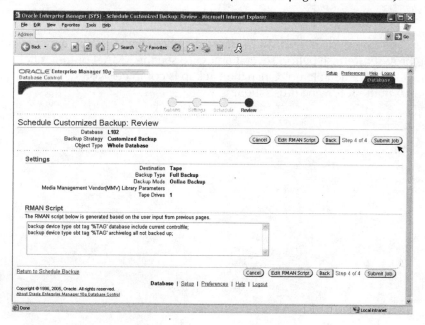

Step 10. On the job Status screen, click View Job.

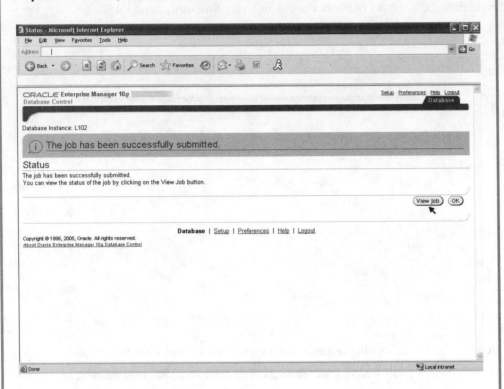

Step 11. The Execution page displays the status of the backup. You may need to click the browser Refresh button several times. To see the RMAN output, click "Backup" in the Name column. Once the backup is complete, you will see the page shown in the following illustration.

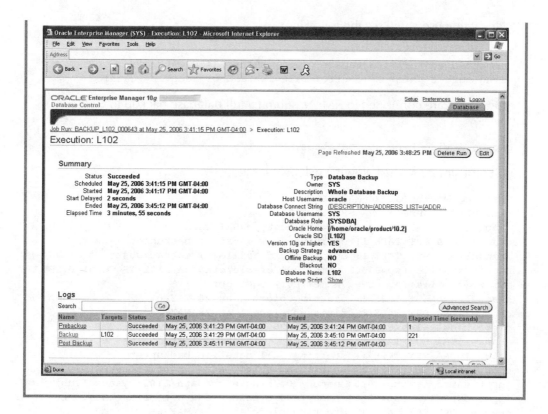

Submitting Oracle Secure Backup Jobs from RMAN

Backup jobs for OSB can also be submitted directly from the RMAN command-line interface. This holds true for Oracle database backups only, and the commands are identical to those used for any other RMAN backup. After you have set the $ORACLE_HOME to the location of the RMAN executable file and $ORACLE_SID to the target database, log in to RMAN and run the following command:

```
rman
connect target /
```

Or, if you are using a recovery catalog, run

```
rman
connect target /
connect catalog <user>/<password>@<catalog_db>
```

Nocatalog users will see the following:

```
RMAN>
connected to target database: L102 (DBID=1234567890)
using target database control file instead of recovery catalog
```

Once you are connected to RMAN, submit a full database backup to OSB as follows:

```
backup device type sbt database;
```

Output similar to the following will be returned:

```
Starting backup at 28-MAY-06
allocated channel: ORA_SBT_TAPE_1
channel ORA_SBT_TAPE_1: sid=133 devtype=SBT_TAPE
channel ORA_SBT_TAPE_1: starting full datafile backupset
channel ORA_SBT_TAPE_1: specifying datafile(s) in backupset
input datafile fno=00005 name=/u04/oracle/oradata/L102/TS_COD01_D.DBF
input datafile fno=00007 name=/u01/rog01.dbf
channel ORA_SBT_TAPE_1: starting piece 1 at 28-MAY-06
channel ORA_SBT_TAPE_1: finished piece 1 at 28-MAY-06
piece handle=1rhk64a9_1_1 tag=TAG20060528T044457 comment=NONE
channel ORA_SBT_TAPE_1: backup set complete, elapsed time: 00:01:17
channel ORA_SBT_TAPE_1: starting full datafile backupset
channel ORA_SBT_TAPE_1: specifying datafile(s) in backupset
input datafile fno=00003 name=/u04/oracle/oradata/L102/sysaux01.dbf
input datafile fno=00004 name=/u04/oracle/oradata/L102/users01.dbf
channel ORA_SBT_TAPE_1: starting piece 1 at 28-MAY-06
channel ORA_SBT_TAPE_1: finished piece 1 at 28-MAY-06
piece handle=1shk64cm_1_1 tag=TAG20060528T044457 comment=API Version
2.0,MMS Version 10.1.0.0
channel ORA_SBT_TAPE_1: backup set complete, elapsed time: 00:01:26
channel ORA_SBT_TAPE_1: starting full datafile backupset
channel ORA_SBT_TAPE_1: specifying datafile(s) in backupset
input datafile fno=00002 name=/u04/oracle/oradata/L102/undotbs01.dbf
channel ORA_SBT_TAPE_1: starting piece 1 at 28-MAY-06
channel ORA_SBT_TAPE_1: finished piece 1 at 28-MAY-06
piece handle=1thk64fd_1_1 tag=TAG20060528T044457 comment=API Version
2.0,MMS Version 10.1.0.0
channel ORA_SBT_TAPE_1: backup set complete, elapsed time: 00:00:03
```

```
channel ORA_SBT_TAPE_1: starting full datafile backupset
channel ORA_SBT_TAPE_1: specifying datafile(s) in backupset
input datafile fno=00001 name=/u04/oracle/oradata/L102/system01.dbf
channel ORA_SBT_TAPE_1: starting piece 1 at 28-MAY-06
channel ORA_SBT_TAPE_1: finished piece 1 at 28-MAY-06
piece handle=1uhk64fg_1_1 tag=TAG20060528T044457 comment=API Version
2.0,MMS Version 10.1.0.0
channel ORA_SBT_TAPE_1: backup set complete, elapsed time: 00:00:25
channel ORA_SBT_TAPE_1: starting full datafile backupset
channel ORA_SBT_TAPE_1: specifying datafile(s) in backupset
including current control file in backupset
channel ORA_SBT_TAPE_1: starting piece 1 at 28-MAY-06
channel ORA_SBT_TAPE_1: finished piece 1 at 28-MAY-06
piece handle=1vhk64g9_1_1 tag=TAG20060528T044457 comment=API Version
2.0,MMS Version 10.1.0.0
channel ORA_SBT_TAPE_1: backup set complete, elapsed time: 00:00:02
Finished backup at 28-MAY-06
```

Configuring Backup Storage Selectors with Enterprise Manager

OSB saves configuration data in database Backup Storage Selectors for RMAN interaction when performing backup or restore operations and to provide users with fine-grained control over database backup and restore operations. Users may define the type of backups that are valid for a database backup, including archive logs, auto backups of the control file and SPFILE, full backups, and incremental backups.

Oracle Secure Backup creates a media family named RMAN-DEFAULT, which may be used to organize backups to specific tape volumes. When executing an Oracle database backup using OSB, RMAN relays the database name and copy number to OSB. Using this information, OSB determines the correct database Backup Storage Selector. It is this Storage Selector that informs OSB what devices, if any, to restrict for this backup and which media family to use, if any.

To configure the Backup Storage Selector from OEM, click the Backup Settings option on the Maintenance tab. Click Configure.

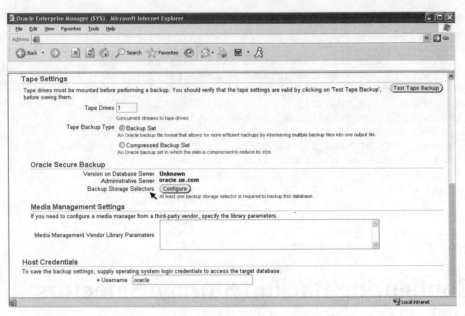

You will be prompted for host credentials. After you click on OK, you'll see the page that allows Backup Storage Selector configuration.

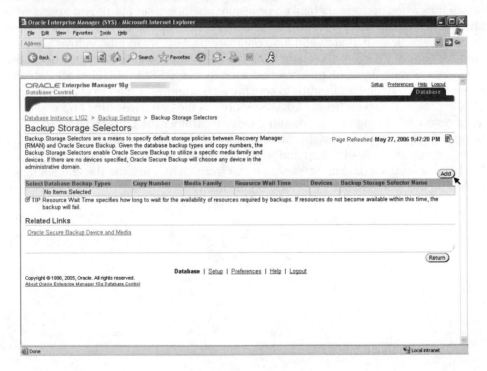

For complete details on configuring Backup Storage Selectors, review the *Oracle Secure Backup Administrator's Guide*.

Configuring the Oracle Secure Backup Administrative Server

The OSB administrative server can also be configured from OEM. From the Maintenance tab, choose Oracle Secure Backup Device and Media to open the Administrative Server page.

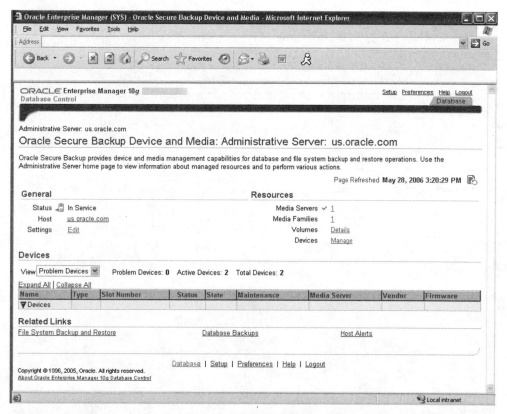

From the Oracle Secure Backup Device and Media screens, you may configure an OSB administrative server and perform procedures such as loading and unloading tape volumes, verifying device connectivity, and so forth. For details on how to configure an OSB administrative server, consult the *Oracle Secure Backup Administrator's Guide*.

Oracle Secure Backup File System Backup and Restore

Oracle Enterprise Manager's Maintenance tab contains a link to the Oracle Secure Backup Web tool for file system backups and restores. The OSB Web tool is an online GUI that allows you to back up and restore file system data, browse the backup catalog, manage operations, and configure administrative domains. For details on using the OSB Web tool, consult the *Oracle Secure Backup Administrator's Guide*. When you click File System Backup and Restore on the OEM Maintenance tab, you will see the page in the following illustration.

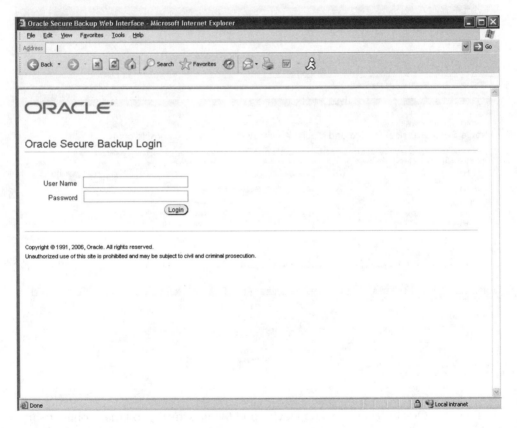

Summary

Oracle Secure Backup delivers high performance and secure data protection crucial for both offsite and local storage of mission-critical data. Complete product support from Oracle Support Services, integration with Oracle Enterprise Manager, and excellent pricing are only a few of the many reasons for employing OSB to meet your file system and Oracle Database backup requirements. For centralized backup tape management in mixed, distributed environments that provides a complete backup solution for the enterprise, OSB is a strong contender.

CHAPTER

6

Enhancing
RMAN with VERITAS
NetBackup™ *for Oracle*

ERITAS NetBackup Server software and Database Agent software work in collaboration with RMAN to manage enterprise backup, recovery, and storage administration. The products run on many operating systems, support popular databases, and integrate easily with an assortment of storage devices. Its tantalizing features coupled with the vendor's close partnership with Oracle make NetBackup a desirable choice. The information and downloads in this chapter are available on Symnatec's website, as Veritas is now part of Symantec.

In this chapter, we will focus on VERITAS NetBackup Version 5.1 running on Unix unless stated otherwise.

Key Features

NetBackup *for Oracle* has many features and benefits that augment the functionality of RMAN. A summary of the key features is listed in Table 6-1.

Some specialty add-ons worth looking into are NetBackup Advanced Client, NetBackup Vault, and NetBackup Bare Metal Restore.

Feature	Benefit
Backup to disk staging area	Provides faster backups and restores by avoiding the overhead of tape latency
Synthetic backups	Conserves network bandwidth by allowing incremental backups
Inline copy	Provides data redundancy by writing multiple copies of the data at the same time
Tape multiplexing	Improves performance by writing parallel streams of data from one or more clients to a single tape drive
Automatic tape device configuration	Reduces the time and effort that would otherwise be required to manually configure tape drives
Data encryption	Secures data as it is written to tape by offering multiple levels of data protection
Backup templates	Simplifies the effort of writing RMAN backup and recovery scripts by providing a graphical tool to assist with script generation and sample scripts preconfigured to run with NetBackup
Proxy copy	Offloads processing power from the database server to a separate media server when doing backups and restores
Checkpoint restart	Allows backups to resume where they left off in the case of a failure

TABLE 6-1. *NetBackup* for Oracle *Key Features*

Necessary Components

The following are the elements that allow successful communication exchanges between RMAN, the NetBackup servers, and the storage devices:

- NetBackup Server software

- NetBackup *for Oracle* agent software—includes a required interface library file (libobk.*)

- Oracle database software—includes the RMAN utility and the Oracle Call Interface (OCI)

- NetBackup licenses—needed for all software, options, and agents being used

Storage/Media Device Configuration

Setting up tape drives, host bus adapters, SCSI IDs, and tape robots (see *NetBackup Media Manager Device Configuration Guide*) is usually left up to Unix or storage administrators. We will not discuss those vendor-specific steps here, but will instead provide a few commands to verify proper configuration of tape media devices.

NOTE
Hardware devices should be set up and tested for proper working order prior to installing the NetBackup for Oracle *agent software.*

Use the following command to query the master server from the client server to verify communications:

```
/<install_path>/netbackup/bin/bpclntcmd -pn
```

Next, query the master server from the client server to verify the version:

```
/<install_path>/netbackup/bin/bpclntcmd -sv
```

View which storage server will be servicing the client server by issuing the following:

```
cat /<install_path>/netbackup/bp.conf
```

Finally, verify that the NetBackup communication daemons are listening for requests:

```
netstat -a |grep bpcd
netstat -a |grep vnetd
```

NetBackup Installation

There are multiple tiers that comprise a networked backup environment. Every layer needs some amount of software configuration to enable component interoperability. The installations are straightforward and should take less than 20 minutes each. Besides doing local installations, it is possible to run remote installs, installs from the Administration Console, and software propagation to the clients from a central master server.

NOTE
NetBackup software should not be installed on a Network File System (NFS)-mounted directory. Doing so could cause interference with its file-locking mechanisms.

NetBackup Server software gets installed on the following servers:

- Master server

- Media server (optional)

- Client (database) server

The NetBackup *for Oracle* agent software gets installed on the client (database) server.

The following list defines the server types just mentioned:

- **Master server**   Orchestrates the NetBackup environment. It is placed in a layer referred to as Tier 1 (top server tier). Tiers are labels for each of the different architectural layers or groupings of architectural components. The role of the master server is to schedule backups, track job progress, manage tape devices, and store backup metadata in a repository. Since the master server plays such a critical role, it is a good idea to cluster this server for high availability (and greater peace of mind).

- **Media servers**   Exist in Tier 2 (middle tier) and are used to back up a group of files locally while other files are being backed up across the network. Media servers are introduced into the environment to boost performance, but they are not required.

- **Client servers**   Reside in Tier 3 (client tier) and are usually the database servers that house the databases to be backed up.

Pre-Installation Tasks for NetBackup *for Oracle* Agent

Before you install NetBackup *for Oracle*, you need to complete the following tasks:

1. Verify that the system administrator has installed and properly configured the NetBackup software on the master server, media servers (optional), and the client database servers.

2. Ensure that the proper license keys for all NetBackup servers, clients, agents, and options have been purchased and are registered on the master server. You can do this from either the Administration Console or the command line. From the Administration Console, launch the following and then choose Help | License Keys:

   `/<install_path>/netbackup/bin/jnbSA &`

   From the command line, run

   `/<install_path>/netbackup/bin/admincmd/get_license_key`

3. Obtain the NetBackup *for Oracle* agent software CD or ask a Unix system administrator to push the software to the client database machine from the master server.

NOTE
On the database server, both the NetBackup Server software and NetBackup for Oracle *agent software need to be the same version. The software on the master server needs to be the same or a higher version as that on the database server.*

NetBackup *for Oracle* Agent Installation Steps

To install the NetBackup *for Oracle* agent, follow these steps:

1. Insert and mount the installation CD.

2. Log in as **root** to the client (database) server.

3. Change to the directory where the CD is mounted.

4. Run the ./install script.

5. Choose NetBackup Database Agent.

6. You are asked whether you want to do a local installation. Enter **y**.

7. Choose NetBackup for Oracle.

8. Enter **q**.

9. Enter **y** to verify your selection.

10. Installation proceeds as following:

  a. A script called /<install_path>/netbackup/dbext/install_dbext is generated.

  b. The file /<install_path>/netbackup/bp.conf is updated with server names.

  c. Entries are added to /etc/services.

  d. Entries are added to the NIS services map if NIS is running on the server.

  e. Entries are added to the server /etc/initd.conf file for bpcd, vopied, and bpjava-msvc.

  f. Startup and shutdown scripts are copied to the /etc/init.d directory.

  g. Installation output is written to /<install_path>/netbackup/ext.

NOTE
In most cases, look for NetBackup to be installed in the /usr/openv/netbackup directory.

How to Link Oracle to NetBackup Media Manager

Following the NetBackup *for Oracle* agent installation is the task of linking Oracle database software with the NetBackup Media Management Library. The link allows RMAN to write files to the media devices or pull files from them. The NetBackup Media Management Library or API will often be found in /<install_path>/netbackup/ bin, while the Oracle library is located in $ORACLE_HOME/lib. Both files will be named libobk*.

The process of linking can be done either automatically or manually, as described next.

Automatic Link Method

NetBackup *for Oracle* includes a script to automate the library link process. Since all steps are automated, using the script is preferred over a manual method. The oracle_link script performs the following actions:

- Retrieves the database version

- Retrieves the operating system version

- Warns if the database is not shut down

- Checks environmental parameter settings

- Applies the appropriate library based on its assessment

The steps to automatically link Oracle9*i* Database and Oracle Database 10*g* with NetBackup *for Oracle* follow:

1. Log in to the Unix server as the oracle account.

2. Set the variables $ORACLE_SID and $ORACLE_HOME.

3. Shut down each Oracle database instance:
   ```
   sqlplus "/ as sysdba"
   shutdown immediate
   exit
   ```

4. Run the <install_path>/netbackup/bin/oracle_link script.

5. View the output that is written to /tmp/make_trace.pid for errors.

Manual Link Method

If you prefer more control over the link process, you may opt for the manual method. The following are the steps to manually link Oracle9*i* Database and Oracle Database 10*g* with NetBackup *for Oracle*:

1. Log in to the Unix server as the oracle account.

2. Set the variables $ORACLE_SID and $ORACLE_HOME.

3. Shut down each Oracle database instance:
   ```
   sqlplus "/ as sysdba"
   shutdown immediate
   exit
   ```

4. Perform the applicable linking steps in Table 6-2.

NOTE
As of 9i and 10g, making a new Oracle executable is no longer required.

For OS version...	...do these steps	If this file exists in ${ORACLE_HOME}/lib...	...then create a symbolic link from the Oracle library to the new NetBackup library

AIX 64-bit using 64-bit Oracle9i Release 9.0.1 and 9.2, Oracle 10g Release 10.1	n/a	libobk.a	`mv libobk.a libobk.a.orig`
			`ln -s /<install_path>/`
			`netbackup/bin/libobk.a64`
			`libobk.a`

Compaq Tru64/ Digital UNIX (OSFI)	Put ${ORACLE_HOME}/ lib in search path On Digital UNIX, set LD_LIBRARY_PATH	libobk.so
		libobk.a
			`mv libobk.so libobk.so.orig`
			`mv libobk.a libobk.a.orig`
			`ln -s /<install_path>/`
			`netbackup/bin/libobk.so.1`
			`libobk.so.1`
			`ln -s libobk.so.1 libobk.so`

HP-UX 64-bit using 64-bit Oracle9i Release 9.0.1 and 9.2, Oracle 10g Release 10.1	n/a	libobk.sl
		libobk.a
			`mv libobk.sl libobk.sl.orig`
			`mv libobk.a libobk.a.orig`
			`ln -s /<install_path>/`
			`netbackup/bin/libobk.sl64`
			`libobk.sl`

Linux	Put ${ORACLE_HOME}/ lib in search path On Digital UNIX, set LD_LIBRARY_PATH	libobk.so	`ln -s /<install_path>/`
			`netbackup/bin/libobk.so`
			`libobk.so`

Solaris (32-bit or 64-bit) using 32-bit Oracle9i Release 9.0.1 and 9.2, Oracle 10g Release 10.1	n/a	libobk.so	`mv libobk.so libobk.so.orig`
			`ln -s /<install_path>/`
			`netbackup/bin/libobk.so.1`
			`libobk.so`

Solaris (32-bit or 64-bit) using 64-bit Oracle9i Release 9.0.1 and 9.2, Oracle 10g Release 10.1	n/a	libobk.so	`mv libobk.so libobk.so.orig`
			`ln -s /<install_path>/`
			`netbackup/bin/libobk.so64.1`
			`libobk.so`

TABLE 6-2. *Manual Link Process*

Architecture

Now that the hardware is configured, the server and agent programs are installed, the daemons are running, and the libraries are linked, we've built a solid foundation (see Figure 6-1) upon which to run RMAN.

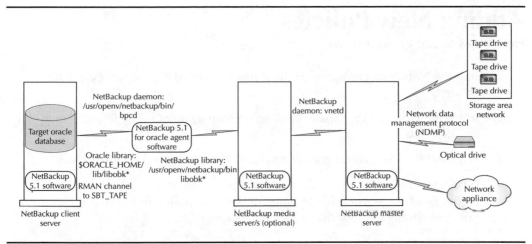

FIGURE 6-1.   *NetBackup architecture*

Configuring NetBackup Policies

NetBackup needs to be given instructions on how and when to execute the backups. These instructions are organized into special groupings called *policies*. Some points to be aware of when configuring policies are

- An RMAN job must be associated with at least one policy in order for it to execute.

- A default policy is provided with the agent software.

- Multiple policies can be created for a single database server.

The NetBackup Administration Console provides a nice and easy interface for configuring the following policy information:

- Attributes

- Schedule

- Clients on which the policy is implemented

- Backup selection

Adding New Policies

Here's how to add a new policy:

1. Start the NetBackup program on the storage server where the policy will be created.

2. Select the Policies tab. Expand NetBackup Management | Policies, as shown in Figure 6-2.

3. In the All Policies pane, right-click Master Server, and then choose New.

4. Type a unique name in the Add a New Policy dialog box, shown in Figure 6-2. Once you add the name of the new policy in the dialog box, the Change Policy dialog box will appear.

As part of the policy definition, you should define the following policy attributes. (See Attributes tab in Figure 6-3.)

- **Policy Types** The Policy Type drop-down list contains many options; for Oracle RMAN backups, you can choose Oracle policy type. The following are the various policy options with the intended use of each option:

  Oracle   Use when the policy will contain only clients with the NetBackup for Oracle option

  DB2   Use when the policy will have only clients with the NetBackup for DB2 option

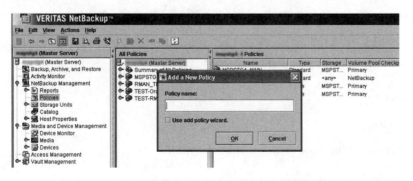

FIGURE 6-2. *Adding new policies*

DataStore	A policy type reserved for use by VERITAS or its partners to provide agents for new applications or databases
Lotus-Notes	Use when the policy will contain only clients with the NetBackup for Lotus Notes option
MS-Windows-NT	Use when the policy will contain only Windows 2000, NT, XP, or Windows Server 2003 clients
MS-Exchange-Server	Use when the policy will contain only clients with the NetBackup for MS-Exchange option
MS-SQL-Server	Use when the policy will contain only clients with the NetBackup for MS-SQL Server option
NCR-Teradata	Use when the policy will contain only clients with the NetBackup for Teradata option
NetWare	Use when the policy will contain only NonTarget NetBackup Novell NetWare clients
NDMP	Use when the policy will contain only clients with the NetBackup for NDMP option
AFS	Use when the policy will be backing up only AFS file systems on clients
DataTools-SQLBackTrack	Use when the policy will contain only clients with the NetBackup for DataTools-SQL-BackTrack option
FlashBackup-Windows	Applies only to NetBackup Enterprise Server; use when the policy will contain only NetBackup FlashBackup-Windows clients on Windows. This policy is available only when the NetBackup Advanced Client is installed.
FlashBackup	Use when the policy will contain only NetBackup FlashBackup clients on UNIX
Informix-On-BAR	Use when the policy will contain only clients that are running the NetBackup for Informix option
MS-SharePoint	Use to configure a policy for NetBackup for SharePoint Portal Server
Split-Mirror	Use when the policy will contain only clients with the NetBackup for EMC option

SAP	Use when the policy will contain only clients with the NetBackup for SAP option
Sybase	Use when the policy will contain only clients with the NetBackup for Sybase option
Standard	Use when the policy will contain any combination of the following: NetBackup Novell NetWare clients that have the target version of NetBackup software UNIX clients (including Mac OS X clients), except those covered by specific policy such as Oracle

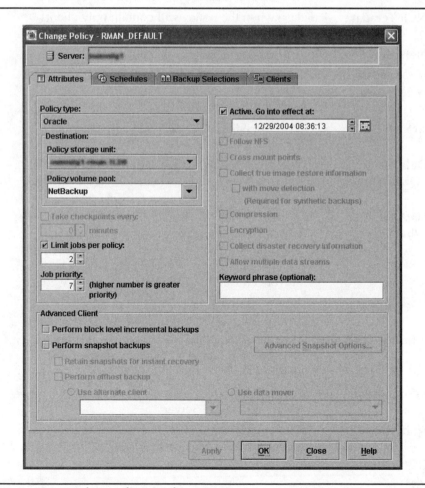

FIGURE 6-3. *NetBackup policy configuration*

- **Backup Destination** Choose settings for Policy Storage Unit and Policy Volume Pool.

- **Active. Go into Effect At** Checking this box and specifying a date and time enables you to turn on at a later date and time a policy that you create in advance.

- **Limit Jobs Per Policy** Checking this box enables you to restrict the number of jobs that can be run in parallel.

Defining Schedules

If you are using the NetBackup scheduler, then you must define when the jobs should run. A single policy can contain more than one job schedule and can be shared by multiple database servers (clients).

Application Backup Schedule and Automatic Backup Schedule options exist for the *Oracle* policy type, as described next. One or more automatic backup schedules will be required depending on the job frequency.

Configure an Application Backup Schedule

Whenever the policy type is "Oracle," NetBackup creates an *Application Backup* schedule. This schedule defines the overall timeframe when any backup job can occur. Unscheduled Oracle backups will default to using this schedule. Special processes, needed for the execution of RMAN jobs, are initiated as part of the Application Backup schedule.

To configure an Application Backup schedule:

1. In the Change Policy dialog box, click the Schedules tab.

2. Double-click Default Application Backup Schedule.

3. Click the Attributes tab, shown in Figure 6-4, and make sure that the Retention setting is set.

4. Click the Start Window tab. The Start Window defines the time boundaries within which a backup job can begin. It is a more granular subschedule within the overall Application Backup schedule. A backup job must start inside the time limits of the Start Window, but will continue to run until it finishes.

NOTE
Set the backup window for the Application Backup schedule to 24 hours a day, seven days a week, in order to perform any unscheduled or schedule backup at any time and for any duration.

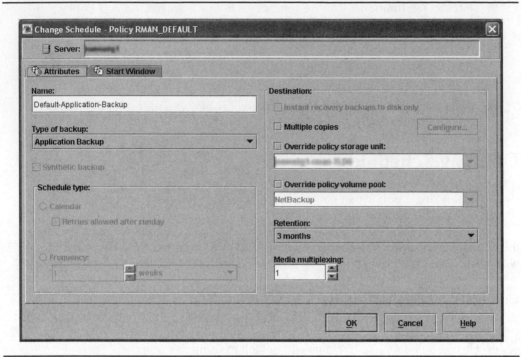

FIGURE 6-4. *Application Backup schedule*

Configure an Automatic Backup Schedule

To configure an Automatic Backup schedule:

1. In the Change Policy dialog box, click the Schedules tab.

2. Click the New button to open the Add Schedule window.

3. On the Attributes tab (refer to Figure 6-5), enter a unique name for the schedule.

4. Select from four different backup types from the Type of Backup drop-down list:

   - **Application Backup** Runs when an Oracle backup is started manually. Each Oracle policy must be configured with one Application Backup schedule.

   - **Automatic Full Backup** Backs up all the database blocks that have been allocated or are in use by Oracle.

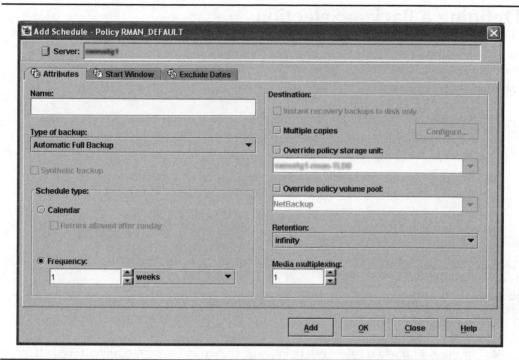

FIGURE 6-5. *Automatic Backup schedule*

- **Automatic Differential Incremental Backup** Backs up database blocks that have changed since the most recent full or incremental backup at level *n* or lower.

- **Automatic Cumulative Incremental Backup** Backs up database blocks that have changed since the most recent full or incremental backup at level *n*-1 or lower.

5. Select from two different schedule types:

   - **Calendar** Specifies exact dates, recurring days of the week, or recurring days of the month.

   - **Frequency** Specifies the period of time that will elapse until the next backup operation can begin on this schedule. Options are hourly, daily, or weekly.

6. Select an appropriate retention period from the Retention drop-down list, which controls how long NetBackup retains the records for scheduled backups.

   To add other schedules, repeat Steps 1 through 6.

Defining a Backup Selection

When running backup jobs, NetBackup will call any custom scripts or templates that are placed in the *backup selection list*. These files will be executed in the order they are listed. In Netbackup, there are two options which can be used to define commands for Oracle RMAN backup or recovery:

- **Templates** Stored in a known location on the central master server so that they do not need to be put on each database server. The filename is entered without a path.

- **Scripts** Located on each database server listed and must be entered with a full pathname.

To add scripts or templates to the backup selections list, follow these steps:

1. From the Administration Console, double-click the policy name in the Policies list.

2. In the Change Policy dialog box, click the Backup Selections tab.

3. Click New.

4. In the Add Backup Selection dialog box, shown in Figure 6-6, enter the shell script or template name. Use the Add button to add the script or template to the selection list.

5. Click OK.

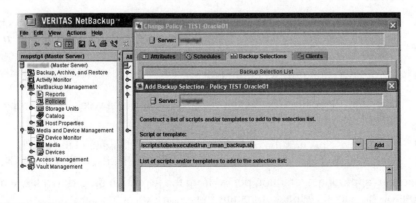

FIGURE 6-6. *Backup selection*

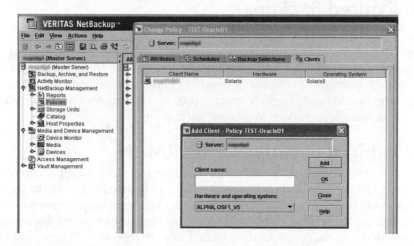

FIGURE 6-7. *Define policy clients*

Defining Policy Clients

To add a database server (client) to a policy, follow these steps:

1. From the Administration Console, double-click the policy name in the Policies list.

2. In the Change Policy dialog box, click the Clients tab.

3. Click New to open the Add Client dialog box, shown in Figure 6-7.

4. In the Client Name field, type the name of the client you are adding.

5. Choose the hardware and operating system type from the drop-down list.

6. Click OK or click Add to set up another client.

Managing Expired Backup Images

The NetBackup Media Manager and RMAN both have the ability to manage backup retention periods. This can be a problem if their retention settings don't match. Automatic expiration of backup images from both repositories is not supported. A workaround is to use the Retention setting in the Application Backup schedule and then synchronize the NetBackup and RMAN repositories.

Delete Expired Backups Using NetBackup Repository

NetBackup controls the expiration of the Oracle backup images from its repository by using the Retention setting in an Application Backup schedule. The setting specifies the length of time before the backup image expires and is deleted. When you use NetBackup retention to delete backup images, you must do regular Oracle repository maintenance to remove references to expired backup files.

Delete Expired Backups Using RMAN

RMAN has a manual command to remove all database and archive log backups that have reached their retention limits. This command can be used to delete database backups from both the RMAN catalog and the NetBackup repository. When a request is issued to delete a backup file from the RMAN repository, RMAN sends the request to NetBackup to delete the corresponding images from its repository, regardless of the retention level. The code for deleting expired backups is shown next:

```
RMAN> allocate channel for maintenance type 'SBT_TAPE';
RMAN> crosscheck backup;
RMAN> delete expired backup;
```

The **crosscheck** command should be used only in cases where files marked with the status Available that no longer exist can be expired and marked deleted. RMAN should control the retention using the following command. If you configure the channel with the tape parameters, there is no need to allocate channels since Oracle does it for you from Oracle9*i*.

```
RMAN> allocate channel for maintenance type 'SBT_TAPE';
RMAN> delete noprompt obsolete;
```

RMAN Sample Scripts

Something particularly clever about the NetBackup *for Oracle* agent installation is that it includes RMAN backup and recovery sample scripts that are pre-instrumented (that is, they already include code snippets or templates) with code for using NetBackup. Look for the sample scripts in /<install_path>/netbackup/ext/db_ext/oracle/samples/rman.

These sample scripts will be included:

```
cold_database_backup.sh
hot_database_backup_proxy.sh
cold_duplex_database_backup_full.sh
hot_tablespace_backup.sh
database_restore.sh
hot_tablespace_backup_proxy.sh
hot_database_backup.sh
pit_database_restore.sh
```

New scripts can be generated from the Administration Console. For anyone who has suffered through the time-consuming effort of trying to locate elusive punctuation errors, these scripts come as a pleasant surprise.

The following is an RMAN code snippet for calling NetBackup:

```
rman target / catalog <user>/<password>@rman_cat_db log=<my_output.log>
run
{
allocate channel t1 type 'SBT_TAPE'
parms="ENV=(NB_ORA_SERV=<storage_server>,
NB_ORA_POLICY=RMAN_DEFAULT, NB_ORA_CLIENT=<db_server>)";
backup database;
}
```

The following is an RMAN code snippet for calling NetBackup that uses **configure** commands:

```
rman target / catalog <user>/<password>@rman_cat_db log=<my_output.log>
rman> CONFIGURE CHANNEL DEVICE TYPE 'SBT_TAPE' PARMS
'SBT_LIBRARY=/<install_path>/netbackup/bin/libobk.so64.1,
ENV=(NB_ORA_SERV=<storage_server>, NB_ORA_POLICY=<policy_name>,
NB_ORA_CLIENT=<db_server>)';
rman> backup database;
```

Troubleshooting

Inevitably, something will break in the environment. Knowing how to prioritize problems in advance helps to make the resolution process go more smoothly. This section highlights steps to help troubleshoot issues.

The following are general troubleshooting steps to take:

1. Verify Oracle agent installation by making sure that the proper libraries exist in /<install_path>/netbackup/bin. Refer to Table 6-2 earlier in the chapter to determine which library (for example, libobk.a) corresponds to your operating system.

2. Check the database server (client) to ensure that the bphdb executable exists. This is used by both the NetBackup scheduler and the GUI to start backups.

3. Check that the following executables exist:

   ■ /<install_path>/netbackup/bin/bpdbsbora

   ■ /<install_path>/netbackup/bin/bpubsora

   ■ /<install_path>/lib/libdbsbrman.so

   ■ /<install_path>/lib/libnbberman.so

4. Check that the following /<install_path>/netbackup/logs directories exist with 777 permissions:

- On the database server (client): bpdbsbora, dbclient, bphdb, and bpcd

- On the master server: bprd and bpdbm

- On the media server: bpbrm and bptm

Use NetBackup Logs

NetBackup generates logs for backup and restore operations. These logs can be used to investigate media manager problems, but RMAN errors will be written to the RMAN logs. There are two types of NetBackup logs:

- **Progress logs** Located in /<install_path>/netbackup/logs/user_ops/username/ logs, these logs are generated for any backup or restore operations. These files can sometimes be large and cumbersome. They contain sizable amounts of data. The key here is knowing how to extract the data you need. There are basically two error types, numbers 16 and 32; 16 is an error failure and 32 is a critical failure. The best way to find them is to search the log files for <16> and <32>.

- **Debug logs** Each debug log corresponds to a NetBackup process and executable. When debugging is turned on, the logs are written to /<install_path>/netbackup/logs. These logs can grow quickly in size, so use debugging only when necessary.

To enable logging on the database server (client), modify the /<install_path>/ netbackup/bp.conf file with this line:

```
VERBOSE = #
```

is a value of 1 to 5 to indicate the level of logging. Keep in mind that a higher value generates a lot of information and could cause the directory to run out of space.

NOTE
Make sure that the debug file permissions are set to 777. Verify that libobk is linked properly if log files are not being created.

Determine Which Library Is in Use

Find out which NetBackup library is interfacing with Oracle:

```
ls -l $( echo $LD_LIBRARY_PATH | sed -e "s/:/ /g")/libobk* | grep libobk
```

Security Best Practices

Since the NetBackup software runs in a networked environment, it is susceptible to vulnerabilities such as denial of service attacks. To prevent these situations from happening, the following best practices are recommended by Veritas, which is now Symantec:

- Allow administrative access to privileged users only

- Allow remote access only from trusted servers

- Apply the latest patches

- Install NetBackup behind a firewall

- Ensure virus protection is running on the servers

- Monitor network traffic for malicious activity

- Block external access to the default ports used by NetBackup

- NetBackup server and clients should face towards the internal network

Cost Justification

It's not always easy to justify the costs of purchasing expensive software and licenses for an information technology department, which is traditionally considered to be a non-revenue generating part of an organization. This section provides some ideas for demonstrating to management the value of purchasing VERITAS NetBackup *for Oracle*.

The NetBackup *for Oracle* software extends the capabilities of RMAN. Since the software allows RMAN to speak directly to storage servers, it automates processes that would otherwise be done by people. It shortens backup and recovery time by eliminating some steps altogether and by cutting out process variation. Essentially, this translates into better overall application performance (since backups take less time), reduced business outages during recovery events, more error-free recoveries, and greater productivity of database and storage administrators.

The NetBackup software could easily pay for itself during just one significant business outage where productivity and revenue are negatively impacted.

Summary

We hope that you have enjoyed our exploration into how NetBackup software is used to facilitate a networked backup and recovery environment. We outlined the ways in which it extends existing RMAN functionality. We described how to configure each layer for direct component communication, which eliminates the need for manual intervention. We discovered that using NetBackup to enhance RMAN results in faster backup and recovery, reduced process variation, and shorter business outages during recovery events. NetBackup *for Oracle* software has been thoughtfully developed for those of us who are excited about easily deployed and feature-rich backup and recovery solutions.

References

- *VERITAS NetBackup 5.1 Media Manager System Administrator's Guide for Windows* http://www.sun.com/products-n-solutions/hardware/docs/pdf/875-3610-10.pdf

- *VERITAS NetBackup 5.1 Troubleshooting Guide for UNIX and Windows* http://www.sun.com/products-n-solutions/hardware/docs/pdf/875-3612-10.pdf

- *VERITAS NetBackup 5.1 Release Notes for UNIX and Windows* http://www.sun.com/products-n-solutions/hardware/docs/pdf/875-3616-10.pdf

- *Oracle Database Backup and Recovery Essentials*, by Paul Massiglia (Symantec Vision Technology Conference presentation) http://www.shobizevents.com/vision2005/presentations/4.45pm-%20Oracle%20Backup_paulmassigila.pdf

- *Oracle9*i *RMAN Backup and Recovery*, by Robert G. Freeman and Matthew Hart (McGraw-Hill/Osborne, 2002)

- The command to find out which NetBackup library is interfacing with Oracle was taken from http://support.veritas.com/docs/250077.

CHAPTER
7

Configuring
EMC NetWorker
Module for Oracle

MC NetWorker Module for Oracle (NMO), formerly Legato NetWorker Module for Oracle, and EMC NetWorker server combine to provide efficient and reliable backup and recovery solutions for the Oracle database and its components. NMO acts as an intermediary between the primary NetWorker server and RMAN. All backups and restores of the Oracle database are initiated by RMAN. In fact, once NMO is set up, little to no interaction is required. The primary mode of operations will be to use RMAN.

This chapter begins with a discussion of the architecture of the Oracle backup and recovery system integrated with NMO. It then describes the basic configuration of NMO for use with Oracle and how to install NMO. You then will learn how to run and schedule RMAN backups in NMO. Finally, you will learn how to set up and run restore operations with NMO.

Architecture of the Oracle and NetWorker Backup and Recovery System

There are six components (two optional) in a backup and recovery system if Oracle and NetWorker have been configured correctly. The Oracle backup and recovery system is comprised of the following:

- The Oracle server
- RMAN
- A recovery catalog (this is optional because the control file can be used)

The NetWorker system consists of the following:

- A NetWorker server
- NetWorker client (in the cases where the NetWorker server resides on a remote host)
- NetWorker Module for Oracle

EMC NetWorker server is the main component of the NetWorker architecture. All the information is stored there, for all backups scheduled and/or performed. The NetWorker server manages all backups and restores and maintains the client indexes and storage medium.

EMC NetWorker client software is how the NetWorker server communicates with the target backup node.

EMC NMO is an add-on module that allows the NetWorker server and NetWorker client combination to communicate with the Oracle backup and recovery system. The client software and the module work hand in hand. NMO allows the NetWorker system to interact with RMAN—in other words, it is the intermediary that passes information from RMAN through to the NetWorker system. The application programming interface (API) that is used between the two systems is Oracle System Backup to Tape (SBT). NMO also links the Oracle Server software with a Media Management Layer (MML). This allows RMAN to back up and restore data directly to the storage media controlled by the NetWorker system. Figure 7-1 shows the architecture of the Oracle backup and recovery system and the NetWorker system.

Backup and Restore Operations

Issuing RMAN commands to the target database starts a backup of the database. Once the backup is started, the Oracle Server reads the appropriate database file, creates a backup data set, and passes it via the SBT API to NMO. NMO translates the object names of the data set into a format that can be recognized by the NetWorker server, and then passes the information to the NetWorker server using the network remote procedure call (RPC) protocol.

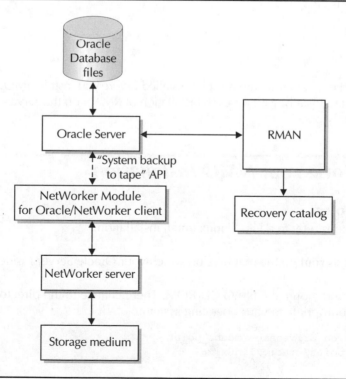

FIGURE 7-1.   *The architecture of the NetWorker and Oracle systems*

Once NetWorker receives the information, it creates an entry in its *client index* file, which contains information about each Oracle object being backed up. The NetWorker server then stores the backup data to the storage media and writes an entry in its *media index* file, which contains information corresponding to the location and content of all storage media.

A restore initiated by RMAN works in a similar way.

Installing NMO

The Oracle Server, NetWorker client, and NMO must be installed on the *same* system; a compatible release of the NetWorker server must be installed on the Oracle Server or a remote host. Similarly, if an Oracle recovery catalog is used, it should reside on a different system. This chapter does not cover the installation procedures for the NetWorker server or the client. For information on the installation procedures, please refer to the appropriate EMC NetWorker documentation.

Before proceeding with the installation of NMO, ensure that EMC Storage Manager bundled with the Oracle Database 10*g* Enterprise Edition software is removed. In Solaris, it includes the following software packages:

- ORCLclnt

- ORCLdrvr

- ORCLnode

The NetWorker client software must be installed *before* you install NMO. Also, you do not need to install NMO for each installation of RMAN on the server—it needs to be installed only once.

RMAN Workshop: *NMO Installation*

Workshop Notes
The following steps refer to a local Linux (Intel) installation.

Step 1. Log in as **root** on the machine on which your Oracle Server resides.

Step 2. Insert and mount the NMO CD-ROM. Then, change to the directory on the CD-ROM appropriate to your operating system.

```
#  mount /dev/cd_drivename /mount_point
#  cd /mount_point/oracle/linux_x86
```

Step 3.   The NMO installation must reside on the *same* directory as the NetWorker client installation. AIX, Linux, and Solaris appear to provide a choice for installing it in a different directory, but the installation will likely fail if you choose a different directory from the one in which the NetWorker client is installed. If installing on Solaris, modify the /var/sadm/install/admin/ default file to specify the parameter **basedir=default**. This ensures that the software is automatically installed in the correct directory.

.Please refer to the EMC *NetWorker Module for Oracle Installation Guide* for other platforms not mentioned here. You can download it once the product is purchased from EMC.

Step 4.   Install the NMO software using the **rpm** command (**pkgadd** for Solaris or **swinstall** for HP-UX). Note: The Oracle database does *not* have to be shut down for this.

```
#  rpm -i lgtonmo-4.2-1.i686.rpm
```

Step 5.   Log in as the owner of the oracle binaries (in other words, the ORACLE_HOME). For example, if the owner of the ORACLE_HOME is "oracle," issue the following command:

```
#  su - oracle
```

Step 6.   Symbolically link the Oracle Server with the NMO libraries. Each platform and each version of Oracle requires a different set of commands to symbolically link the libraries. The following table provides a list of commands for various operating systems and the corresponding Oracle versions:

Operating System	Oracle Release	Command to Change the Symbolic Link
AIX	9.x 64-bit 10.x 64-bit	% cd $ORACLE_HOME/lib % ln -s /usr/lib/libnwora.a libobk.a
HP-UX (Itanium)	9.x 64-bit	% cd $ORACLE_HOME/lib % ln -s /usr/lib/libnwora.so libobk.so
HP-UX (PA-RISC)	9.x 64-bit 10.x 64-bit	% cd $ORACLE_HOME/lib % ln -s /usr/lib/libnwora.sl libobk.sl
Linux (Intel)	9.x 10.x	% cd $ORACLE_HOME/lib % ln -s /usr/lib/libnwora.so libobk.so
Linux (Itanium, AMD64/EM64T)	9.x 64-bit 10.x 64-bit	% cd $ORACLE_HOME/lib % ln -s /usr/lib/libnwora.so libobk.so
Solaris	9.x 9.x 64-bit 10.x 64-bit	% cd $ORACLE_HOME/lib % ln -s /usr/lib/libnwora.so libobk.so
Tru64 UNIX	9.x 64-bit	% cd $ORACLE_HOME/lib % ln -s /usr/shlib/libnwora.so libobk.so

NOTE
*As long as LD_LIBRARY_PATH is set and there is
a soft link to the API or the API is in the Oracle
executable's default search path, the media API will
be loaded dynamically when a channel is allocated
and will be unloaded when released.*

Step 7. Make sure that all the oracle instances associated with the ORACLE_HOME
are shut down. In Oracle9*i* Database and Oracle Database 10*g*, the instances do *not*
have to be shut down.

Step 8. Using the appropriate command from the table in Step 6, soft link
the Oracle Server file with the NMO library file. For Linux, issue the following
command:

```
%   cd $ORACLE_HOME/lib
%   ln -s /usr/lib/libnwora.so libobk.so
```

Configuring NetWorker for Client Operating System Backups

This section does not go into too much detail on configuring NetWorker for a client
operating system backup. Refer to the appropriate EMC documentation for more
detailed information.

CAUTION
*The APIs for the OS backup client and the NMO backup client
are different! Therefore, if OS backups (and restores) are working
correctly and RMAN backups are not, this could indicate that you
have configuration issues. Typically this has to do with environment
variables being incorrectly set, such as LD_LIBRARY_PATH. Refer
to the appropriate Oracle documentation.*

RMAN Workshop: *Configure NetWorker for OS-Level Backups*

Workshop Notes

What follows is a high-level instruction guide for ensuring that your Oracle Server
machine is configured in the NetWorker system as a client for an OS backup.

This is a necessary step before NMO can be configured for use with RMAN. If your Oracle Server machine has already been configured as a client in the NetWorker server, you can skip this section.

Step 1. Configure the NetWorker server by identifying the NetWorker server in the Server Resource section shown in the following illustration. The three most important fields in this dialog box are

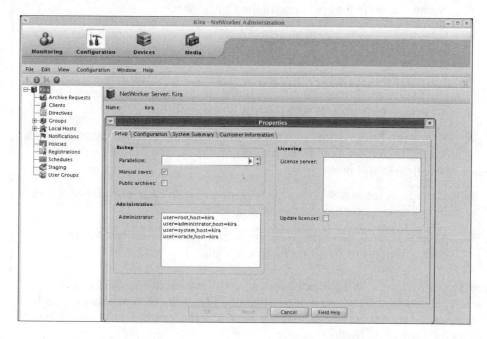

- **Name** Gives the hostname of the NetWorker server: Kira (displayed just above the Properties page).

- **Parallelism** Gives the maximum number of backup data streams between the NetWorker server and the storage device that can exist at the same time.

- **Administrator** Specifies which users should be granted the administrator privilege to modify and update the NetWorker configurations (for example, update client and media indexes, change resource configuration settings, and so on). The owner of the ORACLE_HOME (the Oracle user) should generally be given administrator privileges because when RMAN issues a **change...delete** or **delete expired backup** command, entries will be updated/removed from the client index.

Step 2. Configure appropriate resources and attributes for the Oracle Server, which is registered as a client within the NetWorker server database (as per Step 1). Before NMO can be used, you must configure the Oracle Server client (the NetWorker client—*not* the Oracle client). To do this, select Clients | Client Setup in the main Administrator GUI to open the Clients dialog box. General attributes of concern in this dialog box are the following:

- **Name**   Specify the hostname of the Oracle Server.

- **Schedule**   Use to automate scheduled backups (see "Configuring NMO for Oracle Backups" later in this chapter).

- **Browse Policy**   Specify the length of time the NetWorker server maintains entries for data in the online index file. This is primarily for recovery processes (the default is one month).

- **Retention Policy**   Specify the period of time the NetWorker server keeps the information about backed up data in the online media index file (the default is one year).

- **Group**   A set of NetWorker client resources with preconfigured attributes (for example, start time, retries, and so forth).

- **Save Set**   Specify scripts to be run in conjunction with NetWorker (see "Configuring NMO for Oracle Backups").

Step 3. Configure a storage device for use with Oracle backups and restores. The device can be a stand-alone tape drive or a file, or in an auto-changer. Each device has to be configured in a separate way. The device configuration can be reviewed by selecting Media | Devices.

Step 4. Configure volume pool and label template resources. A *pool* is a collection of backup volumes that NetWorker uses to sort and store data. You can give each pool a meaningful and consistent name by assigning a label template to it. Doing so enables you to organize and track the backing up and labeling of data more easily. In terms of Oracle and RMAN, a volume pool can be useful if you want to back up tablespaces, archived logs, etc., onto different media sets or devices. This can be achieved by using the NSR_DATA_VOLUME_POOL environment variable within the RMAN script.

You need to label and mount each Oracle storage device that has been configured before backup and restore operations take place.

Running and Scheduling RMAN Backups

Now you are ready to run and schedule an RMAN backup with NetWorker. There are a few extra configuration options that are required before this can happen. The configuration scripts have to be created and modified, and the NetWorker server client setup needs additional configuration steps to allow it to interact with NMO and the Oracle Server.

RMAN Workshop: *Configuration of the nsrnmo.SID Script*

Workshop Notes

The nsrnmo.SID script is the main configuration file that contains connection information for the NetWorker and Oracle backup systems.

Step 1.   Connect to the Oracle Server (the NetWorker client server) as the owner of the ORACLE_HOME (the owner is usually "oracle"). The /usr/sbin directory contains a file called nsrnmo.SID. Keeping a copy of the original, rename this file to reflect the name of your SID (such as nsrnmo.TEST). For example:

```
# cd /usr/sbin
# cp nsrnmo.SID nsrnmo.TEST
```

Step 2.   After copying the file, edit the variables in the following table to reflect the environment settings of your site, as well as for your Oracle backup.

Variable	Description
PATH	The directory containing the Networker binaries. This field is mandatory, for example, `PATH=/usr/sbin`
ORACLE_HOME	The home directory of the Oracle Server installation. This field is mandatory, for example, `ORACLE_HOME=/app/oracle/product/8.1.7`
LD_LIBRARY_PATH	The directory containing the Oracle libraries. This field is mandatory on Tru64 only, for example, `LD_LIBRARY_PATH=/app/oracle/product/8.1.7/lib`
NSR_RMAN_ARGUMENTS	Use if parameters are required for the RMAN executable (enclose in a double-quoted string), for example, To output RMAN to a log file, you would use `NSR_RMAN_ARGUMENTS="msglog '/tmp/msglog.log' append"`
NSR_SB_DEBUG_FILE	Path and filename for detailed RMAN-specific debugging information, for example, `NSR_SB_DEBUG_FILE=/tmp/nsrdebug.log`
PRECMD	Specifies whether any pre-processing script needs to be run before the backup commences.
POSTCMD	Specifies whether any post-processing script needs to be run after the backup finishes.
TNS_ADMIN	The directory containing the Net8 configuration files (if it is other than $ORACLE_HOME/network/admin).

Configuring NMO for Oracle Backups

The NetWorker server has to be configured to allow it to interact with the NMO module on the Oracle Server. Previously, we configured the NetWorker server to accept the Oracle Server as a client for OS backups. This section extends this by linking RMAN with the NMO module and the NetWorker client to the NetWorker server (refer to Figure 7-1 for the architecture diagram of data flow).

In Step 2 of the RMAN Workshop "Configure NetWorker for OS-Level Backups," earlier in the chapter, the concept of a *group* was briefly introduced. A NetWorker backup group refers to a particular set of configuration options that can be assigned to NetWorker clients. These configuration options can refer to the start time, cloning, or retries. NetWorker comes with a "Default" backup group.

For ease of administration, create a new group for the Oracle backups with an appropriate name. For example, if the backups are for a customer XYZ, the backup group could be called XYZOracleFull. A new group can be created by selecting Customize | Groups.

Typically, the start time of the Oracle backup should be after or before the time of the OS backup. For network traffic considerations, do not run the Oracle backup at the same time.

Create a backup schedule to automate the scheduled backups for the NetWorker group in question. Preconfigured backup schedules are available that can be modified accordingly.

NOTE
The NetWorker scheduler does not determine the backup level used in an Oracle backup—it is controlled at the RMAN script level. Set the backup as Full whenever the RMAN script should be run (in other words, when a full or incremental Oracle database backup is required) and specify a level of Skip whenever no Oracle database backup is needed. If any level between 1 to 9 is specified, NetWorker treats it as a level of Full.

The final configuration step is to create a new client for the Oracle backups (similar to Step 2 of the RMAN Workshop "Configure NetWorker for OS-Level Backups"):

1. Assign the client the correct Group previously created (for example, XYZOracleFull).

2. In the Save Set field, enter the path and name of the RMAN script that should be used for the scheduled backup. If required, several RMAN scripts can

be specified at this point. However, the order of execution is arbitrary. If an action is required in a particular order, it may be better to use the PRECMD and POSTCMD variables of the nsrnmo.SID file. For details and examples of RMAN scripts, see the following section.

3. Set the appropriate Schedule that you previously created.

4. In the Backup Command field, enter the name of the nsrnmo.SID file that you created and modified earlier in the RMAN Workshop "Configuration of the nsrnmo.SID Script."

Creating RMAN Backup Scripts

An appropriate RMAN script must be created to perform the required type of backup. As mentioned previously, the level and type of backup is determined by the RMAN script and not by the NetWorker settings.

For example, the following script will perform a backup of the entire database to the group XYZOracleFull on the NetWorker server of mycompany.networker4oracle.com:

```
connect target rman-user/password@SQLNetInstance1;
connect rcvcat rcat-user/password@SQLNetInstance2;
run {
    set command id to 'CMD_ID';
    allocate channel t1 type 'SBT_TAPE'
    allocate channel t2 type 'SBT_TAPE';
    send 'NSR_ENV=(NSR_SERVER=mycompany.networker4oracle.com,
    NSR_GROUP=XYZOracleFull)';
    backup full filesperset 4
    format 'FULL_%d_%u'
    (database);
    release channel t1;
    release channel t2;
    }
```

In the RMAN script, providing that the SID is set, one option for establishing a connection to the target database is **connect target rman-user/password**. If more than one instance exists on the server, it may be in your interest to fully qualify the target and catalog/auxiliary (if used) connections; using **connect target rman-user/password@target catalog rman-cat/password@catalog** ensures that you connect to the correct target. The second **connect** command is only required if a recovery catalog is used. An RMAN script must be created for each Oracle instance being backed up, so it is important to use some sort of file-naming convention (for example, SID_full.rcv or SID_inc.rcv). Obviously, since the usernames and passwords are stored in the RMAN script files, a minimal security setting should be granted to the file.

NOTE
*Configuring the channels for backup in Oracle9i and 10g greatly simplifies scripting. So instead of tracking the difficult **send** command strings, add them to the channel configuration using the **configure channel** command:*

```
CONFIGURE CHANNEL DEVICE TYPE SBT PARMS "ENV=
(NSR_SERVER=mycompany.networker4oracle.com,
NSR_GROUP=XYZOracleFull) ";
```

Create the configuration, configure the parallelism to x for SBT, and configure the default device type to be SBT. Then, the value set in parallelism will be spawned automatically with the provided parameters. So the only time they need to be changed is when changing the NetWorker group or server in this case.

The **send** command in the preceding script is what sets the NSR_ environment variables. This command is supported in Oracle8i, 9i, and 10g (for Oracle8, the NSR_ variables are passed through via the **parms** option; see the EMC NetWorker documentation for syntax). The **parms** option is still available in Oracle8i and 9i, but setting the NSR_ variables in this way is not recommended. The following are some things to note about the **send** command:

- All NSR_ environment variables must be written in uppercase.

- When specifying the NSR_ environment variable, no spaces are allowed around the equals sign.

- The commas separating the variables are mandatory.

- The parentheses around the variables are mandatory.

- Comments are not permitted within the variable specification parentheses.

- The command can be run with three options:

  - **No option**   Sets the environment variables for all channels allocated

  - **send device_type 'SBT_TAPE'**   Sets the environment variables for all channels of that backup tape

  - **send channel <channel_name>**   Sets the environment variables for the specified channel

  - The command must be put after the **allocate channel** commands and before the **backup** or **restore** commands of the RMAN script.

RMAN and NMO allow you to *duplex* Oracle backups—in other words, generate copies of the Oracle backup and store them on different media. In Oracle9*i* and 10*g*, this is done through the **configure...backup for device type sbt_tape to...** commands. When using this, individual NSR_ variables of NSR_DATA_VOLUME_POOL must be specified for each duplex stream (up to four copies can be made). For example, if duplex copies of datafiles and archived log files are required, the following script extract can be used:

```
...
run {
...
send 'NSR_ENV=(NSR_SERVER=mycompany.networker4oracle.com,
    NSR_DATA_VOLUME_POOL1=XYZOracleDatafile,
    NSR_DATA_VOLUME_POOL2=XYZOracleArchlogs)';
...
configure datafile backup copies for device type 'sbt_tape' to 2
configure archivelog backup copies for device type 'sbt_tape' to 2;
...
```

Oracle9*i* and 10*g* allow for *backup optimization*, in which RMAN decides whether a file should be skipped based on several criteria. As a result of this optimization, the recovery catalog (if used) and the NetWorker indexes can become out of sync. Therefore, it is recommended that you run the **crosscheck** command on a regular basis to synchronize the two.

Restore Commands

NMO works in conjunction with Oracle and RMAN to restore and recover a database. The restore works in basically the same way as a normal RMAN restore, as all the NetWorker configuration has already been done. Obviously, you can only restore data that has been backed up by NMO.

The first step is to create your restore script. The following is an example. The only difference between a "normal" RMAN restore script and one used by NMO is the environment variables. (Refer to "Creating RMAN Backup Scripts," earlier in the chapter, for some explanation on how to set the variables, and see the upcoming Table 7-1 for a full list.)

```
run {
    set command id to 'CMD_ID';
    allocate channel t1 type 'SBT_TAPE'
    allocate channel t2 type 'SBT_TAPE';
    send 'NSR_ENV=(NSR_SERVER=mycompany.networker4oracle.com,
    NSR_GROUP=XYZOracleFull)';
        restore   (database);
        recover database;
        release channel t1;
        release channel d1;
}
```

The restore script should be run via the command line, such as in the following example:

```
# rman target rman-user/password@SQLNetInstance1 rcvcat rcat-
user/password@SQLNetInstance2 cmdfile '/app/oracle/admin/TEST/
scripts/restore.rcv'
```

NSR Environment Variables

Table 7-1 describes various NSR_ variables that can be set in an RMAN session for an Oracle backup or restore. See "Creating RMAN Backup Scripts," earlier in the chapter, for rules that should be followed when specifying NSR_ environment variables.

Environment Variable	Valid Values	Description
NSR_CHECKSUM	TRUE FALSE	Specifies whether Networker should perform check summing on data.
NSR_CLIENT	Default is the hostname from which the session is initiated; it should be a valid Networker client name.	Specifies the client to be used for the backup or restore session. Recommended for all restores.
NSR_COMPRESSION	TRUE FALSE (default)	Specifies whether Networker should compress the backup data.
NSR_DATA_VOLUME_POOL	Should be a valid Networker pool name; the pool Default is used as the default.	Specifies the name of the volume pool that is to be used for the Oracle backups. It's a mandatory field if duplexing backups. This parameter will override the settings of the Networker Client if they are different.
NSR_DATA_VOLUME_POOLx (where x is 1, 2, 3 or 4)	The name of the volume pool for duplexed Oracle backups; mandatory if duplexing is used.	Each setting of this variable must be different from the other when duplexing is used.
NSR_DEBUG_FILE	Default is undefined (no debugging information is created); should be a valid pathname for the debug file.	Used for specifying a file for dumping debugging information of NMO for the SBT API.

TABLE 7-1.   *NSR Environment Variables*

Environment Variable	Valid Values	Description
NSR_ENCRYPTION	TRUE FALSE (default)	Specifies whether Networker performs encryption on the backup data.
NSR_GROUP	Specify a valid group name.	Specifies a valid backup group name identified in the Networker Client Resource.
NSR_NO_BUSY	TRUE FALSE (default)	Specifies whether the scheduled backup waits for the Networker Server if it is busy. A setting of TRUE means it will fail immediately if the server is busy.
NSR_NWPATH	Valid pathname for the directory of the Networker binaries.	Is mandatory if the Networker installation directory is different from the default installation path.
NSR_SAVESET_ EXPIRATION	Default is the Retention Policy setting in the client configuration; otherwise, specify a valid date.	Specifies the date when the save set becomes recyclable. Primarily used for Networker 6 and above.
NSR_SERVER	Specify a valid Networker Server name; default is the local host.	The hostname of the Networker Server that will perform the Oracle backup; a recommended but *not* mandatory setting.

TABLE 7-1. *NSR Environment Variables* (continued)

Summary

The EMC NetWorker suite of products combined with the Oracle Server and RMAN provides an efficient and relatively simple interface for database backup and recovery.

This chapter has given an overview of how EMC NetWorker and Oracle fit together in terms of data and information flow. We have covered the various components of the two systems and how they should be installed and configured. Using this information, you should now be able to configure RMAN to interact with NMO and create RMAN scripts for your backup and recovery needs.

CHAPTER
8

RMAN and
Tivoli Storage Manager

f you already use Tivoli Storage Manager (TSM) for backing up files in your enterprise, taking the next step and using TSM to back up your Oracle database makes a lot of sense: you not only can leverage an existing data protection asset, but also get a seamless connection from Oracle's RMAN utility to TSM. With only a few minor modifications to your RMAN scripts and a straightforward one-time TSM client installation, you won't even know that the tape or disk drive you're using for backup is on a different server. In your DBA role, you may never even have to run a TSM console command.

In this chapter, we'll cover a number of topics related to TSM, the TSM client in general, and the add-on module known as *Tivoli Data Protection for Oracle (TDPO)*. First, we'll give you a brief overview of the TSM architecture and how an Oracle client connects to it. Next, we'll give you a high-level tour of how to install the components of TSM, including creating storage pools and assigning these pools to a management class. However, your enterprise's storage and backup specialist most likely already set up most of these components. Your in-depth involvement with TSM begins when you must test and configure TDPO on the server where you will perform the RMAN backup commands.

Throughout this chapter, we'll briefly cover a couple of TSM and Oracle client utilities that you will use to perform initial and routine configuration and monitoring tasks.

At the end of the chapter, we'll perform a couple of backups using RMAN and see the effect of this backup in the storage pool assigned to your TSM Oracle client.

Overview of Tivoli Storage Manager

TSM is a multitiered architecture: when you use it to back up an Oracle database, you may have as many as four tiers. In contrast, you could host all tiers on a single server, but this is not recommended in a distributed environment where you want to keep your backup server separate from the server whose data you want to back up.

Figure 8-1 is a diagram of a typical TSM environment. In the next few sections, we'll drill down into each component shown in Figure 8-1 and explain some TSM concepts along the way.

Table 8-1 outlines the nodes shown in Figure 8-1. These nodes are used in the examples throughout this chapter to show you how you can distribute the TSM components across your network.

Table 8-2 lists and briefly describes the disk devices you will use on server tsm01 for your Oracle RMAN backups.

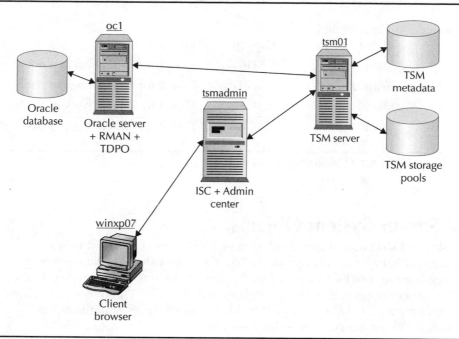

FIGURE 8-1. *TSM architecture*

Node Name	Operating System	Role
tsm01	Linux	TSM server
tsmadmin	Linux	Integrated Solutions Console, Administration Center server
oc1	Linux	Oracle database, Tivoli Data Protection for Oracle; TSM client
winxp07	Windows XP	Integrated Solutions Console/ Administration Center web client

TABLE 8-1. *TSM Node Names and Roles*

Physical Device Name	Linux Mount Point	Capacity	Purpose
/dev/sda1	/tsm01	3.5GB	Disk 1 for Oracle backup pool
/dev/sdb1	/tsm02	3.5GB	Disk 2 for Oracle backup pool
/dev/sdc1	/tsm03	3.5GB	Disk 3 for Oracle backup pool
/dev/sdd1	/tsm04	3.5GB	Disk 4 for Oracle backup pool

TABLE 8-2. *Raw Disks for TSM Storage Devices*

TSM Server System Objects

The multilevel structure of system objects in a TSM server makes it easy to optimally configure your backups for each of the wide variety of data sources in your environment. For the same reason, this flexible hierarchy also makes it easy to assign a specific configuration to unrelated data sources! Figure 8-2 shows the relationship between TSM system objects as well as the types and number of objects that a client uses on any given TSM server.

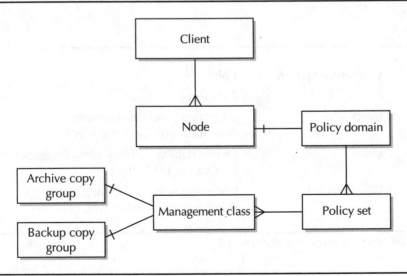

FIGURE 8-2. *Client/TSM relationship and TSM system objects*

At the highest level is the policy domain: a policy domain consists of one or more policy sets, and each policy set consists of one or more management classes. Each management class can have one archive copy group and one backup copy group. We'll tell you more about each of these objects in the following sections.

Policy Domain

A *policy domain* is a group of clients with similar requirements for backing up and archiving data. You might use a policy domain for everyone in a particular department, a particular building or floor, or all users of a specific file server.

A default TSM installation includes one default policy domain called **standard**. For the examples later in this chapter, we will use the **standard** policy domain. You assign backup clients to a policy domain.

Policy Set

A *policy set* is a group of management classes. Each policy domain can contain one or more policy sets, but only one policy set in a policy domain can be active at any given time. You use policy sets to easily switch between available management classes.

Management Class

A *management class* is a collection of zero, one, or two copy groups. You designate one management class within a policy set as the default management class. You typically use management classes to partition client data based on its criticality to the business, how frequently it changes, or whether the data must be retained indefinitely. A management class can have at most one backup copy group and at most one archive copy group.

Backup Copy Groups and Archive Copy Groups

A *copy group* specifies the common attributes that control these characteristics of a backup or archive file:

- **Generation**   How many copies of each file are retained

- **Destination**   Which storage pool will contain the backup

- **Expiration**   When a file will be deleted because the expiration date or retention period has passed

A *backup copy group* contains attributes that control whether a file that has changed since the last backup is backed up again, how many days must elapse before a file is backed up again, and how a file is processed if it is in use during a backup. In contrast, an *archive copy group* contains attributes that control whether a file is archived if it is in use, where the server stores archived copies of the files, and how long the server keeps archived copies of the files. TDPO only uses backup copy groups for Oracle backups.

TSM Client

You install the client piece of TSM, which includes the TSM API, on any server that needs to use a TSM server for backup or recovery. Also included in an installation on an Oracle server is the RMAN library interface to TSM: Tivoli Data Protection for Oracle (TDPO).

Using TDPO, RMAN can back up these database objects to TSM:

- Databases
- Tablespaces
- Datafiles
- Archive log files
- Control files

Plus, you can perform a full database restoration while the database is offline; you can perform tablespace or datafile restores while the database is either online or offline.

The server oc1 is a client node in an Oracle Real Application Clusters (RAC) database in Figure 8-1 and is a client of TSM on server tsm01.

TSM Administration Center and Web Client

The Administration Center is a web-based interface that you use to centrally configure and manage IBM TSM version 5.3 servers. You install it as an IBM Integrated Solutions Console (ISC) component—as a result, you can use ISC to manage a number of heterogeneous systems and applications using a common management interface.

In Figure 8-1, the server tsmadmin hosts ISC and the Administration Center plug-in. TSM administrators use a web browser on the workstation winxp07 to connect to ISC on tsmadmin, which in turn sends console commands and receives status information from the TSM server tsm01. You can administer TSM using this method from any web browser that has a network connection to server tsmadmin.

TSM Installation Tasks

We will not go through each installation step for all the TSM components, but instead we will provide additional details for those steps that are relevant to RMAN in an Oracle environment.

Storage Manager for Linux Server

The first step is to install TSM itself. In all the examples throughout this chapter, we will show you how to do the example on a Linux server; in our sample environment, you will install TSM on the server tsm01. However, the installation tasks are similar for other flavors of Unix and even for Microsoft Windows Server platforms. To start the installer on Linux, mount the installation CD and run this command:

```
/install_server
```

As the installation proceeds, you will see many of the typical steps for any software installation: accepting the license agreement, selecting a language, and choosing one or more packages to install. The primary packages you need to install are TIVsm-server-5.3.0-0 for the server software itself and TIVsm-license-5.3.0-0 to control server licensing. The packages you select are installed during this initial installation session. Other options include SCSI drivers and command-line help files in different languages. When you are done installing packages, select **Q** and the installer exits. If you are familiar with Linux installations using the Red Hat Package Manager (RPM), you can install these packages manually from the installation CD.

The default location for the server files on Linux is /opt/tivoli/tsm. To start the server, run the executable /opt/tivoli/tsm/server/bin/dsmserv. You can use this script to start, stop, or restart the server when required. On Linux, you can use the script dsmserv.rc in the same directory as dsmserv and copy it to the directory /etc/init.d to automatically start TSM when the Linux server boots, and automatically shut down TSM when the Linux server shuts down. If you are using the interactive console, the **halt** command stops the server and exits the console.

You can manage many of your administrative tasks through this command-line interface, but, as you will see later, the Administration Center makes your job easier by enabling you to use the GUI to generate most of the obscure TSM console commands for you.

The server executable and configuration files require approximately 78MB on the file system containing /opt/tivoli/tsm.

IBM Integrated Solutions Console

Your next step is to install the IBM Integrated Solutions Console (ISC). ISC is a highly modular environment that you can use to monitor and manage any applications that use the ISC interface. In our example environment, you will install ISC on the server tsmadmin.

To install ISC, run the installer using the script setupISC on the installation CD. The installer uses /opt/IBM/ISC for the console executables; the console is operational but is not of much use to you until you install the Administration Center in the next section.

ISC requires approximately 470MB of disk space; to complete the installation, you need 982MB of temporary disk space. At the completion of the ISC installation process, the installer creates the user ID iscadmin and prompts you for a password. Keep in mind that this is the user account and password for the administrative console, and not for TSM itself. We will configure the connection from ISC and the Administration Center to TSM later in this chapter.

When the installation is complete, ISC is available at this URL from a web browser anywhere on the network:

http://tsmadmin:8421/ibm/console

If your server supports secure connections via HTTPS, you use port 8422 instead.

Storage Manager Administration

On the server where you just installed ISC, tsmadmin, you will now install the Administration Center. From the Administration Center CD, run the script startInstall.sh, and the installer will automatically pick the executable that is appropriate for your environment.

NOTE
If you are installing the Administration Center on a Windows-based server, use setupAC.exe instead of startInstall.sh.

After the installation process is complete, navigate to http://tsmadmin:8421/ibm/console and you will see a web page (see Figure 8-3) that contains a navigation link on the left side to TSM functions. The Administration Center requires approximately 181MB of disk space.

To start the Administration Center on Linux, navigate to the directory /opt/IBM/ISC/PortalServer/bin and run this command:

```
/startISC.sh ISC_Portal <admin> <admin password>
```

<admin> is an administrator account; as you may remember from earlier in the chapter, the default administrator account created during installation is iscadmin. To stop the Administrator Center, use stopISC.sh instead. If you installed ISC on a

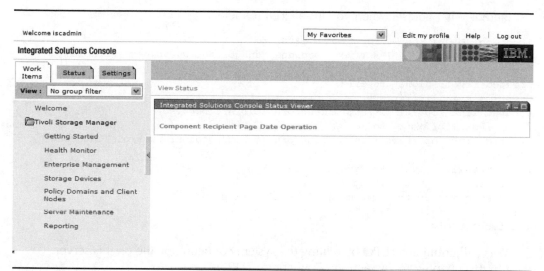

FIGURE 8-3. *ISC with the Administration Center installed*

Microsoft Windows server, the equivalent startup and shutdown scripts are startISC
.bat and stopISC.bat, respectively.

TSM for Databases

The fourth CD you use to establish your TSM environment contains the executables
and libraries for Tivoli Data Protection for Oracle (TDPO). TDPO is an API as well
as a set of library functions that makes it easy for RMAN to create backups on the
TSM server as if the backup destination were a local disk or tape drive. In our
examples that follow, you will install TDPO on the Oracle server oc1 (refer to
Figure 8-1).

To install TDPO on your Oracle server, you need to install the following RPM
packages:

- **TIVguid.i386.rpm**   Creates a globally unique identifier (GUID) to uniquely
  distinguish this server from other servers that will access TSM

- **TIVsm-API.i386.rpm**   Installs the application program interface (API)
  libraries to support TDPO or any other application that will programmatically
  access TSM

- **TDP-Oracle.i386.rpm**   Contains the libraries and link definitions that
  Oracle RMAN will use to connect to TSM

Here is what you see when you install TDP-Oracle:

```
[root@oc1 DPO]# rpm -i TDP-Oracle.i386.rpm
Post Installation of IBM Tivoli Storage Manager for Databases - Oracle.
Checking Tivoli Signature File.
Created Tivoli Signature File.
Creating symbolic links
created link /opt/tivoli/tsm/client/oracle/bin/libobk.so
        /usr/lib/libobk.so
created link /opt/tivoli/tsm/client/oracle/bin/tdpoconf /usr/bin/tdpoconf

Post Installation of IBM Tivoli Storage Manager
for Databases - Oracle Complete.
Be sure to set up the system configuration file
before starting the client!
[root@oc1 DPO]#
```

You will configure TDPO by editing the system configuration file on this server later in this chapter, in the section "Configuring TDPO."

NOTE
The GUID value is stored in /opt/tivoli/guid on Linux.

Configuration Tasks

After you install all software components, you need to connect ISC to all TSMs and configure storage; in this case, we have only one backup client and one TSM server. In addition, you need to perform the initial TDPO configuration steps, which include testing the connection between RMAN and TSM.

One of your configuration tasks is to edit some configuration files: dsm.sys, dsm.opt, and tdpo.opt on Linux; on Windows, you do not have the configuration file dsm.sys.

Creating a TSM Administrator Account

Before you can create a connection to the TSM server from ISC, you want to create an administrator account on the TSM server with permissions commensurate with the tasks the administrator will perform on the TSM server. In this example, you connect to the TSM console on server tsm01 and create an administrator account named **rjb** with a password of **dba** and assign system privileges to this account:

```
TSM:SERVER1> register admin rjb dba passexp=120
ANR2017I Administrator SERVER_CONSOLE issued command:
```

```
     REGISTER ADMIN rjb ?***? passexp=120
ANR2068I Administrator RJB registered.
TSM:SERVER1> grant authority rjb classes=system
ANR2017I Administrator SERVER_CONSOLE issued command:
     GRANT AUTHORITY rjb classes=system
ANR2076I System privilege granted to administrator RJB.
TSM:SERVER1>
```

To create storage groups on the TSM server, you must have system privileges.

Registering a TSM Client

The next step is to register the client oc1 on the TSM server:

```
TSM:SERVER1> reg node oc1_oracle orabakpw maxnummp=2 passexp=0
ANR2017I Administrator SERVER_CONSOLE issued command:
     REGISTER NODE oc1_oracle ?***? maxnummp=2 passexp=0
ANR2060I Node OC1_ORACLE registered in policy domain STANDARD.
ANR2099I Administrative userid OC1_ORACLE defined
     for OWNER access to node OC1.
TSM:SERVER1>
```

Note that we're setting **maxnummp=2**: this specifies the maximum number of parallel sessions that the client can use when backing up to tape. Even though we're using disk drives for backup in these examples, it's a good idea to define the parallelism you need on those occasions when you do back up to tape.

Registering a client node also creates an administrative account that you can use to connect to the TSM server; however, creating individual server accounts for each administrator (such as the rjb account you created earlier) gives you more control over privileges assigned to each administrator as well as more precise auditing information when an administrator changes the TSM server's configuration. In the examples in this chapter, TDPO will use the node name oc1_oracle to connect to the TSM server.

Adding a Server to ISC

Now that you have the client node registered with the TSM server along with an administrator account, you can access the TSM server from the TSM Administration Center in ISC. After you authenticate with ISC, click the Server Maintenance link (shown earlier in Figure 8-3). Next, select Add Server Connection from the drop-down menu and click Go. Figure 8-4 shows the Maintenance Script page, which is where you can enter the TSM connection information.

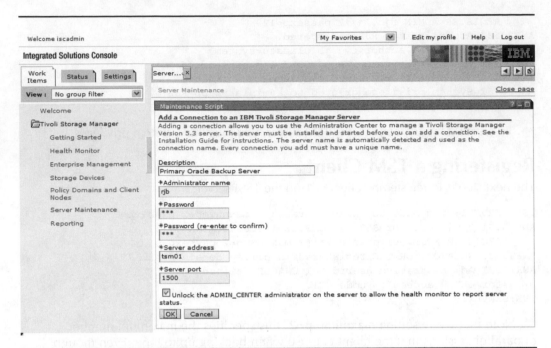

FIGURE 8-4. *Adding a connection to the TSM server*

Unless your TSM server is configured otherwise, the listener port defaults to 1500. Click OK to create the server connection. You now see the TSM server SERVER1 defined in your TSM Administration Center interface, as shown in Figure 8-5.

Adding a Storage Device

For a default installation of TSM, you have three default storage pools defined (ARCHIVEPOOL, BACKUPPOOL, and SPACEMGPOOL), none of which is large enough to hold your Oracle RMAN backups! Therefore, in this section we'll create a storage pool using the four disk devices previously outlined in Table 8-2; the total storage pool size will be 14GB, using all four devices called OraclePool.

To create a new storage pool and add devices to it, click the Storage Devices link, shown in Figure 8-5, and select Add a Storage Device in the drop-down menu for the server SERVER1. On the Select a Device Type page, shown in Figure 8-6, you create a new disk storage device; you will add this storage device to the storage pool in a subsequent step.

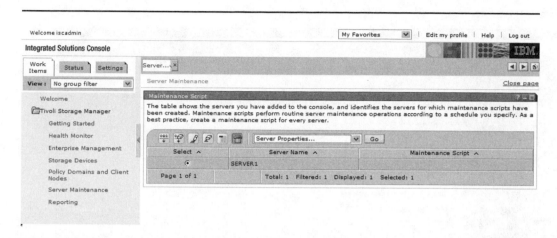

FIGURE 8-5.   *TSM server SERVER1 defined in the TSM Administration Center*

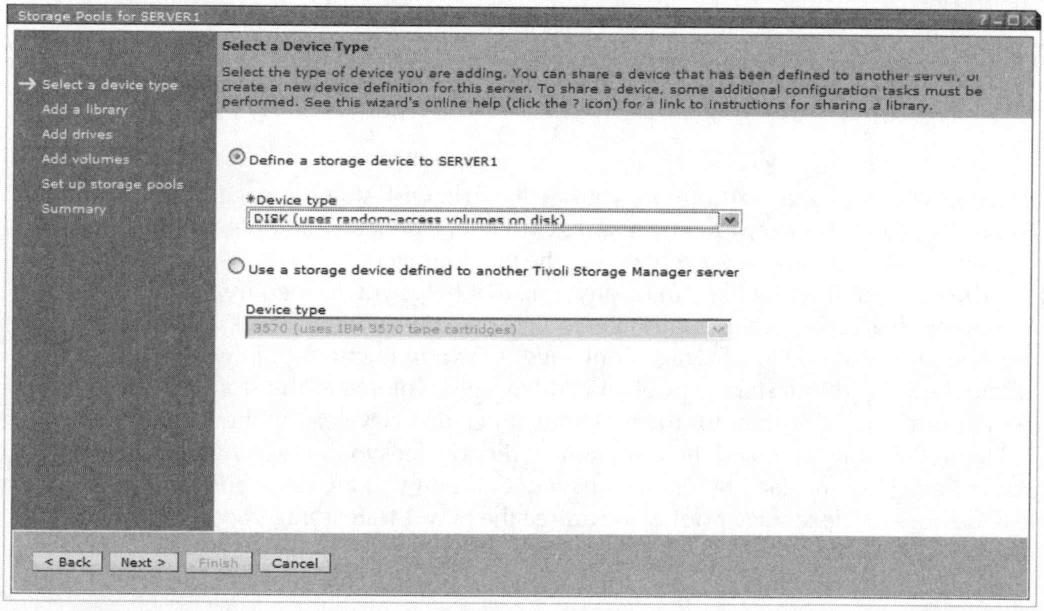

FIGURE 8-6.   *Adding a disk device to a storage pool*

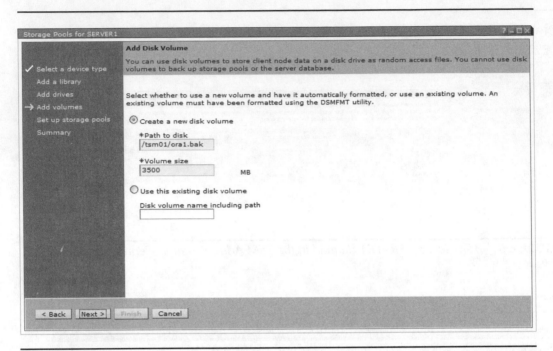

FIGURE 8-7. *Creating a disk volume on a disk device*

After you click the Next button, you see the Add Disk Volume page, shown in Figure 8-7. On this page, you create a disk volume, essentially an operating system file, on the storage device you created in the previous step.

The name of the disk file can be anything that helps you to identify this file as belonging to a TSM storage pool. After you create a disk volume, click Next to open the Add Disk Volume to a Storage Pool page, shown in Figure 8-8, in which you create the OraclePool storage pool and add this disk volume to the storage pool.

Perform the same steps for the remaining three disk devices; on the page shown in Figure 8-8, however, add these remaining disk devices to the existing storage pool OraclePool instead of creating a new one. When you are done adding all four disk devices to the storage pool, you can see the new 14GB storage pool, as shown in Figure 8-9.

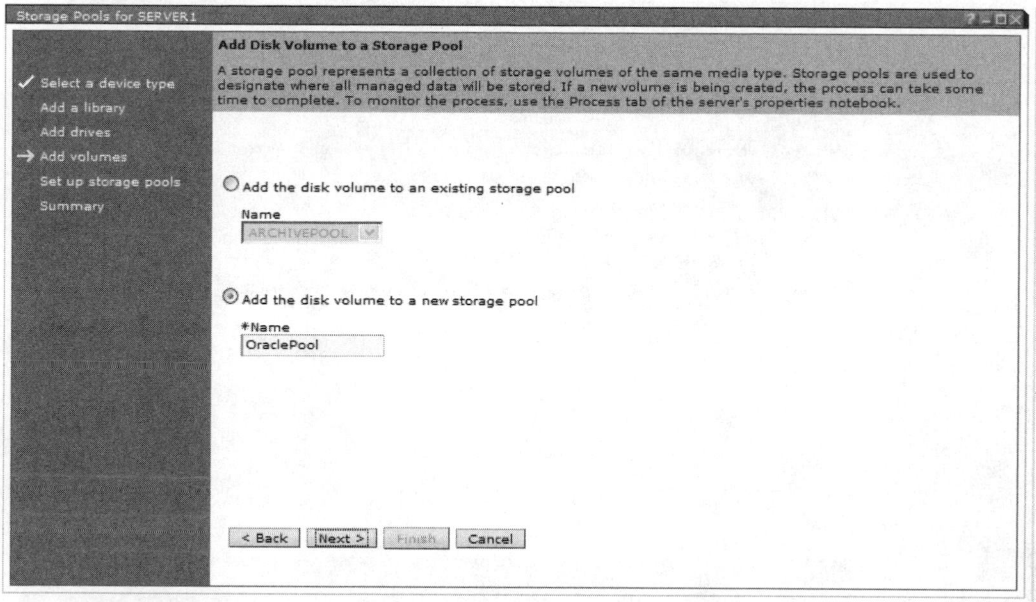

FIGURE 8-8. *Creating a storage pool and adding a disk volume*

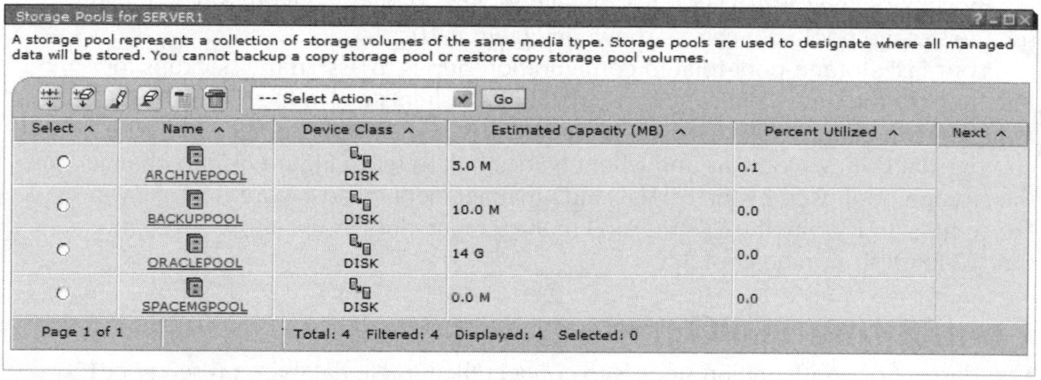

FIGURE 8-9. *Displaying storage pools and capacity*

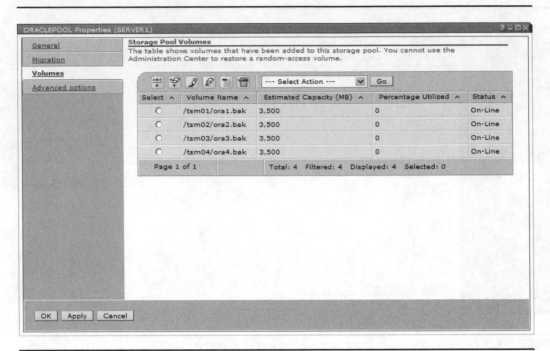

FIGURE 8-10. *Displaying storage pool volumes*

By clicking the ORACLEPOOL storage pool link, shown in Figure 8-9, you can see the storage pool volumes, as shown in Figure 8-10.

Your last storage-pool-related configuration step is to assign the backups for the client to the new storage pool. By default, all clients are in the STANDARD management class, which by default uses the BACKUPPOOL storage pool. You can use the Policy Domains and Client Nodes link (refer to Figure 8-5) to change the storage pool used by the STANDARD management class. Figure 8-11 shows the settings to modify the STANDARD management class to use the ORACLEPOOL storage pool.

Configuring TDPO

Your last set of configuration steps is to connect the Oracle database on server oc1 to the TSM server on tsm01. You do this by

1. Defining the TDPO options in the configuration file tdpo.opt

2. Creating dsm.opt

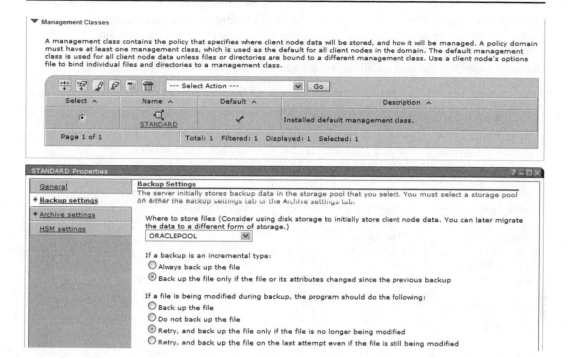

FIGURE 8-11.   *Changing the management class's storage pool*

3. Creating dsm.sys

4. Registering the TDPO node with the TSM server and defining other policy requirements

5. Configuring TSM copy group options

6. Generating the password file for the TSM server

7. Creating symbolic links in the Oracle library directory

8. Testing TDPO connectivity

Defining TDPO Options

On the Oracle client node oc1, change to the directory /opt/tivoli/tsm/client/oracle/bin and copy tdpo.opt.smp (the sample file) to tdpo.opt. The file tdpo.opt, as you might expect, defines the TDPO-specific options such as how TDPO will connect to the TSM server. Uncomment the line beginning with TDPO_NODE and replace <hostname> with the name of the TSM client node you defined earlier in this chapter, oc1_oracle. In addition, uncomment the lines beginning with DSMI_ORC_CONFIG and DSMI_LOG if you installed TDPO in a directory different from the default location. Your tdpo.opt file should now look like this:

```
****************************************************************
* IBM Tivoli Storage Manager for Databases
*     Data Protection for Oracle
*
* Sample tdpo.opt for the Linux86 Data Protection for Oracle
****************************************************************

*DSMI_ORC_CONFIG     /opt/tivoli/tsm/client/oracle/bin/dsm.opt
*DSMI_LOG            /opt/tivoli/tsm/client/oracle/bin

*TDPO_FS             /adsmorc
TDPO_NODE            oc1_oracle
*TDPO_OWNER          <username>
*TDPO_PSWDPATH       /opt/tivoli/tsm/client/oracle/bin

*TDPO_DATE_FMT       1
*TDPO_NUM_FMT        1
*TDPO_TIME_FMT       1

*TDPO_MGMT_CLASS_2   mgmtclass2
*TDPO_MGMT_CLASS_3   mgmtclass3
*TDPO_MGMT_CLASS_4   mgmtclass4
```

Creating dsm.sys

The file dsm.sys defines how to connect to each TSM server, specifying the port number, TCP/IP address, and so forth. Copy the file /opt/tivoli/tsm/client/api/bin/dsm.sys.smp to /opt/tivoli/tsm/client/oracle/bin/dsm.sys and change the values as follows:

```
****************************************************************
* Tivoli Storage Manager                                       *
*                                                              *
* Sample Client System Options file for UNIX (dsm.sys.smp)     *
****************************************************************

* This file contains the minimum options required to get started
* using TSM.  Copy dsm.sys.smp to dsm.sys.  In the dsm.sys file,
* enter the appropriate values for each option listed below and
* remove the leading asterisk (*) for each one.
```

```
*   If your client node communicates with multiple TSM servers, be
*   sure to add a stanza, beginning with the SERVERNAME option, for
*   each additional server.
**********************************************************************

SErvername          SERVER1
COMMmethod          TCPip
TCPPort             1500
TCPServeraddress    192.168.2.69
Passwordaccess      prompt
```

The IP address 192.168.2.69 is the address of the server tsm01. To avoid manually entering a password for every backup, you will use the **tdpoconf** utility later in this chapter to create a password file that TDPO will use to authenticate with the TSM server.

Creating dsm.opt
The file dsm.opt defines the TSM server name you will use for backups on this node. In the directory /opt/tivoli/tsm/client/oracle/bin, create a file with one line, as follows:

```
SERVERNAME SERVER1
```

Registering the TDPO Node with TSM
Earlier in this chapter, you registered the Oracle server with TSM using this command on the TSM console:

```
reg node oc1_oracle orabakpw maxnummp=2 passexp=0
```

To enable the RMAN catalog's archiving and expiration settings to control backup retention on the TSM server, update the configuration for node oc1_oracle on the TSM node using this console command:

```
update node oc1_oracle backdelete=yes
```

Configuring TSM Copy Group Options
Since RMAN creates different backup filenames for each backup file it creates, all backup objects saved to the TSM backup storage pool have unique filenames, and therefore they will never expire. As a result, you must set the copy group attribute **verdeleted** to **0** so that TDPO can remove unwanted backup objects from the TSM backup storage pool when an RMAN command or policy sets the backup object to an inactive or expired state. The parameter **verdeleted** specifies the maximum number of backup versions to retain for files that have been deleted from the client; therefore, setting this value to **0** ensures that the expired backup files on the TSM server are deleted the next time expiration processing occurs.

In this example, you are using the default copy group for your TDPO backups, so you set the option **verdeleted** as follows:

```
TSM:SERVER1> update copygroup standard standard standard verdeleted=0
ANR2017I Administrator SERVER_CONSOLE issued command:
    UPDATE COPYGROUP standard standard standard verdeleted=0
ANR1532I Backup copy group STANDARD updated in policy domain
    STANDARD, set STANDARD, management class STANDARD.
TSM:SERVER1>
```

Generating the tdpo Password File

To ensure that you do not have to interactively specify a password for every RMAN backup to the TSM server, use the **tdpoconf** utility as follows:

```
[root@oc1 bin]# tdpoconf password

IBM Tivoli Storage Manager for Databases:
Data Protection for Oracle
Version 5, Release 2, Level 0.0
(C) Copyright IBM Corporation 1997, 2003. All rights reserved.

**********************************************************
*       IBM Tivoli Storage Manager for Databases Utility *
*  Password file initialization/update program          *
*     ROOT privilege needed to update value             *
**********************************************************

Please enter current password:
Please enter new password:
Please reenter new password for verification:

ANU0260I Password successfully changed.
[root@oc1 bin]#
```

The **tdpoconf** utility creates or updates an encrypted password file called /opt/tivoli/tsm/client/oracle/bin/TDPO.oc1_oracle.

Creating Symbolic Links

In addition to the links created during the installation of the package TDP-Oracle.i386.rpm, you need to create a symbolic link to the TSM library functions in Oracle's default library directory, as follows:

```
ln /opt/Tivoli/tsm/client/oracle/bin/libobk.so
    $ORACLE_HOME/lib/libobk.so
```

The RPM utility has no way of knowing where your Oracle executables and libraries are stored, thus you must define this link manually.

Testing TDPO Connectivity

To ensure that you can establish a connection to the TSM server, use the **sbttest** utility. You can find **sbttest** in the directory $ORACLE_HOME/bin. To run **sbttest**, set the environment variable TDPO_OPTFILE to point to the tdpo.opt configuration file you created earlier, and then run the **sbttest test** command, as in this example:

```
[oracle@oc1 bin]$ export
    TDPO_OPTFILE=/opt/tivoli/tsm/client/oracle/bin/tdpo.opt
[oracle@oc1 bin]$ sbttest test
The sbt function pointers are loaded from libobk.so library.
-- sbtinit succeeded
Return code -1 from sbtinit, bsercoer = 0, bsercerrno = 0
Message 0 not found;  product=RDBMS; facility=SBT
[oracle@oc1 bin]$
```

The output -- sbtinit succeeded and a return code of –1 from the command indicates that the test ran successfully.

Performing an RMAN Backup Using TDPO

Now that the TDPO setup is complete, you're ready to perform your first RMAN backup. You'll use the **allocate channel** command in an RMAN session to define the backup location; even though your channel type is always **sbt_tape**, the actual backup device on the TSM server could be a disk, a writable DVD, or a physical tape drive; RMAN doesn't know and you don't care what physical device will contain the backup, as long as you can recover the database when disaster strikes!

In this first example, you back up just the USERS tablespace to TSM:

```
[oracle@oc1 ~]$ rman target /

Recovery Manager: Release 10.2.0.1.0 -
    Production on Sat Jul 22 21:24:03 2006

Copyright (c) 1982, 2005, Oracle.  All rights reserved.

connected to target database: RAC (DBID=2170964680)
```

```
RMAN> run
2> { allocate channel tdpo type 'sbt_tape' parms
3>      'ENV=(TDPO_OPTFILE=
4>         /opt/tivoli/tsm/client/oracle/bin/tdpo.opt)';
5>    backup tablespace users;
6>    release channel tdpo;
7> }

using target database control file instead of recovery catalog
allocated channel: tdpo
channel tdpo: sid=293 instance=rac1 devtype=SBT_TAPE
channel tdpo: Tivoli Data Protection for
     Oracle: version 5.2.0.0

Starting backup at 22-JUL-06
channel tdpo: starting full datafile backupset
channel tdpo: specifying datafile(s) in backupset
input datafile fno=00004
     name=+DATA/rac/datafile/users.259.582982545
channel tdpo: starting piece 1 at 22-JUL-06
channel tdpo: finished piece 1 at 22-JUL-06
piece handle=02horjvc_1_1 tag=TAG20060722T212604
     comment=API Version 2.0,MMS Version 5.2.0.0
channel tdpo: backup set complete, elapsed time: 00:00:03
Finished backup at 22-JUL-06

released channel: tdpo
RMAN>
```

The only bit of extra work you need to do to back up to TSM is to specify the location of the TDPO options file in the RMAN **env** parameter. In this second example, you back up the entire database:

```
RMAN> run
2> { allocate channel tdpo type 'sbt_tape' parms
3>      'ENV=(TDPO_OPTFILE=
4>         /opt/tivoli/tsm/client/oracle/bin/tdpo.opt)';
5>    backup database;
6>    release channel tdpo;
7> }

allocated channel: tdpo
channel tdpo: sid=293 instance=rac1 devtype=SBT_TAPE
channel tdpo: Tivoli Data Protection for Oracle: version 5.2.0.0

Starting backup at 22-JUL-06
channel tdpo: starting full datafile backupset
channel tdpo: specifying datafile(s) in backupset
```

```
input datafile fno=00003 name=+DATA/rac/datafile/sysaux.257.582982545
input datafile fno=00001 name=+DATA/rac/datafile/system.256.582982545
input datafile fno=00002 name=+DATA/rac/datafile/undotbs1.258.582982545
input datafile fno=00005 name=+DATA/rac/datafile/example.264.582982703
input datafile fno=00006 name=+DATA/rac/datafile/undotbs2.265.582982943
input datafile fno=00007 name=+DATA/rac/datafile/undotbs3.266.582983003
input datafile fno=00004 name=+DATA/rac/datafile/users.259.582982545
channel tdpo: starting piece 1 at 22-JUL-06
channel tdpo: finished piece 1 at 22-JUL-06
piece handle=03hork9s_1_1 tag=TAG20060722T213140 comment=API
   Version 2.0,MMS Version 5.2.0.0
channel tdpo: backup set complete, elapsed time: 00:03:26
channel tdpo: starting full datafile backupset
channel tdpo: specifying datafile(s) in backupset
including current control file in backupset
including current SPFILE in backupset
channel tdpo: starting piece 1 at 22-JUL-06
channel tdpo: finished piece 1 at 22-JUL-06
piece handle=04horkga_1_1 tag=TAG20060722T213140 comment=API
   Version 2.0,MMS Version 5.2.0.0
channel tdpo: backup set complete, elapsed time: 00:00:06
Finished backup at 22-JUL-06

released channel: tdpo

RMAN>
```

Note that you do not have to specify where the backup goes or what disk device to use. TSM automatically puts the backup files into one or more of the storage pool's volumes automatically.

By querying the RMAN catalog, you can see both of the backups you just created:

```
RMAN> list backup;

using target database control file instead of recovery catalog

List of Backup Sets
===================

BS Key  Type LV Size        Device Type Elapsed Time Completion Time
------- ---- -- ---------- ----------- ------------ ---------------
1       Full    2.00M        SBT_TAPE    00:00:02     22-JUL-06
        BP Key: 1   Status: AVAILABLE   Compressed: NO  Tag:
                                        TAG20060722T212604
        Handle: 02horjvc_1_1   Media:
```

```
List of Datafiles in backup set 1
File LV Type Ckp SCN    Ckp Time  Name
---- -- ---- ---------- --------- ----
4       Full 8772169    22-JUL-06
                        +DATA/rac/datafile/users.259.582982545


BS Key  Type LV Size       Device Type Elapsed Time Completion Time
------- ---- -- ---------- ----------- ------------ ---------------
2       Full    1.24G       SBT_TAPE    00:03:24     22-JUL-06
        BP Key: 2    Status: AVAILABLE  Compressed: NO  Tag:
                                                TAG20060722T213140
        Handle: 03hork9s_1_1   Media:
List of Datafiles in backup set 2
File LV Type Ckp SCN    Ckp Time  Name
---- -- ---- ---------- --------- ----
1       Full 8772449    22-JUL-06
                        +DATA/rac/datafile/system.256.582982545
2       Full 8772449    22-JUL-06
                        +DATA/rac/datafile/undotbs1.258.582982545
3       Full 8772449    22-JUL-06
                        +DATA/rac/datafile/sysaux.257.582982545
4       Full 8772449    22-JUL-06
                        +DATA/rac/datafile/users.259.582982545
5       Full 8772449    22-JUL-06
                        +DATA/rac/datafile/example.264.582982703
6       Full 8772449    22-JUL-06
                        +DATA/rac/datafile/undotbs2.265.582982943
7       Full 8772449    22-JUL-06
                        +DATA/rac/datafile/undotbs3.266.582983003


BS Key  Type LV Size       Device Type Elapsed Time Completion Time
------- ---- -- ---------- ----------- ------------ ---------------
3       Full    14.75M      SBT_TAPE    00:00:05     22-JUL-06
        BP Key: 3    Status: AVAILABLE  Compressed: NO  Tag:
                                                TAG20060722T213140
        Handle: 04horkga_1_1   Media:
 Control File Included: Ckp SCN: 8772600       Ckp time: 22-JUL-06
 SPFILE Included: Modification time: 22-JUL-06

RMAN>
```

And finally, you can see how much disk space the backups are using in the storage pool by looking at the properties of the storage pool volumes, as shown in Figure 8-12. You access this page by clicking on the ORACLEPOOL storage pool link in Figure 8-9, then clicking on the Volumes link in Figure 8-10.

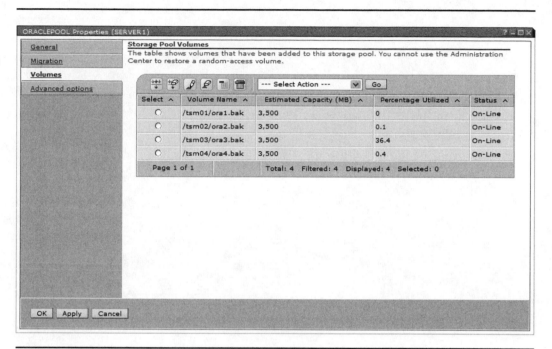

FIGURE 8-12. *Querying storage pool volumes*

Summary

Once you perform the initial installation and setup of TSM, ISC, and TDPO in a few easy steps, it's a case of "set it and forget it," allowing you, the DBA, to focus more on the RMAN scripts themselves than on managing where and how TSM stores the backups. In the environment where you must wear many other hats in addition to the DBA hat, you can use the web-enabled ISC/TSM Administration Center to manage your TSM servers and storage.

TSM and TDPO not only make it easy to back up your Oracle database using the familiar RMAN interface, but also reduce your enterprise's storage management administrative costs because you can use a single storage manager—Tivoli Storage Manager—for all of your backup, recovery, and archival needs.

PART
III

Using RMAN
Effectively

CHAPTER
9

RMAN Backups

ow that we have covered all the startup essentials, we are actually ready to use RMAN to back up something. In this chapter, we are going to talk all about doing backups with RMAN. From offline backups to online backups, backups of archived redo logs to incremental backups, we will cover it all. We will look at how to back up entire databases and individual database datafiles. So, with that in mind, let's move on!

Benefits of RMAN Backups vs. Scripted Backups

So, why use RMAN to back up your databases? You may already be doing online backups with some wonderfully crafted, home-grown scripts, and you may be asking yourself, "Why should I start using RMAN when my scripts work so reliably?" In this section, we hope to answer that question.

Although your scripts may never fail, there are scripts out there that others have crafted that do break. This raises two problems. First, when the script breaks, the database backup fails. Second, when the script fails, someone has to fix it. You might be a wizzo Unix scripter. Unfortunately, after you take that DBA job on the international space station, there is no guarantee that the person following behind you will be an equally gifted Unix scripter. That poor person is going to be sitting there looking at your marvelous code and cussing you up one side and down the other. His or her boss isn't going to be happy, and, most important, the database will be at risk. Of course, the other possibility is that you will be the one having to debug the "Code from the Netherworld" since it was your predecessor, the shell scripter from nether regions, who went to work on the space station. Therein lies one big plus for RMAN—it is supported by Oracle. So, you can go to Oracle with your RMAN woes.

Of course, there are a number of other positives to using RMAN in Oracle Database 10*g*, including:

- RMAN will detect corrupted blocks and report them to you.

- RMAN can back up your database online without having to put the tablespaces in hot backup mode. Thus, the additional (sometimes quite significant) redo generated during a hot backup is reduced.

- RMAN will automatically track new datafiles and tablespaces for you, which means you no longer have to add new tablespaces or datafiles to scripts.

- RMAN will only back up used data blocks (up to the high-water mark [HWM]). Thus, RMAN backup images typically are smaller than those of online backup scripts.

- RMAN offers true compression of backup images.

- RMAN provides easy, automated backup, restore, and recovery operations. RMAN tracks all the backups that you need to recover the database if a restore is required, and will restore only those objects that are needed.

- RMAN can work fairly seamlessly with third-party media management products.

- RMAN supports incremental backup strategies.

- With RMAN, you can actually test your backups without restoring them. Try that with your backup scripts!

- If you use the repository, then RMAN provides a nice, centralized reporting facility.

If you used RMAN in versions prior to Oracle Database 10g, you will find that your earlier RMAN backup commands still work. RMAN is very backward compatible. However, if you don't take the time to review the features that RMAN offers in Oracle Database 10g and implement those that might benefit you, you will not be getting the most benefit out of RMAN.

RMAN Compatibility Issues

Before you haul off and start doing backups, you need to consider some compatibility issues. Your enterprise probably has differing versions of Oracle running, and you need to consider RMAN compatibility issues as you plan your backup strategy. Not all databases are compatible with all RMAN versions, and when you add the recovery catalog into the mix, things get even more complex. Table 9-1 provides a quick reference to the compatibility issues related to RMAN.

In Table 9-1, you can see the RMAN target database version (say your database is version 10.2.0) and the RMAN client that supports backups of that database version (in our example, a 10.2.0 database can be backed up by RMAN versions >=9.0.1.3 and up to version 10.2.0 of RMAN). Also, you will find the version of the RMAN catalog database that must be in place to support the backup of that database (in our 10.2.0 example, the catalog that is required is a 9.0.1 version of the catalog). Finally, the version of the catalog schema that is required is listed (>= the version of the RMAN client being used in our example).

RMAN Target Database Version (with applied patches)	RMAN Client Version (with applied patches)	RMAN Catalog Database Version (with applied patches)	RMAN Catalog Schema (with applied patches)
8.0.6	8.0.6	>=8.1.7	>=8.0.6
8.1.7	8.0.6.1	>=8.1.7	>=8.1.7
8.1.7	8.1.7	8.1.7	>=RMAN client
8.1.7.4	8.1.7.4	>=8.1.7	8.1.7.4
8.1.7.4	8.1.7.4	>=8.1.7	>=9.0.1.4
9.0.1	9.0.1	>=8.1.7	>=RMAN client
9.2.0	>=9.0.1.3 and <=the target database executable version	>=8.1.7	>=RMAN client
10.1.0	>=9.0.1.3 and <=the target database executable version	>=9.0.1	>=RMAN client
10.2.0	>=9.0.1.3 and <=the target database executable version	>=9.0.1	>=RMAN client

TABLE 9-1. *RMAN Compatibility Matrix*

As you can see from Table 9-1, you need to know what version your recovery catalog schema is. The RCVER view in the recovery catalog schema will give you this information. Here is an example:

```
SQL> select * from rcver;
VERSION
------------
10.02.00.00
```

Finally, if you are faced with having to create more than one recovery catalog, there is no reason that all recovery catalogs cannot be maintained in the same database, as long as the database is version 9.0.1 or later. This still makes for a single recovery catalog database, which facilitates easy enterprise-wide reporting from that database.

Monitoring RMAN Backup Status

RMAN produces output during the backup process. If you enable logging when you start RMAN, that output is suppressed. You can monitor RMAN operations by keeping an eye on the log file being generated, or you can use the V$ view V$RMAN_OUTPUT, as shown in this example:

```
SQL> select output from v$rman_output order by stamp;
OUTPUT
-------------------------------------------------------------Starting
backup at 12-NOV-05
using target database control file instead of recovery catalog
allocated channel: ORA_DISK_1
channel ORA_DISK_1: sid=138 devtype=DISK
allocated channel: ORA_DISK_2
channel ORA_DISK_2: sid=154 devtype=DISK
channel ORA_DISK_1: starting compressed full datafile backupset
channel ORA_DISK_1: specifying datafile(s) in backupset
input datafile fno=00001
name=C:\ORACLE\PRODUCT\10.2.0\ORADATA\ROB10R2\SYSTEM01.DBF
input datafile fno=00004
name=C:\ORACLE\PRODUCT\10.2.0\ORADATA\ROB10R2\USERS01.DBF
channel ORA_DISK_1: starting piece 1 at 12-NOV-05
input datafile fno=00003
name=C:\ORACLE\PRODUCT\10.2.0\ORADATA\ROB10R2\SYSAUX01.DBF
channel ORA_DISK_2: specifying datafile(s) in backupset
channel ORA_DISK_2: starting compressed full datafile backupset
input datafile fno=00005name=C:\ORACLE\PRODUCT\10.2.0\ORADATA\ROB10R2\EXAMPLE01.DBF
input datafile fno=00002name=C:\ORACLE\PRODUCT\10.2.0\ORADATA\ROB10R2\UNDOTBS01.DBF
channel ORA_DISK_2: starting piece 1 at 12-NOV-05
```

Offline RMAN Database Backups

Okay, so you think this RMAN thing sounds good, and the first few chapters were sure interesting. Time to really put the beast to work! The first backup topic we will discuss is performing offline (or cold) backups of the Oracle database. An offline RMAN backup is taken with the database mounted, but not open (obviously). If you have set up your default configuration settings for RMAN (as discussed in Chapter 3), then an offline RMAN backup is fairly straightforward.

Offline Backups Using Default Settings

To do an offline backup, first you sign in to RMAN (in the example we provide for this backup, we are not using a recovery catalog). Next, you use the RMAN commands **shutdown** and **startup mount** to mount the database, which is the condition that the database must be in to perform an offline backup. Once the database has been mounted, simply issue a **backup database** command and the backup will occur. Here is an example of the commands you would issue to perform an offline backup via RMAN:

```
shutdown
startup mount
backup database;
startup
```

If you prefer, you could do this as a compressed backup set:

```
shutdown
startup mount
backup as compressed backupset database;
startup
```

RMAN Workshop: *Do an Offline Backup*

Workshop Notes

This workshop assumes that your database has been configured with automatic channels, as shown in Chapter 3. It also assumes that you have configured a database account called backup_admin for backups (as described in Chapter 3). It also assumes that if you are using the Media Management Library (MML) layer, it has been configured.

Step 1.   Start up RMAN:

```
C:\>rman target=backup_admin/robert
```

Step 2.   Shut down the database with the **shutdown immediate** command:

```
RMAN> shutdown immediate
```

Step 3.   Mount the database with the **startup mount** command:

```
RMAN> startup mount
```

Step 4.   Back up the database with the **backup database** command. In this case, to save disk space, we will compress our backup set (since we have not configured compression as a default setting):

```
RMAN> backup as compressed backupset database;
```

Step 5.   Use the **alter database open** command to open the database:

```
RMAN> alter database open;
```

Here is an example of a complete offline RMAN backup following these steps:

```
C:\>rman target=backup_admin/Robert
RMAN> shutdown
using target database control file instead of recovery catalog
database closed
```

```
database dismounted
Oracle instance shut down
RMAN> startup mount
connected to target database (not started)
Oracle instance started
database mounted
Total System Global Area     272629760 bytes
Fixed Size                     1248504 bytes
Variable Size                 83886856 bytes
Database Buffers             184549376 bytes
Redo Buffers                   2945024 bytes
RMAN> backup as compressed backupset database;
Starting backup at 04-NOV-05
allocated channel: ORA_DISK_1
channel ORA_DISK_1: sid=157 devtype=DISK
allocated channel: ORA_DISK_2
channel ORA_DISK_2: sid=155 devtype=DISK
channel ORA_DISK_1: starting compressed full datafile backupset
channel ORA_DISK_1: specifying datafile(s) in backupset
input datafile fno=00001
name=C:\ORACLE\PRODUCT\10.2.0\ORADATA\ROB10R2\SYSTEM01.DBF
input datafile fno=00004
name=C:\ORACLE\PRODUCT\10.2.0\ORADATA\ROB10R2\USERS01.DBF
channel ORA_DISK_1: starting piece 1 at 04-NOV-05
channel ORA_DISK_2: starting compressed full datafile backupset
channel ORA_DISK_2: specifying datafile(s) in backupset
input datafile fno=00003
name=C:\ORACLE\PRODUCT\10.2.0\ORADATA\ROB10R2\SYSAUX01.DBF
input datafile fno=00005name=C:\ORACLE\PRODUCT\10.2.0\ORADATA\ROB10R2\EXAMPLE01.DBF
input datafile fno=00002name=C:\ORACLE\PRODUCT\10.2.0\ORADATA\ROB10R2\UNDOTBS01.DBF
channel ORA_DISK_2: starting piece 1 at 04-NOV-05
channel ORA_DISK_1: finished piece 1 at 04-NOV-05
piece handle=
C:\ORACLE\PRODUCT\10.2.0\FLASH_RECOVERY_AREA\ROB10R2\BACKUPSET\2005_11_04\
O1_MF_NNNDF_TAG20051104T102913_1PQ32XLB_.BKP
tag=TAG20051104T102913 comment=NONE
channel ORA_DISK_1: backup set complete, elapsed time: 00:01:12
channel ORA_DISK_2: finished piece 1 at 04-NOV-05
piece handle=
C:\ORACLE\PRODUCT\10.2.0\FLASH_RECOVERY_AREA\ROB10R2\BACKUPSET\2005_11_04\
O1_MF_NNNDF_TAG20051104T102913_1PQ33J52_.BKP
tag=TAG20051104T102913 comment=NONE
channel ORA_DISK_2: backup set complete, elapsed time: 00:01:11
Finished backup at 04-NOV-05

Starting Control File and SPFILE Autobackup at 04-NOV-05
piece handle=
C:\ORACLE\PRODUCT\10.2.0\FLASH_RECOVERY_AREA\ROB10R2\AUTOBACKUP\2005_11_04\
O1_MF_S_573474457_1PQ357T0_.BKP comment=NONE
Finished Control File and SPFILE Autobackup at 04-NOV-05
Finished Control File and SPFILE Autobackup at 04-NOV-05
RMAN> alter database open;
```

Note that in the preceding example and the RMAN Workshop, we used very few commands. RMAN will automatically use the default configuration settings that we have defined (refer to Chapter 3). We really didn't have to do anything but issue the **shutdown** and **startup mount** commands to shutdown and restart the database. We then issued the **backup as compressed backupset database** command and sat back to watch our backup take off. Pretty easy, huh? RMAN has backed up our database datafiles, our control file, and our SPFILE (assuming we have configured it to do so). Once it's done, all we need to do is issue the **alter database open** command, and our backup is complete.

In this example, Oracle created two backup sets, each of which contains a single backup piece. As you can see from the output, these backup pieces will be created in the flash recovery area (FRA) of this database, which is C:\ORACLE\ PRODUCT\10.2.0\FLASH_RECOVERY_AREA:

```
piece handle=
C:\ORACLE\PRODUCT\10.2.0\FLASH_RECOVERY_AREA\ROB10R2\BACKUPSET\2005_11_04\
O1_MF_NNNDF_TAG20051104T102913_1PQ33J52_.BKP
tag=TAG20051104T102913 comment=NONE
```

NOTE
Oracle only supports backups of SPFILEs. You cannot back up your database text-based init.ora parameter file with RMAN.

Finally, we might have opted to connect to the recovery catalog when we did this backup (and this applies to all backups that we do in this chapter). To connect to the recovery catalog, all you need to do is add the **catalog** parameter when starting RMAN:

```
C:\>set oracle_sid=recover
C:\>rman target=backup_admin/Robert catalog=rcat_owner/password@robt
```

One interesting thing to note here is that when we connected to our recovery catalog owner, we did so using Oracle Net because we had our ORACLE_SID set to the SID of our database rather than the SID of the recovery catalog. When you do a backup with a recovery catalog, you need to use a service name and Oracle Net to connect either to the database you are backing up or to the catalog. We generally recommend using the networking connection to connect to the catalog and connecting directly to the database if possible.

One other thing to note quickly is that if we had not configured automated backups of our control file, RMAN would still back up the control file as long as we were backing up datafile 1. The control file would be backed up into the backup set that contains datafile 1. You would also want to do a separate control file backup after your database backup was complete, so you would have the most current control file backed up (as the control file backed up with the backup set will not have the complete information on the current backup in it). Note that this control file, if it must be recovered, is a bit more complicated to recover if you have not configured control file autobackups. Because of this, we strongly suggest that you configure control file autobackups on your system.

Offline Backups Without Using Configured Defaults

What if we had not configured default settings (see Chapter 3)? Or what if the defaults were not what we wanted to use (maybe we don't want to back up to the FRA)? In this case, we have a few more things that we need to do. Let's look at an example of such a backup and determine what it is doing:

```
shutdown
startup mount
run
{
allocate channel c1 device type disk format 'd:\backup\robt\robt_%U';
allocate channel c2 device type disk format 'c:\backup\robt\robt_%U';
backup as compressed backupset database;
backup current controlfile;
}
```

The next few sections look at this example in a bit more detail.

In the Beginning, Shut Down and Mount the Database

This example looks a bit more complicated than the earlier example. First, we have the **shutdown** and **startup mount** commands that we had in the previous example. These are required for any offline backup. We will discuss online backups later in this chapter.

Run Oracle Run!

Next, we have a **run** block, which is a set of one or more statements, contained within the confines of braces of a **run** command, that is executed together as a block. Oracle will not run any of the statements until the entire block of statements has been entered. After you have entered all the statements, you complete the **run** block with the closing brace (followed, of course, by pressing the ENTER key). The **run** block is then compiled and executed.

NOTE
*This book was written using Oracle Database 10g
Release 2. In this release of RMAN (and 9i and 10g,
in general), many commands that previously had
to run within the confines of a **run** block no longer
need to. We deliberately do not use **run** blocks
unless required by this release. Many of the backup
and restore/recover commands you will see in this
and the next chapter will work in previous versions
but need to be run in the confines of a **run** block.*

Allocate Channels

In the preceding code example, we have several different RMAN commands
within the confines of the **run** block. First, the **allocate channel** commands
allocate a channel each to RMAN for the database backup. We have discussed
channels already (in Chapter 3, for example), but let's look into their use a bit
more for a moment.

First, a word on backup sets and backup set pieces. Each time we create a
channel, this implies that we are going to create one or more backup sets. There
are some exceptions to this statement, but generally this is true, so for the sake of
this discussion, assume this is a true statement. Let's quickly define some terms:

- **Backup sets**   Logical entities, one or more of which will be created for each
  channel you define (generally, it's one backup set per channel).

- **Backup pieces**   The actual physical files that the backed up data resides in.
  One or more backup pieces may be associated with each backup set.

You can control the overall backup set size with the **backup** command
(or, alternatively, you can configure a default value for it), or you can control the
overall backup piece size with the **allocate channel** command (again, this can be
configured when you configure default channels). We will discuss limiting backup
set sizes a bit more later in this chapter.

The **allocate channel** command defines to which device a given channel
(and thus, an individual backup set) is to be allocated. This device might be a
disk (type **disk**) or a tape drive (type **sbt**). If we were allocating a channel to a tape
system, we might also include certain parameter settings required by the MML
vendor that we are using. An example of an **allocate channel** command to tape
using an MML vendor, VERITAS Netbackup, might look like this:

```
allocate channel t1 type sbt parms='ENV=(NB_ORA_CLASS=RMAN_db01)';
```

This particular channel is being allocated to a tape device (refer to Chapters 4 through 8 for more on allocating RMAN channels to MML devices). Having allocated two channels to the backup, RMAN will automatically try to parallelize the backup stream among those channels. Thus, since we have allocated two channels, two different backup sets will be created and each backup set will have one backup piece. The size is defined in bytes, but you can use the *k*, *m*, or *g* specifications to indicate kilobytes, megabytes, or gigabytes, respectively, as required. Here is another example of the **allocate channel** command:

```
allocate channel t1 type disk maxpiecesize=100m;
```

In this example, we have limited the maximum size of each individual piece of a backup set (remember that each channel will create a single backup set) created through that channel to 100MB. This is a great way to ensure that you do not create an individual backup piece that is larger than your tape or file system will handle. Here is another example that we want to look at quickly:

```
allocate channel t1 type disk maxpiecesize=100m
format='d:\backup\robt\robt_%U.bak'
```

In this example, we have used the **format** parameter to define where the backup pieces will be put on the disk and what the naming convention will be for the backup pieces. Note the %U format placeholder. In this case, %U (which is the default value used by RMAN) will be replaced by a set of characters that will make the backup piece name unique. The resulting name will include the database name (robt) followed by an underscore and then an eight-character mnemonic that consists of the following:

- The backup set identifier. Each backup set is assigned a unique identifying number by RMAN when it is created.

- The time the backup set piece was created.

Following the eight-character mnemonic will be an underscore, followed by the backup set piece number. Because the backup set piece number uniquely identifies each piece of the backup set, it is unique to that backup set. Finally, another underscore will be followed by the copy number of the backup set piece. Each multiplexed backup set piece copy has its own unique number assigned to it. If you are not multiplexing, the copy number will be 1.

An example of the resulting backup set piece name might look like this:

```
Rob1_16E112V9_1_1
```

Note in this filename that the time component of the eight-character mnemonic is not readily discernable, but that's not really a problem. The important thing about the use of the %U placeholder is that it guarantees that the name of each backup set piece is unique. Of course, several different mnemonics are available for use with the **format** command, but generally %U will suffice. We added the instance name to the name and the extension just out of habit and good practice. Finally, there are a number of other options with the **allocate channel** command. Check out Appendix A for the entire syntax of the **allocate channel** command.

NOTE
You might have noticed that we are using SBT instead of SBT_TAPE. Earlier versions of RMAN used SBT_TAPE but this is now just SBT. SBT_TAPE is still usable for backward compatibility.

Channels can fail. Perhaps the particular hardware might fail, or some other failure might occur. Many RMAN backups consist of more than one channel going to a different location. If RMAN is using multiple channels and one channel should fail, the remaining channels will attempt to complete the work of the failed channel.

Backup Is the Name of the Game

Moving on now with our example code, after we have allocated the channels, it's time to back up the database with the **backup** command (using the **database** option). The sum result of the **backup database** command is that RMAN will proceed to use the two channels we created and back up the database. The command is a bit different from the **backup database** command we issued earlier, as this **backup database** command is issued within the confines of a **run** command block. We had to perform this backup using a **run** block because we manually allocated the channels with the **allocate channel** command.

The **backup** command also takes care of the control file and server parameter file (SPFILE) for us if datafile 1 is getting backed up (which it always will during an offline backup or any full backup, which is the default). Where this control file backup is stored depends on the setting of the **controlfile autobackup** parameter. If this parameter is set to **off**, then the control file is included in the database backup set along with the server parameter file (if an SPFILE is being used). If the parameter is set to **on**, the control file and SPFILE backup will be made to a separate control file backup piece. You can force RMAN to put the control file in the database backup set by including the **include current controlfile** clause in the **backup database** command (assuming you are not backing up datafile 1). Better yet, as we have done in our example, a separate backup of the control file is a good idea, to ensure that you have a control file backup that is current, including the most recent database backup.

NOTE
*RMAN will only back up a server parameter file
(SPFILE). It will not back up text-based init.ora files.*

The **backup database** command comes with a number of different options
(and is in fact a subset of the larger **backup** command). Let's look at the use of
some of the options of the **backup** command.

Backup Command Options

Now that we have introduced you to the **backup** command, let's look at the number
of different options you can use with it. These **backup** command options can be
used with many of the various **backup** command flavors, such as **backup database**
(which we have just covered), **backup tablespace**, **backup datafile**, and other
backup options, which we will cover later in this chapter. There are a number of
different options available for use with the **backup** command that allow you to do
such things as provide a naming format for individual backup pieces, or limit the
size of those backup pieces. The **backup** command even allows you to manually
decide which channels will be used to back up what, should you wish to override
the choices that RMAN makes otherwise. So, let's look at some of the options that
you can use with the **backup** command.

Compression

As you saw in previous examples, you can actually compress backup sets. By default,
RMAN does NULL data block compression. RMAN also offers true compression of
backup sets, which can reduce the overall storage space consumed by backup images.
We discuss these two different types of compression next.

NULL Data Block Compression

With this form of compression, Oracle does not back up unused data blocks. NULL
data block compression occurs in two different ways:

- Data blocks that have never been used will not be backed up.

- RMAN will also skip backing up blocks that were once used given specific
  criteria.

In the first case, any block that has never had data in it will simply not be backed
up. In the second case, if the database and the associated block meet certain criteria,
then an empty block will not be backed up even if it contained data at one time.

The following are the conditions that must be met to allow RMAN to skip backing up these blocks:

- The compatible parameter is set to 10.2.

- No guaranteed restore points are defined for the database.

- The datafile is locally managed.

- The backup is a backup set and is a full backup or a level zero incremental backup.

- The backup set has been created on disk.

If these conditions are met, Oracle will not back up any unused block and your backups will therefore take up less space on your disks or tape.

RMAN Backup Compression

We provided an example earlier in this chapter of configuring the database to use RMAN compression. RMAN has the ability to apply compression algorithms to your backup sets to help reduce the size of the backup sets RMAN creates. RMAN compression can significantly reduce the size of backup sets. Compression can be significant; for example, in one of our test databases, we saw a 70 percent difference in the size of the backup set images when using compression. If you don't have the database configured to automatically compress backup sets, you can use the **as compressed backupset** parameter to create the backup set as a compressed backup set. If you have compression configured and you do not wish to use it in a given **backup** command, simply use the **as backupset** parameter (without the **compressed** keyword) of the **backup** command.

Tags

Each backup in Oracle can be assigned a tag. This applies to full backups, tablespace backups, datafile backups, incremental backups, and even backup copies (all of which will be discussed in this chapter). Here is an example of assigning a tag to a full backup:

```
backup database tag='test backup';
```

In this example, we used the **tag** parameter to identify this backup. Each tag should be unique, and RMAN will allocate a tag to each backup set using a default naming convention if one is not assigned. The same tag can be applied to multiple backups, and the latest backup will be restored by default.

Limiting Backup Impacts

To assist you in reducing the overall I/O impact of an RMAN backup on other processes, RMAN offers the **duration** parameter of the **backup** command. The **duration** parameter is like an alarm clock; if the backup runs longer than the duration specified, RMAN will cancel the backup. Here is an example of using the **backup duration** command:

```
backup duration 00:30 database;
```

One thing that makes the **duration** parameter a bit less usable is that you cannot use the **backup database plus archivelog** command. The **duration** parameter also helps you to throttle your backups. When defining a duration, you can indicate that RMAN should try to minimize either of the following:

- The time that the backup takes to run

- The I/O load that the backup consumes

If you try to minimize the time that the backup runs, RMAN will back up full speed ahead. This is the default setting. Another feature when you use the default **minimize time** parameter is that RMAN will prioritize the datafiles that are backed up. Those that were backed up recently will have a lower priority than those that have not been backed up recently.

You can also tell RMAN to try to spread out the backup I/O over the duration window that you have established, thus eliminating the overall impact that the backup has on the system:

```
backup duration 00:30 minimize time database;
backup duration 00:30 minimize load database;
```

Finally, with the **duration** parameter, you can indicate how RMAN should treat backups that fail the **backup duration** time restriction. When you use the **partial** parameter, if the backup is terminated because it has exceeded the **duration** parameter, RMAN will not treat it as a failed backup. Thus, remaining commands in any **run** block will continue to be executed. This is handy if you have subsequent **backup** commands like archived redo log backups. Regardless of the setting of **partial**, Oracle will consider any backup set that has been completed successfully to be usable even if the entire backup process did not complete.

Limiting the Size of a Backup Set

The following example builds on our previous example by adding a new parameter, **maxsetsize**:

```
backup database maxsetsize=50m tag='test backup';
```

Using this parameter, we have limited the maximum size of the backup set to 50MB. This is handy if your tape has a size limit or if your disks can only handle datafiles that are a certain size. Oracle will split the backup into multiple backup sets, each no larger than the **maxsetsize** parameter that you defined.

The **maxsetsize** parameter can also lead to a problem in that it limits the overall size of an individual backup set. Thus, if you have a datafile in your backup set that is larger than the defined limit, the backup will fail, as shown in the next example (some output has been removed for brevity):

```
RMAN> set maxcorrupt for datafile 1 to 10;
RMAN> run
2> {
3> allocate channel c1 device type disk format 'd:\backup\robt\robt_%U';
4> allocate channel c2 device type disk format 'd:\backup\robt\robt_%U';
5> backup maxsetsize=50m tag='test backup' database;
6> }
allocated channel: c1
allocated channel: c2
Starting backup at 13-JUN-02
RMAN-00571: ===========================================================
RMAN-00569: =============== ERROR MESSAGE STACK FOLLOWS ===============
RMAN-00571: ===========================================================
RMAN-03002: failure of backup command at 06/13/2002 22:07:47
RMAN-06183: datafile or datafilecopy larger than SETSIZE: file# 1
D:\ORACLE\ORADATA\ROBT\SYSTEM01.DBF
```

So, be careful using this restriction and see whether you instead can use the **maxpiecesize** parameter of the **allocate channel** command.

Also, you can use the **configure** command to create default limits on the size of backup sets and limits on the backup piece size, if that is your preference. Refer to Chapter 3 for more information on this command.

Modifying the Retention Policy for a Backup Set

In the next example, two backup statements are using the **keep** parameter to override the default retention policy (refer to Chapter 3 for more details on using the **configure** command to set a default retention policy):

```
backup database keep forever;
backup database keep until time='sysdate+180';
```

In the first example, we will keep the backup set forever. In the second example, we will keep the backup for only 180 days after the day it was taken. As mentioned in Chapter 3, beware of retention because it is no guarantee that the physical files of your backup will actually be protected. Also, if you back up to disk, somebody can easily go out and physically remove the backup pieces.

Overriding the configure exclude Command

You can configure RMAN to exclude in your backups datafiles that have not changed since the last backup, by issuing the **configure exclude** command (which is discussed in Chapter 3). If you want to ensure that RMAN backs up these datafiles, you can include the **noexclude** parameter in the **backup** command as follows:

```
backup database noexclude keep forever tag='test backup';
```

Checking the Database for Errors with the backup Command

Another handy RMAN feature is the ability to use RMAN to actually scan the database for physical and logical errors without actually doing a backup. This is facilitated through the use of the **validate** parameter of the **backup** command. Here is an example of the use of this option:

```
backup validate database;
```

NOTE
*Even though some of the text generated during an RMAN **validate** run will make it look like a backup set is being created, this is not the case. No RMAN backup file pieces will be generated during the **validate** run.*

Skipping Offline, Inaccessible, or Read-Only Datafiles

Sometimes, you will have a datafile in your database that has a status other than ONLINE. In the case of read-only datafiles, you may not want to back them up every time you do a backup of the database. In the case of offline or inaccessible datafiles, RMAN backups will fail if you don't do something to indicate to RMAN to just skip the missing datafiles. This is what the **skip** parameter is used for. You can skip offline, read-only, or inaccessible datafiles (or all three) as required. Here are some examples of how to do this:

```
backup database skip readonly;
backup database skip offline;
backup database skip inaccessible;
backup database skip readonly skip offline skip inaccessible;
```

The **inaccessible** parameter causes Oracle to skip files that cannot be read at all. These files are not physically on the disk (for example, if the datafiles have been deleted from the disk or moved to another location). Datafiles that are offline but physically still in place are skipped using the **offline** parameter. Finally, the **skip readonly** parameter is used to cause Oracle to skip backing up a read-only datafile. Of course, you can use the **configure** command to indicate that Oracle should not back up read-only tablespaces at all, which leads us to our next section.

Forcing a Backup of Read-Only Datafiles

In the preceding section, we showed you how to cause a backup to skip read-only datafiles, but this can be a bit tedious. Oracle offers backup optimization to make life a bit easier. We talked about backup optimization in Chapter 3 in association with the **configure** command. Backup optimization causes RMAN to not back up unchanged tablespaces (for example, read-only tablespaces) by default. If you want a specific backup to be forced to ignore that configuration setting, you can use the **force** parameter to ensure that all datafiles are backed up. Here is an example:

```
backup database force;
```

Backing Up Datafiles Based on Their Last Backup Time

Oracle allows you to indicate in your backup process if you prefer to only back up database datafiles that have not been backed up since a given time. This is handy if you have added new datafiles (as we discuss first in this section), or if you only want to back up datafiles that have changed in a given number of days. Let's look at each of these choices in a bit more detail.

Backing Up Only Newly Added Datafiles

Here is a neat option you can use. Suppose you have just added four or five new datafiles to the database and you want to back them up without having to back up the entire database. Well, you could just back up the individual datafiles (as we will show you later in this chapter), but there is an easier way. You can use the **not backed up** option of the **backup** command, and RMAN will only back up datafiles that have not been backed up. Here is an example:

```
backup database not backed up;
```

Backing Up Files Not Backed Up in a Specific Time Period

So, perhaps you have a backup strategy in which you back up only specific datafiles on specific nights. The **since time** option is also really handy if you need to restart a failed backup. If the backup fails, you can use this option, after you have corrected the cause of the failure, to restart the backup. For example, let's assume that your tape system died two days ago in the middle of a backup. You finally got the tape system fixed, so how would you restart the backup? Simply issue this command:

```
backup database not backed up since time='sysdate - 2';
```

In this case, RMAN only backs up those datafiles that have not been backed up within the last two days. Note that you can express the time in the format of the database NLS_DATE format, or you can use a SQL date expression such as the one in our example. An additional parameter to the **since time** option applies to archive log backups to ensure that each archive log is backed up a certain number of times before it is removed. We will cover that option later in this chapter.

Some backup strategies include backing up the archived redo logs once, shortly after they are created, and then perhaps later during the nightly backup. Once they are backed up for the nightly backup, they are to be removed. The configured retention defaults don't really allow you to configure the database to meet this requirement, but we can manually define retention criteria in our **backup** commands. As an example, we can perform this kind of backup using the **backup archivelog** command and the **backup database** command, as shown here:

```
-- This command backs up archived redo logs not already backed up.
Backup archivelog all not backed up 1 times;
-- Later in the day, back up the database and archived redo logs, and
-- remove the archived redo logs
backup as compressed backupset database plus archivelog
not backed up 1 times delete input;
```

Checking for Logical Corruption During a Backup

By default, RMAN checks for physical corruption of database blocks. If any corruption is discovered, the backup will fail. If you want even more error checking, you can configure a backup to check for logical corruption using the **check logical** option of the **backup** command. Here are a couple of examples of the use of this option:

```
backup check logical database;
backup validate check logical database;
```

The first example physically backs up the database as it is checking for logical corruption. The second example just validates the database blocks performing a logical database verification without performing an actual physical backup of the database. If you wish the backup to continue through a given number of errors, you need to set the **maxcorrupt** parameter first. This requires using a **run** block, as shown in this example:

```
run {
set maxcorrupt for datafile 1,2,3,4,5,6,7 to 10;
backup validate check logical database;
}
```

Making Copies of Backups on Your RMAN Copier

Perhaps you wish to create multiple copies of the backup pieces of a backup set. While this can be configured by default, you can also use the **copies** parameter to configure a specific backup to create multiple copies of the backup pieces. (You could also use the **set backup copies** parameter.) Here is an example of this option in use:

```
backup database copies=2;
```

Perhaps you have configured different default channels, one to disk and one to tape. You can use the **device type** parameter to define which automatic channel device you wish to use when the backup begins. Here is an example:

```
backup database device type disk;
backup database device type sbt;
```

Capturing the Elusive Control File

The **include current controlfile** option creates a snapshot of the current control file and places it into each backup set produced by the **backup** command. Here is an example of the use of this command:

```
backup database device type disk include current controlfile;
```

By default, if you do a backup of datafile 1, the control file will get backed up anyway. So this parameter comes in much more handy if you are doing tablespace or datafile backups. Furthermore, if automated backup of control files is configured, then this command can cause the current control file to be stored in the backup set also (so you have two copies of the control file, though they might be slightly different if you are running in ARCHIVELOG mode).

Introducing the set Command

Well, we are done with offline backups. We have covered a great deal of material. Before we move on to discuss online backups—and now that you have some idea of how RMAN commands work when backing up—we should take a quick detour and look at the RMAN **set** command.

The **set** command is used to define settings that apply only to the current RMAN session. In other words, the **set** command is a lot like the **configure** command (refer to Chapter 3), but the settings are not persistent. You can use the **set** command one of two ways, depending on the **set** command you need to use. You can use it outside a **run** block for these operations:

■ To display RMAN commands in the message log, use the **set echo** command.

■ To specify a database's database identifier (DBID), use the **set dbid** command.

Certain **set** commands can only be used within the confines of a **run** block. The most common are

■ The **set newname** command is useful if you are performing tablespace point-in-time recovery (TSPITR) or database duplication. The **set newname** command allows you to specify new database datafile names. This is useful if you are moving the database to a new system and the file system names are different. You need to use the **switch** command in combination with the **set newname** command. You will see examples of this in later chapters.

■ Using the **set maxcorrupt for datafile** command enables you to define a maximum number of data block corruptions allowed before the RMAN operation will fail.

■ Using the **set archivelog destination** command allows you to modify the archive_log_dest_1 destination for archived redo logs.

■ Using **set** with the **until** clause enables you to define a specific point in time, an SCN, or a log sequence number, to be used during database point-in-time recovery.

■ Using the **set backup copies** command enables you to define how many copies of the backup files should be created for each backup piece in the backup set.

■ Using the **set command id** setting enables you to associate a given server session to a given channel.

■ Using the **set controlfile autobackup format for device type** command enables you to modify the default format for control file autobackups.

When doing backups, you may well need to use some of these commands. For example, if you wish to do a backup that creates two copies of each backup piece that is created, and you want to allow for ten corruptions in datafile 3, you would craft a backup script that looks like this:

```
run
{
set maxcorrupt for datafile 3 to 10;
set backup copies = 2;
backup database;
}
```

Online RMAN Database Backups

We have spent the first half of this chapter on offline backups and the **set** command. If you are interested in online backups, then this section (and the following one) is for you. Still, don't skip the previous sections, because they present a great deal of foundational information that won't be repeated here. If you are jumping into the chapter at this point, first go back and read the previous sections. If you have read the first half of the chapter already and you find that you are a bit punchy, then take a short break before you forge on.

In this section, we first discuss several different kinds of online backups: backups of the entire database, tablespace backups, and datafile backups. We then look at archive log file backups and, finally, backups of the control file and parameter files.

Online Database Backups

As described in Chapters 1 and 3 in detail, to perform online backups with RMAN, our database must be in ARCHIVELOG mode. If your database is not in ARCHIVELOG mode, RMAN will generate an error if you try to perform an online backup. So, having ensured that we are in ARCHIVELOG mode, we are ready to do our first RMAN online backup.

> **NOTE**
> *From this point on in this chapter, we assume that you have configured default channels (refer to Chapter 3), unless we need to point out something specifically. This saves you typing and allows us to leave out commands such as **allocate channel**, giving us more space to give you important information.*

You will find that online backups are not all that different from offline backups. In fact, they are a bit simpler because you don't have to mess with shutting down and then mounting the database. When you have your defaults configured (refer to Chapter 3), an online backup is as simple as this:

```
backup database plus archivelog;
```

This command does it all. First, the process does a log switch (using the **alter system archivelog current** command). Next, it backs up any existing archived redo logs. Then, the actual database backup occurs. At this point, another log switch occurs (using the **alter system archivelog current** command), and RMAN backs up the remaining archived redo logs (using the **backup archivelog all** command). Finally, the autobackup of the control file and SPFILE occurs. Because a full database backup will always include datafile 1, which belongs to the SYSTEM tablespace, there will always be a backup of the control file and SPFILE.

RMAN Workshop: *Do an Online Backup*

Workshop Notes

This workshop assumes that your database has been configured with automatic channels (as shown in Chapter 3). It also assumes that you have configured a database account called backup_admin for backups (as described in Chapter 3). It also assumes that if you are using the MML layer, it has been configured. Finally, your database must be configured for and operating in ARCHIVELOG mode.

Step 1. Start up RMAN:

```
C:\>rman target=backup_admin/robert
```

Step 2. Start the backup:

```
RMAN> backup database plus archivelog;
```

Here is an example of a complete offline RMAN backup following these steps:

```
C:\>rman target=backup_admin/robert
RMAN> backup database plus archivelog;
Starting backup at 15-JUN-02
current log archived
using target database controlfile instead of recovery catalog
configuration for DISK channel 3 is ignored
allocated channel: ORA_DISK_1
channel ORA_DISK_1: sid=13 devtype=DISK
channel ORA_DISK_1: starting archive log backupset
channel ORA_DISK_1: specifying archive log(s) in backup set
input archive log thread=1 sequence=351 recid=13 stamp=464457020
channel ORA_DISK_1: starting piece 1 at 15-JUN-02
input archive log thread=1 sequence=352 recid=14 stamp=464609012
input archive log thread=1 sequence=353 recid=15 stamp=464609115
channel ORA_DISK_1: finished piece 1 at 15-JUN-02
piece handle=D:\BACKUP\ROBT\BACKUP_20DR2QJ8_1_1 comment=NONE
channel ORA_DISK_1: backup set complete, elapsed time: 00:00:11
channel ORA_DISK_1: starting archive log backupset
channel ORA_DISK_1: specifying archive log(s) in backup set
input archive log thread=1 sequence=357 recid=19 stamp=464610450
input archive log thread=1 sequence=358 recid=20 stamp=464611007
input archive log thread=1 sequence=359 recid=21 stamp=464611921
channel ORA_DISK_1: starting piece 1 at 15-JUN-02
channel ORA_DISK_1: finished piece 1 at 15-JUN-02
piece handle=D:\BACKUP\ROBT\BACKUP_22DR2QJK_1_1 comment=NONE
channel ORA_DISK_1: backup set complete, elapsed time: 00:00:03
```

```
Finished backup at 15-JUN-02
Starting backup at 15-JUN-02
using channel ORA_DISK_1
channel ORA_DISK_1: starting full datafile backupset
input datafile fno=00001 name=D:\ORACLE\ORADATA\ROBT\SYSTEM01.DBF
input datafile fno=00005 name=D:\ORACLE\ORADATA\ROBT\USERS01.DBF
input datafile fno=00004 name=D:\ORACLE\ORADATA\ROBT\TOOLS01.DBF
input datafile fno=00003 name=D:\ORACLE\ORADATA\ROBT\INDX01.DBF
input datafile fno=00002
name=D:\ORACLE\ORADATA\ROBT\ROBT_TEST_RECOVER_02.DBF
input datafile fno=00010 name=D:\ORACLE\ORADATA\ROBT\ROBT_RBS_01.DBF
input datafile fno=00011
name=D:\ORACLE\ORADATA\ROBT\ROBT_TEST_TBS_01.DBF
input datafile fno=00007
name=D:\ORACLE\ORADATA\ROBT\ROBT_TEST_RECOVER_01.DBF
input datafile fno=00006
name=D:\ORACLE\ORADATA\ROBT\ROBT_TEST_RECOVER_03.DBF
channel ORA_DISK_1: starting piece 1 at 15-JUN-02
channel ORA_DISK_1: finished piece 1 at 15-JUN-02
piece handle=D:\BACKUP\ROBT\BACKUP_23DR2QJU_1_1 comment=NONE
channel ORA_DISK_1: backup set complete, elapsed time: 00:04:56
Finished backup at 15-JUN-02
Starting backup at 15-JUN-02
current log archived
using channel ORA_DISK_1
channel ORA_DISK_1: starting archive log backupset
channel ORA_DISK_1: specifying archive log(s) in backup set
input archive log thread=1 sequence=360 recid=22 stamp=464612416
channel ORA_DISK_1: starting piece 1 at 15-JUN-02
channel ORA_DISK_1: finished piece 1 at 15-JUN-02
piece handle=D:\BACKUP\ROBT\BACKUP_25DR2R2K_1_1 comment=NONE
channel ORA_DISK_1: backup set complete, elapsed time: 00:00:04
Finished backup at 15-JUN-02
Starting Control File and spfile Autobackup at 15-JUN-02
piece handle=D:\BACKUP\ROBT_C-3395799962-20020615-02 comment=NONE
Finished Control File and spfile Autobackup at 15-JUN-02
```

We have now completed an entire online database backup! Next, we will look at tablespace backups.

NOTE
A full database backup should be contrasted against an incremental backup (as we will discuss later in this chapter) in that a full database backup cannot be used as a base for application of incremental backups.

Tablespace Backups

Occasionally, you will wish to do tablespace-level backups instead of backups of the entire database. This might be before you drop a partition that is specific to that tablespace, or perhaps just after you have made the tablespace read-only. To do a tablespace-level backup, we simply use the **backup** command with the **tablespace** parameter:

```
backup tablespace users;
```

If we want to back up any archived redo logs at the same time, we would issue the command like this:

```
backup tablespace users plus archivelog;
```

Or perhaps we want to also make sure our current control file is backed up:

```
backup tablespace users include current controlfile plus archivelog;
```

Of course, you are not really backing up a tablespace, but rather the datafiles associated with that tablespace. Oracle just converts the tablespace name into a list of datafiles that are associated with that tablespace. Normally, a control file backup will not occur during these backups unless you have configured automatic control file backups (refer to Chapter 3) to occur (and you are not backing up datafile 1). If you use the **include current controlfile** parameter, then the control file will be backed up.

NOTE
RMAN will not prevent you from doing a tablespace or datafile backup in NOARCHIVELOG mode (as long as the database is not open). However, these backups are not really all that usable when the database is in NOARCHIVELOG mode (unless you back up all the tablespaces and datafiles at the same time).

Datafile Backups

You might want to back up specific database datafiles of the database. Perhaps you are getting ready to move them to a new device and you wish to back them up before you move them. RMAN allows you to back up a datafile using the **backup** command with the **datafile** parameter followed by the filename or number of the datafiles you wish to back up. The following are examples of some datafile **backup** commands:

```
backup datafile 2;
backup datafile 'd:\oracle\oradata\robt\users01.dbf';
backup datafile 'd:\oracle\oradata\robt\users01.dbf' plus archivelog;
```

Again, the control file and the SPFILE will get backed up if datafile 1 is backed up or if automated control file backups are configured. In the last example, the archived redo logs will get backed up as well.

Archived Redo Log Backups

For a number of reasons, you might well want to back up your archived redo logs but not the database. In this event, you use the **backup archivelog** command. To back up all of the archived redo logs, simply issue the command **backup archivelog all**. Optionally, you might want to back up a specific range of archived redo logs, for which you have several options available, including time, SCN, or redo log sequence number (or a selected range of those values). Here are some examples of backing up the archived redo logs:

```
backup archivelog all;
backup archivelog from time 'sysdate - 1';
backup archivelog from sequence 353;
```

Once you have backed up archived redo logs, you may want to have RMAN remove them for you. The **delete input** option allows you to perform this operation. The **delete input** option can also be used with datafile copies (which we will discuss later in this chapter) or backup set copies. Here are a couple of examples of using the **delete input** parameter on an archived redo log backup:

```
backup archivelog all delete input;
backup archivelog from sequence 353 delete input;
```

You can also instruct RMAN to make redundant copies of your archived redo logs. In the following example, we use the **not backed up _n_ times** parameter of the **backup** command to make sure that we have backed up our archived redo logs at least three times. Any archived redo logs that have already been backed up three times will not be backed up again.

```
backup archivelog not backed up 3 times;
```

Also, you can use the **until time** parameter with the **backup** command to ensure that a certain number of days' worth of archived redo logs remain on disk:

```
backup archivelog until time 'sysdate - 2' delete all input;
```

NOTE
Use of the **not backed up** parameter and use of the **delete input** parameter are somewhat mutually exclusive. The **delete input** parameter will remove the archived redo log regardless of how many times it has been backed up.

Control File and Parameter File Backups

Just as with archived redo logs, sometimes you may just want to back up the control file or the server parameter files. RMAN provides specific commands for these functions as well. Use the **backup spfile** command to back up the server parameter file. This is handy if you have made a configuration change to the database, for example. To back up the control file, you can use the **current controlfile** parameter of the **backup** command to generate a copy of the current control file. The **current controlfile** parameter also comes with a **for standby** clause that will create a backup control file for use with a standby database.

You can use the **controlfilecopy** parameter of the **backup** command to create a backup set that contains an externally created backup of the control file. This control file backup might be the result of the **alter database backup controlfile to 'file_name'** SQL command or the use of the RMAN **copy** command (covered later in this chapter) to create a control file backup. Also, you can back up a standby database control file that was created with the **alter database create standby controlfile** command. The benefit of this feature is that you can take external control file backup files and register them with RMAN and create a backup set that contains the control file backup in it. Here are some examples of the use of this parameter:

```
backup current controlfile;
sql "alter database backup controlfile
to ''d:\backup\robt\contf_back.ctl''";
backup controlfilecopy 'd:\backup\robt\contf_back.ctl';
```

Backup Set Backups

Perhaps you like to back up to disk first, and then back up your backup sets to tape. RMAN supports this operation in Oracle Database 10*g* through the use of the **backup** command. Here is an example. Suppose we issued a **backup database** command, and the entire backup set went to disk because that is our configured default device. Now we wish to move that backup set to tape. We could issue the **backup** command with the **backupset** parameter, and Oracle would back up all of our backup sets to the channel that is allocated for the backup.

You can choose to back up all backup sets with the **backup backupset** command, or you can choose to back up specific backup sets. Further, you can only back up from disk to disk or disk to tape. There is no support for tape-to-tape or tape-to-disk backups. The **delete input** option, which we previously discussed in regard to archive log backups, is also available with backup set backups. When used, the **delete input** option will cause the files of the source backup set to get deleted after a successful backup. Here are some examples of this command:

```
backup backupset all;
backup backupset all
format='d:\backup\newbackups\backup_%U.bak'
```

```
tag='Backup of backupsets on 6/15'  channel 'ORA_DISK_1';
backup backupset completed before 'sysdate - 2';
backup backupset completed before 'sysdate - 2' delete input;
backup backupset completed after 'sysdate - 2' delete input;
```

An example of a backup strategy here might be to perform RMAN backups to disk, and then to back up the backup sets to tape with the **backup backupset** command. Perhaps you want to keep two days' worth of your backup sets on disk. You could then issue two commands. First, issue the **backup backupset completed before 'sysdate -2'** command to back up the last two days of backups. Then, to back up and then remove any backup sets older than two days, issue the **backup backupset completed after 'sysdate - 2' delete input** command, which would cause one final backup of the old backup sets and then remove them.

NOTE
Backup set backups are very handy if you want to back up your control file automated backups elsewhere and still have the catalog track the location of the backup set.

Flash Recovery Area Backups

RMAN offers the ability to back up the entire FRA to tape via the **backup recovery area** command. Not all files in the FRA are backed up. Files that are backed up include full and incremental backup sets, control file autobackups, archived logs, and datafile copies. If your backup FRA contains flashback logs, the current control file, and/or online redo logs, these files will not be backed up. Note that files must be backed up to tape.

Copies

Okay, all this new-fangled talk of backup sets and pieces is just blowing your mind. You ask, "Can't I just make a copy of these database datafiles?" Well, we're here to make you feel better. With RMAN, you can just make copies of your different database structures, and that's what we are going to talk about in this section. First, we will review the upside, and downside, to creating copies instead of backup sets. Then, we will look at how we create datafile copies, control file copies, and archived redo log file copies.

Introducing Image Copies

RMAN can create an exact duplicate of your database datafiles, archived redo logs, or your control file. An RMAN image copy is just that—it is simply a copy of the file with the name and/or location changed. There are no backup pieces or anything else to worry about. Image copies can only be made to disk, and you cannot make incremental copies. The database must be either mounted or open to make image copies. A history of the copies made is kept in the database control file, so you can track when copies have been made and where they reside.

You can make image copies of the entire database, tablespaces. or datafiles, just like a regular backup (this is very different from earlier versions of RMAN). The RMAN copy process provides some of the same protections as normal RMAN backup sets, such as checking for corrupted blocks and, optionally, logical corruption. Also, image copies can be combined with normal backup sets such as incremental backups and archived redo log backups to facilitate a complete database recovery.

Database, Tablespace, and Datafile Image Copies

The **backup** command supports the creation of database image copies. Simply use the **backup as copy** command to do image copies, and the process is much like performing backup sets. Here is an example of making a database image copy with RMAN:

```
RMAN> backup as copy database;
```

RMAN will use the FRA to store backup copies, if it is configured. If you are using the FRA, the datafile images will be stored in a directory called datafile, as shown in this partial example output from a datafile image copy:

```
RMAN> backup as copy database;
Starting backup at 12-NOV-05
using channel ORA_DISK_1
using channel ORA_DISK_2
channel ORA_DISK_1: starting datafile copyinput datafile fno=00001
name=C:\ORACLE\PRODUCT\10.2.0\ORADATA\ROB10R2\SYSTEM01.DBF
channel ORA_DISK_2: starting datafile copy
input datafile fno=00003
name=C:\ORACLE\PRODUCT\10.2.0\ORADATA\ROB10R2\SYSAUX01.DBF
output Filename=C:\ORACLE\PRODUCT\10.2.0\FLASH_RECOVERY_AREA\ROB10R2
\DATAFILE\O1_MF_SYSAUX_1QFBPPON_.DBF tag=TAG20051112T205403 recid=
2stamp=574203351
channel ORA_DISK_2: datafile copy complete, elapsed time: 00:01:55
channel ORA_DISK_2: starting datafile copy
```

Image copies of tablespaces work pretty much the same way; just use the **backup as copy** command and the **tablespace** keyword:

```
backup as copy tablespace users;
```

Finally, you can create image copies of datafiles:

```
backup as copy datafile 1;
backup as copy datafile
'C:\ORACLE\PRODUCT\10.2.0\ORADATA\ROB10R2\SYSTEM01.DBF';
```

NOTE
An image copy can be made with the database
mounted or, if the database is in ARCHIVELOG
mode, with the database open.

Control File Copies

Control file copies can also be made with the **backup controlfilecopy** command.
Here is an example of backing up the control file (this will create a backup set with
a control file):

```
backup current controlfile;
```

You can also create copies of control files, as shown here:

```
backup as copy current controlfile;
```

If you wish to create a control file for use with a standby database that you are
creating, then you use the **for standby** clause:

```
backup as copy standby controlfile
```

Further, you can indicate a specific filename when you create a control file
backup:

```
backup as copy current controlfile format 'c:\oracle\controlfilecopy.ctl';
```

ARCHIVELOG Image Copies

Having copies of archived redo logs can be helpful. It's certainly easier to mine a
copy of an archived redo log with Oracle's LogMiner product than to have to first
extract that archived redo log out of a backup set. The **copy** command allows you
to create copies of archived redo logs using the **archivelog** parameter of the **copy**
command. Unfortunately, as we mentioned earlier, the use of **copy archivelog**
requires us to list each archived redo log by name, rather than specify some
temporal range when we make copies of the archived redo logs. Here is an
example of making an ARCHIVELOG file copy:

```
backup as copy archivelog all;
```

Incremental RMAN Backups

We hope you have made it this far through the book without much difficulty, and have
been able to get at least one good backup of your database done. Now we are going to
move on to the topic of incremental backups in RMAN. Through incremental backups,

RMAN allows you to back up just the data blocks that have changed since the last incremental backup. The following are the benefits of incremental backups:

- Less overall tape or disk usage

- Less network bandwidth required

- Quicker backup times

You can do incremental backups either online or offline and in either ARCHIVELOG mode or NOARCHIVELOG mode, which is pretty handy. Keep in mind that if you choose an incremental backup strategy, a give and take exists in terms of the benefits. While you are deriving a benefit in the reduction of overall backup times (and this may be significant), the cost comes on the recovery side. Because Oracle will need to use several backup sets to recover the database if an incremental strategy is used, the time required to recover your database can significantly increase.

NOTE
If you choose to do incremental backups on a NOARCHIVELOG mode database, make sure you shut down the database in a consistent manner each time you back up the database.

The Block Change Tracking File

By default, when doing an incremental backup, any datafile that has changed in any way will be backed up. This can make incremental backups take longer, and will make them larger. RMAN in Oracle Database 10*g* offers the ability to just back up changed database blocks. This can make your incremental database backups much smaller and shorter. To enable block change tracking, issue the command **alter database enable block change tracking**.

If you are using Oracle Managed Files (OMF), Oracle will create the block change tracking file for you. If you are not using OMF, you must define the location and name of the block change tracking file, as shown in this example:

```
alter database enable block change tracking using file
'/u01/app/oracle/block_change/rob10gr2_block_change.fil';
```

If a previous block change tracking file already exists, you need to use the **reuse** parameter:

```
alter database enable block change tracking using file
'/u01/app/oracle/block_change/rob10gr2_block_change.fil' reuse;
```

You disable block change tracking by using the **alter database disable block change tracking** command. The block change tracking file size is pre-allocated and is related to the size of the database and the number of redo log threads. The typical size of the block change tracking file is 1/30,000 of the database size. The block change tracking file can grow, and will grow in increments of 10MB. The minimum size of the block change tracking file is 320k per datafile, so if you have a number of datafiles, the block change tracking file will be larger. Oracle will store enough information in the block change tracking file to allow you to recover your database with up to eight days of incremental backups. Obviously, if you have to go beyond eight days of incremental backups, then the block change tracking file will not be used and you will loose the benefit of the block change tracking file.

You can determine if block change tracking is enabled by checking the V$BLOCK_CHANGE_TRACKING view. The STATUS column indicates if block change tracking is enabled, and the FILENAME column contains the filename of the block change tracking file. You can move the block change tracking file by using the **alter database rename file** command.

```
SQL> select status from v$block_change_tracking;

STATUS
----------
DISABLED
```

The Base Backup

When doing an incremental backup, the first thing you need is an *incremental base backup*. This backup is the backup that all future incremental backups will be based on. Each time you perform a backup of the database, you assign that backup an incremental level identifier through the use of the **incremental** parameter of the **backup** command. A base backup will always have an incremental value of 0, and you must have a base backup to be able to perform any type of incremental backup. If you do not have a base backup and you try to perform an incremental backup (using a backup level other than 0), then RMAN will perform a base backup for you automatically. Here is an example of performing a base incremental backup:

```
backup incremental level=0 database;
```

Differential vs. Incremental Backups

Now, we need to decide how we want to perform our incremental backups. We can use one of two methods:

- Differential
- Cumulative

Each of these is a different method of performing an incremental backup. Let's look at these two different types of incremental backup in a bit more detail.

Differential Backups

This is the default type of incremental backup that RMAN generates. With a differential backup, RMAN backs up all blocks that have changed since the last backup at the same differential level or lower. Understanding how this all works can get a bit confusing. Figure 9-1 should help you better understand the impacts of using different levels.

In this example, we have a level 0 differential backup being taken on Sunday. This backup will back up the entire database. Following the level 0 backup, we perform level 1 differential backups on Monday through Friday (there are no Saturday backups). With a differential backup, each day's backup will contain the changes that occurred since the last differential backup. Finally, on the following Sunday, we do another base-level backup.

Here is an example of a differential backup being executed:

```
backup incremental level=1 database;
```

Cumulative Backups

RMAN provides another incremental backup option, the cumulative backup. When used, this option causes backup sets to back up changed blocks for all backup levels including the backup level that you have selected to back up. This is an optional backup method and requires the use of the **cumulative** keyword in the **backup** command. Again, this can all be somewhat confusing, so let's look at an example. Figure 9-2 is an example of the impacts of cumulative backups using different levels.

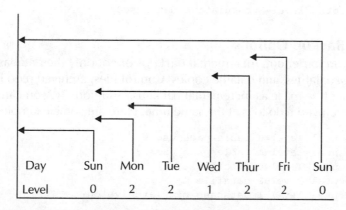

FIGURE 9-1. *Differential backups*

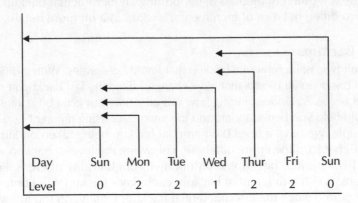

Day	Sun	Mon	Tue	Wed	Thur	Fri	Sun
Level	0	2	2	1	2	2	0

FIGURE 9-2. *Incremental backups*

In Figure 9-2, just as in Figure 9-1, we start with a level 0 differential backup being taken on Sunday. This backup backs up the entire database. Following that, on Monday we perform a level 1 backup. Now things change a little bit. On Tuesday, we perform another level 1 differential backup. This time, the backup will contain not only changed blocks since Monday's backup, but also the blocks that were contained in Monday's backup. Thus, a cumulative backup accumulates all changed blocks for any backup level equal to or less than the level of the backup. As a result, for recovery purposes, we need only Tuesday's backup along with Sunday's base backup. We continue to take level 1 backups over the remainder of the week to complete our backup strategy.

Here is an example of the creation of a level 2 cumulative backup:

```
backup incremental level=2 cumulative database;
```

Incremental Backup Options

Oracle allows you to perform incremental backups of not only the database, but also tablespaces, datafiles, and datafile copies. Control files, archived redo logs, and backup sets cannot be made as incremental backups. Additionally, you can choose to back up the archived redo logs at the same time. Here are some examples:

```
backup incremental level=0 tablespace users;
backup incremental level=1 tablespace users;
backup incremental level=0 datafile 4;
backup incremental level=1 datafile 4;
backup incremental level=1 database plus archivelog;
```

Incrementally Updated Backups

RMAN offers incrementally updated backups. This feature lets you avoid the overhead of taking full image copy backups of datafiles, yet it provides the same recovery advantages as image copy backups. In a sense it's like an incremental backup using image copies. Before we describe incrementally updated backups, let's look at an example of such a backup:

```
RUN {
    RECOVER COPY OF DATABASE WITH TAG 'incr_update';
    BACKUP INCREMENTAL LEVEL 1 FOR RECOVER OF COPY WITH TAG 'incr_update'
    DATABASE;
}
```

The **recover copy of database** command does not actually recover your database, but it causes RMAN to apply any incremental backups to the datafile copies associated with the tag listed (incr_update). The first time you run this command, it will have no effect because there is no incremental backup or datafile copy available. This is not a problem, and RMAN will only display a warning message. The second run will also have no effect because there will be no incremental backup to apply.

After the **recover** command, an incremental backup occurs. The first time this backup runs, it creates a base backup if there is no base backup available. This is true of any incremental level 1 backup; if there is no base backup available, RMAN automatically creates the base backup, even if it's a level 1 backup. The second time you execute this **run** block, the first incremental backup will be performed by the **backup** command.

Once this command has run twice, the third and later executions will be able to apply the previous incremental backups to the datafile copies. Note that it is important that the tags are named the same in both the **recover** and **backup** commands.

RMAN Workshop: *Do an Incremental Backup*

Workshop Notes

This workshop assumes that your database has been configured with automatic channels (as shown in Chapter 3). It also assumes that you have configured a database account called backup_admin for backups (as described in Chapter 3). It also assumes that if you are using the MML layer, it has been configured. Finally, your database must be configured for and operating in ARCHIVELOG mode.

Step 1. Start up RMAN:

```
C:\>rman target=backup_admin/robert
```

Step 2. Perform a level 0 incremental backup. Include the archived redo logs in the backup set, and then remove them after the backup.

```
backup incremental level=0 database plus archivelog delete input;
```

Step 3. The next day, perform a level 1 incremental backup. Again, include the archived redo logs in the backup and remove them after they are backed up.

```
backup incremental level=1 database plus archivelog delete input;
```

That about covers RMAN backups. The next chapter will be even more fun, because in it we discuss how to restore these backups and recover our databases.

Getting Started

We have covered a number of different backup options, and you may be left wondering where you should start. Let us make a suggestion or two. We recommend that you start with a test database, one that is very unimportant (better yet, one you have created for just this process). Here is an RMAN Workshop to get you started!

RMAN Workshop: *Get Your Database Backed Up!*

Workshop Notes

This workshop is more of an overall list of things that you need to accomplish to get your database backed up. We have covered a great deal of ground in the last few chapters and we felt it would be a good idea to summarize everything important up to this point.

Step 1. Set up a special account in your test database that will be responsible for backup operations. Configure the account as described in Chapter 3. Note that you can opt to use the SYS account, but we prefer to use a separate account.

Step 2. Set up your MML layer and be clear on what it requires you to do when performing backup and recovery commands.

Step 3. As we describe in Chapter 3, use the **configure** command to configure a separate default channel for each device that you are backing up to, unless your specific device supports multiple channels (as some do). Set the default degree of parallelism, as shown in Chapter 3, such that each of the channels will be used during the backup. If you need to configure maximum set sizes, do so; otherwise, don't bother with that now.

Step 4. Use the **configure** command to configure automated backups of your control file and SPFILE (if you are using one). For now, let them be created in the default location. You will want to change this later, but for now, just leave it there.

Step 5. Make sure your operating system backup backs up your Oracle RDBMS software (this also makes sure your control file backups will be backed up!).

Step 6. At first, we suggest that you don't use a recovery catalog. Once you have the RMAN basics down pat and are ready to deploy RMAN to the enterprise, then you can consider a recovery catalog.

Step 7. For the first few trials, run your database in NOARCHIVELOG mode if you can. Shut down and mount your database and execute a few **backup database** commands. Make sure the backup sets are getting created where you expect them to.

Step 8. Go to Chapter 10 and recover the database. We suggest you make cold backups of the entire database, control file, and online redo logs (using the **cp** or **copy** command) first, just in case you run into some learning curves.

Step 9. Once you are good at recovering databases in NOARCHIVELOG mode, put the database in ARCHIVELOG mode and do the same thing again. Back up the database using the **backup database plus archivelog** command.

Step 10. Go to Chapter 10 and do some recoveries. Become an RMAN recovery expert before you go any further.

Step 11. Play around with the **crosscheck** command, the **list** command, and the **report** commands (see Chapters 14 and 15 for more details on these commands). Become really comfortable with these commands and their purpose.

Step 12.   If you have a large enterprise environment (say, over ten databases), go ahead and add a recovery catalog to the mix, and connect to it and back up your database with it. We strongly encourage you to use a separate recovery catalog for development/test and production databases. Again, we suggest that you run through the gambit of backup and restore situations while using a recovery catalog before you move on.

Step 13.   Once you are very comfortable with RMAN, create scripts to automate and schedule the process. For example, if you are running on Unix, a script such as the following could be scheduled through **cron** (we include an offline and online script here):

```
# For offline backups, use this script
#!/bin/ksh
# for offline backups, avoid shutdown aborts at all costs!
rman target rman_backup/password<<EOF
shutdown immediate
startup mount
backup database;
alter database open;
quit
EOF
```

If you are doing online backups, use this script:

```
#!/bin/ksh
rman target rman_backup/password<<EOF
backup database plus archivelog;
quit
EOF
```

These are korn shell scripts, which is one of the more commonly used shell scripting languages in Unix. Of course, RMAN works on a number of different platforms, so you can use the scripting language you are most comfortable with. In this script, we use what is known as a *here* document. That's what the EOF is in the fourth line of the first script and the third line of the second script. A here document acts like the user is "here" and typing the input that you see listed from the EOF on the top line, until the closing EOF several lines later. Optionally, you could just use a command script created by a text editor and call it from the RMAN command line, like this:

```
rman target rman_backup/password @backup.cmd
```

In this case, your backup.cmd script would look like this for an offline backup:

```
shutdown immediate
startup mount
backup database;
alter database open;
quit
```

For a hot backup, it would look like this:

```
backup database plus archivelog;
quit
```

You can also store scripts in RMAN using the RMAN **create script** command. We will discuss stored RMAN scripts in Chapter 14, since storing scripts in RMAN requires a recovery catalog.

Step 14. Before you move your backups into production, test restores of the backups you have set up in your test environments. Make sure you are comfortable that everything works as it should. We suggest that you use your old backup strategy in dual until you have successfully tested several restores.

Step 15. Move your RMAN backup strategy into production carefully. Do it one system at a time. Choose your least "visible" systems to convert first. We suggest that you do several test recoveries as you move out into production, and continue (if possible) to do dual backups on each database until you have recovered that production database on a test box with an RMAN backup successfully. Also, you might want to consider separate archived redo log backups, if that is required.

Step 16. Perform disaster recovery and test backups often. We also suggest that, at least once a week, you execute a **restore database validate check logical** command on each database to make sure that the database is recoverable.

You will note that with each of these steps, we err on the side of caution. We leave it up to you to decide when you feel comfortable with your RMAN setup. There is just nothing more disheartening than trying to restore your database and getting the following error message from RMAN:

```
RMAN-00571: ===========================================================
RMAN-00569: =============== ERROR MESSAGE STACK FOLLOWS ===============
RMAN-00571: ===========================================================
RMAN-03002: failure of restore command at 07/07/2006 17:14:55
RMAN-06026: some targets not found - aborting restore
```

Summary

In this chapter, we have covered RMAN backups galore. We looked at how to do offline backups and online backups using RMAN. We also looked at RMAN incremental backups. We also discussed the impact of configured defaults on backups, and how much easier they make the backup process. We also introduced the numerous options you can use with backups, such as using tags, overriding the default retention policy, and forcing backups of read-only datafiles. We looked at methods of detecting database corruption with RMAN. All in all, it's been a full chapter, but we hope you have found it to be a worthwhile one. You are now a step closer to being an RMAN expert, but the real fun is yet to come, and that's recovery. Hang on, because that's coming up next.

CHAPTER
10

RMAN Restore
and Recovery

All of your planning and backing up is about to pay off. This chapter is about restoring your backups and then recovering your database. We will first address some basic issues regarding the overall recovery process. Then, we will look at the different methods that you might need to use to restore your RMAN backups to disk and recover your Oracle database in the event of an outage. We strongly suggest that you test these different types of recoveries on a test database somewhere, as you never quite know when you will need to recover your database, and what the conditions of that recovery will be.

You will find that this chapter is an introduction to foundational restores in RMAN. The number of situational recovery permutations that might exist for a given database is pretty large (we tried to figure it out, but we blew our budget on designing a computer to calculate the answer and it ended up just giving us plans for a bigger computer to do the job), so it's important that you understand not only the mechanics of recovery (as we will discuss here), but also how it works in concert with Oracle's architecture. In this chapter, you will find some rather straightforward recovery situations. In Chapter 12, we will address some of the more advanced recovery techniques. In Chapter 21, we will plow through a number of different recovery case studies. We suggest you read this chapter and test each of the recoveries documented there. Then, look at the more advanced situations in Chapter 12. Once you are really good at recoveries, look at Chapter 21 and try out some of those restores.

RMAN Restore and Recovery Basics

In this chapter, we will be discussing the concepts of restores and recoveries. In RMAN parlance, "restore" and "recover" have different meanings. A *restore* implies that we are accessing a previously made backup set to get one or more objects from it and restore them to some location on disk. A restore is separate from a recovery, then, in that a *recovery* is the actual process of making a database consistent to a given point in time so that it can be opened, generally through the application of redo (contained in online redo logs or archived redo logs).

If the Oracle RDBMS is anything, it is particular. The database is particular about the state of the data within the database and demands that it be consistent to a given state in time when the database is started. If the database is consistent, then it will open; if it isn't consistent, then it will not open. Through the use of rollback segments, this consistency is maintained while the database is up and running. When the database is shut down normally, the datafiles are made consistent again. As you've likely noticed, the ongoing theme here is consistency.

Unfortunately, inconsistency can creep into the database through myriad causes. An abnormal shutdown of the database (as happens with a **shutdown abort**, or due to power loss on the server) will leave it in an inconsistent state.

Oracle hates inconsistency, and it refuses to just start the database in the face of this demon.

Of course, other problems can plague your database. You can lose database datafiles through the loss of a disk, or perhaps lose the entire database. It is because these kinds of losses occur that you back up your database datafiles with RMAN. The problem is that when you restore those datafiles, they are likely to be inconsistent. Worse yet, those restored datafiles are likely to be anywhere from a few hours old to several days old—which safely qualifies as really inconsistent.

As we said, Oracle is a stickler about consistency. When you try to restart the database after recovering datafiles, Oracle is going to detect that those datafiles are in an inconsistent state. How does it do this? Recall from Chapter 1 our discussion of the SCN. Oracle tracks the current SCN in the datafile headers of each database datafile and in the database control file. Oracle goes through three stages when opening the database: nomount, mount, and open. When the database startup enters the open stage, Oracle begins to attempt to open the database. As it opens the database, it checks the SCN in the control file against the SCNs in each of the database datafiles. If the SCNs don't match, Oracle knows that something is amiss with the database and that it is inconsistent.

Other checks occur during startup, as well, and some of these are not consistency checks. For example, Oracle checks each datafile for a bit that indicates the datafile is in hot backup mode. If this bit is set, Oracle will not open the database. In this event, a simple **alter database datafile end backup** command will suffice to restart the database. Oracle might also determine, while trying to open the database, that a given datafile is missing. The solution to this problem might be as easy as mounting the file system the datafile is on, or perhaps a restore of the datafile will be required.

If Oracle discovers that the database is inconsistent, it needs to determine whether it can recover the database based on the online redo logs, or whether it's going to require archived redo logs to do the trick. If It can perform the recovery with the online redo logs, then Oracle will perform crash recovery (or instance recovery in the case of Real Application Clusters). If Oracle cannot make the database consistent with the online redo logs, then it will stop the startup process and report that media recovery is required.

Media recovery is a condition where Oracle will require archived redo logs to recover the database and make it consistent if the database is in ARCHIVELOG mode. If the database is in NOARCHIVELOG mode, then a restore/recovery of a consistent backup of the database will likely be required. This chapter is all about recovery of your database. There are all kinds of recoveries that you can do. Sometimes you will need to recover the entire database, and sometimes you will just need to recover a few datafiles. We will discuss all of these different possibilities in this chapter.

We have highlighted the issues that revolve around restore and recovery of your database. Now it's time to hit the road and see how this all works in practice.

Before You Can Restore the Database

In this chapter, we are going to approach the restore and recovery process from the beginning, assuming you have nothing left of your database except a backup somewhere. So, first we are going to look at restoring the SPFILE, if you are using one, and then we will look at restoring the control file. Once we have those preliminaries out of the way, we will move on to the bigger topic of restoring and recovering the database. Of course, your specific recovery situation may not require recovery to this depth. You might have just lost a few datafiles, or perhaps you want to perform a point-in-time recovery. Some restores will need to use these preliminary steps and others will not. We think that between the layout of this chapter and the case studies later in this book, you will be quite confident as to what you need to restore and when.

Finally, you will note that in most of the examples we use, we do not connect to a recovery catalog unless the operation is different when using the recovery catalog. This lends to some consistency in our examples and saves a few pages with duplicate results. So, keep an eye out for any notes that we might include about recovery catalog issues.

Before RMAN Can Get Going

Before RMAN can do its thing, you need to do a few things first. Preparation is the mother of success, someone once said, and this is so true when it comes to restoring your database. You need to work with your system administrator to make sure the following are done before you attempt your restore/recovery:

- The OS parameters are configured for Oracle.

- Your disks are configured correctly and are the correct sizes.

- The tape drives are installed and the tape software is installed and configured.

- Your network is operational.

- The Oracle RDBMS software is installed.

- The MML is configured.

- Ancillary items are recovered from backups that RMAN does not back up, which include

    - The database networking files (for example, sqlnet.ora and listener.ora)

    - The oratab file, if one is used

■   The database parameter files, if they are not SPFILEs and are not backed up by RMAN

■   Any RMAN control file backups that were made to disk if you have enabled autobackup of control files

Once these items have been restored, then you are ready to begin restoring your Oracle database. If you are using a recovery catalog, you will want to recover it first, of course. Then, you can recover the remaining databases.

When you start recovering databases, you need to start by recovering the SPFILE (if you are using one and it was backed up), followed by the control file. The next two sections cover those topics for you.

Restoring the SPFILE

If you are not using Oracle9*i* Release 2 or later and are not using an SPFILE, then this section really does not apply to you. As a result, you need to restore your SPFILE (or your database parameter file) from an operating system backup. On the other hand, if you have started using SPFILEs and you have backed them up using RMAN's control file autobackup abilities, then you are in good shape!

Recall from Chapter 9 that we suggested that if you are performing RMAN database backups without a recovery catalog, you might want to note the DBID of your database for restore and recovery purposes. This is one of those times that this comes in handy, though it is not 100 percent critical.

SPFILE recoveries come in several flavors, including recoveries that do not use the flash recovery area (FRA) and those that do use the FRA. RMAN offers other ways to recover the SPFILE, as we will find in the following sections.

Recovering the SPFILE from an Autobackup Using RMAN, No FRA

If you have lost your SPFILE, you will want to recover it from the control file autobackup set if you are using this feature. As we have already described, Oracle will by default back up the SPFILE (along with the control file) to the $ORACLE_HOME/dbs or ORACLE_HOME%\database directory (depending on the operating system). If you choose to use the default location (or if you back up to an alternate disk location), you will probably want to back up these backup sets themselves to another backup media such as tape (which RMAN can do for you).

The general procedure to restore the SPFILE is to first set your ORACLE_SID and then log into RMAN. Then you need to set the DBID, so that RMAN will know which database SPFILE it is looking for. We have to start the database instance at this point in the operation. The instance of an Oracle Database 10*g* database will not start on its own without a basic parameter file being present.

Having started the instance, if you are using the default location to back up your control file autobackup to, you can simply issue the **restore spfile from autobackup** command, and RMAN will look for the control file backup set that contains the most current SPFILE backup. Once the SPFILE is recovered, you need to shut down the instance and restart it to allow your new SPFILE parameters to take effect. If you are using a nondefault location, then you will need to allocate a channel pointing to that location, and then you can restore the SPFILE using the same method.

When you issue the **restore spfile from autobackup** command, Oracle looks in the default location for automated control file backup sets (or in the location you defined with the **allocate channel** command). Since you used the **set dbid** command, RMAN knows your database's DBID. It uses the DBID to search through the defined directory to look specifically for the most current control file backup sets for your database. When RMAN creates the control file autobackup pieces, it uses a default naming convention. The following graphic shows an example of an automated control file backup set piece and how the naming convention is used. Note that this naming convention does not apply to the FRA.

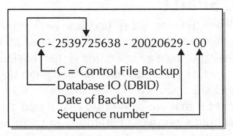

Keep in mind that if we are not using a recovery catalog (and if we are not using a control file, which is likely), Oracle doesn't know for sure what the name of the most current control file backup piece is. Thus, Oracle constructs the name of the control file backup piece based on the default naming standard that is used for those backup sets (which we will document later in this chapter). Oracle will traverse the directory, looking backward in time for a control file backup set for your database. By default, Oracle looks for one created within the last ten days. If it cannot find a backup set created within that time period, it generates an error. If Oracle finds a valid backup set, it proceeds to restore the SPFILE for you.

You can modify how far back RMAN looks for a control file autobackup by using the **maxseq** and **maxdays** parameters of the **restore** command. Here are a couple of examples of recovering control files. First, we use the default settings of the **restore** command:

```
set oracle_sid=recover
rman target sys/robert
set DBID = 2539725638;
startup nomount;
restore spfile from autobackup;
shutdown immediate;
```

We are not that likely to be using the defaults, of course, so let's assume we need to define a specific location for the autobackups in the **restore** command. Here is an example of this type of operation:

```
set oracle_sid=recover
rman target sys/robert
set DBID = 206232339;
startup nomount;
run
{
set controlfile autobackup format for device type disk
to 'c:\oracle\backup\%F';
allocate channel c1 device type disk;
restore spfile from autobackup;
}
shutdown immediate;
```

Next, we use the **maxseq** and **maxdays** parameters to look back beyond the default ten days:

```
set oracle_sid=recover
rman target sys/robert
set DBID = 2539725638;
startup nomount;
run
{
set controlfile autobackup format for device type disk
to 'c:\oracle\backup\%F';
allocate channel c1 device type disk;
restore spfile from autobackup maxseq 200 maxdays 100;
}
shutdown immediate;
```

Restoring an SPFILE to a different location and filename is not terribly complex. In this example, we assume that the database is up and running, so we don't need to indicate the location of the autobackup file sets:

```
set oracle_sid=recover
rman target sys/robert
set DBID = 2539725638;
startup nomount;
restore spfile to 'c:\oracle\spfile.restore' from autobackup;
shutdown immediate;
```

Recovering the SPFILE from an Autobackup Using RMAN, Using the FRA

The process to recover the SPFILE when using the FRA is actually much easier than the process if you don't use the FRA. First, you don't need to worry about all the DBID nonsense or allocating channels, which saves time and headaches. All you need to do to recover the SPFILE is configure your temporary parameter file correctly (make sure the FRA destination directory is properly set), start the Oracle instance, and issue the **restore spfile** command. Here is an example:

```
set oracle_sid=recover
rman target sys/robert
startup nomount;
restore spfile from autobackup;
shutdown immediate;
```

You can still recover the SPFILE using the **maxseq** and **maxdays** parameters, as shown in this snippet:

```
restore spfile from autobackup maxseq 200 maxdays 100;
```

Recovering the SPFILE from a Specific Backup Set

If you used RMAN before Oracle Database 10*g*, you know that recovery of the SPFILE could be difficult if you did not have autobackups configured. In such cases, you needed to write a nasty bit of PL/SQL in order to restore the SPFILE from the RMAN backups.

Oracle Database 10*g* makes this process much easier. Now the **restore** command includes a **from backup** clause that allows you to simply indicate the backup set piece that contains the SPFILE backup in it. Thus, all you need to know is the backup set piece name and where it is located, and you can restore your SPFILE. In some cases, it might take a bit of trial and error to find the backup set piece with the SPFILE backup in it, but once you do, the restore should go like a snap (of course, it would be best to restore the most current control file backup!).

To restore the SPFILE, then, start the database instance and identify the backup set piece that contains the SPFILE (or guess at it). Fire up RMAN. You need to set the DBID of the database also (as we have already discussed). Once you have set the DBID, you also need to allocate a channel to the device you are going to restore from. Having allocated the channel, you issue the **restore spfile from** command, and pass the backup set piece name in at the end of the command. RMAN will then restore the SPFILE to the correct location. Here is an example of this type of restore in action:

```
set oracle_sid=recover
rman target sys/robert
set DBID = 2539725638;
startup nomount;
run
{
 allocate channel c1 device type disk;
 restore spfile
```

```
 from 'd:\backup\recover\C-2539725638-20060629-00';
}
shutdown immediate;
```

You can now perform any additional recovery activities that might be required.

Recovering the SPFILE When Using a Recovery Catalog

If you are using a recovery catalog, restoring the most current SPFILE is as simple as issuing the **restore spfile** command after starting (nomount) the Oracle instance. RMAN will use the recovery catalog to locate the most current control file backup and extract that backup for your use. Here is an example:

```
set oracle_sid=recover
rman target sys/robert catalog rcat_manager/password@robt
startup nomount;
restore spfile from autobackup;
shutdown immediate;
```

Note that we shut down the database after the restore. Again, this is to make sure that the database will be restarted using the correct parameter value settings.

Restoring the Backed Up SPFILE with an Operational Database Online

Extracting a copy of your SPFILE from a database backup with the database up is really easy regardless of whether you are using a control file or a recovery catalog. You should note that this operation will result in a text parameter file, and not an SPFILE, so you will need to convert it if you wish it to be an SPFILE.

If you are not using a recovery catalog and you have enabled automatic backups of control files, just issue the following command:

```
RMAN> restore spfile to pfile 'd:\backup\test.ora' from autobackup;
```

This command restores the SPFILE to a file called test.ora in a directory called d:\backup. Again, with any autobackup restore, RMAN looks only for the past seven days to find a control file autobackup piece unless you supply **maxseq** and **maxdays** parameter values.

If you are not using a recovery catalog and are not using control file autobackups, or if you are using a recovery catalog, then this is the command you would use:

```
RMAN> restore spfile to pfile 'd:\backup\test.ora';
```

In this case, Oracle uses the control file of the database to locate the most current backup set to restore the SPFILE from. So, now that you have your SPFILE back, you are ready to go out and recover your control file.

Restoring the Control File

Restoring the control file is not much different from restoring your SPFILE. First, the database needs to be mounted, so to restore the control file, you should have already restored your SPFILE, or have created one, and mounted your database. Once that occurs, you are ready to proceed to recover the control file for your database.

Control file recoveries come in several flavors, including recoveries that do not use the FRA and those that do use the FRA. In the following sections we deal with additional control file recovery situations.

Recovering the Control File from an Autobackup Using RMAN, No FRA

If you have lost your control file and you are not using the FRA, you will want to recover it from the control file autobackup set (if you are using this feature, which we strongly recommend). As we have already described, Oracle will by default back up the control file (along with the SPFILE) to the $ORACLE_HOME/dbs or $ORACLE_HOME/database directory (depending on the operating system). If you choose to use the default location (or if you back up to an alternate disk location), you will probably want to back up these backup sets themselves to another backup media such as tape (which RMAN can do for you).

When restoring the control file, it is assumed that the instance parameter file has been restored and that the instance can be started (for example, by using **startup nomount**). Once the instance is up and running, the general procedure to restore the control file when not using the FRA is to first set your ORACLE_SID and then log into RMAN (if you have not done so already). As with SPFILE restores, you need to set the DBID so that RMAN will know which database control file it is looking for.

We are now ready to restore the control file. As with the SPFILE restore, if you are using the default location (not likely) to back up your control file autobackup to, you can simply issue the **restore control file from autobackup** command, and RMAN will look for the control file backup set that contains the most current control file backup. Once the control file is recovered, you need to shut down the instance and restart it to allow your new control file parameters to take effect. If you are using a nondefault location, then you need to use the **allocate channel** command to allocate a channel pointing to that location, and then you can restore the control file using the same method.

When you issue the **restore controlfile from autobackup** command, Oracle looks in the default location for automated control file backup sets (or in the location you defined with the **allocate channel** command). Since you used the **set dbid** command, RMAN knows your database's DBID. It uses the DBID to search through the defined directory to look specifically for the most current control file backup sets for your database. See the previous section on SPFILE recoveries for more information about the format of the naming convention that RMAN uses for control file autobackup backup sets. As with SPFILE recoveries, you can modify how far back RMAN looks for a control file autobackup by using the **maxseq** and **maxdays** parameters of the **restore** command.

Let's look at some examples of recovering control files. First, we use the default settings of the **restore** command:

```
set oracle_sid=recover
rman target sys/robert
set DBID = 2539725638;
startup nomount;
restore controlfile from autobackup;
shutdown immediate;
```

Next, we use the **maxseq** and **maxdays** parameters to look back beyond the default ten days. This time we assume that we are not backing up to a default location:

```
set oracle_sid=recover
rman target sys/robert
set DBID = 2539725638;
startup nomount;
run
{
set controlfile autobackup format for device type disk
to 'c:\oracle\backup\%F';
allocate channel c1 device type disk;
restore controlfile from autobackup maxseq 200 maxdays 100;
}
shutdown immediate;
```

Restoring a control file to a different location and filename is not terribly complex. In this example, we assume the database is up and running, so we don't need to define the location of the control file autobackups:

```
set oracle_sid=recover
rman target sys/robert
set DBID = 2539725638;
startup nomount;
run
{
 restore controlfile to 'c:\oracle\control file.restore' from autobackup;
}
shutdown immediate;
```

Recovering the Control File from an Autobackup Using RMAN, Using the FRA

As was the case with SPFILE recoveries, the process to recover the control file when using the FRA is very easy. First, ensure that the parameters defining the location of the FRA are set correctly. Then, start the database instance; issue the **restore control file from autobackup** command and the control file will be recovered. Here is an example:

```
set oracle_sid=recover
rman target sys/robert
startup nomount;
restore controlfile from autobackup;
shutdown immediate;
```

You can still recover using the **maxseq** and **maxdays** parameters, as shown in this snippet:

```
restore controlfile from autobackup maxseq 200 maxdays 100;
```

Recovering Older Control File Backups

You may wish to restore a control file backup that was taken some time ago, such that it's not the most current backup (this is often the case if you issued a **resetlogs** command). The **restore control file from autobackup** command allows you to do this when coupled with the **until time** parameter. For example, we can find and restore the control file backup created on or before 12/09/2005 at 04:11 A.M. by issuing this command:

```
restore controlfile from autobackup until time
"to_date('12/09/2005 13:00:00','MM/DD/YYYY HH24:MI:SS')";
```

You will want to know which control file backups are available to restore if you are going to use this command. We discuss the **list** command in more detail in Chapter 15, but for now you should know that you use the **list backup of controlfile** command to determine which control file backups area available for you to restore. Here is an example:

```
RMAN> list backup of controlfile;
List of Backup Sets
===================
BS Key  Type LV Size        Device Type Elapsed Time Completion Time
------- ---- -- ---------- ----------- ------------ ---------------
38      Full    6.80M       DISK         00:00:05     01-JAN-06
  BP Key: 39   Status: EXPIRED  Compressed: NO  Tag: TAG20060108T183828
        Piece Name: C:\ORACLE\PRODUCT\10.2.0\FLASH_RECOVERY_AREA\TESTOEM
```

```
\AUTOBACKUP\2006_01_08\O1_MF_S_579206308_1W3D485F_.BKP
  Control File Included: Ckp SCN: 3568285        Ckp time: 08-JAN-06

BS Key  Type LV Size        Device Type Elapsed Time Completion Time
------- ---- -- ----------  ----------- ------------ ---------------
40      Full   6.80M        DISK         00:00:06     08-JAN-06
  BP Key: 41    Status: AVAILABLE  Compressed: NO  Tag: TAG20060108T183857
       Piece Name: C:\ORACLE\PRODUCT\10.2.0\FLASH_RECOVERY_AREA\TESTOEM
\AUTOBACKUP\2006_01_08\O1_MF_S_579206337_1W3D5495_.BKP
  Control File Included: Ckp SCN: 3568311        Ckp time: 08-JAN-06
```

In the preceding example, we used the **list** command to discover that we have two different control file backups. The first control file backup (BS Key 38) has a status of EXPIRED because of the current backup retention policy. Since it is expired, RMAN will not try to use it during a restore operation (if the backup set piece is still available, we can change the status with the **change** command and be able to use it). The second control file backup (BS Key 40) is available. RMAN will be able to restore this backup.

Note that the **list** command is only available if you have the database mounted with a current control file. If you do not have a control file available, then the list command will not work. Also, if you do not have a control file available, then the retention criteria will not be an issue and you could restore any control file using the **autobackup** command.

Recover the Control File from a Backup Set

If you used RMAN before Oracle Database 10g, you know that recovery of the control file could be difficult if you did not have autobackups configured. In such cases, you needed to write a nasty bit of PL/SQL in order to restore the control file.

Oracle Database 10g makes this much easier. Now the restore command includes a **from backup** clause that allows you to simply indicate the backup set piece that contains the control file backup in it. Thus, all you need to know is the backup set piece name, and where it is, and you can restore your control file. In some cases, it might take a bit of trial and error to find the backup set piece with the control file backup in it, but once you do, the restore should go like a snap (of course, it would be best to restore the most current control file backup!).

To restore the control file, start the database instance and identify the backup set piece that contains the control file (or guess at it). Fire up RMAN. You will need to set the DBID of the database also (as we have already discussed). Once you have set the DBID, you will also need to allocate a channel to the device you are going to restore from. Having allocated the channel, you issue the **restore controlfile from** command, and pass the backup set piece name in the end of the command. RMAN will then restore the control file and replicate it to the different CONTROL_FILE parameter locations. Here is an example of this type of restore in action:

```
set oracle_sid=recover
rman target sys/robert
set DBID = 2539725638;
startup nomount;
run
{
 allocate channel c1 device type disk;
 restore controlfile
 from 'd:\backup\recover\C-2539725638-20020629-00';
}
shutdown immediate;
```

You can now perform any additional recovery activities that might be required.

Recovering a Control File Using a Recovery Catalog

If you are using a recovery catalog, restoring the most current control file backup is as simple as issuing the **restore controlfile** command. RMAN will use the recovery catalog to locate the most current control file backup and extract that backup for your use. Here is an example:

```
set oracle_sid=recover
rman target sys/robert catalog rcat_manager/password@robt
# Note - We would issue a startup nomount
# and restore control file from autobackup here if we needed to.
# shutdown immediate here if we recovered the control file.
startup nomount;
restore controlfile;
# mount the database in preparation for a restore.
alter database mount;
```

Database Recovery after Restoring a Control File

When you restore a control file with RMAN (and there are no datafiles or online redo logs lost), there are two different things to consider. First, you need to consider how to actually get your database up and running after restoring the control file. Second, you need to recover information related to RMAN, such as registering archived redo logs and backup sets in the newly created control file with RMAN. Let's look at each of these topics in a bit more detail.

Opening the Database after a Control File Recovery   In the event that only your control file was lost, then recovery of the control file and your database is generally pretty straightforward (if any kind of Oracle recovery can be thought of as straightforward). The commands to recover the control file are the same; you just need to simulate incomplete recovery in order to open the database. Note that in some cases you may need to register archived redo logs or even backup sets before you can complete recovery. We discuss this process in the next section.

If you are running in NOARCHIVELOG mode, this would be the method you would use:

```
set oracle_sid=recover
rman target sys/robert
set DBID = 2539725638;
startup nomount;
restore controlfile from autobackup;
alter database mount;
recover database noredo;
alter database open resetlogs;
```

If you are running in ARCHIVELOG mode, recovery is only slightly different:

```
set oracle_sid=recover
rman target sys/robert
set DBID = 2539725638;
startup nomount;
restore controlfile from autobackup;
alter database mount;
recover database;
alter database open resetlogs;
```

Of course, loss of other database physical files can make this complex. Also, if you don't have a recent control file backup, then things can get quite complex and you may end up having to manually re-create the control file with the **create control file** command. This is a horror we hope you never have to face, and you should not need to face it if your backup and recovery strategy is sound.

Restoring RMAN-Related Records to the Control File   Once you have restored the control file, you need to consider the distinct possibility that you have lost RMAN-related data. Since RMAN stores all of its data in the control file, there is a good possibility that you have at least lost some records that relate to archived redo logs (which Oracle needs for a full recovery).

RMAN makes this problem easier to deal with, because you can register various RMAN-related backup files after the restore of a control file just to ensure that you have everything you need for a recovery in the control file. To re-create RMAN-related archived redo log records, you can use the RMAN **catalog** command to register archived redo logs in your control file. The **catalog** command can be used to register a specific backup set piece, as shown in this example:

```
RMAN>Catalog backuppiece 'c:\oracle\product\10.2.0\flash_recovery_area
\testoem\backupset\2005_12_09\O1_MF_ANNNN_TAG20051209T041150_
1SLP386H_.BKP';
```

You can also catalog archived redo logs, as in this example:

```
RMAN>Catalog archivelog
'c:\oracle\product\10.2.0\flash_recovery_area\testoem\archivelog\
2005_12_15\O1_MF_1_2_1T3SVF05_.ARC';
```

Now, if you are thinking ahead, you might sigh and say to yourself, "Who wants to manually catalog the 1000 archived redo logs that I have generated throughout the day?" Fortunately, the RMAN developers had the same thought! With RMAN you can catalog a whole directory without having to list individual files. Simply use the **catalog** command again, but use one of the following keywords:

- **recovery area** or **db_recovery_file_dest**

- **start with**

The **recovery area** and **db_recovery_file_dest** keywords have the same function: they cause the entire FRA to be cataloged by RMAN. If RMAN finds files that are already cataloged, it simply skips over them and continues to catalog any remaining files that are not found in the control file. Here is an example of cataloging all files in the FRA:

```
RMAN> catalog recovery area;
```

If you are not using the FRA, then you will want to use the **start with** syntax instead. The **start with** syntax allows you to traverse a non-FRA backup directory and catalog any RMAN-related files contained in that directory and any subdirectories under that directory. Here is an example of the use of the **catalog start with** command:

```
catalog start with 'c:\oracle\backups\testoem';
```

NOTE
RMAN in Oracle Database 10g R2 automatically catalogs the FRA for you if you perform a restore operation with a backup control file.

Restoring a Control File Online

Extracting a copy of your control file from a database backup while the database is up is really easy regardless of whether you are using a control file or a recovery catalog.

If you are not using a recovery catalog and you have enabled automatic backups of control files, just issue the following command:

```
RMAN> restore controlfile to 'd:\backup' from autobackup;
```

This command restores the SPFILE to a file called test.ora in a directory called d:\backup. Again, with any autobackup restore, RMAN looks only for the past seven days by default to find a control file autobackup piece. Use **maxseq** and **maxdays** to modify this default.

If you are not using a recovery catalog and are not using control file autobackups, or if you are using a recovery catalog, then this is the command you would use:

```
RMAN> restore controlfile to 'd:\backup';
```

In this case, Oracle uses the control file of the database to locate the most current backup set to restore the control file from. Of course, you could use the manual restore process, using the **dbms_backup_restore** procedure, which we discussed earlier in this section.

RMAN Workshop: *Recover Your Control File*

Workshop Notes
For this workshop, you need an installation of the Oracle software and an operational test Oracle database. We also assume that you have the FRA configured and that your backups are being done to that area.

NOTE
For this workshop, the database is in ARCHIVELOG mode.

Step 1. Ensure that you have configured automated backups of your control files:

```
configure controlfile autobackup on;
```

In this case we are accepting that the control file backup set pieces will be created in the default location.

Step 2. Complete a backup of your system (in this case, we assume this is a hot backup). In this workshop, we assume that the backup is to a configured default device:

```
set oracle_sid=recover
rman target rman_backup/password
backup database plus archivelog;
```

Step 3. Shut down your database using the **shutdown immediate** command. Do not use the **shutdown abort** command in this workshop.

```
shutdown immediate;
```

Step 4. Rename all copies of your database control file. Do not remove them, just in case your backups cannot be recovered.

Step 5. Start your database. It should complain that the control file cannot be found and it will not open.

```
startup;
```

Step 6. Recover your control file with RMAN using your autobackup of the control file:

```
restore controlfile from autobackup;
```

Step 7. Mount the database and then simulate incomplete recovery to complete the recovery process:

```
Alter database mount;
recover database;
alter database open resetlogs;
```

The restore and recover Commands

The basic process of recovering a database is a two-step process. The first step is to use the **restore** command to restore the database backups. The second step is to use the **recover** command to recover the database, including the application of archived redo logs. Let's look at each of these commands in a bit more detail before we move on to the details of how to recover your database using them.

The restore Command

While the **restore** command has several ancillary purposes, its main function is to restore files from RMAN backups in preparation for recovery. RMAN and the **restore** command are quite intelligent, and they will choose the most recent backup to restore, in an effort to reduce recovery time. As a result, the **restore** command might restore your datafiles from a backup set, or it might restore them from an image copy, or it might choose to do a little of both, if that will help speed up the restore process.

The **restore** command is used to restore SPFILEs and control files from automated backups. The **restore** command can also be used to create a standby control file for a standby database. You also use the **restore** command to restore the database to any point in time, and in that case, it will find the closest backups to that given point in time to restore. Without a recovery catalog, RMAN can restore the database to any point in time within that database's incarnation (assuming that a backup is available). The **restore** command can also be used to restore databases from previous incarnations, but a control file backed up during that incarnation is required. If you are using a recovery catalog, you can restore the database back to any incarnation.

The **restore** command can also be used to restore a specific backup based on a given tag assigned to that backup. This might be useful in development environments where you might have a "golden" backup that you want to restore to on a regular basis. The **restore** command can also be used to restore archived redo logs, if that is required for operations like LogMiner (but the **recover** command will do this during database recoveries).

Want more? The **restore** command can be used to validate the ability to actually recover the database. It will make sure that backups are available to restore the database and it will validate the integrity of those backups. You can also use the **restore preview** command to identify the backups that will be needed to restore the database (much like the **list** command that we discuss in Chapter 15).

When using the **restore** command, if you are using encryption for your backups, you need to ensure that the encryption method in use is properly configured. Thus, if you are using transparent-mode encryption, the required wallet must be available. (We talked about encryption in Chapter 10.)

When you use the **restore** command, it overwrites any files that already exist without notice, unless you use the **set newname** command (which we document later in this chapter). Because of this, be very careful when restoring files and make sure that you don't mind overwriting what is already out there.

The **restore** command also has a failover feature. If, during a recovery, RMAN finds that a given backup file is not available or is corrupted, it automatically tries to use previous backups to complete the recovery process. In cases where failover happens, RMAN puts a message in the database alert log.

The recover Command

The **recover** command is used to recover the database. It can perform a complete recovery or it can perform a point-in-time recovery of the database. The **recover** command determines which archived redo logs are required and extracts and applies them. Once the application of the redo is complete, all you need to do is open the database with the **alter database open** command.

The **recover** command also determines if any incremental backup images are available to apply. These images can be applied to base incremental backups or to datafile image copies. The **recover** command always tries to use incremental backups first, if they are available, because that will be the quickest way to restore your database (as opposed to applying archived redo logs).

When restoring the archived redo logs, the **recover** command attempts to use any redo logs that are already present on disk. If they are not available on disk, the **recover** command then tries to restore them from the various archived redo log backup sets. Note that you can use the **noredo** parameter in the **recover** command to indicate that RMAN should not try to apply redo to the database. As you will see in an example later in this chapter, the **noredo** parameter is used for recovery of NOARCHIVELOG databases.

Restore and Recover the Database in NOARCHIVELOG Mode

If your database is in NOARCHIVELOG mode, you will be recovering from a full, offline backup, and point-in-time recovery won't be possible. If your database is in ARCHIVELOG mode, read the "Database Recoveries in ARCHIVELOG Mode" section later in this chapter. If you are doing incremental backups of your NOARCHIVELOG database, then you will also want to read "What If I Use Incremental Backups," later in this chapter.

Preparing for the Restore

If you are running in NOARCHIVELOG mode, and assuming you actually have a backup of your database, performing a full recovery of your database is very easy. First, it's a good idea to clean everything out. You don't have to do this, but we have found that in cases of NOARCHIVELOG recoveries, cleaning out old datafiles, online redo logs, and control files is a good idea. You don't want any of those files lying around. Since you are in NOARCHIVELOG mode, you will want to start afresh (of course, it's also a very good idea to make sure that those files are backed up somewhere just in case you need to get them back!).

Having cleaned out your datafiles, control files, and redo logs, you are ready to start the recovery process. First, recover the control file from your last backup, as we demonstrated earlier in this chapter. Alternatively, you can use a backup control file that you created at some point after the backup you wish to restore from. If you use the **create control file** command, you need to catalog the RMAN backup-related files before you can restore the database.

For this example, we assume that you are not using a recovery catalog. We also assume you want to recover from the most current backup, which is the default setting for RMAN. If you want to recover from an older backup, you need to use the **set time** command, which we will discuss later in this section.

The differences in recovery with and without a recovery catalog are pretty much negligible once you are past the recovery of the SPFILE and the control file. So, we will only demonstrate recoveries without a recovery catalog. Also, at this point, there is little difference in how you perform a recovery if you are using the FRA or not. In the upcoming examples, we use the FRA and highlight any issues that arise from this fact in the text.

First, let's look at the RMAN commands you use to perform this recovery:

```
startup mount;
restore database;
recover database noredo;
alter database open resetlogs;
```

Looks pretty simple. Of course, these steps assume that you have recovered your SPFILE and your database control files. The first command, **startup mount**, mounts the database. So, Oracle reads the control file in preparation for the database restore. The **restore database** command causes RMAN to actually start the database datafile restores. Following this command, **recover database noredo** instructs RMAN to perform final recovery operations in preparation for opening the database. Since the database is in NOARCHIVELOG mode, and there are no archived redo logs to apply and the online redo logs are missing, the **noredo** parameter is required. If the online redo logs were intact, the **noredo** parameter would not be needed. Finally, we open the database with the **alter database open resetlogs** command. Since we have restored the control file and we need the online redo logs rebuilt, we need to use the **resetlogs** command. In fact, you will probably use **resetlogs** with about every NOARCHIVELOG recovery you do.

So, let's look at this recovery in action:

```
d:>set oracle_sid=testoem
d:>rman target sys/robert
RMAN> startup mount
connected to target database (not started)
Oracle instance started
database mounted
Total System Global Area      209715200 bytes
Fixed Size                      1248164 bytes
Variable Size                 100664412 bytes
Database Buffers              104857600 bytes
Redo Buffers                    2945024 bytes
RMAN> restore database;
Starting restore at 26-DEC-05
channel ORA_DISK_1: starting datafile backupset restore
channel ORA_DISK_1: specifying datafile(s) to restore from backup set
restoring datafile 00001 to
C:\ORACLE\DATAFILE\TESTOEM\TESTOEM\SYSTEM01.DBF
restoring datafile 00002 to
C:\ORACLE\DATAFILE\TESTOEM\TESTOEM\UNDOTBS01.DBF
restoring datafile 00003 to
C:\ORACLE\DATAFILE\TESTOEM\TESTOEM\SYSAUX01.DBF
restoring datafile 00004 to C:\ORACLE\DATAFILE\TESTOEM\TESTOEM\USERS01.DBF
restoring datafile 00005 to
```

```
C:\ORACLE\DATAFILE\TESTOEM\TESTOEM\CATALOG01.DBF
channel ORA_DISK_1: reading from backup piece
C:\ORACLE\PRODUCT\10.2.0\FLASH_RECOVERY_AREA\TESTOEM\BACKUPSET
\2005_12_26\O1_MF_NNNDF_TAG20051226T085336_1V00ZL3Y_.BKP
channel ORA_DISK_1: restored backup piece 1
piece handle=C:\ORACLE\PRODUCT\10.2.0\FLASH_RECOVERY_AREA\TESTOEM\
BACKUPSET\2005_12_26\O1_MF_NNNDF_TAG20051226T085336_1V00ZL3Y_.BKP
tag=TAG20051226T085336
channel ORA_DISK_1: restore complete, elapsed time: 00:03:26
Finished restore at 26-DEC-05
RMAN> recover database;
Starting recover at 26-DEC-05
using channel ORA_DISK_1
Finished recover at 26-DEC-05
RMAN> alter database open;
```

Well, we now have a happy bouncing baby database back again! Woo hoo!

NOTE
*Use the **restore database noredo** command when your online redo logs are not available. Use the **restore database** command without the **redo** parameter when your online redo logs are available during the recovery.*

Restoring from an Older Backup

You probably have more than one backup that you have taken of your database, and you may well want to recover from some backup other than the most current one. In this case, you need to use the **set** command in conjunction with the rest of the restore process. We will talk about the **set time** command in detail later in this chapter, but here is an example of using it to restore a backup that is a few days older than our default backup:

```
-- If you have issued a RESETLOGS command after the point in time
-- you wish to recover too, you will need to restore a control
-- file previous to that point.
startup mount;
run
{
SET UNTIL TIME "TO_DATE('12/08/05 13:00:00','MM/DD/YY HH24:MI:SS')";
restore database;
recover database noredo;
alter database open resetlogs;
}
```

Note that, in this case, the **set until time** command is in the confines of a **run** block. This is a requirement if you want to use the **set until time** command. Also note that we have established the set time as June 30, 2002, at 13:00:00. This causes Oracle to find the backup taken closest to this time, but not beyond it. Thus, if you took three backups on 6/30/02, one at 8 A.M., the second at 12:50 P.M., and the last at 8 P.M., then RMAN would restore the 12:50 P.M. backup.

If you don't want to have to use a **run** block, you can alternatively set the time restriction in the **restore** command itself, as shown here:

```
-- We assume that we have already recovered the control file
-- If not, you will need to manually use the recover until cancel
-- command as described earlier in the section "A Word About
-- Your Control File".
startup mount;
restore database UNTIL TIME
"TO_DATE('12/08/05 13:00:00','MM/DD/YY HH24:MI:SS')";
recover database noredo;
alter database open resetlogs;
```

NOTE
If you have used RMAN prior to 10g, you might have noticed that RMAN did not re-create your temporary tablespace tempfiles, a rather irritating shortcoming. This has been corrected in Oracle Database 10g, and RMAN will now re-create your tempfiles for you.

Restoring to a Different Location

Of course, we don't always have the luxury of restoring back to the original file system names that the Oracle files resided on. For example, during a disaster recovery drill, you might have one big file system to recover to, rather than six smaller-sized file systems. That can be a bit of a problem, because by default RMAN is going to try to restore your datafiles to the same location that they came from when they were backed up. So, how do we fix this problem?

Enter the **set newname for datafile** and **switch** commands. These commands, when used in concert with **restore** and **recover** commands, allow you to tell RMAN where the datafiles need to be placed. For example, if our datafiles were originally backed up to d:\oracle\data\recover and we wanted to recover them instead to e:\oracle\data\recover, we would first issue the **set newname for datafile** command for each datafile, indicating its old location and its new location. Here is an example of this command's use:

```
set newname for datafile 'd:\oracle\data\recover\system01.dbf'
to 'e:\oracle\data\recover\system01.dbf';
```

Note that we define both the original location of the file and the new location that RMAN should copy the file to. Once we have issued **set newname for datafile** commands for all of the datafiles we want to restore to a different location, we proceed as before with the **restore database** and **recover database** commands. Finally, before we actually open the database, we need to indicate to Oracle that we do, once and for all, really want to have it use the relocated datafiles that we have restored. We do this by using the **switch** command.

The **switch** command causes the datafile locations in the database control file to be changed so that they reflect the new location of the Oracle database datafiles. Typically, you use the **switch datafile all** command to indicate to Oracle that you wish to switch all datafile locations in the control file. Alternatively, you can use the **switch datafile** command to switch only specific datafiles.

If you use the **set newname for datafile** command and do not switch all restored datafiles, then any nonswitched datafile will be considered a datafile copy by RMAN, and RMAN will not try to use that nonswitched datafile when recovering the database. Here is an example of the commands that you might use for a restore using the **set newname for datafile** command:

```
startup nomount
restore controlfile from autobackup;
alter database mount;
run
{
set newname for datafile 'd:\oracle\oradata\recover\system01.dbf' to
'e:\oracle\oradata\recover\system01.dbf';
set newname for datafile
'd:\oracle\oradata\recover\recover_undotbs_01.dbf' to
'e:\oracle\oradata\recover\recover_undotbs_01.dbf';
set newname for datafile 'd:\oracle\oradata\recover\users01.dbf' to
'e:\oracle\oradata\recover\users01.dbf';
set newname for datafile 'd:\oracle\oradata\recover\tools01.dbf' to
'e:\oracle\oradata\recover\tools01.dbf';
set newname for datafile 'd:\oracle\oradata\recover\indx01.dbf' to
'e:\oracle\oradata\recover\indx01.dbf';
restore database;
recover database noredo;
alter database open resetlogs;
switch datafile all;
}
```

Note that if the recovery is not successful but the files were restored successfully, the datafiles restored will become datafile copies and will not be removed.

RMAN Workshop: *Recover Your NOARCHIVELOG Mode Database*

Workshop Notes

For this workshop, you need an installation of the Oracle software and an operational test Oracle database.

NOTE
For this workshop, the database is in NOARCHIVELOG mode.

Step 1. Set the ORACLE_SID and then log into RMAN. Ensure that you have configured automated backups of your control files. Because this is an offline backup, you need to shut down and mount the database.

```
set oracle_sid=recover
rman target rman_backup/password
configure controlfile autobackup on;
shutdown immediate;
startup mount;
```

Note that in this case, we are accepting that the control file backup set pieces will be created in the default location.

Step 2. Complete a cold backup of your system. In this Workshop, we assume that the backup is to a configured default device:

```
backup database;
```

Step 3. Shut down your database:

```
shutdown immediate;
```

Step 4. Rename all database datafiles. Also rename the online redo logs and control files. (Optionally, you can remove these files if you don't have the space to rename them and if you really can afford to lose your database, should something go wrong.)

Step 5. Startup mount your database and restore your control file:

```
startup nomount;
set DBID = <enter the DBID of the database here>;
restore controlfile from autobackup;
alter database mount;
```

Step 6. Recover your database with RMAN using the backup you took in Step 2:

```
restore database;
recover database noredo;
alter database open resetlogs;
```

Step 7. Complete the recovery by backing up the database again:

```
shutdown immediate;
startup mount;
backup database;
```

NOTE
*If your online redo logs had not been removed, you would have used the **recover database** command instead of **recover database noredo**.*

Database Recoveries in ARCHIVELOG Mode

Typically, you will find production databases in ARCHIVELOG mode because of one or more requirements, such as the following:

- Point-in-time recovery

- Minimal recovery time service-level agreements (SLAs) with customers

- The ability to do online database backups

- The ability to recover specific datafiles while the database is available to users

When the database is in ARCHIVELOG mode, you have a number of recovery options that you can choose from:

- Full database recovery

- Tablespace recoveries

- Datafile recoveries

- Incomplete database recovery

We cover the first three items in this section. Later in this chapter, we look at incomplete database recoveries. With each of these types of recoveries, you will find that the biggest difference from NOARCHIVELOG mode recovery is the application of the archived redo logs, as well as some issues with regard to defining when you wish to recover to if you are doing incomplete recovery. For now, let's start by looking at a full database recovery in ARCHIVELOG mode.

 NOTE
Recoveries of SPFILEs and control files are the same regardless of whether or not you are running in ARCHIVELOG mode.

Point-of-Failure Database Recoveries

With a point-of-failure database recovery (also known as a full database recovery), you hope that you have your online redo logs intact; in fact, any unarchived online redo log must be intact. If you lose your online redo logs, you are looking at an incomplete recovery of your database; you should reference Chapter 12 for more information on incomplete recoveries. Finally, we are going to assume that at least one control file is intact. If at least one is not intact, then you need to recover a control file backup, and again you are looking at an incomplete recovery (unless your online redo logs are intact).

So, in this first example, we have lost all of our database datafiles. Our online redo logs and control files are safe, and we just want our database back. In this case, we opt for a full recovery of our database to the point of the failure. Here is the command set we use to perform this restore operation:

```
shutdown;
startup mount;
restore database;
recover database;
alter database open;
```

And here is an actual restore operation:

```
RMAN> restore database;
Starting restore at 09-JAN-06
using target database control file instead of recovery catalog
allocated channel: ORA_DISK_1
channel ORA_DISK_1: sid=156 devtype=DISK
channel ORA_DISK_1: starting datafile backupset restore
channel ORA_DISK_1: specifying datafile(s) to restore from backup set
restoring datafile 00001 to
C:\ORACLE\DATAFILE\TESTOEM\TESTOEM\SYSTEM01.DBF
restoring datafile 00002 to
C:\ORACLE\DATAFILE\TESTOEM\TESTOEM\UNDOTBS01.DBF
restoring datafile 00003 to
C:\ORACLE\DATAFILE\TESTOEM\TESTOEM\SYSAUX01.DBF
restoring datafile 00004 to C:\ORACLE\DATAFILE\TESTOEM\TESTOEM\USERS01.DBF
restoring datafile 00005 to
C:\ORACLE\DATAFILE\TESTOEM\TESTOEM\CATALOG01.DBF
restoring datafile 00009 to C:\ORACLE\TESTDBF\TABLESPACE_NOASSM_01.DBF
restoring datafile 00010 to C:\ORACLE\TESTDBF\TABLESPACE_YESASSM_01.DBF
channel ORA_DISK_1: reading from backup piece
C:\ORACLE\PRODUCT\10.2.0\FLASH_RECOVERY_AREA\TESTOEM
\BACKUPSET\2006_01_08\O1_MF_NNNDF_TAG20060108T224324_1W3THND6_.BKP

channel ORA_DISK_1: restored backup piece 1
piece handle=C:\ORACLE\PRODUCT\10.2.0\FLASH_RECOVERY_AREA\TESTOEM
\BACKUPSET\2006_01_08\O1_MF_NNNDF_TAG20060108T224324_1W3THND6_.BKP
tag=TAG20060108T224324

channel ORA_DISK_1: restore complete, elapsed time: 00:07:46
channel ORA_DISK_1: starting datafile backupset restore
channel ORA_DISK_1: specifying datafile(s) to restore from backup set
restoring datafile 00006 to C:\ORACLE\TESTDBF\TABLESPACE_2K.DBF

channel ORA_DISK_1: reading from backup piece
C:\ORACLE\PRODUCT\10.2.0\FLASH_RECOVERY_AREA\TESTOEM
\BACKUPSET\2006_01_08\O1_MF_NNNDF_TAG20060108T224324_1W3TTCT2_.BKP

channel ORA_DISK_1: restored backup piece 1
piece handle=C:\ORACLE\PRODUCT\10.2.0\FLASH_RECOVERY_AREA\TESTOEM\
BACKUPSET\2006_01_08\O1_MF_NNNDF_TAG20060108T224324_1W3TTCT2_.BKP
tag=TAG20060108T224324
channel ORA_DISK_1: restore complete, elapsed time: 00:00:07
channel ORA_DISK_1: starting datafile backupset restore
channel ORA_DISK_1: specifying datafile(s) to restore from backup set
restoring datafile 00007 to C:\ORACLE\TESTDBF\TABLESPACE_4K.DBF
channel ORA_DISK_1: reading from backup piece
C:\ORACLE\PRODUCT\10.2.0\FLASH_RECOVERY_AREA\TESTOEM
\BACKUPSET\2006_01_08\O1_MF_NNNDF_TAG20060108T224324_1W3TTNWO_.BKP
```

```
channel ORA_DISK_1: restored backup piece 1
piece handle=C:\ORACLE\PRODUCT\10.2.0\FLASH_RECOVERY_AREA\TESTOEM
\BACKUPSET\2006_01_08\O1_MF_NNNDF_TAG20060108T224324_1W3TTNWO_.BKP
tag=TAG20060108T224324

channel ORA_DISK_1: restore complete, elapsed time: 00:00:03
channel ORA_DISK_1: starting datafile backupset restore
channel ORA_DISK_1: specifying datafile(s) to restore from backup set

restoring datafile 00008 to C:\ORACLE\TESTDBF\TABLESPACE_16K.DBF
channel ORA_DISK_1: reading from backup piece
C:\ORACLE\PRODUCT\10.2.0\FLASH_RECOVERY_AREA\TESTOEM
\BACKUPSET\2006_01_08\O1_MF_NNNDF_TAG20060108T224324_1W3TTYJM_.BKP

channel ORA_DISK_1: restored backup piece 1
piece handle=C:\ORACLE\PRODUCT\10.2.0\FLASH_RECOVERY_AREA\TESTOEM
\BACKUPSET\2006_01_08\O1_MF_NNNDF_TAG20060108T224324_1W3TTYJM_.BKP
tag=TAG20060108T224324
channel ORA_DISK_1: restore complete, elapsed time: 00:00:03
Finished restore at 09-JAN-06
RMAN> recover database;
Starting recover at 09-JAN-06
using channel ORA_DISK_1
starting media recovery
media recovery complete, elapsed time: 00:00:12
Finished recover at 09-JAN-06

RMAN> alter database open;
database opened
```

Looks pretty easy, and it is. However, there are a few things to realize about restore operations like this. First of all, Oracle touts that if the file is there already and it doesn't need to be recovered, it will not recover it. After reading the Oracle documentation, you might think that if you lose a single datafile, all you need to do is run the **restore database** command and Oracle will only recover the datafile you lost.

What really happens is that Oracle determines whether the file it's going to restore already exists. If so, and the file that exists is the same as the file it's preparing to restore, then RMAN will not restore that file again. If the file on the backup image is different in any respect from the existing datafile, then RMAN will recover that file. So, if you lose a datafile or two, you will want to do a datafile or tablespace recovery instead, which we will talk about shortly.

Let's take a moment now and look at what's happening during each step of the restore/recovery process. Each of these steps is quite similar for any type of ARCHIVELOG restore. After we have recovered our SPFILE and control files, if that was required, we have the **restore database** command, which causes RMAN to begin restoring all database datafiles. Note that, in this case, the database has to be down because we are restoring critical tablespaces, namely the SYSTEM tablespace. While many ARCHIVELOG recoveries can be done online, a full database point-in-time restore cannot.

Once the datafiles have been restored, Oracle will move on to the next command, the **recover database** command. This command is much like the **recover database** command that you would issue from inside SQL*Plus in that it will cause the Oracle RDBMS to start recovering the database to the point of failure by applying the archived redo logs needed to perform a full point-in-time recovery. An additional benefit that you get from RMAN is that it restores the needed archived redo logs from disk so that they can be applied during the recovery process. Once Oracle has recovered the database, then it's as simple as issuing an **alter database open** command to get Oracle to finish the process of opening the database for use.

NOTE
If you attempt a full database restore and it fails, all recovered datafiles will be removed. This can be most frustrating if the restore has taken a very long time to complete. We suggest that you test different recovery strategies, such as recovering tablespaces (say four to five tablespaces at a time), and see which works best for you and which method best meets your recovery SLA and your disaster recovery needs.

RMAN Workshop: *Complete Recovery of Your ARCHIVELOG Mode Database*

Workshop Notes
For this workshop, you need an installation of the Oracle software and an operational test Oracle database.

NOTE
For this workshop, the database must be configured for and running in ARCHIVELOG mode.

Step 1. Ensure that you have configured automated backups of your control files:

```
set oracle_sid=recover
rman target rman_backup/password
configure controlfile autobackup on;
```

Note that in this case we are accepting that the control file backup set pieces will be created in the default location.

Step 2. Because this is an online backup, there is no need to shut down and then mount the database. Complete an online backup of your system. In this case, we will back up the database and the archived redo logs. Once the archived redo logs are backed up, we will remove them. In this Workshop, we will assume that the backup is to a configured default device.

```
backup database plus archivelog delete input;
```

Step 3. Shut down your database:

```
shutdown immediate;
```

Step 4. Rename all database datafiles. Also rename the control files. Do not rename your online redo logs for this exercise. (Optionally, you can remove these files if you don't have the space to rename them and if you really can afford to lose your database, should something go wrong.)

Step 5. Startup mount your database and restore your control file:

```
startup nomount;
set DBID = <enter the DBID of the database here>;
restore controlfile from autobackup;
alter database mount;
```

Step 6. Recover your database with RMAN using the backup you took in Step 2:

```
restore database;
recover database;
alter database open resetlogs;
```

Step 7. Complete the recovery by backing up the database again:

```
shutdown immediate;
startup mount;
backup database;
```

Tablespace Recoveries

Perhaps you have just lost datafiles specific to a given tablespace. In this event, you can opt to just recover a tablespace rather than the entire database. One nice thing about tablespace recoveries is that they can occur while the rest of the database is humming along. For example, suppose you lose your accounts payable tablespace, but your accounts receivable tablespace is just fine. As long as your application doesn't need to access the accounts payable tablespace, you can be recovering that tablespace while the accounts receivable tablespace remains accessible. Here is an example of the code required to recover a tablespace:

```
sql "alter tablespace users offline";
restore tablespace users;
recover tablespace users;
sql "alter tablespace users online";
```

As you can see, the recovery process is pretty simple. First, we need to take the tablespace offline. We use a new command, **sql**, to perform this action. Enclosed in quotes after the **sql** command is specific SQL that we want the database to execute; in this case, we are taking the USERS tablespace offline with the command **alter tablespace users offline**. Next, we restore the datafiles associated with the tablespace, and then we recover the tablespace. Finally, we use the **sql** command again to issue the **alter tablespace users online** command, and the recovery of the USERS tablespace is complete.

> **NOTE**
> *You cannot recover an individual tablespace or datafile to a point in time different from that of the rest of the database.*

You can also recover multiple tablespaces in the same command set, as shown in this code snippet:

```
sql "alter tablespace users offline";
sql "alter tablespace data offline";
restore tablespace users, data;
recover tablespace users, data;
sql "alter tablespace users online";
sql "alter tablespace data online";
```

Datafile Recoveries

Second cousin to a tablespace recovery is a datafile recovery, which is a very granular approach to database recovery. Here, we can replace lost database datafiles individually, while the rest of the tablespace remains online. Datafile recovery allows the DBA to recover specific datafiles while allowing the rest of the tablespace to remain online for users to access. This feature is particularly nice if the datafile was empty or sparsely populated, as opposed to the entire tablespace. Here is some sample code required to recover a datafile:

```
sql "alter database datafile 3 offline ";
sql "alter database datafile 'd:\oracle\oradata\users01.dbf' offline ";
restore datafile 3;
restore datafile 'd:\oracle\oradata\users01.dbf';
recover datafile 3;
recover datafile 'd:\oracle\oradata\users01.dbf';
sql "alter database datafile 3 online";
sql "alter database datafile 'd:\oracle\oradata\users01.dbf' online ";
```

We recovered a couple of datafiles in this example, using a couple of different methods of defining which datafile we were recovering. First, we used the **sql** command again and took the offending datafiles offline with an **alter database datafile offline** command (they may be already offline in some cases, but we want to make sure).

Before we move on, let's look closer at one component of the **alter database** command: how we reference datafiles. There are two different ways to reference datafiles. The first is to reference the datafile by number, and that's what we did with datafile 3 in the preceding example. The second is to reference a datafile by name, 'd:\oracle\oradata\ users01.dbf'. Either method is acceptable, but we often find that the use of the datafile number is easier. Generally, when a datafile is missing or corrupt, Oracle gives you both the datafile name and number in the associated error message, as shown in this example:

```
ORA-01157: cannot identify/lock data file 4 - see DBWR trace file
ORA-01110: data file 4: 'D:\ORACLE\ORADATA\RECOVER\TOOLS01.DBF'
```

Notice in this listing that datafile 4 is associated with the tools01.dbf datafile. Often, it's much easier to just indicate that you want to restore datafile 4 than to indicate you want to restore d:\oracle\oradata\recover\tools01.dbf.

Once we have taken our datafiles offline, we will restore them (again using either the file number or the filename) and then recover them. Finally, we will bring the datafiles online again, which will complete the recovery process.

What If I Use Incremental Backups?

Oracle will determine automatically if you are using an incremental backup strategy when you restore your datafiles and will automatically apply the required incremental backup sets as required. You do not need to do anything different to recover in these cases.

During a restore using an incremental backup, the **restore** command restores only the base backup. Once that restore is complete, you issue the **recover** command, which causes the incremental backups to be applied to the database, and then the archived redo logs will be applied. Once that is complete, then you can open the database as usual. In all cases, Oracle attempts to restore the base backup and incremental backup that is the most recent. This reduces the amount of redo that has to be applied to fully recover the database, and thus reduces the overall restore time.

Note that since the database will likely be applying multiple backup sets during the recover process, your recovery will likely take longer than you might otherwise expect. However, depending on a number of factors (data change velocity being a large factor), applying incremental backup sets can be faster than the application of a generous amount of redo, and thus the incremental backup solution can be a faster one. Therefore, the ultimate benefit of incremental backups is a quicker backup strategy (and a smaller overall space requirement for the backup set pieces) at the expense of a potentially slower recovery timeline.

Summary

In this chapter, we have looked at the basics of recovering your database with RMAN. We have looked at the many different ways that you can recover your control files and SPFILEs. We have also looked at restoring and recovering your databases from RMAN backups with the **restore** and **recover** commands. We have discussed the different recovery options available, from full database recovery to recovery of specific tablespaces or datafiles. Finally, we have provided some workshops for you to practice your newly learned recovery skills.

There is one big piece of advice that we want to leave you with at the end of this chapter. Practice recoveries, over and over and over. Know how RMAN works and how to recover your database without having to use this book. Become the RMAN expert in your place of work. Then you are poised to be the hero!

CHAPTER
11

Using Oracle Enterprise Manager for Backup and Recovery

p to this point, we have provided guidance on interacting with RMAN strictly from the RMAN client utility itself. This has enabled you to build some confidence using the RMAN command-line syntax. It is critical to become comfortable with this syntax because you will encounter situations in which the command-line syntax of RMAN is the only thing that you have available to get you through a painful downtime.

Oracle does provide a toolset for monitoring all the databases throughout your business, and this toolset includes a graphical user interface for taking backups and performing recoveries. This product, collectively referred to as Oracle Enterprise Manager (OEM), has existed in one form or another since 1998. For most of its history, it has been available as a Java application that could be installed on a client system and used to monitor and administer remote databases.

In *Oracle9i RMAN Backup & Recovery*, Chapter 11 details how to install, configure, and use Oracle 9*i* Enterprise Manager for backup and recovery. It describes the three-tier architecture, the memory requirements, and the job system used to submit RMAN jobs to the target database. But Oracle Enterprise Manager 10*g* bears almost no resemblance to Oracle9*i* Enterprise Manager. It has been completely reengineered from the ground up, and expanded in scope to provide monitoring of more than just your database environments.

Oracle Enterprise Manager 10*g*: The New Paradigm

If you are accustomed to using Oracle9*i* Enterprise Manager, unfortunately, you will be just as lost as everyone else when it comes to using OEM 10*g*. Well, not quite; there are a few similarities in terminology and functionality. But the interface is completely different. More to the point, the underlying architecture is completely different.

Oracle engineered OEM specifically to embrace the new paradigm of enterprise computing: the grid. Oracle built OEM to tame the management chaos unleashed by grid computing. Grid computing enables many compelling business advances, providing an always-up, highly redundant, commodity-based, service-oriented environment in which to deploy enterprise computing resources (enough buzz words for you?). We have already seen the principles of grid computing deployed at customer sites, and it is powerful. But it is also complicated.

To compare how traditional enterprise computing and grid computing differ, it helps to look at some example environments. First, consider the simplified scenario of a traditional enterprise environment shown in Figure 11-1. Configuring this database environment includes the following:

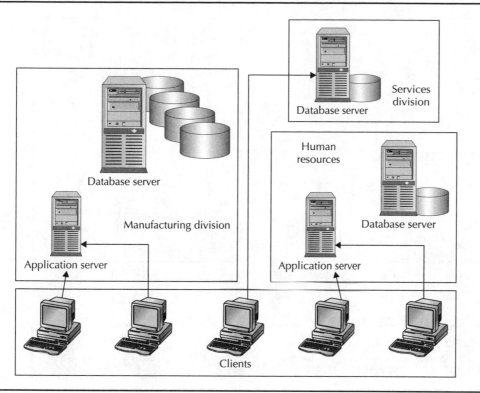

FIGURE 11-1.   *Traditional enterprise computing*

- Requisition as powerful a computer as can be found

- Manage as small a list of computers as can be reasonably grouped

- Manage multiple databases on a single computer

- Segregate data by division and function

- Assign a highly ritualized set of responsibilities to each professional segment (network admin, system admin, database admin, etc.)

If you take the same business needs and deploy them into a grid computing environment, such as that shown in Figure 11-2, configuring the environment includes the following:

- Requisition as many commoditized computers as can be found

- Manage a single database running on many computers

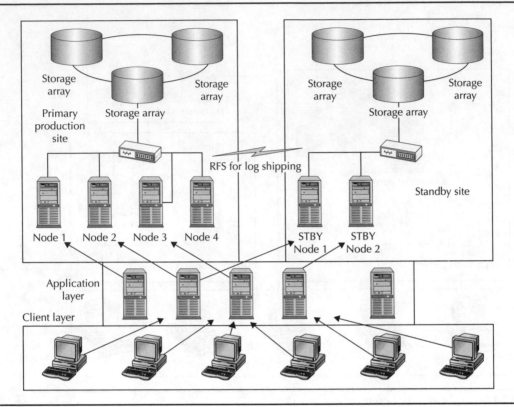

FIGURE 11-2. *The enterprise grid*

- Segregate data as an abstraction (service)

- Take on new professional responsibilities rapidly

- Manage enterprise computing as a single resource, distributed to divisions and functions based on usage requirements

The ability of a grid to add and subtract resources without downtime leads to an ever-increasing level of complexity. DBAs find themselves every day doing more operational architecture work, more network administration work, and more system administration.

OEM 10g was designed to handle this new world order. It was built around the principles of the service-oriented architecture, and its function is far wider than that envisioned for Oracle9i Enterprise Manager. Now, OEM is capable of monitoring and administering the entire "Oracle ecosystem": the host servers, the disk storage, the databases, the application servers, and the applications.

What's the Difference Between Grid Control and Database Control?

OEM 10g Grid Control has the ability to monitor the entire Oracle ecosystem. It has a centralized repository that collects data about multiple targets that exist on multiple computers, and provides an interface that displays collective information for all discovered targets.

OEM 10g Database Control is a subset of Grid Control functionality. It does not monitor anything but a single database, and cannot be used to monitor more than one database. It runs local to the database itself.

From a database administration perspective, the functionality is mostly the same between the two utilities, with Grid Control providing a bit more functionality for operations that involve more than one computer. But the interface is the same, the underlying code is the same, and there is little to differentiate the two. From a backup and recovery perspective, the two utilities are nearly identical.

Coverage of everything that OEM 10g can do would require its own book (or series of books, really). This book is about RMAN, so the coverage of OEM is limited to how it employs RMAN to provide a backup and recovery interface from its console.

OEM 10g takes two forms: Grid Control and Database Control. *OEM 10g Grid Control* is the fully functioning enterprise-wide tool for managing the Oracle ecosystem. *OEM 10g Database Control* is the version of OEM that can be deployed as just a database management utility.

Grid Control

Let's get a few things straight. First, OEM is a web application, with all the power and limitations that come with a web application. The OEM console is a web page that runs on an HTTP server that will be installed and configured as part of the Grid Control install. There is no client install.

What's with the OEM Client Install on the Oracle Client CD?

There is still a "thick" Java client that can be installed as a stand-alone product. This is the old, Oracle9i Enterprise Manager client software, which can be found on the Oracle Client CD. This is still around for a few pieces of functionality that missed the web application integration. This stand-alone OEM client has been stripped down to the barest of functionality, and none of it is for backup and recovery. This thick client is not a front end for OEM 10g Grid Control or Database Control. It is a stand-alone product only. We don't recommend that you use it...for anything.

Second, Grid Control is deployed on Oracle Application Server (OAS). When you install Grid Control, you are installing OAS, and then the Grid Control application is deployed as an Oracle Containers for J2EE (OC4J) application on top of OAS. We point this out so that you realize that a commitment to Grid Control necessitates that you familiarize yourself, to some degree, with the OAS architecture. A discussion of OAS is well beyond the scope of this book, but we will make reference to it occasionally. In fact, a full discussion of Grid Control itself is beyond the scope of this book. Grid Control can monitor many different types of *targets* (as it calls them): databases, application servers, the hosts themselves, even storage devices. In this book, we stick to databases…and mostly to backups of databases only.

Grid Control performs a task that is simple to outline but complicated to realize: it gathers information about computing systems throughout the enterprise, consolidates that information into a central repository, and then displays that information to the DBA from its web console. Based on the information, the DBA can then ask Grid Control to perform tasks on behalf of the DBA at those computing systems.

The Grid Control Architecture

The Grid Control architecture (see Figure 11-3) starts with the Oracle Management Service (OMS), which is the application that is deployed on the application server.

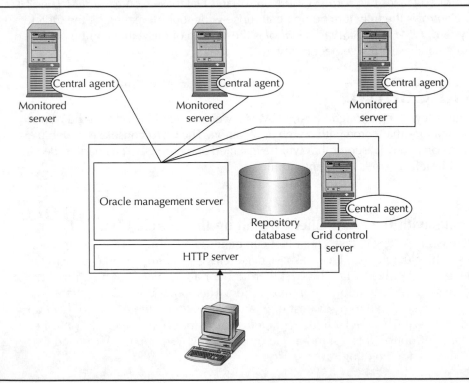

FIGURE 11-3. *Grid Control architecture*

The OMS collects data from registered target servers via the central agent. The agent is installed on a target server, collects information, and pushes the data to the OMS. The OMS loads the data into the repository database. The OMS then builds web pages based on the information in the repository, which can be retrieved from any browser that can hit the OMS server's URL.

The Central Agent

The central agent is installed at each computer that you will be monitoring with Grid Control. The agent is a "dummy" software piece, meaning it cannot make any decisions on its own. It gathers data using Perl scripts and pushes that data over HTTPS to the OMS. The OMS performs any intelligence that is required, and then sends an action to the agent to perform.

The agent is a relatively small footprint, from a memory perspective. However, it can be a visible player on the CPU, depending on what it is you are asking it to do.

The Oracle Management Service

The OMS is a deployed web application on the middle tier of the Grid Control architecture. It is constantly receiving information from agents, in the form of XML files, that it then loads into the tables of the repository. It is responsible for building web content for the HTTP server that provides the console web pages, and as such may ask the agent for specific information. However, the typical data is pushed from the agent, rather than the OMS pulling it.

The Repository Database

The OMS uses an Oracle database for its data source. The repository database is used to store information about the managed targets, as well as Grid Control operations (such as jobs or notifications).

Advanced RDBMS features are put to good use within the repository; Advanced Queuing (AQ) gets a workaround, partitioning is employed heavily, and even the internal DBMS_JOB is used.

Installing and Configuring Grid Control

The Grid Control installation process has many variables, depending on choices you must make about the install. By default, the Grid Control installation creates three ORACLE_HOME directories on the server you provide for the installation: the OMS home, the repository database home, and the central agent home. However, you can choose to install the repository into a pre-existing 10.1.0.4 or 10.2.0.x database that is on the same server as Grid Control, or a different server.

If you choose a pre-existing database, you must provide a host, listener port, and SID for the database. You are also asked for dba credentials (system, for example).

The Oracle Universal Installer then makes a check of the existing database to see if it has all of the required packages and features that Grid Control needs for its repository. If the check succeeds, the install continues. Otherwise, you need to modify the database or choose a different option.

In version 10.1.0.4 of Grid Control, the default database and OMS were in the same home. These have been separated out for patching and upgrading purposes. In Grid Control 10.2, the three homes are all capable of having patches applied separately. This is important when you have uptime considerations. If there is an agent problem that must be patched, for instance, the agent on the Grid Control server can be shut down, and the agent ORACLE_HOME patched, while the OMS and repository database stay up and operational and continue to monitor the other discovered servers.

Resource Considerations

Grid Control is not something you casually install somewhere. If you have already attempted a casual install, you already know this. If you take the default repository database, add in the OMS and its underlying OAS, and top it off with the central agent, you have a good 1.5GB of memory in use—and this is just for Grid Control and does not account for other things running on the computer. So, before you install Grid Control, make sure you've cleared at least 1.5GB of memory on the server. If you have not, you will be swapping. A lot.

Disk storage for Grid Control is not as bad. A couple of gigabytes, what's the big deal? Disks are cheap and storage is ubiquitous. For the record, you should give yourself 5GB, to be safe. And you'll need about 500MB in your temp directory for unjarring files, but this will be checked by the Universal Installers prechecks. So if you don't have it, you won't be able to proceed.

CPU requirements are hard to gauge. The requirements depend on how many targets you are registering and monitoring, and how active your jobs and notifications will be. But from a Linux x86 perspective, at least, don't go with anything that can't clock in at over 1 GHz. That's just to operate, mind you; for actual performance that will make you smile, get yourself as fine a set of chips as you are allowed to procure.

The Oracle Universal Installer

The Universal Installer that provides the installation interface is the same as for any other product from Oracle at this time. It is a wizard-driven process, asking you for input about how you want the install to proceed, punctuated by any number of system checks that actually confirm if the installation you request is feasible.

The prerequisite checks can be annoying, but let's face it, they do all of us a favor. It may be feasible to install a product without the desired requirements, but seriously, how much time do you have to troubleshoot inane OS packages that may be the root of your troubles? Our advice is to pay attention when the Universal Installer tells you that the system is not prepared, make the correction, and then continue.

The Universal Installer begins by asking you what you want to install. There are four choices: Enterprise Manager 10*g* Grid Control Using a New Database, Using an Existing Database, Additional Management Service, and Additional Management Agent. At this point, we are just trying to get Grid Control installed for the first time, so only the first two choices concern us.

Installing the Repository into a New Database

If you choose the Using a New Database option, the Installer builds three ORACLE_HOMEs for you:

- **db10*g***   Stores a prebuilt repository in an Oracle database version 10.1.0.4

- **oms10*g***   Stores the Oracle application server version 10.2.1.2

- **agent10*g***   Stores the central agent

This is by far the simplest and least painful installation. As long as you hit all the system prerequisites, this install is a "sit back and watch" affair.

Installing the Repository into an Existing Database

If you want to use an existing database, choose the Using an Existing Database option in the Universal Installer. There are some requirements:

- SGA_TARGET must be at least 272MB.

- AQ_TM_PROCESSES must be 1 or higher.

- You must install dbms_shared_pool by running the following as the user sys:

```
<DB_HOME>/rdbms/admin/dbmspool.sql
<DB_HOME>/rdbms/admin/prvtpool.plb
```

In addition, the Grid Control repository cannot coexist on a system with the Database Control repository (both desperately want to live in the SYSMAN schema). So, if you are attempting to use a database already monitored by Database Control, either you can drop the SYSMAN user or the Universal Installer will do it for you.

The Configuration Assistants

After the software has been installed, the Universal Installer runs a long series of configuration assistants that perform the arduous task of making all the software play nicely together. The configuration assistant process is divided into three segments to match the three Oracle homes: first, database configuration; second, OMS configuration; finally, agent configuration.

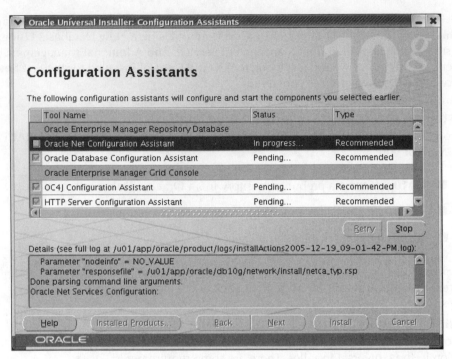

All in all, 12 assistants are run by the Grid Control install, and if you luck out, you won't have to know much about any of them. The bulk of these assistants concern themselves with configuring and deploying the OC4J application that is the OMS. If at any point there is a failure, the installActions.log will have plenty of cryptic information you can dive into (this file is in the ORACLE_BASE/logs directory), but such scrutiny—and what to do after the scrutinizing—is well beyond the scope of this book. If you find yourself with failing configuration assistants, here's the CliffsNotes version of what to do:

1. Make sure you didn't skip a prerequisite warning.

2. Retry the assistant for good measure.

3. Make sure you have enough memory. (Seriously, you can't install this with 512MB!)

4. Scrap the whole thing and try again.

Installing the Central Agent

After you have installed the Grid Control software and have an OMS up and running, you are prepared to start monitoring targets that exist in your enterprise. Well, almost ready: you first must install an OEM agent on all the computers that you want OEM to administer.

The central agent is an independent software install that is used to pass information to the OMS and to receive commands from the OMS. The agent must be installed into its own ORACLE_HOME on all the target hosts that you will be monitoring. There are two ways to install the agent: by manually downloading the entire Grid Control software stack from Oracle Technology Network and using the Universal Installer; or, by using the OMS capabilities to push the agent out to different servers.

The first solution is the most straightforward, but it does require that the entire OEM install disk set be available at every server where you want an agent. This can be a lengthy download process, particularly if you have many different operating systems in your environment. However, the push agent requires a fair amount of configuration as well, all of which is beyond the scope of this book to describe, let alone help you with.

For the sake of this book, we assume you will be manually installing your agents. To do so, you select the fourth and final option, Additional Management Agent, from the first page of the Universal Installer. This goes much quicker than the Grid Control installation.

The Universal Installer then asks you to provide the hostname and port of the OMS server, as shown next. By default, the upload HTTP port is the same as the one you use for the Grid Control console: 4889. You will also be asked for the agent registration password: this is a password that you provide during the Grid Control installation that is required for an agent to authenticate itself as a valid source of data for a particular OMS.

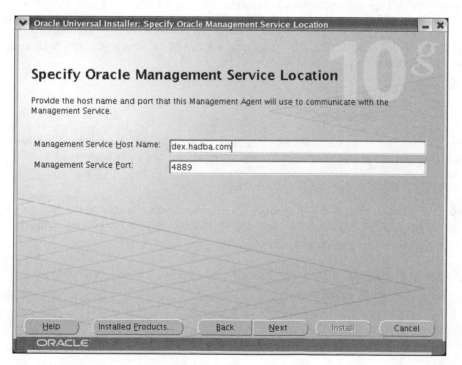

RMAN Workshop: *Starting and Stopping All Grid Control Components*

Workshop Notes

This workshop assumes you have successfully installed Grid Control 10.2 on a Linux machine (a tall order!), and that after this install, everything is currently up and running. Now, it is time to cycle the entire stack—bring it all down, then bring it all back up in the proper order.

Step 1. Stop the central agent. Change directories to the central agent's $ORACLE_HOME/bin directory, and then execute **emctl**:

```
$ORACLE_HOME/bin/emctl stop agent
```

Step 2. Stop the OMS. Change directories to the OMS $ORACLE_HOME/bin directory, and then execute **emctl**:

```
$ORACLE_HOME/bin/emctl stop oms
```

Step 3. Stop the process manager. Change directories to the OMS $ORACLE_HOME/opmn/bin directory, and execute **opmnctl**:

```
$ORACLE_HOME/opmn/bin/opmnctl stopall
```

Step 4. Stop the repository database. Change directories to the repository database's $ORACLE_HOME/bin directory, set the SID to the repository SID, and execute **sqlplus**:

```
Export ORACLE_SID=emrep
sqlplus "/ as sysdba"
sql>shutdown immediate;
```

Step 5. Stop the listener (if it's not listening for any other database). Still in the repository database's $ORACLE_HOME/bin directory, execute **lsnrctl**:

```
Lsnrctl stop
```

Step 6. Now, to start everything back up in proper order, first start the listener. From the repository database's $ORACLE_HOME/bin directory, execute **lsnrctl**:

```
Lsnrctl start
```

Step 7. Start the repository database. Still in the database $ORACLE_HOME, set the SID and execute **sqlplus**:

```
Export ORACLE_SID=emrep
sqlplus "/ as sysdba"
sql>startup
```

Step 8. Start the OMS processes. Change directories to the OMS $ORACLE_
HOME/bin directory, and then execute **emctl**:

```
$ORACLE_HOME/bin/emctl start oms
```

Step 9. Start the central agent. Change directories to the central agent's
$ORACLE_HOME/bin directory, and then execute **emctl**:

```
$ORACLE_HOME/bin/emctl stop agent
```

NOTE
*We have gone to great lengths to keep you oriented
as to which $ORACLE_HOME directory you are in at
each step. This is because an* **emctl** *executable will
exist in the bin directory of every ORACLE_HOME,
but bad things happen if you start running the wrong*
emctl *command in the wrong ORACLE_HOME. We
suggest running a nice set of environment-changing
scripts before any operation.*

Database Control

As we stated previously, Database Control is a subset of Grid Control functionality,
limited to the management and monitoring of a single database. As such, the
functionality is database-centric but not exactly limited to just the database. There
are host statistics gathered for the server on which the database resides, so the host,
while not a separate "target," does have some information reported. In addition,
Database Control can be configured to monitor and administer an Automatic
Storage Management (ASM) instance that the target database uses for storage.

Database Control can also be configured to monitor a RAC database, and thus
to monitor multiple hosts, multiple instances, and multiple ASM instances. Still, it
can monitor only a single database—so the limitation of Database Control is still
the same.

The Database Control Architecture

The Database Control architecture is very similar to that of Grid Control, but the
scale is much smaller. The central agent and the OMS are rolled into the same

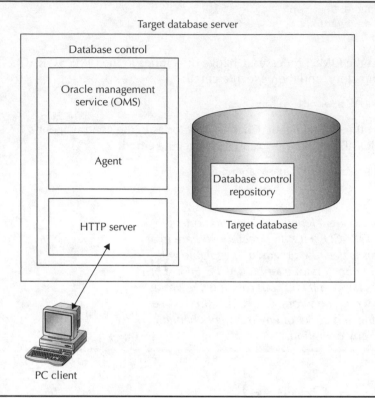

FIGURE 11-4. *Database Control architecture*

OC4J application, and the repository is housed in the target database itself. Figure 11-4 shows how this architecture looks.

Of importance in this diagram is the fact that the Database Control repository is located in the target database that it monitors. So, if the target database is down, Database Control cannot function except to start and stop the database and, of importance to us in this discussion, perform recovery. On a Windows system, the Database Control process is monolithic, and starts and stops as a single service from the Services control panel. On Linux and Unix, you stop and start dbconsole as a single application, but it still spawns separate agent and Java processes.

Database Control is not a separate install from the RDBMS installation. It runs from the same ORACLE_HOME that its target database runs from. Specifically, when dbconsole has been configured for a database, a new subdirectory in the ORACLE_ HOME is created with the name *host_sid*, where *host* is the computer name and *sid* is, well, the SID of the instance being monitored. For instance, if the server is named dex.hadba.com, and we are monitoring the database that is named v102,

then the configuration files would all be located in $ORACLE_HOME/dex.haba
.com_v102.

In a RAC environment, there are always multiple directories named for every
node in the cluster, suffixed by the globalname for the RAC database. So, if you
have a two-node RAC cluster on nodes dex and horatio, and the database is v102c,
then there would be two directories on each node's RDBMS home: ORACLE_
HOME/dex_v102c and $ORACLE_HOME/horatio_v102c. On each node, only the
directory that corresponds in name to that node would actually have any files in it.
The other would be empty. This convention is used in cases where the RAC cluster
shares the same $ORACLE_HOME software tree on a shared drive.

Stopping and starting Database Control is a simple command from the target
database $ORACLE_HOME/bin directory:

```
emctl start dbconsole
emctl stop dbconsole
```

Installing and Configuring
Database Control

There is no specific installation of Database Control software required. It is installed
by default with every 10.2 RDBMS installation that you already have. In fact, you may
already have Database Control up and running on your computer right now, if you
had the Universal Installer provide you with a starter database at the time of install. At
that time, you would have been asked by the Installer how you wanted to manage your
database, and one of the choices is Database Control.

Using the Database Configuration Assistant
to Configure Database Control

Oracle provides a GUI utility to help you build databases, long referred to as the
Database Configuration Assistant (DBCA). This is started by using the executable
dbca out of the $ORACLE_HOME/bin directory; thus, we refer to it hereafter as
lowercase **dbca.**

You can put **dbca** to good use for all kinds of purposes—building a new database,
deleting an old database, and installing database options. You can also use it to add
Database Control functionality to your database. You can use **dbca** to add Database
Control to a new database at the time you build it, or you can use **dbca** to modify an
existing database. This is by far the simplest and most straightforward of all ways to
get Database Control up and running.

The **dbca** executable cannot be used to remove or modify Database Control
after it has been added. It is an addition tool only; for subtraction, you have to use
the command-line tool **emca** (described next).

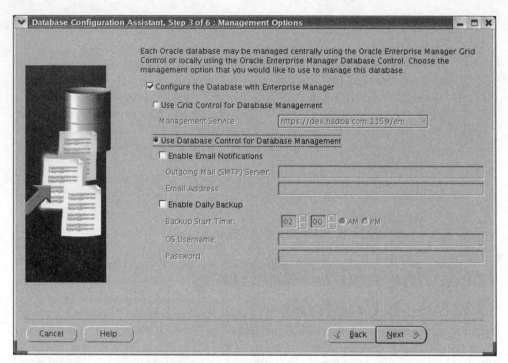

Notice in the preceding illustration the option to specify whether a backup will be scheduled automatically, with the Enable Daily Backup check box. This option enables the Oracle-suggested backup strategy, which we describe later in the chapter in the section "Oracle-Suggested Backup Strategy." This is an out-of-the box backup strategy. You can also configure this with **emca**.

Using Enterprise Manager Configuration Assistant to Configure Database Control

There will be times, as with all things Oracle, when the GUI will simply prove to be too obtuse, too rigid, or too mystifying to serve your purposes when configuring Database Control. In these cases, you can use the command-line utility called Enterprise Manager Configuration Assistant (EMCA), run using the **emca** executable in the $ORACLE_HOME/bin directory of the RDBMS installation (again, we use the lowercase convention **emca** for this utility).

Unlike **dbca**, **emca** is not what you would call intuitive. But it offers all kinds of tweaks and switches that make it powerful and more easily debugged than the GUI **dbca**. Besides which, it's always nice to avoid an X window when you don't really need one. Because of this, **emca** is a valuable tool to spend some time looking at. All the switches and controls are best described in the Oracle documentation; from our perspective, there's only a few worth noting. These are the switches we use to identify the database we want to configure Database Control for, and whether or not we want a default backup strategy put into place:

```
emca -config dbcontrol db -repos  create -backup
emca -deconfig dbcontrol db -repos delete
```

When you fire off a command, **emca** prompts you in an interactive mode for information about what database SID you will be configuring (or deconfiguring), the listener port for the listener that will connect **emca** to the database, and the required user passwords. Note that if you use the **–backup** switch, **emca** will prompt for backup configuration settings.

RMAN Workshop: *Configure Database Control Using emca*

Workshop Notes
This workshop assumes an operational 10.2.0.1.0 database, named v102, running on Linux. This workshop details how to configure a default Database Control application for this database using the command-line utility **emca**.

Step 1.   Use **emca** to drop an existing dbcontrol configuration and the dbcontrol repository:

```
$ emca -deconfig dbcontrol db -repos drop
STARTED EMCA at Dec 20, 2005 9:10:39 PM
EM Configuration Assistant, Version 10.2.0.1.0 Production
Copyright (c) 2003, 2005, Oracle.  All rights reserved.
Enter the following information:
Database SID: v102
Listener port number: 1521
Password for SYS user:
Password for SYSMAN user:
Do you wish to continue? [yes(Y)/no(N)]: yes
Dec 20, 2005 9:11:01 PM oracle.sysman.emcp.EMConfig perform
INFO: This operation is being logged at
$O_H/cfgtoollogs/emca/v102/emca_2005-12-20_09-1039-PM.log.
Dec 20, 2005 9:11:02 PM oracle.sysman.emcp.util.DBControlUtil stopOMS
INFO: Stopping Database Control (this may take a while) ...
Dec 20, 2005 9:11:08 PM oracle.sysman.emcp.EMReposConfig dropRepository
INFO: Dropping the EM repository (this may take a while) ...
Dec 20, 2005 9:13:51 PM oracle.sysman.emcp.EMReposConfig invoke
INFO: Repository successfully dropped
Enterprise Manager configuration completed successfully
FINISHED EMCA at Dec 20, 2005 9:13:52 PM
```

Step 2. Use **emca** to create a new dbcontrol configuration for this database:

```
$ emca -config dbcontrol db -repos create
STARTED EMCA at Dec 20, 2005 9:15:26 PM
EM Configuration Assistant, Version 10.2.0.1.0 Production
Copyright (c) 2003, 2005, Oracle.  All rights reserved.
Enter the following information:
Database SID: v102
Listener port number: 1521
Password for SYS user:
Password for DBSNMP user:
Password for SYSMAN user:
Email address for notifications (optional):
Outgoing Mail (SMTP) server for notifications (optional):
-------------------------------------------------------------
You have specified the following settings
Database ORACLE_HOME ................ /u01/app/oracle/product/10.2.0
Database hostname ................ dex.hadba.com
Listener port number ................ 1521
Database SID ................ v102
Email address for notifications ...............
Outgoing Mail (SMTP) server for notifications ...............
-------------------------------------------------------------
Do you wish to continue? [yes(Y)/no(N)]: yes
Dec 20, 2005 9:15:44 PM oracle.sysman.emcp.EMConfig perform
INFO: This operation is being logged at
/u01/.../product/10.2.0/cfgtoollogs/emca/v102/emca_2005-12-20_09-15
26-PM.log.
Dec 20, 2005 9:15:47 PM oracle.sysman.emcp.EMReposConfig
      createRepository
INFO: Creating the EM repository (this may take a while) ...
Dec 20, 2005 9:20:32 PM oracle.sysman.emcp.EMReposConfig invoke
INFO: Repository successfully created
Dec 20, 2005 9:20:41 PM oracle.sysman.emcp.util.DBControlUtil startOMS
INFO: Starting Database Control (this may take a while) ...
Dec 20, 2005 9:22:23 PM oracle.sysman.emcp.EMDBPostConfig
performConfiguration
INFO: Database Control started successfully
Dec 20, 2005 9:22:23 PM oracle.sysman.emcp.EMDBPostConfig
performConfiguration
INFO: >>>> The Database Control URL is http://dex.hadba.com:1158/em
Enterprise Manager configuration completed successfully
FINISHED EMCA at Dec 20, 2005 9:22:23 PM
```

Configuring Backup Settings in Enterprise Manager

Whew! That was a long-winded explanation of how to get you to this point: where you can use your recently configured OEM Grid or Database Control to take database backups. Hopefully, you have navigated yourself to the point where you are excited about OEM's possibilities, and you are ready to begin scheduling your backups so you can get back to the rest of your day.

First, we need to get our backup settings dialed in. That means a few page clicks in the OEM console. All backup- and recovery-related operations will come from the Maintenance tab, after you have chosen the appropriate database that you wish to configure.

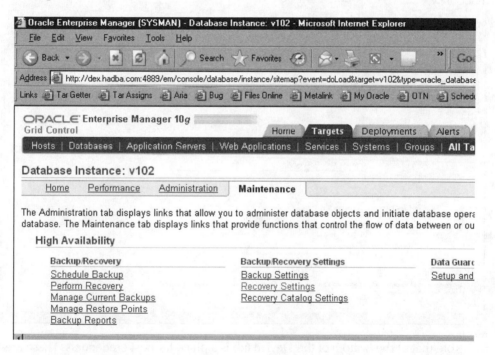

From the Maintenance tab, the first thing that you need to do is configure backup settings, so click the link called Backup Settings. The Backup Settings page has three tabs, Device, Backup Set, and Policy, which are described in the following sections.

Device Configuration

From the Device tab, shown next, you can set up both disk and tape settings. These settings are not for setting which is the default device, but rather are individual settings for all channels on these devices. For disk backups, you set parallelism, the backup location, and the type of backup (backup set or image copy). This is also where you would turn compression on, if you want to use it. For tape backups, you tell OEM how many tape devices will be employed, and the tape backup type (compressed or noncompressed). In addition, for tapes, you can provide any environment settings that are required for the tape backup software to operate (for more on tape backup settings, see Chapters 4 through 8).

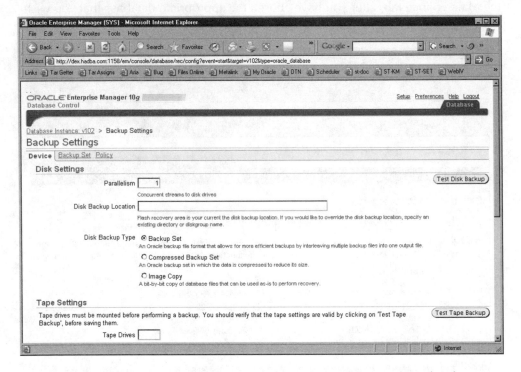

Note that at the bottom of the Device tab is a place for host credentials. These are required in order for OEM to submit a job to make the desired changes on the target database. This same requirement appears at the bottom of each tab of the Configure Backup Settings page.

Backup Set Configuration

After making device configuration decisions, click the Backup Set tab, which allows you to make permanent configuration settings for how the backup sets will be generated. Remember, this only applies to those backups that use backup sets, instead of image copies (disk backups can be either; tape backups are always backup sets).

If you are using disk backups, there is only one thing to configure here: the maximum size of your backup pieces. If you will be backing up to tape, you can set up how many copies of each datafile backup set you will create on the tape devices and the number of copies of each archive log backup to create.

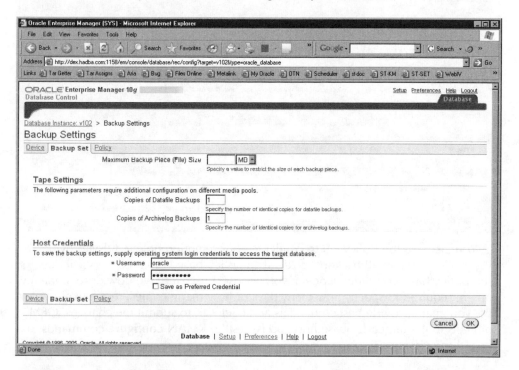

Policy Settings

The Policy tab allows for configuration of those settings that relate to your own business backup policy. This includes turning on autobackups of the control file and SPFILE, and where the autobackups will be located (if disk backups are used). On the Policy tab, you can turn on backup optimization (see Chapter 3 for details on backup optimization). This is also where you turn on block change tracking (see Chapter 16) and configure tablespace exclusions (see Chapter 3).

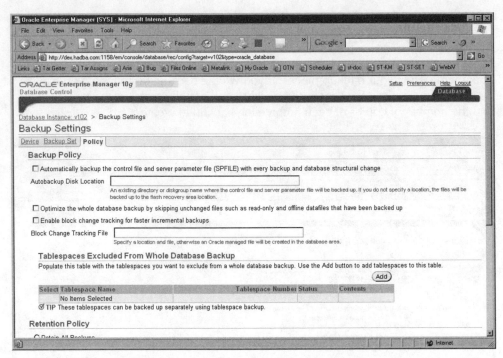

You also use the Policy tab to configure your retention policy. OEM provides three options: retain all backups (ack!), set a policy based on a recovery window, or set a policy based on redundancy. If you choose a recovery window or redundancy, you are required to specify how many days or how many copies, respectively. After this, you again provide host credentials and click OK to submit the changes. OEM connects to the target database host and issues the RMAN **configure** commands to make these changes.

What Is Missing from OEM's Backup Configuration?

Not all things that RMAN can configure are configured in OEM. There are some changes that can be made only from the RMAN command line:

■ **Backup encryption**   There is no interface in OEM for this.

■ **Default device type**   It could be argued that because you schedule backups within OEM to repeat, the default device type is not required. Still, if you are looking for it, stop.

■ **Archive deletion policy**   From RMAN, you can set a specific archive log retention policy that is different from the backup set retention policy. No such option exists in OEM.

- **Snapshot control file location**   RMAN allows you to modify the snapshot control file location, which is handy for RAC configurations. OEM has no way of accomplishing this.

- **Backup throttling**   There is no **rate** command available in any OEM backups, so there is no way to throttle back the RMAN backup speed. This also holds true for the **duration** command that allows you to specify a backup window with the **minimize time** or **minimize load** options.

RMAN Workshop: *Configure Backup Settings in OEM*

Workshop Notes

This Workshop assumes that you have the v102 database and want to configure it to back up to a disk location other than the FRA with two channels, that you want **filesperset** to be 2, and that you want a recovery window of 7 days.

Step 1.   Set up the disk backup settings. Click the database you want to configure, and then click the Maintenance tab. On the Maintenance tab, click the link Backup Settings. The default page that appears is the Device tab. Change Parallelism to **2** and Disk Backup Location to **/u01/backup**. Click the Test Disk Backup button to the right to confirm that the location you have specified exists. The following illustration depicts what the test process looks like while you wait for it to complete.

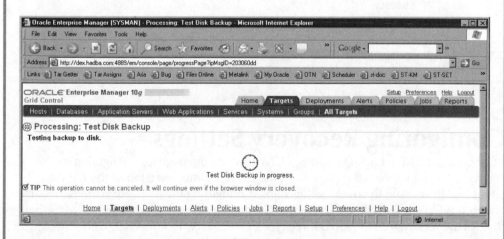

Step 2.   Click the Backup Set tab. Change Maximum Backup Piece (File) Size to **500MB**.

Step 3. Click the Policy tab. Click the Automatically Backup the Control File and Server Parameter File (SPFILE… check box. Set the Autobackup Disk Location to **u01/backup** (the same location as the backups in Step 1).

Step 4. Under the Retention Policy heading, change the policy to the second option, Retain Backups That Are Necessary for a Recovery to Any Time… and set the value to **7** days.

Step 5. Under Host Credentials, set the host server username and password to the user that installed your database software. Then click OK.

Step 6. Confirm that the changes have taken effect for this database. Connect to the host server where this database resides:

```
Export ORACLE_SID=v102
rman target /
RMAN> show all;
using target database control file instead of recovery catalog
RMAN configuration parameters are:
CONFIGURE RETENTION POLICY TO RECOVERY WINDOW OF 7 DAYS;
CONFIGURE CONTROLFILE AUTOBACKUP ON;
...
CONFIGURE CONTROLFILE AUTOBACKUP FORMAT FOR DEVICE TYPE DISK TO
'/u01/backup/%F';
...
CONFIGURE DEVICE TYPE DISK PARALLELISM 2 BACKUP TYPE TO BACKUPSET;
CONFIGURE CHANNEL DEVICE TYPE DISK FORMAT   '/u01/backup/%U'
MAXPIECESIZE 500 M;
...

CONFIGURE CHANNEL DEVICE TYPE 'SBT_TAPE' MAXPIECESIZE 500 M;
...
```

Configuring Recovery Settings

After configuring the backup settings, OEM provides the page for configuring recovery settings. You can access this page from the main Maintenance tab of the database target by clicking the Recovery Settings link. Configuring the recovery settings actually covers a wide scope of different options. On the Recovery Settings page, OEM further divides the recovery settings into three types of recovery, Instance Recovery, Media Recovery, and Flash Recovery, as described in the following sections.

Instance Recovery

There is only one setting that refers to instance recovery, FAST_START_MTTR_
TARGET, as shown next. This is an initialization parameter that determines a target
value, in seconds, that you are interested in hitting when instance recovery is initiated
on the database. MTTR is an acronym for *mean time to recover* and is a common name
for exactly how long it takes for a database to be operational again after it has crashed
for some reason.

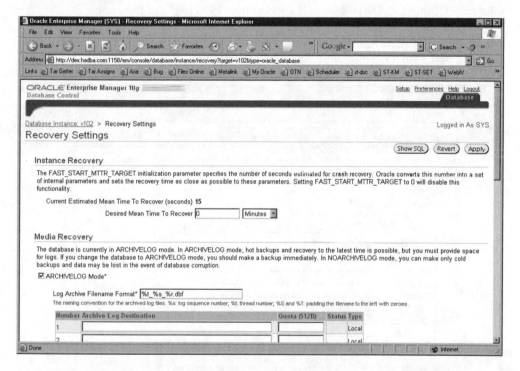

Instance recovery is initiated automatically by Oracle when a database is
started after a hard crash (or a shutdown abort). Instance recovery uses online
redo logs and undo segments to remove any transactions that were uncommitted
at the time of the crash and to set the database to a clean, synchronized state
for further activity. Instance recovery must complete before the database can be
started, so minimizing how long this takes affects how fast your database comes
back to life after a crash.

FAST_START_MTTR_TARGET is a combination of a number of changes that are
made internally to facilitate the speedy recovery of your instance, and is also referred
to as *automatic checkpoint tuning*. This parameter makes the LOG_CHECKPOINT_
TIMEOUT and LOG_CHECKPOINT_INTERVAL parameters obsolete. From OEM,
you can specify this value in seconds. The valid range is 0 to 3600 seconds (or 0 to
60 minutes).

Media Recovery

The ARCHIVELOG mode/NOARCHIVELOG mode switch appears in the Media Recovery section of the Recovery Settings page. It's hard to find if no one has told you to look there—you might start looking in, say, the Archivelogs link from the Administration page of the database target. But here it is, halfway down the Recovery Settings page. It shows up here as a simple check box, but do not think that OEM has fired some magic bullet at the Oracle RDBMS: you still must reboot before this will take effect. In fact, OEM will submit a job to the OS to perform the change.

In addition to enabling ARCHIVELOG mode, you can specify your LOG_ARCHIVE_DEST parameters here. As you can see, the tenth slot is filled by default with USE_DB_RECOVERY_FILE_DEST, also referred to as the flash recovery area (FRA).

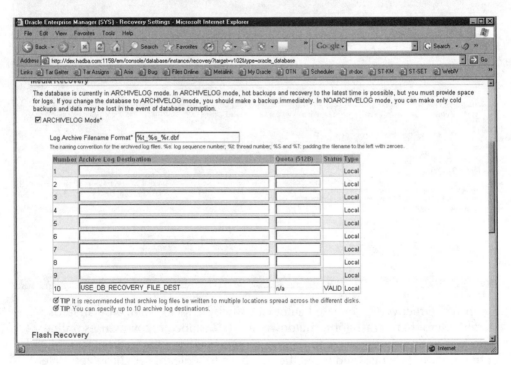

Flash Recovery

Under the heading Flash Recovery, you can configure your FRA, providing both an FRA destination and size. More useful, and unfortunately buried in a configuration page, is an excellent pie graph displaying current used space in the FRA, broken down by file type. This is an excellent quick view of the FRA that is hard to find anywhere else. Remember it is here; it can save you valuable time down the road.

Why Are My Archive Log and Flash Recovery Options Grayed Out?
If you arrived at the Recovery Settings page only to find the options to turn on ARCHIVELOG mode and modify the LOG_ARCHIVE_DEST locations grayed out in OEM (disallowing you from making changes to the mode or the flash recovery options), you have logged in as a user that does not have sysdba privileges. You must log out of Grid or Database Control, and log back in as user SYS with the role SYSDBA, to make changes on the Recovery Settings page.

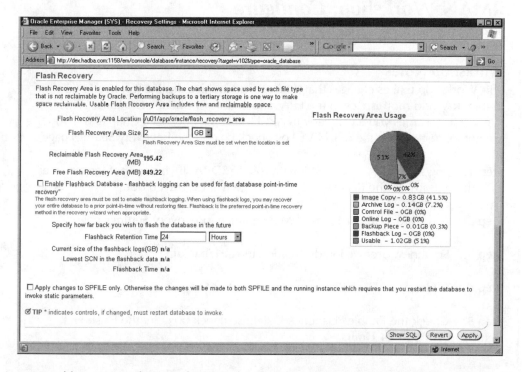

In addition to configuring the FRA, the Flash Recovery area is where you can turn on Flashback Database, a completely new functionality that can radically reduce point-in-time recovery by rewinding the database (literally). Flashback Database, and all of the different configuration requirements and resource needs thereof, are discussed in Chapter 13.

Like ARCHIVELOG mode, turning on Flashback Database requires a database reboot; we suggest that you do them both at the same time to save yourself a bit of hassle. Along with turning on Flashback Database, you can set your flashback retention time target, in hours.

Note, finally, the Apply Changes to SPFILE Only check box. Checking this option is the same as changing parameters like this:

```
alter database set db_recovery_file_dest='/u01/fra' scope=spfile;
```

Note, of course, that checking this box will not "save" the ARCHIVELOG mode and Flashback Database changes. Either you restart the database and change them, or you wait and restart the database and change them later.

RMAN Workshop: *Configure Recovery Settings in OEM*

Workshop Notes

This Workshop makes changes that set a second archive destination in addition to the FRA, add more space to the FRA, and enable Flashback Database. This Workshop assumes you are already in ARCHIVELOG mode (see Chapter 3 if you are not, or just choose the ARCHIVE Log check box on the Recovery Settings page).

Step 1. Log into OEM as user SYS with role SYSDBA. If you are not logged in as SYS, the options on the Recovery Settings page will be grayed out.

Step 2. Navigate to the Database | Maintenance | Recovery Settings page.

Step 3. Set a new archive log destination to **/u01/backup**.

Step 4. Change the Flash Recovery Area Size to **4GB**.

Step 5. Check the Enable Flashback Database check box. Set the Flashback Retention Time to **24 Hours**.

Flash Recovery

Flash Recovery Area is enabled for this database. The chart shows space used by each file type that is not reclaimable by Oracle. Performing backups to a tertiary storage is one way to make space reclaimable. Usable Flash Recovery Area includes free and reclaimable space.

Flash Recovery Area Location /u01/app/oracle/flash_recovery_area

Flash Recovery Area Size 4 GB

Flash Recovery Area Size must be set when the location is set

Reclaimable Flash Recovery Area (MB) **598.46**
Free Flash Recovery Area (MB) **45.29**

☑ Enable Flashback Database - flashback logging can be used for fast database point-in-time recovery*
The flash recovery area must be set to enable flashback logging. When using flashback logs, you may recover your entire database to a prior point-in-time without restoring files. Flashback is the preferred point-in-time recovery method in the recovery wizard when appropriate.

Specify how far back you wish to flash the database in the future
Flashback Retention Time 24 Hours

Current size of the flashback logs(GB) **n/a**
Lowest SCN in the flashback data **n/a**

Flash Recovery Area Usage

- Image Copy – 0.84GB (42.2%)
- Archive Log – 0.48GB (23.8%)
- Backup Piece – 0.05GB (2.5%)
- Control File – 0GB (0%)
- Online Log – 0GB (0%)
- Flashback Log – 0GB (0%)
- Usable – 643.75MB (31.4%)

Step 6.   Click the Apply button. This prompts you to restart the database. Click Yes. You then need to provide host and database credentials for the shutdown.

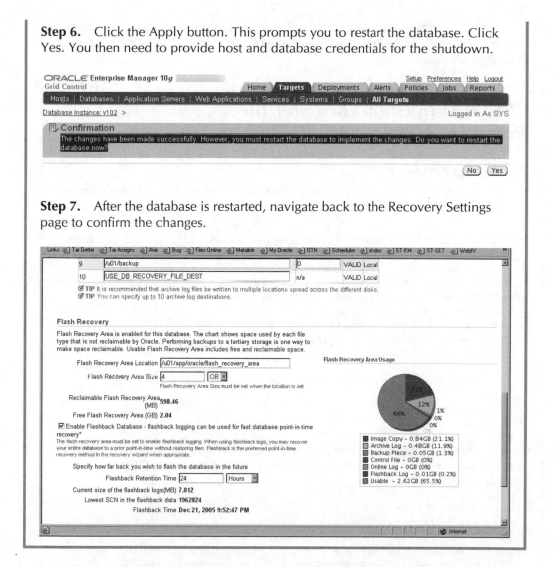

Step 7.   After the database is restarted, navigate back to the Recovery Settings page to confirm the changes.

Configuring Recovery Catalogs in OEM

Enterprise Manager cannot actually create a recovery catalog. You still need to manually create the user, grant the user the RECOVERY_CATALOG_OWNER role, and then connect RMAN to this user and issue the command **create catalog**. There is no wizard or anything for these steps in OEM.

Once the catalog is created, you can inform OEM that you wish to use the recovery catalog. Once you have registered the recovery catalog with OEM, you can register targets in the catalog. If you have registered more than one recovery catalog, you can specify that a particular one be put in use during different backup and recovery operations.

RMAN Workshop: *Register the Recovery Catalog with OEM*

Workshop Notes
This Workshop creates a catalog in the database emrep manually, and then registers it for use in OEM.

Step 1. Connect to the repository database as user sys and create the user for the catalog:

```
SQL> create tablespace reco_cat datafile
'/u01/app/oracle/oradata/emrep/reco_cat1.dbf' size 100m;
Tablespace created.
SQL> create user rman identified by rman
  2  default tablespace reco_cat
  3  temporary tablespace temp;
User created.
SQL> grant connect, resource, recovery_catalog_owner to rman;
Grant succeeded.
SQL> connect rman/rman
Connected.
```

Step 2. Make sure that you source to an Oracle database 10.2 ORACLE_HOME before this step so that the RMAN executable is 10.2. Otherwise, OEM will not be able to register your catalog!

```
$ echo $ORACLE_HOME
/u01/app/oracle/product/10.2.0
[oracle@dex oracle]$ rman catalog rman/rman@emrep
Recovery Manager: Release 10.2.0.1.0 - Production on Wed Dec 21
Copyright (c) 1982, 2005, Oracle.  All rights reserved.
connected to recovery catalog database
RMAN> create catalog;
recovery catalog created
```

Step 3. Now that the catalog is created, go to OEM | Database | Maintenance | Recovery Catalog Settings. Select Use Recovery Catalog, and then click the Add Recovery Catalog button. From Grid Control, you can choose an already discovered database or provide the host, the port, and the sid, and RMAN username and password. From Database Control, you cannot choose from a list, and must provide the host:port:sid combination. Click Next.

Cancel | Next

Add Recovery Catalog: Database

Select a database target for the recovery catalog or specify the host, port, and SID of a database with an existing recovery catalog along with the recovery catalog username and password. The recovery catalog should be stored in a dedicated database that is on a different disk than the target database. Protect the recovery catalog by backing it up.

⦿ Select a database target

Database Target | emrep.hadba.com (Database Instance) ▼

◯ Specify a database that is not an Enterprise Manager target

Host	
Port	
SID	
Recovery Catalog Username	
Recovery Catalog Password	

Cancel | Next

Step 4. The Add Recovery Catalog: Credentials page asks for host and database credentials for the server where the recovery catalog database is located. The database credentials on this page are for the SYS user, not the RMAN catalog user.

Add Recovery Catalog: Credentials

Specify the Host and Database credentials for the recovery catalog database.

Host Credentials

Specify the operating system username and password to log into the recovery catalog database machine.

* Username	oracle
* Password	••••••••

Database Credentials

Specify the credentials for the recovery catalog database.

* Username	sys
* Password	••••••
Database	emrep.hadba.com
* Connect As	SYSDBA ▼

Cancel | Step 1 of 3 | Next

Step 5. Provide the RMAN user and password. Click Next. Review the settings, and then click the Finish button. This will submit a non-cancelable job, as seen here.

⊕ **Processing: Register Database**

Registering Database

Attempting to register database

☑ **TIP** This operation cannot be canceled. It will continue even if the browser window is closed.

Step 6. This returns you to the Recovery Catalog Settings page. Now, your recovery catalog database will appear in the provided box. Click the Use Recovery Catalog check box, and then click OK.

Database Backups from Enterprise Manager

Now that you have configured your database for backups from the OEM interface, you can get to the nitty-gritty of actually taking a backup. From the OEM console, after you have selected your database and clicked the Maintenance tab, click the Schedule Backup link. On the Schedule Backup page, you are given two options: the Oracle-Suggested Backup or Schedule a Customized Backup. You also need to provide host credentials for the OS user on the server where the target database resides.

Oracle-Suggested Backup Strategy

Starting with Oracle Database 10*g*, Oracle has put together a full backup strategy that is "ready to wear" straight from the rack. This is available only via OEM (in both Grid Control and Database Control) and requires the existence of the FRA. The Oracle-suggested strategy checks the settings you've configured for your database and draws conclusions about whether you want a disk-only backup, a tape-only backup, or a combined disk and tape backup.

Disk-Only Oracle-Suggested Backup Strategy

The disk-only backup strategy is the most straightforward. It uses the "incremental apply to database copy" functionality to create a backup strategy that is self-cleaning. Here's an example of how it works. In this example, we start the Oracle-suggested strategy on a Monday evening at 10 P.M. The database is running in ARCHIVELOG mode, has automatic control file and SPFILE backups enabled, and uses the FRA.

- **Monday night**   A full image copy of every datafile is taken for the database. This backup is stored in the FRA.

- **Tuesday night**   A level 1 incremental backup set is created. All blocks that have changed since Monday night at 10 P.M. are backed up.

- **Wednesday night**   First, RMAN applies the Tuesday night incremental backup to the Monday night image copy, which make the full image copy backup a current copy of the database as it looked Tuesday night at 10 P.M. After that is complete, RMAN takes a new level 1 backup.

- **Thursday night**   RMAN applies the Wednesday night incremental backup to the image copy, which makes our database backup current as of Wednesday night at 10 P.M. Then, a new incremental level 1 backup is taken, with all changes since Wednesday night.

- **Friday night**   RMAN does the exact same thing it did on Thursday night. On Saturday, it does the same thing. Same with Sunday. This action repeats every day until you tell it to stop.

There are a few things to notice about this backup strategy. First, a full database backup is taken only once. After that, RMAN takes only level 1 backups. Then, nightly, the previous night's incremental backup is applied. Second, this strategy ensures that the database backup is at least 24 hours behind the current point in time. This allows for a point-in-time recovery to any point in the previous 24 hours, but nothing earlier than that. At most, the database backup is 48 hours behind the current time, so recovery is never that far behind.

There are limitations to this strategy, but that's one of the drawbacks to a "one-size-fits-all" approach to backups.

Tape-Only Oracle-Suggested Backup Strategy

The tape-only suggested strategy differs in many ways from the disk-only suggested strategy. First, no backup will ever be created in the FRA. Sure, archive logs will accumulate there, but all backups will go directly to the tape device. In addition, the tape-only strategy cannot take advantage of the incremental apply feature. Remember, an image copy backup cannot be taken to tape. All backups to tape will be of the backup set type.

When you schedule an Oracle-suggested tape-only backup, two RMAN scripts are generated: a daily backup and a weekly backup. First, the weekly script is run. This creates a full database backup, including all archive logs. Then, the daily script is run. The daily backup does an incremental backup of only changed blocks, along with all archive logs not already backed up. Then, once a week, the full database backup runs again.

During the tape-only backup wizard, if you have not specified a retention policy, OEM asks you to specify one. Then, as part of the daily backup, your retention policy is enforced on the tape channel.

After generating a tape-only suggested strategy, you will find that the scripts might look something like this:

```
Daily Script:
run {
allocate channel oem_sbt_backup1 type 'SBT_TAPE' format '%U' parms
'nb_ora_server=(horatio.hadba.com)';
allocate channel oem_sbt_backup2 type 'SBT_TAPE' format '%U' parms
'nb_ora_server=(horatio.hadba.com)';
backup incremental level 1 cumulative database;
backup archivelog all not backed up;
}
allocate channel for maintenance device type 'SBT_TAPE' parms
'nb_ora_server=(horatio.hadba.com)';
delete noprompt obsolete recovery window of 7 days device type 'SBT_TAPE';

Weekly Script:
run {allocate channel oem_sbt_backup1 type 'SBT_TAPE' format '%U' parms
'nb_ora_server=(horatio.hadba.com)';
```

```
allocate channel oem_sbt_backup2 type 'SBT_TAPE' format '%U' parms
'nb_ora_server=(horatio.hadba.com)';
backup incremental level 0 database;
backup archivelog all not backed up;
```

Combined Disk and Tape Oracle-Suggested Backup Strategy

When you combine disk backups with tape backups, the hybrid solution demands more input from you than either of the previous Oracle-suggested strategies. And, for the first time, you must make a decision.

First, consider the disk part of the strategy. Backups to disk are identical in the combined disk and tape strategy and the disk only strategy: a full image copy in the FRA, and then incremental backups each night that are then applied to the image copy.

As far as the tape part of the strategy, you must decide how much you want backed up to tape on a daily basis. On a weekly basis, the suggested strategy backs up all recovery-related files (with the **backup recovery files** command in RMAN). But, you must choose how much to back up daily: nothing, archive logs only, archive logs and incrementals, or archive logs and the full database copy.

If you decide to back up archive logs and incrementals to tape daily, this would be the resulting daily and weekly script that OEM builds:

```
Daily Script:
run {
allocate channel oem_disk_backup device type disk;
recover copy of database with tag 'ORA$OEM_LEVEL_0';
backup incremental level 1 cumulative
copies=1 for recover of copy with tag
'ORA$OEM_LEVEL_0' database;
release channel oem_disk_backup;
allocate channel oem_sbt_backup1 type 'SBT_TAPE' format '%U' parms
 'nb_ora_server=(horatio.hadba.com)';
backup archivelog all not backed up;
backup backupset all not backed up since time 'SYSDATE-1';
}
allocate channel for maintenance device type 'SBT_TAPE' parms
 'nb_ora_server=(horatio.hadba.com)';
delete noprompt obsolete recovery window of 7 days device type
'SBT_TAPE';

Weekly Script:
run {
allocate channel oem_disk_backup device type disk;
recover copy of database with tag 'ORA$OEM_LEVEL_0';
backup incremental level 1 cumulative  copies=1 for recover of copy with tag
 'ORA$OEM_LEVEL_0' database;
release channel oem_disk_backup;
allocate channel oem_sbt_backup1 type 'SBT_TAPE' format '%U' parms
'nb_ora_server=(horatio.hadba.com)';
backup recovery area;
}
```

```
allocate channel for maintenance device type 'SBT_TAPE' parms
'nb_ora_server=(horatio.hadba.com)';
delete noprompt obsolete recovery window of 7 days device type 'SBT_TAPE';
```

Final Note on Oracle-Suggested Strategies

Taking a default backup strategy "off the shelf" has its benefits and its drawbacks. The benefits come from being able to "set and forget" the backups—they will run forever and clean themselves up. There is some assurance in having this option, particularly for low-priority development databases that typically are operated by someone other than you. If they come to you in a panic, you can always use these backups to fix the problem and save everyone a lot of headaches.

But there is (almost) no customization, and sometimes the default strategy will not match your SLA. The most glaring example of this is in the ability to do point-in-time recoveries to some point in the past (a limitation of the disk-based strategy only). Remember, these strategies are merely Oracle suggestions. You don't have to use them, and if they are giving you any heartburn, there is a simple answer: drop the suggested strategy and build your own.

Scheduling a Customized Backup

From the same Maintenance page where you can choose to schedule an Oracle-suggested backup strategy, you can also choose to build your own customized backup job. This is a wizard-driven process that steps you through the different choices to be made about the backup. When the wizard is finished, you can run the backup as a one-time backup immediately, schedule it for later, or set it up to repeat continually every so often.

It is important that you take the time to develop a full backup strategy ahead of time, but OEM will provide some guidance about how to develop that strategy. These tips appear as small-font hints under some of the choices you will be asked to make in the backup scheduling wizard.

The backup scheduling wizard is divided into four steps:

1. Choose backup options (what do you want to back up?).

2. Choose backup settings (how do you want to back up?).

3. Schedule the backup (when do you want to back up?).

4. Perform a final review (is everything to your liking?).

On the final review page, you will be presented with the RMAN script that the wizard has created, as shown in the following example. At this stage, you can either submit the job for execution or edit the RMAN script from there. This allows you to make any minor tweaks in the script that are to your liking. Note that if you decide to modify the script manually, OEM warns you that you will not be able to go back and make any changes in the backup wizard pages. After you make any of your own changes, you can either cancel them or submit the job.

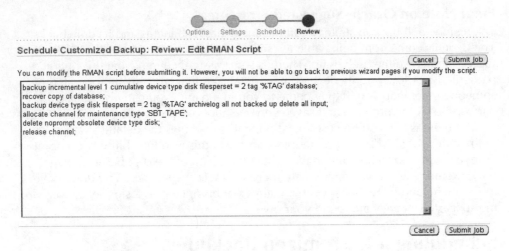

What gives? Well, OEM has this little quirk. If you have, at any point, gone into the Configure Backup Settings page and set the number of tape drives to some value, then OEM has gone to your target database and configured a tape channel in the permanent configuration parameters. Thus, it assumes that any maintenance operation should always check tape and disk. From within OEM, there is no way to change this. You have to go to the RMAN command line and enter the following:

```
configure channel device type 'sbt_tape' clear;
```

Why Does OEM Always Try to Allocate a Tape Channel for Maintenance?

You may notice that when you review your RMAN script after using the OEM wizard to schedule a backup, OEM has the following lines:

```
allocate channel for maintenance type 'SBT_TAPE';
delete noprompt obsolete device type disk;
```

RMAN Script Job vs. Scheduled Backup Wizard

There is another way to use OEM to schedule and run RMAN backups of a target database. If you go to the Jobs tab in Grid Control (or the Jobs link under Related Links in Database Control) and look at the drop-down list of possible job types to create, you will see RMAN Script. This is a specific type of job specification that allows you to use OEM to execute an RMAN script that already exists at the target server.

So what is different from an RMAN script job and a host command job? If you choose an RMAN script job, OEM uses its built-in mechanisms to ensure that the environment is properly configured for your target database before running the script. This is a very nice feature, which you know if you have ever run into the dreaded "compatibility matrix" of RMAN executables versus target databases.

RMAN Workshop: *Create an RMAN Script Job in OEM*

Workshop Notes

This Workshop uses OEM to schedule an RMAN backup. However, the backup will be specified by an RMAN script that already exists as a file on the Linux machine where database v102 exists. In this example, this script already exists in /home/oracle/scripts, named rmanback.rcv, and contains the following code:

```
backup incremental level 1 cumulative device type disk
 filesperset = 2 database;
backup device type disk filesperset = 2 archivelog all not backed up
 delete all input;
delete noprompt obsolete device type disk;
```

Step 1. Go to the Jobs page of OEM. In Grid Control, there is a Jobs tab along the upper-right side. In Database Control, go to the bottom under Related Links to find the Jobs link.

Step 2. Create a new job of type **RMAN Script**. This will take you to a page with multiple tabs.

Step 3. On the General tab, give the job the name **RMAN_BACK_INC_1_ARCH_ DELETE_OBS**, as shown next. On this tab, you also need to add the targets (for Grid Control). Click the Add button and select your desired database.

Create 'RMAN Script' Library Job

(Cancel) (Save to Library)

| General | Parameters | Credentials | Schedule | Access |

* Name RMAN_BACK_INCR_1_ARCH_DELETE_OBS

Description incremental backup plus archivelogs, delete obsolete backup

Target Type **Database Instance**

Targets

Add individual targets or one composite target, such as a Group.

(Remove) (Add)

Select All | Select None

Select	Name △	Type	Host	Time Zone
☐	v102	Database Instance	dex.hadba.com	Central Standard Time

| General | Parameters | Credentials | Schedule | Access |

(Cancel) (Save to Library)

Home | Targets | Deployments | Alerts | Policies | **Jobs** | Reports | Setup | Preferences | Help | Logout

Step 4. Click the Parameters tab. In the box, provide the full path and name to the backup script you created on the target server.

Create 'RMAN Script' Library Job

(Cancel) (Save to Library)

| General | Parameters | Credentials | Schedule | Access |

* RMAN Script @/home/oracle/scripts/rmanback.rcv

Enter RMAN commands or a fully qualified script name on the remote hosts, for example, "@script.rcv"

| General | Parameters | Credentials | Schedule | Access |

(Cancel) (Save to Library)

Home | Targets | Deployments | Alerts | Policies | **Jobs** | Reports | Setup | Preferences | Help | Logout

Step 5. On the Credentials tab, ensure that you have provided SYSDBA Database Credentials, as this is required by RMAN.

Create 'RMAN Script' Library Job

(Cancel) (Save to Library)

| General | Parameters | Credentials | Schedule | Access |

If you choose Preferred Credentials, the job will use your preferred credentials for each target at the time job runs, and therefore requires credentials for all targets to be set. If you choose to override the preferred credentials, one set of credentials will be used for all targets of each type.

Type ⦿ Use Preferred Credentials ○ Override Preferred Credentials

- Database Host Credentials
- Database Credentials [SYSDBA Database Credentials ▾]

| General | Parameters | Credentials | Schedule | Access |

(Cancel) (Save to Library)

Home | Targets | Deployments | Alerts | Policies | **Jobs** | Reports | Setup | Preferences | Help | Logout

Step 6. On the Schedule tab, set a schedule for the job. Your choice is One Time (Immediately), One Time (Later), or Repeating.

Type   ○ One Time (Immediately)   ○ One Time (Later)   ⊙ Repeating

Frequency Type   [Weekly ▾]

Days of Week   ☑ Monday ☐ Tuesday ☐ Wednesday ☐ Thursday ☐ Friday ☐ Saturday ☐ Sunday

Time Zone   [Each target's timezone ▾]

Start Date   [Dec 24, 2005] 🗓

Start Time   [8] : [45]   ⊙ AM ○ PM

Grace Period   ⊙ Indefinite
            ○ End After [   ] Hours [   ] Minutes

Repeat Until   ⊙ Indefinite
            ○ Specified Date
              Date [   ] 🗓
                  (example: Dec 24, 2005)

              Time [   ] : [   ]   ⊙ AM ○ PM

General   Parameters   Credentials   **Schedule**   Access

(Cancel) (Save to Library)

Home | Targets | Deployments | Alerts | Policies | **Jobs** | Reports | Setup | Preferences | Help | Logout

Step 7. Click the Submit button at the top of the page (not shown in the preceding illustration) to send the job to the active jobs page. You can, alternatively, save the job to the library, or submit the job now and save it to the library.

Performing Recovery in Enterprise Manager

After all the backing up that can be done from OEM, it should come as no surprise that you can also perform recovery from OEM. That being said, there are not many situations where we've seen OEM's recovery options being used—even when OEM is used for backups. The decision to use OEM for recovery boils down to one's ability to mitigate the overwhelming sensation typically felt when you realize your database is hosed: panic.

OEM does not help you manage your panic very well. You'd think that a GUI would be the best defense against panic—easy to use, quickly implemented, and all that. But this is actually quite the opposite of all DBA's reactions we've seen in a recovery situation. During the most solemn and distressing recovery situations we've been a part of, the one overwhelming DBA desire that we've noticed is not ease of use, built-in intelligence, or anything like that. What every DBA wants at that time is control. They want complete, total control over everything that they can possibly get control over. Database recovery is no time to be hitting the big red button and hoping for the best.

The Recovery Wizard in OEM is primarily useful in all those databases you deployed in development for people who assured you that they would take care of it themselves. In other words, OEM Recovery is for databases that have Oracle-suggested backup strategies.

This is not to disparage the hard work that went into the OEM Recovery tools. There is a place for such things. But, facing a possible recovery situation with their production database, not many a DBA will turn to their boss and say, with a straight face, "You know what we need right now? A GUI wizard."

Here is the exception: If you have made yourself aware of how OEM Recovery works, you have noticed that it has the capabilities to lead you to the Oracle Flashback Technology, outlined in Chapter 13. Flashback Technology provides a whole new arsenal against downtime, particularly when it comes to user-induced trauma. So, if it is control you seek, it must be stated that you are not in complete control of your recovery situation until you have explored your Flashback Technology options.

What follows is a brief introduction to the recovery options as they appear within OEM. What you do with them will depend on your business requirements and the time you have to invest in testing.

Whole Database Recovery

When the database is still open, you can get to the recovery system within OEM from the same Maintenance tab that you use to configure backup/recovery settings or schedule backups. Clicking Perform Recovery opens a page that provides you with two options: the first is to perform whole database recovery. Under the Whole Database Recovery heading, you have several options: Recover to the Current Time or Previous Point-in-Time; Restore All Datafiles; and Recover from Previously Restored Datafiles. These options are described next, followed by a discussion of the second option on the Perform Recovery page, Object Level Recovery.

Recover to Current Time or Previous Point in Time

The first option is the one that will do what you expect: restore datafiles and recover them using archive logs. The only variable that you decide is the time at which you want the database to be opened. In fact, if you walk through this wizard, you will find that the generated RMAN script is as follows (click the Edit RMAN Script button to see the output):

```
run {
restore database;
recover database;
}
```

Not exactly rocket science.

The other option is to perform point-in-time-recovery (PITR).You can specify the point in time that you want to recover to as, well, a point in time, but also as a log sequence number, an SCN, or a restore point. Note that when you do a PITR and you have Flashback Database turned on, you see a blue-font TIP telling you to consider Flashback Database. There will be a next screen to choose this. When you specify your time (or SCN or log), OEM evaluates whether this point falls within the timeframe that is available for Flashback Database, and offers you the choice: Flashback or Traditional PITR? Choosing Flashback takes you to the Flashback Wizard; choosing Traditional PITR carries you through the present wizard. For more on Flashback Database, see Chapter 13.

Whenever you do any kind of file restore in OEM, you are always allowed to change the location of the restored files to a new location. From the OEM wizard, for a full database recovery, the options are limited to a single new location for all datafiles. You cannot pick and choose different file locations for individual files. However, when you get to the end of the wizard, you can always choose to Edit RMAN Script and make filename changes there.

Restore All Datafiles

From the main Perform Recovery page, the second option is Restore All Datafiles. Choosing this option initiates a datafile restore that does not also perform a recovery. As you may have guessed, following this through to the end of the wizard, and selecting Edit RMAN Script, shows the following:

```
run {
restore database;
}
```

If you choose to rename the datafiles upon restore, you are asked for the single location for all files and are given a check box option to Update the Control File to Use the Renamed Files. Selecting this check box will modify your current control file to point to the datafiles at the new location. This is the same as executing the RMAN command **switch datafile all**. Only do this if you are actually restoring the database, and not just making another set of datafiles in a second location. You can check your script at the end if you want to modify individual filenames.

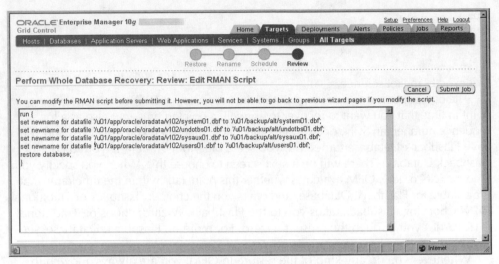

If you choose to restore datafiles to a new location without recovery, OEM still shuts down the target database and then puts it into mount mode. This actually is not required by RMAN, but OEM's intelligence only goes so far, and it sees a database restore as the first step to recovery. Anyway, OEM leaves the database mounted after the file restore. You have to go to the database home page and click Startup to start the database.

A final note about the option Restore All Datafiles. OEM has buried the **backup validate** command at the bottom of the first page of this wizard, under the heading Backup Validation. If you want to simply validate whether a certain type of restore is possible (current point in time or previous point in time), select this option and then follow the wizard as you otherwise would. Note, then, that if you select Edit RMAN Script, it has a slight difference:

```
run {
restore database validate;
}
```

Recovery from Previously Restored Datafiles

Finally, you can choose to recover the database from previously restored datafiles. This simply means that if you choose this option, only a **recover** command will be issued in RMAN. This does *not* mean that if you choose to restore datafiles to a different location, you can then specify those files in this wizard. This is a recovery only. It relies completely on the control file's V$DATAFILE list to determine which files to restore.

There is a check box at the bottom that lets OEM open the database in read-only mode after the recovery so that you can validate the database. This option allows you to confirm that the point in time you specified was correct.

RMAN Workshop: *Perform Database Recovery from OEM*

Workshop Notes
In this Workshop, we perform a PITR to a point in the past, using the backups taken previously in this chapter with OEM. This Workshop uses Grid Control to perform the recovery, which allows us to monitor the recovery job while it is in progress. Recovery from Database Control is slightly different from what is detailed here.

Step 1. Go to the Database | Maintenance | Perform Recovery page. Choose Recover to the Current Time or a Previous Point-in-Time, and then click the Perform Whole Database Recovery button.

Step 2. Select the Recover to a Prior Point-in-Time option. We choose to set this with a date in this example. Click Next.

Point-in-time

You may recover the entire database to the current time or a prior point-in-time.

○ Recover to the current time

◉ Recover to a prior point-in-time

☑ **TIP** Flashback logging has been enabled in this database. Consider using flashback by time or SCN to achieve faster database point-in-time recovery. If you choose to do a recovery by sequence, or if the time to which you want to recover falls out of the range of the flashback logs, Recovery Manager will be used to perform a traditional point-in-time recovery.

Oldest Flashback Time **Dec 23, 2005 12:00:15 AM**
Oldest Flashback SCN **2056840**

◉ Date `Dec 24, 2005` 📅   Time `09` `00` ◉ AM ○ PM
(example: Dec 24, 2005)

○ Restore Point `_____` 🔦

○ SCN `0`

○ Sequence `0`

☐ Open the database in read-only mode to validate data after this point-in-time recovery
If not selected, the database will be opened in read/write mode and the online redo logs will be cleared.

Return to Perform Recovery   (Cancel) Step 1 of 5 (Next)

Home | **Targets** | Deployments | Alerts | Policies | Jobs | Reports | Setup | Preferences | Help | Logout

Step 3. If you have turned on Flashback Database and your point in time falls within the Flashback window, you get a screen asking if you would like to use Flashback Database. Choose No, Use Traditional Point-in-Time Recovery. Click Next.

Step 4. Choose to restore the files to the default location. Click Next. This takes you to the Schedule page, but all recovery jobs run immediately. Click Next.

Step 5. Click the Edit RMAN Script button to look at what RMAN will be running. Click Cancel after your review. Then click Submit Job.

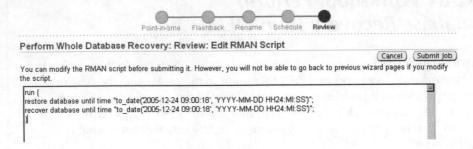

Perform Whole Database Recovery: Review: Edit RMAN Script

Cancel   Submit Job

You can modify the RMAN script before submitting it. However, you will not be able to go back to previous wizard pages if you modify the script.

```
run {
restore database until time "to_date('2005-12-24 09:00:18', 'YYYY-MM-DD HH24:MI:SS')";
recover database until time "to_date('2005-12-24 09:00:18', 'YYYY-MM-DD HH24:MI:SS')";
}
```

Step 6. OEM presents a screen saying, "The job has been successfully submitted." Click the View Job button. The job page shows the history of each job step, known as an *execution*. You can refresh your browser to get up-to-date step and elapsed time values.

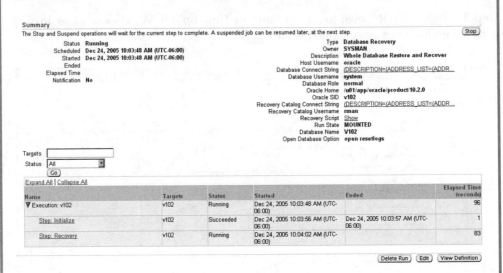

Step 7. Click the Step: Recovery link in the Name column. This allows you to monitor the progress of the RMAN job.

Object Level Recovery

The name "object level recovery" is a bit misleading. On the Perform Recovery page (accessed by clicking the Perform Recovery link on the Maintenance tab), the Object Level Recovery section is ostensibly the place to begin doing any kind of recovery that is some smaller subset of the database. The misleading bit concerns what is meant by "object." The answer: anything that is not the whole database. Tablespaces, datafiles, tables—for anything below the entire database in granularity, you perform recovery from this section.

This means that "object level recovery" refers to both logical objects and physical objects. Some logical objects, such as tablespaces, still require a physical media restore/recovery operation. Selecting other logical objects, such as tables, actually takes you into the Oracle Flashback Technology world, which is completely different from media recovery. Physical objects are straightforward: want to recover a single datafile? That would be a restore and recover. You also can perform block media recovery from the Object Level Recovery area.

Note that when you make a selection from the Object Type drop-down list, the web page refreshes and different suboptions are made available to inform you of your specific suboptions. Handy!

Oracle has done a good job of providing for a complete set of recovery options within OEM, so it would be impossible in this single chapter to review the wizard steps that you walk through based on each type of object level recovery. This chapter would be as long as the rest of this book. We encourage you to go through each of the different types of OEM recovery, to familiarize yourself with the language Oracle uses within OEM for each type of recovery. Often, this language is not the same as that used within RMAN itself.

Backup Management and Reporting

It is perhaps in the area of managing your backups that OEM really proves its worth. Running backups and recoveries from the command line is one thing; reading the output of report and list commands from a terminal is something else completely. From OEM, managing exiting backups is considerably more friendly. The management is divided into three types: managing current backups, managing restore points, and creating backup reports.

Managing Current Backups

On the database Maintenance tab, click the Manage Current Backups link to access the page where you can perform common management activities: run crosschecks, delete obsolete backups, delete expired backups, and so forth.

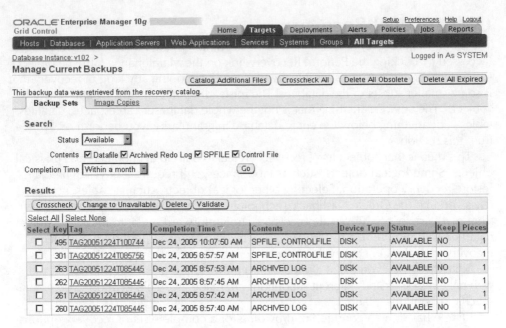

Across the top of the Manage Current Backups page, you will see some quick
link buttons for common tasks: Catalog Additional Files, Crosscheck All, Delete All
Obsolete, and Delete All Expired. These buttons do exactly what they say they do,
and you can read about these options in Chapter 14.

The two tabs below these buttons, Backup Sets and Image Copies, enable you to
manage backups in subsets or individually. The Search area allows you to find a
backup based on certain search vectors. The default is to list all backups. In the Results
area, you can select one or more backups by clicking the corresponding check box,
and then select one of the management options: Crosscheck, Change to Unavailable,
Delete, or Validate.

When you choose one of these options, the Job Creation Wizard helps you to
schedule the maintenance job. This allows you to schedule a particular job, such as
a crosscheck, to occur at a regular interval. You can also click Show RMAN Script
to see what RMAN is doing.

Managing Restore Points

Click Manage Restore Points on the Maintenance tab to open the page on which
you can create new restore points, view existing restore point information, or delete
existing restore points. From OEM, you can look at the restore point creation time,
the amount of storage required, and the creation SCN. If you notice that Guaranteed

Restore Point is grayed out (not shown in the following illustration), this is because you are logged into the target database with NORMAL privileges, and SYSDBA privileges are required for creation of guaranteed restore points. In addition, the Recover Whole Database To button is functional only if you are logged in as SYSDBA user. Clicking this button asks you for confirmation, and then takes you to the Perform Whole Database Recovery page.

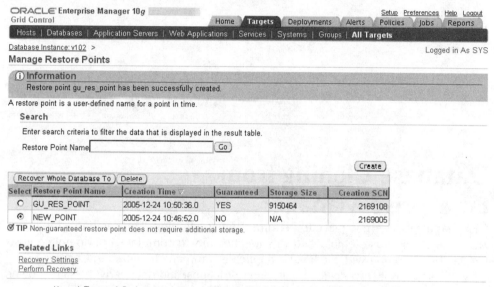

Creating Backup Reports

Clicking the Backup Reports link on the Maintenance tab takes you to the Backup Reports page, which shows all backup jobs known to the database. These are not just those backups taken by an OEM job—OEM is actually querying the recovery catalog (or control file) to find all backups. The Backup Report page enables you to search based on status, start time, and type.

You can click the name of the backup to retrieve specific details about that particular backup, as shown next. This includes a nice summary of the input (what was backed up) and the output (the backup pieces that were created). Then, there is a detailed listing of each input file, its checkpoint information, compression ratio, and so forth. There is enough data here to put anyone to sleep. But, this is valuable stuff, and it's far easier to read and comprehend than the report and list options from the RMAN command line.

Results

Input Summary

Datafile

Files Backed Up	4
Distinct Files	4
Distinct Tablespaces	4
Total Size	968.78M
Oldest Checkpoint Time	Dec 24, 2005 8:52:56 AM
Newest Checkpoint Time	Dec 24, 2005 8:52:56 AM

Archived Log

Files Backed Up	28
Distinct Files	19
Total Size	2.41G
Recovery Range	Dec 10, 2005 8:00:10 PM - Dec 24, 2005 8:54:41 AM

Control File

Files Backed Up	2
Distinct Files	1
Total Size	13.47M
Oldest Checkpoint Time	Dec 24, 2005 8:54:31 AM
Newest Checkpoint Time	Dec 24, 2005 8:57:56 AM

SPFILE

Files Backed Up	2
Distinct Files	1
Total Size	0.00K
Oldest Modification Time	Dec 24, 2005 8:19:03 AM
Newest Modification Time	Dec 24, 2005 8:19:03 AM

Output Summary

Backup Set

Total Backup Sets	22
Total Size	2.00G
Oldest Backup	Dec 24, 2005 8:52:55 AM
Newest Backup	Dec 24, 2005 8:57:56 AM
Compression Ratio	1.688

Inputs

Datafiles

Datafile Number	Output Type	Output Key	File Size	Tablespace	Checkpoint Time	Incremental Level	Compression Ratio	Corrupted Blocks	File Creation Time	File Checkpoint SCN	Resetlogs SCN
1	BACKUPSET	14	500.01M	SYSTEM	Dec 24, 2005 8:52:56 AM CST	1	3.912	0	Jun 30, 2005 7:10:11 PM CDT	2165155	446075
2	BACKUPSET	15	120.01M	UNDOTBS1	Dec 24, 2005 8:52:56 AM CST	1	1.035	0	Jun 30, 2005 7:55:01 PM CDT	2165156	446075

Database Cloning from Enterprise Manager

OEM has a subsystem in place to perform database cloning. The database cloning process that OEM uses employs RMAN functionality to complete, but do not confuse the database cloning with the RMAN **duplicate** command (covered in Chapter 17). OEM cloning has its own logic and its own restrictions, and not nearly the same power, flexibility, or usefulness as RMAN's duplication. That said, cloning from OEM is easy.

OEM may use RMAN behind the curtain, but the database cloning functionality is logically organized in a completely different area of the vast OEM landscape. You need to go to the Deployments tab of Grid Control or the Related Links in Database Control. First of all, cloning to a different server than the target database is only possible in Grid Control. Database Control can only clone to the same server as the target.

On the Deployments page of Grid Control, scroll down and click the link Clone Database. This opens the Cloning Wizard, which gives you multiple choices. First, choose the source database type: a currently running database or an existing working directory. In OEM 10*g* cloning, "working directory" has a specific meaning: it is the location on your source database host where OEM will create the RMAN backup of the source database. The backups can be deleted after they are used for the one clone operation, or they can be saved in the working directory for future OEM clone operations.

Which brings up an important point about OEM cloning: it might use RMAN to do the backups, but *OEM cloning cannot use existing RMAN backups you have taken, even if you took them using OEM.* The cloning system has to take its own backup, in a specific format. So, don't think that cloning will go look at your RMAN catalog and figure out that a backup already exists and use it. It will take its own backup. This means that if you want to be able to use OEM to clone to some point in the past, you will only be able to clone the database back to some previous point where you have already cloned.

OEM cloning has other limitations that don't exist for RMAN duplication: you cannot use it to clone to specific points in time in the past. You also cannot do any type of subsetting of tablespaces. OEM cloning means cloning the entire database or cloning nothing.

After you've chosen to use a running database for this clone and have chosen from the existing list of available databases, the wizard next asks you to choose an existing directory on your source database host for the new working directory. This is where the RMAN backups will be placed temporarily before becoming datafiles at the destination. After specifying the location, you must decide whether you want the working directory to be deleted automatically when the cloning is done or kept for future clones.

And, oh yeah, time to specify host credentials. Just get used to this in OEM.

After ironing out the source database information, next you need to sort out how things will look at the destination: specify a new database global_name, a new instance name, and the storage type of the clone database. This storage type lets you choose if you will lay this database down on a cooked file system, ASM, or raw. After this, provide the destination host credentials. Below this, you will select which destination ORACLE_HOME will be the software used to operate the new clone. OEM has intelligence to provide only a list of those ORACLE_HOMEs it has discovered that match the Oracle version and operating system of the source database.

On the next wizard page, set your new clone database file locations. There are two options: use Oracle Flexible Architecture (OFA) or Oracle Managed Files (OMF). If you choose OFA, you can click the Customize button on the right side to exactly locate for each and every datafile where you would like it to live. After specifying database files, tell OEM where the network files (listener.ora and tnsnames.ora) are located for this database, so it can configure them for your new database. Finally, tell OEM if you want the new clone database to be a monitored OEM target and, if so, provide a dbsnmp password.

Next, schedule the clone to run immediately or at some time in the future. Then, you get a nice review page that provides in clear English what is about to happen. This includes an expandable/contractible tree with all the destination file locations. If everything looks okay, you can submit the job. Things whir and spin in the background, and you should be told the job has been submitted. Then, you can go to the job page itself and watch each execution step. Hint: To keep tabs on each execution step of the clone job, use your browser's Refresh button to refresh the clone job page.

Here are some highlights of the cloning process. First, notice that OEM backs up one datafile at a time on the source database and then restores that datafile to the destination. This takes longer than doing it all at once but enables OEM to break up the job into smaller substeps for better modularity. It also means that the working directory on the source database host will not require enough space to house a complete copy of the source database—because we back up only one file at a time.

If you click the Backup Datafile step and look at the log, you will see that OEM is logging into SQL*Plus, and the output shows the following: pl/sql procedure executed. If this is an RMAN backup, what gives? How can you run a backup from SQL*Plus? The answer is that OEM is skipping the whole RMAN client utility and going straight to the package SYS.DBMS_BACKUP_RESTORE on the source database to back up the files.

After the cloning is all finished, you will have a clone database on your destination server, open and available, and OEM will have discovered it, meaning that you can now manage it from within OEM.

Summary

In this chapter, we discussed the architecture and configuration of Oracle Enterprise Manager 10g Grid Control and Oracle Enterprise Manager 10g Database Control. We provided examples of configuring these utilities to take RMAN backups and configuring a database for recovery in OEM. We discussed the Oracle-suggested backup strategy, and showed how to schedule a customized backup. We touched on how to perform recovery. Finally, we showed how OEM can be used to clone a database using RMAN as the underlying technology.

CHAPTER
12

RMAN Advanced
Recovery Topics

This chapter introduces you to some advanced recovery topics. We start with a topic that tends to cause the most trouble and confusion when it comes to recovery topics, incomplete recoveries. Then, we look at some miscellaneous recovery topics. We will then look at tablespace point-in-time recovery, followed by a look at how you can verify your backups. Finally, we will look at the DBMS_BACKUP_RESTORE package that is associated with RMAN.

Incomplete Recoveries

An incomplete recovery is just what it sounds like—a recovery of the database that is incomplete. It is similar to a complete recovery in many respects; the basic command set is the same, but with a few added wrinkles. The possible causes of an incomplete recovery are numerous, such as the loss of online or archived redo logs or a major user error that has seriously compromised the database. Incomplete recoveries impact the entire database; in other words, you cannot perform an incomplete recovery on just one part of the database because it would result in that part of the database having a different system change number (SCN, or point in time if you prefer) than the remainder of the database.

The point about incomplete recovery impacting the entire database is an important point to make, and many junior DBAs fail to recognize this point. Oracle demands that a database be consistent at startup, and if it is not consistent, Oracle will complain bitterly. To illustrate the point, consider an example in which a user who has his own tablespace has just mistakenly truncated a table in that tablespace, for which he has no backup. He calls a junior DBA in a panic and asks her to recover just that tablespace to the point in time before he issued the truncate operation.

At first thought, the junior DBA might think that she can just restore the datafiles of the offending tablespace and recover them to a time before the truncate operation was executed. Seems somewhat logical, doesn't it? (In fact, that's what a logical backup is for.) So, the junior DBA restores the datafiles and recovers the tablespace to a point in time before the truncate operation. Now she's feeling pretty good about herself. Unfortunately, her euphoria is short lived because when she tries to open the database, RMAN slaps her with this message:

```
ERROR at line 1:
ORA-01113: file 3 needs media recovery
ORA-01110: data file 3: 'D:\ORACLE\ORADATA\RECOVER\INDX01.DBF'
```

Oracle is basically saying (in this case), "You recovered the datafile all right, but you didn't do enough recovery on it, and it's not consistent with the rest of the database!" So, as you can see, incomplete recovery is not the solution to all of your woes, but it can be the solution to some of them. If you need a form of inconsistent recovery (a fancy way of saying you need to restore some database data to a point in time different from the rest of the database), then look at tablespace point-in-time recovery, discussed later in this chapter, or Oracle's Flashback Technology, discussed in Chapter 13.

However, if you want to restore the entire database to some point in time in the past that Flashback Database can't touch, then incomplete recovery is the way you need to go. When you perform a database incomplete recovery, you need to use the **resetlogs** command because it is common to just about every incomplete recovery situation there is. We discuss **resetlogs** next, and then we discuss actual incomplete recovery methods, including time-, SCN-, log sequence–, and cancel-based recoveries.

Using the resetlogs Command

During incomplete recoveries, you pretty much always need to use the **resetlogs** command when opening the database because you are deviating from an already established stream of redo that exists, and you need to indicate this to Oracle. The **resetlogs** command really represents the end of one logical life of your database and the beginning of the next logical life of your database. This logical lifespan of a database is known as an *incarnation*. Each time you use **resetlogs**, you are creating a new incarnation of the database. This can be critical with regard to recovery, as we will discuss later in this section.

With each use of the **resetlogs** command, the SCN counter is not reset. However, Oracle does reset other counters, such as the log sequence number, and resets (and re-creates if required) the contents of the online redo logs.

NOTE
There was a bug in earlier versions of Oracle Database 10g that would cause RMAN to be unable to back up archive logs of a previous incarnation of the database after resetlogs occurred. This could cause a gap in your archived redo logs. Make sure, after a resetlogs command occurs, that all the archived redo logs of the previous incarnation are successfully backed up.

Oracle Database 10g has made recovery through the **resetlogs** command much easier. A new substitution string has been added for the archived redo log names (**%r**), which represents the *resetlog ID number*. When **%r** is included in the **log_archive_dest_format** parameter string, the archived redo log names will remain unique through each **resetlogs** command. This, and other internal Oracle database changes, allows Oracle to easily recover a database through a given **resetlogs** operation. Therefore, the requirement to back up the database immediately after a **resetlogs** operation is relaxed. However, we still think that backing up your database after any incomplete recovery is probably a good idea.

NOTE
In previous versions of RMAN, you needed to re-create any temporary tablespace temp files. This is not required in Oracle Database 10g. RMAN creates these datafiles for you during the recover database process, even during incomplete recoveries!

Establishing a Point to Recover To

One of the things you need to do when performing incomplete recovery with RMAN is to establish a recovery target. The recovery target is the point at which you wish to terminate the recovery process and can be identified based on a point in time, a specific SCN, or a log sequence number. The recovery target can be established in a number of different ways. First, you can use the **set** command along with the **until time**, **until SCN**, or **until sequence** parameter within a **run** block, as shown in this example, which uses the **set until time** command to establish the recovery target as 3 P.M. on July 1, 2006:

```
run
{
set until time "to_date('07/01/06 15:00:00','mm/dd/yy hh24:mi:ss')";
restore database;
recover database
alter database open resetlogs;
}
```

When this command is issued, RMAN looks for the backup set closest to, but not including or after, this period of time and restores the database from that backup set. If the database is in NOARCHIVELOG mode, then recovery will stop at that point; otherwise, during the execution of the **recover** command, Oracle will apply the archived redo logs (and any incremental backups that need to be applied) up to, but not including, the defined recovery target.

NOTE
*If you are trying to recover to the point of completion of a specific backup, you must recover to the CKP SCN or CKP TIME of the files in the backup set as listed in the RMAN **list** command for the different backup sets (for example, **list backupset**). Using the CKP TIME of the backup is not sufficient and can lead to ORA-1152 errors.*

You can also opt to use the **until time**, **until SCN**, or **until sequence** commands directly in the **restore** and **recover** commands, which eliminates the need for the

run block entirely (which we prefer). Here is an example of the use of the **until time** command when restoring and recovering a database:

```
-- We assume that your control file is intact
startup mount;
restore database UNTIL TIME
"TO_DATE('06/28/06 13:00:00','MM/DD/YY HH24:MI:SS')";
recover database UNTIL TIME
"TO_DATE('06/28/06 13:00:00','MM/DD/YY HH24:MI:SS')";
alter database open resetlogs;
```

Time-Based Recovery

In the previous section, we provided some examples of time-based recovery. This type of recovery allows you to recover the database as it looked consistently at a specific time. Of course, if you don't have backups or archived redo logs available to restore the database to the time you are requesting, then Oracle will generate an error somewhat like this one:

```
RMAN-00571: ===========================================================
RMAN-00569: =============== ERROR MESSAGE STACK FOLLOWS ===============
RMAN-00571: ===========================================================
RMAN-03002: failure of restore command at 07/02/2006 21:33:02
RMAN-20207: UNTIL TIME or RECOVERY WINDOW is before RESETLOGS time
```

The bottom line is that you need to make sure you have a backup of your database that was taken before the time you wish to recover to. You also need all of your archived redo logs. In Chapter 15, we discuss the **list** and **report** commands that allow you to determine what backups are available for RMAN to restore from.

SCN-Based Recovery

We talked about the SCN in detail in Chapter 1. Oracle allows you to recover the database to a specific SCN. In practice, this is not a frequently used recovery method, but it's nice to know it's available. We will use it later in this chapter to recover to a previous database incarnation. Here is an example of a recovery to a specific SCN:

```
-- We assume that your control file is intact
startup mount;
restore database UNTIL SCN 10000;
recover database UNTIL SCN 10000;
alter database open resetlogs;
```

In this case, we restore up to, but not including, SCN 10000.

Log Sequence–Based Recovery

RMAN allows you to perform a recovery up to a specific archived redo log sequence number. This is handy if there is a gap in your archived redo logs, which generally means that you can recover only up to the point where the gap begins. Here is the command to perform this recovery in RMAN:

```
-- We assume that your control file is intact
startup mount;
restore database UNTIL SEQUENCE 100 thread 1;
recover database UNTIL SEQUENCE 100 thread 1;
alter database open resetlogs;
```

In this case, we restore up to, but not including, log sequence 100 of thread 1.

Cancel-Based Recovery

RMAN doesn't support cancel-based recovery like SQL*Plus does (though, in a way, cancel-based recovery is much like log sequence–based recovery). RMAN expects you to know what time, SCN, or log sequence number you want to recover to, and that makes sense. If you have some need to perform cancel-based recovery, you need to restore the datafiles from RMAN to some point in time before the point in time you are going to recover to. You need to manually extract the archived redo logs that you will need for the cancel-based recovery, and then you need to perform cancel-based recovery of the database from the SQL*Plus client. Chapter 1 describes the process of performing manual cancel-based database recovery.

Other RMAN Recovery Topics

We have covered a number of different restore operations that you can do with RMAN, but a few more topics remain to go over. In this section, we discuss more of the restore operations that are available to you. First, we look at how to restore archived redo logs from your backup sets. Next, we look at restoring control file copies from backup. Then, we move on to discuss restoring datafile copies and backup set backups. Finally, we discuss validating your backups, an important feature in RMAN.

Read-Only Tablespace Recovery Considerations

By default, RMAN will not restore read-only datafiles when you do a full database restore, even if the read-only datafile is not there. To restore a read-only datafile during a full recovery, you need to include the **check readonly** parameter in the **restore** command:

```
restore database check readonly;
```

Note that the RMAN behavior is different if you issue a **recover tablespace** or **recover datafile** command. When you use either of these two **recover** commands, recovery occurs regardless of the read-only nature of the tablespace.

Archived Redo Log Restores

During the normal course of recovery with RMAN, there is no real need to recover the archived redo logs. However, restoring one or more archived redo logs may be required occasionally. For example, you might want to use Log Miner to mine some information from the archived redo log files stored in your backups. In this event, RMAN allows you to restore specific archived redo logs by using the **restore archivelog** command, as shown in these examples:

```
restore archivelog all;
restore archivelog from logseq=20 thread=1;
restore archivelog from logseq=20 until logseq=30 thread=1;
```

You might want to have Oracle restore the archived redo logs to a location other than the default location. To do this, use the **set** command with the **archivelog destination to** parameter:

```
run
{
set archivelog destination to "d:\oracle\newarch";
restore archivelog all;
}
```

Note that there is no alternative to the **set** command, so a **run** block is required. Finally, be aware that RMAN will not restore an archived redo log to disk if it determines that the archived redo log already exists. Even if you change the destination to a destination other than the default archive log destination, Oracle will not recover an archived redo log to that new destination.

Datafile Copy Restores

You can restore your database datafiles from a datafile copy (as opposed to a backup set). To do this, use the **restore from datafilecopy** command, and then use the **recover** command as you normally would to recover the database (or tablespace or datafile), as shown in this example:

```
restore (datafile 5) from datafilecopy;
recover datafile 5;
sql "alter database datafile 5 online;"
```

Note that when you issue a **restore** command, it will identify the most current copy of the datafiles that need to be restored and then restore those datafiles from that copy. The most current copy of a datafile might be within a datafile copy rather than a backup set. In that case, Oracle will recover the datafile copy. Also note that the use of parentheses is important; if they are not used, this command will fail.

Recovering Corrupted Data Blocks

RMAN offers *block media recovery (BMR)* which allows you to do block-level recoveries to repair logically or physically corrupted blocks in your Oracle database, even while the associated datafile is online and churning away the whole time.

So, just how do you do a block media recovery? It's easy, as demonstrated in the following example. Suppose you receive the following error message when querying an Oracle table:

```
ORA-01578: ORACLE data block corrupted (file # 19, block # 44)
ORA-01110: data file 19: 'd:\oracle\oradata\data\mydb_maintbs_01.dbf'
```

This message is telling you that a block in the MAINTBS tablespace is corrupted. Of course, you need to do something about that. Without BMR, you would have had to recover the datafile from a backup. During this recovery, all data within that datafile would be unavailable to the users.

Instead, you can use BMR to recover just the corrupted blocks. This is facilitated through the **blockrecover** command. In the preceding example, the **blockrecover** command would look like this:

```
blockrecover datafile 19 block 44;
```

You can recover multiple blocks in multiple datafiles at the same time, if you like. Here are two examples of using **blockrecover** for such an operation:

```
BLOCKRECOVER DATAFILE 19 BLOCK 44,66,127;
BLOCKRECOVER DATAFILE 19 BLOCK 44 DATAFILE 22 BLOCK 203;
```

Of course, Oracle tracks block corruption that occurs during backups and copies. If a backup or copy operation has detected corruption, the operation will fail by default because Oracle will allow zero corruption in a backup. You can configure RMAN to allow a set amount of corruption, but this is not a recommended practice.

If you want to see all database corruption that might be detected by RMAN, you can use the **backup validate database** command, which populates the views V$BACKUP_CORRUPTION and V$DATABASE_BLOCK_CORRUPTION with the results of all corrupted blocks. If corruption occurs during a copy operation, the V$COPY_CORRUPTION view indicates which backup sets contain corruption. Note that V$BACKUP_CORRUPTION is a historical view of past corruption. V$DATABASE_BLOCK_CORRUPTION is a view of current block corruption. Once you have corrected the database block corruption, rerun the **backup validate**

database command, and then query V$DATABASE_BLOCK_CORRUPTION to ensure that no further corruption exists.

As we mentioned already, you can query the view V$DATABASE_BLOCK_ CORRUPTION for details on corrupted blocks. To make it easy to correct corrupted blocks in V$DATABASE_BLOCK_CORRUPTION, you can use the **blockrecover** command with the **corruption list restore** parameter:

```
BLOCKRECOVER CORRUPTION LIST RESTORE UNTIL TIME 'SYSDATE - 5';
```

In this case, we restore all corrupted blocks on our corrupt block list that are no older than five days old. You can also use the **until time** and **until sequence** keywords with this command.

Recovering to a Previous Incarnation

Recall from our earlier discussion about the **resetlogs** command that an incarnation of a database is a representation of a specific logical lifetime for that database. As a hotshot DBA, you may find yourself in an odd restore situation in which you need to restore your database using a backup that took place from before the last time you opened the database using the **resetlogs** command, and/or you may wish to restore to a point in time before you issued the last **resetlogs** command. In this section, we discuss how to recover your database from a previous incarnation both with a recovery catalog (a rather easy task) and without a recovery catalog (plan for time and frustration). Finally, we will cover a rather unique recovery situation in which you need to recover through the **resetlogs** command.

Recovering to a Previous Incarnation with a Recovery Catalog

Let's look at an example of recovering from a previous incarnation. In this example, we assume we have done backups using a recovery catalog and that we have recently done a point-in-time recovery using **resetlogs**. Now, we need to recover our database using a backup taken from a point in time before we issued our **resetlogs** command. First, we need to list the database incarnations by using the **list incarnation** command (covered in detail in the next chapter):

```
RMAN> list incarnation;
List of Database Incarnations
DB Key  Inc Key DB Name  DB ID             CUR Reset SCN  Reset Time
------- ------- -------- ---------------- --- ---------- ----------
1       2       RECOVER  2539725638        NO  763059     08-JUL-02
1       123     RECOVER  2539725638        YES 764905     09-JUL-02
```

In this list, we discover that there have been two different incarnations of our database, incarnation key 2 and incarnation key 123. The CUR column indicates that we are on incarnation key 123 right now (since it says YES). So, we need to switch back to incarnation 2 of the database.

Now that we know which incarnation we want to recover, we proceed to do the recovery (we removed some of the output here to make this example clearer):

```
RMAN> startup force nomount
Oracle instance started
RMAN> reset database to incarnation 2;
database reset to incarnation 2 in recovery catalog
RMAN> restore controlfile;
Finished restore at 10-JUL-02
RMAN> restore database until scn 764904;
 Finished restore at 10-JUL-02
RMAN> recover database until scn 764904;
starting media recovery
media recovery complete
Finished recover at 10-JUL-02
RMAN> alter database open resetlogs;
database opened
new incarnation of database registered in recovery catalog
starting full resync of recovery catalog
full resync complete
```

The following steps describe what we have done in this example:

1. Start the instance. We don't mount it, though, because we first want to get a control file that is associated with the incarnation of the database we wish to recover.

2. Use the **reset database to incarnation** command to indicate to RMAN which incarnation's backup sets we wish to be considered for the recovery.

3. Issue the **restore controlfile** command, prompting RMAN to restore the most current control file for us.

4. Mount the database.

5. Restore the database, doing an SCN-based restore (discussed earlier in this chapter). We have decided to restore the database to the SCN just before the last **resetlogs** (which was at SCN 764905), so we issue the **restore database** command, limiting the restore to SCN 764904.

6. Issue the **recover** command, again limiting the recovery of the database to SCN 764904, and wait for the recovery to complete.

7. Open the database, resetting the online redo logs.

Now, when we run the **list incarnation** command, the results are as follows:

```
RMAN> list incarnation;
List of Database Incarnations
DB Key  Inc Key DB Name  DB ID            CUR Reset SCN  Reset Time
------- ------- -------- ---------------- --- ---------- ----------
1       2       RECOVER  2539725638       NO  763059     08-JUL-02
1       123     RECOVER  2539725638       NO  764905     09-JUL-02
1       245     RECOVER  2539725638       YES 764905     10-JUL-02
```

Note the new incarnation of the database that has been created (with incarnation key 245). Also note that the reset SCN for this new incarnation is the same as that of incarnation 123 (which was the active incarnation). The reset time, however, reflects the actual time that this incarnation was created.

Recovering to a Previous Incarnation Without a Recovery Catalog

Oracle has made recovery to a previous incarnation without a recovery catalog so much easier in Oracle Database 10g. No longer are you required to jump through hoops, ask Oracle developers for favors, and send them cookies! No, it's simple!

To recover through a previous incarnation you have a control file that is aware of the previous incarnation. This can be the current control file in most cases. If the current control file is not aware of the incarnation that you need to restore to, you need to restore a control file that is aware of this information to use this method of recovering your database. You can determine which incarnations your control file is aware of by using the **list incarnation of database** command, as shown in this example:

```
RMAN> list incarnation;
List of Database Incarnations
DB Key  Inc Key DB Name  DB ID            STATUS   Reset SCN  Reset Time
------- ------- -------- ---------------- ---      ---------- ----------
4       4       ROB10R2  3753137102       PARENT   3599781    05-FEB-06
5       5       ROB10R2  3753137102       PARENT   3715262    08-FEB-06
6       6       ROB10R2  3753137102       CURRENT  4296046    20-FEB-06
```

In this example, we find that the control file contains information on incarnations (Inc Key) 4, 5, and 6. The current incarnation is incarnation 6. If we needed to restore incarnation 3, we could not use this control file because incarnation 3 does not exist in this control file.

Note that the **list incarnation** output when not connected to a recovery catalog looks slightly different from the **list incarnation** output when connected to a recovery catalog. This is because you are getting your information from the control file, so certain keys (Inc Key, for example) will be different. This is perfectly normal.

If we wish to reset to incarnation 5 and then recover our database, we need to do the following:

1. Run the **list incarnation** command from RMAN and determine which incarnation we wish to reset to.

2. Shut down the database.

3. Startup mount the database.

4. Issue the **reset database to incarnation** command to reset the incarnation.

5. Restore the database using the **restore** command (e.g., **restore until sequence 100 thread 1**).

6. Recover the database (**recover until sequence 100 thread 1**).

7. Open the database using the **resetlogs** command.

Like we said, so much easier! Here is some sample output of a recovery that resets the incarnation. Notice what happens in the **list incarnation** command as we complete the recovery. Also note that if Oracle needed to recover through the **resetlogs** command of incarnation 6, it would have done so automatically without our having to tell it to. We have removed some unneeded output to protect the innocent (trees, that is!).

```
RMAN> list incarnation of database;
List of Database Incarnations
DB Key  Inc Key DB Name  DB ID             STATUS   Reset SCN  Reset Time
------- ------- -------- ----------------- --- ---------- ----------
1       1       ROB10R2  3753137102        PARENT   1          30-AUG-05
2       2       ROB10R2  3753137102        PARENT   534907     03-OCT-05
3       3       ROB10R2  3753137102        PARENT   3586765    04-FEB-06
4       4       ROB10R2  3753137102        PARENT   3599781    05-FEB-06
5       5       ROB10R2  3753137102        PARENT   3715262    08-FEB-06
6       6       ROB10R2  3753137102        CURRENT  4296046    20-FEB-06
RMAN> shutdown immediate
database closed
database dismounted
Oracle instance shut down
RMAN> startup mount
connected to target database (not started)
Oracle instance started
database mounted
RMAN> reset database to incarnation 5;
database reset to incarnation 5
```

```
-- Note the reset SCN on the current incarnation is greater than
-- the SCN we wish to restore to. This is why we had to do a
-- restore to the previous incarnation.
RMAN> restore database until scn 4296041;
Starting restore at 20-FEB-06
allocated channel: ORA_DISK_1
channel ORA_DISK_1: sid=156 devtype=DISK
allocated channel: ORA_DISK_2
channel ORA_DISK_2: sid=155 devtype=DISK
... blah blah blah… more stuff here we don't really need to see...
RMAN> recover database until scn 4296041;
Starting recover at 20-FEB-06
using channel ORA_DISK_1
using channel ORA_DISK_2
... blah blah blah… more stuff here we don't really need to see...
RMAN> list incarnation;
List of Database Incarnations
DB Key  Inc Key DB Name  DB ID            STATUS   Reset SCN  Reset Time
------- ------- -------- ---------------- ------   ---------  ----------
1       1       ROB10R2  3753137102       PARENT   1          30-AUG-05
2       2       ROB10R2  3753137102       PARENT   534907     03-OCT-05
3       3       ROB10R2  3753137102       PARENT   3586765    04-FEB-06
4       4       ROB10R2  3753137102       PARENT   3599781    05-FEB-06
5       5       ROB10R2  3753137102       CURRENT  3715262    08-FEB-06
6       6       ROB10R2  3753137102       ORPHAN   4296046    20-FEB-06
RMAN> alter database open resetlogs;
database opened
RMAN> list incarnation;
List of Database Incarnations
DB Key  Inc Key DB Name  DB ID            STATUS   Reset SCN  Reset Time
------- ------- -------- ---------------- ------   ---------  ----------
1       1       ROB10R2  3753137102       PARENT   1          30-AUG-05
2       2       ROB10R2  3753137102       PARENT   534907     03-OCT-05
3       3       ROB10R2  3753137102       PARENT   3586765    04-FEB-06
4       4       ROB10R2  3753137102       PARENT   3599781    05-FEB-06
5       5       ROB10R2  3753137102       PARENT   3715262    08-FEB-06
6       6       ROB10R2  3753137102       ORPHAN   4296046    20-FEB-06
7       7       ROB10R2  3753137102       CURRENT  4296046    20-FEB-06
```

Tablespace Point-In-Time Recovery

Tablespace point-in-time recovery (TSPITR) is yet another feature of RMAN that is made easier in Oracle Database 10g. Much of the previous hassle with the creation of the auxiliary instance is now done away with, although you can still manually create the auxiliary instance if you choose to. Why use tablespace point-in-time recovery? Consider a case where your user has dropped a table in error…in fact, the user has dropped three tables, truncated two more tables, and then called you asking for your help in getting it all back. Fortunately for you, RMAN allows you to do TSPITR. There are a number of cases where TSPITR might come in handy. Such situations might include accidentally dropping a table, as in our first example of the chapter, or perhaps a big bulk data load program ended up logically corrupting data.

Before you begin performing TSPITR, you need to be aware of some terms related to TSPITR in Oracle Database 10*g*:

- **Auxiliary destination** An optional location where Oracle will create the auxiliary set.

- **Auxiliary instance** A temporary instance that you create. RMAN uses this instance to perform TSPITR. After you complete your TSPITR, you can remove the auxiliary instance.

- **Auxiliary set** The set of remaining target database files that you need to perform TSPITR. This set includes a backup control file, rollback and undo segment tablespace datafiles, the SYSTEM tablespace datafiles, online redo logs of the auxiliary database, and, optionally, a temporary tablespace in the auxiliary database.

- **Recovery set** The set of tablespaces/datafiles that you wish to perform TSPITR on.

- **Target instance** Contains the tablespace(s) to be recovered.

In the next section, we will look at an example of performing automated tablespace point-in-time recovery using RMAN. We will also address manual tablespace point-in-time recovery with RMAN.

Performing Automated TSPITR

In this example, we will have Oracle create the auxiliary instance for us. The basic steps of successful TSPITR are as follows:

1. Prepare for a TSPITR.

2. Perform the actual TSPITR.

Let's look at each of these steps in more detail next. We will also look at performing automated tablespace point-in-time recovery with the auxiliary instance already prepared.

Prepare for a TSPITR

There are some steps you need to complete before you can begin TSPITR, which we discuss in this section:

- Determine what point in time to restore to.

- Make sure the objects are fully contained within the tablespace(s) you wish to restore.

- Preserve objects or data that will otherwise be lost.

Determine the Point in Time to Restore To   The most critical factor here is to determine what point in time you wish to restore your tablespace to. Be cautious here, because recovery of the tablespace is a one-shot deal if you are not using a recovery catalog. If you misidentify the point in time to recover to, you will not be able to retry the recovery. If you are using a recovery catalog, then this restriction does not exist.

Make Sure the Objects in the Transport Set Are Self Contained   You should also use the TS_PITR_CHECK view to make sure your recovery set is complete and identify any other tablespaces that might need to be included. For example, assume that you have a tablespace TEST_RECOVER and need to restore it using TSPITR. You first need to check the TS_PITR_CHECK view to make sure that there are no other dependent tablespaces. Here is an example of a query to check if the TEST_RECOVER tablespace can be transported alone:

```
Set lines 132
Column obj1_owner format a20
column obj1_name format a20
column obj1_type format a20
column reason format a60
SELECT obj1_owner, obj1_name, obj1_type, reason
FROM SYS.TS_PITR_CHECK
WHERE ( TS1_NAME IN ('TEST_RECOVER')
       AND TS2_NAME NOT IN ('TEST_RECOVER') )
OR    ( TS1_NAME NOT IN ('TEST_RECOVER')
        AND TS2_NAME IN ('TEST_RECOVER') );
```

This will return no rows if there are no conflicts. If there were conflicts, you would see a row describing each conflict, as shown here:

```
OBJ1_OWNER    OBJ1_NAME        OBJ1_TYPE    REASON
------------  ---------------  -----------  ------------------------------
SCOTT         TEST_TSPITR      TABLE        Tables and associated indexes
                                            not fully contained in the
                                            recovery set
```

In this case, we have an index that appears to be created in another tablespace. This index is associated with the TEST_TSPITR object. We need to find out what tablespace that index is in and restore that tablespace, too.

Preserve Objects or Data that Might Be Lost in the Recovery   Obviously, if you are going to restore the TEST tablespace to 2 P.M., any changes to that tablespace (new objects, update/insert or delete operations) will be lost after that point. Loosing those objects may be fine, but suppose that you need to preserve that data. If this is the case, you need to export the data to be preserved (or, alternatively, copy it somewhere else in the database). Oracle provides a view, TS_PITR_OBJECTS_TO_BE_DROPPED, that lists all objects that will be lost during the recovery operation. Use this view to determine what the status of the objects in the tablespace will be after the recovery.

For example, if you were going to restore the TEST_TSPITR tablespace to a point in time of 02/20/2006 at 23:40:00, you would loose the TEST_TSPITR_TWO object, as shown in this sample output:

```
SQL>select * from TS_PITR_OBJECTS_TO_BE_DROPPED where
2> tablespace_name='TEST_RECOVER';

OWNER        NAME                  CREATION_TIME        TABLESPACE_NAME
----------   --------------------  -------------------  ----------------
SCOTT        TEST_TSPITR_TWO       02/20/2006 23:42:46  TEST_RECOVER
SCOTT        TEST_TSPITR           02/20/2006 23:26:26  TEST_RECOVER
SCOTT        TEST_TSPITR_THREE     02/21/2006 00:18:29  TEST_RECOVER
```

Perform the Actual TSPITR

Oracle Database 10g will perform automated TSPITR for you, which means that it will create the auxiliary instance for you. In this case, all you need to do is connect to the target database and the optional recovery catalog (if you use one) and issue the **recover tablespace** command. RMAN will do the rest of the work for you.

In the following code snippet, we provide an example of using the **recover tablespace** command to recover the TEST_RECOVER tablespace. In this example, we use the optional parameter **auxiliary destination** to indicate where RMAN and Oracle should create the files associated with the auxiliary database. Using this parameter makes this recovery a *customized TSPITR with an automatic instance*. If you do not use this parameter, the TSPITR is known as a *fully automated TSPITR recovery*.

Note that if you use the **auxiliary destination** parameter, the destination directory should already be created and Oracle must be able to write to that destination. Also note that there is no trailing slash (\ or /, depending on your OS) in the destination pathname. Including a slash will cause TSPITR to fail (and the message you get isn't exactly all that descriptive). Here is an example of the **recover tablespace** command that we used to successfully perform TSPITR in Oracle Database 10*g* Release 2:

```
recover tablespace test_recover
until time "to_date('02/21/2006 00:18:00','mm/dd/yyyy hh24:mi:ss')"
auxiliary destination 'c:\oracle\auxdest';
```

NOTE
To do automatic TSPITR, you must have configured channels on the target. That way, channels used in the auxiliary instance will be the same as those on the target.

Once the TSPITR has been completed, you should be able to look at the objects in the recovered tablespace and find that they have been recovered to the point in time you requested. You need to bring the tablespaces recovered back online to use them. From RMAN, you can issue the command

```
Sql 'alter tablespace test_recover online';
```

If an error occurs, Oracle leaves the auxiliary instance and its related datafiles intact. You can try to correct the problem and restart the recovery. In this case, you would restart RMAN using the **auxiliary** parameter, connecting to the auxiliary instance (as we demonstrate later, in the section "Manual TSPITR").

If the auxiliary instance creation is not entirely successful, it may be easier to just remove the auxiliary instance and its service than to restart the recovery using the manual TSPITR process. First, figure out what failed and then remove the auxiliary instance/service and restart the automated TSPITR process. You can remove the auxiliary instance/service by issuing the following command from SQL*Plus when logged in as sysdba:

```
exec dbms_backup_restore.manageauxinstance('auxiliary_sid_name',1);
```

Note that you need to put the SID that Oracle assigned to the auxiliary instance in the place of the **auxiliary_sid_name** placeholder. The name of the SID will be listed in the RMAN output. This will clean up any old auxiliary instances before you start your TSPITR recovery. You will want to go to the auxiliary destination directory after you execute this command and remove any files that are in that directory.

Customized Automated TSPITR with an Automatic Instance
We already mentioned that you can customize some aspects of the automatic instance creation when performing TSPITR. We demonstrated the use of the **auxiliary destination** parameter to indicate where the recovery set should be created.

Other ways of customizing the creation of the TSPITR, and still allowing Oracle to create the instance for you, include the following:

- Using the **set newname** command to indicate the location of the individual datafiles of the recovery set.

- Using the **configure auxname** command to define the name of the auxiliary instance.

- Creating your own parameter file for the auxiliary instance and supplying parameters such as **db_file_name_convert** in that parameter file. This can be done by creating a file called parms_auxint.ora in $ORACLE_HOME/rdbms/ admin (this filename and location are OS dependent). Optionally, you can use the RMAN command **set auxiliary instance parameter file** to indicate the path on the client where the auxiliary instance parameter file resides. See the next section for more information on parameters that apply when configuring an instance for TSPITR.

Once you have customized your auxiliary instance, you can have RMAN create it for you by issuing the **recover tablespace** command, as shown earlier in the section "Performing Automated TSPITR."

Manual TSPITR

Oracle supports the creation of your own auxiliary instance for TSPITR. You can also use manual TSPITR to complete a failed automatic TSPITR. The steps listed earlier in the preparation phase still apply. You then must prepare the auxiliary instance, and then you execute the TSPITR process. We discuss these steps in the next few sections.

Prepare the Auxiliary Instance

The first thing we need to do is get an auxiliary instance up and running. As already defined, an auxiliary instance is just a temporary instance that RMAN uses to perform TSPITR. The auxiliary instance must reside on the same box as the target database, and you will never be able to execute any type of DML on the auxiliary instance.

Before we can start TSPITR, we need to get the auxiliary instance ready. This is a manual process that RMAN has no part in, but it's not unlike creating a normal database instance. To create the auxiliary instance, perform these actions:

1. Create the password file.

2. Create the database parameter file if you are running the restore from OEM.

3. If you are running Oracle on Windows NT, add the database service with the **oradim** program (for example, **oradim –new –sid recover**).

4. Start the auxiliary instance and check to make sure that you have network connectivity.

You should be familiar in general with each of these steps, as these are typical DBA tasks. Basically, it's a lot like creating an instance in preparation for issuing the **create database** command. We need to note a few issues specific to TSPITR, however, so let's do that quickly.

Configure the Auxiliary Parameter File   The parameter file of the auxiliary database is a separate parameter file from the one used on the target database. You configure the parameter file for the auxiliary instance in much the same way you configure a normal database parameter file. You need to include a few additional parameters in this parameter file, which are listed in Table 12-1.

Parameter Name	Optional/ Required	Comment
db_name	Optional	The same name as the target database.
lock_name_space	Required	Should be a name that is unique among all other databases on the system that you are creating your auxiliary database on. In our examples, we will use aux1.
db_file_name_convert	Optional	Can be used to define a set of file-naming conversion patterns for datafiles in the auxiliary database as they are restored by RMAN. This is an alternative to using the **configure auxname** RMAN command.
log_file_name_convert	Optional	Can be used to define a set of file-naming conversion patterns for redo log files in the auxiliary database as they are restored by RMAN. This is an alternative to using the **set newname** RMAN command.
control_files	Required	The control file parameter defines the names and locations of the auxiliary instance control files. The control files should be unique in name from any existing control file in the location(s) you intend on creating the control files in.
remote_login_passwordfile	Optional/ Required	Used to allow RMAN to connect to the auxiliary database via Oracle Networking services. Requires the presence of a current password file. If you will be connecting to the auxiliary database locally, then this doesn't need to be set.
Compatible	Required	Must be the same as the target database's setting.
db_block_size	Optional/ Required	If set on the target database, must be set in the auxiliary database to the same value.

TABLE 12-1.   *Auxiliary Instance Parameter File Parameters of Interest*

Each of these parameters is further defined in the Oracle reference manual, if you need further information on how to configure them. For our example, we simply copied the target instance parameter file and made a few changes to it. Here is a copy of the resulting auxiliary database instance parameter file:

```
# These parameters already exist in the target database parameter file and
# require no changes.
db_name=rob10r2
db_block_size=8192
db_cache_size=8388608
timed_statistics=TRUE
shared_pool_size=110M
large_pool_size=1M

# Note that remote_loging_passwordfile must be set to exclusive
# if we want to connect to the aux database through RMAN via Oracle Net.
# remote_login_passwordfile=EXCLUSIVE
compatible=10.2.0.1

# These parameters required changes to directory locations
# to reflect the new database instance.
background_dump_dest= c:\oracle\auxdest
core_dump_dest= c:\oracle\auxdest
user_dump_dest= c:\oracle\auxdest
control_files=c:\oracle\auxdest\control01.ctl

# These are new parameters that are exclusive to the aux database
db_unique_name=recover
db_create_file_dest=c:\oracle\auxdest
log_file_name_convert=
('C:\ORACLE\PRODUCT\10.2.0\ORADATA\ROB10R2','d:\oracle\auxdest')
```

NOTE
We dump everything into c:\oracle\auxdest in the parameter file here. This kind of goes with the very temporary nature of the auxiliary database. You can, of course, create more sophisticated directory structures if you like.

Start the Auxiliary Instance and Check Network Connectivity   Now that we have everything in place, we can start our auxiliary instance. To do so, we simply use the **startup nomount** command, as shown in this example:

```
sqlplus "sys as sysdba"
startup nomount pfile=c:\oracle\auxdest\initrecover.ora
```

Once you have started the instance, connect to it using Oracle Net to ensure your network connectivity is correct.

Perform TSPITR with a Manual Auxiliary Instance   To perform the actual recovery, we need to connect to RMAN. The connection string we are going to use is a bit different because we need to connect to the target database, the auxiliary database, and the recovery catalog (if we are using one) all at the same time. To connect to the auxiliary database, we use the **auxiliary** command-line parameter, along with the **target** and **catalog** parameters, as shown in these examples:

```
C:\Oracle\auxdest>rman target=sys/robert@rob10r2 auxiliary=/
Recovery Manager:Release 10.2.0.1.0 Production on Thu Feb 23 10:25:49 2006
Copyright (c) 1982, 2005, Oracle.  All rights reserved.
connected to target database: ROB10R2 (DBID=3753137102)
connected to auxiliary database: RECOVER (not mounted)
```

Now that we have connected to RMAN, we need to be able to mount the auxiliary (clone) database. To do this, we restore a clone control file and then open the auxiliary database. Note that the **alter database archivelog current** command is important here to make sure that we have all the redo we need available for recovery of the clone database. The following is an example of using the **restore clone controlfile** command to restore the control file, and then an example of mounting the clone database. Note that these commands are contained inside of a **run** block. Also note the use of the **sql clone** command to indicate that the SQL commands executed should be on the clone database, as opposed to using the **sql** command without the **clone** parameter, which implies that the command is executed on the target database.

```
Run {
Set until time "to_date(' 02/23/2006 11:42:55','mm/dd/yyyy hh24:mi:ss')";
Restore clone controlfile;
sql clone 'alter database mount clone database';
sql 'alter system archive log current';
}
```

Now, we need to prepare for our TSPITR. First, we need to know which datafiles we need to restore. We need the following tablespace-related datafiles:

- The SYSTEM tablespace datafiles. The SYSTEM tablespace datafile is always at least datafile number 1. (There may be others if you added datafiles to SYSTEM of course.)

- The UNDO tablespace datafiles

- The temporary tablespace (TEMP) tempfiles. These can also be manually created if they are not available.

- The datafiles of the tablespace to be restored (in our case, TEST_RESTORE)

NOTE
We don't have to restore the SYSAUX tablespace in
this case.

So, let's look up these locations in our database using SQL*Plus. We use the
DBA_DATA_FILE view to find the FILE_IDs associated with these tablespace datafiles.
We also need the filename for the tablespace (or tablespaces) that we will be actually
performing the TSPITR on. In our case, here is what the output looks like (yours might
be a bit different, of course):

```
SQL> select tablespace_name, file_id
2> from dba_data_files
3> where tablespace_name in
4> ('SYSTEM','UNDOTBS1','TEST_RECOVER');

TABLESPACE_NAME                      FILE_ID
------------------------------- ----------
UNDOTBS1                                   2
SYSTEM                                     1
TEST_RECOVER                               7

SQL> select file_name from dba_data_files where file_id=7;

FILE_NAME
-----------------------------------------------------------
C:\ORACLE\PRODUCT\10.2.0\ORADATA\ROB10R2\TEST_RECOVER_01.DBF


SQL> select tablespace_name, file_id
2> from dba_data_files
TABLESPACE_NAME                      FILE_ID
------------------------------- ----------
TEMP                                       1
```

Before we start creating the auxiliary database, we need to offline the tablespaces
we are going to perform recovery on. For each tablespace, issue the SQL command
alter tablespace tablespace_name offline for recover; as shown in this example:

```
Sql 'Alter tablespace test_recover offline for recover';
```

We are ready to actually create the auxiliary (clone) database that will be used
for the recovery. First, we use the **until time** parameter again, since this is a new
run block. This way, we are sure to get the correct datafiles. Next, we use the **set
newname for clone** command to make sure these files are correctly named during
the restore. In this example, we are using OMF, so it's easy to do using the **new**
parameter. We also issue a **set newname** command for datafile 7, in preparation

for its restore. We then issue the **switch clone tempfile all** command to rename the temp files. Finally, we restore the datafiles and get the clone database running.

```
Run {
Set until time "to_date('02/23/2006 11:42:55','mm/dd/yyyy hh24:mi:ss')";
Set newname for clone datafile 1 to new;
Set newname for clone datafile 2 to new;
set newname for clone tempfile 1 to new;
Set newname for datafile 7 to
"C:\ORACLE\PRODUCT\10.2.0\ORADATA\ROB10R2\TEST_RECOVER_01.DBF";
Switch clone tempfile all;
restore clone datafile  1, 2, 7;
switch clone datafile all;
sql clone "alter database datafile  1 online";
sql clone "alter database datafile  2 online";
sql clone "alter database datafile  7 online";
sql clone "alter database mount clone database";
}
```

Now, open the clone database in preparation to do the TSPITR:

```
Run {
Set until time "to_date('02/23/2006 11:42:55','mm/dd/yyyy hh24:mi:ss')";
recover clone database
tablespace  "TEST_RECOVER", "SYSTEM", "UNDOTBS1" delete archivelog;
alter clone database open resetlogs;
}
```

We are now ready to perform the final step in the recovery process. We need to export the metadata from the clone database to the host database. Here is that process:

```
C:\Oracle\auxdest>exp 'sys/robert as sysdba' point_in_time_recover=y
tablespaces=test_recover file=tspitr_a.dmp

Export: Release 10.2.0.1.0 - Production on Thu Feb 23 12:44:30 2006
Copyright (c) 1982, 2005, Oracle.  All rights reserved.
Connected to: Oracle Database 10g Enterprise Edition
Release 10.2.0.1.0 - Production
With the Partitioning, OLAP and Data Mining options
Export done in WE8MSWIN1252 character set and AL16UTF16 NCHAR character set
Note: table data (rows) will not be exported

About to export Tablespace Point-in-time Recovery objects...
For tablespace TEST_RECOVER ...
. exporting cluster definitions
. exporting table definitions
. . exporting table                      TEST_TSPITR
. . exporting table                  TEST_TSPITR_TWO
. . exporting table                TEST_TSPITR_THREE
```

```
. exporting referential integrity constraints
. exporting triggers
. end point-in-time recovery
Export terminated successfully without warnings.
```

Now we shut down the clone:

```
C:\Oracle\auxdest>sqlplus "/ as sysdba"
SQL*Plus: Release 10.2.0.1.0 - Production on Thu Feb 23 12:47:05 2006
Copyright (c) 1982, 2005, Oracle.  All rights reserved.
Connected to:
Oracle Database 10g Enterprise Edition Release 10.2.0.1.0 - Production
With the Partitioning, OLAP and Data Mining options
SQL> shutdown immediate
Database closed.
Database dismounted.
ORACLE instance shut down.
```

Finally, we import the metadata into the source database. Note that we already recovered the datafile to the source database earlier, so we don't have to physically move the file.

```
C:\Oracle\auxdest>imp 'sys/robert as sysdba'
point_in_time_recover=y file=tspitr_a.dmp
```

Now, all that remains to be done is to online the tablespace:

```
Alter tablespace test_recover online;
```

Perform Post-TSPITR Activities After a Manual TSPITR

There are a few actions that you need to perform once your TSPITR is complete. First, you should reconnect RMAN to just the target database (and the recovery catalog if you are using one) and back up the tablespaces you just recovered. You will also want to remove the remnants of the auxiliary/clone instance.

TSPITR Restrictions

TSPITR has a number of restrictions, a quick summary of which follows:

- You can't restore tablespaces with objects owned by SYS.

- Any tablespace with replicated master tables cannot be recovered with TSPITR.

- Tablespaces with snapshot logs are not supported.

- You can't restore tablespaces that contain rollback segments.

■ If an object within the tablespace to be recovered has one of the following types, then TSPITR is not supported:

 ■ VARRAY

 ■ Nested tables

 ■ External files

Additionally, TSPITR cannot be used to recover a dropped tablespace. You also will not be able to recover older object statistics.

Finally, there are some restrictions with regard to TSPITR if you are using RMAN without a recovery catalog:

■ The current physical structure of the undo and rollback segments in the target database must be unchanged between the point you wish to recover to and the current point. In other words, the rollback segments can't change during the recovery.

■ Once you have completed TSPITR on a given tablespace, all previous backups of that tablespace are no longer usable for future TSPITR recoveries of that tablespace. This is why a backup of the tablespace after TSPITR is very important, in case you need to run another TSPITR.

Verifying Your Backups Are Recoverable

Of course, backups are not useful if they are not recoverable. RMAN provides a method of checking the restorability of your database without actually restoring it. In fact, RMAN offers you a couple of options. In this section, we look at some different ways to verify that your database backups, and thus your database, are recoverable. First, we will look at the **verify** and **check logical** options of the **restore** command. Then, we will look at the **validate backupset** command.

The restore preview Command

If you want to see which backup sets RMAN will use to perform a particular recovery, you can use the **restore preview** command. This command will detail the backup sets that will be required to perform the restore you indicate on the command line. For example, you can determine which backup set a full restore will apply by using the command **restore database preview**. In the following example, we see the results of the **restore database preview** command. In the output, we find that RMAN will apply an incremental level 0 backup and then an incremental level 1 backup (as shown in the LV column under the individual List of Backup Sets reports). It then also displays the archived redo logs that will be applied. At the end, we also get information that will help us with incomplete recovery if that is what we wanted.

```
RMAN> restore database preview;
Starting restore at 23-FEB-06
using channel ORA_DISK_1
using channel ORA_DISK_2

List of Backup Sets
===================
BS Key  Type LV Size       Device Type Elapsed Time Completion Time
------- ---- -- ---------- ----------- ------------ ---------------
210     Incr 0  66.36M     DISK        00:01:23     23-FEB-06
        BP Key: 210   Status: AVAILABLE  Compressed: YES
Tag: AG20060223T142518
        Piece Name:
C:\ORACLE\PRODUCT\10.2.0\FLASH_RECOVERY_AREA\ROB10R2\BACKUPSET\2006_02_23
\O1_MF_NNND0_TAG20060223T142518_1ZW6KK4H_.BKP
  List of Datafiles in backup set 210
  File LV Type Ckp SCN    Ckp Time   Name
  ---- -- ---- ---------- --------- ----
    2   0  Incr 4471679    23-FEB-06
C:\ORACLE\PRODUCT\10.2.0\ORADATA\ROB10R2\UNDOTBS01.DBF
    3   0  Incr 4471679    23-FEB-06
C:\ORACLE\PRODUCT\10.2.0\ORADATA\ROB10R2\SYSAUX01.DBF
    4   0  Incr 4471679    23-FEB-06
C:\ORACLE\PRODUCT\10.2.0\ORADATA\ROB10R2\USERS01.DBF
    5   0  Incr 4471679    23-FEB-06
C:\ORACLE\PRODUCT\10.2.0\ORADATA\ROB10R2\EXAMPLE01.DBF

BS Key  Type LV Size       Device Type Elapsed Time Completion Time
------- ---- -- ---------- ----------- ------------ ---------------
211     Incr 0  83.30M     DISK        00:01:45     23-FEB-06
        BP Key: 211   Status: AVAILABLE  Compressed: YES
Tag: TAG20060223T142518
        Piece Name:
C:\ORACLE\PRODUCT\10.2.0\FLASH_RECOVERY_AREA\ROB10R2\BACKUPSET\2006_02_23
\O1_MF_NNND0_TAG20060223T142518_1ZW6KYN2_.BKP

  List of Datafiles in backup set 211
  File LV Type Ckp SCN    Ckp Time   Name
  ---- -- ---- ---------- --------- ----
    1   0  Incr 4471684    23-FEB-06
C:\ORACLE\PRODUCT\10.2.0\ORADATA\ROB10R2\SYSTEM01.DBF
    6   0  Incr 4471684    23-FEB-06
C:\ORACLE\PRODUCT\10.2.0\ORADATA\ROB10R2\NEWTBS01.DBF
    7   0  Incr 4471684    23-FEB-06
C:\ORACLE\PRODUCT\10.2.0\ORADATA\ROB10R2\TEST_RECOVER_01.DBF
    8   0  Incr 4471684    23-FEB-06
C:\ORACLE\PRODUCT\10.2.0\ORADATA\ROB10R2\TEST_RECOVER_TWO_01.DBF
```

```
BS Key  Type LV Size       Device Type Elapsed Time Completion Time
------- ---- -- ---------- ----------- ------------ ---------------
216     Incr 1  728.00K    DISK           00:00:38     23-FEB-06
        BP Key: 216   Status: AVAILABLE  Compressed: YES
Tag: TAG20060223T144904
        Piece Name:
C:\ORACLE\PRODUCT\10.2.0\FLASH_RECOVERY_AREA\ROB10R2\BACKUPSET\2006_02_23
\O1_MF_NNND1_TAG20060223T144904_1ZW7Y40G_.BKP
  List of Datafiles in backup set 216
  File LV Type Ckp SCN    Ckp Time   Name
  ---- -- ---- ---------- ---------- ----
  2    1  Incr 4472638    23-FEB-06
C:\ORACLE\PRODUCT\10.2.0\ORADATA\ROB10R2\UNDOTBS01.DBF
  3    1  Incr 4472638    23-FEB-06
C:\ORACLE\PRODUCT\10.2.0\ORADATA\ROB10R2\SYSAUX01.DBF
  4    1  Incr 4472638    23-FEB-06
C:\ORACLE\PRODUCT\10.2.0\ORADATA\ROB10R2\USERS01.DBF
  5    1  Incr 4472638    23-FEB-06
C:\ORACLE\PRODUCT\10.2.0\ORADATA\ROB10R2\EXAMPLE01.DBF

BS Key  Type LV Size       Device Type Elapsed Time Completion Time
------- ---- -- ---------- ----------- ------------ ---------------
217     Incr 1  328.00K    DISK           00:01:10     23-FEB-06
        BP Key: 217   Status: AVAILABLE  Compressed: YES
Tag: TAG20060223T144904
        Piece Name:
C:\ORACLE\PRODUCT\10.2.0\FLASH_RECOVERY_AREA\ROB10R2\BACKUPSET\2006_02_23
\O1_MF_NNND1_TAG20060223T144904_1ZW7Z98D_.BKP
  List of Datafiles in backup set 217
  File LV Type Ckp SCN    Ckp Time   Name
  ---- -- ---- ---------- ---------- ----
  1    1  Incr 4472653    23-FEB-06
C:\ORACLE\PRODUCT\10.2.0\ORADATA\ROB10R2\SYSTEM01.DBF
  6    1  Incr 4472653    23-FEB-06
C:\ORACLE\PRODUCT\10.2.0\ORADATA\ROB10R2\NEWTBS01.DBF
  7    1  Incr 4472653    23-FEB-06
C:\ORACLE\PRODUCT\10.2.0\ORADATA\ROB10R2\TEST_RECOVER_01.DBF
  8    1  Incr 4472653    23-FEB-06
C:\ORACLE\PRODUCT\10.2.0\ORADATA\ROB10R2\TEST_RECOVER_TWO_01.DBF

List of Archived Log Copies
Key     Thrd Seq     S Low Time  Name
------- ---- ------- - --------- ----
300     1    23      A 23-FEB-06 C:\ARCHIVE\ROB10R2ARC00023_0582936761.001

Media recovery start SCN is 4472638
Recovery must be done beyond SCN 4472653 to clear data files fuzziness

Finished restore at 23-FEB-06
```

Some vendors support "recalling" media from a DR site to use for a local restore. The **restore database preview recall** supports this functionality, allowing you to initiate a recall of the required backup files from a remote disaster recovery site in order to perform the restore preview.

Restoring with the verify and check logical Commands

The **restore** command comes with some great options that allow you to verify that your database is recoverable and that the backup itself is valid. First, you can use the **validate** parameter of the **backup** command to cause RMAN to check the backup sets and make sure your database is recoverable. When you use the **validate** option, Oracle checks the most current backup set that will be needed to recover your database, ensuring that it is complete. This option also checks any datafile copies and archived redo log backup sets that will be required for recovery and ensures that they are all complete. Additionally, the **validate** option does a general validation of the backup sets to ensure that they are intact. Validation doesn't take very long, and is one way to ensure that your database is recoverable. Here is an example of a **validate** operation on our database:

```
RMAN> restore database validate;
Starting restore at 05-JUL-02
using channel ORA_DISK_1
using channel ORA_DISK_2
channel ORA_DISK_1: starting validation of datafile backupset
channel ORA_DISK_2: starting validation of datafile backupset
channel ORA_DISK_1: restored backup piece 1
piece handle=D:\BACKUP\RECOVER\BACKUP_4QDSM5IB_1_1
tag=TAG20020703T221224 params=NULL
channel ORA_DISK_1: validation complete
channel ORA_DISK_2: restored backup piece 1
piece handle=D:\BACKUP\RECOVER\BACKUP_4RDSM5IC_1_1
tag=TAG20020703T221224 params=NULL
channel ORA_DISK_2: validation complete
Finished restore at 05-JUL-02
```

Another, more complete check of the most current backup set is the **check logical** parameter of the **restore** command. This command causes RMAN to check the backups of the database, if they pass a physical corruption check, for logical corruption within the data and index segments backed up. If logical errors are found, Oracle responds in one of two ways:

- If the **maxcorrupt** parameter has been set and this count is not exceeded during the restore check logical operation, RMAN populates the Oracle V$ table V$DATABASE_BLOCK_CORRUPTION with a list of corrupted block ranges.

- If **maxcorrupt** is exceeded during the operation, then the operation will terminate.

By default, **maxcorrupt** is set to 0, so any logical corruption will cause the operation to fail. The **maxcorrupt** parameter default is modified via the **set** command and can only be established within the confines of a **run** block. Additionally, **maxcorrupt** is set for each datafile individually, not collectively. The following is an example of setting **maxcorrupt** to allow for some corruption to appear, and then logically validating backups of our database. In this example, we have set **maxcorrupt** for all the datafiles in our database (1 through 5), and we not only are checking that the latest backup sets are present and recoverable, but also are looking for logical corruption within the backup sets.

```
RMAN> run {
2> set maxcorrupt for datafile 1,2,3,4,5,6 to 5;
3> restore database check logical validate;
4> }
executing command: SET MAX CORRUPT
Starting restore at 05-JUL-02
using channel ORA_DISK_1
using channel ORA_DISK_2
channel ORA_DISK_1: starting validation of datafile backupset
channel ORA_DISK_2: starting validation of datafile backupset
channel ORA_DISK_1: restored backup piece 1
piece handle=D:\BACKUP\RECOVER\BACKUP_4QDSM5IB_1_1
tag=TAG20020703T221224 params=NULL
channel ORA_DISK_1: validation complete
channel ORA_DISK_2: restored backup piece 1
piece handle=D:\BACKUP\RECOVER\BACKUP_4RDSM5IC_1_1
tag=TAG20020703T221224 params=NULL
channel ORA_DISK_2: validation complete
Finished restore at 05-JUL-02
```

Using the validate backupset Command

Using the **restore** command with the **validate** and/or **check logical** parameters only checks the most current backup set. There may well be times that you want to check a specific backup set. To do this, you use the **validate backupset** command. To use this command, you first need to determine the backup set key that you want to back up. Each backup set, when it is made, is assigned a unique identifier called the *backup set key*. To determine the key assigned to the backup set you are interested in, you can use the **list backupset** command (covered in Chapter 14), as shown in the following example:

```
RMAN> list backupset;
List of Backup Sets
===================
```

```
BS Key  Type LV Size        Device Type Elapsed Time Completion Time
------- ---- -- ---------- ----------- ------------ ---------------
141     Full    320K        DISK         00:02:09     03-JUL-02
        BP Key: 141    Status: AVAILABLE   Tag: TAG20020703T221224
        Piece Name: D:\BACKUP\RECOVER\BACKUP_4QDSM5IB_1_1
  List of Datafiles in backup set 141
  File LV Type Ckp SCN    Ckp Time  Name
  ---- -- ---- ---------- --------- ----
    2      Full 647435    03-JUL-02 D:\ORACLE\ORADATA\RECOVER\REVDATA.DBF
    4      Full 647435    03-JUL-02 D:\ORACLE\ORADATA\RECOVER\TOOLS01.DBF
    6      Full 647435    03-JUL-02 D:\ORACLE\ORADATA\RECOVER\REVINDEX.DBF

BS Key  Type LV Size        Device Type Elapsed Time Completion Time
------- ---- -- ---------- ----------- ------------ ---------------
142     Full    113M        DISK         00:03:28     03-JUL-02
        BP Key: 142    Status: AVAILABLE   Tag: TAG20020703T221224
        Piece Name: D:\BACKUP\RECOVER\BACKUP_4RDSM5IC_1_1
  List of Datafiles in backup set 142
  File LV Type Ckp SCN    Ckp Time  Name
  ---- -- ---- ---------- --------- ----
    1      Full 647439    03-JUL-02 D:\ORACLE\ORADATA\RECOVER\SYSTEM01.DBF
    3      Full 647439    03-JUL-02 D:\ORACLE\ORADATA\RECOVER\INDX01.DBF
    5      Full 647439    03-JUL-02 D:\ORACLE\ORADATA\RECOVER\USERS01.DBF
```

Here, we are interested in the report's BS Key column, which lists the backup set key number. Notice that the files in the backup set also are listed, as are the date and time of the backup. All of this information should make it easy to identify the backup set you wish to validate. Once you have determined the set you need to check, then validating the backup set is as easy as running the **validate backupset** command, as shown in the next two examples:

```
RMAN> validate backupset 141;
using channel ORA_DISK_1
using channel ORA_DISK_2
channel ORA_DISK_1: starting validation of datafile backupset
channel ORA_DISK_1: restored backup piece 1
piece handle=D:\BACKUP\RECOVER\BACKUP_4QDSM5IB_1_1
tag=TAG20020703T221224 params=NULL
channel ORA_DISK_1: validation complete

RMAN> validate backupset 141 check logical;
using channel ORA_DISK_1
using channel ORA_DISK_2
channel ORA_DISK_1: starting validation of datafile backupset
channel ORA_DISK_1: restored backup piece 1
piece handle=D:\BACKUP\RECOVER\BACKUP_4QDSM5IB_1_1
tag=TAG20020703T221224 params=NULL
channel ORA_DISK_1: validation complete
```

Call the Movers! Cross-Platform Database Movement and RMAN

Oracle Database 10*g* Release 2 supports manually moving database across different platforms, even those of different *endian* formats. The endian formats relate to byte ordering, and there are two different formats, big endian and little endian. If you want to move a database between databases of different endian byte formats, then you have to do so manually, using the RMAN **convert datafile** or **convert tablespace** command along the way to convert the datafiles being transported to the correct endian format.

In this section, we quickly cover cross-platform transportable tablespaces. We then discuss the different endian byte-ordering formats. We then discuss converting tablespaces for transport to platforms with different endian byte formats. We finish with a discussion of using RMAN to move databases between different platforms with the same endian byte format.

Introduction to Cross-Platform Transportable Tablespaces

As DBAs, there have been several occasions where we really wanted to be able to move my tablespaces between my development NT Oracle database and my production Sun Oracle database. We have had cases where we really wanted to move them between a Sun platform and an AIX platform. Until Oracle Database 10*g*, this was just a dream.

Now, Oracle supports transporting tablespaces across almost all platforms of the Oracle database family. This has a number of benefits, including:

- Efficient publication of data between different content providers

- Easy movement of data between data warehouses, data marts, and OLTP systems

- Easy migration of databases across platforms

NOTE
Not all platforms are currently supported for this functionality. Check your platform-specific documentation to determine if your platform is eligible.

There are a few other issues to mention. To be able to move a tablespace between platforms, **compatible** must be set to 10.0.0 or higher. When this occurs, tablespace datafiles will be made platform-aware upon the next startup operation.

Note that read-only and offline datafiles become cross-platform compatible only after they have been made read-write or brought online.

Byte Ordering and Datafile Conversion

In this section, we first introduce you to the concept of byte ordering in Oracle database datafiles and how this impacts transporting your tablespace between different platforms. Then we will look at how to convert these datafiles, if that is required.

Datafile Byte Ordering

Oracle platforms generally use two different byte-ordering schemes (known as the endian formats). If the platforms use the same byte-ordering scheme, then you can transport tablespaces as you always have in the past, no problem.... Go ahead and try it. We will wait for you!

If the byte-ordering scheme is different, then you will need to use the **convert** command in RMAN to convert the tablespace to the format that it will need to be in on the target platform. You can determine the endian format via a join of the dynamic view V$DATABASE and the new V$TRANSPORTABLE_PLATFORM view, as shown in this example:

```
SQL> Select endian_format
  2  From v$transportable_platform tp, v$database d
  3  Where tp.platform_name=d.platform_name;

ENDIAN_FORMAT
--------------
Little
```

In this case, the system we are on is using the little endian format. Thus, if the query returns the same result on both systems, you have a compatible datafile format; if it does not, you need to use RMAN and the **compatible** parameter to transport the tablespaces.

Converting the Tablespace Endian Format with RMAN

If you need to convert a tablespace for another platform, RMAN is the tool you use. First, create the directory that the converted file will be copied to. In our example, we will use the directory path c:\oracle\oradata\betatwo. Next, make the tablespace that you wish to convert read-only. Then, you simply start RMAN and use the new **convert tablespace** command, as shown in this example:

```
Rman target=/
RMAN> convert tablespace users
to platform = ' AIX-Based Systems (64-bit)'
db_file_name_convert='c:\oracle\oradata\betatwo',
'c:\oracle\admin\transport_aix';
```

You can also convert datafiles at the destination site:

```
Rman target=/
RMAN> convert datafile =  c:\oracle\oradata\betatwo\*'
from platform = ' AIX-Based Systems (64-bit)'
db_file_name_convert='c:\oracle\oradata\betatwo',
'c:\oracle\admin\transport_aix';
```

The platform name that we use comes from the PLATFORM_NAME column of the V$TRANSPORTABLE_PLATFORM view. Oracle is very picky about putting the name in just right.

Once you have completed the conversion, you may complete the move by manually moving the datafiles/tablespaces using transportable tablespaces. Note that in cases where the endian format is different, RMAN will not be able to help you. If the endian format is the same, read the next section to see if you can use RMAN's new feature that moves your database across platforms for you!

We Like to Move It! Move It!

RMAN in Oracle Database 10g offers a brand-new feature to assist you in moving your databases across platforms of the same endian byte format. The **convert database** command, in combination with the DBMS_TDP package, can help reduce the overall workload of moving your database between platforms. The process consists of the following steps:

1. Open the database as read only:

   ```
   startup mount;
   alter database open read only;
   ```

2. Use the **dbms_tdb.check_db** procedure to check the database state. You should have already determined your platform name (from the PLATFORM_NAME column of the V$TRANSPORTABLE_PLATFORM view). This program should be run with **serveroutput** turned on, as in this example:

   ```
   set serveroutput on
   declare
        db_ready boolean;
      begin
        db_ready := dbms_tdb.check_db
        ('Microsoft Windows IA (32-bit)',dbms_tdb.skip_readonly);
      end;
      /
   ```

3. Use the **dbms_tdb.check_external** procedure to identify external objects:

   ```
   set serveroutput on
   Declare
        external boolean;
   ```

```
begin
    external := dbms_tdb.check_external;
end;
/
```

4. When the database is ready for transport, use the RMAN **convert database** command. RMAN creates scripts that are required for the database move. RMAN does not actually do the move, but only creates the files that are used for the move.

```
CONVERT DATABASE NEW DATABASE 'copydb'
        transport script 'c:\oracle\copydb\copyscripts'
        to platform 'Microsoft Windows IA (32-bit)';
```

The optional **db_file_name_convert** parameter allows you to define the directory filenames for datafiles that need to be converted. Here is an example:

```
CONVERT DATABASE NEW DATABASE 'copydb'
        transport script 'c:\oracle\copydb\copyscripts'
        to platform 'Microsoft Windows IA (32-bit)'
        db_file_name_convert
        'C:\ORACLE\PRODUCT\10.2.0\ORADATA\ROB10R2','C:\ORACLE\NEWDBDEST';
```

Once the command completes, simply follow the directions that RMAN will give you to complete the conversion process on the target database.

Summary

In this chapter, we have explored point-in-time recoveries that are available in RMAN. Time-based, SCN-based, and cancel-based recoveries are all supported by RMAN. This chapter also touched on RMAN's ability to recover through the **resetlogs** command, a welcome feature to us old-time DBAs who have struggled with this issue in the past.

This chapter also covered some miscellaneous recovery topics. We touched on things like archived redo log recoveries, read-only tablespace recovery considerations, and block level recovery. In short, we covered the wide gambit of RMAN's recovery toolbox.

Finally in this chapter, we explored tablespace point-in-time recoveries. Specifically with tablespace point-in-time recovery, you can run into complexities for various reasons, and thus it might well be that you will need to reference the Oracle documentation for specific implementation details that relate to your case.

CHAPTER
13

Surviving User Errors:
Flashback Technologies

edia recovery with RMAN provides critical safeguards against all kinds of unforeseeable problems—block corruption, hardware failure, even complete database loss. But so far this book has ignored the largest cause of media recovery operations: user error.

User errors can be roughly defined as errors caused by a human mistake (rather than a software or hardware malfunction), such as a table updated with wrong values, a table dropped, or a table truncated. They are the kinds of errors that are far more common than hardware failures (although, let's face it, human errors get *called* hardware errors all the time). In general, user errors are classified as logical errors—the error is logical, within the data itself, and a correction that is done using media recovery options will typically be very expensive.

In this chapter, we will discuss the new means in Oracle Database 10g to programmatically prepare for and recover from logical errors. This includes some functionality that existed already in the Oracle9i Database but has been extended (and made less painful). This also includes brand-new functionality that can radically change the time it takes to recovery from user-induced disasters.

Prepared for the Inevitable: Flashback Technology

When it comes to logical errors, media recovery should not be our first line of attack. It frequently is the line of attack, but this leads to massive outages. Typically, user error is not something that we can recover from, because the action is not interpreted as an error by the database. "Delete * from scott.emp" is not an error; it's a perfectly legitimate DML statement that is duly recorded in the redo stream. So if you restore the datafile and then perform recovery, all you will do is, well, delete * from scott.emp again. Point-in-time recovery can be a solution, but not for the DBA who is committed to avoiding full restore of the database—way too much outage. Tablespace-point-in-time-recovery (TSPITR) offers a toned-down version of media recovery for user error, but it still requires a full outage on the tablespace, has huge space demands for a temporary clone instance, and has object-level limitations (think advanced queuing tables).

To assist with user error recovery, and to complement RMAN's media recovery excellence, Oracle introduced in Oracle Database 10g the concept of Flashback Technology. Flashback Technology refers to a suite of features that gives you a multitude of different ways to survive user errors. These features have as a unifying concept only the simple idea that user errors occur and recovering from them should be simple and fast. The Flashback features are

- Flashback Query
- Flashback Table

- Flashback Drop
- Flashback Database

Flashback Query

If you think you recognize Flashback Query from Oracle9i, you're right: there was some Flashback Query functionality that existed in 9i. In 10g, that functionality has been expanded and simplified to allow you better access. Read: no more PL/SQL interface. Now, it's all built into SQL (and sometimes RMAN!) so you don't have to program a PL/SQL block to look at historical versions of a row.

Flashback and the Undo Segment: A Love Story

The first two types of flashback—Flashback Query and Flashback Table—have their functionality based entirely on technology that has existed in the Oracle database for years: the undo segments (or the segments formerly known as rollback). Undo segments exist to undo transactions that have not been committed. In the past, a committed transaction could not be undone because the associated "before" image of the row in the rollback was freed up to be overwritten.

This is still true: when you commit a transaction, the extent in the undo segment that contains the before image of the row is freed up to be overwritten. However, changes in the way undo space was used in 9i mean that all new transactions look for unused space in the undo tablespace before overwriting previously used segments. Even then, it always goes to the oldest remaining extents first. This means that before images of rows in the database last far longer than they ever have in the past.

This is all very good news, and in 9i and later, Oracle put it to use with the flashback query. Now we can actually control how long we want the undo extents to remain before they are overwritten. After doing so, we can put undo to good use—to help us undo committed transactions that were mistakes.

The ability to query or change objects back to a certain time in the past is predicated on how long our undo extents can remain in the undo tablespace before they are overwritten. Undo extents are used by new transactions based on space pressure in the undo tablespace. Basically, Oracle will not overwrite undo extents until it has exhausted all other possibilities first—that is, until every extent in the undo tablespace has been utilized. Then, it finds the oldest extent and overwrites it. The threshold for how far back you can use a flashback query/table is set by how long Oracle can go from the time a transaction is committed until the time that undo extents for that transaction get overwritten. The period from committed transaction to undo extent being overwritten is the *flashback window*.

There are plenty of factors that go into determining the flashback window, but the most important is your transaction load. You can view statistics for undo usage with the view V$UNDOSTAT. Each row in this view represents the number of undo blocks utilized for a ten-minute period. Running a few analyses of this view through peak usage should provide a decent template by which to guide your settings for undo.

Setting Undo Parameters for Flashback Query and Flashback Table

The guidelines for using Flashback Query demand that you first have automatic undo enabled—no rollback segments are allowed. (Okay, that's a lie. It is feasible to use flashback operations with old-school rollback segments, but Oracle discourages it and so do we. There is no reason to try to set up rollback segments manually anymore.) Oracle is best left to control undo management using new algorithms that emphasize retention of transactional history—algorithms that do not exist in rollback segments. Therefore, you need to set UNDO_MANAGEMENT = AUTO in the PFILE or SPFILE. Second, set your UNDO_TABLESPACE parameter to point to which tablespace will handle undo duties. Finally, set UNDO_RETENTION = *value in seconds*. This sets the desired length of time to keep undo segments around.

Performing Flashback Query

Performing a flashback query of a table is simple, now that it has been integrated into SQL. All you need to know is the point in time in the past for which you would like to view the contents of a table, and then you plug it into your query:

```
select scr_id, head_config from ws_app.woodscrew as of timestamp
  to_timestamp('2003-12-01 09:40:00','YYYY-MM-DD HH:MI:SS')
  where scr_id=1001;

    SCR_ID HEAD_CONFIG
---------- --------------------
      1001 Phillips
      1001 Phillips
```

You can also use an SCN qualifier, if you know the System Change Number (SCN) of the change you are looking for:

```
select scr_id, head_config from ws_app.woodscrew
as of scn 751652 where scr_id=1001;

    SCR_ID HEAD_CONFIG
---------- --------------------
      1001 Slot
      1001 Slot
```

Flashback Version Query with Oracle Enterprise Manager

Implementing Flashback Query—and its relatives, Flashback Transaction Query and Flashback Versions Query—is far simpler when you use Oracle Enterprise

Manager (OEM). OEM allows you to quickly turn a flashback query into an operation that can undo a user-induced error, whether through a flashback table or by applying the undo SQL for the bad transaction.

OEM combines the best features of multiple technologies to provide a user interface that helps you get answers quickly. Underneath the covers, it uses transaction queries to build a more complete investigation into what logical errors have occurred. The first of these is Flashback Versions Query, which also is referred to as row history. Flashback Versions Query provides the ability to look at every version of a row that existed within a specified timeframe. So, you provide a query to look at a row, and a timeframe that you want to review, and Oracle returns a list of every iteration that row has been through. This allows you to see a row morph over time, to determine what may be at the root of the problem.

RMAN Workshop: *Exploring Flashback Versions Query*

Workshop Notes
This Workshop has you build a few tables and populate them with a few dummy rows so that you can watch Flashback Versions Query in action. The following is the DDL and DML for the WOODSCREW table and indices. This code also builds a secondary table with rows for future use in Flashback Drop and Flashback Database. You are obviously not compelled to use our simplistic little test here, and could easily test with existing dummy tables in your system.

```
create table woodscrew (
scr_id            number not null,
manufactr_id      varchar2(20) not null,
scr_type          varchar2(20),
thread_cnt        number,
length            number,
head_config       varchar2(20));

alter table woodscrew add primary key
(scr_id, manufactr_id) using index;

create index woodscrew_identity on woodscrew
(scr_type, thread_cnt, length, head_config);
```

```
create table woodscrew_inventory (
 scr_id          number not null,
 manufactr_id    varchar2(20) not null,
 warehouse_id    number not null,
 locale          varchar2(20),
 count           number,
 lot_price     number);

insert into woodscrew values (
1000, 'Tommy Hardware', 'Finish', 30, 1.5, 'Phillips');
insert into woodscrew values (
1000, 'Balaji Parts, Inc.', 'Finish', 30, 1.5, 'Phillips');
insert into woodscrew values (
1001, 'Tommy Hardware', 'Finish', 30, 1, 'Phillips');
insert into woodscrew values (
1001, 'Balaji Parts, Inc.', 'Finish', 30, 1, 'Phillips');
insert into woodscrew values (
1002, 'Tommy Hardware', 'Finish', 20, 1.5, 'Phillips');
insert into woodscrew values (
1002, 'Balaji Parts, Inc.', 'Finish', 20, 1.5, 'Phillips');
insert into woodscrew values (
1003, 'Tommy Hardware', 'Finish', 20, 1, 'Phillips');
insert into woodscrew values (
1003, 'Balaji Parts, Inc.', 'Finish', 20, 1, 'Phillips');

insert into woodscrew_inventory values (
1000, 'Tommy Hardware', 200, 'NORTHEAST', 3000000, .01);
insert into woodscrew_inventory values (
1000, 'Tommy Hardware', 350, 'SOUTHWEST', 1000000, .01);
insert into woodscrew_inventory values (
1000, 'Balaji Parts, Inc.', 450, 'NORTHWEST', 1500000, .015);
insert into woodscrew_inventory values (
1005, 'Balaji Parts, Inc.', 450, 'NORTHWEST', 1700000, .017);
commit;
```

Step 1. Open the OEM 10g console and choose Administration | Schema | Tables. This opens a view of all tables in the schema of the user you have logged in as. You can change this to the owner of the WOODSCREW table by changing the Schema to the user and then clicking Go. Then, you can select the WOODSCREW table and choose View Data from the Actions drop-down list. After you click View Data, OEM will display the view shown in the following illustration. Note that the value for column HEAD_CONFIG is Phillips for all rows.

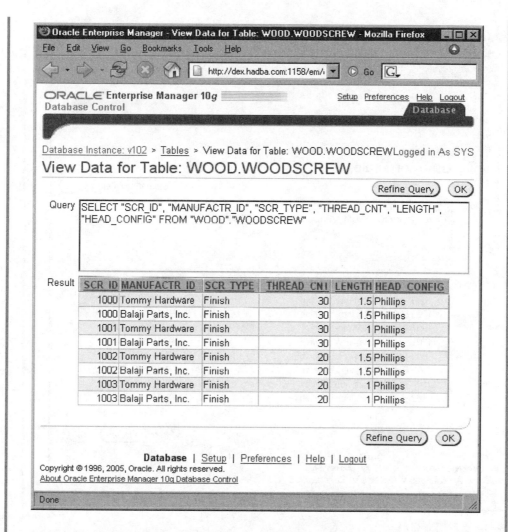

Step 2. Change rows in the table to reflect a different head configuration for the wood screws:

```
update woodscrew set head_config= 'Slot'
where scr_id=1001;
commit;
```

Step 3. View the new data in the table. From Tables, select the WOODSCREW table, choose View Data from the Actions drop-down list, and then click Go. Note in the following illustration that two rows now have Slot instead of Phillips.

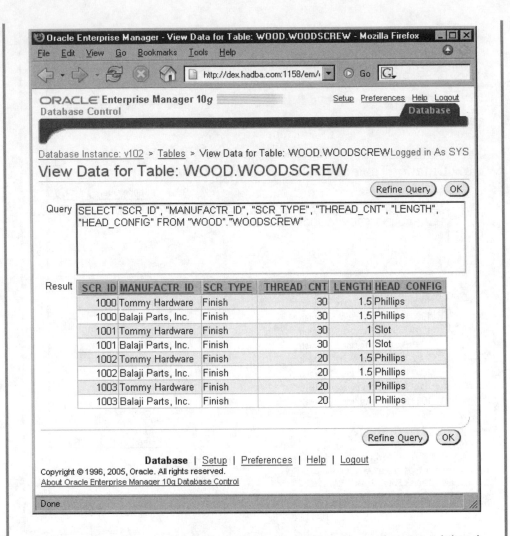

Step 4. Within the woodscrew business organization, it was determined that the screws with scr_id 1001 are *not* slot-headed, but rather Phillips. There has been a logical corruption introduced into the database. Let's review a single row and see what versions the row has been through. From the Tables view, select the WOODSCREW table, choose Flashback Versions Query from the Actions list, and then click Go. This takes you to the Perform Object Level Recovery wizard.

Step 5. In the wizard, we need to provide the parameters of our flashback query. First, choose all columns by selecting Move All under Step 1 of the wizard. Click the Next button from the right side of the page. Under Step 2, specify a clause that isolates a single row. We will use the following WHERE clause:

```
where scr_id=1001 and manufactr_id='Tommy Hardware'
```

After specifying the clause and clicking the Next button, we then choose the timeframe for our row history exploration. You can choose to Show All Row History or specify a specific timeframe. All Row History shows all versions of the row that still exist in the undo tablespace. The following screenshot shows the results of our query, with the transaction that updated the two rows.

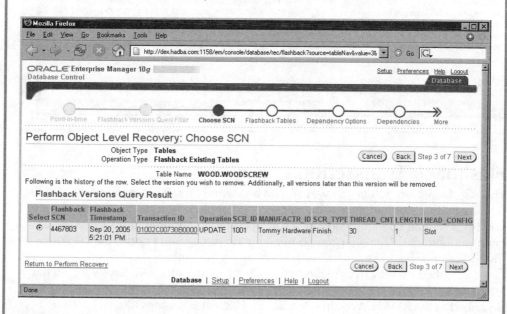

Step 6. Review the different operations that have occurred against this row in the database and determine which row may be in error. From this view, we can continue with the wizard and perform a flashback of the table.

Step 7. If you want proof that OEM is working hard for you, click Back to go to the Recovery: Row History Filter page. At the bottom is a button for Show Flashback Versions Query SQL; after clicking this, you will see the SQL you are blissfully ignoring, as shown next.

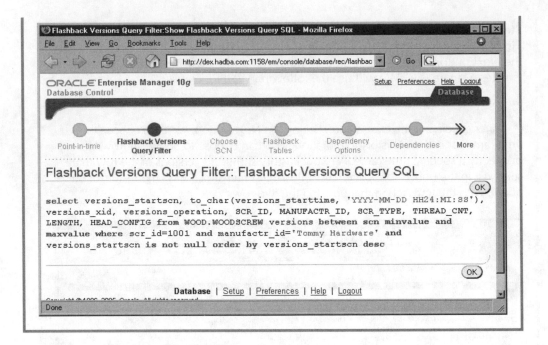

Flashback Transaction Query

There's always more than one way to skin a cat, and there's more than one way to organize a hunt for bad data in the database. Flashback Transaction Query allows you to look at all changes made by a specific transaction, or all transactions in a certain timeframe. Then you can go in and undo just a subset of the transaction, instead of undoing the entire transaction as an atomic unit.

Again, the best way to use Transaction Query is through OEM. Save yourself the grief and log into the OEM Console for the database and use the same set of operations described in the RMAN Workshop "Exploring Flashback Versions Query."

Flashback Transaction Query is compelling because it allows you to review a bad transaction in its entirety, even though the window into the error may be only a single row. For instance, if we found that a row of our WOODSCREW table had been deleted, we could look up that row in Flashback Versions Query. Then, we could get the Transaction ID for the delete operation and see how many other rows were deleted at the same time. This provides a means by which to get a look at the full scope of the problem.

But we can also take it a step further, as Oracle has built into OEM the ability to review the UNDO SQL statement for each row affected in the transaction. So, for the delete against WOODSCREW, each deleted row would be displayed with an INSERT statement that would replace the missing row in the table. In this fashion, you can correct an error without necessarily undoing the entire transaction—perhaps you meant to delete one row, but your SQL was incorrect and you deleted two rows. With OEM, you can undo one delete and leave the other in place. Let's take a look.

RMAN Workshop: *Explore Flashback Transaction Query*

Workshop Notes

This Workshop is an extension of the Workshop "Exploring Flashback Versions Query" in the previous section. The same WOODSCREW table is used.

Step 1. Introduce a fault into the WOODSCREW table:

```
SQL> delete from woodscrew where scr_id='1001';
commit;
```

Step 2. Someone querying for a one-inch finish woodscrew manufactured by Tommy notices that the screw has been deleted from the database, even though these are still offered by the company to customers. What happened? We turn to the OEM Administration | Schema | Tables page. Choose the owner of the WOODSCREW table and click Go.

Step 3. Select the WOODSCREW table, choose Flashback Versions Query from the Actions list, and click Go.

Step 4. Choose all columns, and then put a WHERE clause in to set the boundary of our inquiry. We use the WHERE clause of the user who encountered the fault:

```
where scr_id=1001 and manufactr_id='Tommy Hardware'
```

Then choose a timeframe (we use All Row History for this example) and click Next.

Step 5. You are looking at a row history report. To review the transaction, click the transaction ID for the delete operation. You are now looking at the entire transaction that included the delete of our specified row, as shown in the following screenshot. What is useful is that we can note here any other rows that were also impacted by this transaction to determine if we need to fix just the one row or multiple rows.

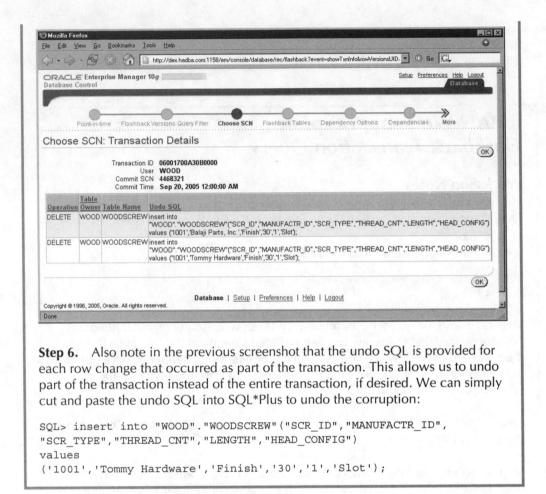

Step 6. Also note in the previous screenshot that the undo SQL is provided for each row change that occurred as part of the transaction. This allows us to undo part of the transaction instead of the entire transaction, if desired. We can simply cut and paste the undo SQL into SQL*Plus to undo the corruption:

```
SQL> insert into "WOOD"."WOODSCREW"("SCR_ID","MANUFACTR_ID",
"SCR_TYPE","THREAD_CNT","LENGTH","HEAD_CONFIG")
values
('1001','Tommy Hardware','Finish','30','1','Slot');
```

Flashback Table

Perhaps the most compelling of the Flashback Technology is the ability to simply revert a table to a previous point in time in a simple and straightforward fashion. The ability to perform point-in-time recovery on a table or group of tables has often been the grounds by which entire clone databases are built—just so that a single table could be extracted and then imported back into production. With Flashback Table, unnecessary cloning operations can be put to pasture.

Flashback Table employs the same mechanisms as Flashback Query—with information stored in the undo segments, Oracle can rewind a database one transaction at a time to put the table back the way it was at a specified time in the past. Because the Flashback Table operation depends on undo, the same restrictions apply: you can only flashback a table as far back as the undo segments allow you.

In addition to undo, the ability to flashback a table requires you to enable row movement for the table. Row movement was initially put in place as a function of partitioned tables, which allowed an updated row to move to the appropriate partition if the update changed the partition key value. Flashback Table employs row movement to assist in the rewind operations. To enable row movement, use the following **alter table** command:

```
alter table woodscrew enable row movement;
```

Flashback Table cannot save you from all user errors. Certain DDL operations that occur against a table cannot be undone. Most importantly, you cannot flashback a table to before a **truncate table** operation, because a **truncate** does not produce any undo—that is why **truncate** exists, versus a **delete * from table**. Also, Flashback Table cannot be used for a dropped table (use Flashback Drop for that—see the section "Flashback Drop").

Performing the Flashback Table Operation from SQL

With row movement enabled, you can move forward with normal operations on the table. Then, when a user-induced corruption occurs in the table, you can use SQL at the command line to perform the Flashback Table operation:

```
flashback table sales.woodscrew to timestamp
to_timestamp('2003-12-01 13:30:00','YYYY-MM-DD HH24:MI:SS')
```

Alternatively, you can use the SCN if you have been able to determine the SCN (through investigation via Flashback Query, for example):

```
flashback table sales.woodscrew to scn 751652;
```

Enabling Row Movement and Flashback Table

It is critical that you foresee possible Flashback Table candidates and enable row movement as soon as possible. You cannot enable row movement and then flashback the table to a point prior to enabling row movement. Such an operation will result in the following error:

```
ORA-08189: cannot flashback the table because row movement is not enabled.
```

In other words, you cannot wait until you need to flashback a table, and then enable row movement as part of the flashback operation. Instead, you would probably want to use Flashback Transaction Query to manually undo each row change.

Like Flashback Query, the performance of a Flashback Table operation is dependent on the amount of data that has to be rewound, and how far back you are rewinding. The more data that has to be undone, the longer the operation will take. But this will always be faster than trying to perform a point-in-time recovery of the table by other methods: you can try TSPITR, or you can try to restore the tablespaces to a different instance and then export the table from the clone instance and import back into production. Nothing can come close to Flashback Table in terms of performance.

Flashback Table with Oracle Enterprise Manager

There is functionality inside OEM to utilize the Flashback Table feature. The added strength of OEM for Flashback Table is the ability to first explore the table via Flashback Versions Query to determine exactly to what time you want to flashback. If you already know the exact time for flashback, using SQL at the command line would be just as simple as using the Flashback Table Wizard in OEM. OEM does, however, provide a way to determine what dependencies are at play, as described in the following RMAN Workshop.

RMAN Workshop: *Explore Flashback Table*

Workshop Notes
In this workshop, we will "accidentally" delete all the rows from the WOODSCREW table and then flashback the entire table to the point in time right before the delete transaction took place.

Step 1.   View the data in WOODSCREW. Because of previous exercises, it might be worthwhile to truncate the table and then reinsert the records manually using the original population script (as shown earlier in the "Explore Flashback Versions Query" RMAN Workshop). Make sure you have all eight rows. Also, make sure you enable row movement prior to inserting the fault:

```
alter table woodscrew enable row movement;
```

Step 2.   Insert the fault. We will delete all the rows in the table using a SQL*Plus DELETE statement. Afterward, select View Data from the Actions drop-down list in OEM to view the empty table.

```
delete from woodscrew;
commit;
```

Step 3. From OEM, choose Administration | Schema | Tables, and then choose the WOODSCREW table. From the Actions drop-down list, choose Flashback Table, and then click Go. This takes you into a Perform Object Level Recovery: Point-in-Time Wizard, which first asks you to specify the point in time to which to recover. We will pretend not to know when the delete took place, so choose to evaluate row changes and transactions—the first choice. Click Next.

Step 4. You will now see a familiar screen for the RMAN Workshops in this chapter—the Flashback Versions Query interface. Here, we have to set our columns (MOVE ALL) and a WHERE clause to narrow down our search. Because the delete affected all rows, we can choose a single row to review here. We will use the same row as in previous Workshops:

```
where scr_id=1001 and manufactr_id='Tommy Hardware'
```

Now we can see the information about the DELETE operation that whacked our poor WOODSCREW table, as shown here:

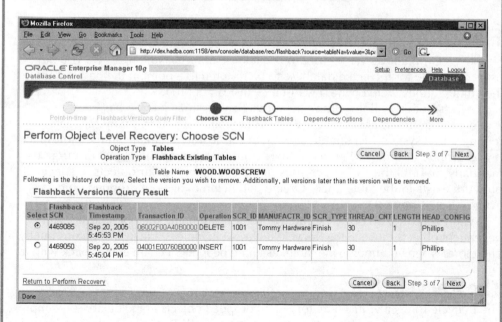

Step 5. You can click the transaction ID to review the entire delete. However, of more importance to us is the Flashback SCN column, which shows us the SCN to set to undo the DELETE operation. With the appropriate DELETE transaction checked from the list, simply click Next to automatically choose the flashback SCN specified on this screen.

Step 6. In Step 4 of 7 in the Flashback Table Wizard, Oracle allows you to specify any logically related objects that should be rewound to the same SCN as this table. Oracle automatically honors all constraints that exist for the table, but you may have logically related tables that should be flashed back. If so, this is your opportunity to specify them. In our example, we do not have any related tables, so click Next.

Step 7. Voila! We are magically transported to Step 7 of 7, where we see the summary of the action that will take place. Of most usefulness here is the Show Row Changes and Show SQL buttons, which will show, respectively, what rows will be changed and what SQL will be executed by OEM on your behalf. Click Submit. If there is any problem, or if you just feel better about it, you can cut the OEM-generated SQL into a SQL*Plus session to run the Flashback Table operation:

```
FLASHBACK TABLE SALES.WOODSCREW TO SCN 804109;
```

Flashback Drop

Flashback Drop allows you to "undrop" database objects. No longer will you have users desperate for the entire database to be restored to a point in the past because they thought they were on the dev instance instead of prod.

There's nothing all that dramatic about how Flashback Drop has been implemented. In Oracle Database 10g, when you drop a table, it merely gets renamed to a system-identifiable string, but the segment remains in the tablespace it was dropped from. It will remain there until you undrop the object or purge it manually, or until the tablespace runs out of space for regular objects. If space pressure exists in the tablespace, Oracle will begin to age out dropped objects from oldest to newest.

When you drop an object, Oracle doesn't just rename the object itself. All dependent objects move to the Recycle Bin as well: indices, triggers, and constraints. Therefore, when you undrop the table, its entire dependent chain comes back with it.

The Recycle Bin

The Recycle Bin is a virtual directory of all dropped objects in the database—simply a list of objects that have been dropped but not purged. The Recycle Bin is a logical container and does not require a specific storage location; actual storage for all dropped objects is in the tablespace the object was in prior to being dropped. Consider an example. User matt drops the table WS_APP.WOODSCREWS. The WOODSCREWS table is in the tablespace WS_APP_DATA, but its two indices are in the WS_APP_IDX tablespace. When WOODSCREWS is dropped, the table is renamed to an internal name, and so are the two indices that existed on the table. Both appear in the DBA_RECYCLEBIN view. However, the actual WOODSCREWS table segment still exists in the WS_APP_DATA tablespace, and the indices still exist in the WS_APP_IDX tablespace. They are logically part of the Recycle Bin, but physically exist in the same place they always have.

The Recycle Bin is quickly viewed via the following two data dictionary views:

- USER_RECYCLEBIN

- DBA_RECYCLEBIN

Purging the Recycle Bin

Manually eliminating dropped objects from the Recycle Bin is not necessary. Objects are purged from the Recycle Bin as the space is required by other segments in the tablespace. In other words, dropped objects continue to take up space in a tablespace until other objects in that tablespace run out of free space elsewhere. Then, the first dropped object is the first object to be purged. Oracle automatically looks to purge indices before tables so that actual data is the last thing to be lost. Recycle Bin objects will also be dropped before a tablespace autoextends, if autoextend is on.

The new **purge** command exists to purge the Recycle Bin. You can purge by user, by object, by tablespace, or the entire Recycle Bin:

```
purge table sales.woodscrews;
purge index sales.woodscrews_pk_idx;
purge tablespace sales;
purge recyclebin;
```

How Long Do Objects Live in the Recycle Bin?

A valid question, but the answer, of course, is: it depends. No, really. It depends. The real question you probably want to hear is, "Can I control how long an object lives in the Recycle Bin?" The answer to this question is no.

You cannot force an object to remain in the Recycle Bin if space pressure exists in the tablespace of the dropped object. Even with autoextend on, the dropped object is purged before the tablespace extends. So, if you want to determine a certain lifespan on objects in the Recycle Bin, you are left with two choices: either make the tablespace overly large to accommodate drops or manually manage the Recycle Bin and purge those objects you don't want to keep, to leave space for those you do want to keep.

You can, therefore, shorten the stay of an object in the Recycle Bin. But you cannot force something to remain, given a shortage of tablespace room.

Undropping Objects in the Recycle Bin

Getting objects back from the Recycle Bin is pretty simple—a simple SQL command renames the object back to its original name, along with any dependent objects:

```
flashback table ws_app.woodscrews to before drop;
```

Of course, sometimes it's not that simple. For instance, if you have multiple dropped objects with the same name, then you would have to refer to the object by its new and improved Recycle Bin name:

```
SQL> select object_name, original_name, droptime,
dropscn from user_recyclebin;
OBJECT_NAME                               ORIGINAL_NAME
------------------------------            ---------------
DROPTIME             DROPSCN
-------------------  ----------
RB$$48623$INDEX$0                         PK_WOODSCREW
2004-01-12:15:21:26      1241651
RB$$48622$TABLE$0                         WOODSCREW
2004-01-12:15:21:26      1241652
SQL> flashback table " RB$$48622$TABLE$0" to before drop;
```

Note the quotes around the Recycle Bin object name. These are required due to special symbols in the name.

If you have dropped an object and then created a new object with the same name, you can still flashback the first object. There is syntax in the flashback SQL to rename the object when you pull it from the Recycle Bin:

```
flashback table ws_app.woodscrews to before drop rename to woodscrews_history;
```

RMAN Workshop: *Explore Flashback Drop and the Recycle Bin*

Workshop Notes

It's time to drop our WOODSCREW table and review the Recycle Bin contents. Although you can do this at the command line, this Workshop shows you how to undrop a table using OEM.

Step 1. Drop the WOODSCREW table. From OEM, choose Administration | Schema | Tables and change the schema to the owner of the WOODSCREW table. Select the WOODSCREW table from the list of tables, and then click the Delete with Options button. A screen offers multiple delete options—drop the table, delete the rows, or truncate. Choose the first option (DROP) and click Yes.

Step 2.   View the list of tables. Note that WOODSCREW is no longer in the list. Click the Recycle Bin link in the lower-right corner of the screen to access the Recycle Bin, shown in the following screenshot. First, under Search, enter the Schema Name of the owner of the WOODSCREW table and click Go.

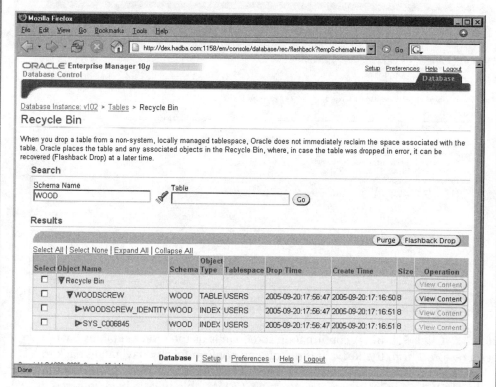

Note in the screen that the table WOODSCREW is in the Recycle Bin, along with the primary key index and the WOODSCREW_IDENTITY index. Also worth noting is the View Content button on the right, which allows you to look at the rows in the dropped table to determine if it is the correct object to be flashback dropped.

Step 3.   Check the box next to the WOODSCREW table, and then click the Flashback Drop button.

Step 4.   The next page enables you to rename the undropped object. After you click Next, you get the impact analysis from OEM explaining what exactly will be flashback dropped, as shown next.

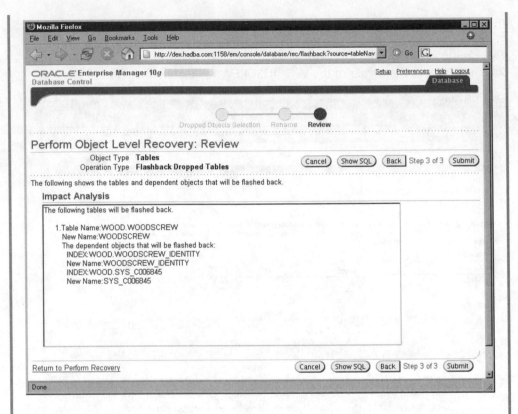

Step 5. Click Submit. A confirmation screen tells us the selected tables have been restored from the Recycle Bin. You can confirm this by navigating back to OEM and choosing Administration | Schema | Tables and choosing the schema of the WOODSCREW owner. The WOODSCREW table will be back in place.

Step 6. Delete the WOODSCREW table again. Click Recycle Bin and find the dropped table again, as outlined in Step 2. Check the box next to WOODSCREW, and then click Purge (next to Flashback Drop).

Step 7. A confirmation screen asks you if you want to purge the selected objects and their dependents. Click Continue. The Recycle Bin of the WOOD user is now empty of the WOODSCREW table and its indices. They have been permanently removed from the database.

Flashback Database

The most revolutionary Flashback Technology may also be the one that gets used the least often. Flashback Database provides the ability to quickly rewind the entire database to a previous point in time. This operation has the same end result as you would get from doing point-in-time recovery using RMAN or user-managed recovery. However, Flashback Database does not require the restore of all of the database's datafiles from the most recent backup, followed by a roll-forward using all the archive logs that have accumulated since that backup. By avoiding these costly operations, Flashback Database can perform a point-in-time recovery in a fraction of the time typically required for such an operation.

Flashback Database works by incrementally recording all blocks that have changed at a timed interval. These flashback "checkpoints" then provide the points to which the database can be "rewound." After rolling back to the flashback checkpoint, you can use archive logs to then roll forward to the exact time or SCN specified by the **flashback database** command. So, the operation uses new technology as well as that old standby, the archive logs, to provide a fast way to perform point-in-time-recovery.

Typically, there are less archivelogs to be applied after a flashback checkpoint than must be applied to the last backup (typically taken every night, versus every few minutes for flashback logs), so the recovery stage of flashback is very quick.

Flashback Logs

Flashback Database implements a new type of log, called the *flashback log*. Flashback logs are generated by the database at regular intervals and accumulate in the flash recovery area (FRA). You must have an FRA for Flashback Database; the logs cannot be created anywhere else. The flashback log contains a copied image of every block that has been changed since the last flashback log was generated. These blocks can then be reinstated into the database when a **flashback database** command is issued to rewind the database back to its state at the time specified in the **flashback** command.

Because entire blocks are being dumped to the flashback logs, they can accumulate very quickly in extremely active databases. Setting an appropriately sized FRA is crucial to the success of meeting your Flashback Database needs. In addition, you can manually turn off flashback logging, as follows, for certain tablespaces that could be manually re-created after a Flashback Database operation, and thereby decrease the amount of logging that occurs:

```
alter tablespace ws_app_idx flashback off;
```

You can turn flashback logging back on at any time, as follows, but it is worth noting that you cannot rewind backward through a flashback logging gap for the tablespace you turned off:

```
alter tablespace sales_idx flashback on;
```

Any tablespace that has flashback logging turned off for any period of time within the **flashback database** command would need to be offlined prior to performing the Flashback Database operation.

Flashback Retention Target

The lifespan of flashback logs correlates directly to how far back in time you would like to have the Flashback Database option. By default, the flashback logs are kept long enough so that you can always flashback 24 hours from the current time. If this is too long or too short of a time, you can change it with an initialization parameter:

```
alter system set db_flashback_retention_target=720;
```

The value is specified in minutes (720 would be 12 hours).

RMAN Workshop: *Configure for Flashback Database*

Workshop Notes

This Workshop walks you through the primary steps required to configure the database initially for using flashback logging for Flashback Database operations.

Step 1. Shut down the database and startup mount. The database must be mounted but not open.

```
SQL> select status from v$instance;
```

In addition, check to make sure the database is in ARCHIVELOG mode, which is required for Flashback Database:

```
SQL> archive log list;
Database log mode              Archive Mode
Automatic archival             Enabled
Archive destination            USE_DB_RECOVERY_FILE_DEST
Oldest online log sequence     62
Next log sequence to archive   64
Current log sequence           64
```

Step 2. Set the flashback retention target to your desired value. We will use 12 hours as the window:

```
alter system set db_flashback_retention_target=720
SCOPE=BOTH SID='*';
```

Step 3. Set the values for DB_RECOVERY_FILE_DEST and DB_RECOVERY_FLE_DEST_SIZE (FRA parameters). Note that if you have already set these for your RMAN backup strategy, you should review the parameters now. Flashback logs increase FRA usage significantly. It would behoove you to at least double the given size of the FRA.

```
SQL> ALTER SYSTEM SET DB_RECOVERY_FILE_DEST_SIZE = 2335825920
SCOPE=BOTH SID='*';
SQL> ALTER SYSTEM SET DB_RECOVERY_FILE_DEST = '/u02/fra/'
SCOPE=BOTH SID='*';
```

Step 4. Turn flashback logging on. This is done in the same fashion as turning ARCHIVELOG mode on—with an **alter database** command when the database is mounted but not open:

```
alter database flashback on;
```

Step 5. Turn flashback logging off for any tablespaces that you deem do not require it:

```
alter tablespace sales_idx flashback off;
```

Step 6. Open the database:

```
alter database open;
```

Flashback Database: Tuning and Tweaking

So, you've determined that Flashback Database provides you with a fallback position you desire for your database, and you have determined how far back you want your fallback position to be. You've set your DB_FLASHBACK_RETENTION_TARGET. Now, the questions come up: "How do I know if I have enough space in my FRA to handle the volume of flashback logs being generated? And, for that matter, how much flashback logging is occurring?" The following sections answer those questions.

Using V$FLASHBACK_DATABASE_LOG

One thing at a time. First, Oracle provides built-in analysis for you to use in determining if you need to increase the size of your FRA. After you enable flashback logging, Oracle begins to keep track of the amount of flashback logging that is occurring, and stores it in the view V$FLASHBACK_DATABASE_LOG. This view actually provides an estimate for the total flashback size:

```
select estimated_flashback_size from v$flashback_database_log;
```

Note that this view gives the size for flashback logs, not for all users in the FRA, so you need to add this value to whatever size you need for archive logs and RMAN backups. This estimated value only gets better with age, meaning that as the database runs through its day-to-day (and then month-to-month) operations, Oracle can provide a better estimate of the size. So, it is a good idea to check back in with this estimator to find out if you still have the right specifications in place.

V$FLASHBACK_DATABASE_LOG also provides you with the actual oldest time that you can flashback the database to, given the current size of the FRA and the currently available flashback logs. You can use this as another indicator of space issues in the FRA. The following select statement will provide you with a basic understanding of the state of the flashback logs.

```
select oldest_flashback_scn, oldest_flashback_time
from v$flashback_database_log;
```

Using V$FLASHBACK_DATABASE_STAT

Oracle has built a monitoring view so that you can keep your eye on flashback logging activity. V$FLASHBACK_DATABASE_STAT provides you with information on flashback data generated over the course of a period of time (typically, a one-hour window extending back from sysdate). In addition to showing how much flashback logging occurred, this view posts the redo generated and the actual database data generated over the same period. The following select shows a sample output of this view.

```
select * from v$flashback_database_stat;
BEGIN_TIM END_TIME  FLASHBACK_DATA    DB_DATA   REDO_DATA
--------- --------- --------------- ---------- ----------
ESTIMATED_FLASHBACK_SIZE
------------------------
19-SEP-05 19-SEP-05         9003008   15294464    3986944
 210247680
19-SEP-05 19-SEP-05        15884288   21225472    5766144
 210247680
19-SEP-05 19-SEP-05        10248192   25772032    5162496
 210075648
```

RMAN Workshop: *Perform Flashback Database*

Workshop Notes

It's time to give it a test drive. We are going to introduce a fault that cannot be handled by any of the other, less-intrusive forms of flashback: the table truncate. Because the truncate does not produce any redo, we cannot do a Flashback Table operation. So, we are forced to do a flashback of the entire database.

Here, we are using the WOOD.WOODSCREW_INVENTORY table that we built earlier, during the "Flashback Versions Query" RMAN Workshop. If you did not build the table yet, do so now.

Step 1. First, get the current SCN from the database. Because we are simply testing, we can prepare for the test by getting the current SCN prior to putting the fault into the database:

```
SQL> select current_scn from v$database;
CURRENT_SCN
----------------
885524
```

Step 2. Introduce the fault:

```
SQL> truncate table wood.woodscrew_inventory;
Table truncated.
```

Step 3. Shut down the database, and then remount. The database must be mounted and not open for flashback.

```
SQL> connect / as sysdba
Connected.
SQL> shutdown immediate;
Database closed.
Database dismounted.
ORACLE instance shut down.
SQL> startup mount;
```

Step 4. Issue the **flashback** command:

```
SQL> flashback database to scn 885524;
Flashback complete.
```

Step 5. Open the database in read-only mode to confirm that the table has been flashed back to the appropriate SCN:

```
SQL> alter database open read only;
Database altered.
SQL> connect wood/wood;
Connected.
SQL> select count(*) from woodscrew_inventory;
  COUNT(*)
----------
         4
```

Step 6. Open the database using the resetlogs operation:

```
SQL> connect / as sysdba
SQL> shutdown immediate;
SQL> startup mount;
SQL> alter database open resetlogs;
```

Summary

In this chapter, we introduced the new means of recovering from user-induced errors, known in Oracle Database 10*g* as Flashback Technology. The new Flashback Technology allows you to recover from logical errors in a faster, less-intrusive way than running a full-bore media recovery. We discussed using Flashback Versions Query and Transaction Query to determine the full scope of the logical corruption. We illustrated using Flashback Table command to recover from a bad DML statement, as well as from a table drop. We ended with a discussion of the new Flashback Database functionality, which allows for a point-in-time recovery of an entire database without requiring a full restore of the datafiles from backup.

CHAPTER
14

Maintaining RMAN

ntropy is a nasty result of the second law of thermodynamics. Basically, *entropy* describes the tendency of an ordered system to become disordered, the result of which is the requirement to maintain that system. RMAN is no different. When using RMAN, you have to maintain a number of things to keep it running smoothly.

In this chapter, we talk all about maintaining RMAN. From the **crosscheck** command to retention policies to redundancy policies, everything you need to know about keeping RMAN from falling apart is provided here. After we have talked about RMAN maintenance issues, we will discuss some issues specific to the recovery catalog, including an introduction to the recovery catalog schema itself.

RMAN Maintenance

You didn't think you could just start using RMAN and not have to do anything to maintain it, did you? The truth is that RMAN is fairly maintenance free, but there are a few maintenance-related things you need to be aware of, which we address in this section. First, we are going to talk about the **crosscheck** command, which is followed by a discussion of retention policies. Next, we discuss the **change** command, and then the **delete** command. Finally, we end this section with a discussion of cataloging your existing database backups in RMAN.

Cross-Checking RMAN Backups

You may encounter situations in which backup set pieces or copies are listed in the control file or recovery catalog but do not physically exist on the backup media (disk or tape). The physical files that comprise the backup or copy might have been deleted, either by some process (for example, a separate retention policy for the tape management system that you are using or a damaged tape) or perhaps by the loss of a physical device that had backup set pieces on it.

In cases where the RMAN catalog and the physical backup destinations are out of synchronization, the **crosscheck** command is used to validate the contents of the RMAN information in the control file or the recovery catalog against the actual physical backup set pieces that are on the backup media.

When using the **crosscheck** command, we are interested in the status of each backup set or copy. Each backup set or copy has status codes that are listed in the STATUS column of the views V$BACKUP_SET for backup set pieces and V$DATAFILE_COPY for copies if you are using a control file, and RC_BACKUP_SET for backup set pieces and RC_DATAFILE_COPY for copies if you want to look in the recovery catalog. There are several different backup status codes, but for now we are interested primarily in two:

■ **A** AVAILABLE; RMAN assumes the item is available on the backup media.

■ **X** EXPIRED; the backup set piece or the copy is stored in the RMAN catalog (meaning the control file or the recovery catalog) but is not physically on the backup media.

It is the purpose of the **crosscheck** command to set the status of the RMAN catalog to either AVAILABLE (status code A) or EXPIRED (status code X). When the **crosscheck** command is executed, RMAN checks each backup set or copy listed in the catalog and determines if it is on the backup media. If it is not, then that piece will be marked as EXPIRED and will not be a candidate for any restore operation. If the piece exists, then it will maintain its AVAILABLE status. If a backup piece or copy was previously marked EXPIRED and it becomes available again (for example, after the recovery of a failed disk drive), then the **crosscheck** command will return that piece's status to AVAILABLE.

In the following example of the execution of the **crosscheck** command, we are checking the status of all backup sets and determining whether they exist on the backup medium:

```
RMAN> crosscheck backup;
using channel ORA_DISK_1
crosschecked backup piece: found to be 'AVAILABLE'
backup piece handle=C:\ORACLE\PRODUCT\10.2.0\FLASH_RECOVERY_AREA\ROB10R2\
BACKUPSET\2006_03_14\O1_MF_ANNNN_TAG20060314T152702_21GF99CV_.BKP
recid=260 stamp=585070025

crosschecked backup piece: found to be 'AVAILABLE'
backup piece handle=C:\ORACLE\PRODUCT\10.2.0\FLASH_RECOVERY_AREA\ROB10R2\
BACKUPSET\2006_03_14\O1_MF_NNNDF_TAG20060314T152713_21GF9QRZ_.BKP
recid=261 stamp=585070039

crosschecked backup piece: found to be 'EXPIRED'
backup piece handle=C:\ORACLE\PRODUCT\10.2.0\FLASH_RECOVERY_AREA\ROB10R2\
BACKUPSET\2006_03_14\O1_MF_ANNNN_TAG20060314T153111_21GFK265_.BKP
recid=262 stamp=585070274

crosschecked backup piece: found to be 'AVAILABLE'
backup piece handle=C:\ORACLE\PRODUCT\10.2.0\FLASH_RECOVERY_AREA\ROB10R2\
AUTOBACKUP\2006_03_14\O1_MF_S_585070278_21GFKB08_.BKP
recid=263 stamp=585070281
Crosschecked 4 objects
```

In this example, we have cross-checked a total of four backup set pieces. Notice that the **crosscheck** command lists all the backup set pieces that were found to be available. It also lists those backup set pieces that were not found on the backup media, shows them to be EXPIRED, and sets their status to EXPIRED at the same time.

Note that the **crosscheck** command will not change a backup set piece with a status of DELETE to AVAILABLE. Any backup marked with a status of DELETE cannot be changed.

You can also cross-check datafile backups, tablespace backups, control file backups, and SPFILE backups. Additionally, you can be selective in the specific backup you want to cross-check by identifying the tag associated with that backup. You can even cross-check all backups taken based on the device used or based on a time period. The following are several examples of cross-checking backups:

```
crosscheck backup of datafile 1;
crosscheck backup of tablespace users;
crosscheck backup of controlfile;
crosscheck backup of spfile;
crosscheck backup tag='SAT_BACKUP';
crosscheck backup completed after 'sysdate - 2';
crosscheck backup completed between 'sysdate - 5' and 'sysdate - 2;
crosscheck backup device type sbt;
```

The first example is a cross-check of backups. As you might expect, you also can cross-check archive log backups:

```
RMAN> crosscheck archivelog all;

using target database control file instead of recovery catalog
allocated channel: ORA_DISK_1
channel ORA_DISK_1: sid=159 devtype=DISK
validation succeeded for archived log
archive log filename=C:\ARCHIVE\ROB10R2ARC00059_0582936761.001
recid=392 stamp=585070021

validation failed for archived log
archive log filename=C:\ARCHIVE\ROB10R2ARC00060_0582936761.001
recid=394 stamp=585070269

validation succeeded for archived log
archive log filename=C:\ARCHIVE\ROB10R2ARC00061_0582936761.001
recid=396 stamp=585071021

validation succeeded for archived log
archive log filename=C:\ORACLE\PRODUCT\10.2.0\FLASH_RECOVERY_AREA\ROB10R2\
ARCHIVELOG\2006_03_14\O1_MF_1_61_21GG8DJL_.ARC recid
Crosschecked 4 objects
```

You can cross-check archived redo log backups based on a number or criteria, including time, SCN (specific or high/low range), or log sequence number. You can even use the **like** parameter, along with wildcards, to cross-check specific archive log backups. Here are some variations in the **crosscheck** command:

```
crosscheck archivelog like 'ARC001.log';
crosscheck archivelog 'D:\ORACLE\ADMIN\RECOVER\ARCH\ARC00012.001';
crosscheck archivelog like '%ARC00012.001';
crosscheck archivelog from time "to_date('01-10-2006', 'mm-dd-yyyy')";
crosscheck archivelog until time "to_date('01-10-2006', 'mm-dd-yyyy')";
crosscheck archivelog from sequence 12;
crosscheck archivelog until sequence 522;
```

To cross-check copies, use the **crosscheck copy** command. You can cross-check datafile copies, control file copies, archive redo log copies, and archived redo logs (on disk). Here are two examples of cross-checking these kinds of objects:

```
crosscheck copy of datafile 5;
crosscheck datafilecopy 'd:\oracle\oradata\recover\recover_users_01.dbf';
```

RMAN Workshop: *Using the crosscheck Command*

Workshop Notes

This Workshop assumes that you have a functional Oracle database running in ARCHIVELOG mode. Additionally, this Workshop assumes that you are backing up your database to disk, that you have a tablespace called USERS in your database, and that one datafile is associated with the USERS tablespace.

Step 1. Using RMAN, back up the USERS tablespace:

```
RMAN> backup tablespace users;

Starting backup at 14-MAR-06
using channel ORA_DISK_1
channel ORA_DISK_1: starting full datafile backupset
channel ORA_DISK_1: specifying datafile(s) in backupset
input datafile fno=00004
name=C:\ORACLE\PRODUCT\10.2.0\ORADATA\ROB10R2\USERS01.DBF
channel ORA_DISK_1: starting piece 1 at 14-MAR-06
channel ORA_DISK_1: finished piece 1 at 14-MAR-06
piece handle=C:\ORACLE\PRODUCT\10.2.0\FLASH_RECOVERY_AREA\ROB10R2\
BACKUPSET\2006_03_14\O1_MF_NNNDF_TAG20060314T162101_21GJGFSD_.BKP
tag=TAG20060314T162101 comment=NONE

channel ORA_DISK_1: backup set complete, elapsed time: 00:00:35
Finished backup at 14-MAR-06

Starting Control File and SPFILE Autobackup at 14-MAR-06
piece handle=C:\ORACLE\PRODUCT\10.2.0\FLASH_RECOVERY_AREA\ROB10R2\
AUTOBACKUP\2006_03_14\O1_MF_S_585073299_21GJHVG0_.BKP comment=NONE
Finished Control File and SPFILE Autobackup at 14-MAR-06
```

Step 2. Look at the output of the backup and determine the backup set piece that has just been created. The backup set piece is highlighted in the output in Step 1. Note that we are not removing the control file autobackup set piece.

Step 3. Remove the backup piece from the disk.

Step 4. Issue the **crosscheck** command to determine the status of the backup set piece. RMAN will detect that the backup set piece has been removed and mark it EXPIRED. Note that the control file autobackup piece is still available.

```
RMAN> crosscheck backup;

using channel ORA_DISK_1

crosschecked backup piece: found to be 'EXPIRED'
backup piece handle=C:\ORACLE\PRODUCT\10.2.0\FLASH_RECOVERY_AREA\ROB10R2\
BACKUPSET\2006_03_14\O1_MF_NNNDF_TAG20060314T162101_21GJGFSD_.BKP
recid=265 stamp=585073261

crosschecked backup piece: found to be 'AVAILABLE'
backup piece handle=C:\ORACLE\PRODUCT\10.2.0\FLASH_RECOVERY_AREA\ROB10R2\
AUTOBACKUP\2006_03_14\O1_MF_S_585073299_21GJHVG0_.BKP
recid=266 stamp=585073307

Crosschecked 7 objects
```

Validation of RMAN Backups

RMAN provides the **validate** command, which allows you to examine a given backup set and verify that it can be restored. With this command, you can choose which backup sets to verify, whereas the **validate** parameter of the **restore** command allows RMAN to determine which backup set to validate.

Here is an example of the use of the **validate** command to get the primary key of the backup set and validate that backup set. Note that you must pass the primary key ID of the backup set that you wish to validate. This primary key can be determined by running the **list backupset summary** command.

```
List of Backups
===============
Key     TY LV S Device Type Completion Time #Pieces #Copies Compressed Tag
------- -- -- - ----------- --------------- ------- ------- ---------- ---
260     B  A  A DISK        14-MAR-06       1       1       NO
TAG20060314T152702
261     B  F  A DISK        14-MAR-06       1       1       NO
TAG20060314T152713
```

```
262      B  A  A DISK          14-MAR-06          1          1          NO
TAG20060314T153111
263      B  F  A DISK          14-MAR-06          1          1          NO
TAG20060314T153118
264      B  A  A DISK          14-MAR-06          1          1          NO
TAG20060314T154657
265      B  F  A DISK          14-MAR-06          1          1          NO
TAG20060314T162101
266      B  F  A DISK          14-MAR-06          1          1          NO
TAG20060314T162139
```

We then validate the backup set. In this case, it's an archive log backup:

```
RMAN> validate backupset 266;
```

Backup Retention Policies

In Chapter 3, we mentioned configuration of a retention policy for RMAN backups and copies. A *retention policy* is a method of managing backups and copies and specifying how long you want to keep them on your backup media. You can define two basic types of retention policies: the *recovery window backup retention policy* and the *backup redundancy backup retention policy*. We will talk more about those shortly.

Each redundancy policy is persistent until changed or removed (or the control file is rebuilt using the **create controlfile** command). Additionally, the two redundancy policies are mutually exclusive. Finally, even with a redundancy policy, physical backup pieces are not removed until you use the **delete** command with the **obsolete** parameter to remove them.

Now, let's look at each of these retention policies in some more detail. After that, we will look at how we manage RMAN backups and copies that are made obsolete as a result of the retention policies.

Recovery Window Backup Retention Policy

The use of this type of retention policy is based on the latest possible date that you want to be able to recover your database to. With a recovery window backup retention policy, you can direct Oracle to make sure that if you want to be able to recover your database to a point in time two weeks ago, you will be able to do so.

For example, assume that today is Monday and you have three backups. The first backup was taken the day before, on Sunday, the second backup was taken on the previous Thursday, and the last backup was taken ten days ago last Saturday. If the recovery window is set to seven days, then the first two backups (Sunday's and Thursday's) would be considered current. However, the backup taken ten days ago, on the previous Saturday, would be considered obsolete. If we wanted to establish this seven-day redundancy policy for RMAN, we would use the **configure** command with the **retention policy to recovery window** parameter:

```
configure retention policy to recovery window of 7 days;
```

Backup Redundancy Backup Retention Policy

When the backup redundancy backup retention policy is used, RMAN will maintain *x* number of database backups, starting with the most current backup. For example, suppose you have configured a backup redundancy of 3 and you did backups on Monday, Tuesday, Wednesday, and Thursday. Because the retention policy is set to 3, Oracle will obsolete the Monday backup as soon as the Thursday backup is successfully completed.

The backup window backup retention policy is enabled using the **configure** command with the **retention policy to redundancy** parameter. If you wanted to set the backup window backup retention policy to 3, you would use the following command:

```
configure retention policy to redundancy 3;
```

Retention Policy Maintenance

When a given backup or copy meets the criteria of a backup retention policy and becomes obsolete, RMAN does not automatically remove that backup or copy. RMAN marks the backup or copy as OBSOLETE. You can determine which backups RMAN has marked as OBSOLETE with the **report obsolete** command (we will look at the **report** command in the next chapter):

```
report obsolete;
```

Of course, when you view the backups that have been made obsolete, you might find that there are some that you want to retain. In this event, you would use the RMAN **change** command with the **keep** parameter to change the status of the backups you want to retain. When you use this command, the backups or copies impacted are considered to be *long-term backups* and are not subject to the chosen retention policy.

With the **change** command, you can modify a backup so that it will be retained forever, or you can define a new date for that backup or copy to be made obsolete by RMAN. Furthermore, you can define that any logs associated with that backup should be retained as well, ensuring the backup will always be recoverable to the current point in time (consider the impact that this might have on storage, however). Finally, you can obsolete a backup manually with the **change nokeep** command. Here are several examples of the **change** command in use to override an established retention policy:

```
-- Run the list backup command to get the backup key we need
-- This is just a partial listing of the list backup output
-- We bolded the backup set key values that we will be using.
RMAN> list backup;
List of Backup Sets
===================
```

```
BS Key   Size        Device Type Elapsed Time Completion Time
-------  ----------  ----------- ------------ ---------------
267      2.92M       DISK          00:00:04    14-MAR-06
  BP Key: 267   Status: AVAILABLE  Compressed: NO  Tag: TAG20060314T164524
Piece Name: C:\ORACLE\PRODUCT\10.2.0\FLASH_RECOVERY_AREA\ROB10R2\BACKUPSET\
2006_03_14\O1_MF_ANNNN_TAG20060314T164524_21GKW8GQ_.BKP

  List of Archived Logs in backup set 267
  Thrd Seq     Low SCN    Low Time   Next SCN   Next Time
  ---- ------- ---------- ---------- ---------- ---------
   1   61      4900588    14-MAR-06 4901437     14-MAR-06
   1   62      4901437    14-MAR-06 4901573     14-MAR-06
   1   63      4901573    14-MAR-06 4903898     14-MAR-06

BS Key  Type LV Size        Device Type Elapsed Time Completion Time
------- -- -- ----------  ----------- ------------ ---------------
268     Full    790.66M     DISK          00:03:35    14-MAR-06
  BP Key: 268   Status: AVAILABLE  Compressed: NO  Tag: TAG20060314T164533
Piece Name: C:\ORACLE\PRODUCT\10.2.0\FLASH_RECOVERY_AREA\ROB10R2\BACKUPSET\
2006_03_14\O1_MF_NNNDF_TAG20060314T164533_21GKWLH6_.BKP

  List of Datafiles in backup set 268
  File LV Type Ckp SCN    Ckp Time   Name
  ---- -- ---- ---------- ---------- ----
   1      Full 4903912    14-MAR-06
C:\ORACLE\PRODUCT\10.2.0\ORADATA\ROB10R2\SYSTEM01.DBF
   2      Full 4903912    14-MAR-06
C:\ORACLE\PRODUCT\10.2.0\ORADATA\ROB10R2\UNDOTBS01.DBF
   3      Full 4903912    14-MAR-06
C:\ORACLE\PRODUCT\10.2.0\ORADATA\ROB10R2\SYSAUX01.DBF
   4      Full 4903912    14-MAR-06
C:\ORACLE\PRODUCT\10.2.0\ORADATA\ROB10R2\USERS01.DBF
   5      Full 4903912    14-MAR-06
C:\ORACLE\PRODUCT\10.2.0\ORADATA\ROB10R2\EXAMPLE01.DBF
   6      Full 4903912    14-MAR-06
C:\ORACLE\PRODUCT\10.2.0\ORADATA\ROB10R2\NEWTBS01.DBF
   7      Full 4903912    14-MAR-06
C:\ORACLE\PRODUCT\10.2.0\ORADATA\ROB10R2\TEST_RECOVER_01.DBF
   8      Full 4903912    14-MAR-06
C:\ORACLE\PRODUCT\10.2.0\ORADATA\ROB10R2\TEST_RECOVER_TWO_01.DBF

BS Key   Size        Device Type Elapsed Time Completion Time
-------  ----------  ----------- ------------ ---------------
269      22.50K      DISK          00:00:02    14-MAR-06
  BP Key: 269   Status: AVAILABLE  Compressed: NO  Tag: TAG20060314T164916
Piece Name: C:\ORACLE\PRODUCT\10.2.0\FLASH_RECOVERY_AREA\ROB10R2\BACKUPSET\
2006_03_14\O1_MF_ANNNN_TAG20060314T164916_21GL3GPM_.BKP

  List of Archived Logs in backup set 269
  Thrd Seq     Low SCN    Low Time   Next SCN   Next Time
  ---- ------- ---------- ---------- ---------- ---------
   1   64      4903898    14-MAR-06 4904000     14-MAR-06
```

```
BS Key  Type LV Size       Device Type Elapsed Time Completion Time
------- ---- -- ---------- ----------- ------------ ---------------
270     Full    7.89M      DISK          00:00:05    14-MAR-06
  BP Key: 270   Status: AVAILABLE  Compressed: NO  Tag: TAG20060314T164923
Piece Name: C:\ORACLE\PRODUCT\10.2.0\FLASH_RECOVERY_AREA\ROB10R2\
AUTOBACKUP\2006_03_14\O1_MF_S_585074963_21GL3P8K_.BKP
  Control File Included: Ckp SCN: 4904009      Ckp time: 14-MAR-06
  SPFILE Included: Modification time: 14-MAR-06
-- change a backup so it will be retained forever. 267 is the backup key
-- that we get from the list backup RMAN command
-- Change backup 267 from an obsolete status to a keep status.
-- Note that this command requires a recovery catalog
change backupset 267 keep forever logs;

-- change a backup so it will be kept for 7  more days
change backupset 267 keep until time 'sysdate + 7' logs;

-- Obsolete a backup
change backupset 33 nokeep;
```

When you change a backup or copy, you have to reference the key that is associated with that backup. As you can see from the example, you find this key by using the **list backup** or **list copy** command, which are described in the next chapter. The **keep forever** option has two important restrictions. First, it's only available if you are using a recovery catalog. Second, it is not available if you are using the FRA.

Once you have reviewed the report, you can then direct RMAN to actually remove the backups with the RMAN **delete** command with the **obsolete** parameter:

```
delete obsolete;
```

If you have a backup that you don't want to make subject to the chosen redundancy policy, you can use the **keep** parameter of the **backup** command to indicate an alternate retention criteria for that backup. For example, here are some **backup** commands that define an alternate retention criteria for the backups being performed:

```
backup database keep forever;
backup database keep until time "to_date('01/01/06','mm/dd/yy')";
backup database keep 5 days;
```

The change Command

We introduced the **change** command earlier in this chapter and explained how it can be used to modify the retention window assigned to a specific backup. The **change** command allows you to change the status of a backup. You might have a case where one of your backup media devices becomes unavailable for a period of time (perhaps someone spilled a drink down the power supply). In this event, you can use the **change** command to indicate that the backups on that device are unavailable.

Once you have properly scolded the employee for fiddling around in your hardware area with a drink and have fixed the device, you can change the status of that backup set with the **change** command again so that it will take on an AVAILABLE status. You can also change a backup status to UNAVAILABLE, indicating that the backup is not currently available. This effectively disqualifies the backup from consideration during restore and recovery operations, but protects the backup record from being removed during the execution of the **delete expired** command. Here are some examples of the use of the **change** command:

```
change backup of database tag = 'GOLD'  unavailable;
change backup of database like '%GOLD%' unavailable;
change backupset 33 unavailable;
change backupset 33 available;
change archivelog 'd:\oracle\mydb\arch\arch_001.arc' unavailable;
```

Using the **change** command, you can modify the status of archived redo log backups. For example, you can modify the status to UNAVAILABLE for all archived redo logs that have been backed up at least a given number of times. You can also change the status of all backups that occurred using a given device. Examples of these operations are shown next:

```
change archivelog all backed up 5 times to device type disk unavailable;
change backup of database device type disk unavailable;
```

You can also use the **change** command to delete backup sets (physically on the backup media and from the control file and recovery catalog). The **delete** parameter is used for this operation. First, you need to identify the RMAN backup IDs of the backups that you wish to remove. Use either the **list backup** or **list copy** command (which are covered in detail in the next chapter) to perform this operation. Here is an example of how to get the backup ID using the **list backup** command (we have modified the output somewhat to save space):

```
RMAN> list backup;
List of Backup Sets
===================

BS Key  Size        Device Type Elapsed Time Completion Time
------- ----------  ----------- ------------ ---------------
267     2.92M       DISK        00:00:04     14-MAR-06
 BP Key: 267    Status: AVAILABLE  Compressed: NO  Tag: TAG20060314T164524
Piece Name: C:\ORACLE\PRODUCT\10.2.0\FLASH_RECOVERY_AREA\ROB10R2\BACKUPSET\
2006_03_14\O1_MF_ANNNN_TAG20060314T164524_21GKW8GQ_.BKP
```

```
   List of Archived Logs in backup set 267
   Thrd Seq     Low SCN    Low Time   Next SCN   Next Time
   ---- ------- ---------- ---------- ---------- ---------
   1    61      4900588    14-MAR-06  4901437    14-MAR-06
   1    62      4901437    14-MAR-06  4901573    14-MAR-06
   1    63      4901573    14-MAR-06  4903898    14-MAR-06

BS Key  Type LV Size       Device Type Elapsed Time Completion Time
------- ---- -- ---------- ----------- ------------ ---------------
268     Full    790.66M    DISK          00:03:35    14-MAR-06
 BP Key: 268    Status: AVAILABLE  Compressed: NO  Tag: TAG20060314T164533
Piece Name: C:\ORACLE\PRODUCT\10.2.0\FLASH_RECOVERY_AREA\ROB10R2\BACKUPSET\
2006_03_14\O1_MF_NNNDF_TAG20060314T164533_21GKWLH6_.BKP

   List of Datafiles in backup set 268
   File LV Type Ckp SCN    Ckp Time   Name
   ---- -- ---- ---------- ---------- ----
   1       Full 4903912    14-MAR-06
C:\ORACLE\PRODUCT\10.2.0\ORADATA\ROB10R2\SYSTEM01.DBF
   2       Full 4903912    14-MAR-06
C:\ORACLE\PRODUCT\10.2.0\ORADATA\ROB10R2\UNDOTBS01.DBF
   3       Full 4903912    14-MAR-06
C:\ORACLE\PRODUCT\10.2.0\ORADATA\ROB10R2\SYSAUX01.DBF
   4       Full 4903912    14-MAR-06
C:\ORACLE\PRODUCT\10.2.0\ORADATA\ROB10R2\USERS01.DBF
   5       Full 4903912    14-MAR-06
C:\ORACLE\PRODUCT\10.2.0\ORADATA\ROB10R2\EXAMPLE01.DBF
   6       Full 4903912    14-MAR-06
C:\ORACLE\PRODUCT\10.2.0\ORADATA\ROB10R2\NEWTBS01.DBF
   7       Full 4903912    14-MAR-06
C:\ORACLE\PRODUCT\10.2.0\ORADATA\ROB10R2\TEST_RECOVER_01.DBF
   8       Full 4903912    14-MAR-06
C:\ORACLE\PRODUCT\10.2.0\ORADATA\ROB10R2\TEST_RECOVER_TWO_01.DBF

BS Key  Size       Device Type Elapsed Time Completion Time
------- ---------- ----------- ------------ ---------------
269     22.50K     DISK          00:00:02    14-MAR-06
 BP Key: 269    Status: AVAILABLE  Compressed: NO  Tag: TAG20060314T164916
Piece Name: C:\ORACLE\PRODUCT\10.2.0\FLASH_RECOVERY_AREA\ROB10R2\BACKUPSET\
2006_03_14\O1_MF_ANNNN_TAG20060314T164916_21GL3GPM_.BKP

   List of Archived Logs in backup set 269
   Thrd Seq     Low SCN    Low Time   Next SCN   Next Time
   ---- ------- ---------- ---------- ---------- ---------
   1    64      4903898    14-MAR-06  4904000    14-MAR-06

BS Key  Type LV Size       Device Type Elapsed Time Completion Time
------- ---- -- ---------- ----------- ------------ ---------------
270     Full    7.89M      DISK          00:00:05    14-MAR-06
 BP Key: 270    Status: AVAILABLE  Compressed: NO  Tag: TAG20060314T164923
Piece Name: C:\ORACLE\PRODUCT\10.2.0\FLASH_RECOVERY_AREA\ROB10R2\
AUTOBACKUP\2006_03_14\O1_MF_S_585074963_21GL3P8K_.BKP
   Control File Included: Ckp SCN: 4904009    Ckp time: 14-MAR-06
   SPFILE Included: Modification time: 14-MAR-06
```

The results of this report provide us with a detailed list of all database backups and the backup piece identifiers. We can then remove either the entire backup set, by using the BS Key identifier, or individual backup pieces, by using the BP Key identifier. Let's assume we want to remove both backup sets. The BP Key IDs for these sets are 117 and 118. Once we have this information, we simply need to use the **change** command with the **delete** parameter, and our backup will be gone. Here is what we would do to remove these backup sets:

```
RMAN> change backupset 267, 268, 269, 270 delete;
using channel ORA_DISK_1
List of Backup Pieces
BP Key  BS Key  Pc# Cp# Status       Device Type Piece Name
------- ------- --- --- ----------- ----------- ----------
267     267      1   1  AVAILABLE    DISK
C:\ORACLE\PRODUCT\10.2.0\FLASH_RECOVERY_AREA\ROB10R2\
BACKUPSET\2006_03_14\O1_MF_ANNNN_TAG20060314T164524_21GKW8GQ_.BKP
268     268      1   1  AVAILABLE    DISK
C:\ORACLE\PRODUCT\10.2.0\FLASH_RECOVERY_AREA\ROB10R2\
BACKUPSET\2006_03_14\O1_MF_NNNDF_TAG20060314T164533_21GKWLII6_.BKP
269     269      1   1  AVAILABLE    DISK
C:\ORACLE\PRODUCT\10.2.0\FLASH_RECOVERY_AREA\ROB10R2\
BACKUPSET\2006_03_14\O1_MF_ANNNN_TAG20060314T164916_21GL3GPM_.BKP
270     270      1   1  AVAILABLE    DISK
C:\ORACLE\PRODUCT\10.2.0\FLASH_RECOVERY_AREA\ROB10R2\
AUTOBACKUP\2006_03_14\O1_MF_S_585074963_21GL3P8K_.BKP

Do you really want to delete the above objects (enter YES or NO)? yes
deleted backup piece
backup piece
handle=C:\ORACLE\PRODUCT\10.2.0\FLASH_RECOVERY_AREA\ROB10R2\BACKUPSET\
2006_03_14\O1_MF_ANNNN_TAG20060314T164524_21GKW8GQ_.BKP
recid=267 stamp=585074728

deleted backup piece
backup piece
handle=C:\ORACLE\PRODUCT\10.2.0\FLASH_RECOVERY_AREA\ROB10R2\BACKUPSET\
2006_03_14\O1_MF_NNNDF_TAG20060314T164533_21GKWLH6_.BKP
recid=268 stamp=585074738

deleted backup piece
backup piece
handle=C:\ORACLE\PRODUCT\10.2.0\FLASH_RECOVERY_AREA\ROB10R2\BACKUPSET\
2006_03_14\O1_MF_ANNNN_TAG20060314T164916_21GL3GPM_.BKP
recid=269 stamp=585074958
deleted backup piece
```

```
backup piece
handle=C:\ORACLE\PRODUCT\10.2.0\FLASH_RECOVERY_AREA\ROB10R2\AUTOBACKUP\
2006_03_14\O1_MF_S_585074963_21GL3P8K_.BKP
recid=270 stamp=585074966
Deleted 4 objects
```

In this example, backup sets 117 and 118, as well as all the associated backup pieces, will be removed. Here are some additional examples of other options for the **change** command that will result in the removal of backup set pieces:

```
change backuppiece 1304 delete;
change archivelog until logseq = 544 delete;
```

Finally, you can use the **change backuppiece uncatalog** command to remove backup set pieces from the catalog. If the **change backuppiece uncatalog** command removes the last remaining backup set piece, then it will also remove the backup set record. Here is an example of using the **change backuppiece uncatalog** command:

```
RMAN> Change backuppiece
'/u01/oracle/RMAN/mydb/mydb_user01_01.bak' uncatalog;
```

RMAN Workshop: *Using the change Command*

Workshop Notes
This Workshop assumes that you have a functional Oracle database running in ARCHIVELOG mode, that you are backing up your database to disk, that you have a tablespace called USERS in your database, and that one datafile is associated with the USERS tablespace.

Step 1.   Using RMAN, back up the USERS tablespace:

```
RMAN> backup tablespace users;
Starting backup at 14-MAR-06
using channel ORA_DISK_1
channel ORA_DISK_1: starting full datafile backupset
channel ORA_DISK_1: specifying datafile(s) in backupset
input datafile fno=00004
name=C:\ORACLE\PRODUCT\10.2.0\ORADATA\ROB10R2\USERS01.DBF
channel ORA_DISK_1: starting piece 1 at 14-MAR-06
channel ORA_DISK_1: finished piece 1 at 14-MAR-06
piece handle=C:\ORACLE\PRODUCT\10.2.0\FLASH_RECOVERY_AREA\ROB10R2\
BACKUPSET\2006_03_14\O1_MF_NNNDF_TAG20060314T171748_21GMRXDL_.BKP
tag=TAG20060314T171748 comment=NONE

channel ORA_DISK_1: backup set complete, elapsed time: 00:00:36
Finished backup at 14-MAR-06
```

```
Starting Control File and SPFILE Autobackup at 14-MAR-06
piece handle=C:\ORACLE\PRODUCT\10.2.0\FLASH_RECOVERY_AREA\ROB10R2\
AUTOBACKUP\2006_03_14\O1_MF_S_585076704_21GMT3X0_.BKP comment=NONE

Finished Control File and SPFILE Autobackup at 14-MAR-06
RMAN>
```

Step 2. Look at the output of the backup and determine the backup set piece that has just been created. The backup set piece is highlighted in the output in Step 1.

Step 3. Use the list **backup of tablespace users** command to determine the backup key of the backup set piece that you need to mark as DELETED in the control file or recovery catalog. Note in the following output that we have highlighted the backup set key and the related backup set piece.

```
RMAN> list backup of tablespace users;

List of Backup Sets
===================
BS Key  Type LV Size       Device Type Elapsed Time Completion Time
------- ---- -- ---------- ----------- ------------ ---------------
277     Full    22.98M     DISK        00:00:33     14-MAR-06
BP Key: 277 Status: AVAILABLE  Compressed: NO  Tag: TAG20060314T172312
Piece Name: C:\ORACLE\PRODUCT\10.2.0\FLASH_RECOVERY_AREA\ROB10R2
\BACKUPSET\2006_03_14\O1_MF_NNNDF_TAG20060314T172312_21GN3116_.BKP

  List of Datafiles in backup set 277
  File LV Type Ckp SCN    Ckp Time  Name
  ---- -- ---- ---------- --------- ----
  4      Full 4905584    14-MAR-06
C:\ORACLE\PRODUCT\10.2.0\ORADATA\ROB10R2\USERS01.DBF
```

Step 4. Exit to the operating system and do a directory listing on the backup set piece. You should see it.

Step 5. Use the **change backuppiece** command to change the status flag of this backup set piece from AVAILABLE to DELETED:

```
RMAN> change backuppiece 277 delete;
using channel ORA_DISK_1
List of Backup Pieces
BP Key  BS Key  Pc# Cp# Status      Device Type Piece Name
------- ------- --- --- ----------- ----------- ----------
277     277     1   1   AVAILABLE   DISK
C:\ORACLE\PRODUCT\10.2.0\FLASH_RECOVERY_AREA\ROB10R2\BACKUPSET\
2006_03_14\O1_MF_NNNDF_TAG20060314T172312_21GN3116_.BKP
```

```
Do you really want to delete the above objects
(enter YES or NO)? yes
deleted backup piece
backup piece
handle=C:\ORACLE\PRODUCT\10.2.0\FLASH_RECOVERY_AREA\ROB10R2\BACKUPSET\
2006_03_14\O1_MF_NNNDF_TAG20060314T172312_21GN3116_.BKP
recid=277 stamp=585076992

Deleted 1 objects
```

Step 6. Use the **list backup of tablespace users** command to determine that the backup set piece is no longer available for use during a recovery:

```
RMAN> list backup of tablespace users;
```

Step 7. Exit to the operating system and do a directory listing on the backup set piece. You should no longer see the backup set piece. Oracle removed it, if it existed.

The delete Command

All good things must come to an end, and the same is true about the life of a given backup set. With a retention policy, we can mark backups whose usefulness and lifetime are at an end. As we mentioned already, enforcement of a redundancy policy does not remove the backups from the catalog, but rather just marks the backups with a status of OBSOLETE. The same is true with the **crosscheck** command, which we discussed earlier in this chapter. The **crosscheck** command marks obsolete backups and copies as EXPIRED, but does not remove them.

Enter the **delete** command, the grim reaper of RMAN. It is the dark raven that swoops down and puts the kibosh on your backups and copies. With the **delete** command, you can remove any backups that have been made obsolete based on a retention criteria, and you can change the status of any expired backups in the recovery catalog or control file to a status of DELETED. Here are a couple of examples of the **delete** command in use:

```
delete expired;
delete obsolete;
```

When you issue a **delete** command, RMAN will request that you confirm your instructions. Once you have confirmed your instructions, RMAN will complete the **delete** operation.

NOTE
*Once a backup has been marked with a DELETED
status, you cannot get it back. You can still recover
the backup, if it's physically available, using the
DBMS_BACKUP_RESTORE procedure.*

RMAN Workshop: *Using the delete Command*

Workshop Notes
This workshop builds on the previous RMAN Workshop, "Using the **change**
Command," which deals with using the **crosscheck** command.

Step 1. Having determined that the backup set piece is missing, we want
to mark it as permanently missing. From the RMAN prompt, issue the **delete
expired backup** command:

```
RMAN> delete expired backup;
using channel ORA_DISK_1
using channel ORA_DISK_2
List of Backup Pieces
BP Key  BS Key  Pc# Cp# Status      Device Type Piece Name
------- ------- --- --- ----------- ----------- ----------
53      53      1   1   EXPIRED     DISK
D:\BACKUP\RECOVER\BACKUP_1VE25VC0_1_1
Do you really want to delete the above objects (enter YES or NO)?
```

Step 2. Review the objects listed to be marked with a DELETED status. If they
can all be marked as DELETED, reply to the prompt with a YES and press ENTER.
Review the output for a successful operation:

```
deleted backup piece
backup piece handle=D:\BACKUP\RECOVER\BACKUP_1VE25VC0_1_1 recid=53
stamp=472055171
Deleted 1 EXPIRED objects
```

Cataloging Other Backups in RMAN

The **catalog** command enables you to record datafile backups, archive log backups,
and control file backups in RMAN, and these backups can later be used to restore
and recover the database. Oracle Database 10*g* allows you to also use the **catalog**
command to catalog existing backup set pieces in the control file. This is a very nice
feature if you have to restore the database with an old backup control file that might
not have the most current RMAN information in it.

Here are some examples of the use of the **catalog** command to catalog old datafile backups:

```
-- first, backup the users tablespace
sqlplus sys/robert as sysdba
alter tablespace users begin backup;
host copy d:\oracle\oradata\recover\users01.dbf
d:\backup\recover\users01.dbf.backup
alter tablespace users end backup;
alter system archive log current;
host copy d:\oracle\admin\recover\arch\*.* d:\backup\recover
-- get a list of archivelog files that were created
host dir d:\backup\recover
alter database backup control file to 'd:\backup\recover.ctl'
quit

-- Now, catalog the backup in rman
rman target sys/robert
catalog datafilecopy 'd:\backup\recover\users01.dbf.backup';
-- Replace arc001.log with the list of archive logs you generated earlier
catalog archivelog 'd:\backup\recover\arc001.log';
-- Now catalog the control file.
catalog controlfilecopy 'd:\backup\recover.ctl';
```

The **catalog** command allows you to enter new backup set–related information into the control file or recovery catalog. RMAN overwrites any pre-existing catalog information that conflicts with the information being cataloged. This command can be handy if you need to move the location of your backup set pieces. In this example, we have moved all our backup set pieces to a new directory. We use the **catalog** command to load the correct directory location for each of the moved pieces in the control file.

```
RMAN> catalog backuppiece '/opt/oracle/oracle-10.0.0/dbs/backup';
```

You can also use the **catalog** command with the **start with** option, which allows you to define the directory that contains the RMAN backup set pieces to be cataloged. RMAN will then catalog all backup set pieces in that directory. Here is an example of using the **catalog** command in this way:

```
RMAN> catalog start with '/u01/oracle/RMAN/mydb';
```

Once you press ENTER, this command prompts you with a list of files to catalog and asks if you wish to catalog the files listed. If you respond in the affirmative, RMAN catalogs all the backup set pieces listed (which will be contained in the /u01/oracle/ RMAN/mydb directory). This command also allows you to catalog several like-named backup set pieces. For example, if you want to catalog several backup set pieces that start with the name backup (e.g., backupset01, backupset02, and so forth), then you could issue the following command:

```
RMAN> catalog start with '/u01/oracle/RMAN/mydb/backup';
```

When you use the **catalog start with** command, it is indiscriminate about which files it tries to catalog; it will try to catalog everything that matches the argument list. However, as the **catalog** process proceeds, files that are not backup set pieces will fail the catalog process and an error will occur. Files that are backup set pieces will be cataloged successfully, in spite of other errors.

Recovery Catalog Maintenance

Use of the recovery catalog involves some additional maintenance activities, which include upgrading the catalog during a database upgrade or migration, manually resetting the database incarnation, and resynchronizing the recovery catalog after certain database operations. This section describes those activities, as well as other maintenance considerations, including removing a database from the recovery catalog and using the Oracle EXP/IMP utilities to back up the recovery catalog. Finally, this section reviews the different recovery catalog views and what they are used for.

Unregistering a Database in RMAN

Prior to Oracle Database 10g, unregistering a database from the recovery catalog was a manual process. Now, Oracle Database 10g makes removing a database from the recovery catalog as easy as issuing the command **unregister database**. Here is an example:

```
RMAN> Unregister database mydb;
```

Note that the backup files for this database are not deleted by this command; only the recovery catalog references to those backup files are deleted. Also note that you only need to be connected to the recovery catalog to issue this command.

Database Migration/Upgrade Issues

As you upgrade your Oracle databases, you need to upgrade your recovery catalog as well. As you saw in Chapter 9, there are some strict rules with regard to the version of the database you are using, the version of RMAN, and the version of the recovery catalog.

You can determine what version your recovery catalog is by querying the VERSION column of the RCVER view in the recovery catalog–owning schema:

```
SQL> select version from rcver;

VERSION
------------
09.02.00
```

As long as the version of the recovery catalog is at the same level or higher than your database, you will be in good shape. Thus, if you are storing multiple databases in the same recovery catalog, it's okay to upgrade the catalog to a higher version, even if only one of the databases stored in the recovery catalog is being upgraded.

To upgrade your recovery catalog, simply issue the command **upgrade catalog** from RMAN. RMAN will prompt you to enter the **upgrade catalog** command again. RMAN will then upgrade the recovery catalog for you.

Manually Resetting the Database Incarnation (reset catalog)

As we have already covered in earlier chapters, each time the **resetlogs** parameter is used when you open an Oracle database, a new incarnation of the database is created. If this is done during an RMAN operation, then the recovery catalog will be correctly updated. However, if you manually issue a **resetlogs** command (through SQL*Plus, for example), you need to reset the database incarnation in the recovery catalog. This is done with the **reset database** command:

```
reset database to incarnation 5;
```

Manually Resynchronizing the Recovery Catalog (resync catalog)

When RMAN uses a recovery catalog, it uses a resynchronization process to ensure that the recovery catalog is consistent with the target database control file. Generally, Oracle performs database resynchronization itself after RMAN operations such as backups and recoveries, so you really don't need to resync the recovery catalog often. One example of the need to resync the recovery catalog is if you are running backups sometimes with and sometimes without a recovery catalog. To manually get Oracle to resync the recovery catalog, use the **resync catalog** command:

```
resync catalog;
```

When Oracle synchronizes the recovery catalog, it first creates a snapshot control file and compares it to the recovery catalog. Once that comparison is complete, Oracle will update the recovery catalog so it is in sync with the database control file.

Purging Recovery Catalog Records

You might have noticed that very few records get removed from the recovery catalog. Unmaintained, old backups will sit forever in the recovery catalog with a DELETED status flag associated with them. So, how do you fix this problem? Oracle provides the solution with the $ORACLE_HOME/rdbms/admin/prgrmanc.sql script, which will remove all records in your recovery catalog with a DELETED status. We recommend that you run this script periodically to control the size of your recovery catalog.

If you want to remove old incarnation records from the recovery catalog, then you will want to remove these incarnations from the DBINC table. Use the RC_DATABASE_INCARNATION view to determine which incarnations you wish to remove. Record the DBINC_KEY value for each incarnation you wish to remove. Then, to remove the incarnation, use SQL*Plus and issue a **delete** command to remove the incarnation from the DBINC table using the DBINC_KEY values you previously recorded. Here is an example of the **delete** SQL command that you would use:

```
DELETE FROM dbinc WHERE dbinc_key=2;
```

Recovery Catalog Schema Objects

There are a number of different objects in the recovery catalog that you can query. Many of these objects have related V$ views that provide the same information from the control file. Appendix B contains a list of the V$ views and their related recovery catalog objects that are related to RMAN.

Backing Up the Recovery Catalog

The procedure for using RMAN to back up a database can be found in Chapter 9, and it just so happens that it is perfectly okay to use RMAN to back up your recovery catalog database. Just make sure you have a sound recovery strategy, so you can restore your recovery catalog as quickly as possible. Also, remember that losing the recovery catalog is not the end of the world. Even if you are using a recovery catalog, you can still recover your databases later without it. All you really need is a backup of the database control file (or, in a really bad situation, some fancy work with DBMS_BACKUP_RESTORE!). The really important thing to note is that you need to test your entire recovery strategy. Only then can you know, and be comfortable with, your ability to recover your databases.

RMAN Stored Scripts

If you find that you are often doing the same RMAN operations over and over, then you would probably like to be able to store those operations somewhere and execute them when needed. Of course, you could create a command file, which is just a text file physically located on disk somewhere, with the RMAN commands and then execute the command file from the RMAN command-line interface using the **cmdfile** parameter, as shown in this example:

```
rman target robert/password cmdfile=run_backup.cmd
```

Or, you can run a command file from within RMAN itself, using the @ command:

```
@@run_backup.cmd
```

RMAN offers another option, which is to store scripts in the recovery catalog. As you might guess, this requires that you use a recovery catalog, so if you are not using one, you will not be able to store RMAN scripts. This section shows you how to store scripts in the recovery catalog and how to manage those scripts.

Creating Stored Scripts

To store a script in the recovery catalog, you use the **create script** RMAN command. Each stored script is assigned a name when you create it. You can create scripts that do backups, recoveries, and maintenance of your databases. To create a script, you must be connected to the recovery catalog. Here is an example of using the **create script** command to create a backup script. RMAN also allows you to store comments related to your stored scripts using the **comment** parameter.

```
create script my_backup_script
comment 'This script backs up the database'
{ backup database plus archivelog;}
```

Changing Stored Scripts

You use the **replace script** command to replace stored scripts in the recovery catalog. Here is an example of using the **replace script** command. Note that we also add a comment to the script.

```
replace script my_backup_script
comment 'This script backs up the database'
{ backup database plus archivelog delete input;}
```

Deleting Stored Scripts

To drop a script, you use the **delete script** command. You must be connected to the recovery catalog to successfully drop a stored script. Here is an example of using the **delete script** command:

```
delete script my_backup_script;
```

Using Stored Scripts

Now that you have created some stored scripts, you probably want to use them. This is what the **execute script** command is for. Simply connect to the recovery catalog and use the **execute script** command within the confines of a **run** block, as shown in this example:

```
run {execute script my_backup_script;}
```

Printing Stored Scripts

If you want to print a copy of your stored script, you can use the **print script** command. Connect to the recovery catalog and run the **print script** command, as shown in this example:

```
RMAN> print script my_backup_script;

printing stored script: my_backup_script
{ backup database plus archivelog;}
```

You can also use the RC_STORED_SCRIPT_LINE recovery catalog view to display the contents of a stored script, as shown in this example:

```
select script_name, text from rc_stored_script_line
order by script_name, line;
SCRIPT_NAME        TEXT
---------------    ---------------------------------------
my_backup_script { backup database plus archivelog;}
```

RMAN Workshop: *Using RMAN Stored Scripts*

Workshop Notes

This Workshop expects that you have an operational Oracle database (called recover) and that you are also using a separate Oracle database to store the recovery catalog in (called catalog).

Step 1. Connect to the target database and to the recovery catalog:

```
rman target rman_account/rman_password catalog rcat_user/rcat_password@catalog
```

Step 2. Create a stored script to back up the target database:

```
RMAN> create script my_backup_script
2> {backup database plus archivelog;}
created script my_backup_script
```

Step 3. Print out the stored script:

```
RMAN> print script my_backup_script;
printing stored script: my_backup_script
{backup database plus archivelog;}
```

Step 4. Execute the stored script to back up your database:

```
RMAN> run {execute script my_backup_script;}
```

Step 5. Delete the stored script:

```
RMAN> delete script my_backup_script;
```

When You Just Can't Take It Anymore

If you are sick and tired of your database and you just can't take it anymore, RMAN offers the perfect response, the **drop database** command. If only terrorists were as easy to get rid of. Simply put the database in restricted session mode, connect to the target database with RMAN, issue the **drop database** command, and watch your database quietly go away. You can add the **including backups** parameter, and all RMAN related backups will be removed, too. When you issue this command, RMAN will confirm the action first and then proceed to remove the database. If you wish to not be prompted, you can use the **noprompt** parameter. Here is an example of the use of the **drop database** command:

```
SQL> alter system enable restricted session;
SQL> quit;
.. log into RMAN ..
RMAN>drop database including backups;
```

Summary

In this chapter, we discussed the various maintenance operations that RMAN may require. We discussed the **crosscheck** command and validating RMAN backups, both very important operations. We also talked about retention policies and how RMAN uses them to control how long your backups will remain available to you for recovery purposes.

We also talked about the **change** and **delete** commands and how they can be used to modify the status of RMAN records in the control file or recovery catalog. We also covered adding backups to the control file or recovery catalog. Finally, we discussed maintenance of the recovery catalog and the use of stored scripts for RMAN operations.

CHAPTER
15

Monitoring and
Reporting on RMAN

ecause everyone wants to know for sure that their databases have been backed up and are currently recoverable, RMAN comes with some good reporting tools. This chapter covers RMAN reporting in some depth. First, we look at the RMAN **list** command, followed by the RMAN **report** command. Each of these commands provides facilities for in-depth analysis of the database that you are using RMAN to back up and on those backups. These commands are the primary ways of extracting information out of RMAN. You will find that lists and reports come in handy not only during recovery, but also when you want to see how RMAN is configured and when you need to perform other administrative tasks (such as determining if a tablespace has been backed up).

The RMAN list Command

The RMAN **list** command is a method of querying either the database control file or the recovery catalog for historical information on backups. Lists provide an array of information, from lists of database incarnations to lists of backup sets and archive log backups. The bottom line is that if you want to know whether the database was backed up and when, then you want to generate a list. The format of lists tends initially to appear to be not very reader friendly. Once you have looked at a few lists, though, they seem a little easier to read. So, let's look at the **list** commands and how they can be interpreted.

Listing Incarnations

The **list incarnation** command provides you a list of each database incarnation for the target database. This list can be used to recover your database to a point in time before your last **resetlogs** command was issued, if this is required (refer to Chapter 12 for more details on this operation). Here is an example of the **list incarnation** command output:

```
RMAN> list incarnation of database;
using target database control file instead of recovery catalog
List of Database Incarnations
DB Key  Inc Key DB Name  DB ID             STATUS   Reset SCN  Reset Time
------- ------- -------  ----------------  -------  ---------- ----------
1       1       ROB10R2  3753137102        PARENT   1          30-AUG-05
2       2       ROB10R2  3753137102        PARENT   534907     03-OCT-05
3       3       ROB10R2  3753137102        PARENT   3586765    04-FEB-06
4       4       ROB10R2  3753137102        PARENT   3599781    05-FEB-06
5       5       ROB10R2  3753137102        PARENT   3715262    08-FEB-06
6       6       ROB10R2  3753137102        ORPHAN   4296046    20-FEB-06
7       7       ROB10R2  3753137102        CURRENT  4296046    20-FEB-06
```

In this listing, we find that our database has had several different incarnations, with each incarnation represented in each row of the report. Each individual incarnation has its own key (Inc Key), which we would use if we wanted to reset the database incarnation (refer to Chapter 12). We also get our database name and ID in this report.

A new column in Oracle Database 10*g* is the STATUS column. This column displays the status of the incarnation listed. It indicates whether the incarnation is an older incarnation (PARENT), the current incarnation, or, if a recovery past **resetlogs** has occurred, an orphan incarnation. Finally, the Reset SCN and Reset Time columns basically indicate when the database incarnation was created (which is why the Reset SCN for the first entry is 1). This column helps support recovery through **resetlogs** and also helps support easier recovery to a previous incarnation.

An important point to note is that output generated with a recovery catalog and output generated without a recovery catalog generally looks somewhat different. For example, this is the output of the **list incarnation** command while attached to a recovery catalog:

```
RMAN> list incarnation of database;
  List of Database Incarnations
DB Key  Inc Key DB Name  DB ID             STATUS   Reset SCN  Reset Time
-------  ------- -------- ----------------  -------  ---------- ----------
1        67      ROB10R2  3753137102        PARENT   1          30-AUG-05
2        68      ROB10R2  3753137102        PARENT   534907     03-OCT-05
3        69      ROB10R2  3753137102        PARENT   3586765    04-FEB-06
4        70      ROB10R2  3753137102        PARENT   3599781    05-FEB-06
5        71      ROB10R2  3753137102        PARENT   3715262    08-FEB-06
6        72      ROB10R2  3753137102        ORPHAN   4296046    20-FEB-06
7        73      ROB10R2  3753137102        CURRENT  4296046    20-FEB-06
```

Note in this example that both the DB keys and the incarnation keys are different from those reported when using the control file. This leads to an important point: Many reports have keys that identify specific items in the reports. You will use these keys in other RMAN commands (such as the **reset database** command). Since the values of the keys change depending on whether or not you are connected to the recovery catalog, you need to be careful about determining which keys you need.

Listing Backups

The **list** command comes with a number of different options that allow you to report on the status of database backups and copies. In this section, we are going to look at several of these reports.

Summarizing Available Backups

Let's first look at a few ways of getting summary backup information. The **list** command provides a couple of options. The first option is the **list backup summary** report:

```
RMAN> list backup summary;
List of Backups
===============

Key  TY LV S Device Type Completion Time #Pieces #Copies Compressed Tag
---- -- -- - ----------- --------------- ------- ------- ---------- ---
156  B  F  A DISK        18-FEB-06       1       1       YES TAG20060218T120509
157  B  A  A DISK        18-FEB-06       1       1       YES TAG20060218T120712
210  B  0  A DISK        23-FEB-06       1       1       YES TAG20060223T142518
216  B  1  A DISK        23-FEB-06       1       1       YES TAG20060223T144904
219  B  F  A DISK        23-FEB-06       1       1       NO  TAG20060223T145029
```

This report provides us with some nice summary information. The backup set key is listed in the Key column. The TY (type) and the LV columns indicate the type of backup listed (B = backup, F = full, A = archive log, and 0 and 1 = incremental backups). The S column indicates the status of the backup (AVAILABLE, UNAVAILABLE, or EXPIRED). The Device Type column let's us know whether the backup is a tape or disk backup. We also have columns for the date of the backup (Completion Time), the number of pieces (#Pieces) or copies (#Copies) that the backup set consists of, if the backup was compressed, and any tag that was assigned to the backup set (Tag).

Most of the **list** commands will accept the **summary** parameter at the end. For example:

```
list backup of database summary;
list expired backup of archivelog all summary;
list backup of tablespace users summary;
```

Listing Backups by Datafile

Another way to summarize backups is to use the **list backup by file** command to list each backup set and backup set piece. Here is an example of this report (we have removed some output to save a few trees):

```
RMAN> list backup by file;

List of Datafile Backups
========================

File Key     TY LV S Ckp SCN    Ckp Time   #Pieces #Copies Compressed Tag
---- ------- -  -- - ---------- ---------  ------- ------- ---------- ---
1    217     B  1  A 4472653    23-FEB-06  1 1     YES TAG20060223T144904
     211     B  0  A 4471684    23-FEB-06  1 1     YES TAG20060223T142518
2    216     B  1  A 4472638    23-FEB-06  1 1     YES TAG20060223T144904
     210     B  0  A 4471679    23-FEB-06  1 1     YES TAG20060223T142518
8    217     B  1  A 4472653    23-FEB-06  1 1     YES TAG20060223T144904
     211     B  0  A 4471684    23-FEB-06  1 1     YES TAG20060223T142518
     204     B  F  A 4468127    23-FEB-06  1 1     YES TAG20060223T125410
```

```
List of Archived Log Backups
=============================
Thrd Seq     Low SCN    Low Time   BS Key  S #Pieces #Copies Compressed Tag
---- -----   ---------  ---------  ------- - ------- ------- ---------- ---
1    13      4109321    17-FEB-06  163     A 1       1       YES        TAG20060221T001459
                                   154     A 1       1       YES        TAG20060218T120458
1    14      4144168    18-FEB-06  163     A 1       1       YES        TAG20060221T001459
                                   157     A 1       1       YES        TAG20060218T120712
1    15      4144575    18-FEB-06  170     A 1       1       YES        TAG20060222T151516
                                   163     A 1       1       YES        TAG20060221T001459
1    16      4209410    19-FEB-06  170     A 1       1       YES        TAG20060222T151516
                                   164     A 1       1       YES        TAG20060221T001459
List of Control File Backups
=============================
CF Ckp SCN Ckp Time   BS Key  S #Pieces #Copies Compressed Tag
---------- ---------  ------- - ------- ------- ---------- ---
4502848    01-MAR-06  220     A 1       1       NO         TAG20060301T071852
4472677    23-FEB-06  219     A 1       1       NO         TAG20060223T145029
4471884    23-FEB-06  213     A 1       1       NO         TAG20060223T142732


List of SPFILE Backups
======================
Modification Time BS Key  S #Pieces #Copies Compressed Tag
----------------- ------- - ------- ------- ---------- ---
01-MAR-06         220     A 1       1       NO         TAG20060301T071852
23-FEB-06         219     A 1       1       NO         TAG20060223T145029
23-FEB-06         213     A 1       1       NO         TAG20060223T142732
```

This report summarizes each backup file that has been created by the type of backup (datafile backup, archive log backup, control file backup, and SPFILE backup) and then by datafile for the datafile backups. In this report, we get the date of the backup and the specific keys associated with the backup file. Depending on the type of backup, we get information that pertains to that type of backup.

Additional Backup Information

If you want as much information reported on your RMAN backups as you can get, then the **list backup** command is for you. It provides detailed information on the backups that you have taken, including backup sets, archived redo log backups, and control file/SPFILE backups. Let's look at an example of the results of the execution of the **list backup** command:

```
RMAN> list backup;

List of Backup Sets
===================
BS Key  Size        Device Type Elapsed Time Completion Time
------- ----------  ----------- ------------ ---------------
154     14.12M      DISK        00:00:08     18-FEB-06
        BP Key: 154    Status: AVAILABLE  Compressed: YES
```

```
Tag: TAG20060218T120458
Piece Name: C:\ORACLE\PRODUCT\10.2.0\FLASH_RECOVERY_AREA\ROB10R2\BACKUPSET\
2006_02_18\O1_MF_ANNNN_TAG20060218T120458_1ZGRGFOP_.BKP

   List of Archived Logs in backup set 154
   Thrd Seq     Low SCN    Low Time   Next SCN   Next Time
   ---- -------  ---------- ---------  ---------- ---------
   1    13       4109321    17-FEB-06  4144168    18-FEB-06
```

This first listing is an archive log backup. The backup set key (BS Key) is number 154. The size of the backup is listed, and we see that it went to disk, instead of SBT. The elapsed time of the backup is pretty short, at eight seconds, and we see that is was completed on February 18. Later in the report we see that the backup is available and that it is a compressed backup. We also find the backup set piece name, which tells us where the backup is physically located. Finally, a list of archived redo logs appears. These are the archived redo logs contained in this backup set. Here is an example of the listing of the rest of this backup:

```
BS Key  Type LV Size       Device Type Elapsed Time Completion Time
------- ---- -- ---------- ----------- ------------ ---------------
155     Full    103.16M    DISK        00:01:39     18-FEB-06
 BP Key: 155    Status: AVAILABLE  Compressed: YES  Tag: AG20060218T120509
Piece Name: C:\ORACLE\PRODUCT\10.2.0\FLASH_RECOVERY_AREA\ROB10R2\BACKUPSET\
2006_02_18\O1_MF_NNNDF_TAG20060218T120509_1ZGRGRWG_.BKP
   List of Datafiles in backup set 155
   File LV Type Ckp SCN    Ckp Time   Name
   ---- -- ---- ---------- ---------  ----
   1       Full 4144179    18-FEB-06
C:\ORACLE\PRODUCT\10.2.0\ORADATA\ROB10R2\SYSTEM01.DBF
   2       Full 4144179    18-FEB-06
C:\ORACLE\PRODUCT\10.2.0\ORADATA\ROB10R2\UNDOTBS01.DBF
   6       Full 4144179    18-FEB-06
C:\ORACLE\PRODUCT\10.2.0\ORADATA\ROB10R2\NEWTBS01.DBF

BS Key  Type LV Size       Device Type Elapsed Time Completion Time
------- ---- -- ---------- ----------- ------------ ---------------
156     Full    45.62M     DISK        00:01:48     18-FEB-06
         BP Key: 156    Status: AVAILABLE  Compressed: YES
Tag: TAG20060218T120509
Piece Name: C:\ORACLE\PRODUCT\10.2.0\FLASH_RECOVERY_AREA\ROB10R2\BACKUPSET\
2006_02_18\O1_MF_NNNDF_TAG20060218T120509_1ZGRHKPP_.BKP
   List of Datafiles in backup set 156
   File LV Type Ckp SCN    Ckp Time   Name
   ---- -- ---- ---------- ---------  ----
   3       Full 4144184    18-FEB-06
C:\ORACLE\PRODUCT\10.2.0\ORADATA\ROB10R2\SYSAUX01.DBF
   4       Full 4144184    18-FEB-06
C:\ORACLE\PRODUCT\10.2.0\ORADATA\ROB10R2\USERS01.DBF
   5       Full 4144184    18-FEB-06
C:\ORACLE\PRODUCT\10.2.0\ORADATA\ROB10R2\EXAMPLE01.DBF
```

```
BS Key  Size        Device Type Elapsed Time Completion Time
------- ----------  ----------- ------------ ---------------
157     338.50K     DISK          00:00:03     18-FEB-06
        BP Key: 157   Status: AVAILABLE  Compressed: YES
Tag: TAG20060218T120712
Piece Name: C:\ORACLE\PRODUCT\10.2.0\FLASH_RECOVERY_AREA\ROB10R2\BACKUPSET\
2006_02_18\O1_MF_ANNNN_TAG20060218T120712_1ZGRLM9W_.BKP

  List of Archived Logs in backup set 157
  Thrd Seq    Low SCN    Low Time   Next SCN   Next Time
  ---- ------- ---------- --------- ---------- ---------
  1    14      4144168    18-FEB-06 4144575    18-FEB-06

BS Key  Type LV Size         Device Type Elapsed Time Completion Time
------- ---- -- ----------    ----------- ------------ ---------------
158     Full    7.08M         DISK          00:00:07     18-FEB-06
 BP Key: 158    Status: AVAILABLE  Compressed: NO  Tag: TAG20060218T120719
Piece Name: C:\ORACLE\PRODUCT\10.2.0\FLASH_RECOVERY_AREA\ROB10R2\
AUTOBACKUP\2006_02_18\O1_MF_S_582725239_1ZGRLWPH_.BKP
  Control File Included: Ckp SCN: 4144584      Ckp time: 18-FEB-06
  SPFILE Included: Modification time: 18-FEB-06
```

This is an actual database backup. The output looks much like the previous output, except that now we get a full list of all the datafiles contained in the backup. We see that the datafile backup actually consists of two backup set pieces (BS Key numbers 154 and 155). How do we know this? Well, we really don't, and this is an important point about RMAN. During this backup, because we watched it (or looked at the time that the backup sets were created and made a good guess), we can tell that two backup sets were created at the time of the backup. RMAN, though, doesn't really care. When it comes to recovery, all RMAN cares about is to what point in time you want to recover. Once it knows that, it will pick the best backups to use to perform the recovery. Perhaps this is a small point, but it's an important one we think.

Back to the previous listing, it does look much like the first listing we showed you. Here we have another backup set being created. It contains three datafiles in it. We also find that there is an archive log backup with a single archive log in it. Finally, on the section of the report, we find an autobackup of the control file/SPFILE. We know this is an autobackup by virtue of the SPFILE Included and Control File Included wording in the output.

Let's look at the archive log backup output a bit more closely:

```
BS Key  Size        Device Type Elapsed Time Completion Time
------- ----------  ----------- ------------ ---------------
157     338.50K     DISK          00:00:03     18-FEB-06
        BP Key: 157   Status: AVAILABLE  Compressed: YES
Tag: TAG20060218T120712
Piece Name: C:\ORACLE\PRODUCT\10.2.0\FLASH_RECOVERY_AREA\ROB10R2\BACKUPSET\
2006_02_18\O1_MF_ANNNN_TAG20060218T120712_1ZGRLM9W_.BKP
```

```
List of Archived Logs in backup set 157
 Thrd Seq     Low SCN    Low Time   Next SCN   Next Time
 ---- -------  ---------- ---------  ---------- ---------
 1    14       4144168    18-FEB-06  4144575    18-FEB-06
```

This backup set has a backup set key of 157. The header information looks the same as in the previous backup set. However, this backup is an archive log backup, so in subsequent lines, RMAN provides a list of the archived redo logs backed up in the backup set. The thread and sequence number of the archive log are listed, along with the low SCN and time, and the next SCN and time. The low time/SCN and high time/SCN ranges allow you to determine when the archive log was created.

So, let's look at an incremental backup set report:

```
BS Key   Type LV Size        Device Type Elapsed Time Completion Time
-------  ---- -- ----------   ----------- ------------ ---------------
216      Incr 1  728.00K      DISK        00:00:38     23-FEB-06
         BP Key: 216    Status: AVAILABLE  Compressed: YES
Tag: TAG20060223T144904
Piece Name: C:\ORACLE\PRODUCT\10.2.0\FLASH_RECOVERY_AREA\ROB10R2\BACKUPSET\
2006_02_23\O1_MF_NNND1_TAG20060223T144904_1ZW7Y40G_.BKP
  List of Datafiles in backup set 216
  File LV Type Ckp SCN    Ckp Time  Name
  ---- -- ---- ---------- --------- ----
   2    1 Incr 4472638    23-FEB-06
 C:\ORACLE\PRODUCT\10.2.0\ORADATA\ROB10R2\UNDOTBS01.DBF
   3    1 Incr 4472638    23-FEB-06
 C:\ORACLE\PRODUCT\10.2.0\ORADATA\ROB10R2\SYSAUX01.DBF
   4    1 Incr 4472638    23-FEB-06
 C:\ORACLE\PRODUCT\10.2.0\ORADATA\ROB10R2\USERS01.DBF
   5    1 Incr 4472638    23-FEB-06
 C:\ORACLE\PRODUCT\10.2.0\ORADATA\ROB10R2\EXAMPLE01.DBF
```

Again, this report is very similar to the other reports. The only differences are that **Incr** is used in the Type field to indicate that the backup is an incremental backup, and the LV (level) column shows the level of the incremental backup. If the incremental backup were a level 0 backup, then the LV column would show the number 0, which corresponds to a level 0 base backup.

Listing Backups Eligible for Recovery

If you want to see all datafile backups or copies that are able to be used to restore and recover your database, then use the **list recoverable** command. This **list** command provides a list of all backups with a status of AVAILABLE that can be used to restore your database (this is only for the current incarnation). Backups, image copies, and incremental backups will all be included. If an incremental backup does not have a valid parent, it will not be included in this backup.

```
RMAN> list recoverable backup of database;
List of Backup Sets
===================
BS Key  Type LV Size       Device Type Elapsed Time Completion Time
------- ---- -- ---------- ----------- ------------ ---------------
166     Full    65.20M     DISK          00:01:00   21-FEB-06
        BP Key: 166   Status: AVAILABLE  Compressed: YES  Tag:
AG20060221T001536
Piece Name: C:\ORACLE\PRODUCT\10.2.0\FLASH_RECOVERY_AREA\ROB10R2\BACKUPSET
\2006_02_21\O1_MF_NNNDF_TAG20060221T001536_1ZOD0CO1_.BKP
  List of Datafiles in backup set 166
  File LV Type Ckp SCN    Ckp Time  Name
  ---- -- ---- ---------- --------- ----
   2      Full 4300709    21-FEB-06
C:\ORACLE\PRODUCT\10.2.0\ORADATA\ROB10R2\UNDOTBS01.DBF
   3      Full 4300709    21-FEB-06
C:\ORACLE\PRODUCT\10.2.0\ORADATA\ROB10R2\SYSAUX01.DBF
   4      Full 4300709    21-FEB-06
C:\ORACLE\PRODUCT\10.2.0\ORADATA\ROB10R2\USERS01.DBF

BS Key  Type LV Size       Device Type Elapsed Time Completion Time
------- ---- -- ---------- ----------- ------------ ---------------
167     Full    83.24M     DISK          00:01:46   21-FEB-06
        BP Key: 167   Status: AVAILABLE  Compressed: YES  Tag:
AG20060221T001536
Piece Name: C:\ORACLE\PRODUCT\10.2.0\FLASH_RECOVERY_AREA\ROB10R2\BACKUPSET\
2006_02_21\O1_MF_NNNDF_TAG20060221T001536_1ZOD1BTT_.BKP
  List of Datafiles in backup set 167
  File LV Type Ckp SCN    Ckp Time  Name
  ---- -- ---- ---------- --------- ----
   1      Full 4300715    21-FEB-06
 C:\ORACLE\PRODUCT\10.2.0\ORADATA\ROB10R2\SYSTEM01.DBF
   6      Full 4300715    21-FEB-06
C:\ORACLE\PRODUCT\10.2.0\ORADATA\ROB10R2\NEWTBS01.DBF
   7      Full 4300715    21-FEB-06
C:\ORACLE\PRODUCT\10.2.0\ORADATA\ROB10R2\TEST_RECOVER_01.DBF
   8      Full 4300715    21-FEB-06
C:\ORACLE\PRODUCT\10.2.0\ORADATA\ROB10R2\TEST_RECOVER_TWO_01.DBF
```

Listing Expired Backups

Using the **list backup** command shows you both available and expired backup sets. If you want to see only expired backups, then you can use the **expired** keyword, as shown in this example:

```
RMAN> list expired backup;
List of Backup Sets
===================
BS Key  Size       Device Type Elapsed Time Completion Time
------- ---------- ----------- ------------ ---------------
154     14.12M     DISK          00:00:08   18-FEB-06
```

```
BP Key: 154    Status: EXPIRED  Compressed: YES  Tag: TAG20060218T120458
Piece Name: C:\ORACLE\PRODUCT\10.2.0\FLASH_RECOVERY_AREA\ROB10R2\BACKUPSET
\2006_02_18\O1_MF_ANNNN_TAG20060218T120458_1ZGRGFOP_.BKP

  List of Archived Logs in backup set 154
  Thrd Seq     Low SCN    Low Time  Next SCN   Next Time
  ---- ------- ---------- --------- ---------- ---------
  1    13      4109321    17-FEB-06 4144168    18-FEB-06

BS Key  Type LV Size       Device Type Elapsed Time Completion Time
------- ---- -- ---------- ----------- ------------ ---------------
155     Full    103.16M    DISK        00:01:39     18-FEB-06
 me: C:\ORACLE\PRODUCT\10.2.0\FLASH_RECOVERY_AREA\ROB10R2\BACKUPSET\
2006_02_18\O1_MF_NNNDF_TAG20060218T120509_1ZGRGRWG_.BKP

  List of Datafiles in backup set 155
  File LV Type Ckp SCN    Ckp Time  Name
  ---- -- ---- ---------- --------- ----
  1       Full 4144179    18-FEB-06
C:\ORACLE\PRODUCT\10.2.0\ORADATA\ROB10R2\SYSTEM01.DBF
  2       Full 4144179    18-FEB-06
C:\ORACLE\PRODUCT\10.2.0\ORADATA\ROB10R2\UNDOTBS01.DBF
  6       Full 4144179    18-FEB-06
C:\ORACLE\PRODUCT\10.2.0\ORADATA\ROB10R2\NEWTBS01.DBF

BS Key  Type LV Size       Device Type Elapsed Time Completion Time
------- ---- -- ---------- ----------- ------------ ---------------
156     Full    45.62M     DISK        00:01:48     18-FEB-06
 BP Key: 156    Status: EXPIRED  Compressed: YES  Tag: TAG20060218T120509
Piece Name: C:\ORACLE\PRODUCT\10.2.0\FLASH_RECOVERY_AREA\ROB10R2\
BACKUPSET\2006_02_18\O1_MF_NNNDF_TAG20060218T120509_1ZGRHKPP_.BKP

  List of Datafiles in backup set 156
  File LV Type Ckp SCN    Ckp Time  Name
  ---- -- ---- ---------- --------- ----
  3       Full 4144184    18-FEB-06
C:\ORACLE\PRODUCT\10.2.0\ORADATA\ROB10R2\SYSAUX01.DBF
  4       Full 4144184    18-FEB-06
C:\ORACLE\PRODUCT\10.2.0\ORADATA\ROB10R2\USERS01.DBF
  5       Full 4144184    18-FEB-06
C:\ORACLE\PRODUCT\10.2.0\ORADATA\ROB10R2\EXAMPLE01.DBF

BS Key  Size       Device Type Elapsed Time Completion Time
------- ---------- ----------- ------------ ---------------
157     338.50K    DISK        00:00:03     18-FEB-06
 BP Key: 157    Status: EXPIRED  Compressed: YES  Tag: TAG20060218T120712
Piece Name: C:\ORACLE\PRODUCT\10.2.0\FLASH_RECOVERY_AREA\ROB10R2\BACKUPSET\
2006_02_18\O1_MF_ANNNN_TAG20060218T120712_1ZGRLM9W_.BKP

  List of Archived Logs in backup set 157
  Thrd Seq     Low SCN    Low Time  Next SCN   Next Time
  ---- ------- ---------- --------- ---------- ---------
  1    14      4144168    18-FEB-06 4144575    18-FEB-06
```

```
BS Key   Type LV Size       Device Type Elapsed Time Completion Time
-------  ---- -- ---------- ----------- ------------ ---------------
158      Full   7.08M        DISK          00:00:07    18-FEB-06
 BP Key: 158   Status: EXPIRED  Compressed: NO  Tag: TAG20060218T120719
Piece Name: C:\ORACLE\PRODUCT\10.2.0\FLASH_RECOVERY_AREA\ROB10R2\
AUTOBACKUP\2006_02_18\O1_MF_S_582725239_1ZGRLWPH_.BKP
   Control File Included: Ckp SCN: 4144584      Ckp time: 18-FEB-06
   SPFILE Included: Modification time: 18-FEB-06
```

This gives you all expired backup set types. With the **list expired backup** command, you can also get a list of expired tablespace and datafile backups and lists of expired archive log backups and control file/SPFILE autobackups by inserting the correct keyword, such as **list expired backup of datafile 3** or **list expired backup of archivelog all**.

Listing Backups by Tablespace Name and Datafile Number

The output of the **list backup of tablespace** or **list backup of datafile** command is very similar to the **list backup** output. These two **list backup** commands allow you to list output specific for a tablespace or a datafile, as shown in this example:

```
RMAN> list backup of tablespace users;
using target database control file instead of recovery catalog

List of Backup Sets
===================
BS Key   Type LV Size       Device Type Elapsed Time Completion Time
-------  ---- -- ---------- ----------- ------------ ---------------
156      Full   45.62M       DISK          00:01:48    18-FEB-06
 BP Key: 156   Status: EXPIRED  Compressed: YES  Tag: TAG20060218T120509
Piece Name: C:\ORACLE\PRODUCT\10.2.0\FLASH_RECOVERY_AREA\ROB10R2\BACKUPSET
\2006_02_18\O1_MF_NNNDF_TAG20060218T120509_1ZGRHKPP_.BKP
   List of Datafiles in backup set 156
   File LV Type Ckp SCN    Ckp Time  Name
   ---- -- ---- ---------- --------- ----
    4      Full 4144184    18-FEB-06
C:\ORACLE\PRODUCT\10.2.0\ORADATA\ROB10R2\USERS01.DBF
```

Note in this example that this particular backup is expired, which might be of particular interest to us, especially if this were the only backup to show up in the output! Again, you can use the **expired** keyword to just list expired backups (**list expired backup of tablespace**).

In much the same way, you can list the backups of a specific datafile with the **list backup of datafile** command:

```
RMAN> list backup of datafile 3;
List of Backup Sets
===================
BS Key   Type LV Size       Device Type Elapsed Time Completion Time
-------  ---- -- ---------- ----------- ------------ ---------------
```

```
156      Full    45.62M    DISK        00:01:48    18-FEB-06
  BP Key: 156   Status: EXPIRED  Compressed: YES  Tag: TAG20060218T120509
Piece Name: C:\ORACLE\PRODUCT\10.2.0\FLASH_RECOVERY_AREA\ROB10R2\BACKUPSET
\2006_02_18\O1_MF_NNNDF_TAG20060218T120509_1ZGRHKPP_.BKP

  List of Datafiles in backup set 156
    File LV Type Ckp SCN    Ckp Time   Name
    ---- -- ---- ---------- ---------- ----
    3       Full 4144184    18-FEB-06
C:\ORACLE\PRODUCT\10.2.0\ORADATA\ROB10R2\SYSAUX01.DBF
```

Listing Archive Log Backups

Several options exist for listing archive log backups in RMAN. To obtain a complete summary of archive logs currently on disk (this does not mean that they have been backed up), the **list archivelog all** command is perfect, as shown here:

```
RMAN> list archivelog all;

List of Archived Log Copies
Key      Thrd Seq     S Low Time    Name
-------  ---- -------  - ---------- ----
298      1    22       A 23-FEB-06 C:\ARCHIVE\ROB10R2ARC00022_0582936761.001
300      1    23       A 23-FEB-06 C:\ARCHIVE\ROB10R2ARC00023_0582936761.001
302      1    24       A 23-FEB-06 C:\ARCHIVE\ROB10R2ARC00024_0582936761.001
303      1    24       X 23-FEB-06 C:\ORACLE\PRODUCT\10.2.0\
FLASH_RECOVERY_AREA\ROB10R2\ARCHIVELOG\2006_02_23\O1_MF_1_24_1ZWCT5SQ_.ARC
304      1    25       A 23-FEB-06 C:\ARCHIVE\ROB10R2ARC00025_0582936761.001
305      1    25       A 23-FEB-06 C:\ORACLE\PRODUCT\10.2.0\
FLASH_RECOVERY_AREA\ROB10R2\ARCHIVELOG\2006_03_01\O1_MF_1_25_20CZBMTZ_.ARC
```

Here we find a list of each archived redo log that Oracle has backed up, along with the thread number and the sequence number of that archived redo log.

If we want a more detailed report, then we use the **list backup of archivelog all** report:

```
RMAN> list backup of archivelog all;

List of Backup Sets
===================
BS Key  Size        Device Type Elapsed Time Completion Time
------- ----------  ----------- ------------ ---------------
154     14.12M      DISK        00:00:08     18-FEB-06
  BP Key: 154   Status: EXPIRED  Compressed: YES  Tag: TAG20060218T120458
Piece Name: C:\ORACLE\PRODUCT\10.2.0\FLASH_RECOVERY_AREA\ROB10R2\BACKUPSET
\2006_02_18\O1_MF_ANNNN_TAG20060218T120458_1ZGRGFOP_.BKP

  List of Archived Logs in backup set 154
  Thrd Seq     Low SCN    Low Time   Next SCN   Next Time
  ---- -------  ---------- ---------- ---------- ---------
  1    13       4109321    17-FEB-06  4144168    18-FEB-06
```

```
BS Key   Size          Device Type Elapsed Time Completion Time
-------  ----------    ----------- ------------ ---------------
215      508.00K   DISK        00:00:06     23-FEB-06
BP Key: 215    Status: AVAILABLE  Compressed: YES  Tag: TAG20060223T144852
Piece Name: C:\ORACLE\PRODUCT\10.2.0\FLASH_RECOVERY_AREA\ROB10R2\BACKUPSET
\2006_02_23\O1_MF_ANNNN_TAG20060223T144852_1ZW7XSPT_.BKP

  List of Archived Logs in backup set 215
  Thrd Seq     Low SCN    Low Time  Next SCN   Next Time
  ---- ------- ---------- --------- ---------- ---------
  1    21      4471659    23-FEB-06 4471873    23-FEB-06
  1    22      4471873    23-FEB-06 4472626    23-FEB-06
```

Note that the first archive log backup set in this report has an EXPIRED status, while the second has an AVAILABLE status. Thus, the second archived redo log backup set is available for RMAN recoveries, while the first is not. If you want to look at expired backup sets only, add the **expired** keyword, as in **list expired backup of archivelog all**.

Listing Control File and SPFILE Backups

As you might expect, you can also list control file and SPFILE backups. The **list backup of controlfile** command provides you with a list of control file backups, and the **list backup of spfile** command provides output for SPFILE backups. Here is an example of each command and its results:

```
RMAN> list backup of controlfile;

List of Backup Sets
===================
BS Key   Type LV Size          Device Type Elapsed Time Completion Time
-------  ---- -- ----------    ----------- ------------ ---------------
33       Full   1M         DISK        00:00:06     14-JUL-06
         BP Key: 33   Status: EXPIRED   Tag:
         Piece Name: D:\ORACLE\ORA912\DATABASE\C-2539725638-20020714-00
  Controlfile Included: Ckp SCN: 402892       Ckp time: 14-JUL-02

BS Key   Type LV Size          Device Type Elapsed Time Completion Time
-------  ---- -- ----------    ----------- ------------ ---------------
39       Full   1M         DISK        00:00:15     14-JUL-06
         BP Key: 39   Status: AVAILABLE  Tag:
         Piece Name: D:\ORACLE\ORA912\DATABASE\C-2539725638-20020714-01
  Controlfile Included: Ckp SCN: 403912       Ckp time: 14-JUL-06

RMAN> list backup of spfile;
```

```
List of Backup Sets
===================
BS Key  Type LV Size       Device Type Elapsed Time Completion Time
------- ---- -- ---------- ----------- ------------ ---------------
68      Full 0             DISK        00:00:09     18-JUL-06
        BP Key: 66    Status: AVAILABLE    Tag:
        Piece Name: D:\ORACLE\ORA912\DATABASE\C-2539725638-20020718-03
  SPFILE Included: Modification time: 26-JUN-06
```

I'll bet you have already guessed that you can use the **list expired backup of archivelog all** command here, too. Also, you can limit the report by time or log sequence number. For example, to list expired archive log backups until a given sequence, you could use the command **list expired backup of archivelog until sequence**.

Listing Image Copies

Just as you can use the **list** command to determine the status of backup sets, you can also use the **list** command to determine the status of database image copies. You can generate a list of all copies with the **list copy** command:

```
RMAN> list copy;
List of Datafile Copies
Key     File S Completion Time Ckp SCN    Ckp Time        Name
------- ---- - --------------- ---------- --------------- ----
60      1    A 01-MAR-06       4502811    01-MAR-06
C:\ORACLE\PRODUCT\10.2.0\FLASH_RECOVERY_AREA\ROB10R2\DATAFILE\
O1_MF_SYSTEM_20C7Q7LN_.DBF
57      2    A 22-FEB-06       4401953    22-FEB-06
C:\ORACLE\PRODUCT\10.2.0\FLASH_RECOVERY_AREA\ROB10R2\DATAFILE\
O1_MF_UNDOTBS1_1ZT3WJPZ_.DBF

List of Control File Copies
Key     S Completion Time Ckp SCN    Ckp Time        Name
------- - --------------- ---------- --------------- ----
56      A 22-FEB-06       4390695    22-FEB-06       C:\ROBERT\CTRL.BAK

List of Archived Log Copies
Key     Thrd Seq     S Low Time   Name
------- ---- ------- - --------- ----
298     1    22      A 23-FEB-06 C:\ARCHIVE\ROB10R2ARC00022_0582936761.001
300     1    23      A 23-FEB-06 C:\ARCHIVE\ROB10R2ARC00023_0582936761.001
302     1    24      A 23-FEB-06 C:\ARCHIVE\ROB10R2ARC00024_0582936761.001
303     1    24      X 23-FEB-06 C:\ORACLE\PRODUCT\10.2.0\
FLASH_RECOVERY_AREA\ROB10R2\ARCHIVELOG\2006_02_23\O1_MF_1_24_1ZWCT5SQ_.ARC
304     1    25      A 23-FEB-06 C:\ARCHIVE\ROB10R2ARC00025_0582936761.001
305     1    25      A 23-FEB-06 C:\ORACLE\PRODUCT\10.2.0\
FLASH_RECOVERY_AREA\ROB10R2\ARCHIVELOG\2006_03_01\O1_MF_1_25_20CZBMTZ_.ARC
```

In addition to this summary list, you can create lists of individual datafile copies, archived redo logs, and control file copies. Let's look at those options in some more detail for a moment.

Listing Datafile Copies

Oracle allows you to generate a summary list of all datafile copies with the **list copy of database** command:

```
RMAN> list copy of database;
List of Datafile Copies
Key      File S Completion Time Ckp SCN    Ckp Time        Name
------- ---- - --------------- ---------- --------------- ----
60       1    A 01-MAR-06       4502811    01-MAR-06
C:\ORACLE\PRODUCT\10.2.0\FLASH_RECOVERY_AREA\ROB10R2
\DATAFILE\O1_MF_SYSTEM_20C7Q7LN_.DBF
57       2    A 22-FEB-06       4401953    22-FEB-06
C:\ORACLE\PRODUCT\10.2.0\FLASH_RECOVERY_AREA\ROB10R2
\DATAFILE\O1_MF_UNDOTBS1_1ZT3WJPZ_.DBF
```

In this output, we have two copies of datafiles that belong to our database, datafile2.copy and datafile3.dbf. While the actual name of the datafile or its assigned tablespace name is not listed, the file number is listed in the second column of the report. We could relate this file number to the associated tablespace by running the **report schema** command, which we discuss later in this chapter.

If you want to know whether you have a datafile copy of a tablespace or a datafile, you can use the **list copy of tablespace** or **list copy of datafile** command, as shown here:

```
RMAN> list copy of tablespace system;

List of Datafile Copies
Key      File S Completion Time Ckp SCN    Ckp Time        Name
------- ---- - --------------- ---------- --------------- ----
60       1    A 01-MAR-06       4502811    01-MAR-06
C:\ORACLE\PRODUCT\10.2.0\FLASH_RECOVERY_AREA\
ROB10R2\DATAFILE\O1_MF_SYSTEM_20C7Q7LN_.DBF
RMAN> list copy of datafile 1;

List of Datafile Copies
Key      File S Completion Time Ckp SCN    Ckp Time        Name
------- ---- - --------------- ---------- --------------- ----
60       1    A 01-MAR-06       4502811    01-MAR-06
C:\ORACLE\PRODUCT\10.2.0\FLASH_RECOVERY_AREA\
ROB10R2\DATAFILE\O1_MF_SYSTEM_20C7Q7LN_.DBF
```

Listing Archived Redo Log Copies

If you want a list of archived redo log copies, you can use the **list copy of archivelog all** command:

```
RMAN> list copy of archivelog all;

List of Archived Log Copies
Key     Thrd Seq     S Low Time   Name
------- ---- ------- - --------- ----
298     1    22      A 23-FEB-06 C:\ARCHIVE\ROB10R2ARC00022_0582936761.001
300     1    23      A 23-FEB-06 C:\ARCHIVE\ROB10R2ARC00023_0582936761.001
302     1    24      A 23-FEB-06 C:\ARCHIVE\ROB10R2ARC00024_0582936761.001
303     1    24      X 23-FEB-06 C:\ORACLE\PRODUCT\10.2.0\
FLASH_RECOVERY_AREA\ROB10R2\ARCHIVELOG\2006_02_23\O1_MF_1_24_1ZWCT5SQ_.ARC
304     1    25      A 23-FEB-06 C:\ARCHIVE\ROB10R2ARC00025_0582936761.001
305     1    25      A 23-FEB-06 C:\ORACLE\PRODUCT\10.2.0\
FLASH_RECOVERY_AREA\ROB10R2\ARCHIVELOG\2006_03_01\O1_MF_1_25_20CZBMTZ_.ARC
```

You can also list copies of specific archived redo logs by time, sequence, or database SCN. Here are some examples of listing archived redo logs based on differing criteria:

```
RMAN> list copy of archivelog from sequence 22;

List of Archived Log Copies
Key     Thrd Seq     S Low Time   Name
------- ---- ------- - --------- ----
298     1    22      A 23-FEB-06 C:\ARCHIVE\ROB10R2ARC00022_0582936761.001
300     1    23      A 23-FEB-06 C:\ARCHIVE\ROB10R2ARC00023_0582936761.001
302     1    24      A 23-FEB-06 C:\ARCHIVE\ROB10R2ARC00024_0582936761.001
303     1    24      X 23-FEB-06 C:\ORACLE\PRODUCT\10.2.0\
FLASH_RECOVERY_AREA\ROB10R2\ARCHIVELOG\2006_02_23\O1_MF_1_24_1ZWCT5SQ_.ARC
304     1    25      A 23-FEB-06 C:\ARCHIVE\ROB10R2ARC00025_0582936761.001
305     1    25      A 23-FEB-06 C:\ORACLE\PRODUCT\10.2.0\
FLASH_RECOVERY_AREA\ROB10R2\ARCHIVELOG\2006_03_01\O1_MF_1_25_20CZBMTZ_.ARC

RMAN> list copy of archivelog from sequence 22 until sequence 23;

List of Archived Log Copies
Key     Thrd Seq     S Low Time   Name
------- ---- ------- - --------- ----
298     1    22      A 23-FEB-06 C:\ARCHIVE\ROB10R2ARC00022_0582936761.001
300     1    23      A 23-FEB-06 C:\ARCHIVE\ROB10R2ARC00023_0582936761.001
```

Listing Control File Copies

Finally, RMAN can report on control file copies with the **list controlfile copy** command:

```
RMAN> list copy of controlfile;

List of Control File Copies
Key     S Completion Time Ckp SCN    Ckp Time        Name
------- - --------------- ---------- --------------- ----
56      A 22-FEB-06       4390695    22-FEB-06       C:\ROBERT\CTRL.BAK
```

The RMAN report Command

The RMAN **report** command is used to determine the current recoverable state of
your database and to provide certain information on database backups. In this
section, we look at reports that tell you which datafiles have not been backed up
in a specified period of time. We also look at reports that tell you when specific
tablespaces need to be backed up because of UNRECOVERABLE operations on
datafiles. Finally, we look at the use of the **report** command to report on database
schemas and obsolete database backups.

Reporting on Datafiles That Have Not Been Backed Up Recently

A question DBAs frequently ask themselves is, "When was the last time I backed up
this tablespace?" RMAN provides some answers to that question with the **report need
backup** command. For example, if you want to know what tablespaces have not been
backed up in the last three days, you could issue the **report need backup days=3**
command and find out. Here is an example of the output of just such a report:

```
RMAN> report need backup days=3;

Report of files whose recovery needs more than 3 days of archived logs
File Days  Name
---- ----- -------------------------------------------------------------
4    2     D:\ORACLE\ORADATA\RECOVER\TOOLS01.DBF
5    2     D:\ORACLE\ORADATA\RECOVER\USERS01.DBF
```

From this report, it appears that two datafiles require application of more than
three days' worth of archived redo to be able to recover them (which implies that
these datafiles have not been backed up in the last three days). In this event, we
might well want to back up the datafiles, or their associated tablespaces.

We can also generate reports based on a given number of incrementals that would
need to be applied, as shown in this example:

```
RMAN> report need backup incremental = 3;

Report of files that need more than 3 incrementals during recovery
```

```
File Incrementals Name
---- ----------- -----------------------------------------------
1     4           D:\ORACLE\ORADATA\RECOVER\SYSTEM01.DBF
2     4           D:\ORACLE\ORADATA\RECOVER\RECOVER_UNDOTBS_01.DBF
3     4           D:\ORACLE\ORADATA\RECOVER\INDX01.DBF
4     4           D:\ORACLE\ORADATA\RECOVER\TOOLS01.DBF
5     4           D:\ORACLE\ORADATA\RECOVER\USERS01.DBF
```

In this example, several database datafiles require four incrementals to be applied. This may well indicate that we need to perform a new backup on these datafiles at a higher incremental level, or even perform a new incremental base backup.

Reporting on Backup Redundancy or Recovery Window

We can use the **report need backup redundancy** command to determine which, if any, datafiles need to be backed up to meet our established backup redundancy policy. The following is an example of the use of this report. In this case, we want a list of all datafiles that do not have at least two different backups that can be used for recovery. These may be backup set backups or datafile copies.

```
RMAN> report need backup redundancy = 2;

Report of files with less than 2 redundant backups
File #bkps Name
---- ----- ------------------------------------------------
1     1     D:\ORACLE\ORADATA\RECOVER\SYSTEM01.DBF
4     1     D:\ORACLE\ORADATA\RECOVER\TOOLS01.DBF
5     1     D:\ORACLE\ORADATA\RECOVER\USERS01.DBF
```

Likewise, we can establish a minimum recovery window for our backups and report on any datafiles whose backups are older than that recovery window. This is done with the **report need backup recovery window days** command:

```
RMAN> report need backup recovery window of 2 days;

Report of files whose recovery needs more than 2 days of archived logs
File Days  Name
---- ----- ------------------------------------------------
1     4     D:\ORACLE\ORADATA\RECOVER\SYSTEM01.DBF
2     4     D:\ORACLE\ORADATA\RECOVER\RECOVER_UNDOTBS_01.DBF
3     4     D:\ORACLE\ORADATA\RECOVER\INDX01.DBF
4     4     D:\ORACLE\ORADATA\RECOVER\TOOLS01.DBF
5     4     D:\ORACLE\ORADATA\RECOVER\USERS01.DBF
```

In this case, several of our datafiles require application of more than two days' worth of archived redo. So, if our recovery policy says we want backups where we only need to apply one day of redo, then we need to back up these datafiles.

Reporting on Unrecoverable Operations on Datafiles

Unrecoverable operations on objects within tablespaces, and the datafiles that make up those tablespaces, lead to certain recoverability issues. For example, if a table is created using the **Unrecoverable** option and is subsequently loaded using the direct load path, then the tablespace needs to be backed up or else the data that was loaded will not be recoverable. It is for these circumstances that the **report unrecoverable** command is used, as shown here:

```
RMAN> report unrecoverable;
Report of files that need backup due to unrecoverable operations

File Type of Backup Required Name
---- --------------------- ---------------------------------------------
5    full or incremental   D:\ORACLE\ORADATA\RECOVER\USERS01.DBF
```

Reporting on the Database Schema

We are using the word "schema" here to mean the physical structure of the database. The schema includes the datafile name and number, the tablespaces they are assigned to, the size of the datafiles, and whether or not the datafiles contain rollback segments. This can be the current schema, or you can generate a report on the database schema at some past point in time. Here is an example of the execution of the **report schema** command:

```
RMAN> report schema;

Report of database schema

List of Permanent Datafiles
===========================
File Size(MB) Tablespace          RB segs Datafile Name
---- -------- ------------------- ------- ------------------------
1    490      SYSTEM              ***
C:\ORACLE\PRODUCT\10.2.0\ORADATA\ROB10R2\SYSTEM01.DBF
2    80       UNDOTBS1            ***
C:\ORACLE\PRODUCT\10.2.0\ORADATA\ROB10R2\UNDOTBS01.DBF
3    350      SYSAUX              ***
C:\ORACLE\PRODUCT\10.2.0\ORADATA\ROB10R2\SYSAUX01.DBF
4    16       USERS               ***
C:\ORACLE\PRODUCT\10.2.0\ORADATA\ROB10R2\USERS01.DBF
5    100      EXAMPLE             ***
C:\ORACLE\PRODUCT\10.2.0\ORADATA\ROB10R2\EXAMPLE01.DBF
6    10       NEW_TBS             ***
```

```
C:\ORACLE\PRODUCT\10.2.0\ORADATA\ROB10R2\NEWTBS01.DBF
7     20       TEST_RECOVER          ***
C:\ORACLE\PRODUCT\10.2.0\ORADATA\ROB10R2\TEST_RECOVER_01.DBF
8     20       TEST_RECOVER_TWO      ***
C:\ORACLE\PRODUCT\10.2.0\ORADATA\ROB10R2\TEST_RECOVER_TWO_01.DBF


List of Temporary Files
=========================
File Size(MB) Tablespace          Maxsize(MB) Tempfile Name
---- -------- ------------------- ----------- --------------------
1     20       TEMP                 32767
C:\ORACLE\PRODUCT\10.2.0\ORADATA\ROB10R2\TEMP01.DBF
```

Reporting on Obsolete Backups

Backups are marked with an OBSOLETE status if you are using a retention policy
(which we discussed in Chapter 14). Here is an example of the execution of **report
obsolete** with a retention policy set to **redundancy 7**:

```
RMAN> report obsolete;

RMAN retention policy will be applied to the command
RMAN retention policy is set to redundancy 7

Report of obsolete backups and copies
Type                  Key    Completion Time    Filename/Handle
------------------- ------ ----------------- --------------------
Backup Set            158    18-FEB-06
   Backup Piece       158    18-FEB-06         C:\ORACLE\PRODUCT\10.2.0\
FLASH_RECOVERY_AREA\ROB10R2\AUTOBACKUP\2006_02_18\
O1_MF_S_582725239_1ZGRLWPH_.BKP
Backup Set            159    20-FEB-06
   Backup Piece       159    20-FEB-06         C:\ORACLE\PRODUCT\10.2.0\
FLASH_RECOVERY_AREA\ROB10R2\AUTOBACKUP\2006_02_20\
O1_MF_S_582936329_1ZO6QFT8_.BKP
Backup Set            160    20-FEB-06
   Backup Piece       160    20-FEB-06         C:\ORACLE\PRODUCT\10.2.0\
FLASH_RECOVERY_AREA\ROB10R2\AUTOBACKUP\2006_02_20\
O1_MF_S_582936815_1ZO76MLD_.BKP
Control File Copy     56     22-FEB-06          C:\ROBERT\CTRL.BAK
Datafile Copy         57     22-FEB-06          C:\ORACLE\PRODUCT\10.2.0\
FLASH_RECOVERY_AREA\ROB10R2\DATAFILE\O1_MF_UNDOTBS1_1ZT3WJPZ_.DBF
```

This report has several different backup sets, datafile copies, control file copies,
and archive log copies that have been marked OBSOLETE by Oracle. If you want to
mark these backups as DELETED, run the **delete obsolete** command, as shown in
Chapter 14.

Summary

Information! We want information! This chapter provides you with the commands you can use to extract information from RMAN. The **list** and **report** commands provide a wealth of information that you can use to administer RMAN and make sure that you are getting good backups of your database. We think it's a good idea to sit down and determine what kinds of reporting you want to do for your databases, and automate that reporting so that you always know the backup and recovery state of your database.

CHAPTER
16

Performance Tuning
RMAN Backup and
Recovery Operations

MAN actually works pretty well right out of the box, and you generally will find that it requires very little tuning. However, there are a number of other pieces that fit into the RMAN architectural puzzle. When all those pieces come together, you sometimes find that you need to tweak a setting here or there to get the best performance you can out of your backup processes. Generally, then, the RMAN tuning you end up having to do usually involves dealing with inefficiencies in the logical or physical database design, tuning of the Media Management Library (MML), or tuning RMAN and the MML layer to coexist better with the physical device that you are backing up to.

If you have used RMAN before Oracle Database 10*g*, you will find some changes to the performance-related commands. In our estimation, these changes make the tuning process easier to understand overall. In this chapter, we look at what you need to tune before you begin to tune RMAN itself. We then provide some tuning options for RMAN.

Before You Tune RMAN

If your RMAN backups take hours and hours to run, it's probably not RMAN's fault. More than likely, it's some issue with your database or with your MML. The last time you drove in rush hour traffic, did you think the slow movement was a problem with your car? Of course not. The problem was one of too many cars trying to move on a highway that lacked enough lanes. This is an example of a bandwidth problem, or a bottleneck. Cities attempt to solve their rush hour problem by expanding the highway system or perhaps by adding a subway, busses, or light rail.

The same kind of problem exists when it comes to tuning RMAN and your backup and recovery process. It's often not the fault of RMAN, although RMAN often gets blamed. More than likely, the problem is insufficient bandwidth of the system as a whole, or some component in the infrastructure that is not configured correctly. RMAN often gets the initial blame, but in the end it is just a victim.

Once you have the architecture working correctly, much of RMAN tuning really turns out to be an exercise in tuning your Oracle database. The better your database performs, the better your RMAN backups will perform. Very large books have already been written on the subject of tuning your Oracle database, so we will just give a quick look at these issues. If you need more detailed information on Oracle database performance tuning, we suggest another title from Oracle Press: *Oracle Wait Interface: A Practical Guide to Performance Tuning & Diagnostics*, by Richmond Shee, Kirtikumar Deshpande, and K. Gopalakrishnan (2004).

NOTE
We make some tuning recommendations in this chapter and in other places in this book. Make sure you test our recommendations on your system before you decide to "fire and forget" (meaning to make a change without checking that the change was positive). While certain configurations may work for us in our environments, you may find that they do not work as well for you.

RMAN Performance: What Can Be Achieved?

So, what is the level of RMAN performance that can be achieved with the currently available technology? Oracle Corporation, in its white paper "Oracle Recovery Manager: Performance Testing at Sun Customer Benchmark Center" (October 2001), available at www.oracle.com/technology/index.html, found that a backup or recovery rate of 1 terabyte (TB) per hour to tape was possible. As tape backup technology continues to improve, rates exceeding this will likely be possible.

Have the Right Hardware in Place

If you want high backup performance, then the first thing to look at is the backup hardware at your disposal. This consists of items such as tape drives, the associated infrastructure such as cabling, robotic tape interfaces, and any MML-layer software that you might choose to employ.

Backup media hardware will provide you with a given speed at which the device will read and write. Of course, the faster the device writes, the faster your backups. Also, the more devices you can back up to, the better your backup timing tests will be. This was clearly pointed out in Oracle's RMAN performance white paper mentioned in the preceding section. The doubling of the number of drives that RMAN could write to causes an almost linear improvement in performance of both backup and restore operations. The ability to parallelize your backups across multiple channels (or backup devices) is critical to quickly backing up a large Oracle database.

RMAN will benefit from parallel CPU resources, but the return diminishes much quicker with the addition of CPUs, as opposed to the addition of physical backup devices. The bottom line, then, is that having multiple backup devices will have a much greater positive impact on your backup and restore windows than adding CPUs will, in most cases.

You will find that most backup devices are asynchronous rather than synchronous. An *asynchronous* device allows the backup server processes to issue I/O instructions without requiring the backup server processes to wait for the I/O to complete. An asynchronous operation, for example, allows the server process to issue a tape write instruction and, while that instruction is being performed, proceed to fill memory buffers in preparation for the next write operation A *synchronous* device, on the other hand, would have to wait for the backup operation to complete before it could perform any other work. Thus, in our example, the synchronous process will have to wait for the tape I/O to complete before it can start filling memory buffers for the next operation. Thus, an asynchronous device is more efficient than a synchronous one.

Because asynchronous operations are preferred, you may want to know about a few of their parameters. First, the parameter BACKUP_TAPE_IO_SLAVES (which defaults to FALSE) will cause all tape I/O to be asynchronous in nature. We suggest you set this parameter to TRUE to enable asynchronous I/O to your tape devices (if that setting is supported). Once this parameter is established, you can define the size of the memory buffers that are used by using the **parms** parameter of the **allocate channel** command or **configure channel** command.

The tape buffer size is established when the channel is configured. The default value is OS specific, but is generally 64KB. You can configure this value to be higher or lower by using the **allocate channel** command. For the best performance, we suggest that you configure this value to 256KB or higher, as shown here:

```
allocate channel c1 device type
sbt parms="blksize=262144, ENV=(NB_ORA_CLASS=RMAN_db01)"
```

If you are backing up to disk, then you need to determine whether or not your OS supports asynchronous I/O (most do these days). If it does, then Oracle automatically uses that feature. If it does not, then Oracle provides the parameter DBWR_IO_SLAVES, which, when set to a nonzero value, causes Oracle to simulate asynchronous I/O to disks by starting multiple DBWR processes.

When either DBWR_IO_SLAVES or BACKUP_TAPE_IO_SLAVES is configured, you may also want to create a large pool. This will help eliminate shared pool contention and memory allocation error issues that can accompany shared pool use when BACKUP_TAPE_IO_SLAVES is enabled. If you are using Automatic Shared Memory Management (ASMM) in 10*g*, Oracle will manage the memory allocation of the shared pool for you. If you want to manually set the large pool, the total size of disk buffers is limited to 16MB per channel. The formula for setting the LARGE_POOL_SIZE parameter for backup is as follows:

LARGE_POOL_SIZE = (number of allocated channels) * (16MB + (size of tape buffer))

NOTE
If DBWR_IO_SLAVES or BACKUP_TAPE_IO_SLAVES is not configured, then RMAN will not use the large pool. Generally, you do not need to configure these parameter settings to get good performance from RMAN unless your OS does not natively support asynchronous I/O.

Tune the Database

A badly tuned database can have a significant negative impact on your backup times. Certain database tuning issues can also have significant impact on your restore times. In this section, we briefly look at what some of these tuning issues are, including I/O tuning, memory tuning, and SQL tuning.

Tune I/O

Most DBAs understand the impact of I/O on basic database operations. Contention on a given disk drive for database resources (say, for example, that the online redo log and a database datafile are on the same device) can cause significant system slowdowns. Just as poor I/O distribution can impact your database performance, it can also impact your backup and restore times. This makes sense, because RMAN is going to be just another process (or, more likely, many processes due to parallel streams) that contends for I/O time on your devices.

Backing up is a read-intensive operation. If you have poor I/O distribution, not only will RMAN performance suffer, but other users will suffer as well, if not even worse, during the backup operation. Recovery may be somewhat easier if all of your recoveries are full database recoveries. However, if you are just recovering a datafile or a tablespace, while the database is open and in use, you may find that poor I/O distribution impacts your recovery window, and your users. The bottom line is that bad I/O distribution impacts not only your day-to-day database users, but also your backups and recoveries, causing them to take longer.

Much has been written on distribution of I/O on an Oracle database and how to do it properly. We suggest that you take a look at the Oracle white paper titled "Oracle Storage Configuration Made Easy" (Juan Loaiza, Oracle Corporation, available at www.oracle.com/technology/index.html). In this paper, Mr. Loaiza makes a compelling argument for using an I/O distribution known as Stripe and Mirror Everything (SAME), discusses current disk speeds and feeds, and then demonstrates the logic of his SAME methodology. This methodology recommends that you stripe your data among the largest number of disks possible, and suggests this is a much better approach than striping across a few disks or using a parity disk approach, such as RAID-5 (mirroring is, of course, more expensive). Further, this paper recommends that a stripe size of about 1MB is generally optimal and demonstrates that such a configuration in Oracle's testing resulted in a 13 percent better read/write from the disk than nonstriped systems, with an associated loss in CPU overhead. This faster disk read/write will translate into faster backup timings.

Tune Memory Usage

Like any Oracle process, RMAN uses memory. When an RMAN operation is started, a buffer is allocated to the operation for RMAN to work out of. The size of the buffer allocated is dependent on a number of different factors, including the following:

- RMAN backup and recovery multiplexing effects
- The device type used
- The number of channels allocated during the operation

Each of these factors has an effect on how much memory RMAN will require. RMAN allocates memory buffers for operations. How it allocates these buffers depends on the type of device you are going to use. Let's look at the different buffer allocation methods in a bit more detail next.

Allocating Memory Buffers for Disk Devices   When backing up to disk devices, RMAN will allocate up to 16MB of memory. This memory is allocated based on the level of multiplexing (based on the **filesperset** setting). If the level of multiplexing is 4 or less, then RMAN will allocate 16 buffers of 1MB each. These 1MB buffers are divided among the number of datafiles to be backed up. So, if **filesperset** is set to 2, then each datafile will be allocated eight 1MB buffers.

If **filesperset** is between 5 and 8, then 512MB buffers are allocated and distributed evenly between the different datafiles. This way, no more than 16MB of buffers will be allocated. Finally, if the level of multiplexing is greater than 8, four buffers of 128MB will be allocated to each datafile, which amounts to 512KB per datafile.

Allocating Memory Buffers for SBT Devices   When backing up to an SBT device, RMAN allocates four buffers for each channel that is allocated. These buffers are 256KB in size generally, and thus the total memory allocated per channel is 1MB. The buffer sizes can be managed using the PARMS and BLKSIZE parameters of the **allocate** or **send** commands.

This memory is generally allocated from the PGA, but if the BACKUP_TAPE_IO_ SLAVES parameter is set to TRUE, then the SGA is used unless the large pool is allocated, in which case the large pool will be used. Thus, if you configure I/O slaves (and generally you should if you back up to SBT devices), then you should configure a large pool to reduce the overall memory requirements on the large pool.

Tune Your SQL

You might ask yourself what bad SQL running in your database has to do with performance tuning your backup and recovery times. It's really quite simple. The negative performance impacts of poor SQL statement operations has an overall negative performance impact on your database and the system the database is on. Anything that has a negative impact on your database is likewise going to have a negative impact on your backup operations. Tune your SQL operations such that they reduce the overall number of I/Os required (logical and physical) and schedule your backups to occur during times of typical low system usage (if that is possible).

Tune Your Environment

Carefully consider your backup schedules and ensure that they do not conflict with I/O-intensive database operations such as data loads or reports. Also, if you find your backups are taking too long, consider an incremental backup strategy and analyze your database to determine whether certain tablespaces might be made read-only so you don't have to continue to back them up often. Further, if you are running in ARCHIVELOG mode, you can consider staggering the backups of tablespaces on different days to reduce the overall timeframe of your backups (at the cost of somewhat longer recovery times, of course).

If you are running your database using Oracle Real Application Clusters, then RMAN can take advantage of the clustered environment to parallelize your RMAN operations (more information on this topic is provided in Chapter 19).

Tune Your Backup and Recovery Strategy

We already talked about tuning when you do your backups, but we also want to discuss tuning how you do your backups. If you have a large database, rather than just issuing a **backup database** command to back up the whole kit and caboodle, consider a more partitioned backup strategy. Consider backing up related datafiles that you are likely to restore together using individual **backup tablespace** or **backup datafile** commands and assign those backups to one specific channel. Why do this? This reduces the need to swap tapes during recoveries and allows the recovery of related datafiles to occur as quickly as possible. Here is an example of such an operation:

```
RMAN> backup (tablespace tools channel 'ORA_DISK_1')
            (tablespace system, undotbs, users, testrbs, indx);
```

We might want to do this if we are backing up a read-only tablespace that we might later want to recover, or perhaps we have a tablespace that we seem to do frequent tablespace point-in-time recoveries (TSPITRs) on. These would be good candidates for such backup strategies.

Another issue to consider is the impact of your backup strategy on your recovery. One of the more painful problems with RMAN is that, depending on the platform (Unix is one example; the following three paragraphs do not apply to Oracle on Windows NT), if you restore an entire database with the **restore database** command, you must be careful to ensure that enough space is available for the restore. Everything is just fine as long as you have enough disk space, but consider for a moment a true disaster recovery situation where you do not have enough disk space in the right places. In this case, RMAN is going to spend perhaps an hour or more recovering your database. Once it runs out of disk space, you would assume that RMAN would just stop at that point, alert you to the lack-of-space problem, and then just stop the restore at that position. The truth, however, is a bit more painful.

Once the restore process fails, RMAN proceeds to remove every single file it restored in that restore session. Thus, if you spend two hours restoring all but one database datafile and then you run out of space during that restore, you are in deep trouble, because RMAN is now going to remove all of those datafiles. This equates to a very unhappy DBA.

One solution to this problem is to restore specific tablespaces with different **restore** commands for each tablespace (or for a number of tablespaces). This allows you to restore your database datafiles in a bit more granular fashion, and the failure of one operation will not cause you to lose hours. Of course, if you use this type of operation, you will want to parallelize the restores and utilize multiple tape or disk devices to reduce contention and tape streaming issues. In this case, you need to run parallel RMAN sessions, each restoring its own set of tablespace data. Note that this type of restore operation is another reason why it's important to try to back up clusters of files that you will likely need to restore on the same channel. That way, you can stream the data off the tape quickly.

Note that some platforms, such as Windows NT, do check for available space before you actually start an RMAN database, datafile, or tablespace restore. In this case, the issue of running out of space, while still a problem, is not as much of a time waster.

Tuning RMAN

As we stated at the beginning of the chapter, RMAN out of the box really works pretty well. Still, you can do a few things to tune it so that you get better performance, which is what this section is all about. First, we discuss the tuning options in RMAN itself. Then, we discuss some MML tuning issues.

Tuning RMAN Settings

There are a few ways to tune RMAN, which we discuss in this section. Tuning RMAN itself can involve tuning parallel operations and also configuring RMAN to multiplex (or not to multiplex, that is the question). This section also covers some things that you can do to actually tune down RMAN.

Parallel Channel Operations

Perhaps the biggest impact you can make when tuning your database backups is to parallelize them by using multiple RMAN channels. Typically, you configure a channel for each device you are going to back up to. Thus, if you back up to three different disks, configure three different channels. You will see little or no benefit of paralleling backups on the same device, of course; so if you have a D drive and an E drive on your Windows NT system but both are just partitioned on the same disk, you will derive no benefit from paralleling backups to those two devices.

NOTE
The memory buffering on tape systems may well make the allocation of additional channels worthwhile, so you should always do some timing tests to decide exactly how many channels you need to use on your system.

Paralleling backups is accomplished by allocating channels to the backup. Channels can have default values configured for them (along with the default degree of parallelization that will determine how many of the channels are used) with the **configure** command, discussed in Chapter 3. For example, if we have two tape devices that we are going to back up to, we'd likely configure two default channels and a default level of parallelization, as shown here:

```
CONFIGURE DEVICE TYPE DISK PARALLELISM 2;
CONFIGURE CHANNEL 1 DEVICE TYPE sbt FORMAT PARMS
'ENV=(NB_ORA_CLASS=RMAN_rs100_tape)';
CONFIGURE CHANNEL 2 DEVICE TYPE sbt FORMAT PARMS
'ENV=(NB_ORA_CLASS=RMAN_rs100_tape)';
```

This would serve to ensure that each **backup** or **recover** command is automatically allocated two channels to parallelize the process.

Of course, depending on your device, you may well be able to run parallel streams to the device. The best thing to do is run several tests and determine from those tests the performance of a varying number of backup streams from both a backup and a recovery point of view. It may be that a different number of streams will be more efficient during your backup than during your recovery, and only testing will determine this.

We have already discussed the multiplexing of backups in RMAN and how to tune this feature. Tuning multiplexing can have significant performance impacts on your backups and recoveries. As we also discussed earlier, how you configure your multiplexing will impact the amount of memory that is allocated to the RMAN backup process. The more memory, the better, as long as you do not start to induce swapping back and forth to disk.

Also, properly configuring multiplexing can make streaming to tape devices more efficient. The more memory you can allocate to RMAN, the more data that can be streamed to your I/O devices. Finally, tape streaming is rarely an issue with newer-generation tape drives. Generally, they have a great deal of onboard buffer memory that is used to ensure that the tape is written to at a constant rate.

RMAN Multiplexing

Before we dive head first into performance considerations, we should take a moment to discuss multiplexing in RMAN. *Multiplexing* allows a single RMAN channel to parallelize the reading of database datafiles during the backup process and write the contents of those datafiles to the same backup set piece. Thus, one backup set piece may contain the contents of many different datafiles.

Note that the contents of a given datafile can reside in more than one backup set piece (which is evidenced by the fact that you can set **maxpiecesize** to a value smaller than that of any database datafile, but **maxsetsize** must be at least the size of the largest tablespace being backed up). However, in a given backup, a given datafile will only be backed up through one channel (or one backup set). Thus, if you allocate two channels (and, as a result, have two backup sets), and your database consists of one large datafile, the ability of RMAN to parallelize that datafile's backup will be limited to a great degree.

The level of RMAN's multiplexing is determined by the lesser of two RMAN parameters. The first is the **filesperset** parameter (established when you issue the **backup** command) and the second is the **maxopenfiles** parameter (established when the channel is allocated).

The **filesperset** parameter establishes how many datafiles should be included in each backup set. The number of datafiles in a given backup set will be some number less than or equivalent to **filesperset**. When you do a backup, RMAN will assign a default value for **filesperset** of either 64 or the number of input files divided by the number of allocated channels, whichever is less. You can use a nondefault value for **filesperset** by using the **filesperset** parameter of the **backup** command, as shown in this example:

```
backup database filesperset 4;
```

The **maxopenfiles** parameter establishes a limit on how many datafiles RMAN can read in parallel (the default is 8). You establish the **maxopenfiles** limit on a channel-by-channel basis. Here is an example of the use of **maxopenfiles**:

```
CONFIGURE CHANNEL 1 DEVICE TYPE DISK MAXOPENFILES 3 FORMAT
  "d:\backup\recover\%U";
```

For example, if I created a backup set with **filesperset** set to 6 and **maxopenfiles** set to 3, RMAN would only be able to back up three datafiles in parallel at a time. The backup sets created would still contain at most six datafiles per backup set (assuming one channel is allocated and a degree of parallelism of 1), but only three datafiles would be written to the backup set at any time.

NOTE
*If you have your data striped on a large number of disks, you will not need to multiplex your backups, and you can set **maxopenfiles** to a value of 1. If you are striped across a smaller set of disks, consider setting **maxopenfiles** to a value between 4 and 8. If you do not stripe your data at all, **maxopenfiles** generally should be set to some value greater than 8.*

Multiplexing, and the establishment of the **filesperset** and **maxopenfiles** parameters, can have a significant impact on the performance of your backups (good and bad). Tuning RMAN multiplexing can decrease the overall time of your backups, as long as your system is capable of the parallel operations that occur during multiplexing. As with most things, too much of a good thing is too much, and certainly you can overparallelize your backups such that the system is overworked. In this case, you will quickly see the performance of your system diminish and your backup times increase quickly.

Multiplexing can also have an impact on tape operations. Since tape systems are streaming devices, it's important to keep the flow of data streaming to the device at a rate that allows it to continue to write without needing to pause. Generally, once a tape has a delay in the output data stream, the tape device will have to stop and reposition the write head before the next write can occur. This can result in significant delays in the overall performance of your backups. By setting **filesperset** high and **maxopenfiles** low, you can tune your backup so that it streams to your tape device as efficiently as possible. Beware, of course, of overdoing it and bogging down your system so much that the I/O channels or CPU can't keep up with the flow of data that RMAN is providing. As always, finding the proper balance takes some patient tuning and monitoring.

Controlling the Overall Impact of RMAN Operations

Sometimes you want to tune RMAN *down* rather than up. Prior to Oracle Database 10*g* you would use the RMAN parameters **rate** and **readrate** to throttle RMAN down, freeing system resources for other operations. These parameters would be set when you allocated channels for RMAN operations. These parameters are still available in Oracle Database 10*g*, but they have been replaced.

Oracle Database 10*g* makes controlling RMAN backups much easier. Now you simply use the **duration** parameter in the **backup** command to control the duration of the backup. The **duration** parameter has an additional keyword, **minimize load**, that allows you to indicate to RMAN that it should minimize the I/O load required to back up the database over the given duration. For example, if the backup typically takes five hours and consumes 90 percent of the available I/O, you can indicate to RMAN that it should use a duration of ten hours for the backup. When this is included with the **minimize load** parameter, you might well expect to see only 45 to 50 percent of available I/O consumed, rather than the 90 percent. The negative side of this is, of course, that your backup will take longer. Here is an example of using the **duration** parameter when starting a backup; in this case, we want the backup to run ten hours:

```
Backup as copy database duration 10:00 minimize load database;
```

Of course, one problem with the use of the **duration** parameter is that the backup could actually take longer than ten hours. Any completed backup set can be used for recovery, even if the overall backup process fails due to duration issues.

You can use the **partial** keyword to suppress RMAN errors in the event that the duration limit is exceeded and the backup fails.

One final thing to note about the use of the **duration** parameter is that the database files with the oldest backups will be given priority over files that have newer RMAN backup dates. Thus, if the backup of a database with 20 datafiles fails after 10 are backed up, the next time the backup runs the 10 that were not backed up would get first priority.

Tune the MML Layer

Each component of RMAN may require some tuning effort, including the MML layer. Refer to Chapter 4 for general information on this topic, and then refer to Chapters 5 through 8 for more detailed information for your specific vendor MML configuration and tuning suggestions for that vendor.

You need to consider a number of things with regard to the MML backup devices. Most are going to be running in asynchronous mode, but if they do not, that may be a big cause of your problems. Also, sometimes DBAs will set the **rate** parameter when they allocate a channel for backups. This is generally something you do not want to do, because this will create an artificial performance bottleneck.

Also, some of the MML vendors provide various configurable parameters, such as a configurable buffer size, that you can configure in vendor-specific parameter files. Look into the tuning possibilities that these parameter files offer you.

There are other factors related to the MML layer, such as the supported transfer rate of the backup device you are using, compression, streaming, and the block size. You must analyze all of these factors in an overall effort to tune the performance of your RMAN backups.

Tuning Views You Can Use

Oracle provides a number of different views that you can use to monitor and tune RMAN performance. Using these views, you can determine how well the database, RMAN, and the MML are performing. You can also use these views to determine how long a backup or recovery process has taken and how much longer you can expect it to take. In this section, we look at these views and how you can best use them.

V$SESSION_LONGOPS and V$SESSION

The V$SESSION_LONGOPS view is useful during a backup or restore operation to determine how long the operation has taken and how much longer it is expected to take to complete. Join this view to the V$SESSION view for additional information about your RMAN backup or recovery sessions. Here is an example of a join between V$SESSION_LONGOPS and V$SESSION during a database backup:

```
SQL> select a.sid, a.serial#, a.program, b.opname, b.time_remaining
from v$session a, v$session_longops b
where a.sid=b.sid
and a.serial#=b.serial#
and a.program like '%RMAN%'
and time_remaining > 0;
 SID SERIAL# PROGRAM  USERNAME  OPNAME                 TIME_REMAINING
 ---- ------- -------- --------- ---------------------- --------------------
   10      8 RMAN.EXE SYS RMAN: aggregate input                         1438
   14      3 RMAN.EXE SYS RMAN: full datafile backup                    7390
```

In this example, we have an RMAN process running a backup. It has connected to the database as SID 14. The time remaining, 7390, is the expected time in seconds that this backup will take. You can thus determine how long your backup will take by looking at this report. Note that we also did a join to V$SESSION to get some additional information on our RMAN session, such as the username and the program name.

V$BACKUP_ASYNC_IO and V$BACKUP_SYNC_IO

The V$BACKUP_ASYNC_IO and V$BACKUP_SYNC_IO views contain detailed information on RMAN asynchronous and synchronous backup operations. These views are transitory in nature and are cleared each time the database is shut down. These views contain a row for each asynchronous or synchronous backup or recovery operation. Perhaps the biggest benefit from this view is the EFFECTIVE_BYTES_PER_SECOND column in rows where the TYPE column is set to AGGREGATE. This column represents the rate at which the objects are being backed up or recovered in bytes per second. This number should be close to the listed read/write rate of your backup hardware. If the EFFECTIVE_BYTES_PER_SECOND column value is much lower than the rated speed of your backup hardware, then you should be looking for some sort of problem with your backup process. The problem could be caused by any number of things, from an overburdened CPU to a saturated network, or perhaps a configuration issue with the MML interface to your vendor's backup solution.

NOTE
If you see data in V$BACKUP_SYNC_IO, this implies that you are not doing asynchronous backups. If this is the case, you need to investigate why your backups are occurring in synchronous fashion.

Here is an example of a query against V$BACKUP_ASYNC_IO and its results after a database backup has been completed:

```
select device_type "Device", type, filename,
to_char(open_time, 'mm/dd/yyyy hh24:mi:ss') open,
to_char(close_time, 'mm/dd/yyyy hh24:mi:ss') close,
elapsed_time ET, effective_bytes_per_second EPS
from v$backup_async_io
where close_time > sysdate - 30
order by close_time desc;

device TYPE      FILENAME                                OPEN
------ --------- ------------------------------- -------------------
CLOSE                          ET       EPS
------------------- ---------- ----------
DISK   OUTPUT    d:\backup\recover\5cdvfjvh_1_1   08/06/2002 20:24:43
08/06/2002 20:28:10     20700    566435

DISK   AGGREGATE                                  08/06/2002 20:24:58
08/06/2002 20:28:09     19100    933288

DISK   INPUT     D:\ORACLE\ORADATA\RECOVER\SYSTEM 08/06/2002 20:24:58
01.DBF
08/06/2002 20:28:09     19100    933288

DISK   OUTPUT    d:\backup\recover\5bdvfjup_1_1   08/06/2002 20:24:18
08/06/2002 20:24:35     1700     24576

DISK   AGGREGATE                                  08/06/2002 20:24:19
08/06/2002 20:24:34     1500     1118481

DISK   INPUT     D:\ORACLE\ORADATA\RECOVER\RECOV  08/06/2002 20:24:19
ER_UNDOTBS_01.DBF
08/06/2002 20:24:34     1500     699051
DISK   INPUT     D:\ORACLE\ORADATA\RECOVER\RECOV  08/06/2002 20:24:26
ER_TESTRBS_01.DBF
08/06/2002 20:24:33     700      748983

DISK   INPUT     D:\ORACLE\ORADATA\RECOVER\TOOLS  08/06/2002 20:24:27
02.DBF    08/06/2002 20:24:29          200      524288

DISK   OUTPUT    d:\backup\recover\5advfjug_1_1   08/06/2002 20:23:55
08/06/2002 20:24:13     1800     18204

DISK   AGGREGATE                                  08/06/2002 20:23:58
08/06/2002 20:24:11     1300     967916
```

```
DISK    INPUT    D:\ORACLE\ORADATA\RECOVER\USERS 08/06/2002 20:24:05
01.DBF
08/06/2002 20:24:11        600      873813

DISK    INPUT    D:\ORACLE\ORADATA\RECOVER\TOOLS 08/06/2002 20:23:58
01.DBF    08/06/2002 20:24:10      1200      436907

DISK    INPUT    D:\ORACLE\ORADATA\RECOVER\INDX0 08/06/2002 20:24:08
1.DBF
08/06/2002 20:24:09        100     2097152
```

In this case, we can see the effective transfer rate from the database to the backup set by RMAN. Further, we can see the name of the datafile that was backed up and the actual start and stop time of the backup itself.

Another way to measure the efficiency of your backup process is to use the V$BACKUP_ASYNC_IO view. This view has several columns of interest, which are listed and described in Table 16-1.

To determine whether there is an I/O problem, we can look at the ratio of I/Os to long waits (LONG_WAITS/IO_COUNTS), as shown in the following code segment:

```
select b.io_count, b.ready, b.short_waits, b.long_waits,
b.long_waits/b.io_count, b.filename
from v$backup_async_io b;
IO_COUNT      READY SHORT_WAITS LONG_WAITS B.LONG_WAITS/B.IO_COUNT
---------- ---------- ----------- ---------- ----------------------
FILENAME
-------------------------------------
         2          1           0          1                     .5
D:\ORACLE\ADMIN\RECOVER\ARCH\ARC00052.001
         2          1           0          1                     .5
```

Column Name	Represents
IO_COUNT	The total number of I/O counts
READY	The number of asynchronous I/O calls for which a buffer was available immediately
SHORT_WAITS	The number of times that a buffer was requested and not available but became available after a nonblocking poll for I/O completion
LONG_WAITS	The number of times that a buffer was requested and not available and Oracle had to wait for the I/O device

TABLE 16-1. *V$BACKUP_ASYNC_IO Column Descriptions*

```
D:\ORACLE\ADMIN\RECOVER\ARCH\ARC00046.001
         2         1         0         1              .5
D:\ORACLE\ADMIN\RECOVER\ARCH\ARC00051.001
         2         1         0         1              .5
D:\ORACLE\ADMIN\RECOVER\ARCH\ARC00050.001
       171       107        12        52       .304093567
D:\ORACLE\ORADATA\RECOVER\SYSTEM01.DBF
        11         8         2         1       .090909091
D:\ORACLE\ORADATA\RECOVER\RECOVER_UNDOTBS_01.DBF
         6         4         0         2       .333333333
D:\ORACLE\ORADATA\RECOVER\TOOLS01.DBF
         6         3         0         3              .5
D:\ORACLE\ORADATA\RECOVER\USERS01.DBF
         6         4         1         1       .166666667
D:\ORACLE\ORADATA\RECOVER\RECOVER_TESTRBS_01.DBF
         3         1         0         2       .666666667
D:\ORACLE\ORADATA\RECOVER\INDX01.DBF
         2         1         0         1              .5
D:\ORACLE\ORADATA\RECOVER\TOOLS02.DBF
```

The numbers returned by this query clearly indicate some sort of I/O bottleneck is causing grief (in this case, it's an overly taxed, single CPU).

Summary

RMAN will support very fast backup and recovery schemes given that the appropriate infrastructure is in place to support it. Often we find the reason that RMAN does not perform well is not because of the database, or because of RMAN, but because of the underlying network or insufficient numbers of backup devices.

We also talked about the times that RMAN is too fast, and takes up too much CPU or floods the network. We discussed the duration parameter and its various options which allow you to reduce the overall run-time impact of RMAN operations.

PART
IV

RMAN in the
Oracle Ecosystem

CHAPTER
17

Duplication: Cloning the Target Database

e've hinted at this chapter's content since the earliest part of the book: RMAN will help you leverage your backups beyond disaster recovery. Indeed, we've already talked about using RMAN for corruption checking and cross-platform database conversion (see Chapter 13). One of the other ways you can leverage your backups is to use them to make copies of the production database for testing and development purposes. In the database world, we refer to this as *cloning* (keep your sheep jokes to yourself).

Database cloning can provide an excellent way to test version upgrades, new application rollouts, and even bug patches. Cloning can also be used to prepare reporting databases that are kept separate from transaction processing databases. In these ways, database backups can be put to work. They can be used to restore the database to another system, or even just to another disk on the same system. We can then do load testing for performance reasons, or try out a new hardware configuration. With clone databases at our disposal, we can leave little to chance and have an almost perfect grasp of what will happen if we change our production environment. RMAN can be also be used to create a standby database that can be kept up to date for disaster recovery. But we are getting ahead of ourselves.

RMAN helps you create clones via the **duplicate** command. This simple little command hides many levels of complexity that are worth knowing about before you begin to use it. In addition, there is a fair amount of prep work required so that a duplication goes smoothly. But once understood, and after you've had a little time to practice, you'll find that database duplication is one of the real "killer apps" within the backup and recovery world. Or perhaps you already know this. But leveraging the RMAN interface will save you hours of scripting pain. Trust me. You'll see.

RMAN Duplication: A Primer

The RMAN **duplicate** command is a simple command that hides a high level of complexity. If you've ever been through the process of restoring image copy backups of your database to another system, you know the amount of information that you have to keep track of: filenames, file locations, backup locations, archive log information, ftp processes, moving tapes around…there's plenty to keep track of. RMAN has a straightforward command:

```
duplicate target database to aux1;
```

This will perform the entire process of cloning your target database to another database. Granted, you have to do a little legwork first, but once you become familiar with the architecture, you'll see that the legwork is minimal and the payoff is huge.

Why Use RMAN Duplication?

Why is duplication necessary? An astute question. Why can't we just copy the control file to a new location and run a restore and recovery? The answer is: you can! There is no reason that this won't work. However, if you use a recovery catalog, you will run into problems if you clone your database without using duplication. You see, RMAN registers databases in the catalog based on the database ID (DBID), which is a number that identifies your database as unique, even if it has the same DB_NAME as another database. If you don't use the **duplicate** command, you will have two databases with the same database ID (DBID). If you try to register your clone in the same catalog as your production system, you will get an error:

```
rman-20002: target database already registered in recovery catalog
```

This error can be a little misleading: you haven't registered the database! If you shrug your shoulders at this and go ahead and try to back up your database, it will give you an even stranger error:

```
rman-20011: target database incarnation is not current
in recovery catalog
```

"Whoa," you say, "what does that mean?" So you go ahead and issue a **reset database**, as you think you should, and this works. You can now back up your database. Sweet. However, you have caused bigger problems. Now, you connect RMAN to your original, production server and try to back it up. But when you do, you get a hauntingly similar error:

```
rman-20011: target database incarnation is not current
in recovery catalog
```

The reason for this error is that RMAN considers your clone no more than a restored version of your production system, and so it now thinks the clone is the current incarnation of your production server, and it has no idea what your production server is. You can reset the incarnation back to the one that actually matches your production database, but you've essentially corrupted your catalog and should unregister your database and reregister it in the catalog (see Chapter 3).

If you don't use a catalog, nonduplicated clones can wreak havoc, as well. Let's lay it out in an example. You clone your database to the same system as your primary database. You are using RMAN to back up both databases to tape, and because you aren't using a catalog, you have automatic control file backups turned on for both instances. One day, you lose a disk array and your entire system goes belly up. Both databases, and all of their control files, are lost. "No problem," you think, "I've got control file autobackup turned on. I'll just use one of those to restore my systems."

But here's the stickler: the command **restore controlfile from autobackup** uses the DB_ID to track down the control file autobackup. Because both of your databases back up to the same tape, it may try to restore the control file from the wrong database, giving you the wrong files with the wrong data.

Obviously, both of these scenarios can be fixed, and they don't cause a loss of data. But they cause a loss of time. They can potentially extend your downtime past your agreement levels. In addition to these problems, using duplication in RMAN provides the power of the RMAN interface to keep things as simple as possible. And simple is good. Simple is wise.

The Duplication Architecture

Here's how duplication works. RMAN connects to your target database and to the catalog, if you use one. This connection is necessary to gain access to the target database control file for details about where to locate backups. After you connect to the target, you must connect to your auxiliary instance (the instance that will house your cloned database). Before duplication starts, you must have already built an init.ora file for the auxiliary instance, and started it in NOMOUNT mode. This way, the memory segment has been initialized, and therefore RMAN can make a sysdba connection to it. The auxiliary instance does not have a control file yet (duplication will take care of that), so you cannot mount the auxiliary instance, even if you want to.

With these connections made, you can issue your **duplicate** command. It can look as simple as this:

```
duplicate target database to aux1;
```

or it can be complicated, depending on where the auxiliary instance is

```
run {
set until time = '08-JUL-2002:16:30:00';
duplicate target database to aux1 pfile=/u02/oracle/admin/aux1/pfile/init.ora
nofilenamecheck
device type sbt parms "env=(nb_ora_serv=rmsrv)"
logfile
'/u04/oracle/oradata/aux1/redo01.log' size 100m,
'/u05/oracle/oradata/aux1/redo02.log' size 100m,
'/u06/oracle/oradata/aux1/redo03.log' size 100m;}
```

The duplication process can be broken down into its distinct phases:

1. RMAN determines the nature and location of the backups.

2. RMAN allocates an auxiliary channel at the auxiliary instance.

3. RMAN restores the datafiles to the auxiliary instance.

4. RMAN builds a new auxiliary control file.

5. RMAN restores archive logs from backup (if necessary) and performs any necessary recovery.

6. RMAN resets the DBID for the auxiliary instance and opens the auxiliary database with **open resetlogs**.

First, RMAN sets any run-time parameters, such as an **until time** clause on the **duplicate** command. Then, based on these parameters, it checks the target database control file (or recovery catalog) for the appropriate backups. It then builds the RPCs for how to access the backups, and which ones to access, but it does not execute the code at the target. Instead, RMAN creates a channel process at the auxiliary instance, referred to as the *auxiliary channel*, and to this channel RMAN passes the call to DBMS_BACKUP_RESTORE. The auxiliary instance, then, accesses the backups and restores all necessary datafiles. Figure 17-1 illustrates how this takes place for both disk backups and tape backups.

Auxiliary Channel Configuration

For duplication to work, RMAN must allocate one or more channel processes at the auxiliary instance. From Oracle9*i* onward, you do not need to manually allocate an auxiliary channel at the time of duplication, as one will automatically be created using permanent configuration parameters stored in the target control file. The makeup of the auxiliary channel mainly comes from parameters you established for target channels: the default device type and the degree of parallelism both get set using the same persistent parameters that set the target channels. Therefore, if you are duplicating using backups taken to disk, you need not do anything to configure your auxiliary channels. However, if you are duplicating your database using backups taken to tape, you need to configure your auxiliary channels to contain any media manager environment parameters that your target channels have. For example, the following code sets the default device type to tape, sets the default level of parallelism to 2, and then configures two auxiliary channels with the correct parameters:

```
configure default device type to sbt;
configure device type sbt parallelism 2;
configure auxiliary channel 1 device type sbt parms
= "env=(nb_ora_serv=mgtserv, nb_ora_class=oracle)";
configure auxiliary channel 2 device type sbt parms
= "env=(nb_ora_serv=mgtserv, nb_ora_class=oracle)";
```

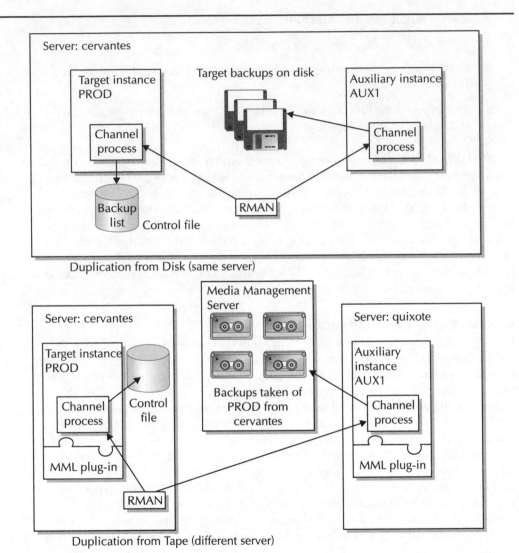

FIGURE 17-1. *A bird's eye view of duplication*

Restoring Datafiles to a Different File Location

After mounting the new control file, RMAN moves forward with the datafile restore. If you are duplicating your database to the same server that your target resides on, it is obviously necessary to change the location to which the files will be restored.

Even when restoring to a different server, differences in mount points and directory structures can require a new file location. The datafile restore step of the duplication process can be modified to point to a new file location in three ways.

First, you can use the **configure** command to configure the auxname for any (or all) datafiles that need a new location. These configurations are stored in the target database control file.

```
configure auxname for datafile 1 to '/u04/oradata/aux1/system01.dbf';
configure auxname for datafile 2 to '/u04/oradata/aux1/undo01.dbf';
...
```

Second, you can specify the new datafile names in a **run** command, as you would in previous versions:

```
run {allocate channel c1 type 'obt_tape';
set newname for datafile 1 to '/u04/oradata/aux1/system01.dbf';
set newname for datafile 2 to '/u04/oradata/aux1/undo01.dbf';
duplicate target database to aux1;}
```

Finally, you can use a parameter in your auxiliary database's init.ora file to set a new location for the files. The parameter is DB_FILE_NAME_CONVERT, and you pass two strings to it: first, the old location of the file on the target, and second, the new location for the file in your auxiliary instance. You can do this in matched file pairs, like this:

```
db_file_name_convert=(
'/u02/oradata/prod/system01.dbf', '/u02/oradata/aux1/system01.dbf',
'/u03/oradata/prod/prd_data_01.dbf', '/u03/oradata/aux1/prd_data_01.dbf')
```

This is a simple string conversion parameter, so you can simply pass a single directory name to be changed. For instance, let's say you have your files spread over four mount points, but they all have prod in the directory structure, so that a select from V$DATAFILE looks like this:

```
Select name from v$datafile;
------------------------------------------------------------
/u02/oradata/prod/system01.dbf
/u03/oradata/prod/prd_data_01.dbf
/u04/oradata/prod/indx_prd01.dbf
/u05/oradata/prod/temp01.dbf
```

Instead of pairing up each file, you can simply do the following:

```
db_file_name_convert=('prod' , 'aux1')
```

This works, so long as everything else about the file location is the same for your auxiliary database, such as the mount point.

Creating the New Control File

The new control file is created for the auxiliary instance after all the files have been restored. RMAN literally just issues a **create controlfile** command at the auxiliary instance, using the parameters you outlined in your **duplicate** command. After creating the control file, the auxiliary database is mounted. Now, RMAN performs a switch operation to switch to the new files. The switch is the means by which RMAN modifies the new control file at the auxiliary site to point to the new location of the datafiles.

Recovery and Archive Logs

After the files are restored and switched, it is time to perform recovery on the database, either to bring it to the current point in time or to bring it to the time specified in the **until time** clause. To perform recovery, RMAN needs access to the archive logs. If they have been backed up by RMAN, then RMAN can simply restore them from the backup location to the LOG_ARCHIVE_DEST specified in the init.ora file of the auxiliary database. You can also manually move archive logs to the location required by the new instance so that they are found on disk by RMAN and no restore is required. If you are duplicating to the same server as the one that the target currently resides on, RMAN can find the archive logs in the LOG_ARCHIVE_DEST of the target.

Once the archive logs are restored, RMAN performs the required amount of recovery. If you did not specify a point in time to end the recovery, RMAN restores up to the last available archive log (as found in the view V$ARCHIVED_LOG) and then stops. During duplication, RMAN cannot check the online redo log files for further recovery information. After it hits the end of the archive logs, it stops recovery. After recovery has completed, if RMAN restored any archive logs from backup, they are deleted.

Changing the Database ID (DBID)

After media recovery is complete, the database is in a consistent state, and it is time for RMAN to change the database ID of the new clone. RMAN has to wait until all other activity in the database has completed, as all operations to this point required the clone database to have the same DBID as the target. The archive logs would not apply to the clone during media recovery if the control file had a different DBID.

The process of changing the DBID is simple. RMAN has at its disposal a little procedure called dbms_backup_restore.zerodbid( ). With the database in a mounted state (not open), this package goes into the file headers and zeros out the DBID in each file header. Then, RMAN shuts down the database and re-creates the auxiliary control file again. When the control file is rebuilt, Oracle checks the file headers for the DBID. When it does not find one, Oracle generates a new one and broadcasts it to every file header.

The zerodbid Procedure: Warning! Achtung!

As you can imagine, the following is a very vulnerable state for a database to be in: shut down without a DBID in the file headers and a control file that is being rebuilt. In the RMAN duplication process, however, elements that could go wrong are tightly controlled, so you don't have to worry too much. We point this out because it is possible to execute this package against any database to generate a new DBID. You just mount the database and run the following code:

```
execute sys.dbms_backup_restore.zerodbid(0);
```

Then, you shut down the database and rebuild the control file using the **set** parameter:

```
create controlfile SET database <db_name> resetlogs…
```

And voila! You have a new DBID. Seems simple enough, doesn't it?

Well, a lot can go wrong if you are trying to do this without the complete control over the environment that RMAN has during duplication. For instance, if you did not get a clean shutdown and you need to perform media recovery before you can open reset logs, you are out of luck. The archive logs have a different DBID. There is no way you will be able to open the database—it is stuck in an inconsistent state, and you cannot fix it. The same thing can happen if a file was accidentally left offline—it won't get the new DBID when you do an **open resetlogs** command, and therefore you will not be able to bring it online. Ever. You will get the following error:

```
ORA-01190: control file or datafile <name> is from before
the last RESETLOGS
```

The moral of the story is to be very careful if you decide to use this procedure manually. There is a better way. As of Oracle9*i* Release 2, Oracle has a utility called DBNEWID, which is a safe and secure way of generating a new ID for a database without making a manual call to the DBMS_BACKUP_RESTORE package. We talk about DBNEWID at the end of this chapter in the section "Incomplete Duplication: Using the DBNEWID Utility."

Log File Creation at the Auxiliary Site

When RMAN issues the final **open resetlogs** command at the completion of the duplication process, it must build brand-new log files for the auxiliary database. This always happens when you issue a **resetlogs** command, but with a **duplicate** command, you need to take into consideration what you want the new redo log files to look like. If you are duplicating to the same system as your target, at a minimum you will have to rename your log files.

You can specify completely new redo log file definitions when you issue the **duplicate** command. Do this if you want to change the size, number, and/or location of the redo logs for the new database. This would look something like this:

```
duplicate target database to aux1
pfile=/u02/oracle/admin/aux1/init.ora
logfile
'/u04/oracle/oradata/aux1/redo01.log' size 100m,
'/u05/oracle/oradata/aux1/redo02.log' size 100m,
'/u06/oracle/oradata/aux1/redo03.log' size 100m;
```

Alternatively, you can use the existing log file definitions from your target and simply move them to a new location using the init.ora parameter LOG_FILE_NAME_CONVERT. This parameter acts exactly like DB_FILE_NAME_CONVERT, so you can convert the log files in coupled pairs, or you can simply use string conversion to change a single directory name:

```
log_file_name_convert=('/u02/oracle/oradata/redo01a.dbf',
'/u03/auxiliary/redo01a.dbf',…)
```

Duplication: Location Considerations

So far, we've completely glossed over one of the biggest stumbling blocks to understanding duplication. You must account for the location of your auxiliary instance in relation to the location of your target instance. Duplicating to the same server is very different from duplicating to a remote server. There are elements unique to each that you must understand before you proceed with duplication.

Duplication to the Same Server: An Overview

You must tread lightly when duplicating to the same server, so that you don't walk all over your existing target database. If you were to simply make a copy of your target init.ora file and then run the following code,

```
duplicate target database to aux1;
```

you would run into a series of problems and errors. These errors would be related to the fact that you already have an instance running with the same name and have the same file locations for two databases.

Memory Considerations

The first memory consideration is the database name. Oracle references memory segments on the server based on the value of the init.ora parameter DB_NAME. Therefore, Oracle cannot allow there to be two instances running on the same system with the same DB_NAME. If you try to startup mount a second instance with the same name, you will get the following error:

```
ORA-01102: cannot mount database in EXCLUSIVE mode
```

Therefore, when duplicating to the same system, you need to change the DB_NAME parameter in the auxiliary init.ora file to be different from the database name of your target:

```
db_name='aux1'
instance_name='aux1'
```

File Location Considerations

Okay, you've squared away your memory problems, but you still have two databases that are trying to write to the same file locations. In fact, you have three different types of files that are all competing for the same name. If you don't account for file locations, duplication will fail at the step of trying to rebuild the control file:

```
RMAN-00571: ===========================================================
RMAN-00569: =============== ERROR MESSAGE STACK FOLLOWS ============
RMAN-00571: ===========================================================
RMAN-03002: failure of Duplicate Db command at 07/02/2002 13:52:14
RMAN-06136: ORACLE error from auxiliary database:
    ORA-01503: CREATE CONTROLFILE failed
ORA-00200: controlfile could not be created
ORA-00202: controlfile:
'/space/oracle_user/OraHome1/oradata/sun92/control01.ctl'
ORA-27086: skgfglk: unable to lock file - already in use
SVR4 Error: 11: Resource temporarily unavailable
```

This is good news for you, because otherwise you would have overwritten your production control file. You must change the auxiliary init.ora parameter CONTROL_FILES to point to a new location on disk, as this is the means by which RMAN determines where to restore the control files to.

After we change the location of the control files, we must change the location of the datafiles. We talked about this previously: your three choices are to use the **configure** command, use the DB_FILE_NAME_CONVERT parameter, or use a **run** block, Oracle8*i*-style. If you fail to change the datafile locations when duplicating to the same server, you will get an error very similar to the preceding control file error, telling you that the files are currently in use and cannot be overwritten.

Finally, you must change the redo log file location. We talked about this previously, when we discussed the different steps that duplication walks through. You can use the **logfile** keyword as part of the **duplicate** command to build completely different redo files, with different sizes, number of groups, and number of members. This option essentially rewrites the similar **logfile** parameter of the **create controlfile** stage of duplication. Alternatively, you can simply use the LOG_FILE_NAME_CONVERT parameter in the auxiliary init.ora file.

Duplication to the Same Server, Different ORACLE_HOME

It is common practice to clone the production database from its location to a different location on the same server but have it be hosted by a different Oracle software installation. When you have a different ORACLE_HOME for the auxiliary instance, there are slightly different rules to conform to. All the rules about hosting on the same system apply as outlined previously. However, you must also consider the location of the backup pieces themselves. If you are duplicating from disk backups, this won't be a problem—just make sure you have your OS permissions worked out ahead of time. If you are duplicating from tape backups, however, you need to make sure that you have your MML file appropriately linked with the auxiliary ORACLE_HOME in the same way as it is linked in your target's ORACLE_HOME. Otherwise, your tape backups will be inaccessible by the auxiliary instance, and duplication will fail because the media manager will be inaccessible.

Duplication to a Remote Server: An Overview

A successful duplication to an auxiliary instance on a different server from the target is no more or less complicated than duplication to the same server. It's just complicated in different ways.

Memory Considerations

Unlike duplication to the same server, you do not have to worry about the DB_NAME parameter in the init.ora file. Because we are on a different server, Oracle has no hang-ups about the LOCK_NAME used for memory.

Of course, it is good operational procedure to always be mindful of the DB_NAME parameter during a duplication process, and crosscheck all other instances running on the same server before beginning the duplication. That way you have no unexpected errors down the road.

File Location Considerations

Again, because we are on a new server, there is not quite the urgency to change any of the file location specifications for your auxiliary instance. There is not a database already running with the same files, so we can leave all file specifications the same as for the target instance, and thus avoid any possible errors in the configuration. Again, we can simplify much of this process when we are on a different system. If you do not change the location of the files, you must specify **nofilenamecheck** in the **duplicate** command. This tells duplication not to confirm that the filenames are different before performing the restore. If this is not specified, RMAN will give you an error.

The one caveat to this simplicity is if the auxiliary host does not have the same file structure and mount point setup that the target host has. If you have different mount points or drive configurations, you still need to change your file specifications for the auxiliary instance so that RMAN can restore to a location that actually exists.

The Backup Location: Disk

The complicating factor for restoring to a different server comes from providing the auxiliary channel process access to backups that were taken at a different server. You must account for whether you backed up to disk or to tape.

If you are duplicating from disk backups, your choices are limited. Remember that RMAN passes the calls to DBMS_BACKUP_RESTORE to a channel process at the auxiliary instance, but it cannot take into account any file system differences. It must look for the backup pieces in the exact location and format that was recorded in the target database control file. For example, suppose you took a full database backup at your target system using the following command:

```
backup database format= '/u04/backup/prod/%U.full.PROD';
```

This created your backup piece as a file called 01DSGVLT_1_1 in the directory /u04/backup/prod. This is recorded in the target control file. Then, during duplication, RMAN passes the **file restore** command to the auxiliary instance and tells it to restore from /u04/backup/prod/01DSGVLT_1_1. That means that on your auxiliary instance, there must be a mount point named /u04, and there must be a directory named backup/prod in which a file called 01DSGVLT_1_1 resides. If not, the duplication will fail with an error:

```
RMAN-03002: failure of Duplicate Db command at 07/02/2002 14:49:55
RMAN-03015: error occurred in stored script Memory Script
ORA-19505: failed to identify file "/u04/backup/prod/01dsgvlt_1_1"
ORA-27037: unable to obtain file status
SVR4 Error: 2: No such file or directory
Additional information: 3
```

There are three ways to make duplication from disk work. The first, and most straightforward, is to simply copy the backups from your target host to the auxiliary host and place them in the same location. Obviously, this involves a huge transfer of files across your network.

The second way to proceed is to NFS mount the backup location on the target host from the auxiliary host. This works only if you can mount the target location with the same mount point name as RMAN will use (in the preceding example, you would have to NFS mount /u04/backup/prod as /u04/backup/prod). For example, you would need to do the following from your auxiliary instance:

```
mount cervantes:/u04/backup/prod /u04/backup/prod
```

That way, from your auxiliary node, you should be able to do the following:

```
cd /u04/backup/prod
ls -l
touch testfile
ls -l
```

If for any reason you get an error when you try to change directories, or when you try to touch a file, you need to sort out your NFS and permissions issues before you proceed with duplication. Figure 17-2 illustrates the mounted file system approach to duplicating to a different server using disk backups.

If you are on a Windows platform instead of NFS, you will be mounting a network drive. The same rule applies: the drive specification must be the same on the auxiliary as it is on the target. So if the backup was written to F:\backup, then you must be able to use F: as a network drive, or duplication will fail. In addition, you will have to set up your auxiliary service (oracleserviceaux1) and your listener service (oracleOraHome92tnslistener) to log on as a domain administrator that has read/write privileges at both the auxiliary host and the target host. Otherwise, you will not be able to access the backups over the networked drive.

As you may have already noticed, it could be difficult to make a network file system operation be successful. If you have the same file systems on both the target

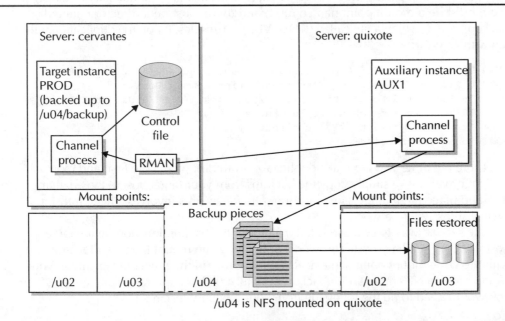

FIGURE 17-2. *Duplication to a different server using disk backups*

and the auxiliary servers, you would not be able to use a straight NFS mount from the auxiliary node to the target location of the backups on disk. Therefore, your only option would be to copy the backup pieces from one node to the other.

The source of these types of headaches, of course, is the fact that RMAN hard codes the backup location when we back up to disk, and this location cannot be changed. In Oracle Database 10g, however, there are now two options for us to change the backup location: the **backup backupset** command and the **catalog backupset** command.

With the **backup backupset** command, we can back up a previous backup set that was on disk and move it to a different disk location. This gives us considerable flexibility. Now, we can move the backup pieces from /u04/backup/prod to, say, /u06/backup/prod, which could then be NFS mounted from our auxiliary system. Or, from the target host, we could NFS mount a drive at the auxiliary host and then use the **backup backupset** command to move the backups to the auxiliary host. For more information on this command, see Chapter 9.

The **catalog backupset** (and **catalog datafilecopy**) command offers another, simpler means of relocating backup sets on a new server. To make RMAN aware that a backup set exists in any location, you need only tell RMAN to catalog a certain file (or a certain directory) and it will look for any valid backups in that location and generate metadata for them. For more details on the **catalog** command, see Chapter 14.

The Backup Location: Tape

By all estimations, duplicating to a remote server using tape backups is far less complicated or demanding than using disk backups, because a tape backup does not have a location, per se, just a file handle. This file handle is all that RMAN knows or cares about; how that file handle relates to a location on a specific tape is completely controlled by the media manager. Therefore, all configuration that occurs for duplication from tape comes from media management configuration.

First, you must configure your MML file at the auxiliary site in the same way as at the target site. Because an auxiliary channel is doing the restore operations, it must be able to initialize the MML, as outlined in Chapter 4. So make sure you've linked your MML at the auxiliary site.

Next, you need to make sure that your media management server is configured correctly. This means that your auxiliary node must be registered as a client in the same media management server that your target node is registered in, and it must have the necessary privileges to access the tapes for restore purposes. In particular, you must enable the auxiliary node to be able to restore backups that were taken from a different server. This functionality is usually disabled by default in most media management software, because allowing files to be restored from one client to another is a potential security hole. The steps for enabling clients to restore files from a different client are outlined in each of our four media management chapters (Chapters 5, 6, 7, and 8), depending on your software vendor.

After configuring your media management server, your final configuration step is to set up your auxiliary channels. As mentioned earlier, RMAN allocates one or more channels at the auxiliary instance to perform the restore and recovery steps of duplication. You configure these channels via the **configure** command when you are connected to your target database from RMAN. The **parms** parameter for the auxiliary channels must contain the usual media management environment control variables. In particular, it needs to specify the client from which the backups were taken. For instance, let's say your target node is named cervantes and your auxiliary node is named quixote. Because you have been backing up from cervantes, this client name is encoded with your RMAN backups at the media management server. So, to be able to access these backups from the client quixote, you must specify from within RMAN that the client name is cervantes. Your auxiliary channel configuration command, then, would look something like this (given a NetBackup media management system):

```
RMAN> configure auxiliary channel 1 device type sbt parms
2> = "env=(nb_ora_serv=mgtserv, nb_ora_client=cervantes)";
new RMAN configuration parameters:
CONFIGURE AUXILIARY CHANNEL 1 DEVICE TYPE 'SBT_TAPE' PARMS
"env=(nb_ora_serv=mgtserv, nb_ora_client=cervantes)";
new RMAN configuration parameters are successfully stored
```

Then, when the auxiliary channel makes its **sbt( )** calls to the MML, it is telling the media management server to access backups that were taken using the client cervantes, instead of checking for backups made by quixote.

Duplication and the Network

Take a deep breath; we're almost through explaining all the intricacies of duplication, and are about to walk you through the steps themselves. There's one more area that you need to prepare prior to running a **duplicate** command from RMAN: the network. By *network*, we mostly mean configuring your Oracle Net files—tnsnames.ora and listener.ora. However, take this opportunity to consider your overall network as well. Make sure that the target node, auxiliary node, and media management server can all access each other okay and that you have plenty of bandwidth.

From an Oracle perspective, we have to configure the Oracle Net files. As discussed in Chapter 2, RMAN must make a sysdba connection to the target database. If you are connecting remotely, you have to configure a password file for the target node. In addition, you need a tns alias that uses a dedicated server process instead of a shared server process. For duplication, this still holds true, but you must also be able to connect to the auxiliary instance as sysdba using only dedicated servers.

This means that, no matter what, you have to create a password file for either your target or your auxiliary machine. You may have been forgoing this step until now by always making a local connection to the target database. But you cannot simultaneously make a local connection to both the target and the auxiliary instance. So now, if you haven't done so already, it's time to build a password file.

RMAN Workshop: *Building a Password File*

Workshop Notes

On Unix platforms, the name of the password file must be orapw<sid>, where <sid> is the value of the ORACLE_SID to which the password is giving access. In this Workshop, the ORACLE_SID = prod. On Windows, the filename must be in the format pwd<sid>.ora. The locations given in this Workshop must be used; the password file cannot be created anywhere else or it will be unusable.

Step 1. Edit the init.ora file and add the following parameter:

```
remote_login passwordfile=exclusive
```

If you are using an SPFILE, you need to execute the following:

```
alter system set remote_login_passwordfile=exclusive scope=spfile;
```

Both operations require a database restart to take effect.

Step 2. Decide what your password will be, and then navigate to your ORACLE_HOME/dbs directory (ORALCE_HOME/database on Windows) and type the following:

```
orapwd file=orapwprod password=<OraclE4ever>
```

Step 3. Check that the file was created successfully, and then test it by making a remote connection as sysdba.

After your password file has been created for your auxiliary instance, you need to configure the listener to route incoming connections to the auxiliary instance. As you may have already noticed, there is no need in 10g for a listener.ora file if you will be connecting only to open databases. This is because the database PMON process automatically registers the database with a running listener daemon on the system. So, you will often see that after a default 10gR2 installation, a listener is running and it is listening for your database, even though you've done no configuration.

While this is excellent news, it does nothing for us in a duplication environment, because we must be able to make a remote connection to an auxiliary instance that is started (in NOMOUNT mode) but not open. Because it is not open, there is no

PMON process to register the auxiliary instance with the listener, so the listener has no idea the auxiliary instance exists. To get past this, you must set up an old-fashioned listener.ora file, with a manual entry for the auxiliary database. We recommend using the Oracle Net Manager utility, shown here, to build this entry:

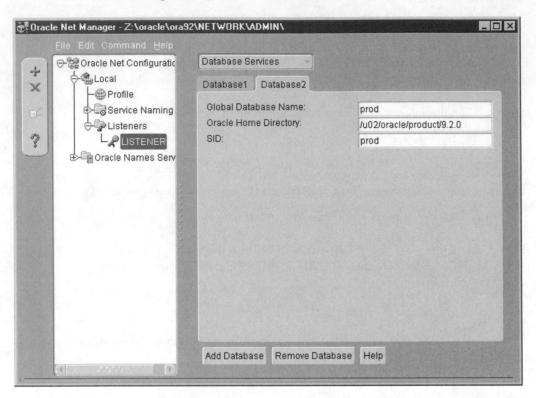

After you have configured the listener.ora at your auxiliary instance location, you must also build a tnsnames.ora entry at the site from which you will be running RMAN. This is the same as almost any other entry, except that when you build it, you must specify the auxiliary SID_NAME instead of the SERVICE_NAME. From the Net Manager, you fire up the Net Service Name Wizard by clicking on "Service Naming" and then going to the menu and choosing Edit->Create . . . . After you give the Net Service Name (Step 1), provide the protocol (Step 2), and provide the hostname and port number (Step 3), you must change from Service Name to SID in Step 4 of 5 of the Net Service Name Wizard, shown next. If you choose Service Name, the listener at the auxiliary site will try to find a service named aux1, but of course there is no service of that name. There is only a SID. Yeah, it's complicated. Do we have time to explain it exactly? Nah. Just take our word for it.

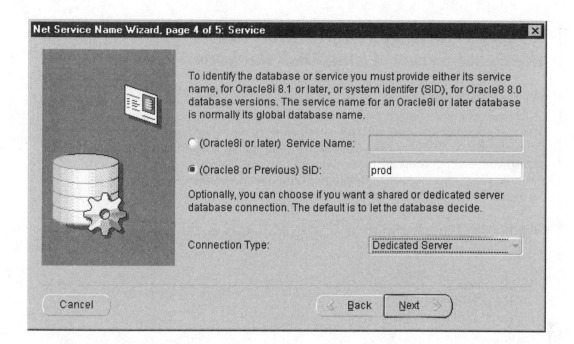

Duplication to the Same Server

Okay, so enough of the explanations, it's time to run through the duplication itself. First, we give a detailed step-by-step workshop for duplicating to the same server on which the target resides, using disk backups. Then, we give a brief explanation of what you would need to do the same thing with tape backups.

Setting an until Clause when Duplicating

When performing duplication, you sometimes will encounter a situation that requires you to specify an **until** clause when duplicating. If you have ever used RMAN to restore your database using a backup control file, and you are now attempting to duplicate that database, you will be required to set an **until** clause. It is recommended to determine the most recent archive log available to duplication and then use it as the ending point during duplication:

```
run { set until sequence n thread 1;
duplicate target database… }
```

Or, as a fix-all, you can set the SCN to an impossibly high value:

```
set until scn  281474976710655;
```

RMAN Workshop: *Duplication to the Same Server, Using Disk Backups*

Workshop Notes

Make sure that your OS has been configured to handle another Oracle instance and that adequate memory and disk space exist. In the following example, our target database, v102, has all of its datafiles, control files, and redo log files located at /u01/app/oracle/product/oradata/v102. All backups have been going to the local flash recovery area (FRA) at /u01/app/oracle/product/flash_recovery_area. We will set the ORACLE_SID for the auxiliary instance to be aux1.

Step 1.   Build your auxiliary database directory structures:

```
$ pwd
/u01/app/oracle/product/oradata
$ mkdir aux1
$ mkdir aux1/arch
$ cd ../admin
$ mkdir aux1
$ cd aux1
$ mkdir pfile bdump udump cdump
$ ls
 bdump  cdump  pfile  udump
```

Step 2.   Copy the target init.ora file to the auxiliary location. If your target database uses an SPFILE, you need to create a PFILE from the SPFILE to capture parameters to move over.

   If you use an SPFILE at your target, enter the following:

```
SQL> connect / as sysdba
Connected.
SQL> create pfile='/u01/app/oracle/product/admin/aux1/pfile/init.ora'
  from spfile;
```

   If you use an init.ora file at your target, enter the following:

```
cp u01/app/oracle/product/admin/v102/pfile/init.ora
   u01/app/oracle/product/admin/aux1/pfile/init.ora
```

Step 3.   Make all necessary changes to your aux1 init.ora file:

```
audit_file_dest='/u01/app/oracle/product/admin/aux1/adump'
background_dump_dest='/u01/app/oracle/product/admin/aux1/bdump'
compatible='10.2.0.1.0'
```

```
control_files='/u01/app/oracle/product/oradata/aux1/control01.ctl',
    '/u01/app/oracle/product/oradata/aux1/control02.ctl',
    '/u01/app/oracle/product/oradata/aux1/control03.ctl'
core_dump_dest='/u01/app/oracle/product/admin/aux1/cdump'
db_block_size=8192
db_file_multiblock_read_count=16
db_name='aux1'
db_recovery_file_dest='/u01/app/oracle/product/flash_recovery_area'
db_recovery_file_dest_size=4294967296
dispatchers='(PROTOCOL=TCP) (SERVICE=aux1XDB)'
job_queue_processes=10
open_cursors=300
pga_aggregate_target=93323264
processes=150
remote_login_passwordfile='EXCLUSIVE'
sga_target=279969792
undo_management='AUTO'
undo_tablespace='UNDOTBS1'
user_dump_dest='/u01/app/oracle/product/admin/aux1/udump'
db_file_name_convert=('v102','aux1')
instance_name='aux1'
```

Step 4. Build your aux1 password file. See the "Building a Password File" RMAN Workshop earlier in this chapter.

Step 5. Startup the aux1 instance in NOMOUNT mode:

```
ORACLE_SID=aux1
export ORACLE_SID
sqlplus /nolog
sql>connect / as sysdba
SQL> startup nomount
pfile=/u01/app/oracle/product/admin/aux1/pfile/init.ora
```

Step 6. Configure your network files for connection to aux1. After making any changes to your listener.ora file, be sure that you bounce your listener or the change will not take effect.

```
$ lsnrctl reload
```

The tnsnames.ora file should have an entry like this:

```
AUX1 =
  (DESCRIPTION =
    (ADDRESS_LIST =
```

```
      (ADDRESS = (PROTOCOL = TCP)(HOST = dex.hadba.com)(PORT = 1521))
    )
    (CONNECT_DATA =
    (SID = aux1)
    (SERVER = DEDICATED)
    )
  )
```

The listener.ora file should have an entry like this:

```
SID_LIST_LISTENER =
  (SID_LIST =
    (SID_DESC =
      (GLOBAL_DBNAME = aux1)
      (ORACLE_HOME = /u01/app/oracle/product/10.2.0)
      (SID_NAME = aux1)
    )
  )
```

Step 7.   From RMAN, connect to the target and auxiliary instance and run the **duplicate** command:

```
$ ORACLE_SID=aux1;export ORACLE_SID
$ rman target /
RMAN> connect auxiliary sys/ora10g@aux1
RMAN> duplicate target database to aux1
 pfile=/u01/app/oracle/product/admin/aux1/pfile/init.ora
 logfile
 '/u01/app/oracle/product/oradata/aux1/redo01.dbf' size 100m,
 '/u01/app/oracle/product/oradata/aux1/redo02.dbf' size 100m,
 '/u01/app/oracle/product/oradata/aux1/redo03.dbf' size 100m;
```

Using Tape Backups

If you were to perform the preceding exercises but with your backups on tape, little would change. In fact, none of the code itself would change; you would simply insert an additional step prior to running the **duplicate** command itself. That step would be to configure your auxiliary channel(s) to resemble the channels that the backups were taken with. In other words, do a **show** command:

```
RMAN> show channel;
RMAN configuration parameters are:
CONFIGURE CHANNEL 1 DEVICE TYPE 'SBT_TAPE' PARMS
"env=(nb_ora_serv=mgtserv)";
CONFIGURE CHANNEL 2 DEVICE TYPE 'SBT_TAPE' PARMS
"env=(nb_ora_serv=mgtserv)";
```

Then, simply create the auxiliary channels to match:

```
CONFIGURE AUXILIARY CHANNEL 1 DEVICE TYPE 'SBT_TAPE' PARMS
"env=(nb_ora_serv=mgtserv)";
CONFIGURE AUXILIARY CHANNEL 2 DEVICE TYPE 'SBT_TAPE' PARMS
"env=(nb_ora_serv=mgtserv)";
```

Duplication to a Remote Server

Duplication to a remote server has many of the same configuration steps as duplication to the same server. In particular, if you are duplicating remotely but will use disk backups, the steps would be identical, although you could forgo all file renaming steps. In addition, you would have to either copy your backups to the remote server or use NFS to mount the backups at the remote site. Covering NFS is outside the scope of this book, so we assume in the following RMAN Workshop that you have the same file systems on both the target and auxiliary servers and have copied the backups to the auxiliary system.

RMAN Workshop: *Duplication to a Remote Server, Using Disk Backups*

Workshop Notes

This Workshop assumes the use of two servers: dex, the target, and proto, the auxiliary. It assumes that you have the same file system on both nodes and have copied your backups from dex to proto. The most important thing to note here is that we maintain the v102 database SID throughout the process (instead of changing it to aux1, which we do when duplicating to the same server).

Step 1. At quixote, build your auxiliary database directory structures:

```
$> pwd
/app/oracle/product/10.1.0/oradata
$> mkdir v102
$> cd ../admin
$> pwd
/app/oracle/product/10.1.0/admin
$> mkdir v102
$> cd v102
$> mkdir pfile bdump udump cdump adump
$> ls
adump  bdump  cdump  pfile  udump
```

Step 2. At dex, make a copy of the target init.ora file so that it can be moved to the auxiliary server. If your target database uses an SPFILE, you need to create a PFILE from the SPFILE in order to capture parameters to move over.

If you use an SPFILE at your target, enter the following:

```
SQL> connect / as sysdba
Connected.
SQL> create pfile='/home/oracle/scratchpad/init.ora'
  from spfile;
```

If you use an init.ora file at your target, enter the following:

```
cp /u01/app/oracle/product/admin/v102/pfile/init.ora
   /home/oracle/scratchpad/init.ora
```

Step 3. Move the target init.ora file to the auxiliary site:

```
cd /home/oracle/scratchpad/
ftp proto.hadba.com
username: oracle
password:
cd /u01/app/oracle/product/admin/v102/pfile
put init.ora
exit
```

You also need a local copy of the init.ora file at the target server dex, for reference by RMAN in the **duplicate** command itself. We will reference the copy that we left in /home/oracle/scratchpad/init.ora when we run the **duplicate** command in Step 10.

Step 4. Start the auxiliary instance in NOMOUNT mode at quixote:

```
ORACLE_SID=v102; export ORACLE_SID
sqlplus /nolog
SQL>connect / as sysdba
SQL>startup nomount
pfile=/u01/app/oracle/product/admin/v102/pfile/init.ora
```

Step 5. Configure the listener.ora at the auxiliary site (proto):

```
SID_LIST_LISTENER =
  (SID_LIST =
    (SID_DESC =
      (GLOBAL_DBNAME = v102)
```

```
      (ORACLE_HOME = /app/oracle/product/10.1.0/db_2)
      (SID_NAME = v102)
    )
  )
```

Step 6. Configure the tnsnames.ora file at the target site (dex):

```
V102_PROTO =
  (DESCRIPTION =
    (ADDRESS_LIST =
      (ADDRESS = (PROTOCOL = TCP)(HOST = proto.hadba.com)(PORT = 1522))
    )
    (CONNECT_DATA =
      (SERVICE_NAME = v102)
    )
```

Step 7. Create a password file at the remote server (proto). Follow the instructions from the earlier RMAN Workshop, "Building a Password File."

Step 8. Move the FRA files from dex to proto. While an NFS mount might suffice, there were enough problems getting past the error:

```
ORA-27054: NFS file system where the file is created
or resides is not mounted with correct options
```

We ultimately took our NFS mount and copied the files to a local directory on proto named to identically match the FRA on the target (dex).

Step 9. From the target system (dex), run your **duplicate** command:

```
ORACLE_SID=v102; export ORACLE_SID
rman target /
RMAN> connect auxiliary sys/password@v102_proto
duplicate target database to v102
pfile=/home/oracle/scratchpad/init.ora
logfile
'/app/oracle/product/10.1.0/oradata/v102/redo01.dbf' size 100m,
'/app/oracle/product/10.1.0/oradata/v102/redo02.dbf' size 100m,
'/app/oracle/product/10.1.0/oradata/v102/redo03.dbf' size 100m;
```

Using Tape Backups for Remote Server Duplication

All the steps in the preceding RMAN Workshop apply if you are using tape backups instead of disk backups; again, the only difference is that you would also have to configure your auxiliary channels to reflect the needs of your media manager.

In addition to specifying the media management server, and any classes or pools that you have for your regular channels, you also need to specify the target client name:

```
RMAN> configure auxiliary channel 1 device type sbt parms
2> = "env=(nb_ora_serv=mgtserv, nb_ora_client=dex)";
```

Incomplete Duplication: Using the DBNEWID Utility

One of the most frustrating elements of performing duplication is that there is no "restartable duplication." What we mean by this is that if you make it through the step that restores all your files—arguably the longest step of the process—but a failure occurs, say, during the recovery, you must restart the duplication process from scratch and restore all the files again. There is no way to correct the recovery process (by making missing archive logs available, for instance) and then pick up where you left off.

With RESTORE OPTIMIZATION turned ON, RMAN will not restore files again that already exist in the restore location with the same datafile header SCN information. This applies to duplication as well: if duplication restores a file, and then duplication restarts, RMAN will not restore the file again. However, if you have applied even one archive log to the file, it will be restored again.

Oracle Database 10*g* includes the DBNEWID utility, which gives your clone database a new DBID in a safe and controlled manner. This allows you to do manual recovery against a duplicated database, prepare all the elements, and then run DBNEWID, which will complete the process started by duplication. This allows you to at least manually complete a duplication.

DBNEWID usage is simple. First, you must make sure you have a good backup taken prior to using DBNEWID. Although it has a verification process, DBNEWID can still encounter unrecoverable errors during the changing of the DBID. After confirming a good backup, you need to get the database shut down in a consistent state and then brought back up to a mounted state:

```
shutdown immediate;
startup mount
```

Then, run the DBNEWID utility from the command line:

```
nid target =/
DBNEWID: Release 10.2.0.1.0 - Production on Sat Sep 3 14:06:43 2005
Copyright (c) 1982, 2005, Oracle.  All rights reserved.
Connected to database AUX1 (DBID=366194736)
Connected to server version 10.2.0
Control Files in database:
 /u01/app/oracle/product/oradata/aux1/control01.ctl
 /u01/app/oracle/product/oradata/aux1/control02.ctl
/u01/app/oracle/product/oradata/aux1/control03.ctl
```

```
Change database ID of database AUX1? (Y/[N]) => Y
Proceeding with operation
Changing database ID from 366194736 to 366203699
    Control File /u01/app/oracle/product/oradata/aux1/control01.ctl
 -modified
    Control File /u01/app/oracle/product/oradata/aux1/control02.ctl
- modified
    Control File /u01/app/oracle/product/oradata/aux1/control03.ctl
- modified
    Datafile /u01/app/oracle/product/oradata/aux1/system01.dbf
- dbid changed
    Datafile /u01/app/oracle/product/oradata/aux1/undotbs01.dbf
- dbid changed
    Datafile /u01/app/oracle/product/oradata/aux1/sysaux01.dbf
- dbid changed
    Datafile /u01/app/oracle/product/oradata/aux1/users01.dbf
- dbid changed
    Datafile /u01/app/oracle/product/oradata/aux1/temp01.dbf
- dbid changed
    Control File /u01/app/oracle/product/oradata/aux1/control01.ctl
- dbid changed
    Control File /u01/app/oracle/product/oradata/aux1/control02.ctl
- dbid changed
    Control File /u01/app/oracle/product/oradata/aux1/control03.ctl
- dbid changed
    Instance shut down
Database ID for database AUX1 changed to 366203699.
All previous backups and archived redo logs for this database are unusable.
Database is not aware of previous backups and archived logs in Recovery
Area.
Database has been shutdown, open database with RESETLOGS option.
Successfully changed database ID.
DBNEWID - Completed successfully.

[oracle@dex oracle]$ sqlplus "/ as sysdba"

SQL> alter database open resetlogs;
```

Summary

In this chapter, we discussed the architecture behind the RMAN duplication process. Using duplication, we can produce clone databases from our RMAN backups to either the local system or a remote server. There are different configuration steps, depending on whether you will be duplicating locally or remotely. In addition, there are specific guidelines to follow depending on whether your backups are on disk or on tape. Two RMAN Workshops gave step-by-step instructions for duplication. We wrapped everything up with a brief discussion of the DBNEWID utility that comes with Oracle Database 10g.

CHAPTER
18

RMAN and Data Guard

any DBAs are already familiar with the functionality known as Oracle Standby Database. It is an architectural feature that adds a little functionality to operations that already take place on your system: the archiving of every single change that happens on a database. The Standby Database was a simple concept, in the beginning, and even though the overall architecture is now referred to as Data Guard, the foundation is still simple: take the archive logs from your production database, move them to another computer that has a copy of that database, and apply the archive logs to the copy. In such a way, Data Guard is able to provide an efficient disaster recovery solution by maintaining transactionally consistent copies of the production database at a remote site. These copies, or standbys, can be one of two types, physical or logical. Which one you choose to include in your Data Guard configuration depends on what business needs you are trying to satisfy.

A physical standby database is kept in sync with the primary database by using media recovery to apply redo that was generated on the primary database. Because media recovery is used, we can be assured that a physical standby is a block-for-block identical copy of the primary database. Because of its nature, a physical standby database is an excellent choice for disaster recovery. In the event of a failure, we can rest assured that our data will be intact and consistent with data that existed on the primary database.

A logical standby database is kept in sync with the primary database by transforming redo data received from the primary database into logical SQL statements and then executing those SQL statements against the standby database. Because we are applying SQL statements instead of performing media recovery, it is possible for the logical standby database to contain the same logical information as the primary database but at the same time have a different physical structure. Because a logical standby database is open for user access while applying changes, it is an ideal solution for a reporting database while maintaining its disaster recovery attributes.

RMAN and Data Guard are complementary technologies that together make a complete Oracle solution for disaster recovery and high availability. RMAN backups can be used to create the underlying standby database, along with providing the initial recovery phase. Then, after you have created the standby database and configured the Data Guard broker, RMAN can connect to the standby database and take backups that can be restored to the primary database. In this way, the resources used to perform a backup can be completely removed from your production environment.

Obviously, this book is about RMAN and not Data Guard. If you have more questions about standby databases or Data Guard, check out the Oracle Press title *Oracle Database 10*g *High Availability: RAC, Flashback, and Data Guard* (2004). From here on out in this chapter, we assume that you are familiar with the basics of Data Guard standby databases and are ready to create one using RMAN.

RMAN and the Standby Database

Primarily, the relationship between RMAN and the standby database is a simple one: RMAN is used to create the standby database. If you are implementing a backup strategy that has RMAN doing all of your backups, you wouldn't really have any choice but to use RMAN, because the standby database must have primary database datafiles copied into place to begin with.

With the release of Oracle Database 10g, RMAN backups can now be used to create both physical and logical standby databases. This was not the case in Oracle9i Database, because the primary database had to be quiesced prior to taking a backup to be used for a logical standby. But in version 10g, a hot backup can now be used as the basis for a logical standby database, and that means RMAN backups can be used.

However, if you were a reader of our *Oracle9i RMAN Backup & Recovery* book, you may find that we haven't changed much in the instructions that follow. This is because RMAN does not discriminate between creating a physical and logical standby database. RMAN does not discriminate because the first step to create a logical standby database is to create a physical standby database. After you create a physical standby database, a conversion takes place to turn it into a logical standby database. And RMAN is only involved in the physical creation, leaving the logical standby conversion to you.

Requirements for Using RMAN for Standby Database Creation

Before RMAN can create the standby database, you have to walk through a few initial steps. These steps are identical to those outlined in the duplication process in Chapter 17:

1. Make all necessary changes in both the primary and standby database init.ora files.

2. Complete all necessary Oracle Net configuration.

3. Start the standby database in nomount mode.

The reason for these steps is that RMAN uses the **duplicate** command to create the standby database, so all rules that apply to duplication also apply to standby database creation. This means that any file-renaming issues are the same, the password file requirement is the same, and the particular way in which you have to configure the listener.ora and tnsnames.ora files is the same. If you're not sure what we're talking about, review Chapter 17 prior to proceeding: everything from here on out is in addition to the duplication requirements and restrictions laid out in Chapter 17.

In addition to reviewing Chapter 17, you must also have a specific kind of control file backup. A regular control file backup is not used when we create a standby database, because a standby database control file is different from a regular control file. It places more stringent conditions on applying archive logs during media recovery. A standby control file also does not allow a standby database to be opened with an **alter database open** command. Instead, you must activate a standby database (and thus make it the primary database) by using **alter database activate standby database**.

To create a standby control file, you can use a SQL command:

```
alter database create standby controlfile as
'/u04/backup/stby_cfile01.ctl';
```

If you create a standby control file in this fashion, you have to catalog it with RMAN before RMAN can use it in a **duplicate…for standby** operation:

```
RMAN>catalog controlfilecopy '/u04/backup/stby_cfile01.ctl';
```

Even simpler, you can use RMAN to create a standby control file. That way, you can create a copy on your tape device (if you use tape backups) using the **backup** command:

```
RMAN>  backup current controlfile for standby;
```

Once you've got a standby control file ready, you can move forward with your standby database creation using RMAN.

Finally, before we discuss the commands for creating your standby database, a little vocabulary lesson will come in handy. As you know from Chapter 17, the RMAN duplication process refers to two databases that must be connected: the target database and the auxiliary database. The *target database* is where the backups came from, and the *auxiliary database* is the clone database being created from the target database backups.

In the language of the standby database architecture, you have two databases, as well: the *primary database*, which is your current production database, and the *standby database*, which is the unopened copy of the primary database that receives the archived redo logs from the primary database. When you are using RMAN to create a standby database, remember this: the target database is the primary database, and the auxiliary database is the standby database.

The duplicate…for standby Command

The **duplicate** command is used a bit differently when you are using it for standby database creation. As we stated previously, all duplication rules apply, but we must add a few caveats and restrictions.

Memory Considerations

First of all, the DB_NAME parameter in the init.ora file of the standby database must match the DB_NAME of the primary database. This is only marginally interesting news if you are creating your standby database on a different server, but it has important implications if you are building the standby database on the same server as the primary database. Oracle uses the DB_NAME to lock memory segments at the OS level, so if you try to mount two instances with the same DB_NAME, you will get an error:

```
<ORA-01102: cannot mount database in exclusive mode>
```

To get around this, you can modify the init.ora file of the standby database and add the parameter LOCK_NAME_SPACE. You set this to a value different from the DB_NAME, and then Oracle uses this to lock memory segments without changing the DB_NAME:

```
lock_name_space='stby'
```

Now, the 10g documentation mentions that LOCK_NAME_SPACE has been deprecated. Upon researching this, we found that its replacement is meant to be SP_NAME. Good luck trying to use that, though—we found that 10.2.0 does not recognize SP_NAME:

```
LRM-00101: unknown parameter name 'sp_name'
```

However, when you use LOCK_NAME_SPACE, it complains that it is deprecated:

```
ORA-32006: LOCK_NAME_SPACE initialization parameter has been deprecated
```

Ignore this. LOCK_NAME_SPACE works fine, and its "replacement" does not.

Because the DB_NAME must be the same, the **duplicate for standby** command does not use the format **duplicate target database to <aux_name>**. This format was necessary to reset the database name in the new control file during duplication, but during standby database creation, we don't create a new control file. Therefore, the command looks like this:

```
duplicate target database for standby;
```

Log File Considerations

In addition to the missing **to** clause of the **duplicate** command, you cannot use the **logfile** clause when creating a standby. The reason for this has everything to do with standby database options, such as the standby redo log file that is available as part of a Data Guard solution. None of these options applies to the duplication process, but because of them, RMAN disallows the **logfile** clause. Instead, if you are doing a straight standby database configuration and need to specify a different location for the log files, you need to use the LOG_FILE_NAME_CONVERT parameter in your standby init.ora file. This parameter acts exactly like DB_FILE_NAME_CONVERT in that it is a simple string conversion and can be used to change a single directory name, or can be used in pairs to make multiple changes.

Datafile Considerations

If you will be creating your standby database to a different server from the one that holds the primary database, you do not have to change anything about the datafile location, so long as the standby database server has the same mount point and directory structure as the primary database server. As with regular duplication, if you will be using the same datafile locations on the standby database that exist on the primary database, you will need to use the **nofilenamecheck** keyword in the **duplicate** command:

```
duplicate target database for standby nofilenamecheck;
```

If you are creating the standby database on the same server as the one that holds the primary database, you are required to change the file locations for the standby datafiles. You can do this in any of the same ways that you would with regular duplication: using the **configure auxname** command, using **set newname** in a **run** block, or using DB_FILE_NAME_CONVERT in the standby init.ora file.

Media Recovery Considerations

A physical standby database is never opened for read/write activity. It is mounted and placed in a state of media recovery, or it is opened in read-only mode and users are allowed to perform SELECT statements only. Because of this peculiarity, the RMAN duplication performs a little differently than it would if you wanted to clone the database. It doesn't re-create the control file; it restores a standby control file. It does not, by default, perform any media recovery on the datafiles after restoring them, and then it skips the steps that reset the DBID and open the database reset logs. So, when the **duplicate... for standby** completes, your standby database is mounted but not open, and you will need to decide how to proceed with media recovery.

If you would like RMAN to perform the initial media recovery and apply archive logs that have been backed up by RMAN, you can use the keyword **dorecover** in your **duplicate** command:

```
duplicate target database for standby dorecover;
```

Typically, you will want to provide an **until** clause along with your **duplicate** command if you will be doing recovery, particularly if you are creating the standby database at a remote site. If you are at a remote site, using **set until time** or **set until sequence** will enable you to make sure that the recovery attempts to use only archive logs that are available at the other site. Of course, because we aren't setting the DBID or opening the clone, a failed media recovery session out of the **duplicate** command is no big deal: you can just pick up manually where it left off.

RMAN Workshop: *Create a Standby Database Using RMAN*

Workshop Notes

This exercise creates a standby database on the same server as the primary database. The ORACLE_SID for the standby database is stby, but the DB_NAME will be the same as for the primary database: v102. We will use both the DB_FILE_NAME_CONVERT and LOG_FILE_NAME_CONVERT parameters, and we will perform media recovery.

Step 1.   Use RMAN to create a standby control file:

```
ORACLE_SID=v102;export ORACLE_SID
rman target /
RMAN> backup current controlfile for standby;
```

You need to specify a point in time after you created this standby control file, so perform a few log switches and then record the last log sequence number from V$ARCHIVED_LOG:

```
SQL> alter system switch logfile;
SQL> alter system switch logfile;
SQL> select sequence# from v$archived_log;
```

Step 2.   Build your standby database directory structures:

```
$ cd $ORACLE_BASE
$ cd oradata
$ pwd
/u01/app/oracle/product/oradata
$ mkdir stby
$ cd ../admin
$ pwd
/u01/app/oracle/product/admin
$ mkdir stby
$ cd stby
$ mkdir pfile adump bdump cdump udump
```

Step 3.   Copy the target init.ora file to the auxiliary location. If your target database uses an SPFILE, you need to create a PFILE from the SPFILE in order to capture parameters to move over.

If you use an SPFILE at your target, enter the following:

```
SQL> create pfile='/u01/app/oracle/product/admin/stby/pfile/init.ora'
  2  from spfile;
```

If you use an init.ora file at your target, enter the following:

```
cp /u01/app/oracle/product/admin/vv102/pfile/init.ora
/u01/app/oracle/product/admin/stby/pfile/init.ora
```

Step 4. Make all necessary changes to your stby init.ora file:

```
*.audit_file_dest='/u01/app/oracle/product/admin/stby/adump'
*.background_dump_dest='/u01/app/oracle/product/admin/stby/bdump'
*.compatible='10.2.0.1.0'
*.control_files='/u01/app/oracle/product/oradata/stby/control01.ctl',
     '/u01/app/oracle/product/oradata/stby/control02.ctl',
     '/u01/app/oracle/product/oradata/stby/control03.ctl'
*.core_dump_dest='/u01/app/oracle/product/admin/stby/cdump'
*.db_block_size=8192
*.db_domain=''
*.db_file_multiblock_read_count=16
*.db_name='v102'
*.db_recovery_file_dest='/u01/app/oracle/product/flash_recovery_area'
*.db_recovery_file_dest_size=4294967296
*.job_queue_processes=10
*.open_cursors=300
*.pga_aggregate_target=93323264
*.processes=150
*.remote_login_passwordfile='EXCLUSIVE'
*.sga_target=279969792
*.undo_management='AUTO'
*.undo_tablespace='UNDOTBS1'
*.user_dump_dest='/u01/app/oracle/product/admin/stby/udump'
lock_name_space='stby'
db_file_name_convert=('v102','stby')
log_file_name_convert=('v102','stby')
lock_name_space='stby'
```

Step 5. Build your stby password file. See the "Building a Password File" RMAN Workshop in Chapter 17.

Step 6. Start up the stby instance in NOMOUNT mode:

```
ORACLE_SID=stby; export ORACLE_SID
sqlplus "/ as sysdba"
sql>startup nomount
pfile=/u01/app/oracle/product/admin/stby/pfile/init.ora
```

Step 7. Configure your network files for connection to stby. After making any changes to your listener.ora file, be sure that you bounce your listener or the change will not take effect:

```
Lsnrctl reload
```

The tnsnames.ora file should have an entry like this:

```
STBY =
  (DESCRIPTION =
    (ADDRESS_LIST =
      (ADDRESS = (PROTOCOL = TCP)(HOST = dex.hadba.com)(PORT = 1521))
    )
    (CONNECT_DATA =
      (SERVICE_NAME = stby)
    )
  )
```

The listener.ora file should have an entry like this:

```
(SID_DESC =
  (GLOBAL_DBNAME = stby)
  (ORACLE_HOME = /u01/app/oracle/product/10.2.0)
  (SID_NAME = stby)
)
```

Step 8. From RMAN, connect to the target and auxiliary instances and run the **duplicate** command:

```
ORACLE_SID=v102; export ORACLE_SID
rman target /
RMAN> connect auxiliary sys/password@stby
RMAN>run {
  set until sequence = 789 thread = 1;
  duplicate target database for standby
  dorecover;}
```

Taking Backups from the Standby Database

After creating your standby database, you can use it for a number of different purposes. Its primary reason for existence, of course, is to provide a disaster recovery solution for your production database. However, you can also suspend media recovery against the standby database, open it as read only, and perform any number of data-mining operations that would suck too many resources away from your production system.

Using the New UR=A Parameter in Oracle Database 10*g*

If you are using instance registration, there will not be any entries in the listener.ora file by default for the database. You can manually configure the database entry in the listener. Or, you can update the tnsnames.ora file with a new Oracle Database 10*g* parameter, UR=A. This is to allow administrative connections only; for example:

```
CONNECT_DATA=((SID=....) (UR=A))
```

From the RMAN perspective, there is another excellent way to put the standby database to work. As you know from Chapter 16, there is a price to pay for running RMAN against your production database in terms of resources used. You utilize precious memory, CPU, and disk I/O resources when the backup is running. So, we recommend running your backups during the off-peak hours of your database. Sometimes, though, there are no off-peak hours. You could be a 24-hour operation, with constant database updates, or your database could be so large that backups are pretty much running around the clock.

If you have a physical standby database, you can take your production backups from the standby database; these backups can then be restored to the primary database if the primary database has a failure of some kind. Because the standby database has the same DBID as the primary database and is always from the same incarnation, the RMAN datafile backups are interchangeable between the standby database and the primary database. The standby database is a true clone of the primary database.

The thing to understand about using a standby database to take production backups is that RMAN will connect to the standby database as the target database. Remember, up to this point we've encouraged you to think of the standby database as the auxiliary database. But that only holds true for duplication operations. Once the standby database is established, you can connect to it as the target database and perform **backup** commands. These backups can then be used for restore operations at the primary database.

To use the standby database in this fashion, you must have a recovery catalog set up. Without a recovery catalog, there is no way to propagate the records of the backups from the standby control file to the primary control file. With a recovery catalog, you resync with the standby control file after a backup, so the records of the backup are put in the catalog. Then, you connect to the primary database as the target and make your catalog connection. To RMAN, the primary and standby databases are indistinguishable, so it accesses the same record set in the catalog when connected to either. Therefore, you can perform a resync operation while connected to the primary database and it will refresh the primary control file with the records of backups taken while connected to the standby database.

Datafile Backups from the Standby Database

Backing up the datafiles from the standby database is the most common activity. To back up the datafiles and then use them at the primary database, you would do something like this:

1. From RMAN, connect to the standby database as the target, and connect to the recovery catalog:

    ```
    RMAN> connect target sys/pswd@stby
    RMAN> connect catalog rman/rman@rcat
    ```

2. Take your database backup. The catalog is automatically resynchronized after any **backup** command.

    ```
    RMAN>backup database;
    ```

3. Exit RMAN and then start it again (this is the only way to disconnect from the target and catalog):

    ```
    RMAN> exit
    $ rman
    ```

4. Connect to your primary database as the target, and connect to the catalog:

    ```
    RMAN> connect target sys/pswd@sun92
    RMAN>resync catalog;
    ```

5. Perform a **restore** operation that utilizes backups taken from the standby database:

    ```
    RMAN> restore datafile 3;
    RMAN> recover datafile 3;
    ```

Archive Log Backups from the Standby Database

Backing up the archive logs from the standby database is a somewhat trickier affair, because of how RMAN determines which archive logs need to be backed up: it checks the view V$ARCHIVED_LOG. On the primary database, this view is incremented with each new archive log after it has been successfully created in the LOG_ARCHIVE_DEST. However, on the standby database, this view is updated only if your standby database is in managed recovery mode (where the archive logs are automatically applied at the standby database). If your standby database is not in managed recovery mode, or due to your setup you will get archive log gaps at the standby database on a regular basis, it may be hard to get all the required archive logs backed up successfully from the standby database. In this case, we recommend using your primary database for its own archive log backups and using the standby database just for datafile backups.

Using Flashback Database for Standby Database Reinstantiation

We weren't sure where to mention this neat little trick that crosses the boundaries of multiple distinct Oracle technologies. We decided that if you were reading this chapter, you were interested in Data Guard implementations, but if you read Chapter 13 on Flashback Technology, you may not be. So here it is.

One of the toughest moments of a Data Guard implementation is failing over your production database to the standby database. Despite all the preparation and testing, failing over still leaves a knot in the belly. When (if!) it happens to you, we hope it all goes well.

The second toughest moment is coming to terms with how to put the Data Guard deployment back into operation. In other words, now that your standby database has become your primary database, what do you do next? This is truly a question for another book, but it's worth mentioning in this context because Oracle used some of its own tricks to help you out with the tough next step: rebuilding a new standby database after failover.

Here's how it went down in Oracle9*i*: Suppose your production database is PROD, and your standby is PROD2. You lose PROD for some reason. You fail over to PROD2, which becomes your new primary database. Then, you take a full new backup of PROD2, move it over to the computer housing PROD, and lay it down over the top of PROD. Next, you start shipping logs from PROD2 to PROD. At some point, perhaps you purposefully fail back over to PROD, and then this labor- and resource-intensive process repeats.

Fast forward to Oracle Database 10*g*, and a new way of rebuilding emerges: you can use Flashback Database for standby database reinstantiation. When a failover occurs from the primary database to the standby database, in the past you were forced to use backups to restore a copy of the new primary database back to the old primary database and make it a standby database, and then fail back over. Now, you can instead use Flashback Database on the old primary database to move it back to the exact SCN at which the standby database was prior to activation. Then, you set up the flow of archive logs from the new primary database to the old primary database, give it a new standby control file, and you are back in business in minutes.

Summary

In this chapter, we discussed the relationship that RMAN can have with the standby database architecture. Primarily, RMAN can be used to create the standby database using the **duplicate...for standby** command. We discussed the means by which you use the **duplicate** command to create the standby database, and included an RMAN Workshop that walked through the steps of creating the standby database on the same server as the primary database. Then, we discussed how you could use an existing standby database to create backups using RMAN that could be restored to the primary database, as a means of offloading the work away from the production environment.

CHAPTER
19

RMAN and Real
Application Clusters

hile it is well beyond the scope of this book to guide you through the intricacies of Oracle Real Application Clusters, we can provide some guidance on preparing your RAC configuration for backup and recovery. As with Data Guard in Chapter 18, we assume that you have a working knowledge of RAC in Oracle Database 10g, and thus our brief discussion of RAC architecture is intended more as a reminder than as an education.

Throughout this chapter, we will use an example cluster database that has only two nodes: winrac1 and winrac2. These nodes share a disk array, which is configured with Oracle ASM as its volume manager. Each node has an instance: prod1 on winrac1, and prod2 on winrac2. While we will limit our explanations to the most simple of RAC environments, a two-node cluster, nothing changes when you scale out to three, four, or more nodes. In our examples, you simply change the number of nodes from 2 to 3, and the number of channels from two to three, and so on. The more nodes you have, the more complex your backup/recovery strategies, but the basic rules apply no matter the number of instances.

In Oracle Database 10g Release 2, there are two ways to share a file system across multiple computers. The first, which was also available with Oracle9i Database, is to use a clustered file system. This is frequently provided by a third-party vendor, such as VERITAS; on Windows and Linux, Oracle provides its own Cluster File System (OCFS). A cluster file system is defined by its ability to properly handle and queue requests for files coming from multiple nodes simultaneously—which is a requirement if you are going to cluster your databases.

The second way to share a file system across multiple computers, introduced in Oracle Database 10g, is to use Automatic Storage Management (ASM). ASM is Oracle's first volume management product and can be used to manage raw disks that have no other formatting on them. Because of its architecture, ASM is built for cluster configurations and can easily handle the demands of RAC. You could say that ASM was built for RAC, because if you decide to deploy RAC on Oracle Standard Edition, ASM is the *only* file system allowed for the shared Oracle database files.

And that is all you're going to get from us on the subject, except to say this: you can still use manually built raw partitions on a shared disk array to arrange your RAC datafiles and log files. So, if you desire, you do not need a cluster file system or ASM. You just need raw, uncooked, shared disks. However, we do not recommend this, nor will we spend more than a fleeting moment explaining how to configure RMAN to back up a RAC database running on raw disks. This is because, given the opportunity to simplify your life with OCFS or ASM, manually maintaining raw disks is folly. There, we said it. In particular, when it comes to backup and recovery on RAC, OCFS and ASM will save your life. Using raw disks will only lead to blood, sweat, tears, and updated resumes.

Real Application Clusters: Unique Backup Challenges

Before we dig any deeper, it's helpful to consider the architectural nature of the RAC cluster. Essentially, you have at least two different servers, each with its own memory and local disks, and each connected to a shared disk array. Oracle uses this hardware by creating two instances, one on each node, with their own SGA/PGA memory areas. Each instance has its own redo logs, but they exist on the shared disk and are accessible by the other nodes. All control files and datafiles are shared between the two instances, meaning there is only one database, with two threads accessing and updating the data simultaneously. Figure 19-1 provides an oversimplified look at RAC.

From the RMAN perspective, this architecture creates interesting challenges for taking backups. First of all, there are multiple instances running, but RMAN can connect to only a single node. This shouldn't pose any problems for backing up the datafiles, but we do have a problem when it comes to archive logs. Each instance is archiving its own redo logs to a local drive rather than to the shared disks, so the issue is how we get to those other archive logs. But let's start by considering the datafile backups.

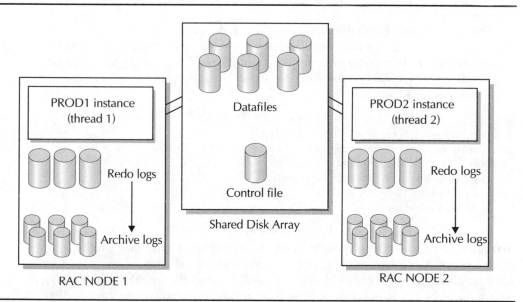

FIGURE 19-1.   *RAC at its most basic*

The RMAN Snapshot Control File and RAC

You need to move the snapshot control file to a shared location if you plan to run backups from more than one node. If you do not move the snapshot control file to a shared file system such as OCFS or an ASM disk group, then you must make sure that the local destination is identical on all nodes. To see the snapshot control file location, use the **show** command:

```
rman> show snapshot controlfile name;
```

To change the value, use the **configure** command:

```
rman> configure snapshot controlfile name to
      '/u02/oradata/grid10/snap_grid10.scf';
```

Datafile Backups

Datafile backups in a RAC environment are pretty much the same as datafile backups in a single-node database: RMAN connects to a node and issues a **backup database** command. The memory that RMAN needs to perform the backup operation will be grabbed from that one node. If backing up to disk, the backups will be local to that node; if backing up to tape, that instance will have to be configured for integration with your MML.

The only problem with this scenario is that it puts quite a bit of load on a single node. This may be what you are after; if not, there is a better way. RMAN can connect to only a single node initially, but it can allocate channels at all of your nodes during an actual backup operation. The following shows an example of how this would be done:

```
configure default device type sbt;
configure device type sbt parallelism 2;
configure channel 1 device type sbt
connect 'sys/password@prod1';
configure channel 2 device type sbt
connect 'sys/password@prod2';
backup database;
```

Then, you can run your backup, and RMAN will spread the work between your two nodes. RAC datafiles sometimes have something known as *node affinity*, where a particular datafile is accessed faster from one node or the other. If this is the case for your cluster, RMAN knows about it and will back up the datafile from the node where it can be read the fastest. If there is no node affinity on your system, RMAN just distributes the work across the two channels as it would any two channels used to parallelize a backup. Obviously, you could allocate two channels at each node, or three, four, or more. How many channels each node utilizes should be based on the same performance parameters we explored in Chapter 16.

In Oracle Database 10g Release 2, RMAN can now utilize information gleaned from Oracle's Cluster Ready Services (CRS) to provide better RAC integration. Of most importance, you no longer have to configure a channel to specifically connect at a particular node. If you have two nodes and you set parallelism to 2, RMAN will query CRS for the node information and automatically spread the two channels across the two nodes. In addition, CRS keeps track of node utilization and will spread RMAN backup jobs out to those nodes that are currently being least utilized, to avoid I/O traffic jams. This is a significant automation improvement, and the lesson to take away is simple: don't try to out-think CRS. Let it do the footwork of determining how to distribute work across your cluster. Just set your level of parallelism equal to the total number of nodes you want involved in your backup and let CRS do the work.

Another feature that is new in 10g is that if you spread out your backup operations across multiple nodes, RMAN is intelligent enough to fail over a backup job if one of the nodes goes down. For instance, in our two-node scenario, let's say we run a backup that allocates channels at both winrac1 and winrac2. We've got 20 datafiles total to back up, and we've set a FILESPERSET value of 2. All our files are the same size, so RMAN will generate a total of ten jobs, five at each node; each job will back up two datafiles.

For the sake of argument, let's say that we've successfully backed up eight of our datafiles, four from each node. RMAN kicks off job number three on winrac1 and job four on winrac2. After these backups run for some time, winrac1 crashes for unknown reasons. RMAN will respond by completing job four on winrac2 and then restarting job three on winrac2 as well. All consecutive jobs will run from winrac2 until the backup is complete. Note that the smallest unit of job failover is the entire backup set. When winrac2 picks up job three, it doesn't pick up at the block that winrac1 left off at. It must restart that entire job. So, if you have FILESPERSET at a very high number, job failover might not do you much good.

Automatic job failover also does no good if the RAC node is already down when the scheduled backup begins. If your scheduled backup assumes that it will connect to two nodes before it runs the backup, but one of the nodes is down, a connection failure will happen at channel allocation time and the backup will abort.

Archive Log Backups

Archive log backups are far trickier than datafile backups because each node is responsible for its own archiving, which means that each node has unshared files that only it can access. If we connect to only one node and issue a **backup archivelog all** command, RMAN will look in the control file and discover the listing for the archive logs from both nodes, but when it looks at the local node, it will find only the archive logs from that node and it will error out.

RMAN, RAC, and Net Connections

RAC comes with many extremely powerful load-balancing and failover features as part of the Net configuration, but this means changes in the listener.ora.file and in the tnsnames.ora files for both the cluster nodes and the clients. RMAN is a little too picky for these features. RMAN can only connect to one node and cannot fail over or be load balanced. Therefore, the Net aliases you use for the target connection and for the CONNECT clause of the channel allocation string must be configured to connect to a single node with a dedicated server. With 10g, however, remember that you no longer have to put CONNECT clauses into your channel allocations.

Of course, the question may be posed, "Why not write archive logs to a raw partition on the shared disk array?" The answer is that you could, if you don't mind the administrative nightmare. Think about it: with raw partitions, you can write only one file per partition, which means you would have to anticipate all of your archive log filenames and create symbolic links to a partition that exists for each archive log. Such a task is simply too labor intensive for even the most scheming Unix scripting mind among us. It is better to use a shared disk volume that has a clustered file system or that is managed by Oracle ASM.

If you insist on leaving archive logs local to each node, there is a solution available that allows RMAN to cope with the non-shared disk locations. First, make sure that each node is archiving to a unique file location. For example, prod1 archives to a directory called /u04/prod1/arch, and prod2 archives to /u04/prod2/arch. Then, you can allocate channels at each node, as you did to load balance the datafile backups earlier, and back up the archive logs:

```
configure default device type sbt;
configure device type sbt parallelism 2;
configure channel 1 device type sbt
connect 'sys/password@prod1';
configure channel 2 device type sbt
connect 'sys/password@prod2';
backup archivelog all delete input;
```

RMAN has a feature known as *autolocate* that identifies which archive logs belong to which node and attempts to back them up only from that node. In this way, you don't have to specify in RMAN which logs you need backed up at which node—RMAN can figure it out for you.

Another option that would allow you to perform your archive log backup from a single node would be to NFS mount the archive log destination of the other node.

For example, at the node winrac1, you have local archive logs located at /u04/prod1/arch. Then, on winrac1, you NFS mount the drive /u04/prod2/arch on winrac2 as /u04/prod2/arch. That way, when you run your archive log backups, RMAN checks the control file for the archive log locations, and it can find both locations while connected to only prod1. Figure 19-2 illustrates this methodology.

The only problem in the scenarios we've provided so far is that you are giving yourself a single point of failure for archive logs. If you archive your logs only to their respective nodes, if you lose a node, you lose the archive logs from that node. That means that you may have to perform point-in-time recovery of the entire database to the point right before the node was lost.

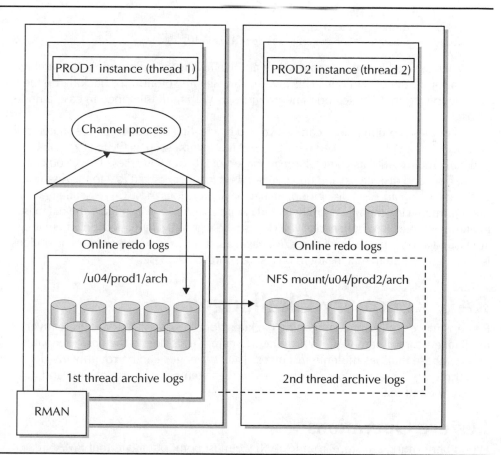

FIGURE 19-2. *Mounting the archive log destination*

A better strategy is to set up each node with a LOG_ARCHIVE_DEST_2 parameter that writes to another node. One way to approach this task is to consider the NFS mount strategies already discussed in this chapter. Instead of just NFS mounting in read-only mode the archive destination of the other node, consider NFS mounting a drive on the other node with write access, and then setting that NFS mount as a second archive destination. Take our two-node RAC database, for example. On winrac1, we could mount the shared directory /u04/prod2/arch from winrac2, and on winrac2, we could mount winrac1's /u04/prod1/arch directory. Then, we could set up the init.ora files for each node, as shown in the following code:

```
winrac1 init.ora file:
log_archive_dest_1='location=/u04/prod1/arch'
log_archive_dest_2='location=/u04/prod2/arch'
...
winrac2 init.ora file:
log_archive_dest_1='location=/u04/prod2/arch'
log_archive_dest_2='location=/u04/prod1/arch'
```

When set up like this, Oracle writes archive logs from each node to the archive destination of the other node. This gives us an elegant solution for backing up the archive logs from a single node and provides us with fault tolerance in case a node is lost.

All of these complications can be avoided by creating a location on the shared disk array that has a volume cooked with a cluster file system, such as OCFS. Even better, you can employ ASM as your volume manager for all your RAC files. Then, you can create a second disk group and deploy your flash recovery area (FRA) to the disk group. With an FRA on an ASM disk group, managing archive logs in RAC is essentially the same as managing them in a single-thread environment. If you configure the database to archive to the FRA, both nodes will deposit the logs in a single location where they are visible to both nodes at all times. Managing archive logs during cleanup operations is no different than managing them on a single-thread database.

RAC Recovery Challenges

Perhaps more confusing than getting backups done is getting restore and recovery tasks taken care of in a RAC environment. Again, this is due to the complex nature of a database that has multiple instances. The challenges can be roughly divided into three areas: restore operations, media management considerations, and recovery challenges.

Restore Operations

When performing a restore from RMAN, we must point out again that RMAN can connect to only one node, but then can allocate channels at each node. This should sound pretty familiar by now; but that's not the tricky part. The part that hangs people up is keeping track of where files were backed up from.

File accessibility is the key to restore success on an RAC node. If you have been backing up to disk using channels allocated at each node, you must allocate the same channels at each node during a restore operation. This is not a problem, unless you've lost a node. If the node is down, your disk backups on that node are inaccessible and restore operations will fail. The lesson is, if you're spending all this time and money on RAC so that you don't have a single point of failure, make sure you apply this philosophy to your backup and recovery strategy, as well. If you back up to disk, duplex the backup to more than one node. This might mean overriding the default autolocate feature so that you can specify where exactly you want your backups to be backed up from. You do this by specifying the channel for datafile sets:

```
configure default device type disk;
configure device type sbt parallelism 2;
configure channel 1 device type disk
connect 'sys/password@prod1';
configure channel 2 device type disk
connect 'sys/password@prod2';
backup (datafile 1,2,3,4,5 channel ORA_DISK_1)
       (datafile 6,7,8,9,10 channel ORA_DISK_2);
# then switch the channels for the datafiles
backup (datafile 1,2,3,4,5 channel ORA_DISK_2)
       (datafile 6,7,8,9,10 channel ORA_DISK_1);
```

Here, again, ASM will save you time and energy. More to the point, running an FRA on a shared ASM disk volume makes disk backups in a RAC environment simple and requires little configuration beyond what you normally do for a single-thread database. Using an FRA on ASM allows you to take advantage of job multiplexing across your nodes yet still have all the backups end up in a location that is always accessible by other nodes during restore. So you no longer need to fear that a disk backup might be left inaccessible on a downed node. Nor do you need to fear a single point of failure, because ASM comes with automatic redundancy, so you can mirror your FRA and have a duplexed copy of your backup without any additional work.

Media Management Considerations During a Restore

Another way to make your backups available to all nodes during a restore is to back up to tape and use a centralized media management server to house your tape backups. If you have tape devices at each node and use them all for tape backup, you're increasing the degree of complexity unnecessarily. If you lose a node in your cluster, you then lose the media management catalog for all backups taken from that node. Chances are that your media management product has an automatic catalog backup, but then you have another restore to do, and where do you do it, and when? You need the catalogs at both of your other nodes for their backup information. So, you have a disaster that is fixable, but valuable minutes are racing by as you stick your nose in manuals, trying to figure it all out.

We prefer to use a centralized media management system, so that all nodes can back up to tape devices that are all managed by the same media manager server, and so that there is a single media management catalog. That way, when a node is lost, you can simply specify the client name in your RMAN channel and do the restores to a different node. This brings us to the most important note to remember when you use RMAN to restore your backup from tape: you must consider the node from which RMAN made the backup when doing the restore.

As an example, suppose that in our two-node cluster we have lost node winrac2, and the disaster that took it out also corrupted some of our datafiles. We've been employing a backup strategy that allocates channels at both nodes to perform the backup, so our restore is going to have to allocate channels from both nodes. Oops! No chance of that! Instead, we can allocate two kinds of channels at winrac1: normal tape channels and channels that specify the client as winrac2. It would look something like this:

```
configure default device type sbt;
configure device type sbt parallelism 2;
configure channel 1 device type sbt
parms="env=(nb_ora_serv=rmsrv)";
configure channel 2 device type disk
parms="env=(nb_ora_serv=rmsrv, nb_ora_client=winrac2)";
restore datafile 5,12,13,18;
```

This is obviously a very simple example of what can be a complex headache. We recommend a backup approach that takes datafile backups from only a single node in the cluster. If the size of your database prohibits such a simplistic approach, try to at least restrict RMAN to a small subset of your nodes. By doing so, you keep the complexity down when it comes time to perform restore operations.

Another option is to utilize new functionality in Oracle Database 10g and first stage your backups to a disk location using an FRA on an ASM disk volume. If you have the space on the disk array to stage your backups to disk first, your ultimate move to tape can happen from one or more nodes at a more controlled time. Using the **backup recovery area** command would allow you to take a consolidated set of backups from the FRA and move them all to tape in a separate operation. This tape operation could occur from any node or any combination of nodes. If you did the tape backup from a single node, then the SBT channel parameters would be simplified during the restore, even if a different node were responsible for the restore.

Recovery Considerations After a Restore

After you get your files restored, it's time to perform media recovery by applying archive logs. Media recovery in a RAC environment has one rule that you must never forget: only one node can perform recovery. Burn it into your brain. This means that one node must have access to all the archive logs on disk. So, if you have been using an archive log strategy that has each node holding its own archive logs in a local disk, you must make that local disk available to the recovery node. You can do this via NFS, if you followed the guidelines specified in "Archive Log Backups" earlier in this chapter. You simply mount the archive log destination of the other node and issue your recover statement from within RMAN. If you're using CFS, this is not a problem and you can ignore all this. If you are using an FRA on ASM, again, access to all archive logs is not an issue.

If you have archive logs that you need to restore from RMAN backups, the same rules and guidelines apply to archive logs that apply to datafile restores. If you allocated channels at each node for the backup, then you need to do so for the restore as well. If you are missing a node, you have to allocate a channel that includes the client name so that the media manager can find the proper backups (see the preceding section, "Media Management Considerations During Restore"). In addition, you may have to restore the archive logs to a directory that exists locally if the LOG_ARCHIVE_DEST parameter that existed on the missing node does not exist on the node doing the restore operation:

```
restore archivelog like '%prod2%' to '/u04/prod1/arch%';
```

While only one node can perform recovery with RMAN, RMAN does media recovery in parallel. You cannot control this level of parallelism, other than to turn it off:

```
rman> Recover database noparallel;
```

By default, though, RMAN automatically selects the degree of recovery parallelism based on the number of available CPUs on the node performing recovery.

Advanced RMAN/RAC Topics

Once you have determined what your backup and recovery strategies will be for your RAC database, you can consider many of the same benefits that RMAN offers you in a single-node database environment: block corruption checking, null compression, block media recovery—all of these benefits are yours in a RAC environment. Advanced functionality such as database duplication exists as well. RMAN backups of RAC databases work for duplication and standby database creation, just as they would for a single-node system. There are some caveats, however, which are discussed next.

Duplication to a Single-Node System

If you administer a RAC cluster and aren't convinced yet that RMAN is the right tool for you, here's a little something to seal the deal: you can use your RMAN backups of your RAC database to create a clone of your RAC database on a single-node database. This gives you a copy of your production database without having to purchase and administer a second RAC cluster. Instead, you have a single-node database running on a cooked file system.

In fact, RMAN cannot actually duplicate from one RAC cluster to another RAC cluster. It can duplicate only to a single-thread database. However, once duplicated, you can easily turn the clone database into a RAC database. Just make sure that you duplicate to an ASM disk group on a node that already has CRS installed.

RMAN Workshop: *Duplicating a RAC Database to a Single-Node Database*

Workshop Notes

This Workshop creates a single-node clone of a two-node database. You can do this either to a new server or to a cooked file system on one of the nodes of the RAC cluster. This example duplicates to a file system on one of the nodes in the RAC cluster. Because duplication must perform recovery, you must remember that a recovery session has access only to the node on which the recovery is being performed, so that node must have access to all the nodes' archive logs. This Workshop assumes that you have NFS mounted the archive destination of each node on each other node so that a full copy of each archive log stream is available at every node.

The two nodes of our cluster are opcbs01 and opcbs02, with instances of V102A and V102B, respectively. We will be connecting to V102B for all RMAN operations.

Step 1. Build your auxiliary database directory structures:

```
mkdir /u02/32bit/app/oracle/oradata/aux1
mkdir /u02/32bit/app/oracle/oradata/aux1/arch
cd /u02/32bit/app/oracle/admin
mkdir aux1
cd aux1
mkdir pfile bdump udump cdump
ls
```

Step 2. Copy the target init.ora file to the auxiliary location. If your target database uses an SPFILE, you need to create a PFILE from the SPFILE to capture parameters to move over.

If you use an SPFILE at your target, enter the following:

```
SQL> connect / as sysdba
create pfile='/u02/32bit/app/oracle/admin/aux1/pfile/init.ora'
from spfile;
```

If you use an init.ora file at your target, enter the following:

```
cp /u02/32bit/app/oracle/admin/V102B/pfile/init.ora
   /u02/32bit/app/oracle/admin/aux1/pfile/init.ora
```

Step 3.   Make all necessary changes to your aux1 init.ora file:

```
control_files=
   '/u02/32bit/app/oracle/oradata/aux1/control01.dbf'
core_dump_dest='/u02/32bit/app/oracle/admin/aux1/cdump'
background_dump_dest='/u02/32bit/app/oracle/admin/aux1/bdump'
user_dump_dest=/u02/32bit/app/oracle/admin/aux1/udump
log_archive_dest_1=
   'location=/u02/32bit/app/oracle/oradata/aux1/arch'
db_name='aux1'
instance_name='aux1'
remote_login_passwordfile=exclusive
db_file_name_convert=
 ('/dev/vx/rdsk/usupport_dg', '/u02/32bit/app/oracle/oradata/aux1')
```

You can remove the following parameters entirely, including those that refer to the other instance:

```
cluster_database_instances=2
cluster_database=true
V102A.instance_name='V102A'
V102B.instance_name='V102B'
V102B.instance_number=2
V102A.instance_number=1
V102B.thread=2
V102A.thread=1
V102B.undo_tablespace='UNDOTBS2'
V102A.undo_tablespace='UNDOTBS1'
```

You can replace them by just having the following:

```
undo_tablespace='UNDOTBS2'
```

Step 4.   Build your aux1 password file. Refer to the "Building a Password File" RMAN Workshop in Chapter 17.

Step 5.   Start the aux1 instance in nomount mode:

```
ORACLE_SID=aux1
export ORACLE_SID
SQLplus /nolog
```

```
SQL>connect / as sysdba
SQL>startup nomount
pfile=/u02/32bit/app/oracle/admin/aux1/pfile/init.ora
```

Step 6. Configure your network files for connection to aux1. After you make any changes to your listener.ora file, be sure that you bounce your listener or the change will not take effect:

```
lsnrctl
LSNRCTL>stop
LSNRCTL>start
```

The tnsnames.ora file should have an entry like this:

```
AUX1 =
  (DESCRIPTION =
    (ADDRESS_LIST =
      (ADDRESS = (PROTOCOL = TCP)(HOST = opcbsol2)(PORT = 1526))
    )
    (CONNECT_DATA =
      (SID = aux1)
      (SERVER = DEDICATED)
    )
  )
```

The listener.ora file should have an entry like this:

```
  (SID_DESC =
    (GLOBAL_DBNAME = aux1)
    (ORACLE_HOME = /u02/32bit/app/oracle/product/10.2.0/db_1)
    (SID_NAME = aux1)
)
```

Step 7. From RMAN, connect to the target and auxiliary instance and run the **duplicate** command:

```
ORACLE_SID=V102B
export ORACLE_SID
rman
rman>connect target /
rman> connect auxiliary sys/password@aux1
rman>duplicate target database to aux1
  pfile=/u02/32bit/app/oracle/admin/aux1/pfile/init.ora
  logfile
  '/u02/32bit/app/oracle/oradata/aux1/redo1.dbf' size 100m,
  '/u02/32bit/app/oracle/oradata/aux1/redo2.dbf' size 100m,
  '/u02/32bit/app/oracle/oradata/aux1/redo3.dbf' size 100m;
```

The Single-Node Standby Database

Of course, if we can duplicate to a single node, then we can also use the **duplicate** command to create a standby database for our RAC cluster on a single node. Perhaps more so than even straight duplication, this feature gives us an excellent cost-to-performance strategy for providing a disaster recovery solution for our RAC database. Instead of purchasing all the hardware and software necessary to have a complete second RAC system set up but unused for a standby database, you can create the standby database on a single-node system. Obviously, it won't have the computing power or load-balancing features of the RAC database, but it gives a reasonable disaster recovery solution so that you can hobble along until the RAC database is restored.

As with the duplication process, the secret lies in using the DB_FILE_NAME_CONVERT parameter to switch the files from OCFS or ASM disk groups to normal, nonclustered file systems. In addition, the single-node standby database can receive archive logs from each of the nodes in the RAC cluster and apply them in the correct chronological order.

RMAN Workshop: *Creating a Single-Node Standby Database from a RAC Database*

Step 1. Use RMAN to create a standby control file:

```
ORACLE_SID=V102B
export ORACLE_SID
rman
rman> connect target /
rman> backup current controlfile for standby
   format= '/u02/backup/stby_cfile.%U';
```

You need to specify a point in time after you created this standby control file, so perform a few log switches and then record the last log sequence number from V$ARCHIVED_LOG. It doesn't matter which thread you choose, because the following command will force a log switch at all nodes:

```
SQL> alter system archivelog current;
SQL> select sequence# from v$archived_log;
```

Step 2. Build your standby database directory structures:

```
mkdir /u02/32bit/app/oracle/oradata/stby
mkdir /u02/32bit/app/oracle/oradata/stby/arch
cd /u02/32bit/app/oracle/admin
mkdir stby
cd stby
mkdir pfile bdump udump cdump
ls
```

Step 3. Copy the target init.ora file to the auxiliary location. If your target database uses an SPFILE, you need to create a PFILE from the SPFILE to capture parameters to move over.

If you use an SPFILE at your target, enter the following:

```
SQL> connect / as sysdba
create pfile='/u02/32bit/app/oracle/admin/stby/pfile/init.ora'
from spfile;
```

If you use an init.ora file at your target, enter the following:

```
cp /u02/32bit/app/oracle/admin/V9232/pfile/init.ora
   /u02/32bit/app/oracle/admin/stby/pfile/init.ora
```

Step 4. Make all necessary changes to your stby init.ora file:

```
control_files= '/u02/32bit/app/oracle/oradata/stby/control01.dbf'
background_dump_dest=/u02/32bit/app/oracle/admin/stby/bdump
user_dump_dest=/u02/32bit/app/oracle/admin/stby/udump
log_archive_dest_1=
    'location=/u02/32bit/app/oracle/oradata/stby/arch'
standby_archive_dest=
    'location=/u02/32bit/app/oracle/oradata/stbyarch'
lock_name_space='stby'
remote_login_passwordfile=exclusive
db_file_name_convert=
  ('/dev/vx/rdsk/usupport_dg', '/u02/32bit/app/oracle/oradata/aux1')
log_file_name_convert=
  ('/dev/vx/rdsk/usupport_dg', '/u02/32bit/app/oracle/oradata/aux1')
```

You can remove the following parameters entirely, including those that refer to the other instance:

```
cluster_database_instances=2
cluster_database=true
V102A.instance_name='V102A'
V102B.instance_name='V102B'
V102B.instance_number=2
V102A.instance_number=1
V102B.thread=2
V102A.thread=1
V102B.undo_tablespace='UNDOTBS2'
V102A.undo_tablespace='UNDOTBS1'
```

You can replace them by just having the following:

```
instance_name='V102B'
undo_tablespace='UNDOTBS2'
```

Step 5. Build your stby password file. Refer to the "Building a Password File" RMAN Workshop in Chapter 17.

Step 6. Start the stby instance in nomount mode:

```
ORACLE_SID=stby
export ORACLE_SID
SQLplus /nolog
SQL>connect / as sysdba
SQL>startup nomount
pfile=/u02/32bit/app/oracle/admin/stby/pfile/init.ora
```

Step 7. Configure your network files for connection to stby. After making any changes to your listener.ora file, be sure that you bounce your listener or the change will not take effect:

```
lsnrctl
LSNRCTL>stop
LSNRCTL>start
```

The tnsnames.ora file should have an entry like this:

```
STBY =
  (DESCRIPTION =
    (ADDRESS_LIST =
      (ADDRESS = (PROTOCOL = TCP)(HOST = opcbsol2)(PORT = 1521))
    )
    (CONNECT_DATA =
      (SID = stby)
      (SERVER = DEDICATED)
    )
  )
```

The listener.ora file should have an entry like this:

```
(SID_DESC =
  (GLOBAL_DBNAME = aux1)
  (ORACLE_HOME = /u02/32bit/app/oracle/product/9.2.0)
  (SID_NAME = aux1)
)
```

Step 8. From RMAN, connect to the target and auxiliary instance and run the **duplicate** command:

```
ORACLE_SID=V102B
export ORACLE_SID
rman
rman>connect target /
rman> connect auxiliary sys/password@stby
rman>run {
  set until sequence = 43 thread = 1;
  duplicate target database for standby
  dorecover;}
```

Backing Up the Multinode RAC Database

Once you have created the single-node standby database, you can take all of your backups from the standby database just as you would in a normal environment. This means that you can offload your production RAC backups from the RAC cluster itself to the node that is set up and running as a standby database. This takes the load off the cluster, gives you a disaster recovery solution, and gives you a simplified backup solution for archive logs because all the archive logs from all nodes will necessarily exist on the standby database.

Again, the secret is in the DB_FILE_NAME_CONVERT parameter. You are taking backups from the standby database that has the datafiles on a cooked file system, but even the standby database control file knows the original location of the files (the raw system). So, when you go to restore a backup taken from the standby on the production RAC database, RMAN checks with the control file and finds the raw locations and places the files there.

In order for such a solution to work for you, you must use a recovery catalog. The recovery catalog acts as the transition agent for the metadata about the backups from the standby database control file to the primary database control file. After you take the backup from the standby database, RMAN resyncs with the recovery catalog, recording the backup metadata. Then, when you connect RMAN to the primary database and perform a manual resync, the backup metadata from the standby database control file is placed in the primary database control file records.

It is important to make sure that you connect to the standby database as the target database when performing backups from the standby database. Then, you connect to the primary database as the target database as well, to perform the resync. RMAN can do this smoothly because it sees no functional difference between the two databases: they have the same DB_NAME, the same DBID, and the same redo stream history.

Summary

In this chapter, we discussed the means by which RMAN interacts with databases in RAC clusters. We discussed how RMAN can allocate channels on each node for backup, but that recovery requires that all backups be accessible from a single node. We discussed the complications caused in archive log backups due to having multiple threads of redo being generated at different nodes. We concluded with examples for duplicating a RAC database to a single-node database and for creating a single-node standby database from a RAC database.

CHAPTER
20

RMAN in Sync and Split Technology

he storage industry never sleeps. With every passing year, new hardware and software storage solutions pour down the pipeline, providing us with interesting new acronyms, tightly coupled buzzwords, and, occasionally, something that is very cool.

Sync and split technology is an example of an innovative (and challenging) solution for storage recovery. Although sync and split technology was available when *Oracle9i RMAN Backup & Recovery* was published in 2002, it was not given coverage because it wasn't widely adopted at that point. Since then, sync and split has become a widely used technology to provide immediate and very fast system recovery at the storage hardware level.

In this chapter, we will provide an overview of what sync and split technology refers to. We won't be discussing any single implementation in particular, but rather discussing the implications for RMAN and database backups. After the overview, we go into the specific steps required to integrate sync and split solutions into an RMAN backup strategy.

Sync and Split: Broken Mirror Backups

In the beginning, doing sync and split backups involved nothing more complicated than extending the functionality of hardware mirroring. The best way to explain this statement is through an example. Suppose we have a disk controller that has two hard drives. For redundancy, we set the RAID level to 0+1 so that we are mirroring everything on disk A to disk B. This gives us immediate protection against any kind of hardware failure on either disk A or disk B.

The next step, then, is to try to leverage the hardware mirror to provide logical fault tolerance. That is the goal of sync and split technology: to provide a fallback position in case of some failure that has occurred on both copies in the mirror. For example, suppose that a user has deleted the entire oracle software tree or the oradata directory. Such a deletion would immediately occur at both copies in our mirror, so having a mirrored copy would do us no good.

So what is the solution? The innovation is any mirrored disk group may have two mirror groups but only one mirror ever currently writing the identical bits as the primary disk group. Let's build an example with three logical volumes, A, B, and C, all dedicated to the same data. Volumes A, B, and C are all mirrored copies of each other. However, at 2 P.M., volume A is split away from the mirror, leaving its bits "stuck" at the split time. Volumes B and C continue to be bit-for-bit copies. After four hours, at 6 P.M., volume C is split from volume B so that it no longer gets writes of data. At this point, there are three different copies of the data on the volume: a copy at 2 P.M., a copy at 6 P.M., and a current copy. There is also no redundancy to protect against a disk failure.

Where Are We in RAID?

Need a primer on RAID? There are hundreds of theories, from the radical to the traditional, that outline the best possible solution for disk failure protection. Typically, we at Oracle have long stood behind the position that nothing beats RAID 0+1, in which you have two disk groups, group 1 and group 2, both of which have two disks. The two disks on group 1 are striped, so that data is evenly spread across both disks. Group 2 is an exact copy, bit for bit, of group 1. This configuration gives us both performance, by striping across disks to avoid hot spots, and redundancy, by writing every bit twice.

Recently, we were reviewing the specs for a RAID 1+0 configuration, which is slightly different from 0+1. Instead of stripe and then mirror, a RAID 1+0 configuration mirrors and then stripes. The difference is best represented visually, as shown in the following illustration. Here, we mirror each disk separately so that we end up with four disk groups. After mirroring each disk, we then stripe across the four mirrors.

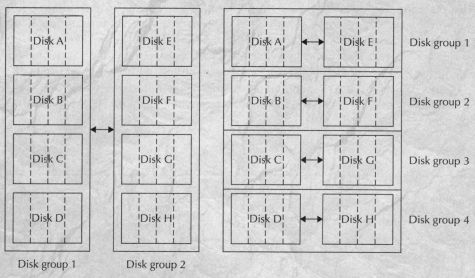

Disk group 1   Disk group 2

RAID 0 + 1 (striped, then mirrored)   **RAID 1+0 (mirrored, then striped)**

It might seem like a small difference, but there is greater fault tolerance in RAID 1+0, because the failure of any one disk does not take down the other mirrored disks. In RAID 0+1, if any disk in group 2 fails, the whole group goes offline. So, RAID 1+0 provides greater tolerance than RAID 0+1 for multiple disk failure, instead of single disk failure.

To get back to our RAID 0+1 configuration, disk volume A will be "resilvered" up to disk B, which runs at the current point in time. This sync up is based on the fact that the volumes have a journaling mechanism in place that records all data changes. This journaling is more I/O on top of the multiple writes to each volume. Volume A will get access to the journals of changes on volume B and apply all the changes until it is getting live writes at the same time as volume B. At this point, then, you have volumes A and B in redundant mode, and volume C is your fallback position, at 6 P.M. Figure 20-1 illustrates this process.

This sync and split cycle goes on and on, ad infinitum. Every four hours a volume is synced up to the primary volume, and another volume is split away to provide a fallback position in case of a logical failure. What happens at the time you actually encounter the logical failure? In our example, let's assume that it is now 8 P.M. Volumes A and B are getting concurrent writes, and volume C is waiting idle at 6 P.M. At 8 P.M., a DBA is doing some system maintenance and deletes the system datafile from the production database. This is when the worrying begins.

Luckily, no unrecoverable data has been added to the database since the end of the day at 5 P.M. However, the nightly batch loads start in about 15 minutes. The DBA has a small window to get the production database back up and running.

With the database running entirely on the mirrored disk volumes A and B, the sync and split architecture has given our DBA an immediate solution. He immediately configures volume C, which was stuck at 6 P.M., as the primary volume and starts up the database. When the database looks for its datafiles, it finds all the files as they appear on volume C, at 6 P.M., and no deletes have taken place. By the time the DBA is finished, it is only 8:05 P.M. The batch processes will kick off on time. Figure 20-2 shows the process.

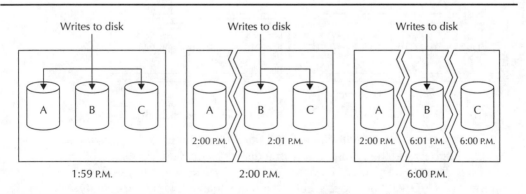

FIGURE 20-1. *Sync and split technology in action*

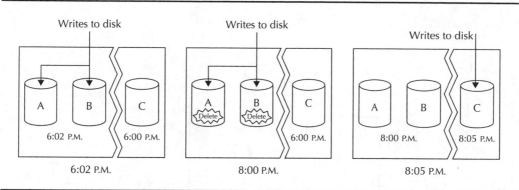

FIGURE 20-2. *Sync and split in action*

Oracle Databases on Sync and Split Volumes

The Oracle software files can reside on a sync and split volume and thus can help protect against logical corruption that occurs in the binaries themselves. No additional configuration is needed, from an Oracle perspective. The files associated with an Oracle database, on the other hand, come with some very specific caveats and disclaimers when you start putting them on sync and split volumes. These caveats and disclaimers relate to the fact that Oracle files are always open and always have active writes taking place (this being the primary importance of a good relational database). So, if you are actively writing to your database and it is mirrored on two drives, there will be consequences if you suddenly break the mirror, unbeknownst to the database.

Each vendor-specific solution is a bit different, but at some point, a volume that is getting active writes must turn off the writes to that volume while continuing to allow writes to another volume. And regardless of how a salesperson might pitch it, the process of breaking a mirror is not instantaneous. Breaking a mirror is more like peeling a banana—you start at the top and separate the peel from the fruit until you get to the bottom. Suppose your Oracle datafile is the fruit and the mirrored copy of the datafile is the peel. If you peel away the mirror copy, you are starting at the beginning of the datafile, and the break is complete when you reach the end of the datafile. However, it is possible (likely) that Oracle will attempt to write to a block while the mirror is in the middle of peeling away. So, on the primary volume, nothing is wrong—the file header knows that an SCN has been advanced in the file and knows which block it was—but on the split mirror, the datafile header knows nothing about the written block. So, after the mirror break is complete, what do we have on the split mirror volume? One fuzzy datafile that is unrecoverable. Check out Figure 20-3 to see this visually.

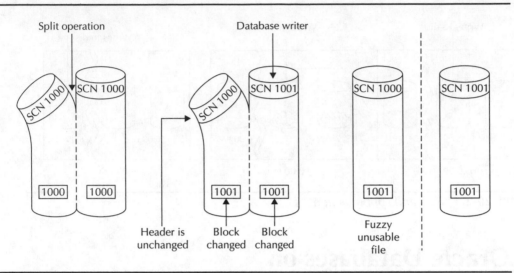

FIGURE 20-3. *Unrecoverable fuzzy datafile*

Fear not, for there are ways to ensure that the split mirror is a healthy copy of the database. It just takes a bit of work first. How you configure Oracle database files in a sync and split environment depends on what type of files you are configuring: datafiles, control file, redo log files, or archive logs. The following sections address each in turn.

Datafiles

The previous section explained what happens to Oracle datafiles if a mirror split takes place without any preparation: the split volume copies of the files are left in a fuzzy, unusable state. This is precisely the same predicament you run into if you simply take a copy of an online datafile without first putting it into hot backup mode. So, before you break the mirror, you must put all datafiles into hot backup mode. This is not an optional step, regardless of which vendor product you are using. Because the split generally takes a very short period of time, the amount of time in hot backup mode is much shorter than it would be if you were doing a copy against the same datafiles. And the I/O hit of running in backup mode (and producing more archive logs) will be relatively small, as well.

To alleviate the headaches of hot backup mode for those implementing sync and split architectures, Oracle has added syntax that allows you to put an entire database into hot backup mode with a single command:

```
alter database begin backup;
```

Previously, you had to put each tablespace into hot backup mode. If there is something preventing the file from going into backup mode, a warning is generated in the alert log, but the **begin backup** command proceeds anyway.

After the split is complete, you pull the database out of hot backup mode with the following command:

```
alter database end backup;
```

Control Files

A split mirror copy of a control file is in an unusable state immediately after the split mirror operation completes. The control file, in general, is up-to-date on the current state of all the datafiles. However, based on the total duration of the split itself, and the overall activity on the database at the time of the split, the control file at the split volume may not reflect much accurate data about the state of the datafiles.

Putting the database into hot backup mode cures most of these ills. With the database in hot backup mode, the control file is aware of a starting point at which recovery will be required, and from which it will be feasible. However, the control file is still at odds with reality: it thinks of itself as a current control file of an active database. This is hardly the case.

We've seen some implementations where a DBA insists on trying to keep the current control file available as such on the split volume, particularly if the split volume will be used for reporting purposes. However, when the time comes to put this control file into service for the sake of recovery, you have to use the **using backup controlfile** command so that the control file understands that some of its checkpoint and SCN information may not reflect reality:

```
recover database using backup controlfile until cancel;
```

If you will be mounting the Oracle database on the split mirror volume for reporting purposes, you may want to use the above command even if you will not be applying any archive logs, just so the control file is flagged as a backup. We discuss this more later in the section "Benefits of the Split Mirror Backup."

Redo Log Files

Split mirror copies of the online redo logs are useless in every way, shape, and form. If possible, don't even bother putting them on the volume that is going through the sync and split. There is no mechanism in the online redo logs to account for writes to the file during the split operation.

Archive Logs

Archive logs are an excellent candidate to be put on a sync and split volume. Doing so gives you a backup of existing archive logs on disk in a second location.

Of course, if you split the archive log volume at the same time as the datafile volume, you do not get all the redo that you need to properly recover your database from the split volume. We suggest that you keep your archive logs on a separate set of sync and split volumes from the set on which you keep your datafiles and control files. That way, you can split the datafiles, take the database out of hot backup mode, force a log switch, and then split the archive log volumes. Then the split mirror volume with the archive logs contains all of the redo required to start the split mirror copy of the database.

One last note on archive logs on split mirror volumes. When the database begins to create an archive log on disk, the split operation may leave behind an unfinished archive log on the split mirror volume. This archive log would be unusable during any recovery operation. This poses a problem only for human-managed backup and recovery operations, where it is unknown if the archivelog that is on-disk is complete or only half-written. Here's why it doesn't pose a problem for RMAN: When an archive log is being generated, the control file is not updated with a record that such an archive log exists until the archive log is complete. Therefore, in a split mirror scenario, if half of an archive log is generated on the split volume, the control file on the split volume has no record of that archive log. During an RMAN operation, then, the control file would be consulted for archive log records, and the half-written file would not exist in the metadata. To RMAN, the half-written file doesn't really exist.

Benefits of the Split Mirror Backup

We've discussed briefly the primary benefit of using the sync and split architecture: a nearly instantaneous fallback recovery point for all files on a particular set of disks. This benefit expands beyond the scope of this book (the Oracle database) to include a fallback point for all files that exist on the volume. There are also other primary benefits of the sync and split, which are discussed next.

Fast Point-In-Time Recovery

From the database perspective, sync and split provides a point-in-time recovery option that can take minutes instead of hours. You simply change the primary disk group to the split mirror, and the datafiles are ready. Then, you apply archive logs up to the point where the failure occurred, and you can open the database.

Speedy-Looking Backups

Another benefit of the sync and split architecture is the relative speed of the backup operation itself. Properly generating copies of the database files at the split mirror side takes only a few moments with the database in hot backup mode. After that, a backup is ready to be pressed into service very quickly. Of course, there's no magic involved with sync and split. I/O is I/O is I/O. It might look like the backup is taking no time at all, but in reality the backup is being taken all the time at the hardware level, because the files are being written to simultaneously prior to the split operation. However, handing the backups over to the hardware architecture can prove to be extremely powerful in many organizations, where the hardware can be responsible for backing up more than just the database.

Mounting a Split Mirror Volume on Another Server

Beyond the simplistic restore and recovery features, much of the true power of sync and split solutions currently in the marketplace comes from what you can do with the split copy of the database. Because the underlying hardware is likely to be a storage array with many computers connected to it, any volume on that storage array can theoretically be associated with any computer connected to it.

For example, let's take a database, PROD. PROD resides on disks in volume A, which is mirrored on volume B. Both volume A and B are connected to server Dex. Volumes A and B both exist on storage array Newton. At 2 P.M., volume B is split from volume A and disassociated from server Dex. Immediately after this, volume B is mounted on a different server, Proto, which is also connected to storage array Newton. After volume B is mounted on Proto, a copy of the database PROD that resided on Dex now resides on Proto, with almost real-time amounts of data. The database copy that is on volume B, and mounted by server Proto, can be recovered and then opened for testing, development, or reporting. Later, at 6 P.M., when it is time to resilver volume B with volume A, Proto can dismount volume B, and then it can be remounted by Dex. The sync operation takes place, overwriting any changes that occurred on volume B after the split at 2 P.M.

Taking Backups from the Split Mirror

Another benefit of sync and split backups, within the framework of this book about RMAN, is the ability to mount the split volume on a different server and, from there, back up the database to tape for long-term backup storage. This allows you to offload the memory, CPU, and I/O operations of the RMAN backup to a completely different server and ensure that there is no impact to your production database.

RMAN and Sync and Split

There are a few different contact points that RMAN has with a sync and split implementation:

- If you use RMAN for recovery, you must make RMAN aware of the datafile copies that are created by the split operation.

- You can use RMAN to take backups from the split mirror volume instead of from the production database itself.

Registering Split Mirror Copies with RMAN

If you are a dedicated RMAN user, then you probably understand the benefits that come from executing all recovery statements from within RMAN, instead of from SQL*Plus or elsewhere. RMAN recovery provides access to the information in the control file so that you are not scrambling to uncover which backups exist where and trying to ensure that you are not missing any files. The control file also aids in archive log management during recovery. When a sync and split system is in place, RMAN doesn't know about everything. The act of splitting the mirror volumes effectively gives you a full datafile copy of every datafile in the database that can be used during a restore/recovery operation, but RMAN has no idea these copies exist.

So, you have to make RMAN aware. You do this by registering the datafile copies with RMAN via the **catalog** command. The **catalog** command can be used against a single datafile copy:

```
catalog datafilecopy '/volumeA/oradata/system01.dbf';
```

Or, starting with 10g, you can catalog an entire directory by the directory name:

```
catalog start with '/volumeA/oradata';
```

By using the **catalog** command, you take the split mirror copies and make them part of any future restore or recovery operation that might be required.

You might be asking yourself, "Why do I need to make RMAN aware of the split mirror copies when I can just remount the entire volume as the primary volume and be up and running without RMAN's help?" A valid question. But what if it makes more sense to switch to only a single copy of the file? Perhaps doing a full database point-in-time recovery would be too expensive, but you still want to leverage the split mirror copy of a subset of files. Beyond that, RMAN also greatly simplifies the recovery stage of any operation, so it makes sense to make RMAN aware of the copies of the archive logs, as well.

Taking RMAN Backups from the Split Mirror

With increasing frequency, DBAs are realizing that with split mirror investments, an additional layer of protection is required, in the form of RMAN backups of the database. The split mirror backup is by definition a short-lived copy—sooner or later, it will be lost when the volume is resilvered with the primary database volume. But what about restoring from last night? Or last week? As you can see, a full-fledged media backup is still required.

With an idle copy of the database simmering on the back burner of the split mirror, a light bulb appears above the DBA's head: "I should just mount the split mirror drive onto a different server, and take the RMAN backup from the split mirror directly to tape (or a different disk volume that can be mounted on the primary)." Great idea! Sounds simple enough, right? Well...there's a few tricky points that need to get worked out first; otherwise, you will have the case of the mysteriously disappearing backups.

Here's the problem: RMAN accesses the control file to determine what to back up, and after the backup is complete, it updates the control file with the details of the backup. If you are connected to a split mirror copy of the control file, that copy gets updated with the details about the backup. So then, of course, when you go to resilver the split volume with the primary, the control file is overwritten with the data in the primary control file and the backup data is lost forever.

The solution, you figure, is to use a recovery catalog when you back up at the split mirror. That is a sound, logical decision: after the backup is complete, the split volume control file is updated with the backup records, which are then synchronized to the catalog. Then, it's simply a matter of syncing the catalog with the primary volume so that the backups can be used. Too cool!

So, suppose that you back up from the secondary volume, you sync the backup records to your recovery catalog, and then you connect RMAN to the primary volume database and to the catalog. You perform a resync. This is where things get really, really weird. Sometimes, when you try to perform an operation, you get the error

```
RMAN-20035: invalid high recid
```

Other times, things work just fine it seems, but the backups you took at the split mirror database have disappeared from the recovery catalog.

The problem, now, has become the internal mechanism of how RMAN handles record building in the control file and the recovery catalog. Every record that is generated gets a record ID (RECID), which is generated at the control file. When the backup occurs at the split mirror database, the control file gets its high RECID value updated, and this information gets passed to the catalog. But the RECID at the primary database control file has not been updated, necessarily. So, when you connect to the catalog and the primary database, if the catalog's high RECID is higher than the one in the control file, you get the "invalid high recid" error. If the RECID in the catalog is lower than the RECID of the primary database control file, RMAN initiates an update of the catalog that effectively eliminates all the records since the last sync operation with the primary control file. Poof! Backup records from the split volume are gone.

The solution to this problem is to set the control file at the split mirror to become a backup control file. If RMAN detects that it is backing up from a noncurrent control file (backup or standby), it does not increment the RECID in the catalog, so that the records are available after a resync with the current control file at the primary database.

You cannot use the control file autobackup feature if you will be taking backups from the split mirror volume. Because the control file in use is a backup control file, autobackup is disallowed.

RMAN Workshop: *Configure RMAN to Back Up from the Split Mirror*

Workshop Notes

This Workshop assumes that you put all the tablespaces into hot backup mode (a requirement) during the period of the split. After the split, you connect the split volume to a new server that has 10g installed, and you now want to take an RMAN backup. Because RMAN will give an error if files are in backup mode, you need to manually end backup for every file, as described in this Workshop. It's best to write a script for this. This Workshop also assumes that you split the archive log destination and bring it across to the clone at the same time for archive log backup.

Step 1. Mount the database on the clone server and prepare the control file for RMAN backup:

```
startup mount;
alter database end backup;
recover database using backup controlfile until cancel;
cancel
exit
```

Step 2. Connect RMAN to the clone instance (as the target) and the recovery catalog and run the datafile backup:

```
rman target /
rman> connect catalog rman/password@rman_cat_db
rman> backup database plus archivelog not backed up two times;
```

Step 3. Connect RMAN to the production database (as the target) and the catalog, perform a sync operation and archive log cleanup, and then back up the control file:

```
rman target /
rman> connect catalog rman/password@rman_cat_db
rman> delete archivelog completed before sysdate -7;
rman> backup controlfile;
rman> resync catalog;
```

Getting Sync and Split Functionality on the Cheap

There is considerable upside to having a hardware solution provide the architecture described in this chapter. Typically, any operation that can be done purely at the hardware level will have performance increases over the same operation done by software. By the same token, a hardware solution is always going to cost you more than a software solution. Sync and split solutions are no different—the more work that is being done at the storage array, the faster it will go…and the more it will cost.

Starting with Oracle Database 10*g* Release 2, Oracle provides a full solution to provide sync and split functionality without paying for any third-party hardware or software solutions. All you need is Oracle Database 10*g* Enterprise Edition, two servers (with the same OS), and a storage array.

Using a Standby Database, Flashback Database, and Incremental Apply for Sync and Split

To implement a sync and split solution using only Oracle software, you need to employ a different feature set within the RDBMS: a standby database, flashback database, and RMAN incremental backup and incremental apply. All of these features have already been discussed to some extent in previous chapters.

Here's how it works. First, you create a standby database of your production database (see the Workshops in Chapter 19). Once you have the standby database fully operational as a disaster recovery solution, you need to implement Flashback Database on both production and standby databases:

```
alter database flashback on;
```

With Flashback Database enabled, you can set a restore point on the primary server:

```
create restore point chapter_20;
alter system switch logfile;
```

Apply changes through the restore point to the standby database. At this point, the standby database can be opened with reset logs for testing or reporting.

```
alter database activate standby database;
```

To resilver your standby database with the primary database, you need to take an incremental backup using the **from scn** keywords to specify the SCN of the restore point. Once this backup is complete, move it to the standby database site.

```
backup database incremental from scn = 120000;
```

At the standby database, shut down and then remount the database again. Perform a flashback database to the restore point specified before the standby database was opened:

```
flashback database to restore point chapter_20;
```

Once the flashback completes, apply the incremental backup from the production database to the standby database, bringing it up to the point of the backup:

```
recover database until scn=1521321;
```

Then, the standby database can go back into managed standby mode and catch up to the production database. Or, it can simply be opened again for reporting, now with all of the latest data imported from the incremental backup. Figure 20-4 illustrates how this process might work.

Benefits of the Oracle Sync and Split Solution

Being less expensive isn't the only thing going for the Oracle sync and split solution. While there are most likely performance drop-offs related to using the standby database/Flashback Database/incremental apply solution, those drop-offs might be less dramatic than you think. This depends entirely on whether you are already using flashback logs for the inherent functionality provided by them. If you are, then you already have two journals of database changes: the flashback logs and the redo logs. Any more journaling at the file system level only adds additional—and redundant—journaling and can be eliminated.

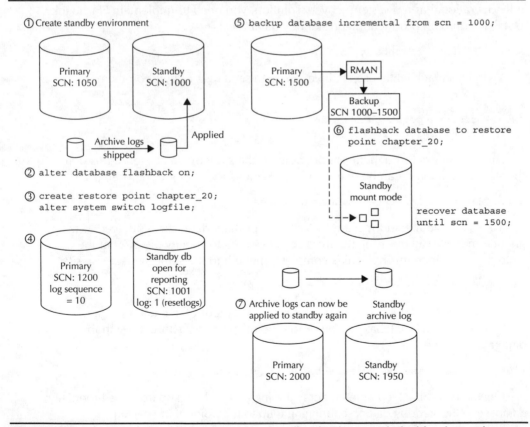

FIGURE 20-4. *Using sync and split with a standby database and Flashback Database*

In addition, you now have a standby database, which you can use for disaster recovery. Although disaster recovery is inherent in the hardware sync and split model as well, having a standby database at your disposal means that much of the manual footwork involved in failing over during an actual disaster is automated and simplified.

Ultimately, deciding between a fully Oracle solution and a hardware solution will come down to other factors as well. Is the sync and split architecture needed for things other than the Oracle databases? Do you have licensing for the additional Enterprise Edition database? Do you have the expertise to use one solution over the other? You would need to address these questions, obviously. More than anything else, though, you would want to test out the solutions. The good news about the Oracle solution is that you probably already have all the requirements to test it right now.

Summary

In this chapter, we covered how a hardware sync and split architecture would impact your backup and recovery solutions. We discussed how to implement sync and split with the Oracle database and how to take RMAN backups from a split mirror copy of the database. Finally, we discussed how to use an existing Oracle RDBMS to implement a software-based sync and split environment.

CHAPTER
21

RMAN in the Workplace:
Case Studies

e have covered a number of different topics in this book, and we are sure you have figured out that there are almost an infinite number of recovery combinations that you might be faced with. In this chapter, we provide numerous different case studies to help you review your knowledge of backup and recovery (see if you can figure out the solution before you read it). When you do come across these situations, these case studies may well help you avoid some mistakes that you might otherwise make when trying to recover your database. You can even use these case studies to practice performing recoveries so that you become an RMAN backup and recovery expert.

Before we get into the case studies, though, the following section provides a quick overview about facing the ultimate disaster, a real-life failure of your database.

Before the Recovery

Disaster has struck. Often when you are in a recovery situation, everyone is in a big rush to recover the database. Customers are calling, management is panicking, and your boss is looking at you for answers, all of which is making you nervous and wondering if your resume is up to date. When the real recovery situation occurs, stop. Take a few moments to collect yourself and ask these questions:

1. What is the exact nature of the failure?

2. What are the recovery options available to me?

3. Might I need Oracle support?

4. Is there anyone else who can act as a second pair of eyes for me during this recovery?

Let's address each of these questions in detail.

What Is the Exact Nature of the Failure?

Here's some firsthand experience from one of the authors. Back in the days when I was contracting, I was paged one night (on Halloween, no less!) because a server had failed, and once they got the server back up, none of the databases would come up. Before I received the page, the DBAs at this site had spent upward of eight hours trying to restart the 25 databases on that box. Most of the databases would not start. The DBAs had recovered a couple of the seemingly lost databases, yet even those databases still would not open. The DBAs called Oracle, and Oracle seemed unsure as to what the problem was. Finally, the DBAs paged me (while I was out trick-or-treating with my kids).

Within about 20 minutes after arriving at the office, I knew what the answer was. I didn't find the answer because I was smarter than all the other DBAs there (I wasn't, in fact). I found the answer for a couple of reasons. First, I approached the problem from a fresh perspective (after eight hours of problem solving, one's eyes tend to become burned and red!). Second, I looked to find the nature of the failure rather than just assuming the nature of the failure was a corrupted database.

What ended up being the problem, pretty clearly to a fresh pair of eyes, was a set of corrupted Oracle libraries. Once we recovered those libraries, all the databases came up quickly, without a problem. The moral of the story is that when you have a database that has crashed, or that will not open, do not assume that the cause is a corrupted datafile or a bad disk drive. Find out for sure what the problem is by investigative analysis. Good analysis may take a little longer to begin with, but generally it will prove valuable in the long run.

What Recovery Options Are Available?

Recovery situations can offer a number of different solutions. Again, back when I was a consultant, I had a customer who had a disk controller drive fail over a weekend, and the result was the loss of file systems on the box, including files belonging to an Oracle database in ARCHIVELOG mode. The DBA at the customer site went ahead and recovered the entire database (about 150GB), which took, as I recall, a couple of hours.

The following Monday, the DBA and I had a discussion about the recovery method he selected. The corrupted file systems actually impacted only about five actual database datafiles (the other file systems contained web server files that we were not concerned with). The total size of the impacted database datafiles was no more than 8 or 10GB. The DBA was pretty upset about having to come into the office and spend several hours recovering the database. When I asked the DBA why he hadn't just recovered the five datafiles instead of the entire database, he replied that it just had not occurred to him.

The moral of this story is that it's important to consider your recovery options. The type of recovery you do may make a big difference in how long it takes you to recover your database. Another moral of this story is to really become a backup and recovery expert. Part of the reason the DBA in this case had not considered datafile recovery, I think, is that he had never done such a recovery. When facing a stressful situation, people tend to not consider options they are not familiar with. So, we strongly suggest you set up a backup and recovery lab and practice recoveries until you can do it in your sleep.

Might Oracle Support Be Needed?

You might well be a backup and recovery expert, but even the experts need help from time to time. This is what Oracle support is there for. Even though I feel like I know something about backup and recovery, I ask myself if the failure looks to be something that I might need Oracle support for. Generally, if the failure is something odd, even if I think I can solve it on my own, I "prime" support by opening a service request on the problem. That way, if I need help, I have already provided Oracle with the information they need (or at least some initial information) and have them primed to support me should I need it. If you are paying for Oracle support, use it now, don't wait for later.

Who Else Can Act as a Second Pair of Eyes During Recovery?

When I'm in a stressful situation, first of all it's nice to have someone to share the stress with. Somehow I feel a bit more comfortable when someone is there just to talk things out with. Further, when you are working on a critical problem, mistakes can be costly. Having a second, experienced pair of eyes there to support you as you recover your database is a great idea!

Recovery Case Studies

Now to the meat of the chapter, the recovery case studies. In this section, we provide you with a number of case studies, a list of which follows, in the order they appear:

1. Recovering from complete database loss in NOARCHIVELOG mode with a recovery catalog

2. Recovering from complete database loss in NOARCHIVELOG mode without a recovery catalog

3. Recovering from complete database loss in ARCHIVELOG mode without a recovery catalog

4. Recovering from complete database loss in ARCHIVELOG mode with a recovery catalog

5. Recovering from the loss of the SYSTEM tablespace

6. Recovering online from the loss of a datafile or tablespace

7. Recovering from loss of an unarchived online redo log

8. Recovering through resetlogs

9. Completing a failed duplication manually

10. Using RMAN duplication to create a historical subset of the target database

11. Recovering from a lost datafile in ARCHIVELOG mode using an image copy in the flash recovery area

12. Recovering from running the production datafile out of the flash recovery area

13. Using Flashback Database and media recovery to pinpoint the exact moment to open the database with resetlogs

In each of these case studies, we provide you with the following information:

■ **The Scenario** Outlines the environment for you

■ **The Problem** Defines a problem that needs to be solved

■ **The Solution** Outlines the solution for you, including RMAN output solving the problem

Now, let's look at our case studies!

Case #1: Recovering from Complete Database Loss (NOARCHIVELOG Mode) with a Recovery Catalog

The Scenario
Thom is a new DBA at Unfortunate Company. Upon arriving at his new job, he finds that his databases are not backed up at all, and that they are all in NOARCHIVELOG mode. Because Thom's manager will not shell out the money for additional disk space for archived redo logs, Thom is forced to do offline backups, which he begins doing the first night he is on the job. Thom also has turned on autobackups of his control file and has converted the database so that it is using an SPFILE. Finally, Thom has created a recovery catalog schema in a different database that is on a different database server.

The Problem
Unfortunate Company's cheap buying practices catch up to it in the few days following Thom's initial work, when the off-brand (cheap) disks that it has purchased all become corrupted due to a bad controller card. Thom's database is lost.

Thom's offline database backup strategy includes tape backups to a local tape drive. Once the hardware problems are solved, the system administrator quickly rebuilds the lost file systems, and Thom quickly gets the Oracle software installed. Now, Thom needs to get the database back up and running immediately.

The Solution

Thom's only recovery option in this case is to restore from the last offline backup, as demonstrated in Chapter 10. In this case, Thom's recovery catalog database was not lost (it was on another server), and his file systems are in place, so all he needs to do is recover the database. First, Thom needs to recover the database SPFILE, followed by the control file. Then, he needs to recover the database datafiles to the file systems.

The Solution Revealed   Based on the preceding considerations, Thom devises and implements the following recovery plan:

1. Restore a copy of the SPFILE. While you will be able to nomount the Oracle instance in many cases without a parameter file at all, to properly recover the database, Thom has to restore the correct SPFILE from backup. Because he doesn't have a control file yet, he cannot configure channels permanently. In this case, Thom has configured his autobackups of the control files to go to default disk locations. Thus, once Thom restored his Oracle software backups, he also restored the backup pieces to the autobackups of the control file. This makes the recovery of the SPFILE simple as a result:

    ```
    rman target sys/password catalog rcat_user/rcat_password@catalogdb
    startup force nomount;
    restore spfile from autobackup;
    shutdown immediate;
    startup nomount;
    ```

2. Restore a copy of the control file. Using the same RMAN session as in Step 1, Thom can do this quite simply. After the restore operation, he mounts the database using the restored control file.

    ```
    restore controlfile from autobackup;
    alter database mount;
    ```

3. Configure permanent channel parameters. Now that Thom has a control file restored, he can update the persistent parameters for channel allocation to include the name of the tape device his backup sets are on. This will allow him to proceed to restore the backup from tape and recover the database.

    ```
    configure default device type to sbt;
     configure channel 1 device type sbt
     parms = "env=(nb_ora_serv=mgtserv, nb_ora_client=cervantes)";
    ```

4. Perform the restore and recovery:

    ```
    restore database;
    recover database noredo;
    alter database open resetlogs;
    ```

NOTE
*Thom used the **alter database open reset logs**
command. He could have used the SQL command
(**sql "alter database open resetlogs"**) too. However,
one benefit of using the RMAN **alter** command is
that the catalog and the database will both be reset.
Using the SQL version, only the database is reset.*

Case #2: Recovering from Complete Database Loss (NOARCHIVELOG Mode) Without a Recovery Catalog

The Scenario
Charles is the DBA of a development OLTP system. Because it is a development
system, the decision was made to do RMAN offline backups and leave the database
in NOARCHIVELOG mode. Charles did not decide to use a recovery catalog when
doing his backups. Further, Charles has configured RMAN to back up the control
file backups to disk by default rather than to tape.

The Problem
Sevi, a developer, developed a piece of PL/SQL code designed to truncate specific
tables in the database. However, due to a logic bug, the code managed to truncate
all the tables in the schema, wiping out all test data.

The Solution
If there were a logical backup of the database, this would be the perfect time to use
it. Unfortunately, there is no logical backup of the database, so Charles (the DBA) is
left with performing an RMAN recovery. Since his database is in NOARCHIVELOG
mode, Charles has only one recovery option in this case, which is to restore from
the last offline backup (see Chapter 10). Because all the pieces to do recovery are in
place (the RMAN disk backups, the Oracle software, and the file systems), all that
needs to be done is to fire up RMAN and recover the database.

The Solution Revealed　Based on the preceding considerations, Charles devises
and implements the following recovery plan:

1. Restore the control file. When doing a recovery from a cold backup, it is
always a good idea to recover the control file associated with that backup
(this prevents odd things from happening). In this case, Charles will be using

the latest control file backup (since he doesn't back up the control file at other times). Since Charles uses the default location to create control file backup sets to, he doesn't need to allocate any channels. He does need to set the DBID of the system, since he is not using a recovery catalog before he can restore the control file. Once Charles restores the control file, he then mounts the database.

```
rman target sys/password
startup nomount
set dbid=2540040039;
restore controlfile from autobackup;
sql 'alter database mount';
```

2. The control file that Charles restored has the correct default persistent parameters already configured in it, so all he needs to do is perform the restore and recovery:

```
restore database;
recover database noredo;
sql "alter database open resetlogs";
```

Case #3: Recovering from Complete Database Loss (ARCHIVELOG Mode) Without a Recovery Catalog

The Scenario
We meet Thom from Case #1 again. Thom's company finally has decided that putting the database in ARCHIVELOG mode seems like a good idea. (Thom's boss thought it was his idea!) Unfortunately for Thom, due to budget restrictions, he was forced to use the space that was allocated to the recovery catalog to store archived redo logs. Thus, Thom no longer has a recovery catalog at his disposal.

The Problem
As if things have not been hard enough on Thom, we also find that Unfortunate Company is also an unfortunately located company. His server room, located in the basement like so many server rooms are, suffered the fate of a broken water main nearby. The entire room was flooded, and the server on which his database resides has been completely destroyed.

Thom's backup strategy has improved. It now includes tape backups to an offsite media management server. Also, he's sending his automated control file/SPFILE backups to tape rather than to disk. Again, he's salvaged a smaller server from the wreckage, which already has Oracle installed on the system, and now he needs to get the database back up and running immediately.

The Solution

Again, Thom has lost the current control file and the online redo logs for his
database, so it's time to employ the point-in-time recovery skills discussed in
Chapter 12. Thom still has control file autobackups turned on, so he can use them
to get recovery started. In addition, he's restoring to a new server, so he wants to be
aware of the challenges that restoring to a new server brings; there are media
management, file system layout, and memory utilization considerations.

Media Management Considerations   Because he's restoring files to a new server,
Thom must first make sure that the MML file has been properly set up for use on
his emergency server. This means having the media management client software
and Oracle Plug-In installed prior to using RMAN for restore/recovery. Thom uses
the sbttest utility—a good way to check to make sure that the media manager is
accessible.

Next, Thom needs to configure his tape channels to specify the client name of
the server that has been destroyed. As discussed in Chapter 4, he needs to specify
the name of the client from which the backups were taken. In addition, he needs to
ensure that the media management server has been configured to allow for backups
to be restored from a different client to your emergency server.

File System Layout Considerations   Thom's new system has a different file system
structure from his original server. The production database had files manually striped
over six mount points: /u02, /u03, /u04, /u05, /u06, and /u07. His new server has
only two mount points: /u02 and /u03. Fortunately, Thom employed directory
structure standards across his enterprise, and all data directories are /oradata/prod/ on
all mount points. In addition, he has a standard that always puts the ORACLE_HOME
on the same mount point and directory structure on every server.

Memory Utilization Considerations   Thom's emergency server has less physical
memory than his lost production server. This means he will have to significantly
scale back the memory utilization for the time being in order to at least get the
database up and operational.

The Solution Revealed   Based on the preceding considerations, Thom devises and
implements the following recovery plan:

1. Determine the DBID of the target database. Thom can do this by looking
    at the file handle for his control file autobackup. He needs to be able to
    view the media management catalog to do so; even easier, Thom has every
    DBID for all his databases stored somewhere in a log—a notebook, a PDA,
    whatever. Whatever you decide to use, just make sure it's accessible in an
    emergency.

2. Restore a copy of the SPFILE. As you may remember, Thom will have to force an instance to be opened using a dummy SPFILE, and then restore the correct SPFILE from backup. Because Thom changed the default location for his control file/SPFILE autobackups to tape, he needs to manually configure the channel for this backup because he doesn't have a control file yet, and thus he cannot configure channels permanently. Instead, he has to imbed **channel allocation** commands in a **run** block, and then issue the **startup** command to start the database with the correct SPFILE.

```
rman target /
set dbid=204062491;
startup force nomount;
run {
allocate channel tape_1 type sbt
parms='env=(nb_ora_serv=rmsrv, nb_ora_client=cervantes)';
restore spfile from autobackup;}
shutdown immediate;
startup nomount;
```

3. Make changes to the SPFILE. Thom must modify his SPFILE to take into account the new server configuration. This means changing memory utilization parameters and setting filename conversion parameters. He must connect to the newly started instance from SQL*Plus and make the necessary changes.

```
alter system set control_files= '/u02/oradata/prod/control01.dbf',
'/u03/oradata/prod/control02.dbf' scope=spfile;
alter system set db_file_name_convert= ('/u04' , '/u02' ,
'/u05' , '/u02' ,
'u06' , ' u03' ,
'u07' , 'u03') scope=spfile;
alter system set log_file_name_convert= ('/u04' , '/u02' ,
'/u05' , '/u02' ,
'u06' , ' u03' ,
'u07' , 'u03') scope=spfile;
alter system set log_archive_dest_1=
'location=/u02/oradata/prod/arch' scope=spfile;
alter system set db_cache_size=300m scope=spfile;
alter system set shared_pool_size=200m scope=spfile;
shutdown immediate;
startup nomount;
```

NOTE
*You could also choose to use the **set newname** option here.*

4. Restore a copy of the control file. Using the same RMAN session as the preceding, Thom can do this quite simply (he's already set the DBID). Then mount the database using the restored control file.

```
run {
allocate channel tape_1 type sbt
parms='env=(nb_ora_serv=rmsrv, nb_ora_client=Cervantes)';
restore controlfile from autobackup; }
alter database mount;
```

5. Configure permanent channel parameters. Now that Thom has a control file restored, he can update the persistent parameters for channel allocation to include the name of the lost server as the media management client. This serves two purposes: it allows RMAN to access the backups that were taken from the lost server, and RMAN will pass this client name to the media management server when any backups are taken from the new server. That way, when the lost server is rebuilt, any backups taken from this stopgap system will be accessible at the newly reconstructed production server.

```
configure default device type to sbt;
configure device type sbt parallelism 2;
configure auxiliary channel 1 device type sbt parms
= "env=(nb_ora_serv=mgtserv, nb_ora_client=cervantes)";
configure auxiliary channel 2 device type sbt parms
= "env=(nb_ora_serv=mgtserv, nb_ora_cient=cervantes)";
```

6. Determine the last archive log for which there is a copy. Because Thom lost the entire server, he also lost any archive logs that had not yet been backed up by RMAN. So, he must query RMAN to determine what the last archive log is for which a backup exists.

```
list backup of archivelog from time = 'sysdate-7';
```

7. With the last log sequence number in hand, Thom performs his restore and recovery and opens the database:

```
restore database;
recover database until sequence=<number>;
alter database open resetlogs;
```

Case #4: Recovering from Complete Database Loss (ARCHIVELOG Mode) with a Recovery Catalog

The Scenario
Charles is taking over for Thom, because management recognized that Thom was a hero of a DBA and thus sent him and his wife to Hawaii for two weeks of R and R.

Before he left, Thom's company added additional disk storage and decided that using the RMAN recovery catalog was probably a good idea.

Unfortunately for Charles, disaster seems to follow him around. At his last company, a huge electrical fire caused all sorts of mayhem, and this time it's gophers. Yes, gophers. Somewhere outside the computer room, a lone gopher ate through the power cable leading to the computer room. This resulted in an electrical fire and a halon release into the computer room. As a result of the electrical fire, the server and disks on which his database resides have been completely destroyed…again.

The Problem

Charles reviews Thom's backup strategy. Again, Charles has salvaged a smaller server that survived the fiasco, which already has Oracle installed on the system, and now he needs to get the database back up and running immediately. Fortunately, the recovery catalog server is intact, so Charles can use it during the recovery.

The Solution

Again, Charles has lost the current control file and the online redo logs for his database, so it's time to employ the point-in-time recovery skills discussed in Chapter 12. The backup strategy still has control file autobackups turned on, so Charles can use them to get recovery started. In addition, he's restoring to a new server, so he wants to be aware of the challenges that restoring to a new server brings; there are media management, file system layout, and memory utilization considerations.

Media Management Considerations   Because Charles is restoring files to a new server, he must first make sure that the MML file has been properly set up for use on his emergency server. This means having the media management client software and Oracle Plug-In installed prior to using RMAN for restore/recovery. Charles uses sbttest to check to make sure that the media manager is accessible.

Next, Charles needs to configure his tape channels to specify the client name of the server that has been destroyed. As discussed in Chapter 4, he needs to specify the name of the client from which the backups were taken. In addition, he needs to ensure that the media management server has been configured to allow for backups to be restored from a different client to his emergency server.

File System Layout Considerations   On Charles's new system, the file system structure is different from that on his original server. The production database had files manually striped over six mount points: /u02, /u03, /u04, /u05, /u06, and /u07. His new server has only two mount points: /u02 and /u03. Luckily, directory structure standards exist across his enterprise, and all data directories are /oradata/prod/ on all mount points. In addition, he has a standard that always puts the ORACLE_HOME on the same mount point and directory structure on every server.

Memory Considerations   Charles's emergency server has less physical memory than his lost production server. This means he has to significantly scale back the memory utilization for the time being in order to at least get the database up and operational.

The Solution Revealed   Based on the preceding considerations, Charles devises and implements the following recovery plan:

1. Get a copy of the SPFILE restored. First, Charles will nomount the database instance without a parameter file, since Oracle supports this. Then, he will restore the correct SPFILE from backup. Because he doesn't have a control file yet, he cannot configure channels permanently. Instead, he has to embed **channel allocation** commands in a **run** block, and then issue the **startup** command to start the database with the correct SPFILE. Since he has a recovery catalog, he doesn't need to set the machine ID as he did earlier.

    ```
    rman target / catalog rcat_user/rcat_password@catalog
    startup force nomount;
    run {
    allocate channel tape_1 type sbt
    parms='env=(nb_ora_serv=rmsrv, nb_ora_client=cervantes)';
    restore spfile from autobackup;}
    shutdown immediate;
    startup nomount;
    ```

2. Make changes to the SPFILE. Charles must modify his SPFILE to take into account the new server configuration. This means changing memory utilization parameters and setting filename conversion parameters. He must connect to the newly started instance from SQL*Plus and make the necessary changes.

    ```
    alter system set control_files= '/u02/oradata/prod/control01.dbf',
    '/u03/oradata/prod/control02.dbf' scope=spfile;
    alter system set db_file_name_convert= "('/u04' , '/u02' ,
    '/u05' , '/u02' ,
    '/u06' , '/u03' ,
    '/u07' , '/u03')" scope=spfile;
    alter system set log_file_name_convert= "('/u04' , '/u02' ,
    '/u05' , '/u02' ,
    '/u06' , '/u03' ,
    '/u07' , '/u03')" scope=spfile;
    alter system set log_archive_dest_1=
    'location=/u02/oradata/prod/arch' scope=spfile;
    alter system set db_cache_size=300m scope=spfile;
    alter system set shared_pool_size=200m scope=spfile;
    shutdown immediate;
    startup nomount;
    ```

3. Restore a copy of the control file. Using the same RMAN session, Charles can do this quite simply (he's already set the DBID). Then, he must mount the database using the restored control file.

```
run {
allocate channel tape_1 type sbt
parms='env=(nb_ora_serv=rmsrv, nb_ora_client=Cervantes)';
restore controlfile from autobackup; }
sql 'alter database mount';
```

4. Configure permanent channel parameters. Now that Charles has a control file restored, he can update the persistent parameters for channel allocation to include the name of the lost server as the media management client. This serves two purposes: it allows RMAN to access the backups that were taken from the lost server, and RMAN will pass this client name to the media management server when any backups are taken from the new server. That way, when the lost server is rebuilt, any backups taken from this stopgap system will be accessible at the newly reconstructed production server.

```
configure default device type to sbt;
configure device type sbt parallelism 2;
configure auxiliary channel 1 device type sbt parms
= "env=(nb_ora_serv=mgtserv, nb_ora_client=cervantes)";
configure auxiliary channel 2 device type sbt parms
= "env=(nb_ora_serv=mgtserv, nb_ora_cient=cervantes)";
```

5. Determine the last archive log for which there is a copy. Because Charles lost the entire server, he also lost any archive logs that had not yet been backed up by RMAN. So, he must query RMAN to determine what the last archive log is for which a backup exists:

```
list backup of archivelog from time = 'sysdate-7';
```

6. With the last log sequence number in hand, Charles performs his restore and recovery and opens the database:

```
restore database;
recover database until sequence=<number>;
sql "alter database open resetlogs";
```

Case #5: Recovering from the Loss of the SYSTEM Tablespace

The Scenario

Nancy, an awesome DBA, is in charge of a large database installation. She shut down her database so the system administrators of her Unix system could do some file system maintenance.

The Problem

Unfortunately, during the maintenance operation, the system administrators at her company managed to drop a file system her database is sitting on. They have since restored the file system, but none of the files from her database are on it, so she must recover them. Nancy lost all datafiles from the following tablespaces: USERS, SYSTEM, and INDEX.

The Solution

Fortunately for Nancy, this is not a complete loss of her system. Her online redo logs and control file are all intact. Because she has to recover the SYSTEM tablespace, she has to do her recovery with the database closed, not open. Otherwise, the recovery is a pretty easy one.

The Solution Revealed   Based on the preceding considerations, the recovery plan that Nancy devises and implements simply requires her to restore the database, as follows:

```
rman target / catalog rcat_user/rcat_password@catalog
startup force mount;
restore tablespace users, system, index;
recover tablespace users, system, index;
alter database open;
```

Case #6: Recovering Online from the Loss of a Datafile or Tablespace

The Scenario

Yang was working on his database the other day when a power surge caused a media failure.

The Problem

Unfortunately for Yang, he lost one file system. This file system contained the following:

■ All the datafiles for a tablespace called WORKING_DATA

■ One datafile for a tablespace called HISTORICAL_DATA

Several other tablespaces in this database are not related to the tablespace he is recovering, so Yang needs to do this recovery with the database up and running.

The Solution

Yang will restore the WORKING_DATA tablespace and the lone datafile missing from the HISTORICAL_DATA tablespace via RMAN. He first will take offline the tablespace and datafile so that others may continue to work.

The Solution Revealed   Based on the preceding considerations, Yang devises and implements the following recovery plan:

1. Take offline the WORKING_DATA tablespace:

   ```
   sql "alter tablespace working_data offline";
   ```

2. Take offline the HISTORICAL_DATA datafile needed to recover (Yang has already queried the V$DATAFILE view to determine that it is datafile 13):

   ```
   sql "alter database datafile 13 offline";
   ```

3. Restore and recover the tablespace and datafile using RMAN, and then bring them online:

   ```
   restore tablespace working_data;
   restore datafile 13;
   recover tablespace working_data;
   recover datafile 13;
   sql "alter tablespace working_data online";
   sql "alter database datafile 13 online";
   ```

NOTE
If either tablespace contains active rollback segments, this recovery case may not work. In the event of the loss of active rollback segment tablespaces, you may well be required to do an offline recovery of that tablespace or datafile.

Case #7: Recovering from Loss of an Unarchived Online Redo Log

The Scenario

Today is not Bill's day. A large thunderstorm is raging outside, and Bill has forgotten that his car's soft top is down. To make Bill's day worse, a strike of lightning hits the data center and fries several disk drives that Bill's database calls home.

The Problem

Once the hardware is repaired, Bill is horrified to find that he has lost all of his online redo logs, in addition to some of his datafiles. Fortunately, his control file is intact.

The Solution

Bill needs to restore his database using incomplete recovery. Since the online redo logs are not available, Bill has to accept that there will be some data loss as a result of the recovery.

The Solution Revealed   Based on the preceding considerations, Bill devises and implements the following recovery plan:

1. Determine the last archive log for which there is a copy. Because Bill has to do incomplete recovery, he must query RMAN to determine what the last archive log is for which a backup exists.

   ```
   startup mount;
   List backup of archivelog from time = 'sysdate-7';
   ```

   The output will look something like the following output—note the log sequence number (log sequence number 3, in bold at the bottom of the report). Since this is the oldest backed up archived redo log, this is as far as Bill can recover to.

   ```
   List of Backup Sets
   ===================
   BS Key  Size       Device Type Elapsed Time Completion Time
   ------- ---------- ----------- ------------ ---------------
   216     48K        DISK         00:00:03     16-AUG-02
           BP Key: 247   Status: AVAILABLE   Tag: TAG20020816T095848
           Piece Name: D:\BACKUP\RECOVER\75E08R2P_1_1

     List of Archived Logs in backup set 216
     Thrd Seq     Low SCN    Low Time  Next SCN   Next Time
     ---- ------- ---------- --------- ---------- ---------
     1    2       1271924    16-AUG-02 1272223    16-AUG-02

   BS Key  Size       Device Type Elapsed Time Completion Time
   ------- ---------- ----------- ------------ ---------------
   218     2K         DISK         00:00:02     16-AUG-02
           BP Key: 249   Status: AVAILABLE   Tag: TAG20020816T100344
           Piece Name: D:\BACKUP\RECOVER\77E08RC1_1_1

     List of Archived Logs in backup set 218
     Thrd Seq     Low SCN    Low Time  Next SCN   Next Time
     ---- ------- ---------- --------- ---------- ---------
     1    3       1272223    16-AUG-02 1272321    16-AUG-02
   ```

2. With the last log sequence number in hand, perform the restore and recovery and open the database. Bill first restores the database using the **until sequence** parameter. This ensures that all database datafiles will be restored to a point in time no later than log sequence 3. Also note the use of the **force** parameter, which ensures that all datafiles are restored. Recall that one of the requirements for point-in-time recovery is that all database datafiles must be restored to the same consistent point in time. Thus, it's important to restore all datafiles to at least a point in time prior to the point in time Bill wants to recover to.

```
restore database until sequence=4 thread=1 force;
```

3. Recover the database until sequence 4 (since the **until sequence** recovers up to but not including the listed sequence number, Bill added one number to the last sequence number, and thus gets 4):

```
recover database until sequence=4 thread=1;
```

4. Open the database:

```
sql "alter database open resetlogs";
```

NOTE
*If Bill's database had been shut down normally (via **shutdown normal**, **immediate**, or **transactional**) before the online redo logs were lost, he may well have been able to open the database without needing to recover it.*

Case #8: Recovering Through resetlogs

The Scenario
Bill spent all night doing his recovery and then called in Tim to monitor the restore and finish the database recovery. Once the recovery was done, Tim was supposed to back up the database. One problem is that the business requirement demanded that the database be open and available during the backup.

Tim came in and finished the recovery. Following that, he opened the database using the **resetlogs** command (as previously described in Case #7). Following the business requirements, Tim began the backup, but allowed users access to the database.

The Problem
Unfortunately, on this troubled day, a power surge hit Tim's system and one of the disk drives of Tim's database was damaged. After another hardware repair, Tim finds that

several datafiles were lost. To make matters worse, he has no complete backup of these datafiles since he issued the **resetlogs** command. Fortunately for Tim, this database was upgraded to Oracle Database 10*g* about three months ago. So, Tim is in luck. In Oracle Database 10*g*, Oracle has made recovery through the **resetlogs** command much easier.

When the database was upgraded to Oracle Database 10*g*, the LOG_ARCHIVE_ FORMAT parameter was changed. The DBA added the new %R parameter so that LOG_ARCHIVE_FORMAT now looks like this:

```
SQL> show parameter log_archive_format
NAME                                 TYPE         VALUE
------------------------------------ ------------ -----------
log_archive_format                   string       ARC%S_%R.%T
```

So, now the LOG_ARCHIVE_FORMAT parameter includes the %R placeholder, which means the reset logs ID is contained in the archived redo logs' filenames. This will save our intrepid DBAs much time during this recovery!

The Solution

Tim is going to use RMAN to recover the database through **resetlogs**. For the most part, this is a recovery that is easy to complete in Oracle Database 10*g*.

The Solution Revealed   Based on the preceding considerations, Tim devises and implements the following recovery plan:

1. Mount the database:

   ```
   /u01>Rman target=/
   RMAN>startup mount;
   ```

2. Tim knows that datafile 4 is missing. It is part of the USERS tablespace. He therefore restores datafile 4:

   ```
   restore datafile 4;
   ```

NOTE
Tim didn't even have to reset the incarnation of the database! This is totally new in Oracle Database 10g and makes cross incarnation recovery so much easier.

3. Having restored the datafile, Tim now recovers it, and then opens the database:

   ```
   recover datafile 4;
   alter database open resetlogs;
   ```

NOTE
Did it occur to you that Tim could have opened the database by just taking the datafile offline? He then could have restored the datafile and brought it online after the recovery. Here is an example of the commands he would have used to do an online recovery:

```
rman>startup mount
rman>sql 'alter database datafile 4 offline'
rman>alter database open;
rman>restore datafile 4;
rman>recover datafile 4;
rman>sql 'alter database datafile 4 online'
```

Case #9: Completing a Failed Duplication Manually

The Scenario
Tim decided to use RMAN duplication to create a clone of his production database on a different server. He ran the **duplicate** command, and the datafiles were successfully restored to the new server. The database is very large, and this file restore process took six hours to complete.

The Problem
Tim forgot to move the archive logs over to the auxiliary server for media recovery, so the duplication failed. This means that the cloned database is not fully recovered and does not have a new DBID.

The Solution
Tim isn't worried, though, and he certainly isn't going to take another six hours to perform the file restore. As described in Chapter 17, Tim can manually perform the media recovery and then use the DBNEWID utility on the clone database to create a new DBID and finish the duplication process without RMAN's assistance.

The Solution Revealed   Based on the solution he decided upon, Tim will implement the following action plan to complete his failed duplication:

1. Move the archive logs from the production to the auxiliary site.

   ```
   cd /space/oracle_user/OraHome1/oradata/sun92
   tar -cvf arch.tar arch
   gzip arch.tar
   ```

2. Use FTP to move the arch.tar file to the auxiliary system, and then enter the following:

```
cd /space/oracle_user/OraHome1/oradata/sun92
gunzip arch.tar.gz
tar -xvf arch.tar
```

3. Perform manual recovery on the database. Tim needs to note the sequence number of the last archive log available on his target database and then set the recovery to stop at that sequence number. The %s variable in the LOG_ARCHIVE_FORMAT parameter signifies the sequence number and will be in the archive log name. Tim will perform manual recovery from SQL*Plus, connecting locally to his auxiliary database (at the auxiliary site).

```
ORACLE_SID=aux1
export ORACLE_SID
Sqlplus /nolog
SQL> connect / as sysdba
SQL> recover database using backup controlfile until sequence 11 thread 1;
```

4. Use DBNEWID to create a new DBID for the clone database. Tim's auxiliary database has been mounted, but it has not yet been opened. This is the right state in which to use DBNEWID. If you are unsure of the database state, you can go ahead and remount it without doing any harm.

```
SQL> Shutdown immediate;
SQL> startup mount;
SQL> exit
$ nid target=/
$ sqlplus /nolog
SQL> connect / as sysdba
SQL> Shutdown immediate;
SQL> startup mount;
SQL> alter database open resetlogs;
```

Case #10: Using RMAN Duplication to Create a Historical Subset of the Target Database

The Scenario

Svetlana is a DBA at an online toy-train reseller. Her production database is under heavy load, with constant updates, inserts, and deletes. Over time, Svetlana has noticed that performance is starting to trail off for data-mining operations against certain inventory-tracking tables.

The Problem

She suspects foul play from the Cost-Based Optimizer, thinking that the Explain Plan might be changing in an adverse way. To test things out, she is looking for a way to get a historical snapshot of a subset of production tables. She's considered duplication in the past, but doesn't have enough room on any server to clone the entire production database.

The Solution

Svetlana can use the Oracle Database 10*g* feature of being able to specify tablespaces to skip during duplication. In this way, she can include only tablespaces that are part of the subset that she needs to test. In addition to skipping tablespaces, she can specify an **until** clause in the **duplication** command itself to set the historical point in time that she would like to test against.

The Solution Revealed   Chapter 17 has excellent RMAN Workshops for performing duplication. For Svetlana to have success with her point-in-time duplication subset, she needs to do all the same duplication footwork described in Chapter 17 prior to performing the duplication. Svetlana will be duplicating to the same server that runs her target database, so she needs to make sure that she has her file renaming strategy worked out. Then, she needs to get an auxiliary database started in nomount mode. After that, she runs her duplication code.

```
$ rman log=/space/backup/pitrdup.out
connect target /
connect auxiliary sys/password@aux1
duplicate target database to aux1
 pfile=/space/oracle_user/OraHome1/admin/aux1/pfile/init.ora
 skip tablespace 'CWMLITE' , 'USERS' , 'ODM' , 'TOOLS'
 until sequence = 11 thread = 1
 logfile
 '/space/oracle_user/OraHome1/oradata/aux1/redo01.dbf' size 5m,
 '/space/oracle_user/OraHome1/oradata/aux1/redo02.dbf' size 5m,
 '/space/oracle_user/OraHome1/oradata/aux1/redo03.dbf' size 5m;
```

The outcome would look something like the following RMAN log. This output has been truncated to save space; we've left the highlights that show what RMAN is doing to get rid of unneeded tablespaces. Remember that when you set an **until sequence** clause in RMAN, the sequence you specify is not included as part of the recover set. So, in Svetlana's code, she has archive logs through sequence 10, but not sequence number 11.

```
Recovery Manager: Release 10.2.0.1.0
Copyright (c) 1982, 2005, Oracle.  All rights reserved.
connected to target database: V102 (DBID=2188245167)
connected to auxiliary database: aux1 (not mounted)
Starting Duplicate Db at 24-DEC-05
```

```
using target database controlfile instead of recovery catalog
allocated channel: ORA_AUX_DISK_1
channel ORA_AUX_DISK_1: sid=14 devtype=DISK
Datafile 3 skipped by request
Datafile 7 skipped by request
Datafile 8 skipped by request
Datafile 9 skipped by request
printing stored script: Memory Script
{   set until scn 1122792;
    set newname for datafile  1 to
 "/space/oracle_user/OraHome1/oradata/aux1/system01.dbf";
…
    set newname for datafile  10 to
 "/space/oracle_user/OraHome1/oradata/aux1/xdb01.dbf";
    restore
    check readonly
    clone database
    skip tablespace  USERS, TOOLS, ODM, CWMLITE    ;
}
executing script: Memory Script
executing command: SET until clause
executing command: SET NEWNAME
…
Starting recover at 24-DEC-05
datafile 3 not processed because file is offline
datafile 7 not processed because file is offline
datafile 8 not processed because file is offline
datafile 9 not processed because file is offline
starting media recovery
…
media recovery complete
Finished recover at 24-DEC-05

{   Alter clone database open resetlogs;}
executing script: Memory Script
database opened
printing stored script: Memory Script
{# drop offline and skipped tablespaces
sql clone "drop tablespace  USERS including contents";
# drop offline and skipped tablespaces
sql clone "drop tablespace  TOOLS including contents";
# drop offline and skipped tablespaces
sql clone "drop tablespace  ODM including contents";
# drop offline and skipped tablespaces
sql clone "drop tablespace  CWMLITE including contents";}
executing script: Memory Script
sql statement: drop tablespace  USERS including contents
sql statement: drop tablespace  TOOLS including content
sql statement: drop tablespace  ODM including contents
sql statement: drop tablespace  CWMLITE including contents
Finished Duplicate Db at 24-DEC-05
Recovery Manager complete.
```

Case #11: Recovering from a Lost Datafile (ARCHIVELOG Mode) Using an Image Copy in the Flash Recovery Area

The Scenario

Tim, a senior DBA for a large manufacturing firm, has long lived by the maxim: "Just because you are paranoid doesn't mean they aren't out to get you." In this vein, he has fought hard up the management chain to garner the resources to keep a full database backup on disk, instead of streaming directly to tape. There is not enough room for every datafile backup on disk, so he has chosen those datafiles that represent the data that is most important to operations and that would be the most impacted by a prolonged outage.

After the database was migrated to 10.2, Tim set up his flash recovery area and created an image copy of his most important files in the FRA. He now takes a nightly incremental backup and applies the incremental to the image copy of those files.

The Problem

Disaster strikes, as it invariably does, near the end of month when massive data processing is taking place. Tim's pager starts chirping only moments before a deluge of angry department heads start calling him. Tim turns off his phone and checks the database. He finds that one of the critical tablespaces has a corrupt datafile, file number 5. The file shows up on disk as 0 bytes. The end-of-month processing cannot continue until the file is recovered.

The Solution

Tim will switch to the datafile running in the FRA, which is current as of the level 1 incremental backup the night before. Then, it's just a matter of applying archive logs to the file to bring it up to the current point in time.

The Solution Revealed Tim's preparation means his outage will be significantly minimized. Here is his action plan:

1. Switch datafile 5 to the copy in the FRA:

    ```
    [oracle@dex oracle]$ rman target /
    Recovery Manager: Release 10.2.0.1.0
    Copyright (c) 1982, 2005, Oracle.  All rights reserved.
    connected to target database: V102 (DBID=2188245167)

    RMAN> switch datafile 5 to copy;
    using target database control file instead of recovery catalog
    ```

```
datafile 5 switched to datafile copy
"/u01/… /V102/datafile/o1_mf_payroll_21v9dhtp_.dbf"
```

2. Recover datafile 5:

```
RMAN> recover datafile 5;

Starting recover at 19-MAR-06
allocated channel: ORA_DISK_1
channel ORA_DISK_1: sid=124 devtype=DISK
allocated channel: ORA_DISK_2
channel ORA_DISK_2: sid=132 devtype=DISK

starting media recovery

archive log thread 1 sequence 208 is already on disk as file
/u01/app/oracle/flash_recovery_area/V102/archivelog/2006_03_19/o1_mf_1_208_
1v9hwr2_.arc
archive log thread 1 sequence 209 is already on disk as file
/u01/app/oracle/flash_recovery_area/V102/archivelog/2006_03_19/o1_mf_1_209_
1v9hzvb_.arc
archive log thread 1 sequence 210 is already on disk as file
/u01/app/oracle/flash_recovery_area/V102/archivelog/2006_03_19/o1_mf_1_210_
1v9j3ts_.arc
archive log thread 1 sequence 211 is already on disk as file
/u01/app/oracle/flash_recovery_area/V102/archivelog/2006_03_19/o1_mf_1_211_
1v9j4jz_.arc
archive log thread 1 sequence 212 is already on disk as file
/u01/app/oracle/flash_recovery_area/V102/archivelog/2006_03_19/o1_mf_1_212_
1v9j59g_.arc
archive log thread 1 sequence 213 is already on disk as file
/u01/app/oracle/flash_recovery_area/V102/archivelog/2006_03_19/o1_mf_1_213_
1v9jc07_.arc
archive log
filename=/u01/app/oracle/flash_recovery_area/V102/archivelog/2006_03_19/o1_
f_1_208_21v9hwr2_.arc thread=1 sequence=208
archive log
filename=
/…/flash_recovery_area/V102/archivelog/2006_03_19/o1_mf_1_209_21v9hzvb_.arc
thread=1 sequence=209
archive log
filename=
/…/flash_recovery_area/V102/archivelog/2006_03_19/o1_mf_1_210_21v9j3ts_.arc
thread=1 sequence=210
archive log
filename=
//flash_recovery_area/V102/archivelog/2006_03_19/o1_mf_1_211_21v9j4jz_.arc
thread=1 sequence=211
media recovery complete, elapsed time: 00:00:03
Finished recover at 19-MAR-06
```

3. Bring datafile 5 online:

```
sql>alter database datafile 5 online;
```

Case #12: Recovering from Running the Production Datafile Out of the Flash Recovery Area

The Scenario
Tim used his FRA setup to significantly minimize the outage due to a corrupted datafile 5. However, now he is running a production datafile out of the FRA, the bad disk has been replaced, and it is time to get the datafile properly restored to its normal location.

The Problem
Using the datafile switch methodology to decrease MTTR is, of course, a very good thing. But it means that the production database is running live with a datafile that is in the Flash Recovery Area. This can hold for a short period, but ultimately the file has to be switched back to the correct, standard location.

The Solution
Tim needs to make a new backup of datafile 5, restore it to the original file location, and then take a temporary outage while he switches back to this datafile and recovers it.

In order for Tim to restore the production datafile to the production environment, he has to plan a temporary outage. One of the trade-offs of a quick recovery time is this preplanned temporary outage. But, Tim can plan for it to occur deep in the night, when few users will be affected, and can absolutely minimize the amount of time the outage requires.

The Solution Revealed   Tim will use the following action plan:

1. Take a new image copy backup of datafile 5. (Alternatively, Tim could use a previous backup of datafile 5 from tape, but Tim felt that taking a new backup of the file and restoring it from disk would actually be faster than trying to get the tape loaded and restored.)

```
RMAN>  backup as copy datafile 5 format
'/u01/app/oracle/oradata/v102/payroll01.dbf';

Starting backup at 19-MAR-06
using channel ORA_DISK_1
using channel ORA_DISK_2
channel ORA_DISK_1: starting datafile copy
input datafile fno=00005
name=/u01/app/oracle/flash_recovery_area/V102/datafile/o1_mf_payroll_21v9dh
p_.dbf
output filename=/u01/app/oracle/oradata/v102/payroll01.dbf
tag=TAG20060319T124728 recid=27 stamp=585492453
```

```
channel ORA_DISK_1: datafile copy complete, elapsed time: 00:00:07
Finished backup at 19-MAR-06
```

2. Restore datafile 5 to the original file location. In the code displayed previously, the file was backed up directly to the original location, so the restore is not required.

3. Switch datafile 5 to the copy in the original location:

```
RMAN> switch datafile 5 to copy;

datafile 5 switched to datafile copy
"/u01/app/oracle/oradata/v102/payroll01.dbf"
```

4. Recover datafile 5 and bring the file online:

```
RMAN> recover datafile 5;

Starting recover at 19-MAR-06
using channel ORA_DISK_1


starting media recovery

archive log thread 1 sequence 221 is already on disk as file
/u01/app/oracle/flash_recovery_area/V102/archivelog/2006_03_19/o1_mf_1_221_
1v9x6vv_.arc
archive log thread 1 sequence 222 is already on disk as file
/u01/app/oracle/flash_recovery_area/V102/archivelog/2006_03_19/o1_mf_1_222_
1v9xbvk_.arc
archive log thread 1 sequence 223 is already on disk as file
/u01/app/oracle/flash_recovery_area/V102/archivelog/2006_03_19/o1_mf_1_223_
1v9xj15_.arc
archive log thread 1 sequence 224 is already on disk as file
/u01/app/oracle/flash_recovery_area/V102/archivelog/2006_03_19/o1_mf_1_224_
1v9xk6m_.arc
archive log
filename=/u01/app/oracle/flash_recovery_area/V102/archivelog/2006_03_19/o1_
f_1_221_21v9x6vv_.arc thread=1 sequence=221
media recovery complete, elapsed time: 00:00:02
Finished recover at 19-MAR-06
...
SQL> alter database datafile 5 online;

Database altered.

SQL> select name from v$datafile where file#=5;

/u01/app/oracle/oradata/v102/payroll01.dbf
```

Case #13: Using Flashback Database and Media Recovery to Pinpoint the Exact Moment to Open the Database with resetlogs

The Scenario

Farouk did not notice the problem for all of Monday and part of Tuesday morning, because it was not brought to his attention. Finally, Tuesday morning, one of the managers for the Woodscrew Dept. called him to say that the Woodscrew database was missing records for some of the most popular woodscrew models. Farouk checked the database and, sure enough, found that someone had deleted rows from a primary table.

The Problem

Finding out who did it, and why, would have to wait. First, it was time to act. The manager said he had noticed the problem around lunchtime on Monday. Farouk checked his Flashback Query option but found that the transaction was already older than his undo segments. He checked his Flashback Database option and found that he could still flashback nearly 48 hours.

The Solution

Farouk will use Flashback Database to do a point-in-time recovery of his entire database. There is no other option at this time. However, Farouk does not know the exact moment of failure, so he needs to be able to move back and forth in time to pinpoint the very last transaction before the failure. He will use Flashback Database and archive log recovery to scroll back and forth until he finds the correct moment to open the database. He will open the database in read-only mode to check the table.

The Solution Revealed   Farouk devises the following plan:

1. Flashback the database to the approximated first point of the failure:

    ```
    RMAN> run {
    2> flashback database to time "to_date('2006-03-19 13:30:00',
    'YYYY-MM-DDHH24:MI:SS')";
    3> }
    Starting flashback at 19-MAR-06
    allocated channel: ORA_DISK_1

    starting media recovery

    archive log thread 1 sequence 225 is already on disk as file
    /u01/app/oracle/flash_recovery_area/V102/archivelog/2006_03_19/o1_mf_1_225_
    1vcwlnx_.arc
    ```

```
archive log thread 1 sequence 226 is already on disk as file
/u01/app/oracle/flash_recovery_area/V102/archivelog/2006_03_19/o1_mf_1_226_
1vcwnlv_.arc
archive log thread 1 sequence 227 is already on disk as file
/u01/app/oracle/flash_recovery_area/V102/archivelog/2006_03_19/o1_mf_1_227_
1vcwt8h_.arc
archive log thread 1 sequence 228 is already on disk as file
/u01/app/oracle/flash_recovery_area/V102/archivelog/2006_03_19/o1_mf_1_228_
1vczqgf_.arc
...
media recovery complete, elapsed time: 00:00:24
Finished flashback at 19-MAR-06
```

  2. Select from the affected table to see if the values are in place:

```
sql> alter database open read only;
sql> select count(*) from ws_app.woodscrew where thread_cnt=30;
```

  3. Farouk finds the values are not there, so he flashes back again:

```
sql> shutdown immediate;
sq> startup mount;

rman> run {
flashback database to time "to_date('2006-03-19 13:20:00',
'YYYY-MM-DD HH24:MI:SS')";}
```

  4. He checks the values again:

```
sql> alter database open read only;
sql> select count(*) from ws_app.woodscrew where thread_cnt=30;
```

  5. The values are there but missing a few rows that can be gained. So Farouk can shut down the database again and recover a bit further.

```
sql> shutdown immediate;
sql> startup mount;

RMAN> recover database until sequence=227 thread=1;

sql> alter database open read only;
sql> select count(*) from ws_app.woodscrew where thread_cnt=30;
```

  6. The values are the best they can be, under the circumstances. Farouk opens the database in read/write mode.

```
sql> shutdown immediate;
sql> startup mount;
sql> alter database open resetlogs;
```

Summary

We hope you found these case studies helpful. We have done our best to provide you with a number of different circumstances that might come your way and solutions you can practice on a test system so that you will be ready to implement them in real life, should the occasion arise. This is also the last chapter in this book on RMAN. We had a ball putting it together, and we hope that you find it useful. Thanks for buying it, and please let us know if you found it to be helpful. We welcome any suggestions for the next revision!

PART
V

Appendixes

APPENDIX
A

RMAN Syntax
Reference Guide

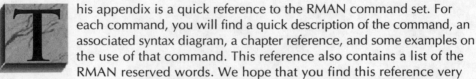

his appendix is a quick reference to the RMAN command set. For each command, you will find a quick description of the command, an associated syntax diagram, a chapter reference, and some examples on the use of that command. This reference also contains a list of the RMAN reserved words. We hope that you find this reference very useful. We expect that it will become very dog-eared from heavy use and will be the main reason you do not loan this book out to anyone!

RMAN Reserved Words

The following table provides a list of reserved words, which you should avoid using when performing RMAN operations.

abort	affinity	after	all
allocate	alter	and	append
archivelog	at	atall	autobackup
autolocate	auxiliary	auxname	available
backed	backup	backuppiece	backupset
before	between	block	blockrecover
blocks	by	cancel	catalog
change	channel	charset	check
clear	clone	clone_cf	clonename
cmdfile	command	compatible	completed
configure	connect	consistent	controlfile
controlfilecopy	copies	copy	corruption
create	crosscheck	cumulative	current
database	datafile	datafilecopy	days
dba	dbid	debug	default
define	delete	destination	device
disk	diskratio	display	dorecover
drop	dump	duplex	duplicate
echo	exclude	execute	exit
expired	file	files	filesperset
final	for	force	forever
format	from	full	g
get	group	high	host
id	identifier	immediate	inaccessible
incarnation	include	incremental	input

io	job	k	kbytes
keep	level	libname	libparm
library	libtext	like	limit
list	log	logfile	logical
logs	logscn	logseq	low
m	maintenance	mask	maxcorrupt
maxdays	maxopenfiles	maxpiecesize	maxseq
maxsetsize	maxsize	misc	mount
msglog	msgno	name	need
new	new-line	newname	nocatalog
nocfau	nochecksum	noexclude	nofilenamecheck
nofileupdate	nokeep	nologs	nomount
none	noprompt	noredo	normal
not	null	obsolete	of
off	offline	on	only
open	optimization	orphan	packages
parallelism	parms	pfile	pipe
plsql	plus	policy	pool
print	proxy	put	quit
rate	rcvcat	rcvman	readonly
readrate	recover	recoverable	recovery
redundancy	register	release	reload
remove	renormalize	replace	replicate
report	reset	resetlogs	restart
restore	resync	retention	reuse
rpc	rpctest	run	save
schema	scn	send	sequence
set	setlimit	setsize	show
shutdown	since	size	skip
slaxdebug	snapshot	spfile	spool
sql	standby	startup	step
summary	switch	tablespace	tag
target	test	thread	time
timeout	times	to	trace
transactional	txt	type	unavailable
uncatalog	unlimited	unrecoverable	until
unused	up	upgrade	validate
verbose	window		

RMAN Command List

The following table documents each RMAN command. Details on each command are provided in the upcoming section "RMAN Command List Syntax Details."

			ALLOCATE CHANNEL FOR MAINTENANCE
@	@@	ALLOCATE CHANNEL	
ALTER DATABASE	BACKUP	BLOCKRECOVER	CATALOG
CHANGE	CONFIGURE	CONNECT	CONVERT
CREATE CATALOG	CREATE SCRIPT	CROSSCHECK	DELETE
DELETE SCRIPT	DROP CATALOG	DROP DATABASE	DUPLICATE
EXECUTE SCRIPT	EXIT	FLASHBACK	HOST
LIST	PRINT SCRIPT	QUIT	RECOVER
REGISTER	RELEASE CHANNEL	REPLACE SCRIPT	REPORT
RESET DATABASE	RESTORE	RESYNC	RUN
SEND	SET	SHOW	SHUTDOWN
SPOOL	SQL	STARTUP	SWITCH
TRANSPORT TABLESPACE	UNREGISTER DATABASE	UPGRADE CATALOG	VALIDATE

RMAN Specifier and Operands Lists

The following table provides the names of the various RMAN specifiers and operands. Documentation for each can be found later in this appendix in the section "RMAN Specifier and Operands Syntax Details."

allocOperandList	archivelogRecordSpecifier	completedTimeSpec
connectStringSpec	datafileSpec	deviceSpecifier
fileNameConversionSpec	formatSpec	keepOption
listObjList	maintQualifier	maintSpec
obsOperandList	recordSpec	releaseForMaint
tempfileSpec	untilClause	

RMAN Command List Syntax Details

This section provides detail information on each of the RMAN commands. For each command you will find

- A summary description of the command

- The syntax diagram for the command

- The relevant chapter in the book in which you can find more details on the command

- Examples of the use of the command

Some commands also make use of RMAN specifiers and operands. You will find documentation on these items in the section "RMAN Specifier and Operands Syntax Details."

@ and @@ Commands

The @ and @@ commands allow you to run a command file (RMAN script) from within RMAN or from within another RMAN command file. If the @@ command is used, then the script called will be executed from the same location as the calling script.

Syntax Diagram

Chapter Reference

Chapter 14 provides more information on these commands.

Examples

```
@/usr/oracle/rman/script/rmanbackup.scr
@@rmanbackup2.scr
```

allocate channel Command

The **allocate channel** command establishes a channel, which is a connection between RMAN and a database instance. At least one channel must be allocated for any backup, recovery, or maintenance operation, though channels are often preconfigured.

Syntax Diagram

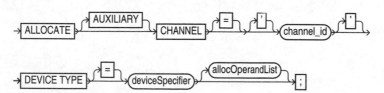

Chapter References

Several chapters reference the **allocate channel** command. Chapter 3 discusses automatic channel configuration, which eliminates the need for **allocate channel** most of the time. Chapters 9, 10, and 11 in particular provide direction on the use of the **allocate channel** command.

Examples

```
allocate channel c1 device type disk format '/u01/orabackup/robprod/robprod_%U';

allocate channel t1 DEVICE TYPE 'SBT_TAPE' PARMS
'ENV=(TDPO_OPTFILE=/opt/oraback/rman/delta_${ORACLE_SID}.opt)'
RATE 1 G FORMAT '${ORACLE_SID}_%U' MAXPIECESIZE 20 G MAXOPENFILES 64;
```

allocate channel for maintenance Command

The **allocate channel for maintenance** command is used to allocate a channel in preparation for issuing maintenance commands such as **change**, **crosscheck**, or **delete**. If you have automated channels configured, you should not need to use this command.

Syntax Diagram

Chapter Reference

We do not cover the **allocate channel for maintenance** command in this book, since we expect you are using automated channel allocation.

Example

```
allocate channel for maintenance device type sbt;
```

alter database Command

The **alter database** command allows you to mount or open the target database that RMAN is connected to.

Syntax Diagram

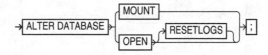

Chapter References

The **alter database** command is demonstrated in Chapters 9, 10, and 12.

Example

```
alter database open resetlogs;
```

backup Command

The **backup** command allows you to back up the database. The **backup** command supports online and offline backups and also supports backups of database files, copies of database files, archived logs, and backup sets.

Syntax Diagram

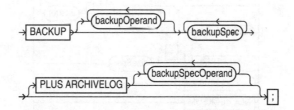

backupOperand Parameter Syntax Diagram

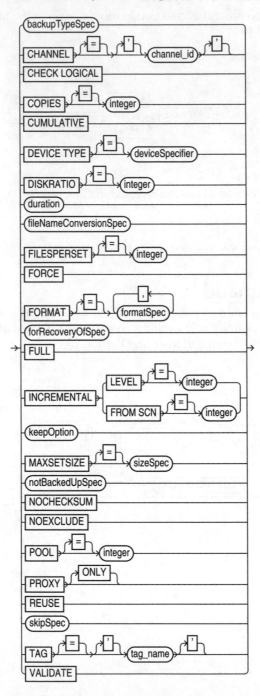

backupSpec Parameter Syntax Diagram

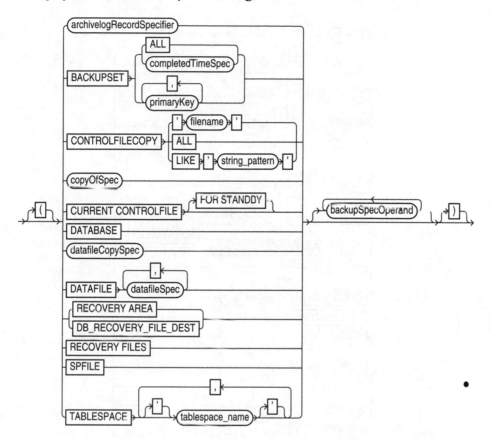

backupSpecOperand Parameter Syntax Diagram

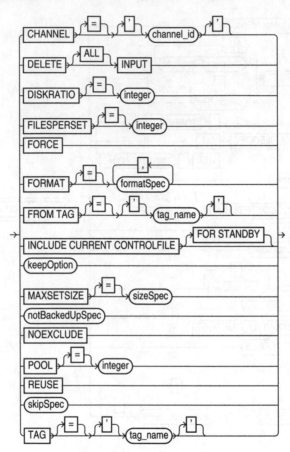

backupTypeSpec Parameter Syntax Diagram

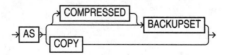

copyOfSpec Parameter Syntax Diagram

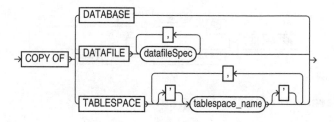

datafileCopySpec Parameter Syntax Diagram

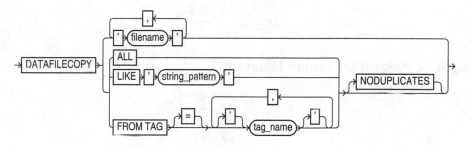

duration Parameter Syntax Diagram

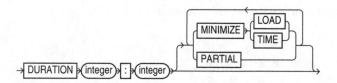

forRecoverOfSpec Parameter Syntax Diagram

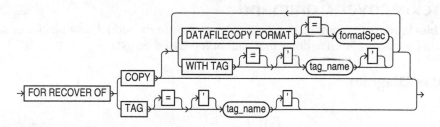

notBackedUpSpec Parameter Syntax Diagram

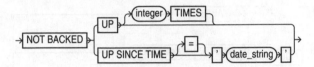

sizeSpec Parameter Syntax Diagram

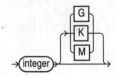

skipSpec Parameter Syntax Diagram

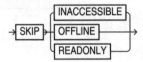

Chapter Reference

The **backup** command is covered in detail in Chapter 9.

Examples

```
backup database plus archivelog delete input;
backup tablespace users, system;
backup as copy datafile 1,2,3;
backup incremental level=0 check logical database plus archivelog;
```

blockrecover Command

The **blockrecover** command enables RMAN to restore individual data blocks, or sets of data blocks, online. Try doing that with home-based scripts!

Syntax Diagram

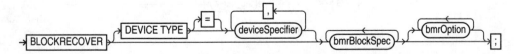

bmrBlockSpec Parameter Syntax Diagram

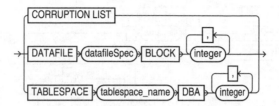

bmrOption Parameter Syntax Diagram

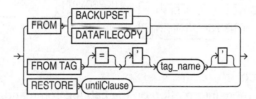

Chapter Reference

The **blockrecover** command is covered in Chapter 12.

Example

```
blockrecover datafile 19 block 44,66,127;
```

catalog Command

The **catalog** command allows you to do the following:

- Add metadata about backup pieces and image copies to the database control file and recovery catalog

- Catalog valid backup sets, datafile copies, and archived redo logs in the flash recovery area (FRA)

- Catalog valid backups in ASM, OMF, and user-defined disk locations

- Record a datafile copy as a level 0 backup in the RMAN repository so you can use that backup as the source of an incremental backup

Syntax Diagram

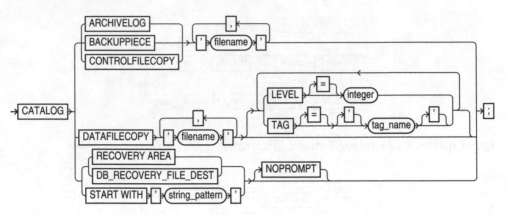

Chapter Reference

Chapter 14 provides more information on the **catalog** command.

Examples

```
catalog recovery area noprompt;

catalog datafilecopy 'd:\oracle\oraback\system01.bak'
'd:\oracle\oraback\users01.bak' level 0;
```

change Command

The **change** command is used to mark backup pieces, image copies, and archived redo logs with a status of AVAILABLE if they currently have a status of UNAVAILABLE. Additionally, this command can totally remove a backup or copy from a repository, and can also be used to modify the retention policy that is effective for a given backup or copy.

Syntax Diagram

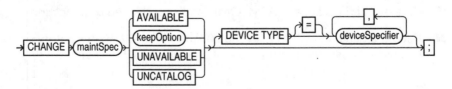

maintSpec Parameter Syntax Diagram

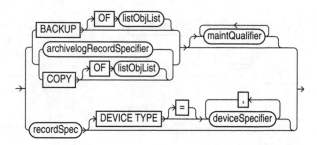

Chapter Reference

Chapter 14 contains a discussion on the use of the **change** command.

Example

```
change backup tag 'Gold_Backup' keep forever nologs;
```

configure Command

The **configure** command allows you to configure persistent RMAN configuration settings. These settings apply to all RMAN sessions unless they are changed or disabled. These settings are stored in the database control file.

Syntax Diagram

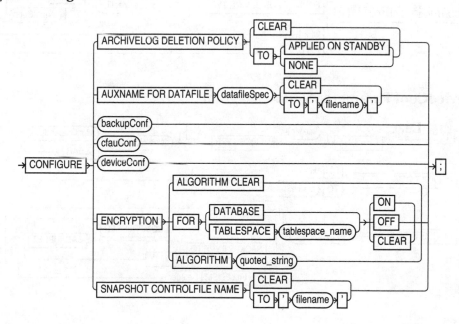

backupConf Parameter Syntax Diagram

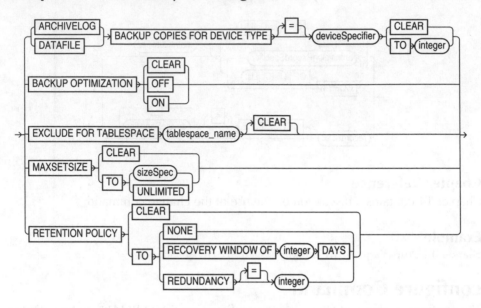

cfauConf Parameter Syntax Diagram

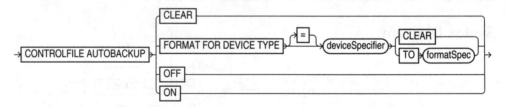

deviceConf Parameter Syntax Diagram

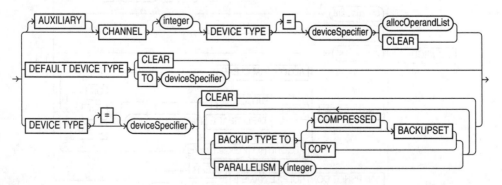

Chapter Reference

The **configure** command is covered in Chapter 3 in detail.

Examples

```
configure retention policy to recovery window of 180 days;
configure backup optimization off;
configure default device type to 'sbt_tape';
configure controlfile autobackup on;
configure controlfile autobackup format for
device type 'sbt_tape' ''%f'';
configure controlfile autobackup format for device type disk to
'/oradata/oraback/rman/robone/%f';
configure device type 'sbt_tape' parallelism 4;
configure device type disk parallelism 2;
configure datafile backup copies for device type 'sbt_tape' to 1;
configure datafile backup copies for device type disk to 1;
configure archivelog backup copies for device type 'sbt_tape' to 1;
configure archivelog backup copies for device type disk to 1;
configure channel device type 'sbt_tape' parms
'env=(tdpo_optfile=/opt/oracle/rman/tdpo_a273.opt)'
rate 9 g format  'a273_%u' maxpiecesize 20 g maxopenfiles 64;
configure channel device type disk format
'/oradata/orabck01/rman/a273/ora_a273_df%t_s%s_s';
configure auxiliary channel device type 'sbt_tape' parms
'env=(tdpo_optfile=/opt/oracle/rman/tdpo_a273_dup.opt)'
rate 99 g format  'a273_%u' maxpiecesize 20 g maxopenfiles 64;
configure maxsetsize to 20 g;
configure snapshot controlfile name to
'/oradata/orabck01/rman/a273/snapcf_a273.f';
configure channel 1 device type sbt
connect 'sys/robert@test1' parms 'env=(nsr_server=bktest1)';
```

connect Command

The **connect** command is used to connect to the target database, the recovery catalog, or the auxiliary instance from the RMAN prompt.

Syntax Diagram

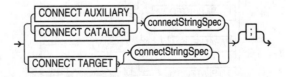

Chapter References
Examples of the **connect** command can be found in many of the chapters in this book.

Examples
```
connect target sys/Robert@maindb
connect catalog rman/rman@rmancat
```

convert Command

The **convert** command is used when moving tablespaces and databases across platforms. If the source and destination platforms are of a different byte-ordering format (endian), then the **convert** command must be used to make the datafiles compatible with the new platform. The **convert** command can also be used to move datafiles in and out of ASM storage.

Syntax Diagram

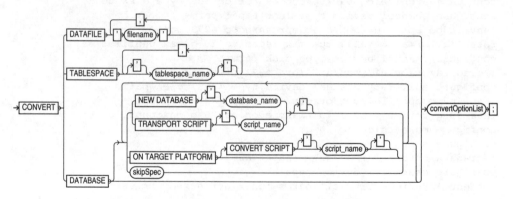

convertOptionList Parameter Syntax Diagram

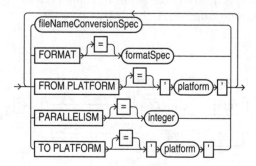

Chapter Reference

The **convert** command is covered in Chapter 12 in more detail.

Examples

```
-- Copy regular datafiles into ASM storage
convert datafile '/disk1/oracle/dbs/my_tbs_f1.df',
'/disk1/oracle/dbs/t_ax1.f'
format '+asmfile';

-- Copy a tablespace from ASM storage to disk.
convert tablespace tbs_2 format '/tmp/tbs_2_%U.df';

-- Convert a database, moving it to a new platform
convert database new database 'convdb'
transport script '/ora01/scripts/transport/transportscript'
to platform 'Microsoft Windows IA (32-bit)'
db_file_name_convert '/ora01/oracle/dbs' '/newora/converted';
```

create catalog Command

The **create catalog** command is used to create the recovery catalog schema.

Syntax Diagram

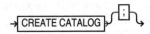

Chapter Reference

The **create catalog** command is covered in Chapter 3.

Example

```
create catalog tablespace rec_cat;
```

create script Command

The **create script** command allows you to create a stored command script within RMAN. You must have a recovery catalog to use this command.

Syntax Diagram

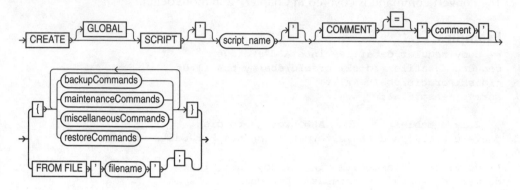

Chapter Reference

The **create script** command is referenced in Chapter 14.

Example

```
create script backup_db {backup database plus archivelog delete input;}
```

crosscheck Command

The **crosscheck** command is used to verify that existing backup sets and backup set pieces listed in the control file or recovery catalog exist on the backup media. Any physical backup file (backup set piece, copy, and so forth) that is not found on backup media is marked as EXPIRED and will not be considered by RMAN for recovery operations. If the backup file later appears, then it will be marked AVAILABLE during a subsequent **crosscheck** operation.

Syntax Diagram

maintSpec Parameter Syntax Diagram

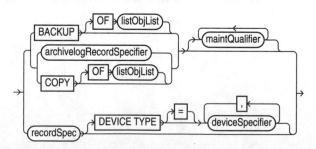

Chapter Reference
The **crosscheck** command is covered in Chapter 14.

Examples
```
crosscheck backup;
crosscheck backup completed between 'sysdate' and 'sysdate-30';
crosscheck archivelog all;
crosscheck archivelog time between 'sysdate' and 'sysdate-30';
```

delete Command
The **delete** command allows you to mark backups and copies in the recovery
catalog or control file with a status of DELETED. Once backups or copies are
marked DELETED, the status cannot be changed. Objects that are marked as
EXPIRED (via the **crosscheck** command) or OBSOLETE (via predefined retention
criteria) can be marked DELETED with the **delete** command.

Syntax Diagram

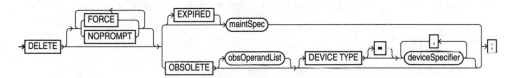

maintSpec Parameter Syntax Diagram

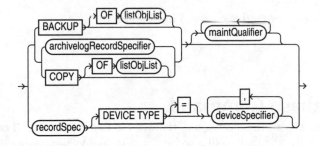

Chapter Reference
The **delete** command is covered in Chapter 14.

Examples
```
delete expired backup;
delete expired archivelog;
```

delete script Command

The **delete script** command allows you to delete any existing RMAN script stored in the recovery catalog.

Syntax Diagram

Chapter Reference

The **delete script** command is covered in Chapter 14.

Example

```
delete script backup;
```

drop catalog Command

The **drop catalog** command is used to drop the recovery catalog schema.

Syntax Diagram

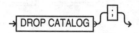

Chapter Reference

The **drop catalog** command is covered in Chapter 3.

Example

```
drop catalog;
```

drop database Command

The **drop database** command is used to remove the target database. If connected to a recovery catalog, the database will also be unregistered. When dropped, RMAN will remove all datafiles, online logs, and control files belonging to the target database.

Syntax Diagram

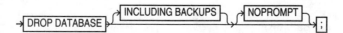

Chapter Reference

The **drop database** command is discussed in Chapter 14.

Example

```
drop database;
```

duplicate Command

The **duplicate** command is used to create either a duplicate database (with a new DBID) or a standby database (with the same DBID) using RMAN backups of a given target database.

Syntax Diagram

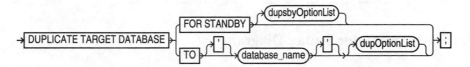

dupOptionList Parameter Syntax Diagram

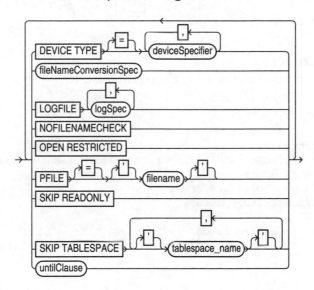

dupsbyOptionList Parameter Syntax Diagram

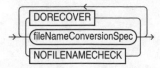

logSpec Parameter Syntax Diagram

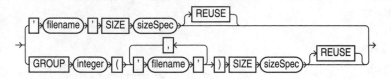

sizeSpec Parameter Syntax Diagram

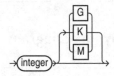

Chapter References

The **duplicate** command is covered in Chapters 17 and 18.

Example

```
duplicate target database to copydb
db_file_name_convert=
('/ora01/oracle/oradata/olddb/','/ora02/oracle/oradata/newdb/')
    until time 'sysdate- 5'
    skip tablespace oldusers, test
    pfile = ?/dbs/initcopydb.ora
    logfile
      group 1 ('/ora01/oraredo/newdb/redo01_1.f',
               '/ora02/oraredo/newdb/redo01_2.f') size 200k,
```

```
group 2 ('/ora01/oraredo/newdb/redo02_1.f',
        '/ora02/oraredo/newdb/redo02_2.f') size 200k,
group 3 ('/ora01/oraredo/newdb/redo03_1.f',
        '/ora02/oraredo/newdb/redo03_2.f') size 200k reuse;
```

execute script Command

The **execute script** command is used to execute a stored RMAN script.

Syntax Diagram

Chapter Reference

The **execute script** command is covered in Chapter 14.

Example

```
execute script my_script;
```

exit Command

The **exit** command terminates the operation of your RMAN session and returns you to the OS prompt.

Chapter References

The **exit** command is covered in Chapter 3.

flashback Command

The **flashback** command allows RMAN to manage Oracle Flashback Database operations. This allows you to reset the database to some previous time or SCN.

Syntax Diagram

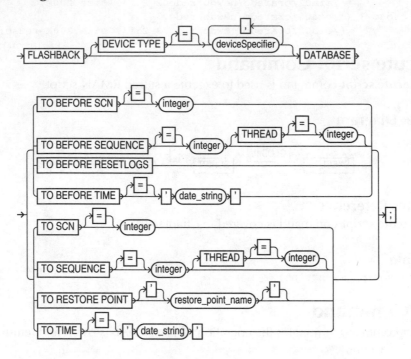

Chapter Reference

Chapter 13 contains a great deal of information on the **flashback** command.

Examples

```
flashback database to scn 669605;
flashback database to timestamp (sysdate-2);
flashback database to timestamp
   to_timestamp('2006-01-03 15:00:00', 'yyyy-mm-dd hh24:mi:ss');
flashback database to restore point "gold_copy";
flashback database to before resetlogs;
```

host Command

The **host** command invokes the OS command-line subshell from within RMAN. The **host** command also allows you to run a specific OS command from the RMAN prompt.

Syntax Diagram

Chapter Reference

Examples of the **host** command can be found in Chapter 14.

Examples

```
host 'dir';
Host 'ls -al';
host
```

list Command

The **list** command provides information on RMAN backups, such as when they occurred, what files they contain, and how long they took.

Syntax Diagram

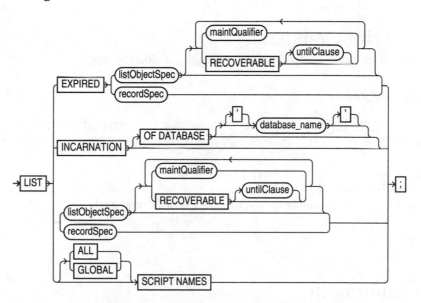

listObjectSpec Parameter Syntax Diagram

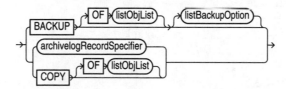

listBackupOption Parameter Syntax Diagram

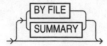

Chapter Reference

Chapter 15 contains information on the RMAN **list** command.

Examples

```
list backup of database;
list backup of database summary;
list backup of datafile;
list backup of archivelog all;
```

print script Command

The **print script** command allows you to display a stored script.

Syntax Diagram

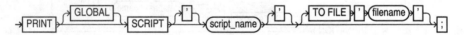

Chapter Reference

Chapter 14 provides more detail on the **print script** command.

Example

```
print script booga_booga;
```

quit Command

Use the **quit** command to exit the RMAN executable.

Syntax Diagram

Chapter Reference

The **exit** command is covered in Chapter 3.

recover Command

The **recover** command is used after a restore to complete recovery of a database, tablespace, or datafile. The **recover** command will extract needed archived redo logs during the recovery process and apply the undo as required.

Syntax Diagram

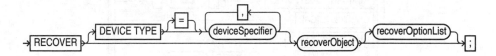

recoverObject Parameter Syntax Diagram

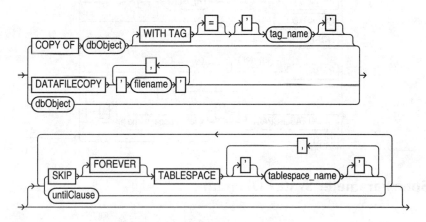

dbObject Parameter Syntax Diagram

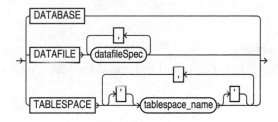

recoverOptionList Parameter Syntax Diagram

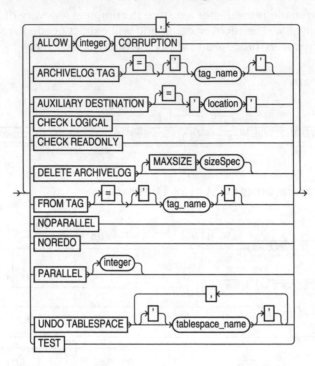

sizeSpec Parameter Syntax Diagram

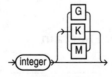

Chapter References

The **recover** command is documented in several chapters, such as Chapters 10 and 12.

Examples

```
recover database;
recover tablespace users;
recover datafile 1;
```

register Command

The **register** command registers the target database in the recovery catalog.

Syntax Diagram

→| REGISTER DATABASE |→| ; |

Chapter Reference

The **register** command is covered in Chapter 3.

Example

```
register database;
```

release channel Command

The **release channel** command is used to release an allocated channel (regular and maintenance). Channels are generally released automatically by RMAN so this command is rarely needed in practice.

Syntax Diagram

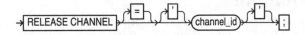

releaseForMaint Parameter Syntax Diagram

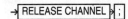

Example

```
release channel c1;
```

replace script Command

The **replace script** command is used to replace command scripts stored in the recovery catalog.

Syntax Diagram

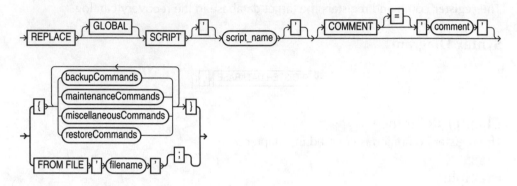

Chapter Reference

Chapter 14 contains information on this command.

Examples

```
replace script backup_full
{ backup device type sbt database plus archivelog; }
```

report Command

The **report** command is used to provide reporting functionality based on the metadata in the recovery catalog or the database control file. The output from the **report** command can be used to determine the recovery status of the database and its component parts.

Syntax Diagram

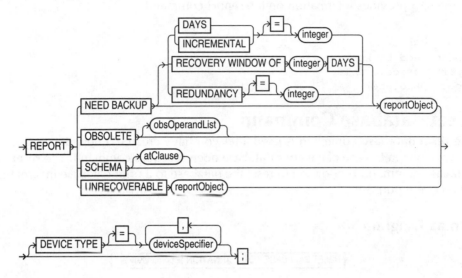

reportObject Parameter Syntax Diagram

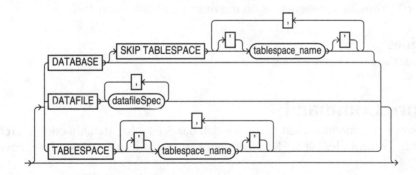

atClause Parameter Syntax Diagram

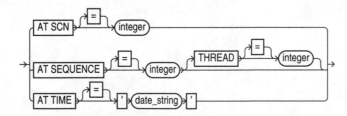

Chapter Reference

Chapter 15 provides information on the **report** command.

Examples

```
report need backup days=3;
report unrecoverable;
report obsolete;
```

reset database Command

The **reset database** command is used after you have created a new database incarnation via the use of the **alter database open resetlogs** command. The **reset database** command is also used to reset the database to a prior database incarnation for recovery purposes.

Syntax Diagram

Chapter Reference

Chapter 12 provides more details on the **reset database** command.

Examples

```
reset database to incarnation 3;
reset database;
```

restore Command

The **restore** command is used to restore database datafiles, datafile copies, archived redo logs, control files, or SPFILEs from backup media in preparation for recovery.

Syntax Diagram

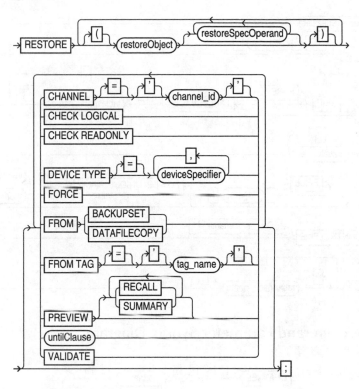

restoreObject Parameter Syntax Diagram

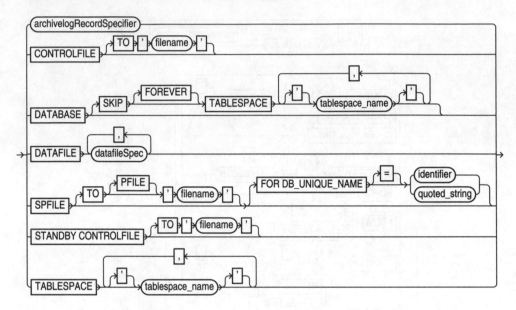

restoreSpecOperand Parameter Syntax Diagram

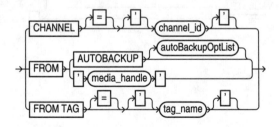

autoBackupOptList Parameter Syntax Diagram

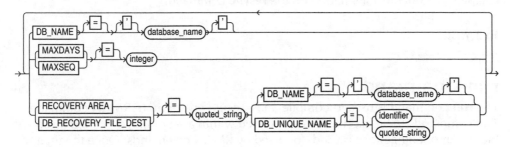

Chapter References

The **restore** command is covered in detail in Chapters 10 and 12.

Examples

```
restore database;
restore tablespace user_data, user_index;
restore datafile 1,2,3,4,5;

CONNECT TARGET /
STARTUP NOMOUNT;
SET DBID 660055374;
RESTORE CONTROLFILE FROM TAG 'monday_cf_backup';
ALTER DATABASE MOUNT;

RMAN> RUN
{
  SET ARCHIVELOG DESTINATION TO '/oratmp/arch_restore';
  RESTORE ARCHIVELOG ALL;
}
```

resync Command

The **resync** command is used to resynchronize the recovery catalog with the database control file.

Syntax Diagram

Chapter Reference

Chapter 14 contains information on the **resync** command.

Example

```
resync catalog;
```

run Command

The **run** command is used to compile and execute one or more RMAN commands. The commands to be executed are contained within a set of braces, called a **run** block. An opening brace is used, followed by RMAN commands. Once the final RMAN command is listed, a closing brace causes the entire set of commands to execute when you press ENTER.

Syntax Diagram

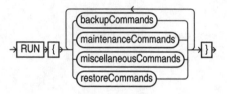

backupCommands Parameter Syntax Diagram

restoreCommands Parameter Syntax Diagram

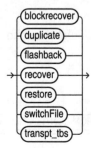

maintenanceCommands Parameter Syntax Diagram

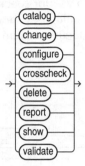

miscellaneousCommands Parameter Syntax Diagram

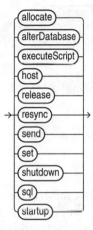

Chapter References

The **run** command is demonstrated in many chapters in this book, such as Chapter 9.

Example

```
RMAN> RUN
{
  set archivelog destination to '/oratmp/arch_restore';
  restore archivelog all;
}
```

send Command

The **send** command is used to send a vendor-specific string to one or more channels. Because these strings are vendor specific, they should be documented in your vendor-supplied media management layer documentation.

Syntax Diagram

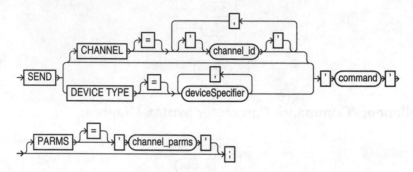

Chapter References

See Chapters 4 through 8 for more on the MML layer and valid vendor strings.

Example

```
send 'env=serv_bck01';
```

set Command

The **set** command configures RMAN settings for the current RMAN session. It is used to configure settings that are not persistent, or temporarily change persistent settings for a given session. The **set** command comes in two different flavors. The **set_run_option** parameters can be used within the confines of a **run** block. The **set_rman_option** parameters are set from the RMAN prompt.

Syntax Diagram

setRmanOption Parameter Syntax Diagram

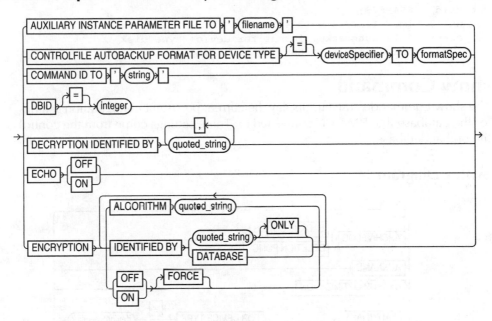

setRunOption Parameter Syntax Diagram

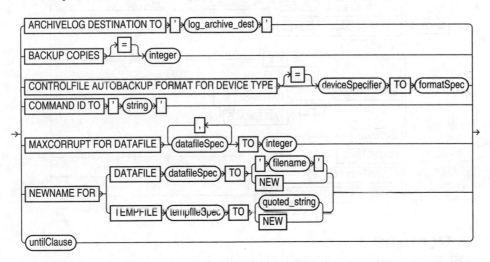

Chapter Reference

The **set** command is documented in Chapter 9.

Examples

```
set dbid 676549873;
set until time '1/10/2006 13:45:00';
set controlfile autobackup format for device type disk
to '/u01/oraback/cntrlf_%f.bak';
```

show Command

The **show** command is used to display the current persistent configuration settings for the database that RMAN is connected to. These settings come from the control file of that database.

Syntax Diagram

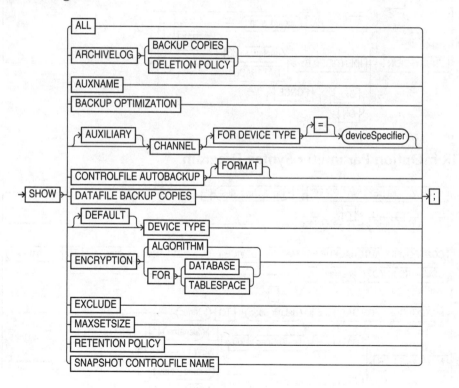

Chapter Reference

The **show** command is documented in Chapter 3.

Examples
```
show all;
show retention policy;
```

shutdown Command

The **shutdown** command is used to shut down the target database and is equivalent to the SQL*Plus **shutdown** command.

Syntax Diagram

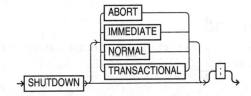

Chapter References

The **shutdown** command is demonstrated in several chapters in this book.

Examples
```
shutdown abort;
shutdown immediate;
```

spool Command

The **spool** command is used to spool the output of RMAN operations to an operating system file.

Syntax Diagram

Example
```
spool log to 'rmanoutput.log'
```

SQL Command

The **SQL** command is used to execute a SQL statement from the RMAN prompt. Single SQL statements are placed within single quotes.

Syntax Diagram

Chapter References

This command is documented in many places in this book.

Examples

```
sql 'alter tablespace mytbs offline immediate';
```

startup Command

The **startup** command is used to start the target database and is equivalent to the SQL*Plus **startup** command.

Syntax Diagram

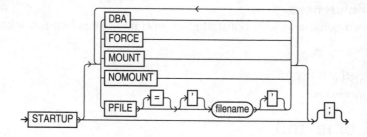

Chapter References

The **startup** command is documented in several chapters of this book.

Examples

```
startup nomount;
startup;
```

switch Command

The **switch** command causes an RMAN datafile copy to become the current database datafile. This command is used frequently if the database datafiles must be restored to a location other than their original location, and is generally associated with an RMAN **set newname** command. This command is equivalent to the SQL statement **alter database rename file** when applied to database datafiles.

Syntax Diagram

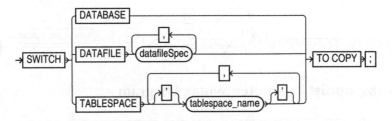

switchFile Parameter Syntax Diagram

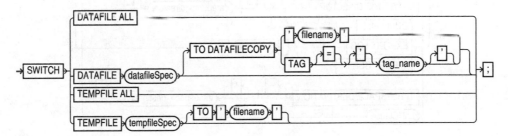

Chapter Reference

Chapter 10 provides details on this command.

Example

```
run
{
  set newname for datafile '/disk7/oracle/tbs11.f'
    to '/disk9/oracle/tbs11.f';
  restore tablespace tbs_1;
  switch datafile all;
  recover tablespace tbs_1;
  sql "alter tablespace tbs_1 online";
}
```

transport tablespace Command

The **transport tablespace** command is used to create transportable tablespace sets from RMAN backups, instead of using the actual datafiles of the source database. You can also use the **transport tablespace** command to create transportable tablespace sets that can be recovered to a specific point in time.

Syntax Diagram

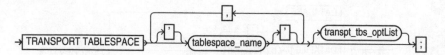

Transp_tbs_optlist Parameter Syntax Diagram

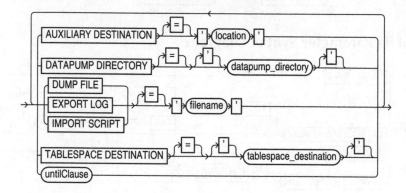

Chapter Reference

Chapter 12 covers transportable tablespaces and RMAN.

Example

```
transport tablespace tbs_2, tbs_3
    tablespace destination '/disk1/transportdest'
    auxiliary destination '/disk1/auxdest'
    UNTIL SCN 251982;
```

unregister database Command

The **unregister database** command removes a database and its associated records from the recovery catalog.

Syntax Diagram

Chapter Reference
The **unregister database** command is covered in Chapter 3.

Examples
```
unregister database;
unregister database oldprod;
```

upgrade catalog Command
The **upgrade catalog** command is used to upgrade the recovery catalog from an older version of RMAN to a newer version of RMAN.

Syntax Diagram

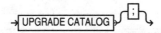

Chapter Reference
Chapter 14 contains information on the **upgrade catalog** command.

Examples
```
upgrade catalog;
```

validate Command
The **validate** command is used to check and validate that a given backup set can be restored. All pieces of that backup set will be scanned by RMAN during the operation.

Syntax Diagram

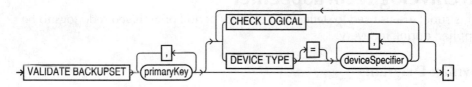

Chapter Reference
Chapter 14 contains information on the **validate** command.

Example
```
validate backup set 1330;
```

RMAN Specifiers and Operands Syntax Details

These specifiers and operands appear in a number of different RMAN commands, so they are all listed in this common section for ease of reference. See the corresponding section of any related commands for examples on the use of these operands and specifiers.

allocOperandList

This operand specifies control options related to a channel.

Syntax Diagram

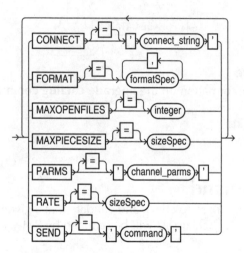

archivelogRecordSpecifier

This subclause is used to define the recovery period or archived redo logs to be applied during recovery.

Syntax Diagram

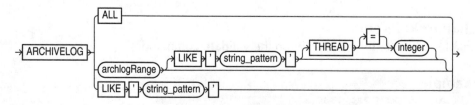

archlogRange Parameter Syntax Diagram

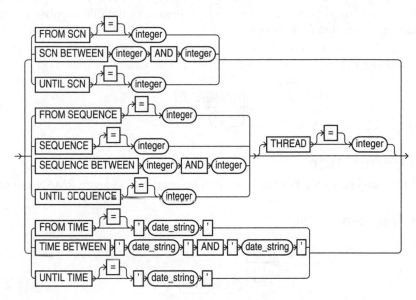

completedTimeSpec

This command is used to define when a backup or copy was completed. It is commonly used with the **list**, **crosscheck**, and **delete** commands.

Syntax Diagram

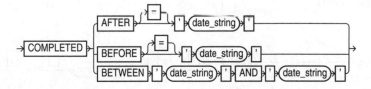

connectStringSpec

This subclause is used to define the username, password, and Oracle Net service name when connecting to a target database, a recovery catalog, or an auxiliary database.

Syntax Diagram

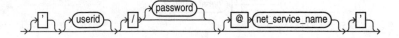

datafileSpec

This subclause is used to define a datafile by filename or datafile number for various operations, such as datafile recovery.

Syntax Diagram

deviceSpecifier

This subclause defines the type of storage to be used by the given RMAN operation.

Syntax Diagram

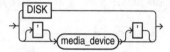

fileNameConversionSpec

This specification defines patterns that should be used to generate new datafile names based on old datafile names. See the sections for the **backup**, **convert**, and **duplicate** commands for more details.

Syntax Diagram

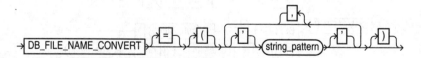

formatSpec

This specifier is used to define a specific filename format. This can include normal file names or ASM disk groups.

Syntax Diagram

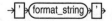

keepOption

This subclause is used to define the retention policy related to a given backup
or copy.

Syntax Diagram

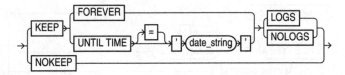

listObjList

This subclause is used to indicate specific datafiles and archived redo logs to be
affected by the parent command.

Syntax Diagram

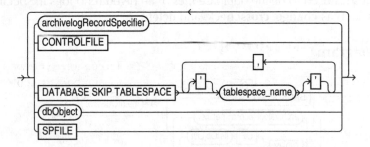

Syntax Diagram

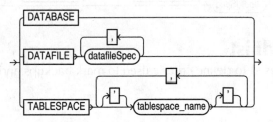

maintQualifier

This subclause is used to define database files or archived redo logs in specific RMAN commands such as **list**, **crosscheck**, **delete**, and **switch**.

Syntax Diagram

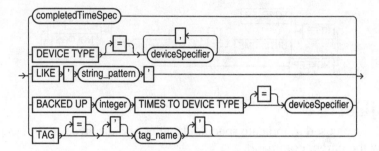

maintSpec

This subclause is used to define database files or archived redo logs in specific RMAN commands such as **change**, **crosscheck**, and **delete**.

Syntax Diagram

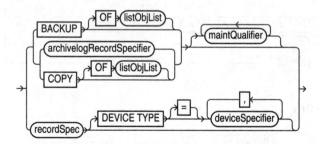

obsOperandList

This subclause is used to define criteria used to mark backups and datafile copies as OBSOLETE.

Syntax Diagram

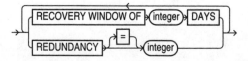

recordSpec

This subclause defines which objects that commands such as **change**, **crosscheck**, **delete**, and **list** will work on.

Syntax Diagram

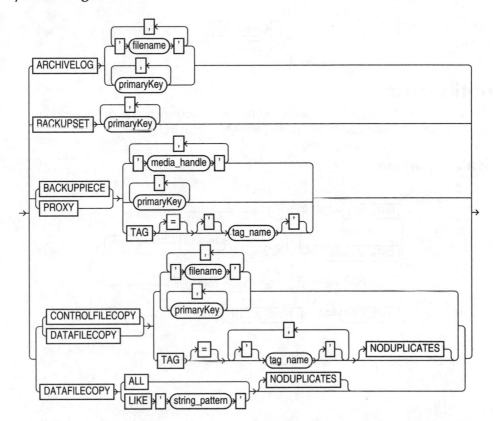

releaseForMaint

This subclause is used to release channels previously allocated for maintenance.

Syntax Diagram

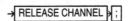

tempfileSpec

This subclause is used to define tempfiles by name or file number that should be operated on by the parent command.

Syntax Diagram

untilClause

This subclause defines a limit based on time, SCN, restore point, or log sequence number that is referenced by the parent RMAN command.

Syntax Diagram

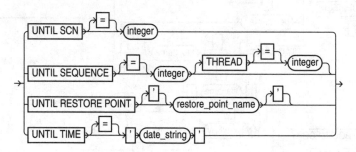

APPENDIX B

Exploring the Recovery Catalog

he recovery catalog provides a series of views that can be used to explore the metadata being produced by your RMAN backup strategy. These views have base tables that are populated when you register your database, and then on any subsequent **resync** command from the catalog. The naming convention for these views is RC_*; for example, RC_BACKUP_SET or RC_BACKUP_REDOLOG.

As RMAN operations have grown increasingly independent of the recovery catalog, many of the views that were unique to it in the past have been incorporated into tables in the target database control file. This means that there is now a corresponding v$view for every RC_* view in the catalog. For instance, if the recovery catalog view is RC_BACKUP_SET, the v$view would be V$BACKUP_SET. The only difference will be a primary key column in the recovery catalog that does not exist in the v$view.

This appendix provides a list of the critical RC_* (and corresponding V$) views in the catalog, along with brief explanations. It is beyond the scope of this book to give a complete rundown of each column in each view; the Oracle-provided documentation does this excellently. Instead, we give a brief explanation of what the view might mean to you and how you might use it. We've left out all views that deal with proxy copies, because they are not covered in this book, and all views that deal with stored scripts.

Having access to these views is a critical tool when setting up and refining a backup strategy; no doubt you will also want access prior to any restore and recovery operation. It is extremely useful to put together a series of scripts that you can run on demand, or even schedule a report output on a regular basis. We provide an example of a few useful catalog queries that can prove useful to you during backup and recovery operations.

It is worth noting that some of the examples in this appendix select against the v$view of the target database, while others refer to the RC_* views in the catalog. If you are making selections against the catalog and have more than one database registered, you always need to limit your query based on the DBID or the DB_NAME (if it's unique within the catalog). Otherwise, you will get information for more than one database, which won't be that useful unless you are trying to gather enterprise-wide information.

RC_ARCHIVED_LOG (V$ARCHIVED_LOG)

The archive log history in V$ARCHIVED_LOG will be one of the most heavily utilized views you have at your disposal. Due to the confusing nature of backing up archive logs and restoring them for recovery purposes, having access to their metadata is critical. Bear in mind that RC_ARCHIVED_LOG does not hold information about any backups you have of your archive logs (see RC_BACKUP_REDOLOG for that); it holds only information about all archive logs that have been generated by the target.

Because archive logs are constantly being generated, whereas catalog resyncs are relatively less frequent, you will find yourself most often at the V$ARCHIVED_LOG version of this view, instead of RC_ARCHIVED_LOG. The kind of code that would give you the most out of this view would look something like this:

```
column name format a50
column completion_time format a25
alter session set nls_date_format= 'DD-MON-YYYY:HH24:MI:SS';
select name, sequence#, status, completion_time
from rc_archived_log;
```

RC_BACKUP_CONTROLFILE (V$BACKUP_DATAFILE)

This view provides information about backups you have taken of your control file. This does not include control file copies; there is a different view for copies that have been made with the **copy** command or cataloged with the **catalog** command. This view is an excellent source to reference if control file restore operations are behaving strangely, particularly if you are trying to duplicate for standby database creation.

To review control file copies in V$BACKUP_DATAFILE, you would look at records with a file number of 0—this represents the control file:

```
select file#, creation_time, resetlogs_time,
blocks, block_size, controlfile_type
from v$backup_datafile where file#=0;
```

The following query would give you information about all the control file backups for the database V102, with the completion time, the status, the type of control file (B for a normal backup and S for a standby control file backup), and the date of the autobackup (this will be null if you do not have the control file autobackup configured):

```
column completion_time format a25
column autobackup_date format a25
alter session set nls_date_format= 'DD-MON-YYYY:HH24:MI:SS';
select db_name, status, completion_time, controlfile_type,
autobackup_date from rc_backup_controlfile
where db_name= 'V102';
```

RC_BACKUP_CORRUPTION (V$BACKUP_CORRUPTION)

This view lists the corruption that exists in datafile backups. To tolerate corruption, the value of MAXCORRUPT must be set to a non-zero value, which indicates how many corrupt blocks RMAN will back up before it throws an error and aborts. The corrupt blocks are not discarded, but rather are backed up as is.

Do not confuse this view with RC_DATABASE_BLOCK_CORRUPTION (described later in this appendix), which lists blocks that are corrupt in the database based on the last backup operation (or **backup validate**). RC_BACKUP_CORRUPTION lists blocks that are corrupt in the backup, not in the database itself.

The following code provides a list of corrupt blocks, with block number, file number, backup piece in which the corruption exists, and the type of corruption for the database V102:

```
select db_name, piece#, file#, block#, blocks, corruption_type
from rc_backup_corruption where db_name='V102';
```

RC_BACKUP_DATAFILE (V$BACKUP_DATAFILE)
This view has extensive information about datafiles that exist in backup sets. If you are interested in viewing specific information about datafiles that have been backed up, use this view.

RC_BACKUP_FILES (V$BACKUP_FILES)
This view most completely corresponds to the information provided by the commands **list backup** and **list copy** from the RMAN command-line interface. This view provides details about all backup files known to the recovery catalog, regardless of whether the file is a backup set, datafile copy, or proxy copy.

To use this view, you must first call DBMS_RCVMAN.SetDatabase to indicate which database you are looking for:

```
CALL DBMS_RCVMAN.SETDATABASE(null,null,null,2283997583,null);
select backup_type, file_type, status, bytes from rc_backup_files;
```

RC_BACKUP_PIECE (V$BACKUP_PIECE)
Reference this view for information about specific backup pieces that have been created during normal backup operations. Remember that a backup set contains more than one backup piece, and that the backup piece is the physical file that corresponds to the logical unit of the backup set.

RC_BACKUP_REDOLOG (V$BACKUP_REDOLOG)
The name of this view is something of a misnomer: RMAN cannot back up online redo logs; it can back up only archived redo logs, which most often are simply referred to as archive logs. This view lists archive logs that exist in backup sets. There is a record for each archive log that has been backed up; if the same archive log is backed up twice, there will be two records.

The following query provides information for a particular range of archive logs, with backup set information, the status of the backup set, and the completion time:

```
alter session set nls_date_format= 'DD-MON-YYYY:HH24:MI:SS';
select db_name, bs_key, sequence#, thread#, first_change#, status
from rc_backup_redolog;
```

RC_BACKUP_SET (V$BACKUP_SET)

Information in this view refers to each logical backup set. You have to specify what type of backup set you would like to review: full backups, incremental backups, or archive log backups.

RC_BACKUP_SPFILE (V$BACKUP_SPFILE)

In this view, you will find information on SPFILE backups that exist in backup sets.

RC_CONTROLFILE_COPY (V$DATAFILE_COPY)

Like RC_BACKUP_CONTROLFILE, the corresponding view here, V$DATAFILE_COPY, also includes information about control files, encoded as file number 0. In the catalog, this view contains control file copy information for control files created with the **copy** command or cataloged with the **catalog** command.

RC_COPY_CORRUPTION (V$COPY_CORRUPTION)

This view is the same as RC_BACKUP_CORRUPTION except that it reports blocks that are corrupt in copies instead of in backup sets. The **select** statement, then, would omit a **piece#** but would otherwise be identical:

```
select db_name, file#, block#, blocks, corruption_type
from rc_COPY_corruption where db_name='V102';
```

RC_DATABASE (V$DATABASE)

This view contains basic information about each database registered in the catalog: the database name, DBID, current incarnation number, and last RESETLOGS time and SCN.

RC_DATABASE_BLOCK_CORRUPTION (V$DATABASE_BLOCK_CORRUPTION)

This view provides the corruption list that is populated when a **backup** or **backup validate** operation discovers corrupt blocks. Remember that these are the actual corrupt blocks in the database, and not in the backups or copies themselves. This view is refreshed on each backup operation to reflect current corruption (if any).

V$DATABASE_BLOCK_CORRUPTION is the view used during block media recovery when you specify **blockrecover corruption list** and is therefore the one that you will most often be referencing. The following code is an example select statement against this view.

```
select file#, block#, corruption_type
from v$database_block_corruption;
```

RC_DATABASE_INCARNATION (V$DATABASE_INCARNATION)

This view contains a record for each incarnation of each database registered in the catalog. The most important information here is the RESETLOGS information, which by definition defines each incarnation. The following code is an example select statement against this view.

```
select dbid, name, dbinc_key, resetlogs_time, current_incarnation
from rc_database_incarnation
where db_key = <database key>
and dbinc_key = <current incarnation key number>;
```

RC_DATAFILE (V$DATAFILE)

This view exists so that the catalog has access to the same schematic information as does the control file about the location and specifics of each datafile in the database. You are much more likely to use V$DATAFILE when you want to look at your datafile information; however, in a recovery situation, this view can be extremely helpful if a current control file is not available. It also contains tablespace information in addition to datafile information, and in that way resembles the fixed view DBA_DATA_FILES. In addition, this view contains permanent configuration information for the commands **configure exclude** and **configure auxname**. The following code is an example select statement against this view.

```
SQL> select db_name, ts#, tablespace_name, file#, name,
bytes, included_in_database_backup, aux_name
from rc_datafile
where db_name='V102';
```

RC_DATAFILE_COPY (V$DATAFILE_COPY)

This view provides metadata about datafile copies created by the **copy** command or OS copies that have been registered with the **catalog** command.

RC_LOG_HISTORY (V$LOG_HISTORY)

V$LOG_HISTORY is the view that contains historical information about online redo logs, such as when they switched and what the SCN was at the time of the switch.

This is a little redundant with V$ARCHIVED_LOG, but V$LOG_HISTORY does not concern itself with any current files, just the historical log switching information.

RC_OFFLINE_RANGE (V$OFFLINE_RANGE)

Offline ranges set the parameters for when a datafile went offline or read-only, and when it came back to read/write mode (if ever). It is important for RMAN to know this about a file when doing backups and restores. From a recoverability standpoint, it is critical to know the entire time range when a file was offline. If a backup of a datafile exists from before a transition from online to offline (or read-only), archive logs will be required from the moment the file was taken offline or read-only until the current point in time.

RC_REDO_LOG (VLOG, VLOGFILE)

From a schematic point of view, this is the same for RMAN as knowing the information in V$DATAFILE—on rebuilds, it needs to know where the online redo log files are located. This view is a combination of both V$LOG and V$LOGFILE, so that thread and group membership is available alongside the name of each log.

RC_REDO_THREAD (V$THREAD)

Thread information is really only important in RAC environments, where there is more than a single thread of redo being generated at once. This view lists a record for each separate thread in the current database incarnation, along with the status of the thread and its redo stream. The following code is an example select statement against this view.

```
select db_name, thread#, status, sequence# from rc_redo_thread
where db_name='V102';
```

RC_RESYNC

This view provides information for each catalog resync operation that occurs. Obviously, there is no corresponding v$view for this one. You can use this view to determine if any of your enterprise databases need a resync, or to troubleshoot possible resynchronization problems. The following code is an example select statement against this view.

```
SQL> select db_name, controlfile_time, controlfile_sequence#,
resync_type, resync_time
from rc_resync where db_name='V102';
```

RC_RMAN_CONFIGURATION (V$RMAN_CONFIGURATION)

This view is equivalent to a **show all** command, giving the name and value for each configuration parameter that is set for each of your target databases.

It is worth noting that three configuration parameters are not stored here: **configure exclude** information is found in RC_TABLESPACE (V$TABLESPACE), **configure auxname** information is found in RC_DATAFILE (V$DATAFILE), and **configure snapshot controlfile** information is found only in the target database control file (there is no catalog equivalent).

It is also important to point out that RC_RMAN_CONFIGURATION does not have a DB_NAME column, so you have to use the primary key DB_KEY value from RC_DATABASE to get the values for the appropriate database registered in your catalog.

Furthermore, no values are listed in either V$RMAN_CONFIGURATION or RC_RMAN_CONFIGURATION for default values. Only values that have been manually changed will appear in this list. The following code is an example select statement against this view.

```
SQL> select name, value from rc_rman_configuration where db_key=1;
```

RC_TABLESPACE (V$TABLESPACE)

Tablespace information is included in this view. The real benefit of this view over V$TABLESPACE is that historical information about dropped tablespaces is kept in the catalog. Therefore, you can use this view to look back and see when a tablespace was dropped. In addition, this view contains the information recorded for any **configure exclude** commands.

RC_TEMPFILE (V$TEMPFILE)

RMAN, with version 10g, now is tempfile aware and can rebuild tempfiles upon restore so that you do not have to do it manually, as in the past. RC_TEMPFILE provides the bridge for this functionality, and a window into the existing tempfiles for a database.

New Catalog Views Intended for Use by Oracle Enterprise Manager

A series of new views in the recovery catalog were created specifically to provide performance and functionality enhancements to the OEM Console and thus have limited functionality for end users. Most of these views do not have corresponding v$views in the target database control file. It is worth taking a look at these views and identifying their parts, to dispel any misunderstanding that might arise from their existence. If you are looking for a way to leverage the information in these views, you can find the same information in them in OEM's backup and recovery functionality. The following table lists and briefly describes the RC_* views that are built primarily for use by OEM.

RC_* View	Note
RC_BACKUP_ARCHIVELOG_DETAILS	Detailed information about backed up archive logs.
RC_BACKUP_ARCHIVELOG_SUMMARY	Summarized archive log backup information.
RC_BACKUP_CONTROLFILE_DETAILS	Detailed control file backup information.
RC_BACKUP_CONTROLFILE_SUMMARY	Summarized information about all control file backups known to RMAN.
RC_BACKUP_COPY_DETAILS	Detailed information regarding all control file and datafile copies.
RC_BACKUP_COPY_SUMMARY	Summarized control file and datafile copy information.
RC_BACKUP_DATAFILE_DETAILS	Detailed information about all datafile backups—in backup sets as well as image copies.
RC_BACKUP_DATAFILE_SUMMARY	Summary information about datafile backups.
RC_BACKUP_PIECE_DETAILS	Detailed information about available backup pieces in the catalog.
RC_BACKUP_SET_DETAILS	Detailed information regarding available backup sets in the catalog. This includes backups created with the **backup backupset** command.
RC_BACKUP_SET_SUMMARY	Aggregated information about available backup sets.
RC_BACKUP_SPFILE_DETAILS	Detailed information about available SPFILE backups.
RC_BACKUP_SPFILE_SUMMARY	Summarized information about available SPFILE backups.
RC_RMAN_OUTPUT	Assists OEM with job status tracking. The corresponding v$view is V$RMAN_OUTPUT.
RC_RMAN_BACKUP_JOB_DETAILS	Detailed information on individual backup job sessions, combining all operations in the same session.
RC_RMAN_BACKUP_SUBJOB_DETAILS	Details concerning groups of similar operations within an RMAN session.
RC_RMAN_STATUS	A historical view of RMAN sessions for all databases in the recovery catalog. It does not contain current session information, as does its corresponding v$view, V$RMAN_STATUS.
RC_UNUSABLE_BACKUPFILE_DETAILS	A list of all backup files of any type that have been marked as UNAVAILABLE or EXPIRED.
RC_RMAN_BACKUP_TYPE	Provides filtering information to OEM during its report building.

APPENDIX
C

Setting Up an RMAN
Test Environment

s the complexity of production enterprise environments grows with each passing year, we DBAs are finding the same complexity creeping into our test environments. For example, in *Oracle9i RMAN Backup & Recovery*, the test environment was seemingly complex for us: a Windows laptop for minor tweaks and screenshots, another Windows server for more robust testing, and a Sun Blade 150 for multi-OS interaction and unix commands. Between these three machines, we were able to do all technical reviews (combined with years of actual experience in the workplace, of course).

For this book, the test environment included two Linux boxes with a shared FireWire disk drive (running RAC, of course), my trusty Windows laptop, that old Sun Blade, and a stand-alone Linux box. And we still went hunting with my colleagues looking for other RAC clusters, tape storage jukeboxes, and Oracle Enterprise Manager repositories.

As stated in *Oracle9i RMAN Backup & Recovery*, test environments can be tricky to describe or provide advice about. Every shop has its own concept of what testing is required, and at what level, for application design, quality assurance, version control, and so forth. And with RMAN playing a more integral role in a wider array of DBA activities, it's increasingly difficult to separate an RMAN test environment from other test environments. But, you are looking at this book now, and we have opinions on testing backup strategies. As we like to say, everyone has a backup strategy. Few have a recovery strategy. Testing backups is only a fraction of the work. If you do not test your recovery strategies, then you don't have backups, no matter how many files you've written to how many thousands of dollars' worth of equipment.

A test environment for backup and recovery is different from other testing environments. First of all, you have to be able to remove datafiles, or even the entire database, on a whim, without having to clear it with other users. In other words, you need your own database. Or two. If you begin testing RMAN functionality on a shared database, pretty soon you'll either start getting angry phone calls from other users or find yourself locked out of the machine by the SA. A backup and recovery test environment is simply too volatile to share. Think about it from the other end: you're busy testing a backup yourself, when suddenly the backup aborts because someone started removing datafiles in order to test their own restore and recovery.

On the other hand, you need to test your strategies in an environment that most closely matches that of your production databases. Therefore, you can't always run in isolation, because you might need to tune your backup on a large, production-grade server that has the same kind of load as production.

What we suggest, then, is that you approach RMAN backup and recovery testing as a two-tier investigation: first, get comfortable with functionality and behavior in the isolation of a small test server; second, take the lessons you've learned and schedule time to test on a larger, production-grade database server. That way, you can schedule time on a test box for a backup/recovery test outage and avoid spending that valuable time trying to learn lessons that you could have figured out on your workstation.

So what does this approach look like more specifically? The answer is provided in this appendix.

The Test Box

The first-level test machine for RMAN functionality doesn't need to be a supercomputer. In fact, you should think of the first level of testing as just a rehearsal—you're reading through your lines, getting the placement right, and talking through the steps with the other actors and the director.

Match Your Production Environment

If possible, your RMAN testing should take place on the same operating system that you run in production. This is a rather humorous thing to say, we know: who has a single OS in their environment anymore? Anyway, if you will be backing up only Solaris servers, it makes sense to invest a little money in a Sun workstation. That way, you can begin production environment matching as soon as possible.

Go Cheap

It's not that critical to have your first wave of testing take place on the same OS as your production environment. RMAN acts the same on all platforms, and the exercises in this book work on all platforms. So, if you're in the market for an RMAN test box, we have only two words: go cheap. Buy a commodity-priced computer that runs Windows or Linux. I've grown quite fond of my cut-rate Linux cluster that Scott Jesse outlined in the Oracle Press book *Oracle Database 10g High Availability with RAC, Flashback, and Data Guard* (2004). It is a two-node RAC tester for under $1500, bought refurbished from Dell's Outlet. As far as what to look for in a cheap test environment, we provide the following advice:

- **Processor speed**   Don't worry about processor speed at the RMAN proof-of-concept level. RMAN simply does not rely on CPUs that heavily. As you move into heavy parallelization in production, CPU speeds might grow in testing importance. Even if you monitor for performance at this level, the data is meaningless when compared to your production environment. Instead, spend money on other resources, mainly disk space and memory.

- **Memory**   You need enough memory to run three Oracle instances simultaneously, along with your media management software. If you will be testing with OEM or some other management software package, factor that in as well. Any more, this means that you need 2GB minimum. Don't cut corners on memory or you will get sucked down into time-consuming swap rat holes from which there is no escape.

■ **Disk space** Disks are cheap, and you don't need some SCSI disk or anything, just space. Speed, again, is not important at this level. A 200GB hard drive should be sufficient. You're doing concept testing at this level, so you can control the size of databases to keep things under control. But keep in mind that you're going to have more than one database, and you will also be backing up to disk (most likely), so you need space for RMAN backup pieces, as well. So load up on disk space if you can.

If you decide to do a RAC tester, you need an external SCSI or FireWire drive in addition to whatever you load internally into your box. Again, consult *Oracle Database 10*g *High Availability with RAC, Flashback, and Data Guard* for a blow-by-blow description of RAC home clusters.

The Oracle Configuration

After you get your test box up and running, you need to think about your Oracle installation and configuration. This step depends on what exactly you need to test: Will you be backing up multiple versions of Oracle? Will you be using OEM?

Multiple Homes

If you will be testing multiple versions of Oracle, be sure to install them in chronological order from oldest to newest; for example, install version 9.2.0 before 10.1.0, and 10.1.0 before 10.2.0. Before you get very far, patch Oracle to the latest patch level. There are always RMAN bugs getting fixed, so it makes sense to be at the most recent patch level.

Creating Databases

Obviously, you need at least one database created in each ORACLE_HOME that you have installed. These databases may be default databases created during Oracle installation, but an even better scenario would be to use databases that are configured somewhat like production databases. From a size perspective, that may not be possible, but you can scale datafile sizes down while keeping the same number of datafiles and tablespaces.

In addition, try scaling down the memory utilization of these test boxes to be as low as possible. You won't actually be doing that much processing, so you don't need a lot of buffer cache available. The smaller you keep the System Global Area (SGA), the better off your little test box will be.

You also need a recovery catalog database that is separate from the target databases that you are using for testing. We always recommend that your recovery catalog database be the most recent version, so put this in a 10.2 home. In a pinch, this can also be used as a target database, but try to keep your recovery catalog database out of the mix of databases that you blow away and rebuild.

It just makes life easier. If at all possible, put your recovery catalog database on a different server. Put it on a Windows workstation or an old Linux box. Keep it out of the crash-and-burn destruction path.

Using Oracle ASM

If you plan to test out Oracle's volume manager, Automatic Storage Management (ASM), you have to make preparations when you first configure your RMAN test box. In a production environment, you would simply add full, raw disks to an ASM disk group. In a test environment, if you want to test multiple ASM disk groups, you can simply use logical partitions on a single disk. But this means you have to think ahead and create some unused, raw partitions on your disks before you get too far into your OS setup.

Oracle Enterprise Manager

If you plan to use OEM, make sure there is enough memory to do so. As you learned in Chapter 11, there are two flavors of OEM you can choose from: Database Control and Grid Control. From a testing perspective, it might make sense to go with Database Control to save on resources and administration headaches. However, make the choice that matches your production environment: If you deploy Grid Control management in production, use Grid Control to manage RMAN backups in the test environment.

That being said, try to avoid using production Grid Control for RMAN test environments. The databases will be down, up, down, lost, trashed, crashed, and lost. This means lots of alerts will be sent to the Oracle Management Service (OMS) and, consequently, e-mailed out to people. Avoid bot spam! If you have not already deployed a test Grid Control environment for your enterprise, get one set up for your RMAN backups and then offer it to others for testing purposes.

For Database Control, expect a memory hit of 150 to 200MB per instance. Also, Database Control makes heavy use of CPUs and uses up database space. Database Control generates about 200MB of archive logs per day just by itself, with an idle database.

For Grid Control, you need a 2GB system all by itself for the repository database and OMS. Factor it in as a separate system. On the RMAN test system itself, the agent will use only about 60MB of memory and enough CPU to run its Perl scripts.

OEM, either Database or Grid Control, is highly dependent on a stable and predictable networking sublayer, which means you cannot constantly change the hostname or IP address. Sorry. It's just easier that way. If you have to, create your own subnet and manually assign dummy IP addresses in the hosts files. The easiest check you can implement to ensure everything will operate correctly is the **nslookup** command on the hostname, and a reverse lookup on the IP address.

Media Management Considerations

If possible, you should install a version of the media management client that you will be using in production. Then, install the Oracle Plug-In and do the backups to tape the same as you would in production. This gives you the best opportunity to anticipate what to expect when you implement your strategy in your enterprise.

If you can't get access to the media management product that is used for your enterprise, there is little alternative left. The best option is to try out Oracle Secure Backup, as outlined in Chapter 5 of this book.

If you simply need to test tape channel allocations, or the process of staging the flash recovery area to tape, you still have access to the Oracle SBT API, which enables you to write "tape" backups to a disk location. This is described in the RMAN Workshop "Test Tape Channels with the Oracle Default SBT Interface" in Chapter 4.

The RMAN Configuration

Now that you have your system set up with Oracle installed and databases built, we have a few hints on the testing process itself:

- *Have a cold backup that remains untouched.* Before you do any RMAN testing, shut down your database and take a cold OS copy backup and place it in a folder that doesn't get touched. This is your last line of defense if you completely mess everything up during your RMAN testing.

- *Switch your redo logs a lot.* One of the biggest mistakes that happens with RMAN testing is that the timeframe between the backup and restore is unrealistically short. Confusion sets in because there is no space between the completion time of the backup and the "until time" of the restore operation. So, after any backup, make sure you switch the log file three or four times, just to put a little "distance" between operations.

- *Set the NLS_DATE_FORMAT environment variable.* This is good advice for RMAN in general, but particularly in a test situation, where the timeframe between a backup and a restore will be unrealistically short and you will want to know the timeframe of a backup to the second. So, before starting RMAN, be sure to run the following:

```
export NLS_DATE_FORMAT='mon-dd-yyyy hh24:mi:ss'
```

Then, when you start RMAN and issue a **list backup** command, the time will always show details to the minute and second.

■ *Leave your catalog database alone.* You will be tempted to use the database that houses your catalog as a target and perform some tests with it. That is fine—that's why it's called a test environment. But you can seriously undermine your testing if you foul up your catalog. Do yourself a favor and leave the catalog database alone. And export your catalog schema with a user-level export before any new test session begins.

■ *Keep up with catalog maintenance.* This may be your test environment, but you will be creating a lot of backups over time, and you have a limited amount of space on your little test box. Take the opportunity to test out using retention policies to get rid of old backups.

■ *Remove clones as soon as possible.* Attack of the clones! If you use the **duplicate** command, you can end up with numerous different instances running and taking up precious memory and disk space. Hey, it's a clone, and you're in a test environment—get rid of it as soon as you make it.

■ *Leave a clone file system in place.* You don't need to go through the steps of building the file system and the init.ora file for your duplicate database every time you want to test the **duplicate** or **duplicate... for standby** command. Leave the file system and supporting files in place, and use the same DB_NAME and SID. On Windows, be sure to leave the Oracleservice<sid> in place in the Services control panel.

■ *Don't get attached to your test environment.* Sometimes you need to just blow everything away and start over from scratch, particularly if you don't have good maintenance habits. Eventually, your database will get to the point that it has had tablespaces dropped, has had re-created, dropped, and forgotten files placed in the wrong directory, has had archive logs stored all over the place—basically a rambling mess. Don't worry. That's why they call it testing. Don't get too wrapped up in the environment you have; just whack everything and start over from the cold backup you took prior to testing.

You'll surely find some of your own valuable lessons after you've done a bit of testing. After you go through the conceptual learning, take the scripts you've built and the knowledge you've gained and schedule some time on a production-grade system to make sure that everything is going to scale up to your enterprise. You'll be glad you took the time to learn it before you went live.

Index

651

O

P

S